LAW AND THE MEDIA

D1635296

LAW AND THE MEDIA

SECOND EDITION

BY

PROFESSOR DUNCAN BLOY,
B.A., L.L.M., P.G.C.E.
*School of Journalism, Media and Cultural Studies and Law
at Cardiff University*

AND

SARA HADWIN
M.A. (OXON)
*Lecturer, School of Journalism, Media and Cultural Studies at
Cardiff University (former newspaper editor)*

SWEET & MAXWELL  THOMSON REUTERS

First Edition 2007
Second Edition 2011

*Published in 2011 by Sweet & Maxwell, 100 Avenue Road, London NW3 3PF
part of Thomson Reuters (Professional) UK Limited
(Registered in England & Wales, Company No 1679046.
Registered Office and address for service:
Aldgate House, 33 Aldgate High Street, London EC3N 1DL)*

Typeset by Servis Filmsetting Ltd, Stockport, Cheshire

**For further information on our products and services, visit
www.sweetandmaxwell.co.uk*

*No natural forests were destroyed to make this product;
only farmed timber was used and re-planted.*

A CIP catalogue record for this book is available from the British
Library.

ISBN 978 0 414 04610 8

Thomson Reuters and the Thomson Reuters logo are trademarks of
Thomson Reuters. Sweet & Maxwell ® is a registered trademark of
Thompson Reuters (Professional) UK Limited

PREFACE

"Lawyers tell it how it is; journalists how they would like it to be." Since we became colleagues more than seven years ago that simple aphorism seems to have permeated most of our conversations. In trying to instil best practice into budding journalists, we have regularly had to put both sides of the argument. The journalist can see no obvious reason why something cannot be broadcast or printed yet the lawyer urges caution.

A good example is the law on contempt. The Contempt of Court Act 1981 warns journalists not to create a substantial risk of serious prejudice to pending legal proceedings in pre-trial reporting. Yet in early May 2011 the High Court gave permission to the Attorney General to commence proceedings against two national newspapers for contempt of court. The proceedings relate to the arrest in late 2010 of Chris Jefferies on suspicion of the murder in Bristol of Joanna Yeates. The media's response was to put into the public domain every conceivable piece of information that could be gleaned about the suspect including the fact that, when a student, he coloured his hair blue. The Act warns against trial by media. In the event another man has been charged with causing the young woman's death. Jefferies is no longer on police bail. He is an innocent man. At the time the information was put into the public domain the media had to assume that this man could be facing a trial for murder or manslaughter. However the decision-making falls to the media as to whether anything published when proceedings are active complies with the law. This type of situation reflects what we attempt to achieve in this book. The legal principles are well established but it is for the media to interpret those principles in practice.

The law has the capacity to change unbelievably quickly. The developing law in favour of greater art.8 (ECHR) protection causing the corresponding restrictions on freedom of expression is perhaps the best recent example. Throughout this book, we have endeavoured to state the current legal principles in many of the everyday situations faced by journalists. We are conscious of the fact that copyright has not been given prominence but space limitations have meant that certain intellectual property issues had to be sacrificed.

The text essentially offers two perspectives. The major legal principles are stated together with a number of pertinent quotations from major cases. An experienced editorial eye is then cast over those principles in an endeavour to explain just what could or should not be attempted without risking a breach of the law. The text is aimed at both trainee journalists and those studying media law at undergraduate level, but we hope that it may prove to be of interest to a wider media audience as a reference text. A healthy democracy requires both an acceptance of the rule of law and a thriving and responsible fourth estate. Lawyers and journalists may not always agree but at least we can keep the dialogue open, ongoing and friendly!

We would both like to thank our Cardiff University students for demanding answers to many of the questions addressed in this book. Staff at Sweet & Maxwell have been wonderfully supportive.

We have endeavoured to state the law as at June 30, 2011

Duncan Bloy
Sara Hadwin

Dedicated to the memory of
Arnold Hadwin
Newspaper editor and evader of the litigious
(1929–2011)

ACKNOWLEDGMENTS

Grateful acknowledgment is made to the following authors and publishers for permission to quote from their works:

European Court of Human Rights: *Selisto v Finland* [2004]; *B and P* [2001].

Frankel, Maurice, Director of Campaign for Freedom of Information, *www.cfoi.org.uk*

Guardian, quotations from Duncan Lamont, Mary Riddell and Simon Jenkins, *www.guardian.co.uk*

Incorporated Council of Law Reporting: various cases.

Information Commissioner's Office, Richard Thomas', "What Price Privacy?" Report May 2006.

Information Policy (PSI), Report of the House of Commons Culture, Media and Sport Committee on Press standards, privacy and libel.

Judicial Communications Office, quotation from Sir Nicholas Wall, *www.judiciary.gov.uk*

Judicial Studies Board, Reporting Restrictions in the Magistrates' Courts, *www.judiciary.gov.uk*

Media Lawyer, Mostyn Memorial Lecture at Gray's Inn, (Lord Falconer); and Commons Constitutional Affairs Committee, (Munby J.), *www. media lawyer.press.net*

Nigel Hanson, "Libel Reform—what's in it for me?", March 29, 2011 *www.holdthefrontpage.co.uk*

Ofcom, Ofcom Broadcasting Codes 7 & 8, *www.ofcom.org.uk*

Press Complaints Commission, PCC Report on Subterfuge and Newsgathering, and PCC Editors Code of Practice *www.pcc.org.uk*

Society of Editors, Paul Dacre's speech to the Society of Editors Conference, Bristol, 2008 and Sir Igor Judge Keynote Speech to Society of Editors conference, Stansted 2009, *www.societyofeditors.org*

Thomas, Richard, Information Commissioner's Office, "What Price Privacy", *www.ico.gov.uk.*

CONTENTS

TABLE OF CASES

TABLE OF STATUTES

INTRODUCTION: IT'S THE HUMAN RIGHTS ACT, STUPID

Law is learnt as a litany of bans and restrictions; terrible tales of journalists' undoing, massive legal bills and expensive apologies. It is good, and indeed vital, that those lessons are learnt. Warning bells need to ring for journalists, but learning law must not end with a list of stories that can't be told. Journalists need to turn to statute and to informed legal judgments in order to realise what is required in terms of investigative procedure and the wording of their reports so that a story can be safely put in the public domain. Media law is something journalists can't avoid, but we can learn to work more effectively within it.

Ignorance of the law can certainly be expensive in terms of damages, costs and even a spell in prison. Adopting an informed attitude to working within the law will protect a responsible journalist seeking genuinely to serve the public interest where a legal challenge arises. This greatly improves their chances of telling the stories that need to be told and providing the public with the fullest possible story within the law.

Most stories can be told in a legally safe form by employing legal insights, ingenuity and rigorous journalistic method. But this requires judgment. Risk must be acknowledged but it can be minimised with the benefit of legal advice. Ignore it at your peril but use it to your advantage.

The implications of the law must be borne in mind for all stories, for it applies to all. Journalists have a tendency to see defamation, for instance, as applying only to in-depth exposés rather than to seemingly innocuous club reports or letters to the editor.

They recognise that legal training is required for reporting courts but fail to see its significance for health, education, council or human interest coverage.

Law is not a series of absolutes. Grey areas increase uncertainty but also create room for manoeuvre in individual cases. Media law is about much more than relevant legislation. Case law, especially in the wake of the Human Rights Act, has significant impact on journalists. Barely a week goes by without a hearing which challenges the boundaries of journalistic activity; what can and can't be printed and increasingly the behaviour expected of journalists claiming any protection from the law for what they publish.

Law is changing at a sometimes alarming pace, mainly by virtue of judicial rulings more than legislation. As a result, journalists need to keep up to date with the ramifications of these decisions for their work. They also need to know where they can take advantage of methods and wordings which will keep them on the right side of the law.

Journalists may wish that legislation and case law were less intrusive in our work, but the trend is strongly towards greater scrutiny not less. Journalists who want to push the limits of the law to tell stories that the public really do have a right to know can expect to have to justify their working practices as well as what they say.

This trend is set to continue and even accelerate for some time to come given the enormous impact of the adoption into the Human Rights Act of the principles of the European Convention on Human Rights, which now lie at the heart of all media law. All legislation and related judicial rulings are now required to be convention-compliant. So the Act has ushered in a series of judgments seeking to create a new methodology for resolving media-related cases. Since 2000 and from now on, cases will be judged in terms of pitting the journalist's art.10 rights against other human rights, particularly the art.8 rights of individuals to protect their privacy and the art.6 rights to a fair trial.

These responses to the Human Rights Act have largely determined the contents of this book in that we have focused on those areas of direct impact, primarily defamation, privacy and contempt, but also looked at associated questions of regulation and statutory developments such as the Freedom of Information Act.

We have featured the areas of media law which are changing most in the 21st century and where emerging case law is having the most significant impact on working journalists and their news organisations. Those areas of media law which are relatively "fixed" in comparison have been left to existing textbooks to outline.

Only by keeping abreast of these developments can a journalist expect to operate within the law while not allowing it to create more curbs on reporting than need be.

Journalists respect the law and would generally seek to work within it. They are certainly not above it and are likely to face swift retribution where they behave as if they were. The jailing of News of the World royal editor Clive Goodman in 2007 for phone-hacking provided a stark reminder to journalists of the price they may pay for breaking the criminal law. And the fall-out from the hacking allegations continues with more journalists suspended and police investigations renewed in 2011.

Journalists claim their rights to freedom of expression as individuals and it is, generally, as individuals that they are called to account, as anyone else would be, if they disobey the law. Many journalists, and editors, will come across a story that they want to tell badly enough—for principled and/or commercial reasons—to take that risk. Some will pay a heavy price.

But far more frequently massive legal bills are racked up because the legal ramifications of a story are not thought through, because defences are not marshalled or because, when it comes to the crunch, the journalistic process as a whole does not stand up to scrutiny. Don't let that happen to you.

Each chapter of this book aims to capture not just the 21st-century trends in media law but the continuing debate and tensions between the law and the journalist. Each chapter commences with Duncan Bloy in Part One discussing the major legal principles and concludes with Sara Hadwin in Part Two providing a practical journalistic perspective. While neither of us can claim to be typical of our "breed", we both consciously and sub-consciously interpret media law in ways which reflect our respective callings. We hope this will prove illuminating and go some way to stimulating the dialogue between the law and the media which remains crucial to democratic debate, and to what kind of democratic society we will become.

For each chapter of the book, relevant legislation and the thinking behind it are discussed. Key definitions and landmark cases are given. These legal underpinnings are then viewed from a working journalist's perspective in an attempt to illustrate the impact on day-to-day practice, including general pointers on how stories can be run without falling foul of the law. The inclusion of recent case law provides the most up-to-date guidance we can for journalists. We acknowledge the time constraints of any textbook and would strongly urge journalists to adopt our habit of tracking relevant judgments which are published on a variety of legal websites as they emerge. See Bibliography for details.

This volume is part source book for budding media lawyers, part advice guide for practising journalists and, hopefully, a catalyst for informed debate about the interrelationship between the law and the media in the 21st century.

As the authors we can inform. We can challenge. We can urge that any risk taken be a calculated risk and we can help you to make that assessment. But, however much legal advice is sought, the ultimate decision on what to run remains with your editor.

We believe this is a crucial time for journalists to grapple with the issues raised by the judicial responses to the Human Rights Act. If the right to freedom of expression is to be upheld, journalists need to know where it can be advanced and where it is under threat. They need to think long and hard about their role in a democratic society and know how the law protects or hinders it. Hopefully by tracking 21st-century media case law, we can provoke journalists and their news organisations into playing a still more active role in testing the boundaries of our freedom of expression and the public's right to know.

CHAPTER 1: INTRODUCTION TO THE LEGAL SYSTEM

PART ONE: THE LEGAL SYSTEM

All journalists need to have as part of their training an introduction to the workings of the legal system. It is after all the context within which journalists in this country have to practise their art. We shall see later in this book that the law interacts very closely with the way journalists operate and on numerous occasions will act as a constraint on the exercise of rights to freedom of expression and therefore the concept of a free press.

This chapter is designed to introduce readers to the underpinning knowledge of the English and Welsh legal system. This is designed to ensure that journalists understand and appreciate how the system works so that this can be conveyed, when necessary, accurately and professionally in their everyday reporting. There are numerous sources of information readily available on the internet and this is where we shall start with this overview of the legal system.

The first point to note is that throughout this book any reference to English law means we are referring to the law applicable to England and Wales. Avoid referring in reports to the British or United Kingdom legal system simply because there isn't one. The Scottish Legal system is different from England and Wales.

Each jurisdiction has Law Officers whose job is to advise the respective governments. So the United Kingdom government is advised by the Attorney General and the Solicitor General. The Scottish government's Law Officers are the Lord Advocate and the Solicitor General. At the time of writing Dominic Grieve QC MP is the Attorney General and Edward Garnier QC MP is the Solicitor General. In Scotland Frank Mulholland QC is the Lord Advocate and Lesley Thomson is the Solicitor General. In addition, reflecting the fact that we have a United Kingdom government, Scottish legal interests are promoted in London by the Advocate General for Scotland who is currently the Rt Hon Lord Wallace of Tankerness QC. Dominic Grieve QC MP acts as the Advocate General for Northern Ireland.

1. Law Officers of the Crown

England and Wales

Attorney General

The Attorney General is the chief legal advisor to the government. While the role is generally to ensure the effectiveness of the major prosecuting authorities in England and Wales it will be obvious that at times it can be intensely political when, for example, giving advice to government on the legality of a declaration of war or the invasion of another country. The most obvious example in recent times is the advice tendered by the then Attorney General Lord Goldsmith QC on the legality of the invasion of Iraq in 2003.

The Attorney General seeks on occasions to remind the media of their responsibilities under relevant legislation in respect of, for example, pre-trial reporting in highly publicised cases. The intention is to avoid having to prosecute the media for contempt of court by avoiding publishing anything that might create a substantial risk of serious prejudice to any upcoming criminal proceedings. In a speech to the Law for Journalists conference in 2003 the Attorney General opined that the reporting in the lead up to the trial of Ian Huntley for the Soham murders was "frankly unacceptable."[1] However despite the criticism of the reporting no prosecutions for contempt were brought against any media outlet.

A more recent example was the reporting surrounding the death of Joanna Yeates in Bristol in late 2010. The arrest of her landlord Chris Jefferies sparked a frenzy of media activity with a whole range of uncomplimentary views and opinions expressed about Mr Jefferies. Such reporting prompted the Attorney General to state:

"We need to avoid a situation where trials cannot take place or are prejudiced as a result of irrelevant or improper material being published in newspapers and also online, where the case has been subject of intense commentary on Twitter."

Speaking on BBC Radio 4's *The World at One* programme he went on:

". . . it is important to understand that the contempt of court rules are there to protect the rule of law and the fair trial process and they require newspapers, and indeed anyone who is covering material, to do that in a way that doesn't prejudice the possibility of a fair trial taking place at a later date."[2]

---

[1] Law for Journalists Conference November 2003.
[2] *The World at One*: BBC Radio 4. December 31, 2010.

Mr Jefferies was released on police bail and subsequently another person was charged with the murder.

Solicitor General

The Solicitor General is in effect the Attorney General's deputy. The Attorney General's website states simply that *"The Solicitor General supports the Attorney across the range of his responsibilities."*

Information relating to the activities of the Law Officers can be found at *www.attorneygeneral.gov.uk/TheLawOfficers*

Clearly the work of the Attorney General and his relationship with the media is of great importance to journalists.

Scotland

The *www.scotland.gov.uk* website describes the role and functions of the two law officers as follows:

Lord Advocate

- Head of the systems of prosecution and investigation of deaths.
- Principal legal advisor to the Scottish Government.
- Representing the Scottish Government in civil proceedings.
- Representing the public interest in a range of statutory and common law civil functions.

Solicitor General

"The Solicitor General is the Lord Advocate's deputy. He may discharge any of the Lord Advocate's functions where the office of Lord Advocate is vacant, the Lord Advocate is unable to act owing to absence or illness, or the Lord Advocate authorises the Solicitor General to act in any particular case."

Further detailed information as to the respective roles of the two officers can be found on the above website.

2. Criminal Justice System

It is the duty of the police to investigate criminal behaviour and hopefully gather enough evidence to bring the perpetrators to justice. Until 1986, the police had the responsibility to both investigate criminal activity and to prosecute defendants. As a result of the Prosecution of Offences Act 1985 a prosecution service independent of the police was established named the Crown Prosecution Service (CPS). This is a service applicable only to England and Wales and is headed by the

Director of Public Prosecutions, a post held since November 2008 by
Keir Starmer QC.

The service advises police on what charges may be appropriate
in light of the evidence held by the police and eventually deciding
whether to authorise a prosecution. The CPS operates a two-stage test.
The first stage is referred to as the evidential stage. Prosecutors "must
be satisfied that there is sufficient evidence to provide a realistic prospect of a conviction against each suspect on each charge." The second
element is known as the "Public Interest Stage." This is a balancing
exercise pitting the public interest factors in favour of proceeding to
trial against the public interest factors opposing such a decision. In
simple terms the more serious the offence or the alleged offender's
criminal record the more likely it is that it is in the public interest to go
ahead with the trial rather than deal with it out of court. The Code for
Crown Prosecutors identifies some 19 public interest factors in favour
of and 11 against prosecution. It should be remembered that the CPS
is also under an obligation to take into account the views of the victims
and/or their families. This centres on considering the *impact* that the
offence has had, but prosecutors are reminded that they must form an
overall view of the public interest and the victim's or family's view is
unlikely to be the decisive factor in deciding whether to take the case
to trial.[3]

Once the decision is taken to proceed to trial, whether in the
Magistrates' Court or Crown Court, the Crown Prosecution Service will
prepare the case and has the responsibility for prosecuting at the trial.
For journalists wishing to know more about how the Crown Prosecution
Service works please visit the *www.cps.gov.uk* website and access the
CPS Code for Crown Prosecutors; the latest version was published in
2010. This is a public document and can be freely accessed.

Scotland

In Scotland the responsibility for the prosecution of those involved in
criminal activity rests with the Crown Office and the Procurator Fiscal
Service. The Office also deals with complaints against the police. This
office is the sole prosecuting authority for Scotland. Scotland is divided
into 11 Procurator Fiscal areas in the same way that there are Crown
Prosecution Service Offices throughout England and Wales. As in
England and Wales the police carry out the initial investigation and
then submit an official report to the local Procurator Fiscal's Office.
After assessing the evidence a decision will be taken on public interest
grounds whether to take the case to trial but the final decision rests with
Crown Counsel.

It will be evident that the procedure is similar to that in England and
Wales. For more information visit the *www.copfs.gov.uk* website.

---

[3] The Code for Crown Prosecutors. February 2010. Section 4.

Criminal Justice Process

The criminal justice process provides extensive copy for our newspapers and also more than the occasional reference on our television and computer screens. Therefore every journalist and broadcaster needs to have a working knowledge of the courts from which the reports will emanate.

The court structure is hierarchical in the sense that the Supreme Court is at the pinnacle and the Magistrates' Courts at the bottom. It is also useful to subdivide the structure into the courts where the offences are tried and those that deal with appeals from the "lower" courts. The Magistrates' Courts are where the vast majority of "minor" offences are tried. It is estimated that some 95 per cent of all criminal cases are tried in the Magistrates' Courts of England and Wales.[4]

Magistrates' Court and Categorisation of Offences

The cases are usually heard by a panel of three magistrates supported by a legally qualified clerk to the court. Magistrates are referred to as Justices of the Peace (JP). They are volunteers from all walks of life and, as a consequence, do not receive payment although reasonable expenses can be claimed for travel and subsistence. Magistrates can be appointed from the age of 18 although this will be a relatively rare occurrence and have to retire at the age of 70. As members of a community they will sit in their local Magistrates' Court dealing primarily with criminal matters although there will be some civil work. (See the Civil Justice section of this chapter.)

Their duties include deciding whether a defendant is guilty and if so passing sentence. Magistrates have more or less exclusive jurisdiction to try and to determine **SUMMARY** offences. A *summary* offence is one that is regarded as relatively minor where on a finding of guilt the defendant cannot be sentenced to more than six months imprisonment or fined more than £5,000. In simple terms these are cases that are disposed of quickly and do not involve a jury. Examples are common assault, driving without insurance and drink driving.

All crimes in England and Wales fit into one of three categories. In addition to summary offences the criminal law recognises what are called **EITHER-WAY** offences and finally the most serious crimes are labelled **INDICTABLE** offences. *Indictable* offences are the most serious offences such as murder, rape and robbery, and may be tried only in the Crown Court where guilt or innocence will be determined by a jury.

Either-way offences are those that can be tried either in the Magistrates' Court or at Crown Court. The decision on whether the case should be heard in the Magistrates' Court or Crown Court will be determined at a "Mode of Trial" hearing. If the decision is that the case can be dealt with by the magistrates the defendant can decide not to accept the decision

---

[4] *www.hmcourt-service.gov.uk* (February 2011).

and opt for trial at the Crown Court. The sort of offences categorised as triable either-way include burglary, sexual assault, theft involving large amounts of money and fraud offences. The potential complexity of a case may also be a factor in deciding that the Crown Court is the appropriate venue.

Needless to say that what has just been stated is very much an overview of the current situation. There are numerous exceptions to the principles stated above. Some either-way offences MUST be tried in the Magistrates' Court; for example criminal damage where only low-value damage has resulted from the activities of the defendant. (See s.22 Magistrates' Courts Act 1980.)

The Magistrates' Courts Act 1980 decrees that some summary offences MAY be tried in the Crown Court. Other summary matters may be **sent** to the Crown Court for example when magistrates believe their sentencing powers are inadequate in the particular case. There are instances when some either-way offences are triable only on indictment. An example is a charge of trafficking a Class A drug where the accused has at least two previous convictions for such an offence. Another example is burglary of a dwelling house.

The crucial point to note is that journalists really don't need to be au fait with **all** the specific details of which courts try which cases. However a broad understanding of the criminal court structure and the categories of offences is necessary particularly when considering whether there any specific reporting restrictions in operation. (See Ch.7 on Reporting Restrictions.)[5]

The open justice principle applies generally to proceedings in the adult Magistrates' Court with certain exceptions. However please note that the youth court, which is the Magistrates' Court for young people under the age of 18, is covered by automatic reporting restrictions preventing any material being published that will identify the young defendant in criminal cases.

Crown Court

There are a number of basic duties undertaken by the Crown Courts in England and Wales.

Firstly, defendants charged with serious criminal offences are tried by judge and jury. Secondly, appeals from the Magistrates' Courts are heard by the Crown Court judges. Thirdly, sentences are imposed on defendants who have been tried in the Magistrates' Courts when the sentencing powers of that court are deemed inadequate.

The Crown Courts were established in 1971 and replaced the "old" system of Assizes. There are approximately 80 court centres across England and Wales. They are allocated to one of three categories. First-tier centres are visited by High Court Judges for Crown Court and High Court civil work. The second-tier centres are visited by High Court

---

[5] Detailed information is available from the Crown Prosecution Website: *www.cps.gov.uk*

judges for Crown Court criminal work only. The third-tier centres are not normally visited by High Court judges and handle Crown Court criminal work.

Offences tried in the Crown Court are sub-divided into three classes of seriousness. Class 1 offences are the most serious, for example murder, and are normally tried by a High Court judge. Class 2 offences, such as rape, are usually heard by a Circuit judge. Class 3 offences include all other offences such as burglary, grievous bodily harm and robbery, and these are normally tried by a Circuit judge or Recorder. It will be evident that the vast majority of cases heard in the Crown Court will be tried by Circuit judges with the occasional appearance of a High Court judge to try the Class 1 cases. Circuit judges are appointed to one of seven regions of England and Wales. Circuit judges must be lawyers who have had the right to appear in court as advocates for at least 10 years. The overwhelming majority of Circuit judges will have been barristers rather than solicitors in their professional careers before becoming members of the judiciary.

Circuit judges can be visually distinguished from High Court judges in court by the robes they wear. Circuit judges will wear a violet robe with a short wig and when hearing criminal cases will wear a red sash (tippet) over the left shoulder. A High Court judge presiding over a criminal trial at a Crown Court will wear a red robe (hence the nickname the Red Judges). From a journalist's viewpoint the crucial thing to remember is to give the judge in the case you are reporting the correct appellation. It is very unprofessional to refer to a High Court judge as "Judge" as this is the appellation given to Circuit judges. In effect you have instantly demoted the High Court judge. Conversely, while Circuit judges might be pleased to see their status elevated in a court report, a print journalist can hardly claim to be meeting the requirements of the first clause of the Press Complaints Commission Editors' Code of Practice.[6] So High Court judges are referred to as Mr (Mrs) Justice . . . or simply Justice.

Juries

In a criminal trial at the Crown Court the decision on whether the defendant is found guilty or acquitted rests with the jury. Juries are the arbiters of fact and must make their decision based upon the evidence presented in court. In a criminal trial the burden of proof rests upon the prosecution. The defendant is entitled to be acquitted if the prosecution cannot convince the jury that it has proved the case beyond all reasonable doubt. It will be explained later in the book why juries are a relative "no-go" area for journalists and broadcasters. Suffice at this stage to say that s.8 of the Contempt of Court Act 1981 makes it a criminal offence to do anything that breaches the confidentiality of the jury's deliberations. Specifically it is an offence to:

[6] Clause 1: Accuracy: "The press must take care not to publish inaccurate, misleading or distorted information . . ."

"... obtain, disclose or solicit any particulars of statements made, opinions expressed, arguments advanced or votes cast by members of the jury in the course of their deliberations in any legal proceedings."

The Times newspaper was recently fined £15,000 for breaching this provision when deliberately publishing the concerns expressed by the foreman of the jury some time after a manslaughter case had concluded. The foreman of the jury was fined £500. [7]

Jurors are chosen from the electoral roll and must be aged between 18 and 70. The Juries Act 1974 establishes the criteria for jury service and specifically excludes those suffering from a mental disorder or subject to a community treatment order.[8] This restriction has been the subject of much criticism given that it is thought that some 40 per cent of the UK population have suffered some form of mental illness. A spokesperson for the Criminal Bar Association stated:

"Trial by jury is a vital component of our criminal justice system and, in order to work at its best, juries should represent a cross-section of society ... it is inappropriate to impose a blanket ban that prevents anyone with a history of mental illness from sitting on a jury without assessment of their capacity."[9]

At the time of writing the Ministry of Justice has ruled out any revision to the rule.

The Trial

It is most unlikely that you will attend court every day of a major trial but that of course may depend on the nature of the crime or the identity of the defendant or both. Media representation was ever present at the trial of Ian Huntley and Maxine Carr and long periods can be spent covering terrorism trials. Broadcasters will be familiar with the routine of watching a trial for a couple of hours and then engaging in a live two-way from outside the court building on the national lunchtime news programmes. Jury deliberations in the vast majority of cases are concluded fairly quickly but in some cases, often involving a number of defendants, the decision-making can be complex and time consuming. The UK record for jury deliberation was set in April 2007 by the jury trying the so-called "Fertiliser Bomb Plot" case when seven men were accused of conspiracy to cause explosions with intent to endanger life. The jury deliberated for 27 days, eventually convicting five of the seven defendants. [10]

Reporting needs to be accurate and succinct and therefore an understanding of the criminal trial process is important.

Before entering the court always check the screens outside the court

---

[7] *Attorney General v Seckerson & Times Newspapers* [2009] EWHC 1023 (Admin).
[8] Mental Health Act 2007.
[9] Quoted in the Observer January 10, 2010.
[10] *R v Khyam & Others* [2007].

which are likely to indicate any reporting restrictions in place. If so find out from the court administrators, listings officer or usher exactly what they are. Also remember that the principle of open justice means that you are entitled to report on anything said in court in the presence of the jury. On occasions the judge may request that the jury leaves the court while legal argument is conducted. This will often relate to whether or not certain evidence is admissible at the trial. Normally you will not be permitted to report on what you hear unless permission is given. When the jury is recalled you will then be able to report on any comments the judge makes to the jury relating to what had taken place.

All participants in a trial, members of the public and of course journalists are meant to show due respect to the court. One issue that is currently under review is whether or not to allow the use of live text-based communication for the purposes of fair and accurate reporting. Rather than reporters having to use shorthand and then return to the office with their notes it will clearly assist the "rolling news" agenda if reporters and broadcasters are allowed to communicate directly from court to their respective newsrooms or direct to the public.

In December 2010 the Lord Chief Justice addressed the question by publishing an Interim Practice Guidance concerning this issue. The guidance relates to court proceedings which are open to the public and to those parts of the proceedings which are not subject to reporting restrictions.

Live text-based communications include mobile email, social media including Twitter and internet-enabled laptops. The Lord Chief Justice has indicated that a consultation exercise relating to such communications being allowed from courts will take place during 2011. Pending the outcome of the consultation the guidance issued on December 20, 2010 will apply. Reporters intending to use live text-based communication should bear in mind the existing restrictions to be found in the Contempt of Court Act 1981. (See Ch.4 and s.41 of the Criminal Justice Act 1925 which prohibits the taking of photographs in court.)

The interim guidance notes a number of "general principles." The main one is the acknowledgement that:

"a fundamental aspect of the proper administration of justice is the principle of open justice and that fair and accurate reporting of court proceedings forms part of that principle. It reminds us that the prohibition on photography in court is absolute. There is no judicial discretion to suspend or dispense with that element of the 1925 Act. Sound recordings are also prohibited UNLESS the court permits such equipment to be used in which case any recording will be used on as an aide memoire i.e. as a substitute for a short or long hand note. It will be obvious that the ability to check a recording should in theory at least lead to greater accuracy in reporting the trial".[11]

---

[11] *Reporting Restrictions in the Criminal Courts*. October 2009. Joint publication by the Judicial Studies Board, Newspaper Society, Society of Editors and Times Newspapers Ltd. See cl.5.3.

This desire for fair and accurate reporting underpins the current approach contained in the guidance. The paramount question in deciding whether or not to allow text-based reporting is whether it may interfere with the proper administration of justice. The perceived danger is that witnesses who have yet to give evidence may be informed of what has already happened in court or reference to inadmissible evidence may be placed on Twitter. The approach seems to be that judges will consider requests on a case-by-case basis. One option is that the judge may limit the use of such text-based communication to ". . . representatives of the media for journalistic purposes but to disallow its use by the wider public in court."

There is also the remote possibility that the number of devices in use at any one time could interfere with the court's electronic sound recording equipment. In February 2011 the Supreme Court announced that it was to permit text-based communication from the court. This is a far less controversial development as there are no witnesses or jurors involved in cases that reach the Supreme Court.

So having obtained permission to use your iPhone or Blackberry in court and having checked whether there are reporting restrictions in place, you are ready for the commencement of the trial. The charges will be read to the defendant and these should be noted carefully as some of the "counts" may have been dropped since the pre-trial hearings for example in the Magistrates' Court. Once the defendant pleads not guilty the trial will commence. As might be expected it is for the prosecution to outline the facts of the case against the defendant. Prosecuting counsel (note the spelling!) will then call witnesses whose evidence is designed to support the prosecution case. Prosecution witnesses will then be cross-examined by defence counsel. It is these early encounters that are usually reported by the media. Whether the case attracts the ongoing support of the media will depend on the local or national interest in the case.

It is always possible that after the prosecution evidence has been completed defence counsel could submit that the prosecution case is so weak that there is "no case to answer." If the judge agrees that is the end of the matter and a formal not guilty verdict is recorded.

If the case is permitted to continue then defence counsel will call witnesses to support the defence argument. They in turn may be cross-examined by the counsel for the prosecution. Each side will know who is being called as a witness as this information has to be disclosed in advance of the trial. The defendant can remain silent and need not give evidence. However it is open for the prosecution to draw this fact to the attention of the jury but it must not be suggested that the failure to take the stand is an admission of guilt.

The penultimate part of the trial process involves counsel making their closing statements to the jury outlining reasons why the jury ought to regard their arguments the stronger and asking for a verdict of guilty or acquittal in the case of defence counsel.

Finally the judge must sum up the evidence, direct the jury on the law in respect of the charge or charges against the defendant and remind the jury of the standard of proof. The jury should only return a guilty verdict if the case is proved to its satisfaction beyond all reasonable doubt.

The hope is that a jury will return a unanimous verdict but the judge may direct the jury that a majority verdict of either 11–1 or 10–2 is acceptable if it appears after lengthy deliberation (of at least two hours and 10 minutes) that a unanimous verdict is going to prove impossible.

If the jury acquits the defendant then he or she simply walks free from the court. If a guilty verdict is returned then the sentencing phase commences. The judge will reveal whether the defendant has any previous convictions and will also ask the defence counsel to make a plea in mitigation. Sentencing may be postponed while reports are made on the defendant. Go into any Crown Court and you will see on the daily lists a number of short sentencing hearings where the decision has been postponed from the date of conviction.

When reporting on sentencing it is vitally important to ensure that the details of the sentence are correct. An obvious example is where the court has imposed a sentence of imprisonment but has suspended that sentence for a period of say 18 months. In some circumstances a defendant may have been found guilty of more than one offence. The judge will pass sentence for each offence and then determine whether the sentences should run *concurrently* or *consecutively*. In the former case the defendant stays in prison for the length of time of the longest sentence. In the latter the sentences are totalled and the defendant will serve the total less any time already spent on remand and deducted for good behaviour.

Judges are occasionally severely criticised by the press for imposing what the public believes is an unduly lenient sentence. Judges though have limited discretion when it comes to sentencing in the majority of cases. In order to "promote a clear, fair and consistent approach to sentencing" the government has established a Sentencing Council[12] under the Chairmanship of Lord Justice Levesen who was appointed to the position in April 2010.

Journalists and broadcasters wishing to gain a broader understanding of how the sentencing process works should consult the sentencing guidelines available to download from *www.sentencingcouncil.org.uk.* At the time of writing there are 19 "definitive" guidelines available to download covering all the major crimes. For example when sentencing for *theft or burglary* from a building other than a dwelling the guidelines outline seven stages in the decision-making process.

I. Identify the appropriate starting point.
II. Consider relevant aggravating factors, both general and those specific to the type of offence. (This element may of course result in a sentence higher than the suggested starting point.)

---

[12] Established under the Coroners and Justice Act 2009.

III.   Consider mitigating factors and personal mitigation.
IV.   Reduction for a guilty plea. (See the Council's Guideline-*Reduction in Sentence for a Guilty Plea* which was revised in July 2007.)
V.   Consideration of ancillary orders.
VI.   The totality principle. (This means that the judge should "review the total sentence to ensure that it is proportionate to the offending behaviour and properly balanced".)
VII.   Reasons. (If the judge imposes a sentence that is outside the range provided or of a different type then reasons need to be given for the decision.)

An extremely valuable inclusion in the list of guidelines is the one relating to the Magistrates' Court covering virtually every offence tried in these courts. This is a valuable document not only because it explains the sentences available for the crimes but also states at the outset whether the offence is one that can only be tried summarily or whether it is an either-way offence.

Please note that the maximum sentence for any particular offence is usually set out in the relevant legislation. For example the Theft Act 1968 states that the maximum sentence for theft shall be seven years. In the case of causing death by dangerous driving the Road Traffic Act 1988 makes the maximum sentence fourteen years. In the case of murder, which is a common law offence, there is a mandatory sentence of life imprisonment. The judge however will set a minimum term that the offender must serve before consideration for release by the Parole Board. Reference should be made to Sch.21 of the Criminal Justice Act 2003 which sets out examples of the different types of cases and the starting point which would usually be applied. For extremely serious offences where the offender is over the age of 21 a whole life tariff is deemed to be appropriate, for example, where the offender is a serial killer. Since the whole life tariff was introduced in 1983 there have been approximately 70 offenders issued with such sentences.[13]

Reference was made at V above to ancillary orders. These are orders made in addition to the sentence often aimed at redressing the harm caused by the offender.

An obvious example is a compensation order or an anti-social behaviour order. In certain circumstances an ancillary order MUST be made as, for example, when a person is convicted of causing death by dangerous driving then a driving disqualification of a minimum of two years must be imposed. In practice the disqualification period is often higher.

---

[13] Sentencing Guidelines: Mandatory Life Sentences.

Appeals

From the Crown Court

If an appellant is appealing against conviction it is usually on the grounds that the conviction is "unsafe." This could be on the basis that the judge summed up the law incorrectly and therefore the jury came to its decision having taken account of the wrong legal principles. Alternatively it could be alleged there has been some discrepancy during the trial, for example, that the judge incorrectly ruled certain evidence inadmissible.

Alternatively the appeal could be against the sentence imposed by the judge. Usually this will be an allegation that the judge has misinterpreted the Sentencing Council's Guidelines in respect of the particular crime and has imposed a too severe sentence. In the case of co-defendants one may be given a lesser sentence than the other even though they were each part of a joint enterprise in carrying out the crime for which they have been convicted.

From a media viewpoint it must be remembered that if the Court of Appeal (Criminal Division) agrees to accept the appeal this does NOT involve a rehearing of the case. There is no jury and it is rare for there to be any witnesses called. However if evidence is given it is usually from expert witnesses in the form of medical specialists or forensic experts.

An appeal against conviction will normally be heard by three judges; a Lord/Lady Justice of Appeal and two High Court judges. If reporting from the Appeal Court please ensure that you use the correct appellation for the judges. Court of Appeal judges are referred to as Lord Justice or Lady Justice (Surname). A list of all the judges sitting in the Court of Appeal is available on the *www.judiciary.gov.uk* website. There are currently four female and more than thirty male members of the court. A sentencing appeal can be heard by two judges.

On occasions an important point of law may be argued before the court and in those circumstances five judges may hear the appeal. A recent example is *R. v Gnango* [2010] EWCA 1691, a case dealing with murder and the concept of a joint enterprise. An innocent passer-by had been shot and killed when the appellant and another man had been involved in a "shoot-out" in a car park. The appellant had not fired the fatal shot. His conviction for murder was quashed by the Court of Appeal (Criminal Division).

Four Lord Justices, Thomas, Hooper, Hughes and Gross, sitting with Mr Justice Hedley decided the appeal. At the time of writing this case may well be subject to a further appeal to the Supreme Court given that the current law on criminal joint enterprises needs to be clarified.

Supreme Court

Appeals from decisions of the Court of Appeal go to the Supreme Court. Until September 30, 2009 the final appeal court was the House of Lords sitting in its judicial capacity. That court is now no longer in existence and the new Supreme Court started hearing cases on October 1, 2009. There are currently eleven members of the court, ten male and one female, Baroness Hale of Richmond. The senior judge is Lord Phillips of Worth Matravers. This court hears a small number of cases each year when points of law of general public importance need to be decided. The panel is usually constituted of five judges although in extremely important cases seven and even nine judges may hear the case.[14] The Supreme Court also hears appeals against decisions that originated in the Magistrates' Court and went on appeal to the High Court (Queens Bench Division).

Criminal Cases Review Commission

The Criminal Cases Review Commission is an independent body established in 1997 as a result of the Criminal Appeal Act 1995. Its job is to review possible miscarriages of justice and where appropriate refer such cases to the Court of Appeal. Its main aim is to "... *enhance public confidence in the criminal justice system and to give hope and to bring justice to those wrongly convicted* . . ."[15] All those intending to pursue a career in the media need to know a little about this process. Some high-profile cases have attracted a large measure of public interest. For example, the quashing in 2003 of Sally Clark's conviction for the murder of two of her children received enormous publicity. One of the most notorious criminal law convictions for murder was that of Derek Bentley hanged for the murder of a police officer in January 1953. The problem in this case was that Bentley did not fire the gun that killed the police officer. That act was carried out by Christopher Craig but, as a juvenile, he escaped the gallows. Bentley, his co-defendant, was 19 and pleas for clemency failed. In 1997, 44 years after his death his case was referred by the Criminal Cases Review Commission to the Court of Appeal and his conviction quashed.

The work of the Criminal Cases Review Committee is often of interest to journalists because on occasions the media has campaigned on behalf of families of defendants who have firmly believed that a miscarriage of justice has been perpetrated. Perhaps the most famous was the BBC's *Rough Justice* programme that ran for 27 years until 2007. The series was credited with contributing to the creation of the Criminal Cases Review Commission.

Appeals from Magistrates' Courts

Those reporting on cases in the Magistrates' Court should note that if a defendant pleads guilty there can be an appeal only against *sentence* not conviction.

In cases where the defendant has been found guilty any appeal must be by way of re-hearing in the Crown Court. The defendant has 21 days from conviction to lodge a notice of appeal. Please note that just

---

[14] See *A & Others v Secretary of State for the Home Department* [2004] UKHL 56.
[15] *www.ccrc.gov.uk*

because the appeal is heard in the Crown Court it does NOT mean that a jury will be involved. The case will be determined by a Crown Court judge (Circuit judge) usually sitting with two magistrates. If the appeal is dismissed then the original conviction remains and it is possible that the sentence could be increased. It follows that appeals against sentence only will be less time-consuming than an appeal against conviction. In this case the prosecutor will outline the facts of the offence for which the defendant has been found guilty and also detail any previous convictions. The defendant, or his legal representative, will then try to make the most persuasive case possible to persuade the judge that the sentence was too harsh.

Case Stated

In the same way that an appeal from the Crown Court can be taken to the *Court of Appeal* (*Criminal Division*) on the basis that the particular legal principles have been incorrectly explained to the jury a case can be made that an opinion of the *High Court* is needed on a question of law. This is referred to as the "case stated" process and demands that the magistrate or district judge states a case upon which the opinion of the High Court will be sought. This procedure is also available for the Crown Court to state a case for the High Court to consider.[16]

Criminal Offences

Before moving away from criminal law procedures mention must be made of the types of crime that journalists are most likely to routinely report. The crucial point to remember is to be accurate when describing the crime for which the defendant is facing trial. Confusion can be caused to those reading newspaper reports or hearing broadcasts if the details of an offence are not stated correctly. The most obvious examples relate to "theft" offences. The overwhelming majority of "serious" crimes require two elements to be proved by the prosecution before there can be a conviction. The term "actus reus" is used to refer to that part of the definition of an offence that refers to the act or omission that the criminal law is aimed at preventing. To simply bring about the "actus reus" of an offence is not enough to establish guilt. The act or omission must be accompanied by a state of mind on the part of the defendant that would indicate that his or her actions were carried out intentionally or recklessly. Occasionally an act or omission perpetrated as a result of grossly negligent behaviour will be enough to secure a conviction. The major example of this is the crime of manslaughter. The term used to refer to the state of mind of the accused at the time of carrying out the offence is "mens rea".

---

[16] For both courts see Pt. 64 of Criminal Procedure Rules 2010 which came into force on April 5, 2010.

Theft/Robbery/Burglary

Theft

The prosecution in a theft case must prove five things. From the *actus reus* viewpoint there must have been an *appropriation*[17] of *property*[18] *belonging to another*.[19] It may seem a simple task to prove these elements but in practice it may prove very difficult. If there are potentially difficulties surrounding proof of the elements of the *actus reus* then there are corresponding problems associated with proving the *mens rea* of theft. The Theft Act 1968 requires two elements to be proved. Firstly, that the defendant must have acted with the *intention to permanently deprive*[20] the other of the property. Secondly, that when doing so he must have been acting *dishonestly*.[21]

Robbery

When reporting on an apparent theft if force or the threat of force is used in order to steal then the event should NOT be described as *theft* but as a *robbery*. Section 8 of the Theft Act 1968 provides the definition of robbery:

> (1) A person is guilty of robbery if he steals, and immediately before or at the time of doing so, and in order to do so, he uses force on any person or puts or seeks to put any person in fear of being then and there subjected to force.[22]

Thus, for example, if a person takes a handbag from a table and in order to escape then knocks over the owner this would not be robbery as the force was used after, not before or during, the theft. Depending on the nature of any injuries suffered by the owner there may also be additional charges relating to assault or causing bodily harm to the victim.

Burglary

Property removed from a building without lawful authority may seem like theft but is more than likely to amount to burglary providing the person who removes the property is a trespasser. Section 9 of the Theft Act 1968 provides the legal context for the offence of burglary:

> (1) A person is guilty of burglary if—
>
>> (a) he enters a *building or part of a building* as a *trespasser* and with *intent* to commit any such offence as is mentioned in subsection (2) below; or

---

[17] See s.3 of the Theft Act 1968 for the statutory definition of the word "appropriation."
[18] See s.4 of the Theft Act 1968 for the statutory definition of "property."
[19] See s.5 of the Theft Act 1968 for the statutory definition of "belonging to another."
[20] See s.6 of the Theft Act 1968 for the statutory definition of "intention to permanently deprive."
[21] See s.2 of the Theft Act 1968 for guidance on when a person does not act dishonestly.
[22] See s.8 Theft Act 1968.

(b) having entered any building or part of a building as a trespasser he steals or attempts to steal anything in the building or that part of it or inflicts or attempts to inflict on any person therein grievous bodily harm.

(2) The offences referred to in subsection (1)(a) above are offences of stealing anything in the building or part of a building in question, of inflicting on any person therein any grievous bodily harm therein, and of doing unlawful damage to the building or anything therein.[23]

While there may be evidential and legal difficulties proving who is or is not a trespasser it will be appreciated that terms such as *theft* and *robbery* are inappropriate to describe what happens when property is entered without permission and items removed without authority. Clearly the crime of burglary may embrace theft but in practice the charge of burglary will always be more appropriate when a dwelling is entered without authority for the purposes of stealing. However if there are doubts about whether or not the prosecution can establish that the "taker" was a trespasser, a charge of theft may be sanctioned by the Crown Prosecution Service.

Please note that there is a second offence relating to burglary, that of Aggravated Burglary found in the Theft Act 1968. A person is guilty of this offence if he commits burglary and "... *at the time has with him any firearm or imitation firearm, any weapon of offence, or any explosive*".[24]

The Theft Act 1978 created additional offences that might on the surface look like the offence of theft but for legal reasons do not necessarily amount to the crime. The most obvious example is the crime of Making off Without Payment.[25] This offence is committed when a person "... *knowing that payment on the spot for goods supplied or service done is required or expected of him, dishonestly makes off without having paid ... and with the intent to avoid payment of the amount due ...*"

A most obvious example is when a person fills the car at a self service petrol pump and then races away without making payment. In fact many garage forecourts contain notices warning customers that they should not proceed to draw petrol unless they have the means to make payment.

It follows that great care needs to be exercised when reporting on such "theft related" offences and that the correct name for each offence is used in any report.

Harm to the Person

Given the range of offences that relate to harm perpetrated against the person it is hardly surprising if some confusion may be caused when reporting on these offences.

---

[23] See s.9 Theft Act 1968.
[24] See s.10 Theft Act 1968.
[25] See s.3 Theft Act 1978.

Homicide

The term homicide refers to the most serious offences against the person.

Murder

In very simple terms murder relates to the killing of a human being (the *actus reus*) by a person or persons who at that time have the requisite mental element (the *mens rea*) required by law. This latter element can be one of three elements. Firstly, an intent to kill, secondly, an intent to cause really serious harm and thirdly the intent to carry out an act or omission knowing the consequence is virtually certain to result in death. The so called "specific intent" required to be proved to establish murder can be very difficult to prove and discussion of this element goes beyond the scope of this book.

Manslaughter

Manslaughter is the word used to describe an act or omission that has caused death but the defendant did not possess the mental element needed to proceed with a charge of murder. Manslaughter has to be considered from two perspectives. The term *involuntary manslaughter* refers to this element. For example the defendant has acted recklessly— he took an unjustified risk— and that action has resulted in the death of another. In simple terms death was not intended or desired but it would have been foreseeable if the defendant had turned his mind to thinking about the consequences of his actions.

The Court of Appeal said in 2003 ". . . in cases of involuntary manslaughter the offender has not intended to either kill or even to cause really serious bodily harm to his victim."[26] This differs from the crime of *voluntary manslaughter* where the defendant admits he had the intent required for murder to be proved but pleads the existence of circumstances that should reduce any conviction to one of manslaughter. The partial defences of Diminished Responsibility, Provocation and Suicide Pact were originally to be found in the Homicide Act 1957.[27] Diminished responsibility referred to a defendant who at the time of the killing was suffering from an *abnormality of mind* and that substantially impaired his mental responsibility for his acts and omissions. Please note that abnormality of mind was a different legal concept from insanity. For example the defendant still had reasoning powers but suffered from arrested or retarded development of mind.

The limits of the provocation defence were listed at s.3 of the Homicide Act and centred on a defendant losing self control as a result of being provoked by things said or things done or by both together. It was then to be left to the jury to decide whether in all the circumstances a reasonable man would have reacted in the same way as the defendant resulting in death.

[26] *Regina v Parnham* [2003] EWCA Crim 416 at para.14 per Jackson J.
[27] See s.2-4 Homicide Act 1957.

However, the Coroners and Justice Act 2009 has updated the two defences to take into account decisions of courts over the past 50 years. Section 2 of the Homicide Act has been amended in the following way:

(1) A person who kills or is a party to the killing of another is not to be convicted of murder if D was suffering from an abnormality of mental functioning which—

   (a) arose from a recognised medical condition,
   (b) substantially impaired D's ability to do one or more of the things mentioned in subsection 1(A) and
   (c) provides an explanation for D's acts and omissions in doing or being a party to a killing.

1(A) Those things are

   (a) to understand the nature of D's conduct;
   (b) to form a rational judgment;
   (c) to exercise self control.[28]

Section 2 of the Homicide Act is amended but s.3 has been abolished. As a result of s.54 of the 2009 Act the defence of *provocation* no longer exists and has been replaced by the following provision—

Partial Defence to Murder: Loss of Control

(1) Where a person (D) kills or is a party to the killing of another, D is not to be convicted of murder if—

   (a) D's acts and omissions in doing or being a party to the killing resulted from D's loss of self-control,
   (b) the loss of self-control had a qualifying trigger, and
   (c) a person of D's sex and age, with a normal degree of tolerance and self-restraint and in the circumstances of D, might have reacted in the same or in a similar way to D.[29]

This partial defence will not apply if D's actions have been motivated by the desire for revenge.

Reference is made to the "qualifying trigger" which covers a range of circumstances including the defendant's fear of serious violence against him or things done or said that caused him to have a justifiable sense of being seriously wronged. It is worth noting though that "the fact that a thing done or said constituted sexual infidelity must be disregarded".[30]

---

[28] See s.52 of the Coroners and Justice Act 2009.
[29] See s.54 of the Coroners and Justice Act 2009 the provisions of which came into force on October 4, 2010, along with the s.52 provision relating to Diminished Responsibility.
[30] See s.55 of the Coroners and Justice Act 2009.

Suicide Pact

If two people agree to commit suicide and one survives after helping the other to die then liability will be for manslaughter even though the defendant had an intention to bring about the death of the other and did in fact achieve that objective.

Corporate Manslaughter

As a final comment on manslaughter it is worth noting that the law was expanded in April 2008 with the coming into force of the Corporate Manslaughter and Corporate Homicide Act 2007. The Ministry of Justice describes the purpose of the legislation in the following way:

> "*The Act sets out a new offence for convicting an organisation where a gross failure in the way activities were managed or organised results in a person's death. This will apply to a wide range of organisations across the public and private sectors.*"[31]

So the focus is on an organisation and the way it is managed. At the heart of the offence is proof beyond all reasonable doubt that a gross breach of a duty of care owed to the victim has occurred and this in turn has resulted in death. A substantial failure within the organisation must have been at a senior level and this embraces all those who make significant decisions about the way the organisation operates.

There will need to be a high degree of precision when reporting on this offence because the facts may also lead to charges under health and safety legislation and under the existing law of manslaughter—a charge of gross negligence manslaughter being the most likely. To date cases centring on this legislation have been few and far between.

Causing harm

The major piece of legislation which criminalises this type of behaviour is the Offences Against the Person Act 1861. The definition of the most serious of the crimes is to be found at s.18 which makes it an offence to cause grievous bodily harm with intent to do so. The maximum punishment is life imprisonment. Section 20 created the offence of unlawfully and maliciously wounding or inflicting grievous bodily harm. Here it will be noted that no intent is required and this is the key feature that differentiates it from the s.18 offence. Section 47 is the offence of assault occasioning actual bodily harm. The final offence is that of common assault or battery.[32] Where very minor injuries are caused then this will be the appropriate offence to charge and will be tried in the Magistrates' Court.

---

[31] Ministry of Justice: Understanding the Corporate Manslaughter and Corporate Homicide Act 2007. *www.justice.gov.uk*
[32] See s.39 of the Criminal Justice Act 1988.

Sexual Offences

The existing law relating to sexual offences was consolidated in the Sexual Offences Act 2003 and the opportunity was taken to introduce new provisions, for example, dealing with people trafficking for sexual purposes and offences involving a breach of trust which results in sexual activity with a child. The crucial point to remember when reporting is that the victim of all offences of a sexual nature, including non-contact offences, is entitled to lifelong anonymity and nothing should be published that will result in identification.

Motoring Offences

There is a plethora of offences aimed at those who drive carelessly to those who cause death by dangerous driving. A conviction for *careless driving* will ensue if the prosecution can prove that the driving fell below the standard expected of a reasonably competent driver taking into account all of the circumstances.

Dangerous driving shares many of the characteristics of the offence of careless driving. However the distinguishing feature will be whether the careful competent driver would regard the driving as dangerous. This could include driving at high speed in speed restricted areas and generally failing to comply with road traffic requirements. The consequences can be serious. On conviction a court must disqualify the driver for at least 12 months unless there are exceptional personal circumstances making such a penalty unjust.

Causing death by dangerous driving is the most serious motoring offence and this is reflected in the fact that it can be tried only on indictment. The maximum sentence was increased from 10 years to 14 years in February 2007.[33] There is a minimum disqualification period of two years.

Drink driving. It is an offence to attempt to drive or be in charge of a motor vehicle while over the legal limit. For this offence the legal limits are:

i)   35 micrograms per 100 millilitres of breath;
ii)   80 milligrams per 100 millilitres of blood; or
iii)   107 milligrams per 100 millilitres of urine.

Media representatives should note the offence of *being unfit to drive through drink or drugs* and make a mental note not to confuse the two offences. In the case of the latter offence this may be proved even though the defendant's alcohol levels are within the legal limits. The

[33] S.285 Criminal Justice Act 2003.

offence also covers people who are in charge of a vehicle in such a condition even though they are not actually driving the vehicle.

Taking Without the Owner's Consent (TWOC). If someone takes a vehicle without the owner's consent then theft may seem the appropriate offence to charge. In many cases this will be true providing the Crown Prosecution Service accepts that the intention to permanently deprive the owner of the vehicle can be proved. However with many TWOC cases the perpetrator requires the vehicle for only a short period and therefore the *mens rea* may be impossible to prove. In such circumstances the offence of taking without the owner's consent will be the fallback charge.[34]

If the vehicle is taken without consent and is driven dangerously, or injury or damage is caused while being driven dangerously, or an accident occurs owing to the driving of the vehicle, then the offence of *Aggravated Vehicle-Taking* is committed. This is subject to the proviso that the person taking the vehicle unlawfully was actually in or on the vehicle or in the immediate vicinity when the accident or damage occurred.[35]

3. Civil Justice System

Whereas the criminal justice system involves interaction between the state and the individual, the civil justice system exists to resolve disputes between people, companies and other organisations. If a person "sues" or is "sued" then the legal action will take place in the civil courts. Usually this means the County Court and the High Court. Most reporters will spend relatively little time in the County Courts simply because the majority of disputes between citizens have little or no public interest component.

County Courts
The County Courts will deal with claims for personal injury, breach of contract, debt repayment, bankruptcy, insolvency and recovery of land matters. Disputes over wills and trusts where the fund or estate does not exceed £30,000 can be settled in this court. The *small claims* procedure is also available through the County Courts where the sums claimed are relatively small.

There are also family cases heard in the County Courts of which there are 216 in England and Wales. Undefended divorce petitions are processed through these courts. Cases involving disputes over children as a result of divorce proceedings or where a local authority may be

---

[34] See s.12 Theft Act 1968.
[35] See s.12A Theft Act 1968.

considering adoption proceedings are heard in these courts. The family justice system has been labouring under allegations that it lacks transparency and organisations such as Families need Fathers have done much to bring the issue to the attention of government.[36]

Family Justice
The government is undertaking a review of the family justice system. The need for such a review is based on the rising volume and duration of cases which carries with it a cost to the state of more than £800 million per annum. The review, which is regarded as a "root and branch" exercise, aims to produce recommendations that will allow families to reach "easy, simple and efficient agreements which are in the best interest of children whilst protecting children and vulnerable adults from risk of harm."[37] It is expected that the review panel's final report will be published in autumn 2011.

The family justice system has been largely ignored by the media mainly because of the legal restrictions imposed by the Administration of Justice Act 1960 and the Children Act 1989. The fact that judges imposed reporting restrictions on the media in respect of the "private law" cases meant it was often impossible to give sufficient detail about a case to make it intelligible to the public. The last government sought to present a more media friendly environment when in April 2009 it announced that accredited media would be able to attend all levels of family courts thus removing ". . . the inconsistency of access between magistrates' courts, and the county and high courts."[38]

The government attempted to fulfil its promise by introducing legislation immediately prior to Parliament being dissolved in May 2010. Part II of the Children, Schools and Families Act 2010 deals with the reporting by authorised press representatives of Family Proceedings. Given that the legislation was meant to provide a means of ensuring greater transparency in family court reporting there seems to have been remarkably little support for the provisions. In October 2010 the new coalition government announced that the provisions of the Act would not be implemented until the family law review panel's findings are published in late 2011. Sir Nicholas Wall, the President of the Family Division of the High Court, is on record as saying that the legislation ". . . is not popular with the press, it's not popular with the judges and it's not popular . . . with most litigants."[39] The major difficulty from the media's viewpoint is that, if implemented, journalists will still be prevented from naming virtually anyone appearing in a family proceedings case.

---

[36] *www.fnf.org.uk*
[37] *www.justice.gov.uk/reviews/family-justice*
[38] *www.justice.gov.uk/news*
[39] *Law in Action*: BBC Radio 4. October 19, 2010.

High Court

The High Court comprises three divisions: Queen's Bench; Chancery and Family. High Court judges are allocated to one of three divisions and they deal with differing categories of work. There are currently 73 judges in the Queen's Bench Division, 18 in Chancery and 19 in the Family Division. [40]

The Queen's Bench Division has a series of specialist courts within it. These are the Divisional Court, the Admiralty Court, the Commercial Court and the Technology and Construction Court. Excluding the work of these specialist courts, the Queen's Bench Division concentrates on adjudicating upon claims that seek damages for personal injury, negligence, breach of contract and defamation. Actions for non-payment of debt and recovery of land or property are also determined in the Queen's Bench Division.

The "core" business of the Chancery Division is the resolution of disputes involving property including intellectual property, insolvency and bankruptcy. While there may be some overlap with the Queen's Bench Division regarding property disputes, the main "property" business is carried out in the Chancery Division. Most of the Chancery business is dealt with in London but with assistance from eight provincial High Court centres.

The Family Division of the High Court deals with a range of both contentious and non-contentious business relating to family matters including probate. The Divisional Court of the Family Division hears appeals from the County Courts and Magistrates' Courts on matters connected with family proceedings.

Reporting on Civil Justice

There are a number of straightforward requirements with which every journalist needs to comply when reporting from the civil as opposed to the criminal courts.

Terminology

The simple maxim is to avoid using "criminal" terminology when reporting on civil matters. So for example the defendant who loses a defamation action should not be described as being found *"guilty* of defamation" even though a jury may have been involved in reaching a verdict in favour of the claimant. In civil cases litigants are not *prosecuted*—no-one is *charged* in respect of a civil claim.

At the outcome of a civil trial one party will often be awarded financial compensation which is referred to as *damages*.

So for example it is correct to write that "the claimant was awarded £25,000 in damages against the defendant" not "the defendant was fined £25,000." Reference might also be made to the issue of costs. The usual

---

[40] Accurate as at February 14, 2011. Figures obtained from *www.judiciary.gov.uk*

rule is that the defeated party pays the costs on top of any damages that may be awarded. Costs can easily escalate and the matter has recently been exercising the minds of the judiciary and the government. If one takes by way of example the case of *Campbell v Mirror Group Newspapers* [2004].[41] The supermodel Naomi Campbell won £3,500 in damages from the *Daily Mirror* after it published photographs taken surreptitiously of her exiting from a branch of Narcotics Anonymous. The case commenced in 2002 in the High Court, then went to the Court of Appeal and finally to the House of Lords. The claimant was funded despite her apparent great wealth on a conditional fee arrangement. In essence this means that in return for taking the risk of losing a case lawyers will be allowed to claim up to 100 per cent in addition to their normal fees. This is referred to as the *success fee*. The costs in the Campbell case were in the order of £1,000,000.

The case also spawned two other high profile cases relating to costs, the most recent in the European Court of Human Rights.[42] The newspaper argued that the "success fee regime" contravened art.10 of the European Convention on Human Rights in that it potentially inhibited the media from fully exercising its right to freedom of expression. In simple terms the possibility of having to pay such huge costs was a deterrent to publishing controversial stories where a person's privacy might be breached. It is also pertinent to note that the law of the misuse of private information is still developing and this is an additional deterrent to publishing. The European Court of Human Rights, while accepting that Ms Campbell's "privacy" rights had been breached, nevertheless accepted that the costs regime was contrary to art.10. The government is currently considering the ramifications of this judgment and has pledged to reform the conditional fee arrangements which apply to a range of civil actions, not just those affecting the media.

At the time of writing *Times Newspapers* is engaged as defendant in a defamation action brought by Gary Flood, a detective in the Metropolitan Police. The defendants have recently lost in the Court of Appeal[43] and would like to take the case to the Supreme Court. In an unusual step the Supreme Court has indicated it is prepared to hear the case providing that an assurance is given that, irrespective of the outcome, the newspaper will be responsible for all the costs.[44]

Standard of Proof
In a criminal trial the prosecution in order to succeed must convince the jury that the case has been proved *beyond all reasonable doubt*. This is deemed to be a higher standard of proof than required to be proved

---

[41] *Campbell v Mirror Group Newspapers* [2004] UKHL22.
[42] *Campbell v MGN Ltd* [2005] UKHL 61 and *Mirror Group Newspapers v The United Kingdom* [2011] ECHR 66.
[43] *Flood v Times Newspapers Ltd* [2010] EWCA Civ 804.
[44] See generally Ch.3 on Defamation and Ch.5 on Privacy.

by a claimant in a civil case where the test is based upon proving a case on the *balance of probabilities*. The existence of two standards does mean that on occasions a defendant in a criminal trial may be acquitted but has to pay damages when sued by the victim/claimant. A good example is the case of *EB v Haughton* [2011].[45] In this case the defendant in 2006 had been acquitted of sexual assault upon a young girl. A separate civil action for damages for assault commenced in December 2009. The case against him was proved and the court awarded the claimant £28,000 in general damages and £3,640 in special damages.

The *standard of proof* must be differentiated from the *burden of proof*. The burden of proof in a criminal case falls upon the prosecution. In civil cases it will fall upon the claimant with the exception that in libel cases it is up to the defendant when pleading the defence of justification (truth) to prove that the publication is substantially true.

Damages

As mentioned above the civil courts provide compensation through the award of damages. There are three types of damage claims that may be made. The majority of claims are for *general damages*. This may be relatively easy to calculate when dealing with personal injury cases but less so for example in the law of defamation when trying to assess the value of one's reputation or in privacy cases when the media has misused private information. The upper level for compensatory damages in defamation cases is £200,000 although higher sums can be obtained as a result of out of court settlements. For example, *Express Newspapers* agreed a settlement of Kate and Gerry McCann's libel action for the sum of £550,000 and a front page apology in the *Daily Express* after the newspaper published a series of "utterly false and defamatory" allegations implicating them in the disappearance of their daughter Madeleine.[46]

Aggravated Damages

There can be a penal element in the award of aggravated damages for example to indicate that the media should not engage in a particular type of behaviour such as completely fabricating a story. Lord Woolf M.R. in *Thompson v Commissioner of Police of the Metropolis* [1999][47] held that aggravated damages are primarily awarded to compensate the claimant for injury to his pride and dignity and the consequences of being humiliated.

---

[45] *EB v Haughton* [2011] EWHC279 (QB).
[46] *www.guardian.co.uk* March 19, 2008.
[47] *Thompson v Commissioner of Police of the Metropolis* [1999] Q.B. 498.

Special Damages

In the case of *EB v Haughton* special damages were awarded to the claimant in order to pay for the cost of therapy sessions recommended by her mental health practitioner.

4. Tribunals

In addition to covering the proceedings in the established courts of law journalists are also likely to spend some time covering cases that arise at the many and varied number of tribunals in this country. Figures released by the Ministry of Justice[48] show that at September 30, 2010 there were 706,200 cases waiting to be heard with 60 per cent being multiple claims to the Employment Tribunal. This tribunal is likely to be the one that is visited most by journalists, particularly from the tabloid press given the nature of its work. Discrimination and unfair or constructive dismissal cases abound. The threat of taking a case to a tribunal can often be a major bargaining tool for disgruntled employees against an employer who does not wish to spend time and money on defending a case in the tribunal.

The tribunal system is administered by the Tribunal Service which was established in April 2006 as an executive agency of the Ministry of Justice. A major task for the service has been to implement the restructuring of tribunals as a result of the Tribunals, Courts and Enforcement Act 2007. The result is a streamlined system that places tribunals into one of two tiers, either the First–tier or Upper Tribunal each of which are split into chambers.

So for example the First-tier Tribunal chambers are: Social Entitlement; Health, Education and Social Care; War Pensions and Armed Forces; General Regulatory; Immigration and Asylum; and Tax. Each tribunal is placed within a chamber. So under the Social Entitlement "umbrella" are found the Asylum Support, Social Security and Child Support and Criminal Injuries Compensation tribunals.

The tribunal system represents the government's attempt to provide a quick dispute resolution service which does not attract the costs associated with conventional court-based dispute resolution. Lawyers are not necessarily involved in the cases but that does not mean to say that the obligation to act fairly and within the rules of natural justice are absent from the tribunal system.

The open justice principle applies to tribunals just as it does to the conventional court systems. As Jackson J. said, the principle of Open

---

[48] Ministry of Justice: Quarterly Statistics for the Tribunals Service: 2nd Quarter 2010-2011.

Justice applied to employment tribunals with just as much force as it applied to court proceedings.[49]

Reporting Restrictions and Contempt of Court

The media is attracted to employment tribunals in particular because there are occasionally human interest stories centred on sexual misconduct allegations. Employment tribunals have the ability to issue Restricted Reporting Orders.[50] If the tribunal should accede to a request for such an order it must specify in the order the persons who are not to be identified. A tribunal has the power to revoke the order at any time if it thinks fit. It is important to note that a distinction should be made between allegations of sexual *harassment* and allegations that a sexual *offence* has been perpetrated. The legislation that bestows anonymity for life upon a victim of a sexual offence applies when reporting tribunal proceedings irrespective of whether a Restricted Reporting Order is in force. The tribunal must in these circumstances ensure that nothing is recorded or documented that is likely to lead members of the public to identify any person affected by or making such an allegation.[51] It follows therefore that a Restricted Reporting Order can be made in either case but the additional "burden" under the Sexual Offences (Amendment) Act 1992 will apply to cases only where a sexual offence is alleged.

Contempt

The Contempt of Court Act 1981 defines a court as "any tribunal or body exercising the judicial power of the state."[52] This does not mean that every tribunal is covered by the contempt laws but the major ones certainly will be. In *R (Mersey Care NHS Trust) v Mental Health Review Tribunal* [2004][53] Beaton J. said:

> **"A mental health review tribunal is a "court" within section 19 of the Contempt of Court Act 1981 to which the law of contempt applies: Pickering v Liverpool Daily Post & Echo Newspapers plc [1991] 2 AC 370,417. Accordingly the High Court has the jurisdiction to commit for the contempt of an order of a mental health review tribunal."**

The potential problem is caused by the fact the Contempt of Court Act does not define the words "judicial power of the state." As a consequence it requires a court to determine on a case-by-case basis

---

[49] *R v Secretary for Central Office of Employment Tribunals ex parte Public Concern at Work* (CO/191/00) April 19, 2000.
[50] Sch.1 r.50: Employment Tribunals (Constitution and Rules of Procedure) Regulations 2004.
[51] See s.1 Sexual Offences (Amendment) Act 1992 and Sch.1 r.49 of the Employment Tribunals (Constitution and Rules of Procedure) Regulations 2004.
[52] See s.19.
[53] [2004] EWHC 1749 (Admin).

whether the contempt laws apply to a particular tribunal.[54] The position of Employment tribunals is not however in doubt it having been determined that they exercise a judicial function.[55] Factors taken into account in reaching that decision were:

- Established by Parliament.
- Sits in public.
- Decisions affect the rights of subjects.
- Power to compel witnesses to attend.
- Can order discovery of documents.
- Can award costs.
- Must give reasons for its decisions.
- Decisions can be appealed to the Court of Appeal.

PART TWO: THE LEGAL SYSTEM IN PRACTICE

Law and the media are inextricably linked—both are often reviled but both are essential pillars of democracy.

As Lord Chief Justice Sir Igor Judge told the Society of Editors:

"An independent press and an independent judiciary are twin cornerstones, and bulwarks, of a free society. I choose the words carefully; cornerstones because the entire fabric of a free society is dependent on an independent press and an independent judiciary; bulwarks because these are the institutions which must defend a free society when it is threatened.

Name me a country, state, or community where there is a subservient press and an independent judiciary. There is none. Name me such a place where there is a subservient judiciary and an independent press. There is none either. That is why we must work to preserve both. All of us must work to preserve both. It is not quite love and marriage. That cannot be. A degree of tension is inevitable and healthy if only because we are independent of each other. But, the entire fabric of a free society is dependent on an independent press and an independent judiciary. In that sense we are mutually depend-

---

[54] See for example the recent case of *Tel-Ka Talk Ltd v Commissioners of Her Majesty's Revenue and Customs and the Law Society of England and* Wales [2010] EWHC 90175 (Costs) discussing the status of the VAT and Duties Tribunal.

[55] See *Peach Grey & Co v Sommers* [1995] 2 All ER 513.

ant. Nevertheless we cannot compromise on our independences but in any democratic society they must work together."[56]

We need to understand each other's rights and responsibilities. We need to argue over the interplay between media, judiciary, Government and the people. We will not always agree but we need to have the continuing debate. The press is currently at loggerheads with the judiciary over anonymised and super-injunctions, but the dialogue continues.

Also at a practical level journalists need to know their way around the legal system. We need to know who's who in the pecking order; their powers and the limits on them. We need to understand the principles and jargon of judicial processes so we can make sense of them for the public. This chapter has introduced readers to the key players, the institutions, procedures and hierarchy of the legal system to provide a basic context for journalistic inquiry and reporting.

5. Law Officers of the Crown in Practice

The Attorney General has a special significance for journalists being the officer with the power to bring prosecutions under the Contempt of Court Act 1981 which relates not just to court reporting but potentially to all kinds of issues, particularly the reporting of crime. In practice prosecutions are rare as Attorney Generals tend to prefer to issue public or private warnings to the media so as to avoid bringing action for reasons which will be discussed more fully in Ch.4 on Contempt.

The Director of Public Prosecutions can loom large too as head of the CPS, the ultimate arbiter of whether a prosecution is brought and an overall monitor of how the criminal justice system is operating. The present encumbent Keir Starmer has determined to deal more transparently with journalists and the public. This helps to improve accountability and understanding of the process but can also foster controversies.

Mr Starmer focused on four main issues in an address to media editors in 2009.

1. Decisions whether to prosecute or not
These can be highly controversial and Mr Starmer is committed to explaining the decisions in plain English to the public. So ten pages of reasoning was produced to show how the balance came down in favour of NOT prosecuting Damian Green, a Conservative MP and then

---

[56] Society of Editors, Stansted, 2009 *http://www.societyofeditors.co.uk/page-view.php? pagename=KeynoteAddress2009* [Accessed April 2011].

Shadow Immigration Minister controversially arrested and accused of leaking information from the Home Office, nor the civil servant allegedly involved, Christopher Galley. Within the public announcement, Mr Starmer said:

"There is a high threshold before criminal proceedings can properly be brought for misconduct in public office. In considering whether the conduct of Mr Galley and Mr Green reached that threshold and in particular whether it represented such a serious departure from acceptable standards, and abuse of trust as to constitute a criminal offence, I have considered the extent to which there has been any actual damage arising, or the extent of any potential damage that could have arisen, as a result of their conduct.

"I have also had regard to the freedom of the press to publish information and ideas on matters of public interest.

"I have concluded that there is evidence upon which a jury might find that there was damage to the proper functioning of the Home Office. Such damage should not be underestimated. However, it has to be recognised that some damage to the proper functioning of public institutions is almost inevitable in every case where restricted and/or confidential information is leaked.

"In this case, therefore, I have considered whether there is evidence of any additional damage caused by the leaks in question. I have concluded that the information leaked was not secret information or information affecting national security: It did not relate to military, policing or intelligence matters. It did not expose anyone to a risk of injury or death. Nor, in many respects, was it highly confidential. Much of it was known to others outside the civil service, for example, in the security industry or the Labour Party or Parliament. Moreover, some of the information leaked undoubtedly touched on matters of legitimate public interest, which were reported in the press.

"I have therefore decided there is insufficient evidence for a realistic prospect of conviction against Mr Galley or Mr Green.

"This should not be taken to mean that in future cases, a prosecution on other facts would not be brought. My decision is made on the particular facts of this case and the unauthorised leaking of restricted and/or confidential information is not beyond the reach of the criminal law."[57]

A decision whether or not to prosecute an MP is always controversial and Mr Starmer's policy of putting reasoning in the public domain has helped in a string of cases since he took office in November 2008, notably those related to the MPs' and House of Lords expenses scan-

---

[57] *http://www.cps.gov.uk/news/press_releases/122_09/index.html* [Accessed April 2011].

dals. The policy also improves the chances of those decisions being made without fear or favour.

2. Access to court material

Mr Starmer pledged a review to see if the media could be given access to more material, such as documents, videos and exhibits, relied on in court cases. Access was extended partially under a 2005 protocol but reporters often remain limited to describing rather than sharing the evidence put before juries, particularly because photography/filming is generally not allowed in UK courts. This inhibits the public appreciation of the evidence and can make it difficult for justice to be seen to be done.

3. Reporting restrictions

In a most welcome assertion Mr Starmer said: "We (the CPS) are no longer neutral on reporting restrictions. Unless there is an absolute necessity for a restriction by the defence, we will actively oppose it." (See also Ch.7 on Reporting restrictions in court.)

4. Public consultation

Mr Starmer said the CPS would "up its game" on public consultation, such as on the issue of assisted suicide, which attracted 2,000 responses. During his tenure there have been consultations on human trafficking and domestic violence and on the CPS's own code of principles on whether to prosecute or not.

Sceptical editors know there can be a huge gulf between fine words from the top and actual practice on the ground, but these were welcome examples of a more transparent approach which Starmer has worked to maintain since, as evidenced at *http://www.cps.gov.uk*.

The DPP has been back in the spotlight most recently in the continuing controversy over phone hacking by inquiry agents on behalf of journalists, particularly at the *News of the World*, amid demands to know why more prosecutions were not brought based on earlier phases of the ongoing investigation. (See also Ch.7 on Journalists' Sources.)

Mr Starmer has also taken a pro-active response on potential miscarriages of justice in the case of environmental campaigners prosecuted in connection with attempts to close a power station at Ratcliffe-on-Soar. In April 2011 he wrote to the legal representatives of 20 protesters convicted of conspiracy to commit aggravated trespass inviting them to appeal the convictions, in the wake of revelations regarding the role of an undercover police officer in their arrest.

6. Criminal and Civil Justice Systems in Practice

Journalists have a vital role in delivering the principle of open justice. This can involve challenging any of an array of reporting restrictions if they are unreasonable. Day in, day out it is about simply being there—being in court to record trials and sentencing, and impart that information to the public.

As Lord Chief Justice Sir Igor Judge said:

"It is my personal belief that in any society which embraces the rule of law it is an essential requisite of the criminal justice system that it should be administered in public and subject to public scrutiny. And for these purposes the representatives of the media reflect the public interest and provide and embody public scrutiny."[58]

But he went on to express concerns shared widely that already fewer courts are being covered by reporters and that the challenges to the local newspaper business model might lead to titles closing and to a far more drastic fall off in court reporting. He said:

"The best way I can put this to you is to ask myself how representatives of the local press can be present in court, or for that matter in local councils, or anywhere else where the press should be, if there is no local press? I am not comforted with the thought that the press can be admitted to court and report if it wishes. I am not content if there is no one to go into court and observe and write up. If there is no one to walk in, the public interest is damaged. That is the harsh reality.

Some weeklies are relying on council press offices too much. If that is true, it should send a shiver down all our spines. Experience of local government reporting is being lost. Court reporting has suffered too, with 64% of newspapers covering fewer court's sessions than before. The decline in local government and court reporting has led to an overall decline of the number of court reports appearing. These are self-explanatory and important considerations. If you are talking about survival, then this information matters hugely to the fabric of our society."[59]

Such concerns raised the possibility of public subsidy being provided for the creation of "independently financed news consortia" to secure provision of grassroots level coverage of key judicial and local

---

[58] Speech to Society of Editors, Stansted 2009 — *http://www.societyofeditors.co.uk/page-view.php?pagename=KeynoteAddress2009* [Accessed April 2011].

[59] Speech to Society of Editors, Stansted 2009 — *http://www.societyofeditors.co.uk/page-view.php?pagename=KeynoteAddress2009* [Accessed April 2011].

government functions. Labour's defeat in the 2010 election scuppered one source of funding but various experiments are being tried, mainly using digital platforms, to fill the gap and there is some prospect of public subsidy for those comfortable with taking it.

Journalists covering court should remember that they are the eyes and ears of the public and may have to challenge reporting restrictions imposed in a specific case, to defend the principle of open justice. Judges and magistrates share that responsibility but can be persuaded, usually by the defence, to impose restrictions which the media would deem unreasonable. Understanding the principles at stake and knowing the detailed legal requirements are vital if a journalist is to uphold the public's right to know.

So be prepared to make an informed challenge. Being able to cite some of the legal precedents covered in this book will help but the Judicial Studies Board guidelines[60] on reporting the courts should be enough. (See also Ch.7, Reporting Restrictions.)

Journalists should understand the legal hierarchy, topped by the Supreme Court. Judges and juries must apply precedent, legal principles and logic to try each case before them on its merits. Higher courts examining appeals and points of law can look more broadly, and thus generate more general guidelines. They do consider the bigger picture.

Civil actions such as those for defamation and abuse of private information are plagued by uncertainty. The media, most frequently in the position of defendant, craves more clarity. Some seek this in statute—welcoming the new definitions proposed in the Defamation Bill or calling for a Privacy Act. Others believe that no law can remove uncertainty as all legislation is open to judicial interpretation. Judges will ultimately need to look case by case at the balance of rights—in our instances, between freedom of expression and the right to privacy, reputation or fair trial. The other source of clarity is Supreme Court ruling and media organisations may actively seek to take controversial cases all the way as they did in *Spiller*[61] and as *The Times* is paying to do in *Flood*[62] after losing in the Court of Appeal. The outcome may not necessarily be to the media's liking but at least it provides the framework and authority on which future decisions in the lower courts will be based.

The legal system looms large in the lives of citizens, and particularly of journalists whether reporting the courts directly or investigating any matters of public interest. Some will find the workings and dilemmas of the legal system fascinating; others may read more grudgingly on the basis of "better the devil you know". Either way a journalist can't afford not to find out more.

---

[60] *Reporting Restrictions in the Criminal Courts.* October 2009. Joint publication by the Judicial Studies Board, Newspaper Society, Society of Editors and Times Newspapers Ltd.
[61] *Spiller & Anor v Joseph & Ors* [2010] UKSC 53.
[62] *Flood v Times Newspapers Ltd* [2010] EWCA Civ 804.

CHAPTER SUMMARY: THE LEGAL SYSTEM

- **Law officers**—note the roles of the Attorney General and the Director of Public Prosecutions for England and Wales; and that of their counterparts in Scotland.
- **Criminal justice**—note the path proceedings take through the hierarchy of courts topped by the Supreme Court, which replaced the House of Lords in 2009.
  - A defendant can be convicted of a crime only if the prosecution can prove guilt beyond reasonable doubt.
  - Juries are at the heart of the criminal law across the UK. In jury trials, the jury determines guilt/innocence; the judge determines sentence.
  - Note the role of sentencing guidelines.
  - The Criminal Cases Review Commission has particular significance as a source of media stories.
  - Be aware of the definitions of crime and which are more serious.
- **Civil actions**—note the hierarchy of county court and High Court, and the differences in language between criminal and civil law.
  - A claimant brings an action against a defendant for damages.
  - Civil cases are decided on the balance of probabilities.
- **Tribunals**—note their particular status. Some are effectively undertaking judicial functions and journalists covering them face many of the same freedoms and restrictions as in court.

CHAPTER 2: FREEDOM OF EXPRESSION

PART ONE: FREEDOM OF EXPRESSION

In December 1948 the United Nations General Assembly "adopted and proclaimed" the Universal Declaration of Human Rights. Member countries at that time were invited to disseminate the Declaration principally through educational institutions. The young of each nation were to be asked to embrace the terms of the Declaration in the hope that future generations would benefit from the foresight of their elders. Sadly there have been many examples over the years of breaches of many of the Articles. However, nations have consistently reaffirmed the commitment to freedom of expression enshrined in art.19 which states:

"Everyone has the right to freedom of opinion and expression; this right includes freedom to hold opinions without interference and to seek, receive and impart in-formation and ideas through any media regardless of frontiers."[1]

The International Federation of Journalists reported in January 2011 that "Over the past 12 years more than 1,100 journalists and media staff have been killed in the line of duty. They died because someone did not like what they wrote or said, or because they were in the wrong place at the wrong time." The unsurprising conclusion was that "the killing of journalists threatens everyone's human rights by closing the door to free expression."[2]

The first part of each of the chapters in this book endeavours to describe and comment upon the legal context within which the press has to operate in this country. We then comment on the practical impli-cations of the law for the working journalist and broadcaster. In discuss-ing freedom of expression and the value of a free press to a modern western democracy, we examine the legislation, case law and judicial comments relevant to these concepts. The United Nations Universal Declaration of Human Rights was closely followed in Europe when,

---

[1] United Nations Declaration of Human Rights 1948.
[2] International Federation of Journalists: *www.ifj.org*

in 1950, the European Convention on Human Rights was signed. The signatories proclaimed that they were:

"Reaffirming their profound belief in those Fundamental Freedoms which are the foundations of justice and peace in the world and are best maintained on the one hand by an effective political democracy and on the other by a common understanding and observance of the Human Rights upon which they depend."[3]

We are primarily concerned with art.10 of the Convention:

"1. Everyone has the right to freedom of expression. This right shall include freedom to hold opinions and to receive and impart information and ideas without interference by public authority and regardless of frontiers.

2. The exercise of these freedoms, since it carries with it duties and responsibilities, may be subject to such formalities, conditions, restrictions or penalties as are prescribed by law and are necessary in a democratic society, in the interest of national security, territorial integrity or public safety, for the prevention of disorder or crime, for the protection of health or morals, for the protection of the reputation or rights of others, for preventing the disclosure of information received in confidence, or for maintaining the authority and impartiality of the judiciary."

Even the most cursory examination of this provision tells us that freedom of expression is subject to limitations. That in itself does not undermine its value to a democratic society of the first part of art.10 but is more a reminder to governments that, while freedom to express views and opinions may be legitimately curtailed, it should only occur when absolutely necessary. *Necessary* is indeed the defining word. An illustration of how the word is interpreted in this context is found in the case of *MGN Ltd v United Kingdom* [2011].[4]

Two major issues had to be addressed each involving the application of art.10 rights. The first related to the decision of the House of Lords in the case of *Campbell v MGN Ltd* [2004][5] when the court held by a 3:2 majority that the claimant's privacy had been breached as a result of being surreptitiously photographed as she left a branch of Narcotics Anonymous. The photographs were subsequently published in the *Daily Mirror*. The decision was a case of art.8 rights to privacy trumping art.10 rights to freedom of expression. The claimant in this case was the model Naomi Campbell. Her case had been funded as a result of a conditional fee arrangement (see p.29). Under such arrangements lawyers acting for a successful claimant can claim a success fee of up to 100 per

---

[3] Preamble European Convention on Human Rights, Rome, November 1950.
[4] [2011] ECHR 66.
[5] [2004] UKHL 22.

cent of the normal fee from the defendants. This is meant to reflect the risk in taking on the case without the certainty of gaining any remuneration for their efforts should the case be lost.

Mirror Group Newspapers had failed to have this order overturned in the House of Lords in 2005[6] and now argued that the potentially huge financial penalties under such arrangements acted as a deterrent to free expression.

The court stated that the adjective 'necessary' implies the existence of a pressing social need. It is recognised that the contracting States have what is known as a 'margin of appreciation' when assessing whether such a need exists. The key question is whether any restriction is reconcilable with freedom of expression as protected under art.10. The court states its approach this way:

> "... what the court has to do is to look at the interference complained of in the light of the case as a whole and determine whether the reasons adduced by the national authorities to justify it are "relevant and sufficient" and whether it was "proportionate to the legitimate aimed pursued." In so doing the court has to satisfy itself that the national authorities applied standards which were in conformity with the principles embodied in Article 10 and moreover, that they relied on an acceptable assessment of the relevant facts."[7]

In the context of this case the question was whether the UK's success fee regime within the provisions of the conditional fee arrangement system were necessary in a democratic society. The court concluded that there were a number of flaws within the scheme which meant the scheme "exceeded even the broad margin of appreciation to be accorded to the State in respect of general measures pursuing social and economic interests." (See section on CFAs on p.66 for more detail about the case.)

These strong statements of principle are hardly something new.[8] European Court of Human Rights cases usually reiterate the general principles to be applied whenever the issue to be determined revolves around alleged breaches of art.10. They are:

1   That freedom of expression constitutes one of the essential foundations of a democratic society.
2   Safeguarding the press is of particular importance. However the press must not "overstep the bounds set."
3   It is incumbent on the press to "impart information and ideas of public interest."
4   There is a corresponding right on behalf of the public to receive such information and ideas.
5   The press has a vital role to play as "public watchdog."

---

[6] *Campbell v Mirror Group Newspapers Ltd* (costs) [2005] UKHL 61.
[7] [2011] ECHR 66 at para.139.
[8] See in particular *Sunday Times v United Kingdom* [1979] ECHR 1.

6   It is incumbent on the Court of Human Rights to engage in the "most careful scrutiny" when a national authority has acted in such a way as to discourage "the participation of the press in debates over matters of legitimate public concern."

7   The right to freedom of expression includes the right to communicate ideas and opinions that ". . . offend, shock or disturb the State or any section of the community."

8   Journalistic freedom ". . . covers possible recourse to a degree of exaggeration, or even provocation."[9]

The Court is always at pains to confirm that art.10 does not admit of "unrestricted freedom of expression" even when matters of serious public concern are being highlighted. The press must be aware of the "duties and responsibilities" listed in art.10(2). These duties and responsibilities said the court in the Moldova case "assume significance when . . . there is a question of endangering national security and the territorial integrity of the State."

There is a long line of well-established authorities to support the above propositions. For example, the principle of the media's role as public watchdog is supported by the *Observer and Guardian v United Kingdom* (1991)[10] (the aftermath of the *Spycatcher* litigation in the United Kingdom) and more recently *Gutierrez Suarez v Spain* [2010].[11]

The court's approach when press freedom is under challenge by national authorities is supported by the precedents of *Lingens v Austria* (1986),[12] *Bladet Tromso and Stensaas v Norway* (1999)[13] and *Thorgeir Thorgeirson v Iceland* (1992).[14]

Freedom to express views forcefully and to offend the State is regarded as a "right" within the proper ambit of art.10. For example see the case of *De Haes and Gijsels v Belgium* [1997][15] as authority for the proposition. The strongly held views of the authors, the editor and a journalist with HUMO magazine criticising the decision of the judges in the Antwerp Court of Appeal were held to be consistent with art.10.

"Although Mr De Haes' and Mr Gijsels' comments were without doubt severely critical, they nevertheless appear proportionate to the stir and indignation caused by the matters alleged in their articles. As to the journalist's polemical and even aggressive tone, which the Court should not be taken to approve, it must be remembered that Article 10 protects not only the substance of the ideas and information expressed but also the form in which they are conveyed."[16]

[9] See, for example, *Kommersant Moldovy v Moldova* [2007] ECHR 9.
[10] [1991] ECHR 49 at para.59.
[11] [2010] ECHR 2225 at para.25.
[12] [1986] ECHR 7 at para.59.
[13] [1999] ECHR 29 at para.64.
[14] [1992] ECHR 51 at para.63.
[15] [1997] ECHR 7, para.46.
[16] [1997] ECHR 7, para.48.

Of course, art.10 does not give a guarantee of wholly unrestricted freedom of expression. The duties and responsibilities of the press are likely to be drawn into sharper focus when writing about issues that the state believes could adversely affect national security or territorial integrity.[17] It is worth pointing out that, whatever safeguards are comprehended by art.10, they are subject to the proviso that journalists are *". . . acting in good faith in order to provide accurate and reliable information in accordance with the ethics of journalism."*[18]

The numerous decisions of the ECHR leave us in no doubt about its views on the importance of a free press to a democratic society. What of the English judiciary? This is what Lord Justice Brooke said in *Greene v Associated Newspapers Ltd* [2004]:

> **"**In this country we have a free press. Our press is free to get things right and it is free to get things wrong. It is free to write after the manner of Milton, and it is free to write in a manner that would make Milton turn in his grave. Blackstone wrote in 1769 that the liberty of the press is essential in a free state, and this liberty consists in laying no previous restraints on publication. 'Every freeman,' he said, 'has an undoubted right to lay what sentiments he pleases before the public: to forbid this is to destroy the freedom of the press.**"**[19]

Lord Hoffmann was typically forthright in *Campbell v MGN Ltd* [2004]:

> **"**. . . the press is free to publish anything it likes. Subject to the law of defamation, it does not matter how trivial, spiteful or offensive the publication may be.**"**[20]

The Master of the Rolls in *Loutchansky v Times Newspapers Ltd* [2004] is of the opinion that there is a public interest:

> **"**. . . in a modern democracy in free expression and, more particularly, in the promotion of a free and vigorous press to keep the public informed. The vital importance of this interest has been identified and emphasised time and again in recent cases and needs no restatement here.**"** [21]

In *Flood v Times Newspapers* [2009] Tugendhat J. quoted with approval from Lord Nicholls speech in *Reynolds v Sunday Times* [1999]:

> **"**Without freedom of expression by the media freedom of expression would be a hollow concept . . . there is no need to elaborate on the importance of the role discharged by the media in the expression and

---

[17] See, for example, *Han v Turkey* [2005] ECHR 588.
[18] *Moldova* case at [2007] ECHR 9 at para.32.
[19] [2004] EWCA 1462, para.1.
[20] [2004] UKHL 22, para.56.
[21] [2001] EWCA 1805.

communication of information and comment on political matters. It is through the mass media that most people today obtain their information on political matters."[22]

The current Master of the Rolls Lord Neuberger said in a speech at Eton College in April 2010:

"Freedom of expression whether by individuals or by the media, and the ability to exercise it, is an essential feature of any open, liberal and democratic society."[23]

Judicial support in the UK for a free press is strong and consistent. Perhaps it all the more surprising then that Sir Christopher Meyer, when chairman of the Press Complaints Commission, should tell his audience that press freedom was "being eaten away." He went on:

"I believe the boundaries of freedom of expression seem to be closing in a bit on newspapers and magazines in a way that may not be healthy. I'm not a conspiracy theorist, I don't believe in government plotting to curb freedom of expression but when you read that after two years, there are proposals to make it more difficult to obtain information under the Freedom of Information Act, you have to worry."[24]

It needs to be considered how far a free press can go in pursuing the aims of freedom of expression. In April 2011, the *News of the World* admitted that it had hacked into the voice messages of a number of celebrities and had set up a fund of some £15 million in order to compensate them for breaches of their privacy:

"We have written to relevant individuals to admit liability in these civil cases and we apologise unreservedly and will do the same to any other individuals where evidence shows their cases to be justifiable."[25]

The police are carrying out an investigation to see whether the actions of some employees of the *News of the World* have contravened the criminal law. In 2007, the royal correspondent of the newspaper went to prison together with a private investigator after admitting phone hacking.

The information they were trying to gain had little or nothing to do with the pursuit of genuine public interest stories, but more to do with obtaining information about the private lives of celebrities and royalty to feed the apparently voracious appetite the British public has for scandal on Sunday mornings.

---

[22] [2009] EWHC 2375, para.147.
[23] Lord Neuberger of Abbotsbury: Privacy and Freedom of Expression: A Delicate Balance: Eton College April 28, 2010. Speech available at *www.judiciary.gov.uk*
[24] Quoted in the *Guardian*, November 14, 2006.
[25] *News of the World*, April 10, 2011.

So it is right to ask, 'what are the responsibilities cast upon the media in seeking to uphold the principles of a free press?' Rights and responsibilities do, after all, tend to go hand in hand. The issue was graphically raised by the 2005 publication in *Jyllands-Posten*, a Danish newspaper, of cartoons which depicted the Prophet Mohammed. The editor of the newspaper was bound to be aware that graphic depictions of the Prophet would provoke extreme reactions from Muslims, particularly as one of the cartoons showed the Prophet with a bomb in his turban. The implication was obvious . . . Islam, and therefore all Muslims, are linked to terrorism. The Danish government responded to criticism by commenting that, in a democratic country which embraced freedom of expression, the newspaper was free to publish what it liked subject to any laws which specifically prohibited the publication of such material. Protests spread throughout the Islamic world and this led to damage to property and loss of life.

The cartoons were reprinted in many newspapers throughout Europe and the western world as part of the process of disseminating the news and, in some cases, simply to demonstrate the right to freedom of expression. The cartoon issue raised a number of questions about the interrelationship between a free press, freedom of expression and a government's duty to protect religious freedom and promote religious tolerance.

A government that appears to suppress speech that it finds distasteful or offensive will inevitably lead to accusations of censorship and political interference. One might do well to heed the words of Lord Nicholls of Birkenhead when dealing with the limits of the defence of fair comment in English Law:

> ". . . the comment must be one which could have been made by an honest person, however prejudiced he might be, and however exaggerated or obstinate his views: see Lord Porter in *Turner v Metro-Goldwyn-Mayer Pictures Ltd* [1950] . . . It must be germane to the subject matter criticised. Dislike of an artist's style would not justify an attack upon his morals or manners. But a critic need not be mealy-mouthed in denouncing what he disagrees with. He is entitled to dip his pen in gall for the purposes of legitimate criticism."[26]

Without, at this stage, entering into a discourse on the defence of Fair Comment (Honest Opinion as it will become known if the Defamation Bill becomes law) the purpose of such a defence is to:

> ". . . facilitate freedom of expression by commenting on matters of public interest. This accords with the constitutional guarantee of freedom of expression. And it is in the public interest that everyone should be free to express his own, honestly held views on such matters . . ."

[26] *Cheng v Tse Wai Chun Paul* [2000] HKCFA 88.

Lord Nicholls goes on to state:

"The public interest in freedom to make comments within these limits is of particular importance in the social and political fields. Professor Fleming stated the matter thus in his invaluable book on The Law of Torts, 9th edition, p.648: '. . . untrammelled discussion of public affairs and of those participating in them is a basic safeguard against irresponsible political power. The unfettered preservation of the right of fair comment is, therefore, one of the foundations supporting our standards of personal liberty."[27]

Under art.10(2) of the European Convention one accepts that, through the due process of law, a state may seek to inhibit or proscribe particular aspects of free speech. In the United Kingdom, Parliament has made it a criminal offence intentionally to stir up religious hatred. This may be achieved by the use of words or behaviour written material or publishing or distributing the same. However, under the schedule to the Racial and Religious Hatred Act 2006 which inserts a new Pt 3A into the Public Order Act 1986, Parliament, through s.29J, reaffirms its commitment to freedom of expression:

"Protection of Freedom of Expression
   Nothing in this Part shall be read or given effect in a way which prohibits or restricts discussion, criticism or expressions of antipathy, dislike, ridicule, insults or abuse or particular religions or the beliefs or practices of their adherents, or of any other belief system or the beliefs or practices of its adherents, or proselytising or urging adherents of a different religion or belief system to cease practising their religion or belief system."[28]

So would the publishers of the cartoons have committed an offence under the Act if published initially in the UK rather than Denmark? In all likelihood the answer would be "no" because there was no evidence that the publishers intended to stir up religious hatred, although that would depend very much on whether the editor foresaw that "religious hatred" would be the consequence of his actions. Also the offence is committed if a person uses *threatening* words or behaviour or displays any written material that is threatening, if he intends thereby to stir up religious hatred. *Threatening* is the operative word so possession, publication or distribution of inflammatory material is also an offence. On that basis the publication of the cartoons might have constituted the act required by the offence but it would still be argued that the publication was not meant to stir up religious hatred. The publishers would also be able to fall back on the freedom of expression defence in s.29J.
   The theoretical perspective in favour of freedom of speech rests

---

[27] *Cheng v Tse Chun Paul*, 2000, HKCFA, para.38.
[28] Racial and Religious Hatred Act 2006, Sch.1: s.29J.

squarely with John Stuart Mill (1806–1873). Arguably the most famous British philosopher of the 19th century, he embraced logic, philosophy, economics, politics, ethics and religion. His treatise *On Liberty*, published in 1859, was one of his most controversial works. He expressed the view that society should not have to keep defending the "liberty of the press." Press freedom was necessary to protect society "against corrupt or tyrannical government." Referring to the suppression of free expression as a "particular evil" he opines that the human race is being "robbed" of something of value. If the opinion is "right" then the people are "being deprived of the opportunity of exchanging error for truth: if wrong, they lose, what is almost as great a benefit, the clearer perception and livelier impression of truth, produced by its collision with error . . .".[29] He goes on to advocate that "the necessity to the mental wellbeing of mankind (on which all other wellbeing depends) of freedom of opinion and freedom of expression of opinion . . ." is well recognised. There are four distinct grounds:

1. Truth should never be denied a platform.
2. Through expressing opposing opinions the truth may emerge.
3. The truth should be "vigorously and earnestly contested."
4. Suppression of opinion inhibits the growth of "any real and heartfelt conviction." Both the individual and the nation are the losers.

Professor Eric Barendt's classic work *Freedom of Speech*[30] takes a modern-day perspective on the notion of free speech pitting the "purely" philosophical arguments in favour of freedom of speech against the more "specific" arguments that courts have to take into account when acting constitutionally. The theoretical nature of the discussion is underpinned by reference to four justifications of free speech which warrant the conclusion that free speech deserves special legislative protection. The first drawing upon Mill's analysis resonates around the idea that opinions should never be suppressed otherwise individuals will rarely be able to discover the truth. Even falsehoods should be articulated so that they can be shown up for what they are. As Wendell Holmes J. so famously stated in his dissenting judgment in *Abrams v United States*[31]:

". . . the ultimate good desired is better reached by free trade in ideas—that the best test of truth is the power of the thought to get itself accepted in the competition of the market, and that truth is the only ground upon which their wishes safely can be carried out . . . we should be eternally vigilant against attempts to check the expression of opinions that we loathe and believe to be fraught with death, unless they so imminently threaten immediate interference with the lawful

---

[29] *On Liberty*, Ch.2.
[30] Oxford University Press, 2nd edn, March 2007.
[31] [1919] USSC 2.

and pressing purposes of the law that an immediate check is required to save the country."

The pursuit of truth as an overriding justification for supporting a principle of free expression is shown by Barendt if not to be fallacious, then certainly to be a principle that can be challenged on grounds of logic alone. He points out that the Weimar Republic in the 1920s generally supported free political expression yet led to the Nazi regime establishing itself in Germany in the early 1930s. The collective myopia of much of the German nation to the holocaust bears testimony to the fact that the free expression of opinions is not enough. It was the exposure to graphic images and newsreels that was the catalyst to the ultimate acceptance of the truth.

The second argument put forward by Barendt is that free speech makes a contribution to individual self-development and fulfilment. That aspect of freedom of expression would seem to complement the recognition inherent in art.8 of the European Convention on Human Rights that the right to a private life includes a person's physical and psychological integrity. Over-zealous reliance by the media upon art.10 rights to reveal information about private lives has recently come under critical surveillance not just from the European Court of Human Rights but also the English courts including the House of Lords.[32] A primary objective of the Convention is to ensure "the development, without outside interference, of the personality of each individual in his relations with other human beings . . . There is therefore a zone of interaction of a person with others, even in a public context, which may fall within the scope of 'private life'."[33] The amount of money that the state pours into education would seem to suggest that government accepts the need for intellectual self-fulfilment through the development of ideas, opinions and the ability to communicate one's views to others.

Eric Plutzer tells us that "most young citizens start their political lives as habitual non-voters but they vary in how long it takes to develop into habitual voters."[34] This sentiment would strike a chord with Barendt's third argument in favour of freedom of speech that of encouraging people to take an inclusive approach to the democratic processes of their country. As he says: ". . . citizen participation in a democracy . . . is probably the most easily understandable, and certainly the most fashionable, free speech theory in Western democracies."

In order to make an informed choice at the ballot box, one must not only be capable of intellectually comprehending the various manifestos on offer, but also be aware of the detail contained in the manifestos through extensive publicity and debating of the issues. This is the argument that sustains the major rationale for the First Amendment to the

---

[32] See Ch.5 on Privacy and Confidentiality.
[33] *von Hannover v Germany* [2004]ECHR 294 para.50.
[34] Plutzer, "Becoming a Habitual Voter: Interia, Resources and growth in Young Adulthood. American Political Science Review" (2002) 96 Cambridge University Press.

American Constitution—the desire for the populace to embrace self-government through representation and the ballot box.

Finally, and perhaps not unexpectedly, the notion of free speech permits the populace to be vigilant against governmental attempts to "limit radical or subversive views." This section of Barendt's first chapter is headed "Suspicion of Government" and the author rightly poses the question of whether in this all pervasive media age we need to be any more suspicious of government than we do of other organisations which have the power to censor free speech such as the huge media conglomerates.

It is ironic that the very organisations upon whom we depend for information may in fact be disseminating information that is itself selective and non-critical. This in turn brings us back to the Millian argument that we need to hear as many opinions as possible to be able to determine where the truth lies.

Unlike the United States, this country has an unwritten constitution and therefore freedom of expression apparently has no greater standing than any other principle in English law. However, the Human Rights Act 1998 does include a section entitled "Freedom of Expression" which purports to emphasise to the judiciary the importance of the concept. In assessing whether to grant any relief which might affect the exercise of art.10, the court has to take a number of factors into account. When the respondent in any action is not present or represented in court, no relief is to be granted unless all reasonable steps have been taken to notify the respondent of the action, unless there are *compelling* reasons for not so doing. A court is directed to have "particular regard" to "the importance of the convention right to freedom of expression" when the respondent wishes to publish "journalistic, literary or artistic material."

In 2004, the House of Lords had the opportunity to consider the meaning of s.12(3) of the Human Rights Act. This sub-section appears to support the rule against prior restraint (see p.57). This means that a publication will not be subject to injunctive relief prior to publication unless a court is satisfied that the applicant's prospects of success at any subsequent trial "are sufficiently favourable to justify such an order being made in the particular circumstances of the case."[35]

The UK position should be contrasted with the United States where freedom of speech is protected by the First Amendment to the United States Constitution. Ratified on December 15, 1791, it reads:

"Congress shall make no law respecting an establishment of religion, or prohibiting the free exercise thereof; or abridging the freedom of speech, or of the press; or of the right of the people peaceably to assemble, and to petition the Government for a redress of grievances."

---

[35] *Cream Holdings v Banerjee* [2004] UKHL 44.

It is worth noting that the Amendment doesn't actually refer to the word "expression." The "freedoms" protected are speech, assembly and the ability to petition government but arguably the use of the word "expression" covers all three rights identified by the First Amendment. Freedom of speech is clearly protected but only against interference by Congress and by the 14th Amendment of the Constitution, not state legislatures. In *New York Times v Sullivan* [1964][36] the Supreme Court was required for the very first time to decide the extent to which "the constitutional protections for speech and press limit a State's (Alabama's) power to award damages in a libel action brought by a public official against critics of his official conduct."

The newspaper had carried an advertisement urging its readers to "Heed Their Rising Voices." Its purpose was to elicit funds to assist with the promotion of civil rights campaigns in the southern states of America. The respondent was one of three elected Commissioners of the City of Montgomery in Alabama and held the position of Commissioner of Public Affairs. He sued on the basis that he had been libelled by statements in the advertisement. Although he was not identified by name, he claimed that the criticism of the police force in Montgomery were a direct reflection on him. Here is an example of what was written:

> "In Montgomery, Alabama, after students sang "'My Country, 'Tis of Thee'" on the State Capitol steps, their leaders were expelled from school, and truckloads of police armed with shotguns and tear-gas ringed the Alabama State College Campus. When the entire student body protested to state authorities by refusing to reregister, their dining hall was padlocked in an attempt to starve them into submission. Again and again, the Southern violators have answered Dr King's peaceful protests with intimidation and violence. They have bombed his home, almost killing his wife and child. They have assaulted his person. They have arrested him seven times—for speeding, loitering and similar offences. And now they have charged him with perjury—a felony under which they could imprison him for ten years ..."

The threat of civil action for libel undoubtedly induces the potential for the "chilling effect" on the media to raise its head. The Court in *Sullivan* determined that a public official could only succeed in an action for libel if it could be shown the newspaper in question was actuated by malice. Lest it be thought that *Sullivan* has no influence on the English courts one needs to consider the speech by Lord Keith in *Derbyshire County Council v Times Newspapers Ltd* [1993].[37] The House of Lords agreed that it was of vital importance in a democratic society to be able to criticise public bodies without the constant fear of a defamation action hanging over the media. Not only did he endorse the decision in *Sullivan*, he

[36] [1964] 376 US 254.
[37] [1993] 1 All E.R. 1011.

quoted with approval from the earlier US decision in *City of Chicago v Tribune Co* (1923),[38] in which it was held that the city could not bring an action for libel against the media. Thompson C.J. stated:

"The fundamental right of freedom of speech is involved in this litigation and not merely the right of liberty of the press. If this action can be maintained against a newspaper it can be maintained against every private citizen who ventures to criticise the ministers who are temporarily conducting the affairs of his government."

The judge was of the opinion that the threat of civil action against the media was "as great if not a greater restriction than a criminal prosecution." He went on to say:

"It follows, therefore, that every citizen has a right to criticise an inefficient or corrupt government without fear of civil as well as criminal prosecution. This absolute privilege is founded on the principle that it is advantageous for the public interest that the citizen should not be in any way fettered in his statements, and where the public service or due administration of justice is involved he shall have the right to speak his mind freely."[39]

1. Public Interest

The above statements reinforce the view that free speech/expression is in the public interest. This raises the question of what is legally meant by the words *public interest* because it is this very concept that the media consistently relies upon to justify publication of, sometimes, extremely contentious material.

When the media applied to intervene in the *McKennitt v Ash* case,[40] one of the issues identified by counsel was that the definition of public interest needed to be restated particularly when balancing personal privacy against the media's right to expose what might be regarded as essentially private information. That, of course, is a narrow issue whereas the original point was that the media consistently relies upon the concepts of freedom of expression and "public interest" to defend its right to publish. The context is very often the legal basis upon which a judge will decide between two competing public interests. There can be no doubt about the Parliamentary expenses 'scandal' being a matter of public interest especially as it is taxpayers money that goes to pay the expenses. When the *News of the World* exposed Winchester MP Mark

---

[38] (1923) 307 Ill 595.
[39] (1923) 307 Ill 595, pp.607–08.
[40] [2005] EWHC 3003 and [2006] EWCA 171.

Oaten's predilection for rent boys it could only be justified on the basis
that the newspaper was exposing his hypocrisy in promoting his image
of being a happily married family man.[41]

In the privacy field the balance is likely to be between the public interest in protecting confidentiality, whether personal or commercial, and
the public interest in publishing information, i.e. utilising the right of
free expression and free speech. The recent trend in privacy cases is to
grant injunctions to prevent 'intimate' details of a person's relationships
and to preserve the anonymity of the applicant. The courts are sending
a clear message to the tabloid press in particular that publishing such
information is not in the public interest.[42] As Lord Justice Stephenson
said in *Lion Laboratories v Evans*[43] the countervailing interest is of the
public being kept informed of matters that are of "real public concern."
There were, he said, four further considerations:

> "1. There is a wide difference between what is interesting to the
> public and what it is in the public interest to make known.
> 2. The media have a private interest of their own in publishing what
> appeals to the public and may increase the circulation or the numbers
> of their viewers or listeners and as a result they are 'particularly vul-
> nerable to the error of confusing the public interest with their own
> interest.'
> 3. The public interest may be best served by an informer giving
> information not to the press but to the police or other responsible
> body.
> 4. It is in the public interest to disclose grave misconduct or wrong-
> doing or to put it another way there is no confidence 'as to the disclo-
> sure of iniquity.'"[44]

In this case two ex-employees of Lion Laboratories had released, to the
press, information based upon confidential company documents that
indicated that Lion, the maker of breath-testing equipment, was aware
there were doubts as to the reliability and accuracy of the instruments.
The court held that injunctions granted to the company to prevent
publication of the information should be lifted. The court confirmed
that it was "well accepted" that there was a public interest defence to
actions of breach of confidence and breach of copyright providing that it
could be shown that it was in the public interest to publish confidential
information.

Much the same reasoning applied in the *McKennitt* case albeit in a
different context. McKennitt was a folk singer of some repute whose
erstwhile friend was intent on publishing a book about her life.

For commercial reasons publishers will expect revelations in such

---

[41] January 2006.
[42] See, for example, *JIH v News Group Newspapers* [2011] EWCA Civ 42.
[43] [1984] 2 All E.R. 417.
[44] [1984] 2 All E.R. 417, p.423.

a book and Ash was intent upon not disappointing them. McKennitt sought an injunction and damages for breach of confidence. In this chapter we are not concerned with the current state of the privacy laws (see Chapter 5 on Privacy and Confidentiality), but looking at whether such a publication would be construed as being in the public interest. It will be obvious that much of what Ash intended to publish could have been gleaned only because of her close friendship with McKennitt. In other words it was argued by the applicant that there had been a breach of confidentiality. The trial judge, Eady J. took the view that there was "little public interest in the matters addressed in the book" and "certainly no public interest sufficient to outweigh Ms McKennitt's art.8 right to respect for her private life."

In response, Ms Ash argued that McKennitt was a public figure and "for that reason alone" there was a legitimate public interest in her affairs. The second argument centred on "putting the record straight." This is based on the premise that 'if a public figure misbehaves' then the public have a right to have the record corrected. The premise is not in doubt and has been supported by the courts for many years. In precedent terms, the most influential case is the decision of the House of Lords in *Campbell v MGN Ltd* [2004].[45] All five Law Lords held that it was in the public interest that the *Daily Mirror* informed its readership of Ms Campbell's use of drugs. Not only was she a public figure but she had maintained that, unlike other supermodels, she did not use drugs; a fact that the *Daily Mirror* exposed as a lie when she was photographed by long lens coming out of Narcotics Anonymous in London. However the House went on to conclude by a 3:2 majority, that the *Daily Mirror* was breaching Ms Campbell's privacy by using a surreptitiously obtained photograph to illustrate the story.

The Court of Appeal in rejecting Ms Ash's arguments expressed surprise that McKennitt should be considered a public figure. The court followed European jurisprudence from the Court of Human Rights[46] in reaching that conclusion. The "European" view is that while it is accepted that the press has an:

" . . . *important role . . . in dealing with matters of public interest . . . a distinction was then to be drawn between the watchdog role in the democratic process and the reporting of private information about people who, although of interest to the public, were not public figures.*"[47]

In 2008 the *News of the World* told its readers that Max Mosley, the head of the Formula 1 racing organisation (FIA), engaged in sado-masochistic activities with '5 hookers.' How could this revelation possibly be justified on public interest grounds? The newspaper claimed that the orgy had or was intended to have a Nazi theme. Mosley is the

---

[45] [2004] UKHL 22.
[46] *von Hannover v Germany* [2004] ECHR 294.
[47] [2006] EWCA 171 at para.58.

son of Oswald Mosley (the leader of the fascist movement in the 1930s in the UK). On that basis it sought to justify the publication, of which no notice had given to Mosley of its intention to expose this behaviour, because he was an elected official of the FIA. The court roundly rejected the newspaper's justification for publishing. The judge held there was no evidence that the participants intended their actions to reflect Nazi behaviour or attitudes. There was no public interest for the publication and damages of £60,000 were awarded for breach of Mosley's art.8 rights.[48]

It follows that there will always be a degree of subjectivity when assessing whether a publication is in the "public interest." However, what seems to be clear is that, if the media is exercising its "watchdog" role, then there is every likelihood that the publication will be deemed to be in the public interest. Exposing corruption, examining the actions of state-funded bodies, matters of constitutional importance, rooting out crime and, of course, keeping a watchful eye out for potential abuses of trust or office by politicians is in all probability going to serve the media well if challenged by an aggrieved applicant.

The Press Complaints Commission (PCC) Code of Practice provides a definition of public interest. After stating the various elements of best practice for newspaper and magazine journalists, the Code makes the following assertions:

1   The public interest includes, but is not confined to:
    i   detecting or exposing crime or serious impropriety
    ii protecting public health and safety
    iii preventing the public from being misled by an action or statement of an individual or organisation.

The Code goes on to confirm that, in the PCC's view, there is a public interest in freedom of expression itself. (In fact, it would have been difficult to have made any other statement, given the strong endorsement from the English and European courts.) As a matter of good practice, once an editor has invoked the public interest as a justification for publication, then the onus is placed upon the editor to justify that decision. In other words there must be tangible evidence to support the conclusion. One factor that will clearly influence editors is whether or not the information is already in the public domain. One day after the *News of the World* published the "Mosley" revelations the video of the "orgy" had been seen more than one million times courtesy of the newspaper's website. This amount of exposure in the public domain resulted in the court refusing an injunction to prevent further dissemination of the material.[49]

The Broadcast Code takes a slightly different approach.[50] Nowhere

[48] *Mosley v News Group Newspapers Ltd* (No 3) [2008] EWHC 1777 (QB).
[49] [2008] EWHC 687 (QB).
[50] See *www.ofcom.org.uk* The latest amended version of the Broadcasting Code is February 2011. Amended to take account of the changes permitting product placement on

is there to be found a "generic" definition of public interest. Rather the Code identifies certain situations where the public interest is a necessary concomitant of good broadcasting practice. For example at cl.8.13, which deals with surreptitious filming and recording, broadcasters are told that such filming will only be warranted if "there is prima facie evidence" of a story in the public interest. Another example at cl.8.1 works on the same assumption as 8.13. In this case, a breach of privacy may be warranted if it is in the public interest and "the broadcaster should be able to demonstrate that the public interest outweighs the right to privacy."

As one might expect, discussion of the public interest concept is evident in a number of cases. We have already mentioned *Campbell v MGN Ltd*. It is also fruitful to refer to the House's decision in *Cream Holdings Ltd v Banerjee [2004]*.[51] As Lord Nicholls said, the material the newspaper wished to publish was "incontestably" a matter of serious public interest and the story was one that no court could properly suppress. The case hinged upon whether the former finance officer of Cream Holdings was acting in the public interest to remove confidential documentation when dismissed by the company.

The documentation was delivered to the *Liverpool Post* and *Echo* and purported to show that there was illegal and improper activity by the company including an allegation of a corrupt relationship between a director of the company and a local council official. The House denied injunctive relief to the company. The newspaper was undertaking its "watchdog" role in bringing into the open the allegation of impropriety.

In *Jameel v Wall Street Journal Europe* [2006][52] Lord Bingham quoted Lord Hobhouse's comment from the *Reynolds* case to the effect that "No public interest is served by publishing and communicating misinformation." He also said that "what engages the interest of the public may not be material which engages the public interest."

So the concept of the public interest goes to the very heart of media operations. This and the right to exercise freedom of expression are vital factors to consider if the media is faced with an application for an injunction to prevent the publication or broadcasting of material that the applicant would rather did not receive a public airing.

2. The Rule Against Prior Restraint

Lord Justice Brooke, in the case of *Greene v Associated Newspapers Ltd* [2004][53] was blunt in his defence of free speech. Our press, he said:

---

television. (February 28, 2011).
[51] [2004] UKHL 44.
[52] [2006] UKHL 44 at para.30 and 31.
[53] [2004] EWCA Civ 1462.

"... is free to get things right and it is free to get things wrong. It is free to write after the manner of Milton, and it is free to write in a manner that would make Milton turn in his grave."

This sentiment has its historical roots in the writings of the English jurist Sir William Blackstone (1723–1780) and his famous *Commentaries on the Laws of England* published in four volumes from 1765–1769. He wrote:

"The liberty of the press is indeed essential to the nature of a free state: but this consists in laying no previous restraints upon publications, and not in freedom from censure from criminal matter when published. Every free man has an undoubted right to lay what sentiments he pleases before the public: to forbid this is to destroy the freedom of the press: but if he publishes what is improper, mischievous or illegal, he must take the consequences of his own temerity."[54]

The principle therefore seems to have strong foundations. The US courts are not averse to quoting the principle in support of the First Amendment to the Constitution. "Any system of prior restraints of expression comes to this court bearing a heavy presumption against its constitutional validity."[55] The Government "thus carries a heavy burden of showing justification for the imposition of such restraint."[56] In *New York Times v US* (1971),[57] the government had sought injunctions to prevent *The New York Times* and *The Washington Post* from publishing government documents relating to the conduct of the Vietnamese war. The Supreme Court was having none of it.

As Brennan J. so forcefully put it:

"The error that has pervaded these cases from the outset was the granting of any injunctive relief whatsoever, interim or otherwise. The entire thrust of the Government's claim throughout these cases has been that publication of the material sought to be enjoined 'could,' or 'might,' or 'may' prejudice the national interest in various ways. But the First Amendment tolerates absolutely no prior restraints of the press predicated upon surmise or conjecture that untoward consequences may result."[58]

Of course the UK does not have the benefit of a written constitution, but the rule against prior restraint was given judicial acknowledgement in respect of libel in *Bonnard v Perryman* (1891).[59] Lord Coleridge C.J. stated:

---

[54] *Commentaries on the Laws of England*, Volume 4, p. 151.
[55] *Bantam Books Inc v Sullivan* (1963) 372 US 58, p. 70.
[56] *Organisation for a Better Austin v Keefe* (1971) 402 US 415, p. 419.
[57] [1971] 403 US.
[58] [1971] 403 US, p. 714.
[59] (1891) 2 Ch 269.

"... it is obvious that the subject matter of an action for defamation is so special as to require exceptional caution in exercising the jurisdiction to interfere by injunction before the trial of an action to prevent an anticipated wrong. The right of free speech is one which it is for the public interest that individuals should possess, and, indeed that they should exercise without impediment, so long as no wrongful act is done; and, unless an alleged libel is untrue, there is no wrong committed; but on the contrary, often a very wholesome act is performed in the publication and repetition of an alleged libel. Until it is clear that an alleged libel is untrue, it is not clear that any right has been infringed; and the importance of leaving free speech unfettered is a strong reason in cases of libel for dealing most cautiously and warily with the granting of injunctions ..."

The rule is still as potent now as it was in 1891. Lightman J. in *Service Corporation International Plc v Channel Four Television* [1999][60] said:

"The reason that defamation is not and cannot be invoked is because no interlocutory injunction could be granted on this ground in view of the defendant's plain and obvious intention to plead to any such claim the defence of justification."[61]

Additionally an intention to plead honest opinion (fair comment) and qualified privilege will invariably lead to the same conclusion.[62] The prevailing view is that it is up to the media to publish at their own risk. As Lord Denning said in *Fraser v Evans*[63] if the media is guilty of libel or breaches of confidence or copyright, then that can be determined by a post-publication action and damages awarded against the media organisation. In light of the developments in privacy protection under art.8 of the Human Rights Convention the part of Lord Denning's statement relating to breach of confidence no longer appears to represent the law.[64] The rule against prior restraint would therefore seem to sit easily with the idea of a free press and freedom of expression. In legal terms it would appear to be compatible with art.10 of the European Convention of Human Rights.

The European Court in its judgment in the notorious Spycatcher case (*The Observer and the Guardian v United Kingdom* [1991])[65] stated:

"... the dangers inherent in prior restraints are such that they call for the most careful scrutiny on the part of the Court. This is especially so as far as

---

[60] [1999] EMLR 83.
[61] [1999] EMLR 83, p.89.
[62] See, for example, *Fraser v Evans* (1969) 1. Q.B. (349).
[63] *Fraser v Evans* (1969) 1. Q.B. (349), p.363.
[64] See *JIH v News Group Newspapers* [2011] EWCA Civ 42 and other "no name" cases cited in Ch.5 on Privacy and Confidentiality.
[65] [1991] ECHR 49.

the press is concerned, for news is a perishable commodity and to delay its publication, even for a short period, may well deprive it of all its value and interest."[66]

However the court did add, by reference to art.10(2), that the imposition of prior restraints was not prohibited under art.10. A number of the judges expressed the opinion that any such restraint should only be imposed in "wartime and national emergency."

The approach that had been adopted in respect of the granting of interim injunctions was that the applicant had to establish a prima facie case. In practice, this meant that it had to be proved on the evidence before the court *at that time* and on the balance of probabilities the applicant would succeed at any subsequent trial. The so-called "balance of convenience" test was then conceived by the House of Lords in the non-media case of *American Cyanamid v Ethicon Ltd* [1975].[67] In essence judges were to be satisfied that the applicant's claim for an injunction was not "frivolous or vexatious." If that "threshold" was passed then the court had to consider where the "balance of convenience" lay. As Lord Nicholls said in the *Cream Holdings* case, where matters were evenly balanced then a court was likely to take "such measures as are calculated to preserve the status quo."[68] In other words, to grant the interim injunction. Enter the Human Rights Act and s.12(3), a section designed to "allay (the) fears" that, if the conventional Cyanamid test was applied, then prior restraint could almost become a formality. As Lord Nicholls so eloquently put it:

> "Its principal purpose was to buttress the protection afforded to freedom of speech at the interlocutory stage. It sought to do so by setting a higher threshold for the grant of interlocutory injunctions against the media . . ."[69]

So what is the current position and what will an applicant have to establish to obtain an interim restraint order against the media? Lord Nicholls again:

> "Section 12(3) makes the likelihood of success at the trial an essential element in the court's consideration of whether to make an interim order . . . There can be no single, rigid standard governing all applications for interim restraint orders . . . the court is not to make an interim restraint order unless satisfied the applicant's prospects of success at the trial are sufficiently favourable to justify such an order being made in the particular circumstances of the case." [70]

---

[66] [1991] ECHR 49, para.60.
[67] [1975] A.C. 396.
[68] *Cream Holdings v Banerjee* [2004] UKHL 44, para.1.
[69] *Cream Holdings v Banerjee* [2004] UKHL 44, para.15.
[70] *Cream Holdings v Banerjee* [2004] UKHL 44, para.22.

Two recent cases have explained the current position. In *Allister v Paisley & Others* [2010][71] Gillen J. said that he had "(from the authorities) . . . distilled the following principles governing the jurisdiction to grant interim injunctions to restrain publication of alleged defamatory statements:

(i) The jurisdiction ought to be exercised only in the clearest of cases. The reluctance to grant peremptory injunctions is rooted in the importance attached to the right of free speech. The statement above at note 60 from *Bonnard v Perryman* is quoted with approval.

(ii) These sentiments are now underpinned by Art.10 of the European Convention on Human Rights pursuant to the Human Rights Act 1998.

(iii) An applicant seeking an interim injunction must be prompt in his application. The relief is discretionary and if he is dilatory he will probably fail.

(iv) An interim injunction will only be granted where four basic conditions prevail. These are:
   (a) The statement is unarguably defamatory
   (b) There are no grounds for concluding the statement may be true.
   (c) There is no other evidence which might succeed
   (d) There is evidence of an intention to repeat or publicise the defamatory statement."

The other factors relate to the application of s.12(3) making the likelihood of success at the trial an essential element in the court's consideration and that the defendant should be present or represented unless there are good reasons not to be in court. As was pointed out in the *Cream Holdings* case there can be no single rigid standard governing all applications for interim injunctions. Attention should also be paid to the statement which must be a statement of fact and not merely of opinion. Moreover the statement must relate to the personal character or conduct of the applicant. However as Gillen J. said ". . . the dividing line between what is personal and what is political is not always readily apparent or easy to draw".[72]

In *ZAM v CFW and TFW* [2011][73] the judge summed up the evidence when deciding if an interim injunction should be granted. This represents an application of the principles outlined in the *Allister* case. He said:

"On the information before me I am satisfied that there is a prima facie case of libel, that there remains the threat by the defendants to publish or further publish the words complained of, and that if

---

[71] [2010] NIQB 48.
[72] *Allister v Paisley & Others* [2010] NIQB 48, paras 14–22.
[73] [2011] EWHC 476 (QB).

publication or further publication occurs the claimant will suffer injury which cannot be fully compensated in damages. I am in no doubt that the words complained of are defamatory. Nothing has been stated by the defendants personally to the effect that they have a defence of justification or any other defence. Nor am I able to regard the fax of 2 March 2011 as providing any or any sufficient basis for saying that there may be a defence that will succeed at trial."[74]

The issue of prior restraint has taken on a new dimension in recent years because of the increasing influence of the European Convention on Human Rights upon English law. Many of the applications for interim injunctions resulted in judges having to decide between the respective public interest in maintaining confidentiality and supporting free expression. The "modern" dimension has encompassed the twin rights of freedom of expression under art.10 and the right to respect for private life under art.8. If there is a story to tell, why should a person be prevented from informing the public of the details with the active support of the media?

The prior restraint principle is well established as far as defamation is concerned. Courts applying the above principles will be most reluctant to impose interim injunctions restraining the media from putting material into the public domain unless there is the clearest evidence that the clamant is likely to succeed at trial. However, the position with applications for interim injunctions in respect of breaches of privacy or confidentiality raises different issues. In most cases the availability of damages at a subsequent trial, as in the *Mosley* case, is of no benefit to the applicant. He or she simply wishes to keep private the material which the media intends to publish. Section 12(3) will be applicable to claims based on breaches of privacy. However, a major issue is that the claimant is unlikely to be aware of the impending publication until very close to the publication date.

There is no legal obligation upon editors to inform the subject of an expose that publication is due to occur as shown in the *Mosley* case. The court will also have to take into account the provisions of section 12(4) (b) of the Human Rights Act which requires the court to consider the provisions of any relevant privacy code. Max Mosley has taken the issue of prior notification on appeal to the Grand Chamber of the European Court of Human Rights arguing that UK law cannot provide applicants with an effective remedy in privacy cases unless the applicant has prior notification within a reasonable time to enable him to take legal advice.

It will be apparent from the cases cited in Ch.5 on Privacy and Confidentially that the courts are more readily prepared to grant interim injunctions in this area of the law than when dealing with defamation.

[74] *Zam v CFW and TFW* [2011] EWHC476 (QB), para. 24.

3. Forum Shopping

The vast majority of legal actions affecting the media will commence in the High Court in London. The assumption is that the correct forum to resolve a dispute is that in which the "wrong" occurred. Therefore, if we are discussing the "tort" of defamation, it would appear to be relatively straightforward to determine which jurisdiction should be seized of the case. If the alleged defamatory comments are contained in a national newspaper or broadcast on the BBC or another national broadcaster then it should be relatively straightforward to work out where to bring a claim.

However, with the advent of online journalism and the rapid expansion of the internet there is more likely to be a degree of uncertainty as to where any legal action may be commenced. This problem was addressed for the first time in 2004 by the Court of Appeal in the case of *Lennox Lewis v Don King*."[75] This case is a fertile source of information about the legal criteria upon which jurisdictional issues will be determined. The background is that King, a boxing promoter with an international reputation, alleged he had been defamed. Two articles had appeared on boxing websites hosted in California. They had been placed there by Judd Bernstein, a New York lawyer, among whose clients were Lennox Lewis and his production company Lion Promotions. In the articles Bernstein referred to the "clearly anti-Semitic tone" of his (King's) comments. King argued that the articles portrayed him as a ". . . persistent, bigoted, and unashamed or unrepentant anti-Semite."

King wished to bring an action in the High Court in London basing his claim on the fact that he had a reputation within this jurisdiction. Yet the facts are that a New York lawyer posted articles on Californian websites criticising a United States citizen. We are entitled to ask what this has to do with London.

The answer of course is that Don King is well known in this country. His reputation could, as a result of the postings, be damaged in this country. Logically, therefore, a person with an "international" reputation could literally sue in any jurisdiction in the world if he could prove that his reputation has been damaged.

The Court of Appeal examined the relevant law in order to determine the appropriate *forum conveniens*. The following is a digest of the court's assessment of the law.

1. Two points are to be established at the outset based upon the reasoning of the House of Lords in the case of *Spiliada Maritime Corp v Consulex Ltd*.[76] The first is that the matter of which jurisdiction is

---

[75] [2004] EWCA 1329.
[76] [1987] A.C. 460.

"pre-eminently a matter for the trial judge . . . An appeal should be rare and the appellate court should be slow to interfere."[77]

The second proposition is that the burden of proof rests upon the claimant to persuade the court that England ". . . is the appropriate forum for the trial of the action (and) that he has to show that this is clearly so."

2 Other authorities, particularly *The Albaforth*[78] establish three "strands" which in essence are discretionary matters. The first "strand" is that there is an initial assumption that the appropriate forum for trial will be the courts of the place where the tort is committed. Lord Steyn approved this statement in the *Berezovsky v Michaels & Others* case[79] stating that the approach was "unobjectionable in principle." The second strand follows from the first and it is that "the more tenuous the claimant's connection with this jurisdiction (and the more substantial any publication abroad) the weaker this consideration becomes." The third strand deals with so called "transnational" libels. This includes libels originating from the internet. The court refused a request to adopt special rules for the internet. It must be remembered that no media organisation is forced to utilise cyberspace. Those that do, choose to do so and for a variety of reasons. The old English authority of *Duke of Brunswick v Harmer*[80] established the principle that in respect of defamatory material each publication constituted a separate tort. Therefore actions could lie in numerous jurisdictions assuming the claimant has a reputation and there has been a publication of the alleged defamatory material within the jurisdiction. The European Court of Human Rights in 2009 refused to hold that the application of the multiple publication rule was contrary to the art.10 rights of the UK media.[81]

This in turn has led the government to propose that the rule should be abolished and clause 6 of the Defamation Bill is set to bring about that result. The multiple publication rule will be replaced by a single publication rule if the clause in its current form becomes law. The recent concern about the existing rule has been in the context of online archives. The multiple publication rule relates to "access" rather than "publication." So at the moment every time an online archive is accessed then there is potential for a defamation action to result. This puts tremendous pressure on the newspapers to maintain their archives in such a way as to ensure that any defamatory material is removed. (See Ch.3 on Defamation and the *Flood v Times Newspapers* case).

---

[77] *Spiliada Maritime Corp v Consulex Ltd* [1987] A.C. 460, p.465 F-G.
[78] [1984] 2 Ll LR 91.
[79] [2000] 1 W.L.R. 1004.
[80] (1849) 14 (QB) 185.
[81] *Times Newspapers v United Kingdom* [2009] ECHR 451.

The converse argument is that the existence of the multiple publication rule means that the media has to act more responsibly. The limitation period in defamation is one year from the publication of the material or "access." This could mean that both the traditional media and internet web and search aggregators may take a less responsible approach to content if they realise that the limitation period runs for 12 months from the date of the original publication.

It is obvious that with no global boundaries to the internet an online publisher can be sued in literally any jurisdiction in the world where he or she had a reputation. In *Cairns v Modi* [2010][82] the defendant had "tweeted" that the claimant, a professional cricketer, had been involved in match fixing. The High Court gave Cairns permission to commence his action in London on the basis that he had a reputation in this country having played top level cricket here for some eight years. The case is interesting as it involved expert witnesses trying to predict how many Twitter followers would have accessed the material. There was also evidence that the alleged defamatory material had been published in an online cricket magazine. Three guiding principles in these cases will be:

1. In which jurisdiction was the 'tort' committed?
2. How many people in that jurisdiction accessed the material? Although the courts emphasise the fact that it is not a numbers game if the numbers are very low it may lead to a finding of 'abuse of process.' In *Dow Jones & Co Inc v Jameel*[83] the libel action against the company related to an article posted on web servers in New Jersey. The company claimed that there was no publication in England, arguing that the publication took place in the United States. The court recognised that Dow Jones had removed the article from its website and from the archive and therefore no repetition was likely to occur. There had been what the court called "insignificant publication" in this jurisdiction (five people, of whom three were known to the claimant) but recognised that this jurisdiction could nevertheless be the *forum conveniens*. However adopting a pragmatic approach it ruled that it would be an abuse of process to proceed as damage to reputation was unlikely in the circumstances. The proceedings were stayed.
3. Has the claimant established a reputation in this jurisdiction?

Perhaps the action that has had the most profound impact on this aspect of the law is the case of *Mahfouz v Ehrenfeld* [2005].[84] The claimant and his two sons sued the defendant for libel on the basis that of parts a book suggested that he and his family were involved in funding terrorism. The book was published in the United States and was not meant to be

[82] [2010] EWHC 2859 (QB).
[83] [2005] EWCA 75.
[84] EWHC 1156 (QB).

sold outside of the jurisdiction. However, 23 people from the UK using the *Amazon.com* website bought copies. Mahfouz was given permission to commence his action here and as the defendant failed to appear a default judgment was made in his favour. He then proceeded to the United States to enforce the judgment. The response was for a number of states to pass laws preventing the enforcement of foreign libel judgments against US citizens. The reasoning was that they would have lost First Amendment protection for free speech. In July 2010, the United States Congress passed the Speech Act making it impossible for foreign judgments to be enforced in defamation cases unless the overseas jurisdiction subscribed to principles similar to the First Amendment to the US constitution.

The Defamation Bill 2011 seeks to limit the impact of libel tourism/forum shopping in the UK. Clause 7 states that a court does not have jurisdiction to hear and determine an action for defamation unless satisfied that, of all the places in which the statement has been published, England and Wales is clearly the most appropriate place in which to bring an action based upon that statement. This applies only to those who are not domiciled in the United Kingdom or a Member State or a state that for the time being is a 'contracting party to the Lugano Convention.'[85]

It is likely that a court interpreting this clause will take account of a number of factors including the strength of the claimant's reputation in the jurisdiction and also whether the person may get a fair trial in another jurisdiction.

Overall the warning to the media is clear. Be aware of the potential legal consequences of what is published given the global reach of the internet. This is particularly important as newspapers are now being offered via iPads and other tablet devices and some predict the print editions will disappear altogether in the near future to be replaced by electronic versions. Whatever the process, the solution as Lord Goff's speech in *Spilida* emphasised was that the venue should reflect the interests ". . . of all the parties and for the ends of justice" to be achieved.

4. Conditional Fee Arrangements

Conditional fee arrangements are discussed within the ambit of freedom of expression because they have had a profound impact on the overall cost of defending actions brought against the news media which may have a "chilling" effect on its reporting as demonstrated by the decision of the European Court of Human Rights in *MGN Ltd v UK* [2011].[86]

---

[85] Lugano Convention: Convention on Jurisdiction and Enforcement of Judgments in Civil and Commercial Matters 1988.
[86] [2011] ECHR 66.

To mount an action against a media organisation requires a fair amount of resource. Legal aid is not available for defamation suits. Over the past decade, conditional fee arrangements have become widespread. The scheme was introduced by the Courts and Legal Services Act 1990 and modified by the Access to Justice Act 1999. The idea is to provide greater access to justice as in cases such as defamation where legal aid is not available to claimants.

In broad terms, such agreements permit lawyers to engage in "no win, no fee" arrangements. The benefit to the client is that if he or she loses the case no fee would be charged although the claimant would be liable for disbursements and the winning side's costs. If the claimant is successful then fees are payable but in practice the losing side will be liable for the costs of the case. In addition, the lawyer will also be able to claim a "success" fee which is calculated on a percentage basis of the normal professional fees.

This may sound like a good deal for the litigant and indeed, it is. It can also be rewarding for the lawyers involved because although they have to shoulder the risk of losing, if they were to win the case, the "success" fee can be has high as 100 per cent.

However, it will be obvious that this is not such good news for the defendant media organisation faced, as it will be, with a massive hike to the conventional fees that would be paid if the claimant were not acting under a CFA. Media organisations argued forcefully that the mere existence of the success fee regime is contrary to the principles of art.10 of the European Convention on Human Rights and this was confirmed by the European Court of Human Rights in the *MGN* case in January 2011. The court accepted the argument that the higher the costs that a media organisation has to pay if successfully sued will act as a deterrent to publication, i.e. freedom of speech will be restricted.

Lord Justice Jackson was appointed to carry out a review of civil litigation funding and costs and, in March 2011, the government published its response to his recommendations.[87] The government claims that it is seeking to 'reduce the unfair costs suffered by the many businesses, individuals and other organisations that have been faced with CFA actions. We aim to restore greater proportionality to the costs of civil cases as demanded in the recent European Court of Human Rights case of *MGN v UK*.'[88] The government believes that the right way forward is to abolish the recoverability of CFA success fees and after the event insurance premiums. In practice it will mean that any success fees will be recoverable from the damages paid to the claimant. It was suggested by the Secretary of State that damages awards could be increased by 10 per cent to "ease the bill."

---

[87] Reforming Civil litigation Funding and Costs in England and Wales-Implementation of Lord Justice Jackson's Recommendations: The Government's response March 2011. Available at *www.justice.gov.uk*

[88] ibid: Ministerial Foreword: Kenneth Clarke: Lord Chancellor and Secretary of State for Justice.

These proposals impact upon personal injury claims as well as actions against the media. It remains to be seen whether the proposals mean that it will be almost impossible to find a lawyer who is willing to take on a defamation case unless funded entirely by the client. There has been a 'traditional' imbalance between the amounts awarded in damages and the costs incurred to achieve them. The classic example is the *Campbell* case from which MGN Ltd took its grievance to the European Court of Human Rights. It will be recalled that she won £3,500 in damages for breach of confidentiality. The case had 'travelled' through the three levels of the court structure.

Ms Campbell's solicitors claimed the following in costs:

1   £377,070 for the trial;
2   £114,755 for the appeal to the Court of Appeal;
3   £594,470 for the appeal to the House of Lords.

Total Costs: £1,086,295.

There can be no doubts about the need for reform as a number of cases in the past decade have shown. One issue had been who controls the costs and the time frame for pending litigation? It is surely in the claimant's solicitor's best interests to prolong the pre-trial process while at the same time racking up the costs. A good example of this latter point is the first case in the *Henry v BBC* litigation.[89] The BBC applied for a cost capping order which was refused by Gray J. on the basis that the application was made too late in the process. The judge identified the "predicament" the BBC found itself in:

"If the case goes to trial, the BBC's own costs will be £515k. If the BBC wins at trial . . . the BBC will not be entitled to recover more than 20% of its costs (under the ATE insurance). The combined assets of the claimant and her husband come to about £235,000 most of which consists in the equity in the matrimonial home. The claimant's share is therefore only £117,000. Conversely if the claimant wins at trial the BBC will be faced with a bill of the claimant's costs which, inclusive of uplift, will total in the region of £1.6 million. On the other hand the BBC will also have to pay its own costs."

In March 2007, a claimant withdrew her action against Associated Newspapers after claiming that she had been libelled by the *Evening Standard*. An undercover investigation had claimed that the nursing home that she owned mistreated its patients. In 2005, the case had been subject to a cost capping order when the claimant's lawyers working on a CFA had accumulated costs that were estimated to be in the region of £500,000. This was another case where there was no ATE insurance

---

[89]   [2005]EWHC 2503 (QB).

in place. As it was, the newspaper would have to absorb its own costs estimated to be around £100,000.[90]

At the heart of the costs regime was the issue of proportionality in relation to the amount of damages at issue. In *Cox and Carter v MGN Ltd* [2006],[91] this issue was considered by the court as the aftermath of the privacy claim against MGN by Sara Cox and her husband in which a settlement of £50,000 was agreed without the need for a trial of the issues. The case is instructive as it focused attention on how quickly costs may escalate. The claimants were represented under a CFA agreement. There was a dispute over the hourly fees charged by the claimant's lawyer. Should it be £300–£315 per hour or £400–£450 per hour? Also under contention was the "correct" percentage for the success fee. The Costs judge thought 40 per cent, the claimant's solicitor 95 per cent uplift and the newspaper 5 per cent. There was not much basis for compromise when one looked at the different aspirations of those involved. The court dismissed each of the appeals but the judgment is instructive as it reviews the main factors to be considered, including the potential "chilling effect" upon the media, in determining the appropriate costs level. Reference should be made to the "proportionality test" in the case of *Lownds v Home Office* [2002].[92]

The above cases are cited to illustrate the problems that have arisen over the past decade culminating in the decision of the European Court of Human Rights in the *MGN Ltd* case in January 2011. It is assumed that the government will have to use primary legislation to implement the proposals and so it is likely to be the 2011–2012 legislative programme that contains these reforms. It will be interesting to see whether the principles underpinning the Access to Justice 1999 survive the reforms.

PART TWO: FREEDOM OF EXPRESSION IN PRACTICE

Freedom is 2011's rallying cry as citizens in numerous countries rise up against their despotic regimes. Some are now on their way to creating a more democratic state; others are still fighting for their basic rights. Freedom of expression has been a central demand of these protest movements which condemn state censorship and state-controlled media as emblems of repression. Those determined to challenge the powers-that-be also evaded controls on freedom of speech by using modern media platforms, such as Twitter and Facebook, which can add momentum to their cause.

---

[90] *Matadeen v Associated Newspapers* (unreported) March 17, 2005.
[91] [2006] EWHC 1235.
[92] [2002] EWCA Civ 365.

Yet in the UK, and much of Europe, freedom of speech, like many of our civil liberties, is at worst derided and, at best, predominantly taken for granted. A UK journalist adopting the moral high ground by claiming to be upholding a fundamental human right is likely to provoke hollow laughter in most circles. The trivialisation of the news agenda, particularly but not exclusively in print, has strengthened the sense that little of significance is at stake. The concept of media ethics is dismissed as an oxymoron and the "me" generation assumption is that self-interest is the only genuine driver of the actions of journalists.

But the commitment to freedom of expression is genuine. A journalist has to believe that, as a general rule, disclosure is the best policy. People want and need to know what is happening in their world, if they are to understand it and be able to play their part in it, not just in an overtly political context but in a day-to-day, sometimes mundane, way of using information to improve their lot, to seize opportunities, to make sense of the world, to develop their own opinions and to make the most of their lives.

Upholding the public right to know inevitably involves exercising freedom of expression. For many journalists this is manifested in the daily battle to overcome the welter of obstacles put in the way of placing information in the public domain. The vast majority of journalists working up and down the country 24/7 will never bring down a government or even topple a corrupt local official but that does not make their contribution insignificant. Journalists toiling away in the backwaters may not even themselves consider their work fundamental to the successful workings of democracy but that must not obscure the fact that it is.

5. The Human Rights Act in Practice

Asked if they have had "a good day at the office, dear", journalists are certainly not likely to say what a cracking time they have spent exercising their art.10 rights. Even now many will not realise what an impact the Human Rights Act is having, and will increasingly have, on their ways of working and their role in society. Its operation challenges the journalistic mindset and news values and marks a significant shift in the whole field of media law.

Traditionally, journalists, like any other citizens, could pretty much act as they liked except in those areas specifically subject to legal sanction. This partly explains why media law is synonymous with restraint. Media law has historically told us what we can't do; or at least what we can expect to be punished for doing.

The Human Rights Act challenges that pattern. Journalists should arguably welcome it with open arms as, in the absence of a written constitution, it comes as close as we can get to a fundamental declaration of the right to freedom of expression. It falls a long way short of the US First Amendment but it is more than we have had in the past. It includes a variety of phrases to gladden any journalist's heart by recognising a free press as an essential player in a healthy democracy. This provides a strong legal card and means the public interest in freedom of expression per se and in any particular case has to be recognised by the courts.

But we certainly don't get it all our own way. All the freedoms 'guaranteed' by the Act's adoption of the European Convention on Human Rights are subject to limitations and these aren't even in the 'small print.' All the Articles—particularly those establishing the right to privacy and the right to a fair trial—have specific implications for journalists which will be discussed throughout this book. However, taken as a whole, the message of the Convention means that media law now relies explicitly on a balancing act. Exercising any fundamental right, such as freedom of expression, can involve impinging on the rights of others and where it does, it is for the courts to decide where the balance lies; where and when one must yield to the other.

This is, in many ways, startlingly obvious. A key challenge for any healthy democracy is to operate a complex system of checks and balances on power. The Articles of the Convention provide the check and, where rights compete or where grounds for restricting those rights are advanced, the courts will decide the balance to be struck. The work of journalists so often butts up against the rights of others, our right to exercise freedom of expression is bound to be challenged frequently in court where judges will decide our fate.

Although journalists may recognise the absolute value of an independent judiciary, we remain nervous of our fate being in the hands of individual judges. We fear they tend to the view of a Tom Stoppard character in his play *Night and Day*: "I'm with you on the free press; it's the newspapers I can't stand."[93]

Any statute is open to interpretation and that task has always been a matter for the courts. However, the Human Rights Act, whatever the original intention of Parliament, is founded on the concept of a balancing act, of what the courts call proportionality, which means it is inevitably going to be even more dependent on judicial views and, for journalists, effectively a small group of media specialists. Names such as Baroness Hale, Lord Phillips, Lord Chief Justice Igor Judge, Master of the Rolls Lord Neuberger, Lord Justice Sedley, Mr Justice Eady and Mr Justice Tugendhat are set to loom large in journalists' lives as they will in this book. The legal future of journalism and freedom of expression is in their hands.

---

[93] Stoppard, Tom, *Night and Day* quoted by himself in *My love affair with newspapers*, British Journalism Review, Vol.16, No.4, 2005, pp.19–29 (interestingly as not being indicative of his general attitude to newspapers. Nevertheless it remains a pithy encapsulation of the kind of ambivalence towards the news media in the upper echelons of British society).

6. The Lessons of Case Law

The range of the latest key judgments relating to Freedom of Expression explored earlier in this chapter highlight the trends in the application of the Convention and thereby our UK Human Rights Act. Article 10 rights do not give journalists anything like free rein to publish whatever they deem to be in the public interest. Countervailing rights will put a check on that. But the Act provides the framework for decision-making in the courts. Any 20th century (or earlier) judgment can be re-assessed or even dismissed as not Convention-compliant so the 21st century has become a whole new world for media law. These are early days in legal terms, but each case that goes all the way to the Supreme Court establishes a powerful legal authority which can have a significant impact on how we exercise our freedom of expression—what sorts of stories we run, who and what we cover and what we can report within the law.

Journalists can reasonably celebrate the outcome of *Kommersant Moldovy v Moldova* (2007), where a newspaper successfully fought back against State efforts to close it down. This was a classic case of the news media standing up to effective censorship by a Government, one of the more blatant challenges to art.10 rights as exercised by journalists.

But there are concerns too. Moldova, like many governments, tried to rely on the exemption clause, art.10(2), specifically that it could restrain freedom of expression in the interest of *national security, territorial integrity or public safety*. These are the standard opt outs which governments, particularly the more repressive ones, rely on more or less disingenuously to justify suppression of the media. There is a deep-set suspicion among journalists that playing the "national security" card is all too often the last resort of a government desperate to keep embarrassing secrets hidden.

The national security or territorial integrity exception is also why journalists are right to challenge catchphrases such as the War on Terror. One doesn't have to apply the full Orwellian conspiracy to see that it could be tempting for those in power to fall back on such justifications to save themselves under the cloak of national security: "If you run that you'll undermine national security and, oh dear, we can't tell you why, that would undermine national security too." There are situations where national security is genuinely at stake but striking the balance is tough. Language should be used with precision. To use the terminology of war when the country is not at war is inimical to civil and media liberties.

The European Court of Human Rights made some supportive moves in finding against Moldova, partly by dwelling on the proviso in the exception clause that it must be necessary—that there must be a pressing social need for the restraint and that it must be proportionate. Its main complaint was that the State had not done enough to explain how the material run by the newspaper jeopardised national security.

Unfortunately this suggests that, had the State been slightly less high-handed and come up with a more detailed justification, its action could have been upheld.

The tone of the judgment is less than complimentary of the newspaper and there is much stress on duties and responsibilities, good faith, ethics, accuracy and reliability. Cavalier journalists are warned not to expect a sympathetic hearing.

7. Public Interest in Practice

Few concepts are more to the fore in current media law judgments than the notion of public interest. Yet there is no one all-embracing definition of it and often its meaning is almost assumed as in the Ofcom broadcasting code.

Information is power and information empowers the public, particularly as voters but also in their daily lives. There is a public interest in the free flow of information. There is recognition of a public interest in freedom of expression itself, but given that there is a public interest in upholding all the other human rights too, this does little to advance the journalist's cause because in practice most disputes involve a clash of rights.

The limitations outlined in *Lion Laboratories v Evans* suggest a scepticism on the part of the courts regarding media claims to be running a story in the public interest. Obviously, for a journalist, there would be no point running any story if it wasn't of some public interest, but that is nowhere near enough for the courts. When the news media seeks to defend a story, its case tends to be considered more in terms of its (commercial) interest in telling it rather than in the public's interest in knowing it.

Certainly there is a temptation to be disingenuous and confuse self-interest with public interest, but the vast majority of news organisations deserve a more sophisticated appreciation of their arguments than that.

Selling newspapers, or attracting "eyeballs" to any platform, is not just a matter of self-interest. It is only by attracting an audience that the news media can inform the public. There is no public interest in covering stories in such a way that they are ignored. The pursuit of audience may have led some to abandon genuine issues in favour of celebrity gossip and other trivia, but it is not an ignoble aim in itself. One of the greatest challenges for any journalist committed to serving the public's right to know is that of "making the significant interesting."[94]

Information about weighty issues has to be communicated successfully and that may involve telling stories in a human interest style,

---

[94] Bill Kovach and Tom Rosenstiel, *The Elements of Journalism*, p.13.

perhaps using celebrity examples, which will draw the public to the story and engage their attention. Without a consideration of how to make issues accessible, a high-minded journalist may not be serving the general public any better than one devoted entirely to "tittle-tattle."

One of the most encouraging contributions was from Lord Nicholls in *Reynolds v Times Newspapers Ltd* [1999] where he said:

> "The court should be slow to conclude that a publication was not in the public interest and, therefore, the public had no right to know. . . . Any lingering doubts should be resolved in favour of publication."[95]

More generally, and particularly in privacy rather than defamation actions, the higher courts are reining back on various fronts and creating effective hierarchies of public interest depending on the topic of any story, who it involves and the scope and level of detail it reveals. The idea of resolving lingering doubts in favour of publication has most definitely not survived the application of strict "proportionality".

In *Campbell v MGN*, in the context of freedom of expression, Baroness Hale advances a hierarchy of different types of speech. She says:

> "There are undoubtedly different types of speech, just as there are different types of information, some of which are more deserving of protection in a democratic society than others. Top of the list is political speech. The free exchange of information and ideas on matters relevant to the organisation of the economic, social and political life of the country is crucial to any democracy. Without this, it can scarcely be called a democracy at all. This includes revealing information about public figures, especially those in elective office, which would otherwise be private but is relevant to their participation in public life.
>
> Intellectual and educational speech and expression are also important in a democracy, not least because they enable the development of individuals' potential to play a full part in society and in our democratic life. Artistic speech and expression is important for similar reasons, in fostering both individual originality and creativity and the free-thinking and dynamic society we so much value. No doubt there are other kinds of speech and expression for which similar claims can be made."[96]

But she goes on to say:

> "But it is difficult to make such claims on behalf of the publication with which we are concerned here. The political and social life of the community, and the intellectual, artistic or personal development of

---

[95] [1999] UKHL 45.
[96] *Campbell v MGN* [2004] UKHL 22, para.148.

individuals, are not obviously assisted by pouring over the intimate details of a fashion model's private life."[97]

She did, however, acknowledge that using a model's story as an example of the battle to overcome drug addiction could have a "beneficial educational effect."

This is an example of the courts' somewhat high-brow approach to the public sphere which places the emphasis effectively on political dialogue and those who hold formal public office.

Yet celebrities wield considerable influence on attitudes and behaviours. Their role in society cannot be so easily dismissed. Comedian Eddie Izzard fronted the 'Yes campaign' in the Alternative Voting referendum. A BBC 4's *Moral Maze* programme in April 2011 was devoted to the question: "Is celebrity activism good for democracy?" It noted that the tweets of Stephen Fry's (actor/presenter/commentator) were followed by 2.45 million people, which is more than the printed copies of *The Times, Daily Telegraph, Financial Times, Guardian* and *Independent* combined. As many charities and other causes know, celebrity endorsement and involvement can have a considerable impact on the public. Many people crave fame and will go to considerable, sometimes, dubious lengths to achieve it. Surely the public should know the reality of being famous; not just the airbrushed version. Celebrities are, for better or worse, a reality of public life and, thus, should not escape scrutiny and debate of their behaviour.

The Press Complaints Commission Code of Practice[98] provides the most frequently quoted examples of what is in the public interest, although it pointedly uses the phrase "includes but is not confined to" to keep the door open to argue for a wider definition. The three areas are broadly: wrongdoing, health and safety, and preventing the public from being misled. The BBC Editorial Guidelines expand on the similar basic principles.[99]

The PCC factors all help to establish the area of public interest, but the extent of the public interest accepted by judges depends on the circumstances in each case. A whole matrix is building up. A small misdemeanour by a Government Minister might help art.10 rights to "win", but even a serious impropriety by a B-list celebrity might not, and the chances are diminishing with every landmark judgment. If the impropriety involves criminal activity, such as drug-taking, celebrity might be enough, but if it is only sexual shenanigans, again it probably won't. Even putting the record straight is not the trump card it used to be; it depends how actively the public is being misled and how much judges deem it matters whether they have accurate knowledge or not.

The wrongdoing element of the PCC Code refers to "serious impropriety". Criminal behaviour is still covered, but a much more relaxed

---

[97] *Campbell v MGN* [2004] UKHL 22, para.149.
[98] PCC Code of Practice, *www.pcc.org.uk*
[99] BBC Editorial Guidelines, available to journalists and the public, *www.bbc.co.uk/editorial guidelines.*

view is taken by the courts about sexual misdemeanour. Commercial abuses can also be included and courts have accepted there is a public interest in the affairs of corporations. Shareholders have a right to know if they are being misled about the company they part-own but football, music or movie fans have no corresponding right to know as much about those they pay to watch.

This divergence between journalists and the courts in the interpretation of 'impropriety' is becoming more marked. It was at the heart of an emphatic challenge from *Daily Mail* Editor-in-Chief Paul Dacre to privacy rulings made by Eady J., particularly in the aftermath of the Max Mosley decision. Dacre told the Society of Editors in Bristol in November 2008:

> "In the Mosley case, the judge is ruling that there is no public interest in revealing a public figure's involvement in acts of depravity. What the judge loftily calls the 'new rights-based jurisprudence' of the Human Rights Act seems to be ruling out any such thing as public standards of morality and decency, and the right of newspapers to report on digressions from those standards."

He went on:

> "I personally would rather have never heard of Max Mosley and the squalid purgatory he inhabits. It is the others I care about: the crooks, the liars, the cheats, the rich and the corrupt sheltering behind a law of privacy being created by an unaccountable judge.
>
> "All this has huge implications for newspapers and, I would argue, for society. Since time immemorial public shaming has been a vital element in defending the parameters of what are considered acceptable standards of social behaviour, helping ensure that citizens – rich and poor – adhere to them for the good of the greater community. For hundreds of years, the press has played a role in that process. It has the freedom to identify those who have offended public standards of decency – the very standards its readers believe in – and hold the transgressors up to public condemnation. If their readers don't agree with the defence of such values, they would not buy those papers in such huge numbers."[100]

One doesn't have to be a friend of the *Daily Mail* to see the gulf in the mindsets of the mainstream media and senior judges when it comes to challenging the 'morality' of people in the public eye. The flurry of privacy injunctions to which the mass-circulation tabloids (and others) are subject is another indicator of unresolved tensions over how 'public interest' is defined in respect of the activity to be exposed and the 'importance' of the person involved in it.

---

[100] Speech by Paul Dacre, Editor-in-Chief of the *Daily Mail* at the Society of Editors conference, Bristol, 2008. Available at *www.societyofeditors.org*

A further gulf is opening up when it comes to the Code of Conduct's assertion that there is a public interest in preventing the public from being misled by an action or statement of an individual or organisation. There is a presumption that it is good for society to expose deceptions.

The courts are considerably more piecemeal in their approach. We are again in the realms of 'it depends' – on who is doing the misleading, whether they can claim the deception relates to private information and whether the courts deem it sufficiently important for the public to know the truth.

There was a worrying aside from Baroness Hale in *Campbell*. Although she accepted the newspaper's right to put the record straight in the instance of drug abuse, she says:

> "It might be questioned why, if a role model has adopted a stance which all would agree is beneficial rather than detrimental to society, it is so important to reveal that she has feet of clay."[101]

Why is it important? It is so important because the public should not be deceived even where that deception might be convenient for some. The public are not there to be fed a line and kept in compliant ignorance. Healthy public discourse has to be based on honest, rational foundations; anchored in reality not pretence.

It is of great concern when judges take the view that it doesn't really matter if the public are misled as long as it isn't about anything the courts consider important. That is dangerous territory to enter. There is enough that is phoney about the public sphere already without providing the pedlars of myths with the protection of the law. No-one has to lie to the media; they can always decline to comment.

Wherever public interest is relied upon as justification for putting into the public domain material considered defamatory or in breach of confidence, the degree of damage done has to be proportionate to the importance of the matter. So in *Campbell*, readers were entitled to know that Campbell had made misleading statements about drug use, but the newspaper should not have gone so far as to run a photograph of her outside Narcotics Anonymous which is by the nature of the organisation a private activity.

Judgments examined in the emerging appeals to uphold art.8 rights, suggest a move to define public interest in predominantly political terms. So infringements may be justified affecting the lives of those holding public office or involved in the implementation of public policy, but footballers, actors and other celebrities are generally off-limits. This comes through strongly in *McKennitt* where a woman who makes a living from performing publicly is judged not even to be a public figure and in the alphabet soup of anonymous privacy injunctions secured in the past few years which has been causing such a heated debate.

---

[101] *Campbell v MGN Ltd* [2004] UKHL 22, para.151.

Accusations of any impropriety have to be judged against what claims that person has made of themselves and what expectations there are of them. If a cabinet minister is caught committing adultery, abusing position or lying to the public, then an intrusion into an intimate area of his life and in greater detail could be acceptable. The cabinet minister claims to be a fine, upstanding family man in his election material so he has misled the public who can reasonably expect him to live up to his claims, behave within the law and meet the required standards of public life. His abuse of power undermines the political system and there is a clear public interest in exposing him. He may even resign.

If a pop singer has an extra-marital affair what justification do we have to publish? There is no criminality, hardly an impropriety in this day and age and he won't necessarily have said much on public record about his family life. The public has no particular expectations of him and no obvious harm has come of his fling. Even if the "other woman" or the wronged wife wants to tell her story, in the weighing of their art.10 rights against his art.8, the courts consider very little personal or public benefit can be claimed in the name of freedom of expression to counterbalance the damage to him from the intrusion into his privacy.

When it comes to putting the record straight, the PCC Code includes any attempt to mislead by anyone. There is no threshold regarding the type of person doing the misleading. The public is entitled to honesty across the board. Lying should be challenged—there is a public interest in honesty and in challenging dishonest versions of events.

Perhaps media lawyers in time will be able to establish a series of sliding scales with a points system. Take one backbench MP worth eight points, times a cocaine habit worth nine points, times fronting up a "Just Say No" drugs campaign worth eight points, making a total of 576 points. Victory to art.10 is possible.

Take one minor league footballer worth one point, times an extra-marital affair (barely worth anything in the courts these days), times no media profile worth speaking of, worth one point, making a total of one, heading towards zero. Defeat for art.10. Injunction granted.

This is not that much of a stretch from the principles being laid down by the higher courts in 21st century privacy cases. Some journalists might prefer the greater clarity of a Privacy Act but the other side of the coin is that codified statute can be rigid. News organisations want some "wriggle room" themselves to reflect the unique circumstances of each case. Much depends on whether we think MPs or judges more sympathetic to Freedom of Expression.

Certainly the news media can expect to have to work a great deal harder to justify the right to run intrusive stories and be clearer about why a story matters and why it needs to be in the public domain. We will return to this in greater detail in Ch.5 on Privacy and Confidentiality.

There is one further concern in the great proportionality debate over competing human rights. Apart from all the caveats and the accent being on the right to express, rather than the right to know, there is also a downside from the central, albeit understandable, focus on the rights of the individual rather than the collective. This opens up the risk that general, shared "public interest" may be downplayed.

Sir Christopher Meyer, then chairman of the Press Complaints Commission, made the point well with regard to moves to restrict coverage of inquests. He said:

"There will surely be a temptation for coroners, when faced with applications for anonymity from the bereaved, to side with those vulnerable individuals who appear before them against the interests of the general public—who will of course be absent and anonymous."[102]

The very suggestion of anonymity in some inquests would entirely negate its purpose —which is to uphold the rights of those who die in unusual circumstances to have a public investigation into the circumstances of their death (thankfully the Government backed off). Sir Christopher went on:

"The right of journalists to report on inquests is not to be defended solely in terms of press freedom, although that is of course important. Such a right is also a key feature of an open society in which the public as a whole has a right to know what is going on and be reassured that there are no cover-ups of unusual or premature deaths.

"As with evidence given in other courts, the possibility of public scrutiny also focuses the minds of those appearing before the coroner on the importance of giving accurate evidence."[103]

These are the kinds of other "public interest" benefits which need to be accounted for in demonstrating why freedom of expression should prevail in any particular circumstance.

8. Prior Restraint in Practice

Publish and be damned has always been a potentially expensive policy but it is vital that it remains an option. In less inflammatory terms, it means journalists retain the freedom to run any story, as long as we are prepared to accept the consequences. Anticipation of those consequences can for ethical, or purely financial, reasons lead to a story being spiked but at least that is the journalist's decision.

---

[102] Sir Christopher Meyer, "PCC in plea against Coroner gagging powers", *Press Gazette*, September 5, 2006.
[103] Sir Christopher Meyer, "PCC in plea against Coroner gagging powers", *Press Gazette*, September 5, 2006.

To intervene to prevent the story being run at all is the most draconian infringement of freedom of expression and yet we are seeing more of it thanks to the Human Rights Act.

The debacle over the attempt to injunct an email in the 2007 cash for honours inquiry demonstrates the practical difficulty of restraining media across the board. If an injunction is sought against one news organisation, as it was against the BBC here, other media may not even be aware as there may well be a bar even on reporting the existence of the injunction. In this case, as the BBC fought to ease the scope of the injunction, its battle came to dominate the television news and details were gradually released. Meanwhile, the *Guardian* went ahead with a fuller version of the claims and attempts to impose an injunction failed because, by the time restraint was sought, the edition carrying the story was already in circulation.

Once a story begins to emerge it can be difficult to put the brakes on it in our digital age. Even though a police inquiry was held to be at stake, the central involvement of leading Government figures made it almost impossible to keep the lid on the information, which ended up in the public domain despite the best efforts of the Attorney General.[104]

Injunctions have been a feature of our law for centuries, as some commentators during the present clamour have been at pains to point out. They were not invented by the Human Rights Act but as more cases are being fought on art.8 privacy grounds, the demand for injunctions has inevitably risen. No-one wants defamatory material to run, but at least it can be corrected after publication if untrue and damages paid to compensate. Where the main concern is secrecy, logically prior restraint will be to the fore as the whole purpose is to stop information entering the public domain.

And, not surprisingly, the courts are often persuaded to protect not just the information in dispute but also the identities of those seeking injunctions. Presumably, the moment we heard a Premiership footballer was seeking an injunction everyone would jump to the same conclusion. Certainly once the media knew the name of the person with a secret, it would be tempting to try to find out the nature of the secret. But the media is trusted to withhold information and/or avoid jigsaw identification in many other legal proceedings, so why not here? The penalties for breaching an injunction include imprisonment and unlimited fines, so why is the extra layer of secrecy required?

Worse still are super injunctions whereby the applicant and the courts are so concerned about setting the rumour mill in motion that secrecy is applied to the very existence of the action. In these cases the media can be barred from even mentioning that an action is taking place. The imposition of a super-injunction in the *Trafigura* case[105] was thwarted by a combination of fast-spreading tweets hinting that something was up and the attempt to extend the gagging order to reporting questions

---

[104] *Attorney General v BBC* [2007] EWCA Civ 280.
[105] *RJW & SJW v Guardian News and Media Ltd & persons unknown*, [2009] Q.B. HQ09.

in Parliament which caused outrage among MPs. This case will be discussed further in Ch.5 on Privacy and Confidentiality but two points are worth mentioning here.

1 Attempts at prior restraint are not limited to celebrities trying to keep quiet about their infidelities.
2 The anarchic nature of digital communication makes enforcement of orders much harder. Mainstream journalists are expected to obey injunctions, and risk a combination of imprisonment and unlimited fines for any breach. Yet in many high-profile cases, the identities can be found easily online often in a far more damaging, salacious and unreliable format. Judges are almost obliged to downplay the significance of these alternative informal sources because otherwise the private information would be deemed to be in the public domain and the injunction would be invalid.

Super injunctions and anonymised rulings are significant departures from the principle of open justice and their proliferation caused sufficient concern to trigger an inquiry by Master of the Rolls Lord Neuberger. He encouraged courts to be more selective in their use of super-injunctions.

The Human Rights Act has clearly provided momentum to the emergence of what is tantamount to privacy law in the UK and this inevitably puts greater emphasis on issues of prior restraint.

As leading privacy lawyer Hugh Tomlinson said in 2009:

"The new law of privacy has come a long way in a short time. Many issues remain unresolved or only partially clear. What is clear is that kissing and telling and "public photography" have become a lot more legally hazardous. The law of privacy is slowly having an impact on the staple fare of the British tabloid reader. We are gradually moving from a position where anything could be published unless it was forbidden to the opposite – nothing about an identifiable individual can be published unless it can be justified. Under the influence of human rights case law from Strasbourg we are moving slowly but inescapably towards the stricter privacy protection of French or Italian law."[106]

Max Mosley's continuing bid to require prior notification[107] would be a major step towards the media requiring permission for any mention of individuals which would stifle debate massively and crucially. Prior restraint is at odds with freedom of expression and any extension of its application is a matter of immense concern to journalists.

---

[106] Times/Matrix Privacy Forum in April 2009. Accessed at: *http://inforrm.wordpress.com/2010/04/30/revisited-opinion-privacy-the-way-ahead-part-3-options-for-the-future*
[107] *Mosley v UK* [2011] ECHR 774, lost by Mosley but subject to appeal as of July 2011.

9. Forum shopping in practice

The transfer of journalism online has moved the question of forum shopping up the agenda. Although jurisdictional issues are technically platform-neutral, online material is more likely to offer claimants a choice of where to sue. The global spread of audience driven by the web makes it even easier to demonstrate that, although material may be generated in one country, it is consumed all around the world. In defamation terms, if the subject has a reputation in a particular country where the relevant material has been accessed, a writ may be issued.

Lawyers assessing the chances of success may decide one forum is likely to be more sympathetic than another in terms of whether they win or lose, are awarded higher damages and/or face lower costs.

Thanks to the American constitution, journalists are generally in a stronger position in the US courts, so European jurisdictions are more attractive for claimants. London, despite its relatively high costs, has been a popular choice particularly for American litigants who have little prospect of achieving remedy at home.

Some cases went ahead based on the letter of the law but involving minimal exposure. These contrived actions in which the UK has a 'bit' part in terms of both the creation and consumption of the material at issue will hopefully become a thing of the past. The new Defamation Bill[108] proposes to raise the bar to make it easier to reject claims which do not naturally relate to Britain.

The *Ehrenfeld* case discussed earlier[109] caused political as well as legal fallout with much outrage in the US at the suggestion of its authors or journalists falling prey to more draconian legal environments. The clamour and condemnation of Britain's defamation laws as overly restrictive hopefully helped to shame politicians into finally taking action.

Significantly, action can be taken in multiple jurisdictions, although the costs and risks obviously multiply too. While this could be seen to deter the actions, the rich and famous may be prepared to take their chances, meaning the potential costs to news organisations which fight and lose would be even more daunting.

Lord Chief Justice Sir Igor Judge told the Society of Editor's Stansted conference in 2009:[110]

> "I am not proud of reading, as I frequently do, that 'London is the libel capital of the world'. I do not regard it as a badge of honour. I am deeply unsympathetic to 'forum shopping'. I believe that justice should be done where justice needs to be done. If you commit a

---

[108] Available on the Ministry of Justice website: *www.justice.gov.uk.*
[109] *Mahfouz v Ehrenfeld* [2005] EWHC 1156 (QB).
[110] Society of Editors, Stansted, 2009 *http://www.societyofeditors.co.uk/page-view. php?pagename=KeynoteAddress2009* [Accessed April 2011].

murder in Bristol, it should normally be tried in Bristol. Forum shopping has no appeal to me. Forum shopping means that a case is litigated, not where the alleged wrong occurred, or has caused serious damage, but in the country or before the courts which might advantage one of the litigants."

As he pointed out, it was not within his power to change the practice: the remedy would require legislation which may now materialise. The changes envisaged in the Defamation Bill would offer some protection in this regard, but journalists need to remain alert to the legal implications of their work being accessed in many different countries, thus making it subject to many different regimes of media law and regulation. For most UK titles the main external audience is in the freer US environment so there have been fewer nasty legal shocks for British journalists but the global spread of content requires global legal awareness too.

10. Conditional Fee Arrangements in Practice

Despite the noble sentiments of "justice for all" behind the introduction of CFAs they don't appear to have widened the range of media litigants much beyond the usual suspects among the rich and powerful. In practice CFAs have just upped the bill for media defendants. In the days of outrageously high damages awards, news organisations only got stung if they lost. Now defending a claim for libel or misuse of private information is potentially a prohibitively expensive undertaking, win or lose. Damages have been capped but costs have soared, making them the prime consideration in whether to proceed with any action.

A losing defendant in these "no-win, no-fee" actions pays all costs plus a success fee, but even if the media wins, and even if costs are awarded these can be claimed only from the claimant, who may not have the assets and is not required to take out "after the event" insurance. The main gainers would appear to be the lawyers.

As the *Daily Mail*'s Editor in Chief Paul Dacre complained in his Society of Editors speech:

"Costs in CFA cases, as many of you here know, can be almost infinite with lawyers entitled to 'success fees' of up to 100% on top of their actual bills. This gives them a positive financial incentive to take relatively straight-forward cases, worth just a few thousand pounds, and run them as long as possible. Adding insult to injury, CFA claimants can take out very expensive ATE (after the event) insurance policies to protect themselves against costs. If they win, the paper has to pay the claimant's premium, but if they lose - and this is the cynicism of it all – the insurer rarely enforces the charges because the claimant invariably cannot afford to pay.

Let me give you an example: Martyn Jones, an .. MP, sued the Mail on Sunday over their claim that he had sworn at a Commons official. The Mail on Sunday believed it had rock-solid witnesses and decided to fight the case. In the event, they lost and were ordered to pay £5,000 in damages. The MP's lawyers claimed costs of £388,000 – solicitor's costs of £68,000, plus 100% success fees, barrister's costs of £63,000, plus 100% success fees, VAT and libel insurance of £68,000. Associated's costs were £136,000 making a total of £520,000 costs in a case that awarded damages of just £5,000 in a dispute over a simple matter of fact.

Can it really be right for a QC in a libel case to be paid £7,000 for a day in court whilst the same QC, prosecuting or defending a serious case at the Old Bailey, may receive less than £600 a day – less than a tenth?

The result is that today, newspapers – even wealthy ones like the Mail – think long and hard before contesting actions, even if they know they are in the right, for fear of the ruinous financial implications. For the provincial and local press, such actions are now out of the question. Instead, they stump up some cash, money they can't afford, to settle as quickly as possible, to avoid court actions – which, if they were to lose, could, in some case, close them. Some justice!"[111]

Again there is legislation in the pipeline which could redress the balance here – although its main target is the ambulance-chasing personal injury claim sector. Attempts to control costs in claims brought against the media have had limited success, so most media would probably trade the 10 per cent increase in damages envisaged in return for the end to success fees. As the examples given here and earlier in the chapter show, the amounts involved in damages tend to be a fraction of the total costs so for the media in particular, this is looks like a better deal.

The move to a legislative solution follows not only a welter of complaints from the media but also some recognition of the dilemma within the judiciary and now the ECHR in *MGN v UK*.[112]

In *Tierney v News Group Newspapers Ltd* [2006],[113] Eady J. cited Brooke L.J. in *Musa King v Telegraph Group Ltd* [2005]:

"It cannot be just to submit the defendant in these cases where their right to freedom of expression is at stake, to a costs regime where the costs they will have to pay if they lose are neither reasonable nor proportionate and they have no reasonable prospect of recovering their reasonable and proportionate costs if they win."[114]

---

[111] Speech by Paul Dacre, Editor in Chief, *Daily Mail*, to Society of Editors, Bristol, 2008. Available at *www.societyofeditors.org*.
[112] [2011] ECHR 66.
[113] [2006] EWHC 3275 (QB).
[114] [2005] 1 W.L.R. 2282 para.101.

In *Tierney*, a legislative solution was seen as the appropriate route. Cost capping procedures were tried but the judiciary was concerned that severe cuts would make it harder for a claimant without the resource for other than a CFA-funded action to attract lawyers to take a case. With damages awards reduced, the costs and success fees are what make the risk worth their while. But, as the Dacre figures suggest, the legal representatives have some room for manoeuvre on civil actions without putting themselves on the breadline. The new Government line is that worthy claimants will still find lawyers to take their case and that putting an end to easy money will deter the commercial firms who whip up claims artificially.

It would also not be fair under the principle of "equality of arms" for the media defendant to weigh in with top-notch counsel and the CFA claimant not to be able to match it. Horse-trading can take place where both sides agree to deals such as to instruct only junior counsel to keep costs down. In *Tierney*, Eady J. speaks favourably of the tendency, not shown in *Tierney*, to impose costs capping on both sides rather than on the CFA claimant only, which would uphold the "equality of arms" principle. It cannot be healthy for media organisations to throw in the towel and fail to defend their rights to freedom of expression because the costs of fighting their corner are so high.

This "chilling" effect facing journalists and their employers means the handling of civil actions has been driven more by issues of cost than principle. One of the most galling experiences for any editor is to pay out under advice from insurers who play safe and would rather accept a dent to the news organisation's reputation by admitting fault than a dip in the bank balance of paying to fight. Indeed, the temptation grows not to run contentious stories in the first place, especially when the outcome seems so unpredictable and the costs so high, win or lose.

What it definitely means is that the cost of making legal mistakes is rising. Consequently it becomes even more important for journalists to understand how to tell stories in legally-safe ways—and for organisations to have the courage to stand up for their freedom to tell them. Hopefully the planned abolition of CFAs will make that more likely.

11. Freedom of Expression Around the World

Our discussion on Freedom of Expression should end with a reminder of the appalling price many journalists pay for exercising that right. Journalists in many parts of the world don't just suffer embarrassment or upset by upholding their art.10 rights. They die for them.

And it isn't just the state that suppresses news and deprives the public of information. BBC Gaza correspondent Alan Johnston survived his kidnapping ordeal. Many journalists do not.

Gangsterism is rife, especially in countries where the traditional forces of law and order are disrupted, as they were in Northern Ireland and as they are in many countries of the world, including Russia and the Philippines. In too many countries, the restraint on a journalist's freedom of expression is a bullet in the head. Masked gunmen executed 11 employees of a fledgling TV channel in Baghdad in October 2006, the year of the murder of Russian journalist Anna Politkovskaya, who exposed human rights abuses in Chechnya. Barely one in ten murders of a journalist has led to a prosecution.[115]

Significantly, an Asian editor, forced recently to operate with soldiers in his newsroom, came up with an interesting answer to the question: What is the greatest threat to press freedom?

"Self-censorship" was his reply. He likened freedom of speech to an elastic band—it only fulfils its purpose when in use; when stretched. Journalists must exercise their freedom, investigate its limits or it withers. His greatest fear was of journalists playing safe; not asking the awkward questions, not running stories that ruffle feathers within the corridors of power and thereby selling the public short.

Journalists must stand up for art.10 rights, pushing the boundaries of freedom of expression and pursuing the cause of a free press. The greater our knowledge of the law, the greater our chances of success. But we cannot afford to stand idly by as celebrities, officials and politicians look to the law to gag us.

CHAPTER SUMMARY: FREEDOM OF EXPRESSION

Freedom of expression is a fundamental human right and cornerstone of democracy now enshrined in Britain's Human Rights Act. Our claim is laid out in art.10 of the European Convention of Human Rights which states:

"1. Everyone has the right to freedom of expression. This right shall include freedom to hold opinions and to receive and impart information and ideas without interference by public authority and regardless of frontiers."

But like all rights it can be outweighed as outlined in art.10(2):

"2. The exercise of these freedoms, since it carries with it duties and responsibilities, may be subject to such formalities, conditions,

---

[115] "What price world press freedom when journalists die?" *International News Safety Institute*, May 2007, *www.newssafety.com*

restrictions or penalties as are prescribed by law and are necessary in a democratic society, in the interest of national security, territorial integrity or public safety, for the prevention of disorder or crime, for the protection of health or morals, for the protection of the reputation or rights of others, for preventing the disclosure of information received in confidence, or for maintaining the authority and impartiality of the judiciary."

The right to Freedom of Expression also has to be weighed against the specific convention rights of others, notably art.8 to privacy and art.6 to fair trial. This balancing act is at the heart of media law. It is a core responsibility of a journalist to uphold the right to freedom of expression.

- **Public interest** is a key concept and justification employed in cases when journalists need to argue that freedom of expression outweighs other individual rights such as to privacy and reputation. The Press Complaints Commission Code of Conduct definition has wide currency in the media but judges tend to interpret it more narrowly.
- **The rule against prior restraint** allows for a free flow of information on the basis that any damage deemed to be caused unjustifiably can be compensated for after publication. Journalists and their media organisations must pay the price of infringements of the law or claimants' rights but should not be told what can and cannot be printed in advance by a court or the state. Injunctions preventing publication clearly breach this rule. Privacy rights granted under the Human Rights Act are making injunctions to prevent the misuse of private information more common.
- **Forum shopping.** Britain had become the "libel capital" of the world because claimants expected more favourable treatment under our Defamation Act than elsewhere, certainly in the US. This led to cases being pursued here despite publication and audience being mainly outside the UK. The Defamation Bill aims to raise the threshold so as to limit the scope for forum shopping.
- **Conditional fee arrangements.** No-win, no-fee arrangements in civil actions, including those against the media, were introduced to allow people who could not afford full costs to bring actions. But the success fees involved saw costs spiralling way beyond the level of damages involved in the case. The "chilling effect" of costs exceeding £1 million was accepted by the European Court of Human Rights as a breach of art.10 rights. The current coalition Government has to work out how to change the system to achieve compliance and make costs "proportionate".

CHAPTER 3: DEFAMATION

PART ONE: DEFAMATION

In the first edition of this book we highlighted the case of Rupert Lowe the then chairman of Southampton Football Club who had taken action against *The Times* newspaper for defamation for publishing the following words:

" . . . a chairman whose idea of crisis management was to remove his manager over a court case that collapsed within 24 hours . . . How would Lowe approach the issue of an England player accused of breaking the law, when he so shabbily handled the case of David Jones, his manager?"

The point we were making was that journalists, or indeed anyone who puts information into the public domain, do not have to use seemingly strong or abusive words to prompt an action for defamation or indeed to convince a jury that the "sting" was defamatory.

In April 2010 Mrs Justice Sharp had to rule on whether the *Daily Telegraph* had libelled a claimant Dee in referring to him as the ". . . worst professional tennis player in the world . . ."[1] The judge ruled that the comment had to be linked to the fact that he had lost 54 consecutive games on the professional tennis circuit—a fact made abundantly clear in the *Telegraph* article. She went on to say: "There can be no rational conclusion other than that the claim of justification must succeed." The point to emphasise though is that this clamant was willing to bring the action in the first place when it must have been obvious that he had only a remote chance of winning the case because his record of consecutive defeats was the world record equalling worst ever run of consecutive losses on the international professional circuit.

Indeed the litigation came before the courts three times. On the first occasion in 2009 Mr Justice Eady had offered his view on the matter:

"The object of any libel action is to restore reputation. It is difficult to see what the claimant hopes to gain from this litigation. It may be true that the newspaper was 'having a laugh' at his expense, but it is not immediately apparent how the claim is likely to restore or enhance his reputation. Nonetheless the solicitors have lodged a costs estimate

---

[1] *Dee v Telegraph Media Group Ltd* [2010] EWHC 924 (QB).

of over £500,000. To an outside observer, it may seem difficult to understand how the case could give rise to such expenditure."

The lessons from this are obvious. One never knows when an action for defamation may be commenced and at what cost in terms of money and time. The two cases mentioned above relate to what one might call conventional media offerings. The advent and global reach of the internet places professional journalists, so called citizen journalists and bloggers at risk of a defamation action.

The most innocuous of words could be the catalyst to legal action.

The protection of reputation is at the very core of the defence of defamation but it may sit uneasily with the desire of journalists and others to express their views in the context of their art.10 rights. Lord Nicholls in the vitally important case of *Reynolds v Times Newspapers* [2001][2] spoke of the interaction of two fundamental rights; freedom of expression and protection of reputation.[3] The traditional role of the press is to be both watchdog and bloodhound in the pursuit of information in which the public has a legitimate interest. In *Sanoma Uitgevers BV v The Netherlands* [2010][4] it was expressed in these terms by the European Court of Human Rights:

> "Freedom of expression constitutes one of the essential foundations of a democratic society and the safeguards to be afforded to the press are of particular importance. Whilst the press must not overstep the bounds set, not only does the press have the task of imparting such information and ideas: the public also has a right to receive them. Were it otherwise, the press would be unable to play its vital role of 'public watchdog'."[5]

In this chapter we look first at the legal context within which journalists will operate. The defamation laws have been under critical scrutiny on a number of levels over the past few years. The government has just produced a new Defamation Bill[6] in 2011. While it doesn't amount to a radical reappraisal of the totality of defamation principles it is wide ranging and reflects the concerns expressed in a number of quarters about the operation of the current law. Reference will be made to the proposed changes and amendments to the law as we deal with each of the areas of law. However the Bill will not become law before this book is published and therefore readers should ensure they refer to the new Defamation Act that is likely to result. The standard defences have come under particular scru-

---

[2] [1999] UKHL 45.
[3] [1999] UKHL 45 at para.1.
[4] [2010] ECHR 1284.
[5] [2010] ECHR 1284 at para.50.
[6] Available on the Ministry of Justice website: *www.justice.gov.uk* Consultation period ended on June 10, 2011. See also Appendix 3.

tiny as has the multiple publication rule which it is proposed will be abolished. Clause 1 of the Bill provides that a statement will not be defamatory unless its publication has caused or is likely to cause substantial harm to the claimant's reputation. The intention is to send out the message that trivial claims will not be countenanced. However this is hardly a radical departure from the current position where trivial cases rarely make it to trial as shown in the *Dee* case referred to earlier.

1. Freedom of Expression

We made the point in the introductory chapter that freedom of expression as defined in art.10 of the European Convention on Human Rights is the foundation from which all journalists operate. The general principles are not in doubt and a neat summary is to be found in the case of *Selisto v Finland* [2004][7]:

General Principles
"According to the court's well-established case-law, freedom of expression constitutes one of the essential foundations of a democratic society and one of the basic conditions for its progress and each individual's self-fulfilment. Subject to paragraph 2 of Article 10, it is applicable not only to "information" or "ideas" that are favourably received or regarded as inoffensive or as a matter of indifference, but also to those that offend, shock or disturb. Such are the demands of pluralism, tolerance and broadmindedness, without which there is no "democratic society.". . . This freedom is subject to the exceptions set out in Article 10(2) which must, however, be construed strictly. The need for any restrictions must be established convincingly.

The Court further recalls the essential function the press fulfils in a democratic society. Although the press must not overstep certain bounds, particularly as regards the reputation and rights of others and the need to prevent disclosure of confidential information, its duty is nevertheless to impart—in a manner consistent with its obligations and responsibilities— information and ideas on all matters of public interest. Not only does it have the task of imparting such information and ideas: the public also has a right to receive them. In addition, the Court is mindful of the fact that journalistic freedom also covers possible recourse to a degree of exaggeration, or even provocation . . ."

[7] [2004] ECHR 634.

This "theme" is also reflected in statements of the UK judiciary at the highest level. Thus in the key House of Lords decision of *Reynolds v Times Newspapers Ltd* [1999][8] Lord Nicholls said:

> "My starting point is freedom of expression . . . At a pragmatic level freedom to disseminate and receive information on political matters is essential to the proper functioning of the system of parliamentary democracy cherished in this country . . . The common law is to be developed and applied in a manner consistent with Article 10 . . . and the court must take account of relevant decisions of the European Court of Human Rights.
>
> Likewise, there is no need to elaborate on the importance of the role discharged by the media in the expression and communication of information and comment on political matters . . . Without freedom of expression by the media, freedom of expression would be a hollow concept. The interest of a democratic society in ensuring a free press weighs heavily in the balance in deciding whether any curtailment of this freedom bears a reasonable relationship to the purpose of the curtailment. In this regard it should be kept in mind that one of the contemporary functions of the media is investigative journalism. This activity, as much as the traditional activities of reporting and commenting, is part of the vital role of the press and the media generally."

We make no apology for quoting this passage at length because with these words you have the explicit support of the highest court in England and Wales and the European Court of Human Rights. It should be noted but not with any particular concern that the press must not "overstep certain bounds" and that must include reference to the laws on defamation.

However a distinction can be drawn between private citizens and politicians whose reputations *as politicians* will undoubtedly come under greater press scrutiny that any ordinary citizen has a right to expect. Examples of politicians taking court action based upon media criticism of their work are rare. One exception is *Lait v Evening Standard* [2010].[9] The claimant was the MP for Beckenham. She, along with other MPs, had written a letter to *The Times* in which they criticised proposed changes to the parliamentary expenses system. The *Evening Standard* published an article commenting on the contents of the letter. In the article it was stated that the claimant was ". . . forced to pay back nearly £25,000 after it emerged she had made a major capital gain on the sale of a house funded by the taxpayer . . ."

It transpired that the writer of the article had got his facts wrong as the claimant had not been forced to pay back £25,000 nor did she in fact do so. The *Standard* issued a correction some 16 days later in the following terms:

---

[8] [1999] UKHL 44.
[9] [2010] EWHC 642 (QB) and *Lait v Evening Standard (No 2)*[2010] EWHC 3239 (QB).

"In an article . . . the name of Ms Jacqui Lait MP was, due to mistake, wrongly connected with the sale of a home funded by the taxpayer. We apologise for this error."

The apology was not relevant to the claim for defamation. The basis of the claim for defamation was that the reference to being forced to pay back £25,000 meant that she was "milking" the expenses system and that to comment as she did in the letter amounted to hypocrisy. Eady J. concluded that although the words were not capable of bearing the defamatory meaning alleged by the claimant they were capable of bearing one or more other defamatory meanings. Further pleadings were made and the case came before Mr Justice Eady for a second time in December 2010. The defendants pleaded fair comment by way of defence. Each party asked for summary judgment. It was held that the defence of fair comment was "bound to succeed" if the case went to trial. In accordance with the advice given by the Court of Appeal in *Burstein v Associated Newspapers* [2007][10] the judge dismissed the application. The Court of Appeal had ruled in 2007 that it was generally for a jury to decide on whether a claim succeeds of fails:

"But if this court is firmly of the view that only one answer is available to any reasonable jury and that the defence of fair comment must succeed, then it is the court's duty so to rule. Anything else would not be judicial self-restraint but an abdication of judicial responsibility."[11]

It goes without saying that all is not lost even if an action is commenced. The time and costs involved in defending an action must act as an incentive to keep well away from the court and therefore to be wary before publishing. There is no need to practise defensive journalism.

2. Public Interest and Responsible Communication

The first chapter made reference to the overriding importance to the media of the public interest concept. It would be helpful to take a moment to revisit Ch.2 and reacquaint yourself with the legal and industry context to public interest. In the key areas of privacy and defamation the public interest can be the determining factor in defeating the claimant's case. For example it was mentioned in Ch.2 and in

---

[10] [2007] EWCA Civ 600.
[11] [2007] EWCA Civ 600 at para.29.

the privacy chapter that it was in the public interest to "put the record straight" as illustrated by the *Daily Mirror's* article relating to Naomi Campbell's use of drugs after she had publicly denied taking drugs. In respect of defamation the Reynold's defence is essentially a public interest justification for publishing defamatory material providing the journalism that underpinned the feature was deemed to be "responsible." (See later in this chapter).

Clause 2 of the Defamation Bill creates a new defence of responsible *publication* on matters of public interest. This is essentially the *Reynolds* defence put onto a statutory basis but recognising that the defence should be open to a wider audience than just mainstream journalists. This seems to be following the lead in Canada when in late 2009 the Supreme Court recognised a defence of responsible *communication* on matters of public interest rather than responsible *journalism*.[12] The defence was described in these terms in the *Quan* case:

"The defence of responsible communication on matters of public interest recognised in *Grant v Torstar Corporation* is applicable where the publication is on a matter of public interest and, having regard to the relevant factors, the publisher was diligent in trying to verify the allegations." [13]

The Supreme Court stated the various components of the defence to be:

I.   The publication is on a matter of public interest.
II.   The publisher was diligent in trying to verify the allegation, having regard to:
        • the seriousness of the allegation;
        • the public importance of the matter;
        • the urgency of the matter;
        • the status and reliability of the source;
        • whether the plaintiff's side of the story was sought and accurately reported;
        • whether the defamatory statement's public interest lay in the fact that it was made rather than its truth (reportage); and
        • any other relevant considerations.

These two cases acknowledge that it is not only professional journalists who are in the business of communicating ideas and opinions in the internet and digital economy eras. As the court said in the *Grant* case:

"The press and others engaged in public communication on matters of public interest like bloggers must act carefully, having regard to the injury that a false statement can cause."[14]

---

[12] See *Grant v Torstar Corporation* [2009] SCC 61 and *Quan v Cussons* [2009] SCC 62.
[13] See generally *Quan* at para 28–32.
[14] See the *Grant* case at para.62.

If one compares the Canadian principles to that put forward in the new Defamation Bill one sees a close similarity of approach. It is deemed to be a defence to an action for defamation for the defendant to show that the statement made is on a matter of public interest and that the defendant acted responsibly in publishing the statement. In deciding whether the defendant acted responsibly the court is entitled to take the following matters into account:

I.   The nature of the publication and its context.

II.   The seriousness of any imputation about the claimant that is conveyed by the statement.

III.   The extent to which the subject matter of the statement is of public interest.

IV.   The information the defendant had before publishing the statement and what the defendant knew about the reliability of that information.

V.   Whether the defendant sought the claimant's views on the statement before publishing it and whether the publication included an account of any views the claimant expressed.

VI.   Whether the defendant took any other steps to verify the accuracy of the statement.

VII.   The timing of the publication and whether there was reason to think it was in the public interest for the statement to be published urgently.

VIII.   The tone of the statement (including, whether it draws appropriate distinctions between suspicions, opinions, allegations and proven facts).

A defendant is to be treated as having acted responsibly in publishing a statement if it was published as part of an accurate and impartial account of a dispute between the claimant and another person. This would appear to be a codification of the current law on reportage. (See later in this chapter).

The approach is very similar to the Canadian approach although the UK version adds a little more detail than its Canadian counterpart.

3. Reputation

On this voyage of initial discovery, we now come to reputation. Even journalists have reputations to lose although that proposition may be a matter of some debate! It was reported in 2009 that journalism is not held in high esteem by the public with only 15 per cent of respondents in a YouGov poll believing that "red-top" journalists could be relied upon to tell the truth.[15] When a publication or broadcast amounts to an attack upon reputation then you are at risk of being sued for defamation. The risk is always there. However, the success rate will be massively lower than the risk might suggest. Please remember it is not only individuals who have reputations to lose. A company has the right to sue for defamation and therefore attacks upon a company, its products and performance should always be underpinned by accurate and verifiable information. The other vital piece of information to bear in mind is that, as the law stands, there is an automatic presumption of damage to reputation as far as libel proceedings are concerned.

If the words are proved to have been defamatory then the claimant will succeed without any need to prove that the person or company has actually suffered a negative consequence to their reputation as a result of the "sting." This fairly contentious position was reviewed by the House of Lords in the case of *Jameel v Wall Street Journal Europe Ltd* [2006].[16] The current law was upheld albeit by a 3:2 majority.

As Lord Bingham succinctly put it:

> "The first (question raised by the appeal) concerns the entitlement of a trading corporation . . . to sue and recover damages without pleading or proving special damage."[17]

The majority were of the opinion that the good name of a company is a valuable commodity. The loss of reputation can have damaging consequences for a company that may not be apparent immediately after the alleged defamatory material is published or even when proceedings are commenced. The minority view was represented by Lord Hoffmann and Baroness Hale. It could be argued that their approach is the more enlightened and reflects the view that the press should be free to challenge the actions of large corporations just as much as they have a duty to criticise the actions of government.

As Baroness Hale points out:

> "These days the dividing line between governmental and non-governmental organisations is increasingly difficult to draw. The power wielded by the major multi-national corporations is enormous and growing. The freedom to criticise them may be at least as important in a democratic society as the freedom to criticise the government."[18]

To be fair Lord Bingham did state that, if it could be shown that a corporation had suffered no financial loss, the measure of damages should be kept "strictly within modest bounds."

---

[15] Media Standards Trust: A More Accountable Press: January 2009.
[16] [2006] UKHL 44.
[17] [2006] UKHL 44 at para.1.
[18] [2006] UKHL 44 at para.158.

The decision of the majority in *Jameel* on the damages point should be regarded as somewhat conservative. The Faulks Committee, in considering the future of the defamation laws way back in 1975, proposed:

"That no action in defamation should lie at the suit of any trading corporation unless such corporation can establish either: (i) that it has suffered special damage, or (ii) that the words were likely to cause it pecuniary damage."

In 1964, Lord Reid had expressed the view that "a company cannot be injured in its feelings; it can only be injured in its pocket."[19]

Yet as a consequence of the *Jameel* decision, at least for the foreseeable future, that issue is settled in favour of the presumption of damage to reputation irrespective of whether the claimant is an individual or trading corporation.

It remains to be seen what impact if any the "substantial harm" test proposed in the Defamation Bill will have in practise upon the current law. A claim will be ruled out unless it can be shown that the publication "has caused or is likely to cause substantial harm to the reputation of the claimant." It is upon the latter category that companies are likely to frame their claims. So evidence will need to be forthcoming that the company's profits have been adversely affected as a result of the attack upon its reputation and/or that of its products. The debating point of course will be what amounts to substantial harm. This cannot be determined purely by the reduction in profit. Companies will also have to prove the causal link between the alleged defamatory comments and the reduction in profits.

Few companies sue for defamation and the current common law position is unlikely to change if this proposal becomes the statutory test for defamation. The intention to reduce trivial claims for defamation is laudable but the price to pay for that may well be that there will be more trials at the initial stages of whether the substantial harm test is likely to be satisfied. This could push up the cost of litigation at a time when the overall objective is to reduce the cost of defamation actions.

We now refer you to a number of judicial statements to establish the importance of reputation in the eyes of the law.

In *Berkoff v Burchill & Another* [1996][20] Neill L.J. quoted from the Canadian case of *Manning v Hill* [1995][21]:

"... the protection of reputation remains of vital importance ... reputation is the 'fundamental foundation on which people are able to interact with each other in social environments.' At the same time it serves the equally or perhaps the more fundamentally important purpose of fostering our self-image and sense of self-worth. This sentiment was eloquently expressed by Stewart J. in *Rosenblatt v Bear* (1966) 383 US 75

[19] *Lewis v Daily Telegraph* [1964] A.C.234 at p.262.
[20] [1996] EWCA Civ 564.
[21] (1995) D.L.R. (4th Issue) 129.

at 92: "The right of a man to the protection of his own reputation from unjustified invasion and wrongful hurt reflects no more than our basic concept of the essential dignity and worth of every human being - a concept at the root of any decent system of ordered liberty."

In the landmark *Reynolds* case Lord Nicholls said this:

"Reputation is an integral and important part of the dignity of the individual. It also forms the basis of many decisions in a democratic society which are fundamental to its wellbeing: who to employ or work for, whom to promote, whom to do business with or to vote for. Once besmirched by an unfounded allegation in a national newspaper, a reputation can be damaged forever, especially if there is no opportunity to vindicate one's reputation . . . Protection of reputation is conducive to the public good. It is in the public interest that the reputation of public figures should not be debased falsely."

Mr Justice Gray commented in *Charman v Orion Publishing Group Ltd (No 3)* [2006][22]:

". . . there is a clear public interest in the promotion of (a) free and vigorous press to keep the public informed and journalists should be permitted a good deal of latitude in how they present the material; but reputation is an integral and important part of the dignity of the individual, the protection of which is conducive to the public good. In some cases the reputations of other individuals than the claimant may be engaged."

It must not be thought that reputation is an "all or nothing" concept. You either have a good reputation or you don't. The Dublin Circuit Court held in November 2010 that a man serving a jail sentence for child pornography offences was entitled to a declaration under the Irish Defamation Act 2009 that a story in the *Star on Sunday* was false and defamatory. It had been argued on behalf of the newspaper that because of his conviction he could have no reputation in the eyes of right-thinking people. The judge took the view that simply because the plaintiff had a conviction did not mean that he was "beyond the pale of reputation." It was pointed out that he had admitted his guilt, made efforts to address his addiction and rehabilitate himself, and was seeking to be open and honest with his family. He concluded that the plaintiff had a "residual" reputation which was capable of being damaged. It was accepted that if an early voluntary admission of guilt was a mitigating factor in sentencing it could also be a factor in helping to determine whether an element of a person's reputation was still intact. The story in

---

[22] [2006] EWHC 1756 Q.B. at para.108.

which the plaintiff was described as a "twisted pervert" was deemed to be both defamatory and inhibited his attempts to rehabilitate himself.[23]

This decision is not binding in England and Wales but there is no reason in principle why a court in this jurisdiction should not come to the same conclusion. So in essence there are two "types" of reputation that can be harmed by defamatory statements: "Full" and "Residual."

So to summarise, reputations are worth protecting in law. That process is for the public good. The preservation and encouragement of freedom of expression is also deemed to be for the public good. There, in a nutshell, you have the journalists' dilemma. Which will take precedence? According to Gray J., a journalist will be allowed a fair measure of latitude when presenting a story but in so doing he or she must not exceed the bounds of what a responsible journalist would do. Unless, of course, the journalist is fully aware that the story is untrue and the intention is to attack the individual and his reputation regardless of the likely consequences.

4. General Principles of Defamation

In our opinion, if a journalist is aware of the basic legal principles of defamation that knowledge should assist in making informed choices about what to publish with minimal risk of a defamation action resulting. Initially, consider the matter from any claimant's viewpoint.

The first stage is that the claimant has taken umbrage at what has been published. It has been regarded as an unwarranted attack on the person's reputation. Everyone is presumed to have a good reputation. As the libel law stands at the moment the claimant doesn't need to prove damage has resulted from the "sting" although the opposite is true if the action for defamation is based upon slander. Cases dealing with slander and the proof of damage to reputation are rare. An exception though is the case of *Noorani v Calver* [2009].[24] The litigants were respectively the deputy chairman and chairman of a local Conservative Association. The defendant was alleged to have said to the claimant's wife and daughter:

> "No wonder you have depression married to an Islamist terrorist. He is a refugee. He is a troublemaker. We should get rid of these people and rebuild the country."

The judge had to decide whether there was any damage to the claimant's reputation because the words were heard only by his wife and daughter. Although the daughter mentioned the conversation to her father

---

[23] *Barry Watters v Independent Star Ltd*, November 3, 2010, Dublin Circuit Court.
[24] [2009] EWHC 561.

his wife did not. Neither appeared to think any worse of the claimant as a result of the comments (which incidentally the defendent strenuously denied ever making). Coulson J. concluded "I must recognise that evidence to the damage, if any, done to the claimant's reputation by the alleged conversation . . . is at least, open to very serious doubt."

Reputation is assumed in law to have a value. A key factor to remember is that the claimant *doesn't* have to prove that what you have written is untrue. In legal terms, the burden of proof is on the publisher. So the onus is upon the publisher to justify what has been written. Section 5 of the Defamation Act 1952 demands only that what has been written or broadcast is *substantially* true. *The standard of proof is on the balance of probabilities.* Section 5 is set to be repealed if cl.3 of the Defamation Bill becomes law. The "updated" version of the justification defence is "truth" and it is a defence to an action for defamation for the defendant to show that the imputation conveyed by the statement complained of is substantially true.

Publication

The next point is a pretty obvious one. A claimant will need to prove that the material upon which the claim is based has been published. This means that the communication has been seen or heard, as lawyers say by a "third party." This clearly is not going to cause a problem when the material forms part of a newspaper, magazine or broadcast irrespective of whether it is locally, regionally or nationally targeted. If the circulation of a newspaper is 15,000 then there has been a publication.

If it is 15 then there has still been a publication in law providing the link has been made between the content and the claimant irrespective of whether that is an individual, group of individuals, a company or organisation. This issue has attracted the attention of the courts on a number of occasions since the last edition of this book. It was the key factor in the *Noorani* case cited above. The legal term is *abuse of process.* In simple terms it means that so few people were aware of the publication that it could not possibly have had an adverse effect on the claimant's reputation and makes any ensuing legal action for defamation redundant.

The leading case on this topic is *Jameel v Dow Jones & Co Inc.*[25] In this case it was held that where only five people were known to have accessed a website (three of whom were friends or associates of the claimant and not likely to be influenced by the content) containing alleged defamatory material it was an abuse of process to allow the case to continue because it was most unlikely that the complainant's reputation would have been affected. However (and this is not meant to worry you) the Court of Appeal endorsed a view that where a person was identifiable then *in principle* it could still lead to an action being brought even though the persons concerned had no prior knowledge of the claimant.

[25] [2005] EWCA Civ 75.

The assumption here is that both the print and broadcast media can create and then besmirch a reputation at one and the same time.

The courts have consistently stressed that it is not a numbers game.[26] The task is to discover on a case-by-case basis whether or not the claimant's reputation is likely to have been adversely affected by the publication. To put it in legal terms—no real and substantial tort had been committed within the jurisdiction. At best if a case were to proceed and use up valuable court resources to achieve vindication for the damage done to reputation both damage and consequently vindication will be minimal. As Lord Phillips so eloquently put it:

"*The costs of the exercise will have been out of all proportion to what has been achieved. The game will not merely not have been worth the candle, it will not have been worth the wick!*"[27]

In *Noorani* the claimant lost the case on this point. The judge found that there was only limited publication to the wife and daughter of the claimant and lack of any proper evidence of damage to reputation led to the conclusion that this was a ". . . clear case where the slander allegation should be struck out as an abuse of process".[28]

In *Wallis & Another v Meredith* [2011][29] the publication relied upon was to one person who was the claimant's solicitor. The court thought it unlikely the solicitor would think any worse of his client, particularly in light of his denial of the allegations. There was no evidence of any harm resulting from the communication. On that basis no real and substantial tort had been committed.

A similar question was posed in the case of *Cairns v Modi* [2010][30] which dealt with a Twitter communication sent from India stating that the claimant, a New Zealand test cricketer, had been involved in match fixing. The allegation had been repeated on a cricket website. The question was whether the case could be commenced in the High Court in London. Cairns had played cricket for Nottinghamshire for a number of seasons and the court found little difficulty in concluding that he had established a reputation in this jurisdiction.

However the court was faced with conflicting evidence from expert witnesses as to how many of the defendant's Twitter "followers" would have read the "tweet." The estimates in this case ranged from 2 to 800! The responsibility falls upon a claimant to establish there was a publication within the jurisdiction and the judge concluded that the action should be allowed to proceed. Tugendhat J. also emphasised that

---

[26] See for example the comments of Eady J. in *Mardas v New York Times* [2008]EWHC 3135 at para.15.

[27] *Mardas v New York Times* [2008] EWHC 3135 at para.19.

[28] See also *Bezant v Rausing* [2007] EWHC 1118 (QB) and *McBride v Body Shop Int Plc* [2007] EWHC 1658 (QB).

[29] [2011] EWHC 75 (QB).

[30] [2010] EWHC 2859 (QB).

there was more to abuse of process than "the number of publishees." Reference was made to the likelihood of there being re-publication of the alleged defamatory material. That could be a material factor in permitting a case to go to trial and permitting the claimant to seek vindication in order to prevent future dissemination of the material.

The words complained of must be capable of being regarded as defamatory. In the absence of agreement to that effect between the parties then a judge will have to decide this issue of capability. If the judge agrees that the words are capable of being defamatory then the final decision in the case will rest with the jury. There are cases where a jury may be dispensed with because the judge decides that the case is too complex for the matter to be fully understood by them. The continuing use of juries in defamation causes may be coming to an end. When announcing the Defamation Bill and consultation exercise the Ministry of Justice stated that research had shown that over the previous 12 months all defamation trials had been heard by a judge alone. The consultation document asks for comments on whether jury trial should be abolished or as at present the judges should continue to have discretion on whether a jury hears the case. If the latter option is agreed the evidence suggests that judges are keen to take control of such trials.

In *Cook v Telegraph Media Group* [2011][31] the judge decided against jury trial. The legal context is provided by s.69 of the Senior Courts Act 1981. This says that when there is a claim for defamation then the mode of trial will be with a jury unless the court is of the opinion that the trial "... requires any prolonged examination of documents, or accounts ..."

Guidance on how this is to be interpreted is given by Lord Neuberger M.R. in *Fiddes v Channel Four Television Corporation* [2010].[32] There are four factors that will guide judicial discretion. Firstly that the emphasis is against jury trials. Secondly, in favour of a jury is when the case involves prominent figures in public life and questions of great national interest. Thirdly, the fact that the case involves issues such as credibility and a party's honour and integrity should be taken into account. However this is not seen as an overriding factor in favour of a jury. Finally the advantage of a reasoned judgment is a factor properly taken into account. The court considered that a fifth factor could be relevant and that is where the claimant is bringing the action against the state or a public authority. In this contest it is argued the claimant, if an individual, has a constitutional right to have his case determined by his peers.

The court determined that any trial should be without a jury. A similar conclusion was reached by Sharp J. in *Bowker & Another v The Royal Society for the Protection of Birds* [2011].[33] Section 69 of the Senior Court Act 1981 also makes reference to whether scientific investigation is part of the action. As the judge said:

---

[31] [2011] EWHC 763 (QB).
[32] [2010] EWCA Civ 730.
[33] [2011] EWHC 737 (QB).

"It is plain . . . that the trial will involve scientific investigation; and that the investigation cannot conveniently be made by a jury."

So the trend continues against jury trial which could well become a thing of the past if the consultation exercise shows overwhelming support for its abolition in defamation cases.

The "sting"

How will a judge decide whether the "sting" is potentially defamatory? The answer is to be found in the case of *Gillick v BBC* [1996][34] and in subsequent decisions that have endorsed the approach such as *Gillick v Brook Advisory Centres* [2001][35] *Jameel v Times Newspapers* [2004][36] *Noorani v Calver* [37] and *Bowker & Another v The Royal Society for the Protection of Birds* [2011].[38]

The onus is cast upon the "hypothetical reader or viewer" to make that important decision. The Court of Appeal in *Gillick v Brook Advisory Centres* expressed it in these terms:

1 The courts must give to the material complained of the natural and ordinary meaning that it would have conveyed to the ordinary reasonable reader.

2 The hypothetical reasonable reader is not naïve but he is not unduly suspicious. He can read between the lines. He can read in an implication more readily than a lawyer and may indulge in a certain amount of loose thinking. But he must be treated as being a man who is not avid for scandal and someone who does not, and should not, select one bad meaning where other non-defamatory meanings are available.

3 While limiting its attention to what the defendant has actually said or written the court should be cautious of an over-elaborate analysis of the material in issue because an ordinary reader would not analyse the article as a lawyer or accountant would analyse documents or accounts.

4 The court should not be too literal in its approach: (see *Lewis v Daily Telegraph Limited* [1964] A.C. 234 at 277 per Lord Devlin and in particular "the lawyer's rule is that the implication must be necessary as well as reasonable. The layman reads in an implication much more freely; and unfortunately, as the law of defamation has to take into account, is especially prone to do so when derogatory").

5 A statement should be taken to be defamatory if it would tend to

34 [1996] EWCA Civ 46.
35 [2001] EWCA Civ 1263.
36 [2004] EWCA Civ 983.
37 [2009] EWHC 561 (QB) at para.10.
38 [2011] EWHC 737 (QB).

> lower the claimant in the estimation of right-thinking members
> of society generally or affect a person adversely in the estimation
> of reasonable people generally.[39]
>
> [6] In determining the meaning of the material complained of the
> court is not limited by the meanings which either the claimant or
> the defendant seeks to place upon the words.

Look closely at point 5, above. That is the standard test to apply. Has the
claimant's reputation been lowered in the estimation of right-thinking
members of society generally or affected a person adversely in the
estimation of reasonable people? Our advice is that when a journalist
has written a story they should assume the position of the hypothetical
viewer or reader and ask whether in light of the test any of the content
is potentially defamatory. If journalists get into the habit of reflecting
on what they have written, making all allowances for the time pressures that they may well be under, then they may well end their careers
without having crossed the threshold of the High Court as a participant
in a defamation case rather than being there to report on one.

It should not be assumed that just because a journalist fails to name
the claimant in the publication then there is no possibility of a writ
landing on the doorstep. The crucial question is whether or not from
the information that has been published the "hypothetical reasonable
reader or viewer" will understand that the "sting" relates to or includes
the claimant. You do not need to name the individual members of a
premiership soccer team for people to conclude that your story is about
those players who regularly appear in the first team. To comment on
the activities of a vicar of a church in the village of X who it is alleged is
having sexual relationships with parishioners hardly obscures identity
if there is only one church in the village. While we are on the subject
it should be made absolutely clear that the simple device of using the
word *"allegedly"* when revealing information about an individual that
he or she would rather wasn't in the public domain will not necessarily
protect the writer from a defamation action. The legal authority for that
proposition is *Lewis v Daily Telegraph* [1964].[40]

> "I agree, of course, that you cannot escape liability for defamation by
> putting the libel behind a prefix such as 'I have been told that . . . ' or
> 'It is rumoured that . . . ' and then asserting that it was true that you
> had been told or that it was in fact being rumoured. You have . . . 'to
> prove that the subject matter of the rumour was true'".

Innuendo

The Concise Oxford Dictionary defines the meaning of innuendo as:

[39] See *Sim v Stretch* [1936] 2 All E.R. 1237.
[40] [1964] A.C. 234 at p.283–284.

"1. An allusive or oblique remark or hint. **2.** A remark with a double meaning usually suggestive.**"**

The issue for a judge will be to decide whether the words complained of are capable of bearing either the natural and ordinary meaning or any innuendo meanings pleaded in the particulars of claim. It will only be in certain cases that the innuendo meaning is pleaded. The courts recognise two types of innuendo meaning. The first is known as "reference innuendo" and the second "meaning innuendo."

In *Baturina v Times Newspapers* [2011][41] the Master of the Rolls gave the following definitions:

Reference Innuendo: "A reference innuendo arises where the statement is, on its face defamatory but where knowledge of extrinsic facts is needed to link them to the claimant."

Meaning Innuendo: "Meaning innuendo arises where the statement does NOT appear to be defamatory on its face, and is only rendered defamatory by knowledge of extrinsic facts."[42]

The majority of authorities concerning innuendo have been reference innuendos. In *Cassidy v Daily Mirror Newspapers Limited* [1929][43] the newspapers published a photograph of the claimant's husband with his "fiancee". The claimant was living apart from her husband but sued for defamation on the basis that people who knew her would assume that her husband was free to marry and therefore she had been maintaining the pretence of being married. She was successful. This was a case where the statement or in this case photograph and caption were deemed defamatory "on its face."[44]

The *Baturina* case is one of meaning innuendo. The newspaper had published an article in which it claimed that "Russia's wealthiest woman" had purchased a house in London for £50 million, the house being second only in size to Buckingham Palace. This was in fact untrue and *The Sunday Times* subsequently published a "clarification" albeit tucked away on page 24 of the particular edition.

The Master of the Rolls made it clear there was "nothing inherently defamatory" in publishing a story that a person has bought a house even though she had not in fact done so. However this case was not based on the ordinary and natural meaning scenario. The case was brought on the basis of an alleged innuendo. This arose from the fact that Mrs Baturina's husband was the Mayor of Moscow and under Russian law officials and civil servants had to make a declaration of their assets. The information was posted on an official government website accessible

---

[41] [2011] EWCA Civ 308.
[42] [2011] EWCA Civ 308 at para.23.
[43] [1929] 2 K.B. 331.
[44] See also *Hulton v Jones* [1910] A.C. 20 and *Hough v London Express Newspapers Ltd* [1940] 2 K.B. 507.

to the public. Mrs Baturina's claim was based upon the fact that people reading *The Sunday Times* article and then checking the website would not find the house listed. They would therefore assume that she was deliberately flouting the law.

The newspaper argued that at the time it published the article it was unaware of the legal requirements of Russian law and therefore should not be liable for defamation. The court rejected that assertion on the basis of authority from the *Cassidy* case and followed in *Hough*. Lord Justice Russell said that ". . . liability for libel should not depend on the intention of the defamer; but on the fact of defamation."[45]

The Court of Appeal permitted the case to progress on the basis of innuendo but with the proviso she would have to identify specific readers who had appreciated the innuendo. These readers would have to be prepared to be witnesses at any future trial. [46]

Context

As will be seen when we consider the fair comment/honest comment defence (see p.122) the sting must be considered within the context of the article as a whole. On occasions this may seem a little unfair. The passenger on the London underground that takes a look at a fellow passenger's newspaper will in all probability only have the ability to note the headlines rather than read the article as a whole. This can of course be very misleading given that the headline is the "hook" upon which to catch the potential purchaser of the newspaper. The law refers to the concept of *bane and antidote.*

In 1995 two of the stars of the Neighbours television programme sued the *News of the World* for defamation. The newspaper had carried a headline: *"Strewth! What's Harold up to with our Madge?"*[47] Another smaller but still prominent headline read: *"Porn Shocker for Neighbours Stars."* The feature also contained photographs of what appeared to be the two *Neighbours* stars engaging in sexual acts. The text accompanying the photographs explained that computer games had been produced which superimposed the heads of famous actors onto the bodies of pornographic film actors. Anyone reading the full text would be well aware that the two *Neighbours* actors had no knowledge of this and had certainly not consented to their images being used in this way.

The House of Lords was sympathetic to the claimant's plight and warned the press that they were treading on dangerous ground when publishing headlines of this nature that carried defamatory implications. However it was stated that the headlines had to be judged against the article as a whole and not taken out of context. The reading public must be aware of the fact that headlines were often exaggerated in order

---

[45] [1929] 2 K.B. 331 at 343.

[46] For another recent example of a defamation claim based on innuendo see *Johnson v MGN Ltd* [2009] EWHC 1481 (QB).

[47] [1995] UKHL 6.

to promote the sale of the newspaper. The general public apparently must not place any great faith in headlines as they could be potentially misleading. The positioning of the "antidote" within an article or feature might also be a deciding factor. In this case it was apparent almost from the start of the article that the two stars were not involved.

Another example is *Norman v Future Publishing* [1999].[48] The defendants were the publishers of the magazine *Classic CD*. The claimant was Jessie Norman a famous opera singer. In a feature on her the author wrote:

> "While her Salome is released this month on Phillips, it is still hard to envisage the grand, statuesque 49-year-old as the libidinous adolescent on stage stripping off the seven veils. This is a woman who got trapped in swing doors on her way to a concert, and when advised to release herself by turning sideways replied: 'Honey, I ain't got no sideways.'"

She claimed that the ordinary and natural meaning of the words was:

> i) "That she had used a mode of speech which was a) vulgar and undignified and/or b) conformed to a degrading racist stereotype of a person of African-American heritage; alternatively
> ii) she had been guilty of patronising mockery of the modes of speech stereo-typically attributed to certain groups or classes of black Americans and was therefore guilty of hypocrisy."

The Court of Appeal found against her. Lord Justice Hirst pointed out that the whole feature that comprised 47 paragraphs was "extremely complimentary" to the claimant. Emphasis had been laid on her education and her stable family life. Adjoining the paragraph complained of on either side were quotations from interviews with her in which she spoke in clear grammatical and idiomatic English. In other words the "sting" had to be read in the context of the article as a whole and ordinary readers would be left with a highly favourable impression of her. There was no obvious damage to her reputation.

5. Defamation Defences

The best time to think about the working of the legal defences to defamation is when the story is being constructed. One should ask: "If this piece were to be challenged on the basis that it is potentially defamatory would I have a reasonable prospect of succeeding by pleading an established defence?" In practice, the more likely outcome is that the claimant will not pursue the case if his or her lawyers are of the opinion

---

[48] [1999] EWCA Civ 1800.

that, on the basis of information supplied to them, the media will win the case. We now discuss the legal principles underpinning the stand-ard defences of privilege, justification and fair comment.

i)   Absolute and statutory qualified privilege

Journalists have long enjoyed protection from defamation actions because Parliament has recognised that in certain circumstances the right to free expression prevails over protection of reputation. The situations are however relatively limited. All journalists should be acquainted with the terms of s.14 of the Defamation Act 1996 entitled Absolute Privilege. This section of the Act bestows total protection upon a journalist when report-ing court proceedings *providing* the report is a "fair and accurate report of proceedings in public before a court to which the section applies, if published contemporaneously with the proceedings . . ."

"Contemporaneous" means as soon as possible after the proceedings for the day have finished or even while they are going on if you are report-ing, for example, on the lunchtime news or in an edition of a newspaper.

Section 14(3) applies this absolute privilege to:

(a) any court in the United Kingdom;
(b) the European Court of Justice or any court attached to that court;
(c) the European Court of Human Rights; and
(d) any international criminal tribunal established by the Security Council of the United Nations or by international agreement to which the United Kingdom is a party.

However if the provisions of cl.5 of the Defamation Bill become law s.14(3) will be redrafted in the following terms:

(a) any court in the United Kingdom;
(b) any court established under the law of a country or territory outside of the United Kingdom; and
(c) any international court or tribunal established by the Security Council of the United Nations or by any international agreement.

"Court" means any tribunal or body exercising the judicial power of the state. Amendments are also proposed to paras 9, 10, 12, 13, 14, 15, 16 and 17 and readers are invited to visit the provisions of the Defamation Act (2011?) at *www.legislation.gov.uk* in order to ascertain whether or not the changes proposed have become law.

That is absolute privilege offering total protection from defamation proceedings providing the reports are fair and accurate and contempo-raneous. A current issue for which there is no judicial precedent relates to online court copy. It will be common practice for court reports to be placed online in addition to the hardcopy newspaper. If the court copy online is archived and accessed at a later date and it is claimed the report contains defamatory material will the media outlet still be protected by s.14? A literal interpretation of s.14 would suggest the answer is no because the material could not be regarded as a "contemporaneous" publication. However, although there is no judicial authority, under s.15 qualified privilege is given to fair and accurate reports from courts anywhere in the world.

Protection is also offered by s.15 of the Defamation Act 1996. This section deals with statutory qualified privilege. Schedule 1 of the Act identifies a number of reporting situations where journalists can expect to be protected from the consequences of inadvertently including defamatory material in the report. The protection is offered providing the publication can be shown to be made without malice. The other major point to remember is that this protection only applies if the publication relates to something of public concern and the assumption is that the publication is "for the public benefit." There are eight different situations identified in Sch.1, Pt 1. They cover fair and accurate reports of legislatures anywhere in the world, courts anywhere in the world, public inquiries and so on. You should become familiar with these situations and the list can be found by accessing the *www.legislation.gov.uk* website and clicking on "legislation."

Part II of the Schedule offers protection for fair and accurate reports of proceedings at any meeting in the UK of a local authority so "cutting your teeth" at local council meetings can be done safe in the knowledge that, providing your report is a fair and accurate reflection of the proceedings, then you need have no particular worries about the laws on defamation. This second part also covers reports of public meetings and according to a House of Lords decision in 2000 this also covers press conferences and press releases. (*McCarten, Turkington & Breen v Times Newspapers* [2000])[49]

Finally note that in the situations mentioned in Pt 1 of the Schedule the protection is offered without the media outlet having to offer the opportunity to a "claimant" to explain or contradict what has been published. However in the second part the statements made by the journalist are subject to explanation or contradiction.

It has to be remembered that in principle a reporter is allowed to summarise and to be selective without losing the benefits of absolute and qualified privilege. "Summarise" in this context must be synonymous with "fair and accurate" in terms of reporting the proceedings.

In *Curistan v Times Newspapers Ltd* [2008][50] the claimant brought proceedings over an article in the *Sunday Times* that had quoted from a statement made in the course of Parliamentary proceedings by a Member of Parliament. It alleged that the claimant had been involved in money laundering activities in support of the IRA. The article was referred to in court as a "hybrid" article because it contained other

[49] [2000] UKHL 57.
[50] [2008] EWCA Civ 432.

material that related to his business activities that had not be referred to in parliament.

The question was whether the article as a whole was protected by statutory qualified privilege. The Court of Appeal was disinclined to accept the view that privilege would be lost simply because the article contained a mixture of parliamentary comment and material discovered through the newspaper's own investigations.

The claimant's argument was that the repetition rule should apply to the non-privileged parts of the reports. The Court of Appeal's view was that if this approach were to be adopted it would undermine the protection offered by s.15 of the Defamation Act 1996. Critical to this approach is a finding that the protection offered by s.15 does indeed apply to the "parliamentary" part of the report. If that is lost then it would appear that the repetition rule would apply and the s.15 context would prove irrelevant.

ii) Common law qualified privilege, Reynolds, Jameel and responsible publication

The House of Lords decision in *Reynolds* is often heralded as a landmark ruling in that the court took the opportunity to emphasise the importance of freedom of expression in light of the Human Rights Act 1998 having received royal assent immediately prior to the case being heard. (It was not to come into effect until October 2000). It will be recalled that parliament had expressly included s.12 in the Act intended to stress the importance of freedom of expression. The House was therefore balancing two fundamental rights: freedom of expression against protection of reputation.

According to the House of Lords, common law qualified privilege protection was dependent upon the report and reporter meeting a number of criteria. The first related to the story. This had to be one of public interest in the sense that the media organisation is under a social, moral or legal duty to publish and the audience had a corresponding interest in receiving the information. In simple terms the story must be clearly one of public interest as distinct from being of interest to the public. It will usually be fairly evident if that is the case. The subject matter may concern corruption in high places, misinformation of a public nature, politicians abusing power or conflict of interest situations. The recent MPs' expenses "scandal" and the phone hacking allegations that have been made against the *News of the World* are prime examples of public interest stories.

Gray J. said in *Charman v Orion Publishing Group* [2006][51]:

". . . in order to determine whether publication was in the public interest, it is first necessary carefully to analyse the information which has been provided to the public and to pose and answer the ques-

---

[51] [2006] EWHC 1756 at para.106.

tion whether the public had a right to know or a legitimate interest in knowing the facts alleged, even if they cannot be shown to be true."

If the first "hurdle" was cleared, then the second one related directly to journalistic conduct.

The question was whether the journalism that went into creating the story was "responsible." In *Reynolds*, Lord Nicholls identified ten "non-exhaustive" factors to help judges to decide whether the journalism passed muster. The common law said Lord Nicholls:

"... does not seek to set a higher standard than that of responsible journalism, a standard the media themselves espouse. An incursion into press freedom which goes no further than this would not seem to be excessive or disproportionate. The investigative journalist has adequate protection."

It was the practice of judges to take into account **all** ten factors when deciding the issue of responsible journalism. That approach was relaxed as a result of the *Jameel v Wall Street Journal (Europe)* [2006][52] case and *Reynolds* factors are now treated as being much more flexible. However it is worth journalists familiarising themselves with the ten factors because their professionalism is still likely to be judged by reference to some if not all of them. The factors are:

i.   The seriousness of the allegation. The more serious the charge, the more the public is misinformed and the individual harmed, if the allegation is not true.

ii. The nature of the information, and the extent to which the subject matter is of public concern.

iii. The source of the information. Some informants have no direct knowledge of the events. Some have their own axes to grind, or are being paid for their stories.

iv. The steps taken to verify the allegation.

v.   The status of the information. The allegation may have already been the subject of an investigation which commands respect.

vi. The urgency of the matter. News is often a perishable commodity.

vii. Whether comment was sought from the claimant. He may have information others do not possess or have not disclosed. An approach to the claimant will not always be necessary.

viii. Whether [the book] contained the gist of the claimant's side of the story.

ix. The tone of the [book] and [author] can raise queries or call for an investigation. It need not adopt allegations as statement of fact.

x.   The circumstances of the publication, including its timing.

---

[52] [2006] UKHL 44.

The media's difficulty with these factors related not to their existence but the fact that it was alleged that trial judges had turned them into ten "tests" to be passed or "hurdles" which all had to be jumped before the defence could succeed. This was not what Lord Nicholls had intended when he established the factors. Gray J., in the *Charman* case [2006] made that clear:

"The requirements of responsible journalism will vary according to the particular circumstances. Depending on the circumstances, factors other than those identified by Lord Nicholls may come into play. It is necessary always to bear in mind that the publication is defamatory and cannot be shown to be true. The standard of conduct by which the responsibility of the journalism is judged must be applied in a practical, fact-sensitive and elastic manner . . . this will be determined by reference to the information which is known to the publisher at the time of publication."[53]

Yet why should a publisher have to prove that the journalism that created the story was "responsible." The answer is to be found in Lord Nicholls comments in *Bonnick v Morris* [2002][54]:

"Stated shortly, the Reynolds privilege is concerned to provide a proper degree of protection for responsible journalism when reporting matters of public concern. Responsible journalism is the point at which a fair balance is held between freedom of expression on matters of public concern and the reputations of individuals. Maintenance of this standard is in the public interest and in the interest of those whose reputations are involved. It can be regarded as the price journalists pay in return for the privilege."

The importance of this is the fact that if successful the case may never come to court or if it does it will be a complete defence to a claim for libel.

The *Jameel* case is the most recent authoritative review of the ambit of *Reynolds* privilege although at the time of writing the *Flood* case is set to be heard by the Supreme Court in late 2011. The Law Lords took into account the inter-relationship between arts 8 and 10 of the European Convention on Human Rights. This has become more of an issue since the European Court of Human Rights held in *Pfeifer v Austria* [2007][55] that reputation falls within the ambit of art.8. This means that in defamation cases just as much as privacy disputes the court will need to recognise that neither article takes precedence and that an intense focus

---

[53] [2006] UKHL 44 at para.108.
[54] [2002] UKPC 31 and quoted with approval in *Flood v Times Newspapers Ltd* [2010] EWCA Civ 804 at para.18.
[55] [2007] ECHR 935.

is needed on the facts of the case before deciding which article should prevail.

The situation was summed up by Mr Justice Gray in Charman[56]:

"... the touchstone being that of the public interest and responsible journalism, it is then necessary to ask whether in the particular circumstances of the case the publisher has demonstrated that he was acting responsibly in communicating the information to the public. For that exercise the starting point is to consider such of the factors set out by Lord Nicholls in Reynolds at [208] as are applicable."

In summary then the claimant will lose the action if a judge determines (and it is a question for the judge not a jury) that both the duty/interest test and the responsible journalist "test" have been established. To put it another way if the journalism is palpably "responsible" the legal advice received by a claimant is likely to suggest that the chances of success are not great and the claim is unlikely to be pursued. The less responsible the journalism, the more cause for optimism from the claimant.

Key cases post Reynolds

There have been a number of cases since the *Reynolds* decision in which the "defence" has failed. The key to understanding these cases and consequently the criticisms of the media is to identify why the journalists were not able to convince the judge that they had been responsible in the legal sense of the word and whether the judge was too "rigid" in assessing the impact of the ten factors. It has been said that of 15 cases that went to trial prior to the *Jameel* decision only three succeeded when using the defence.[57] One of these was *GKR Karate v The Yorkshire Post* [2000].[58] The defence of qualified privilege was used by the defendants in respect of articles in a Leeds "freesheet" owned by them that alleged the karate club was "ripping off" its members. The judge was asked at the pre-trial stage to rule on whether the defence was applicable. It was held that the journalist concerned had acted honestly and despite there being some inaccuracies these did not defeat the purpose of the public interest *Reynolds* defence.

However, the defence was lost in the *Galloway v Telegraph Group Ltd* [2004][59] case and arguably rightly so. The claimant was a Member of Parliament and had been accused by the *Daily Telegraph* of being in the pay of Saddam Hussein's regime. The first rule of course is that the media should be able to plead justification especially when making such serious allegations against a serving member of Parliament. The *Telegraph* did not. Instead it relied upon *Reynolds* privilege. Eady J. had

[56] [2006] EWHC 1756 at para.108.
[57] Richard Rampton QC, *The Times*, October 24, 2006.
[58] [2000] 2 All E.R. 931.
[59] [2004] EWHC and [2006] EWCA Civ 17.

no hesitation in deciding that the defence should not succeed. Looked at from the *Telegraph's* point of view the newspaper had a public interest story particularly as the story broke within weeks of the invasion of Iraq. However the judge held that the newspaper failed the duty/interest test because it was not under a social or moral duty to publish the story at that time. If the newspaper had held the story for a few more days that would have allowed further investigation to have occurred and possibly then a defence of justification might had been used. The *Telegraph* had rushed to publish when there was no need to do so. No other media outlet was aware of the story.

The judge reserved his major criticisms for when asked to decide whether the *Telegraph's* journalism had been responsible. He was not impressed. The *Telegraph* had not taken any steps to verify the information it was putting into the public domain. Remember there is deemed to be no public interest in receiving misinformation. Also, the tone of the coverage was "dramatic and condemnatory." Allegations had been adopted as statements of fact. Instead of simply adopting a neutral tone (what is known as reportage) the *Telegraph* had chosen to sensationalise the material. If it had simply raised queries or called for an investigation by the appropriate authorities it would have been on firmer ground. Galloway was awarded £150,000 in damages. The *Telegraph's* subsequent appeal to the Court of Appeal was emphatically dismissed, the court agreeing with virtually every conclusion reached by the trial judge. If there is a better case study on how not to comply with the responsible journalism test we have yet to come across it.

It is worth contrasting the *Galloway* case with one where the journalism was deemed to have failed to have met the responsible journalism "test" but was not as blatantly irresponsible as that in the *Galloway* case. In *Henry v BBC (No.2)* [2005][60] the claimant, Mrs Henry, had alleged that she had been defamed by the regional BBC Points West news programme. The programme had used unedited footage of a press conference in which the speaker had named the claimant as a manager who had instructed her to manipulate waiting list figures when she had worked at a local hospital. The BBC relied on *Reynolds* privilege arguing that this was a local news story that had to be broadcast to coincide with the release of an official report into the allegations.

The Judge ruled against the BBC. Once again, a key question was whether the public needed to be informed at that time with that particular piece of information. In addition the BBC had not had time to put the allegations to Mrs Henry with the consequence that the judge believed there was not a proper "balance" in the news item.

This decision may seem a little harsh. The time scale from recording the press conference to going on air was something like three hours. The reporter had to travel more than 20 miles to go back to the studio before he could start to assemble his material. In between, he also had

---

[60] [2005] EWHC 2787 (QB).

to present a "slot" on local radio. Could it not have been argued that just like the reporter in the *GKR* case he was doing his best to be as professional as possible in the time-limited circumstances he found himself in?

Look also at *Loutchansky v Times Newspapers* [2001].[61] Here *The Times* had published an article which suggested the claimant was involved in criminal activities. The allegations were published in both the print and online editions of the newspaper. The newspaper relied on *Reynolds* privilege in that it maintained that it was in the public interest to publish the story. This argument was accepted for the print edition but not the online edition. The matter that concerned the Court of Appeal, was the presence of the alleged defamatory material in the newspaper's online archive. This was available to the public and the court took the view that this was "stale news" and could not therefore enjoy the same protection as contemporary news material.

It is often said that history repeats itself and so it was nearly a decade later when *The Times* found itself relying on the *Reynolds* defence when the claimant brought an action for libel for an archived online story. In the case of *Flood v Times Newspapers Ltd* [2010][62] the claimant was an officer with the Metropolitan Police. The newspapers reported that allegations had been made to the police that he had been giving information to Russian exiles in return for bribes. It was also stated that the allegation had been taken seriously and was being investigated.

The claimant brought an action for libel based on the story in the print edition of June 2, 2006 and the online report from that date onwards. A year later the newspaper was informed of the outcome of the investigation and that Flood had been exonerated. *The Times* did not update its online report from June 2006 despite knowing that no action was being taken against him. A hearing took place where the judge had to decide whether the *Reynolds* defence applied to the publications. It was held that the defence did apply to both print and online copies of the article on June 2, 2006. However, the continued publication of the article on the website after *The Times* had been informed of the outcome of the investigation meant that the defence failed in respect of this version of the story. Both parties appealed against the rulings.

The Court of Appeal dismissed *The Times'* appeal and allowed Flood's cross appeal. The journalism that had underpinned the article when first published in June 2006 was deemed irresponsible. *The Times* had simply been repeating the allegations of a third party rather than carrying out an independent investigation in order to verify as far as possible that the allegations were credible. The importance of this decision is that newspapers need to be extra careful when simply repeating information from an unnamed third party source. A responsible journalist would seek independent verification of the allegation before going into print. Also, the continued presence of the online version meant that the newspaper had not acted responsibly because it had not amended or

---

[61] [2001] EWCA Civ 1805.
[62] [2010] EWCA Civ 804.

removed the original article even after it became aware of the result of the investigation carried out by the police.

The conclusion in the context of European Human Rights Convention jurisprudence is that Flood's art.8 rights prevailed over the newspaper's art.10 rights. This is not the final word on the matter because the Supreme Court has agreed to hear the appeal by the newspaper on the basis that win or lose *The Times* will be liable for all the costs of the case.

What will have become apparent is that despite trial judges taking a more "holistic" approach to the ten factors there will always be a significant level of subjectivity in the decision-making process. This subjectivity will embrace the circumstances of the case and a consideration of whether the journalist has done his best to act in a professional manner.

The question now posed is whether the Supreme Court will take the opportunity to redefine the approach to common law qualified privilege as the House of Lords did in the *Jameel* case in 2006.[63]

In *Jameel*, the Wall Street Journal had pleaded the *Reynolds* defence in response to the claimant's allegation that he had been named and therefore defamed as a result of an article entitled *"Saudi Officials Monitor Certain Bank Accounts. Focus Is On Those With Potential Terrorist Ties."*

The High Court rejected the defence and this was subsequently confirmed by the Court of Appeal. There were two major grounds supporting the rejection. The first was the questionable reliability of the sources relied upon by the author and secondly the fact that Jameel had not been given sufficient opportunity to comment on the allegations. The Journal appealed to the House of Lords.

Lord Hoffmann said that the *Reynolds* decision was intended to provide ". . . greater freedom for the press to publish stories of genuine public interest." However he went on to state:

> "But this case suggests that Reynolds has had little impact on the way the law is applied at first instance. It is therefore necessary to restate the principles."[64]

The lack of success of the *Reynolds* defence was of major concern because of the potential to inhibit good investigative journalism carried out in the public interest. In such circumstances, any story or report might well contain defamatory statements but that should not of itself prevent the publication of a story that was clearly justified by reference to the public interest. Lord Hoffmann and Baroness Hale were of the opinion that the defence should no longer be referred to as *Reynolds* privilege. It was, said the latter, "a defence of publication in the public interest." In assessing whether the report was in the public interest there was no reason to dispense with the reference to the duty/interest test but essentially the task will be to distinguish that which is of public interest from that which is of

---

[63] [2006] UKHL 44.
[64] [2006] UKHL 44 at para.38.

interest to the public. The assessment of the public interest will encompass the elements of reciprocal duty and interest.

As Baroness Hale commented, ". . . the most vapid tittle-tattle about the activities of footballers' wives and girlfriends . . ." might interest the public but ". . . no-one would claim there is any real public interest in being told all about it."[65]

The House took the opportunity to emphasise the key role of the editor in the publishing process. Even though the story may prove to be of public interest, the editor will still have to justify the inclusion of the alleged defamatory material. The approach, said Lord Hoffmann, was to consider the article as a whole and not isolate the defamatory statement. If the public interest test is passed, then one moves on to an assessment of whether the journalism underpinning the story was responsible. That, said Lord Hoffmann, may be divided into three topics:

- The steps taken to verify the story.
- The opportunity given to the claimant to comment.
- The propriety of the publication at that particular time.

So what of the ten hurdles or non-exhaustive factors to use Lord Nicholls' words? The House was of the opinion that they had been applied too strictly.

A more liberal or flexible approach was needed. The trial judge said Lord Hoffmann had assumed that ". . . the defence can only be sustained after "the closest and most rigorous scrutiny" by the application of what he called "Lord Nicholls' ten tests." He went on:

"... That is not what Lord Nicholls meant. As he said in Bonnick (at page 309) the standard of conduct required of a newspaper must be applied in a practical and flexible manner. It must have regard to practical realities."[66]

In conclusion, it is fair to assume that trial judges should in the future take a more "relaxed" approach in assessing whether journalists have acted in a legally responsible manner. However, as Richard Rampton QC said in October 2006:

"So, for editors, lawyers and judges, the future looks interesting but not necessarily easier. Flexibility is no doubt a good thing. But so is certainty."[67]

From Jameel to Flood

There was a flurry of activity immediately post the *Jameel* decision dealing with the redefined approach to the *Reynolds* defence. In four

---

[65] [2006] UKHL 44 at para.147.
[66] [2006] UKHL 44 at para.56.
[67] *The Times*, October 24, 2006.

cases in 2007 the defence had mixed success. In *Malik v Newspost Ltd & Others* [2007] the court held that the journalism employed by the newspaper could not "remotely be classed as investigative journalism". The story relating to the alleged threats to intimidate voters at a local election was without doubt in the public interest but the newspaper failed on the grounds that its reporting was not responsible.[68] In *Radu v Houston & Another* (No 3) [2007][69] the defence was lost because ". . . some of the allegations came from a source that was not impartial and proper steps to verify the information were not taken".[70] *Roberts & Another v Gable & Others* [2007][71] was a case where the defence was successful. The journalism was deemed responsible because the defendants, reporting two sides of the story, had refrained from adopting allegations of wrongdoing. Finally *Charman v Orion Publishing Group* [2007][72] was the first case to decide that the *Reynolds* defence could apply to a book rather than only to conventional pieces of journalism. The court held that the book as a whole was entirely responsible journalism.

Then there was nothing of significance until the *Flood* litigation commenced in 2009.

iii) Truth (Justification)

The simplest way to view this defence is that, if one can prove that what has been published is substantially true, the claimant has no chance of success. The critical issue is to remember that it can take a substantial amount of time for a case to come to court and it may be very difficult to prove that something you knew at the time to be true can be proved to be true to the satisfaction of a judge or jury. It is not something that any journalist should underestimate. In fact, it is an experience which one would do well to avoid.

However here are the basic principles:

1   The burden of proving the defence of justification rests upon the defendants on the balance of probabilities.

2   The "quality" of the evidence to be adduced will depend on the nature and gravity of the "sting." The law generally seeks to put the publication into one of three categories know as the Chase[73] "levels" from the case of that name in 2002. Do not think that they are dated because both the High Court and Court of Appeal have

---

[68] [2007] EWHC 3063 (QB).
[69] [2007] EWHC 2735 (QB).
[70] *www.5rb.com/casereports*
[71] [2007] EWCA Civ 721.
[72] [2007] EWCA Civ 972.
[73] *Chase v News Group Newspapers* [2002] EWCA Civ 1772 (The "levels" originating in the case of *Lucas Box v News Group Newspapers* [1986] 1 W.L.R. 147).

recently confirmed their usefulness in the cases *Horlick v Associated Newspapers* [2010][74] and *Curistan v Times Newspapers* [2008].[75]

In *Fallon v Mirror Group Newspapers* [No2] [2006][76] Eady J. neatly summed up the approach to the Chase levels:

"This case requires consideration of the disciplines imposed in the context of pleading a Lucas-Box meaning which is pitched at Level 2 or Level 3 on the scale identified in *Chase v News Group Newspapers Ltd* [2003] EMLR 11 at [45] and *Musa King v Telegraph Ltd* [2005] 1 WLR 2282 at [21]-[22]. It may be a somewhat artificial scale in the sense that defamatory words are capable of bearing an infinite variety of meanings and implications and, correspondingly, a range of levels of gravity which do not necessarily lend themselves to classification in one or other of these three categories. 'It is not perhaps an entirely satisfactory distinction': per Simon Brown L.J. *Jameel v Wall Street Journal Sprl* [2004] EMLR 6 at [19]; see also *Armstrong v Times Newspapers Ltd* [2006] EMLR 9 at [23]-[25]. Nevertheless, the categorisation is currently found useful primarily because it represents a convenient way of identifying what should be pleaded if it is sought to advance a defence of justification to some defamatory allegation falling short of a direct attribution of guilt. Moreover, it appears to have had the imprimatur of Lord Devlin in *Lewis v Daily Telegraph Ltd* [1964] AC 234, 282, 285."[77]

In our opinion the best and probably the most succinct statement in respect of the Levels is to be found in the *Elaine Chase v News Group Newspapers* case:

"The sting of a libel may be capable of meaning that a claimant has in fact committed some serious act, such as murder. Alternatively it may be suggested that the words mean that there are reasonable grounds to suspect that he/she has committed such an act. A third possibility is that they may mean that there are grounds for investigating whether he/she has been responsible for such an act." (per Brooke L.J.)[78]

Therefore, when composing a story, a good journalist will make a mental note to decide whether or not it is a Level One, Two or Three story. It sounds easy but as Eady J. said in *Fallon* (above), the sting is "capable of bearing an infinite variety of meanings and implications and, correspondingly, a range of levels of gravity which do not necessarily lend themselves to classification in one or other of these three categories . . .".

---

[74] [2010] EWHC 1544 (QB).
[75] [2008] EWCA Civ 432.
[76] [2006] EWHC 783.
[77] [2006] EWHC 783 at para.1.
[78] [2002] EWCA Civ 1772 at para.45.

The first issue is whether it is a Level One story. Has the reasonable reader been left in no doubt about the veracity of the statement? Presumably there is no room for ambiguity? To take Brooke L.J.'s example: Does the story make it clear that the public is being told that Mr X has committed murder? This is clearly a massive attack on his character and reputation. Can it be proved to be true? What evidence is there for making that statement? Remember a Level One statement is not an allegation. It purports to be a statement of fact. Take this example from *Purnell v Business F1 Magazine* [2007][79]:

> "Purnell bribed top journalist to puff achievements."

No-one would doubt that those words constituted a Level One statement. There is no ambiguity in the wording. There is no suggestion of any reasonable doubt or that the author of those words merely suspected that was the case. Therefore, the evidence to support the claim would have to be impeccable in order to succeed with the defence of justification. It wasn't and the case was lost with damages set at £75,000.

A Level Two story is one in which the wording used conveys to the reader or viewer that there are reasonable grounds to suspect that what is stated is true. You might look at the *Fallon* case cited above and read in full the article published by the *Racing Post*. The claimant pleaded that the words used meant that he had agreed with another person (MR) to "throw" races and thereby engaged in behaviour that would amount to a criminal conspiracy. The judge held, after considering all the evidence, that the words were consistent with a Level Two meaning. It follows from this that the higher the "level", with 1 being the highest, the stronger the evidence needed to support the defendant's case. No attempt should be made to move the burden of proof onto the claimant. In this case the evidence of the defendants would have had to establish a "bridge" between the claimant and MR. In the telling words of Eady J.:

> "It need not be a particularly robust construction at this stage, but it must at least be strong enough to support 'reasonable grounds'."

The conclusion was that the evidence relied on by the defendants was insufficient to support the case of reasonable grounds to suspect. To put it simply, the words published suggested to the ordinary reader that there were reasonable grounds to suspect that the claimant had been involved in race fixing, but MGN Ltd's evidence could not support the claim.

Level Three is where a report states there are grounds for investigating allegations relating to the claimant. The media organisation is stating that it has enough evidence to suspect the claimant has been

---

[79] [2007] EWCA Civ 744.

involved in certain activities, e.g. race fixing, and is calling upon the relevant authorities to investigate. It will be evident that, while the "sting" will still need to be supported by the best available evidence, that does not have to be of the same "quality" as that required to back up a Level One or Two assertion.

It will be instructive to consider the notorious litigation between Tommy Sheridan and the *News of the World* in 2006. Sheridan, a former member of the Scottish Parliament, had been accused by the newspaper of committing adultery and attending "swingers" parties. He sued the *News of the World* for libel and the case was heard by the High Court in Edinburgh. The newspaper brought 18 witnesses to court to support its defence of justification. They gave evidence on oath. The jury chose not to believe them and Sheridan was awarded £200,000 in damages prompting the paper's Scottish editor to announce an immediate appeal on the basis that it implied that 18 witnesses had come to court and had "committed monstrous acts of perjury."

The appeal was later suspended while the police investigated perjury allegations. In December 2010 Sheridan was convicted of perjury in the defamation trial and sentenced to three years imprisonment.

If there is anything to be learned from this case it is that there is nothing certain about the outcome when justification is pleaded before a jury even if the defendant appears to be "holding all the aces."

Section 5 of the Defamation Act 1952 makes it clear that the defendant does not have to prove the truth of every single allegation. If it is stated that a high-ranking politician consorted with prostitutes at hotel X when in fact it was at hotel Y the defence would not fail simply because the latter part of the "sting" was false.

Section 5 will be repealed if the Defamation Bill becomes law. The defence is to be renamed truth (cl.3 of the Bill) and the "substance" of the defence expressed in this way:

> "It is a defence to an action for defamation for the defendant to show that the imputation conveyed by the statement complained of is substantially true."

The thrust of the "old" s.5 is carried over into the new Bill in cl.3(3):

> "If one or more of the imputations is not shown to be substantially true, the defence under this section does not fail if, having regard to the imputations which are shown to be substantially true, the imputations which are not shown to be substantially true do not materially injure the claimant's reputation."

There appears to be nothing of a radical nature in this recasting of the existing defence other than it is renamed "truth." As the Bill proposes to "abolish" the common law defence of justification and repeal s.5 does this mean that the existing body of case law knowledge is now to become redundant? It would appear that if we are in for a "fresh start" then the existing precedents have no status. It is hard to imagine that Parliament intends this consequence and it can be expected that this is a step too far and will be remedied before the Bill becomes law.

Perhaps a neat way to summarise the law on justification is to refer to a comment in the *Dee v Telegraph Media Group* [2010] case. The judge accepted the contention from counsel that "meaning and justification are so bound together."[80] If the defence is pleaded and the meaning is uncontroversial then no problem exists in deciding whether the defence is bound to succeed. However if the issue of meaning is controversial then the court has to consider whether the defence would succeed in respect of ANY defamatory meaning the words are capable of bearing.[81]

iv)   Honest opinion (fair comment)

Since the first edition of this book, the law on fair comment has been developed significantly through case law and now through changes proposed in the Defamation Bill. It is probably fair to say that while there have been changes these have not been of a particularly radical nature. If the Bill becomes law the defence will be renamed honest opinion. However at the moment the defence has lost the name fair comment and is referred to as honest comment as a result of the decision of the Supreme Court in *Spiller & Another v Joseph & Others* [2010].[82] Throughout this Chapter we refer to cases prior to *Spiller* by reference to the existing defence of fair comment. Post *Spiller* we refer to honest comment. Post the Defamation Act (2011?) the defence will be known as honest opinion. The case law on fair comment will cease to have importance in a number of respects should the current proposals become law. (See later in this chapter.)

Background

The premise underpinning the defence of fair comment was straightforward. Journalists were permitted to exercise their right to comment on matters of public interest and if in so doing they inadvertently defamed someone then the defence was available to the media organisation.

This appeared to be consistent with the principles of freedom of expression. As Lord Nicholls said in the leading case of *Tse Wai Chun Paul v Albert Cheng* [2001]:

> "The purpose for which the defence of fair comment exists is to facilitate freedom of expression by commenting upon matters of public interest. This accords with the constitutional guarantee of freedom of expression." [83]

---

80   [2010] EWHC 924 (QB) at para.101.
81   [2010] EWHC 924 (QB) at para.99.
82   [2010] UKSC 53.
83   [2001] E.M.L.R. 777.

The basic ground rules for running a defence of fair comment were contained in this judgment. Lord Nicholls regarded the following as "non-controversial." They are:

- The comment must be on a matter of public interest. Public interest is not to be confined within "narrow limits."
- The comment must be recognisable as comment and distinct from imputations of fact. Clearly the context of what is written or spoken will be all important in reaching a conclusion as to whether the reasonable reader or viewer would regard the information as comment.
- Any comment must be based upon facts which are either true or have the protection of privilege.
- The reader or viewer should be able to glean the facts from what has been published. In other words, the reader or hearer will be able to establish a causal connection between the facts and the comment upon which he can base a conclusion.
- The comment must be one which an "honest person" could hold however "prejudiced he might be and however exaggerated or obstinate his views". As Lord Nicholls emphasised, the comment:

". . . must be germane to the subject matter criticised. Dislike of an artist's style would not justify an attack upon his morals or manners. But a critic need not be mealy mouthed in denouncing what he disagrees with. He is entitled to dip his pen in gall for the purposes of legitimate criticism."

So there you have it. These are the rules upon which the judiciary decided whether or not what had been published was amenable to the defence of fair comment. However, remember this is still the case, that the "burden of establishing that a comment falls within these limits and hence within the scope of the defence, lies upon the defendant who wishes to rely upon the defence." (per Lord Nicholls).

To have a full understanding of the recent developments in the law on fair comment up to the decision of the Supreme Court in *Spiller* consider the following cases. The *Galloway* analysis (see p.137) provides a good example of how these rules were applied in practice. You may also care to peruse the decision of the High Court in *Lowe v Associated Newspapers Ltd* [2006].[84] This case decided that to sustain a successful fair comment defence the words used must be assessed objectively and not subjectively. There is of course a subjective element in that the journalist needs to be aware of the facts that prompted the comment.

The objectivity assessment echoes what we said earlier that journalists should place themselves in the position of the reasonable (objective) reader or viewer. It may have been the intention to say one thing but looked at objectively that may not be the impression given. The case

---

[84] [2006] EWHC 320.

also decided that, while comments should be based upon facts, all the facts do not need to be explicit in the piece.

Clearly facts not mentioned in an article must exist and be known to the journalist at the time of writing. Eady J. summarised the position by identifying the following nine statements of principle in respect of the commentator's state of knowledge at the time of publication. The argument is centred on the assumption that there cannot be "fair comment" in respect of facts that are unknown to or not at the forefront of the commentator's mind at the time of writing:

1   Any fact pleaded to support fair comment must have existed at the time of the publication.

2   Any such facts must have been known, at least in general terms, at the time the comment was made, although it is not necessary that they should all have been in the forefront of the commentator's mind.

3   Any general fact within the commentator's knowledge (as opposed to comment itself) may be supported by specific examples even if the commentator had not been aware of them.

4   Facts may not be pleaded of which the commentator was unaware (even in general terms) on the basis that the defamatory comment is one he would have made if he had known them.

5   A commentator may rely upon a specific or a general fact (and, it follows, provide examples to illustrate it) even if he has forgotten it, because it may have contributed to the formation of his opinion.

6   The purpose of the defence of fair comment is to protect honest expressions of opinion upon, or inferences honestly drawn from, specific facts.

7   The ultimate test is the objective one of whether someone could have expressed the commentator's defamatory opinion (or drawn the inference) upon the facts known to the commentator, at least in general terms, and upon which he was purporting to comment.

8   A defendant who is responsible for publishing the defamatory opinions or inferences of an identified commentator (such as a newspaper column or letters page) does not have to show that he, she or it also knew the facts relied upon provided they were known to the commentator.

9   It is not permitted to plead fair comment if the commentator was doing no more than regurgitating the opinions of others without any knowledge of the underlying facts—still less if he was simply echoing rumours.

As a final point, Mr Justice Eady went on to state:

"It would plainly be unacceptable to dredge up a "welter" of factual allegations after the event of which he knew nothing at the time and upon which he might have written a different article—if only it had been drawn to his attention. Nor, as a matter of principle, can it be right to find the material for one's comment ex post facto by interrogating the Claimant or by obtaining order for disclosure, whether from him or third parties."[85]

We will return to this list later as it came under review by Lord Phillips in the *Spiller* case. Lord Phillips acknowledged the importance of *Lowe* case in these words:

"That decision merits attention, for it contains the carefully considered views of a judge whom has great experience of the law of defamation on the subject matter of the present appeal."

In addition to the knowledge of the writer and the public interest nature of the facts upon which the comments are based the distinction between the use of "fact" and "opinion" words is critical to the success of the defence. The reader needs to be able to distinguish between fact and opinion, and context becomes important. In *Convery v Irish News Ltd* [2008][86] the owner of a restaurant took exception to the review in which food had been described as "inedible" although there was much more detail about the restaurant including the fact that it was very busy with people queuing waiting for a table to become free. The newspaper pleaded fair comment but a jury awarded the claimant significant damages. The appeal was allowed. The Northern Ireland Court of Appeal warned that words should not be taken out of context and that the review as a whole had to be considered. The judge considered that "sufficient factual substratum existed for the comment which constituted the preponderance of the article."[87]

A similar approach was adopted by Tugendhat J. in Elton John's action against the Guardian Media group in 2008.[88] The claimant took exception to a "spoof" diary article entitled "A peek at the diary of Elton John." The allegation was that the ordinary reader would have concluded that he was insincere in promoting charitable causes, doing it for self-promotion rather than altruistic motives. The judge concluded that the pleaded meaning could not be sustained. A major reason was that ordinary readers would realise this was satire rather than an examination of Sir Elton's John actual diary for the particular week in question. In that context no-one would believe that they were reading the truth.

In *British Chiropractor Association v Singh* [2010][89] the defendant had contributed an article to the *Guardian*'s Comment and Debate section which included the following passage:

---

[85] [2006] EWHC 320 at para.74-5.
[86] [2008] NICA 1.
[87] [2008] NICA at para.41 per Kerr L.C.J.
[88] *Elton John v Guardian Media Group Ltd* [2008] EWHC 3006 (QB).
[89] [2010] EWCA Civ 350.

"The British Chiropractor Association . . . is the respectable face of the chiropractic profession and yet it happily promotes bogus treatments."[90]

The trial judge determined that these words were assertions of fact and not comment and therefore the defence was not open to be pleaded by the defendant. The Court of Appeal stated the question to be determined was:

". . . whether its meaning includes one or more allegations of fact which are defamatory of the claimant, or whether the entirety of what it says about the claimant is comment (or to adopt the term used by the European Court of Human Rights in its Article 10 jurisprudence, value-judgment)."[91]

The Court of Appeal concluded that the statement was an expression of opinion. An opinion may be mistaken but nevertheless is still an opinion. The court roundly rejected the premise that before fair comment could succeed as a defence the defendant had to make good his assertion.[92] The academic and scientific community would have been wary of expressing views at conferences or in published research if the threat of legal action had not been lifted by the decision of the Court of Appeal.

Spiller

The claimants were a music group. The defendants acted as agents in obtaining work for them. The defendant posted on its website critical comments about the reliability of the claimants in fulfilling contracts. The defendants pleaded fair comment. The trial judge struck out the fair comment defence on the grounds that it was not capable of amounting to comment. The judge also ruled that defendant's response had not been in response to a matter of public interest. The Court of Appeal confirmed that the defence of fair comment should be struck out but not for the reasons relied upon by Eady J. at first instance.

The Court of Appeal found that the comment did not sufficiently set out the facts upon which the response was based. There was evidence that there had been a breach of contract by the claimants some 14 months before a second breach which had prompted .the website posting. There was "no nexus between it (the first breach) and the comment."[93] The second breach was not referred to and therefore could not be relied upon. In conclusion the Court could find no link between the comment and any fact referred to in the publication.

The Supreme Court took the opportunity to review the law on fair

---

[90] April 19, 2008.
[91] [2010] EWCA Civ 350 at para.16 per Lord Judge L.C.J.
[92] [2010] EWCA Civ 350 at para.24.
[93] See *www.5rb.co.uk/case reports*

comment. Its decision takes the law forward in two respects. First Lord Nicholls' comment in the *Cheng* case to the effect:

". . . the comment must explicitly or implicitly indicate, at least in general terms, what are the facts on which the comment is being made. The reader or hearer ought to be able to be in a position to judge for himself how far the comment was well founded."

It was held that the second part of Lord Nicholls' statement should no longer be followed. All that was needed was the inclusion of information which met the first part of the statement. The question therefore is whether the comment explicitly or implicitly indicated in general terms at least the facts upon which the comment is based. So the implication is that the commentator need not provide as much information as previously was the case in order to rely on the defence. A balance has to be maintained between freedom of expression and protection of reputation. The defence supports the principle of free expression and in its new form still means that the reader will have sufficient information to understand why the defendant has made those comments.

The second point is the renaming of the defence. In the *Singh* case the Court of Appeal had decided it should be called "honest opinion" but the Supreme Court has now renamed it "honest comment." The continued use of the word comment provides the link with the "old" principles but this is not destined to last for long given Parliament's current preference for "honest opinion" as expressed in the Defamation Bill. Lord Phillips queried points 3 and 5 of the Eady "list" in the *Lowe* case but the Supreme Court does not seem to have overruled them.

The Defamation Bill

It is hard to imagine that anyone would regard the Bill's proposals for a renamed fair comment defence to be radical. The name is new-ish given the Court of Appeal's view in *Singh*. The key elements of the defence are distilled into three conditions:

1   The statement complained of is a statement of opinion.
2   The opinion is on a matter of public interest.
3   An honest person could have held the opinion on the basis of
   (a) a fact which existed at the time the statement complained of was published;
   (b) a privileged statement which was published before the statement complained of.
     • The defence is defeated if the claimant shows that the defendant did not hold the opinion.
     • If the statement published was made by another person the defence is not lost but if the defendant knew or ought to have known the other person didn't hold that opinion then the defence is lost.

Evidence of malice will defeat the defence.

However, the Bill's provisions would suggest that the old subjective/objective assessment has been consigned to history and the test will now be purely objective. Currently it is important for the defendant to establish awareness at some stage of the facts upon which the comment was based, even if in the interim those facts had been forgotten or were not at the forefront of his mind at the time of writing the comments. (See the Eady list above). Now it appears that what is to be established is the honest person could have held that opinion providing that the fact upon which the comment was based actually existed when the statement was published.

If this is true then it would appear to undermine the decision of the Supreme Court which is, at the time of writing, only five-months old. Query therefore the balance between protection of reputation and freedom of expression. Is this going to be open season for anyone to express any views about anything/anyone at all providing there are facts in existence at the time the comment was published? The only element of the Bill that might limit this interpretation is the fact the comment must be on a matter of public interest.

Under the bill, the common law defence of fair comment is abolished and section 6 of the Defamation Act 1952 is repealed.

v) Offer of Amends

This is a popular way to bring defamation proceedings to a reasonably speedy conclusion. The basis of the defence is found in ss.2–4 of the Defamation Act 1996. A person who has published an alleged defamatory statement may make an offer of amends. The offer must be in writing and make it clear whether the offer relates to the statement— "generally" or in relation to a specific defamatory meaning that the offeror accepts the statement conveys. This latter situation is referred to as a "qualified offer".

The purpose of the offer is to:

a   make a suitable correction of the statement complained of and make a sufficient apology to the aggrieved party;

b   to publish the correction and apology in a manner that is reasonable and practicable in the circumstances; and

c   to pay to the aggrieved party such compensation (if any) and such costs, as may be agreed or determined to be payable.

The media organisation should have in place a robust system to determine complaints as quickly as possible. Many correspondents will simply wish to correct something that is inaccurate and most newspapers will remedy an inaccuracy within hours. However, as the case of *Campbell-James v Guardian Media Group* [2005][94] illustrates, there can be

[94] [2005] EWHC 893.

severe penalties for a failure to respond quickly enough. In this case, the claimant was a serving Army officer who had been accused by the newspaper of being involved in the Abu Ghraib prison scandal in Iraq where prisoners were, according to the report, "systematically abused and humiliated." Colonel Campbell-James responded by stating: "I was not even in Iraq until two months after the abuses had been exposed."

The *Guardian* eventually published an apology some three months after the original piece by which time the allegations had been reprinted in the French newspaper, *Le Matin*. The *Guardian* considered defending its position by reference to all three established defences. The judge, Mr Justice Eady, was plainly unimpressed by the *Guardian*'s stance. He had the task of assessing damages and as is normal in these circumstances was prepared to make a discount for "the belated offer of amends and apology". There is no standard percentage discount and therefore each case must be assessed on its own facts. The 35 per cent discount was towards the lower end of the discount range. The judge awarded the claimant £58,500 and his costs. Perhaps the best way to sum up the approach is to quote from the decision of Eady J. in *Tesco Stores Ltd v Guardian News and Media Ltd* [2008][95]:

> "Litigation is no longer intended to be a game for lawyers; it is a means provided by the state of achieving justice for the parties, which almost always is going to be imperfect and to involve compromises. It was the need for compromise which underlay the offer of amends regime."

PART TWO: DEFAMATION IN PRACTICE

Few working journalists will have spent much time reading formal court judgments unless directly involved in the case. Yet these daunting-looking documents are very informative about far more than the specific details of each case and indeed about more than pure media law. Developments in defamation cases, particularly the emergence of the *Reynolds* defence in qualified privilege, raise key issues about what it means to be a responsible journalist. Judges are discussing and defining acceptable investigative methods in at least as much detail as most journalism textbooks.

The chilling effect of libel decisions which go against media outlets cannot be ignored but there are some encouraging developments which can help the working journalist, including, it would appear, the 2011

---

[95] [2008] EWHC B14 (QB) at para.48.

Defamation Bill. Understanding the risks and responsibilities imposed by defamation law is not just about staying out of court; it is about having the confidence and expertise not to be frightened of running stories which should rightly be put in the public domain even where they may impact on reputation.

The number of libel cases which actually go to trial represents the tip of an iceberg. Few journalists will be directly involved in a court room clash. However, nearly all will find their work subject to claims of defamation at some point in their career. Every journalist has to bear that threat in mind in every story covered, however innocuous it may appear. A good journalist will know enough about the law to be aware of those risks and to take advice on how to avoid them. Only very rarely should that have to mean abandoning the story. The skill is in crafting a story which avoids being defamatory or proceeding in such a manner as to construct a robust defence to any subsequent action. Many people threaten to sue for libel. Few proceed if met with a convincing defence. Most discussion here focuses on procedures before publication which will protect you against claims.

Many complaints are resolved without recourse to the courts, including by offer of amends. If the newspaper has made a mistake, it is best corrected. Apologising may stick in the craw of many editors but some defamation claims result from an error which is obvious after the event. Doing the decent thing means correcting it. If legal action is a possibility, making this a formal offer of amends is advisable. (It is then necessary to find better ways of spotting errors before publication.) Trying to defend the indefensible is pointless and potentially very costly.

If the journalist's newsgathering procedure or sources cannot be relied upon, the advice will be to settle as cheaply as possible. If a defence is in place with evidence and procedural probity, the complaint may well be withdrawn. The lack of certainty in defamation cases may increase the caution on journalists, but it also weighs against claimants. They can also lose and face considerable costs.

The other key requirement on good journalists protecting themselves against the threat of libel action is that the methods they employ in chasing and presenting the story stand up to scrutiny. As one in-house media lawyer put it, pursue and write every story as if you were defending your actions to a judge.

Online journalism
Broadly speaking, websites are subject to the same laws as any other media, but the explosion of web-based journalism, message boards and other public contributions has thrown up a welter of new questions as to how the law is applied to these platforms.

These include, for defamation purposes, where discussion hosts sit within the definition of "publisher" and where the "audience" now is which affects where actions are taken in terms of forum shopping. In general terms, the law has struggled to cope with the explosion in the volume of publishing and thus of the potential for defamatory material reaching the public domain. We will see later how this has affected, for example, the defence of fair/honest comment.

A significant downside in terms of exposure to defamation actions has arisen from the easy availability of news archives to the public. Journalists had benefited from the time limit on defamation actions being reduced from six years from publication to just one. But the approach under the multiple publication rule that every new online "hit" counts as a new "publication" for defamation purposes effectively removed any time limit to action. This generated a welter of actions regarding online archive material which, as the law stands, remains actionable as long as it can be accessed.

The new Defamation Bill[96] proposes a single publication rule under which action would be limited to 12 months from the date of first publication, unless the article changed materially or was displayed prominently. Standard archive material would thus cease to be the ticking timebomb it has become.

Loutchansky[97] was one of a growing number of cases where a judgment was platform-specific. A print version of a story was cleared of defamation, but the action was upheld against the online version because it persisted so much longer than a single edition of the newspaper which was also given more leeway for having been published under considerable time pressure. This judgment has caused headaches for the industry faced with huge legal and logistical problems of managing digital archives.

In principle, the situation has not changed, as newspapers have generally always allowed public access to their dusty, bound volumes of newspapers dating back, in some cases, for centuries. Actionable material would not have been ripped from their covers but may have had a warning note attached. But in practice, making these archives electronic and searchable has made the level of access much higher and the chances of the public re-accessing defamatory material so much greater. The modern requirement upholds the principle for correcting inaccuracies, whereby in many cases the material challenged can remain in the archive, but is tagged with the changes made after first publication. Where material is defamatory, the court may demand its removal from the archive.

A further headache arises from discussion boards. To date, if a member of the public has posted defamatory material, the "host" has generally been thought likely to avoid an action as long as the offending material is removed as soon as it is brought to the host's attention. Newspapers, for instance, wanting to encourage interaction with and between readers, have created all kinds of avenues for public comment. But are they responsible for anything that appears online under the

---

[96] Available on the Ministry of Justice website: *www.justice.gov.uk.* Consultation period ended on June 10, 2011.

[97] *Loutchansky v Times Newspapers* [2001] EWCA Civ 1805.

banner of the newspaper? If so, everything would have to be moderated before publication which imposes severe restrictions on the volume and speed of the exchanges. The attitude to date of trying to assume the limited "hosting" role effectively encouraged a hands-off approach. It is far easier for the host to limit liability if the off-shoot sites are not moderated than if they are. Yet this, in practice, is more likely to allow defamatory material to be published. What is a "responsible" newspaper to do?

This is certainly what one could call an "emerging" area of the law. The courts have tended to treat websites as minor adjuncts to mainstream news organisations or as low-level irritants. The rapid expansion of traffic to the web makes many of the existing positions untenable.

There have been various attempts to quell the potential rush of defamation actions arising from the blogosphere. Eady J. has developed the concept of "vulgar abuse" whereby some of the slanging matches conducted on bulletin boards can evade action. Such ravings are not to be taken seriously or literally, he argues, and thus do not have to be deemed defamatory. The terminology was historically associated with slander cases, and Eady argued that such online exchanges were more akin to slander than libel.

This may discourage actions between bloggers but is unlikely to be of much help to paid journalists who will not get away with claiming that remarks were made "off-the-cuff".

This expansion has potential implications for internet service providers. Complainants who find it is not worth suing members of the public who have contributed defamatory material to message boards or blogs, say, may turn their attention to the facilitators. The High Court decision in *Bunt v Tilley* [2006][98] has now offered ISPs a reasonable degree of protection against such claims. ISPs will be viewed as "secondary publishers" within the terms of s.1 of the Defamation Act 1996. However ISPs should not become complacent because the protection could be lost if the ISP has reason to believe that defamatory material has been posted and does not take steps reasonably quickly to remove the offending content.

This grey area could be hindering freedom of expression. The cautious approach is to remove any material subject of complaint. But that means those with the media nous and resources to complain can stifle remarks about them. It is now much easier to trawl the digital universe to find references to a person or company and raise an objection to it. This concern has been raised, among others, by Justine Roberts, founder of the influential Mumsnet social networking website which faced defamation action from childcare expert Gina Ford over comment posted on Mumsnet's bulletin board which receives more than five million postings a year. The case was settled out of court.

Roberts told the *Guardian*,[99]: "The law regards a bulletin board just as

---

[98] [2006] EWHC 407 (QB).
[99] The *Guardian*, Monday December 10, 2007, p.3.

it does a newspaper or a book, which is a bit like trying to use a set of railway signals to control the air traffic over Heathrow. The principles may be fine but different forms of communication, just like different forms of transport, require a different approach."

She said: "What it has done is make us more trigger happy with the delete button. We pull anything that anyone complains about—because you can't take a risk as to what constitutes defamation when you don't have the resources to seek legal advice or go to court."

6. Defamation Defences in Practice

i) Absolute privilege and statutory qualified privilege in practice

These defences generate relatively little case law because they have been established in statute for many years. The new Defamation Bill aims to extend their reach. So, for example, journalists will enjoy absolute privilege for fair, accurate and contemporaneous reports of courts anywhere in the world if the Bill is enacted as it stands.

These can be very strong defences to employ as they derive directly from statute and are relatively clear cut in their definitions and in their demands on the journalist.

Reporting the criminal courts would not be possible without the benefit of absolute privilege, as clearly derogatory claims are made against the defendant and sometimes others. The requirement is that reports are a fair, accurate and contemporaneous account of the proceedings held in public. Accuracy is a must so take particular care when reporting court. Reports should provide some balance of prosecution and defence, and be published promptly. The standard understanding of "contemporaneous" is publication in the next available edition.

Indeed some reporters are eager to turn contemporaneous into instantaneous by tweeting coverage from court. This could be a cumbersome way of reporting the trial as a whole but would be very appealing in major trials where readers are hanging on a verdict or sentence. To date, use has been limited and is at the discretion of individual judges. There is some understandable nervousness about the instant reporting of proceedings from the relatively closed atmosphere of the court. An ill-advised remark, for instance, could hardly be struck from the record if it had already whizzed round on Twitter. The general judicial aversion to filming, sound recording and photography in court signals a desire to control the version of events which reaches the public. The whole topic was out to consultation as we went to print. (See also the discussion in Ch.1 on the Legal System.)

Statutory qualified privilege can also be a godsend for the journalist. It can offer a very solid defence—the sort that a media lawyer (or well-briefed editor) can use to deter potential claimants from even issuing a writ. The attention in case law is on the "responsible journalism" more often variant of qualified privilege because the grey area is where court battles are fought. Statutory qualified privilege offers greater clarity and is generally preferred as a more reliable defence where available.

Under the existing Defamation Act of 1996, the privilege was attached very much to certain occasions—to the meetings of particular public bodies, public inquiries, press conferences and the like. These are set out in the Schedule to the Act, as explained in Part One of this chapter.

Case law gradually extended the reach of statutory qualified privilege in a most welcome way so as to embrace press releases and a great deal of material placed in the public domain. (But do read the argument over a lost statutory privilege defence in Case Study Two: *Henry*.)

The new Defamation Bill proposes to expand the remit of the Schedule. So rather than just protecting public statements by UK police, it would cover police forces "anywhere in the world" which would be of great reassurance when covering the antics of Brits abroad. As Nigel Hanson of Foot Anstey commented on *Holdthefrontpage*:[100]

> "This change was prompted because, for fear of being sued, local papers in England had declined to publish defamatory statements made by a Thai police chief – including an appeal for witnesses based in England – about a UK citizen arrested in Bangkok for alleged sex offences."

In similar recognition of our globalised world, the privilege would also be extended to reports of public meetings anywhere in the world and to proceedings at a general meeting of a "quoted company" to include overseas companies rather than just UK public companies.

A good journalist is likely to rely frequently on these statutory privileges to protect a huge range of reporting in the public interest. It is well worth becoming familiar with the details of the schedules in terms of their scope and the requirements of maintaining the defence, as outlined in Part One. A solid defamation defence can be built by pushing organisations to make public statements, to issue documents or call meetings which would put the material under the protection of statutory qualified privilege. These are techniques well worth developing to avoid the uncertainties and costs of relying on a responsible publication defence.

ii) Responsible publication in practice

The responsible journalism defence is hugely influential and has great potential. However, it comes with a health warning. Some media

---

[100] Libel Reform—what's in it for the regional press? *www.holdthefrontpage.co.uk* March 29, 2011 [Accessed April 2011]

organisations, believing it offers more protection than it does, have gone to trial relying on it and lost. It is worth remembering too that despite Lord Nicholls helpfully expanding upon the legal onus on a journalist, he found in favour of the claimant in the original *Reynolds* case. The newspaper lost.

The law remains highly protective of individual reputations. Qualified privilege under common law will tend to be complex and unpredictable to rely on. In the absence of a justification defence, the *Reynolds* defence specifically does not provide carte blanche for any stories in the public interest to be run whatever their defamatory content. The public interest must be there in terms of the right to know test but there must be evidence too of journalistic rigour and an open mind.

Here the definition of reportage could also be significant for the working journalist. Simon Brown L.J. described it as "neutral reporting of attributed allegations rather than their adoption by the newspaper" (*Al Faghi v HH Saudi Research & Marketing (UK) Ltd*).[101] This was the basis of the successful defence in *Roberts v Gable*.[102] (See Case Study Four later in this chapter.)

But reportage was ruled out in the judgments to date on *Flood*,[103] which is due to reach the Supreme Court later this year.

There is also the argument that, because the defence of freedom of expression in areas of public interest is now so strong, as outlined in Ch.1, judges feel it right to rein us in, partly by generous interpretation of art.8 privacy rights, but also, within libel, by making those freedoms subject to evidence of "responsible" journalism.

At one level, this is to be welcomed with open arms for strengthening "serious" journalism genuinely driven by the public right to know but, at another, one cannot help feeling more than a faint whiff of judicial disapproval, particularly for the "popular" press. Journalists may have to be "responsible" but they will never be entirely respectable, and nor should they be. Only those with an unhealthy devotion to the status quo would ever achieve that standing. So perhaps we are destined always to cause judges, and the rest of the establishment, some degree of offence.

Moreover, the very fact that we use the term "popular" as one of the range of pejorative labels attached to newspapers sneered at by the establishment and academics, masks a deeper dilemma for the UK, which is that far more of the population choose to buy those papers, despite having a wide range of weightier alternatives.

Also, being from a regional newspaper background, where tabloids have dominated for decades, the generic word "tabloid" grates when used to indicate a paper devoted to trivia and sensationalism. While it is not even a reasonable shorthand to describe the mass-market national newspapers, it is certainly not applicable regionally. There is no simple association between the format of a newspaper, per se, and its core

---

[101] [2001] EWCA Civ 1634.
[102] *Roberts & Another v Gable & Others* [2007] EWCA Civ 721.
[103] *Flood v Times Newspapers Ltd* [2010] EWCA Civ 804.

values and approach to content; nor its commitment to "responsible" journalism.

Whatever your platform, you will have to convince judges that the material is in the public interest and has been gathered, verified and published in a responsible, fair manner. Or as media lawyers have been known to put it:" In a *Reynolds* defence, the person on trial is the journalist."

iii) Truth (justification) in practice

To pursue a defence of justification, a journalist will have to produce evidence that the sting of the libel is substantially true. Do note the concept of Chase Levels outlined in Part One under iii) which can help a journalist decide how to pitch a story so as not to limit the requirements of a justification defence.

Information may be true, but proving it can be very demanding. A journalist has to consider what would be available if a claim went to court. A reassuring combination for any defence lawyer is a credible source backed by some documentary evidence. Working in anticipation of a libel action, a journalist will secure a sworn affidavit from any source who may later have to stand up to be counted in court.

Seeking a sworn affidavit may seem overly elaborate but it can be vital and is an effective way of weeding out poor sources. A refusal to sign at best means a source cannot be relied upon in court but it should also ring alarm bells for a journalist. Is the source genuine? Are they who they say they are? Do they have evidence for their claim? Are they in a position to know what they claim to know? These are the questions any journalist should ask themselves about a source but where a story is potentially defamatory they become essential.

A signed statement, or better still signed draft article, is no guarantee that a source will go to court but most who have made the commitment have followed through when required. There is, however, little point in persuading a source to sign a statement only to run a story that goes way beyond its contents, especially if the way beyond includes the sting of the libel. An overblown story makes it easy for the source to wriggle out of giving evidence and, even if they are still prepared to go to court, their evidence is unlikely to go far enough.

The lack of availability and/or credibility of witnesses has often been the basis of media defeat in a justification defence. Juries can be completely unconvinced by a string of witnesses, as they were in the original action brought by Tommy Sheridan, an SMP, against the *News of the World*. Sheridan was ultimately convicted of perjury but it took considerable nerve and money for the newspaper to persevere with the case after such a resounding early failure.

The mundane matter of record keeping can make or break a defence too. Documents and tapes must be stored so they can be easily retrieved, if called upon to mount a defence. Key interviews should be transcribed, partly for security but also to guard against journalists hearing what they want to hear. Sources can seem more convincing and categorical in the heat of the moment than when their words are scrutinised later. Only rely on the actual quotes. It should go without saying, but a refusal to comment is not an admission. Never treat it as such.

Paid sources can still provide evidence in civil cases, but the payment will always be an issue in court and can easily undermine credibility. A source will be asked if payment was offered in such a way that changing or exaggerating their evidence earned them more. It doesn't help either if they haggled. Juries don't like the idea that someone made a fortune from their revelations.

iv) Honest opinion (fair comment) in practice

Honest opinion, previously known as fair comment, is involved in several of the key cases considered in defamation. The defence was clarified considerably in *Lowe*[104] but has undergone change via *Singh*[105] and *Spiller*.[106] It had been considered an "easier" defence than justification or *Reynolds* privilege but in *Galloway*, for example, it failed as a defence too. The court was not prepared to protect comment based on allegations rather than fact and the *Daily Telegraph* never attempted to prove that the claims were true.

There was also considerable debate on the distinction between fact and comment. Our attitude to freedom of expression is such that claimants tend to be less likely to challenge a story which is clearly opinion, such as a newspaper's leader column. It is therefore tempting for a publisher to claim material falls under comment rather than fact in attempting to defend it against defamation actions. Judges are well aware of this and will thus give very careful scrutiny to which is which. This can lead to complex semantic as well as legal debate.

Just as comment frequently creeps into news stories, so not everything in an opinion column will be accepted as comment. The judge in Galloway decided the sting of the leaders was fact not comment. Talk of treason, for instance, relates to fact. Treason is a crime; it is not a matter of opinion. The leader also referred to the discovery of prima facie evidence. As the judge said: "That is not comment."

Judicial rulings in the area of honest opinion provide both greater clarity and a greater challenge to journalists. Judges are, seemingly intentionally, in particular cases providing frameworks for their judgments to set out general principles in those areas which are ECHR-compliant. These have some potential to act as guidelines for journalists working on other stories and lend at least a degree of predictability to the likely outcome in other cases. The principle of deciding each case on its merits is clearly vital for the interests of justice, but it can create a quagmire for journalists seeking to reveal the strongest, fullest possible

---

[104] *Lowe v Associated Newspapers Ltd* [2006] EWHC 320 (QB).
[105] *British Chiropractic Association v Singh* [2010] EWCA Civ 350.
[106] *Spiller & Anor v Joseph & Ors* [2010] UKSC 53.

story without falling foul of the law. While even those frameworks are subject to reinterpretation in subsequent cases, they can provide some help to the journalist in determining the legal boundaries and in outlining what will be required to mount a successful defence to any claim, especially where they are endorsed by higher courts.

Comment is a growth area in UK media, in print, online and effectively in broadcast too, where specialist reporters are increasingly being called upon to "interpret" events which can raise the question of where facts end and comment begins. Some newspapers are actively adopting a policy whereby, given the preponderance of "breaking news" in 24/7 broadcast and online platforms, their role is predominantly to provide considered analysis and place events in perspective. What that means in practice, is an explosion of punditry which goes well beyond analysis and clearly into the realms of opinion and advocacy.

That alone is likely to bring fair comment defences to the fore. Prior to the Human Rights Act, fair comment tended to feature less than justification in key libel judgments. Claims for defamation arising from opinion pieces were often not brought because it was felt the fair comment defence would be too strong. Even before art.10, it was harder to censure a journalist for expressing a genuinely held opinion based on fact than it was for getting their facts wrong in a news story. So we might have expected the defence to have been strengthened by UK adoption of the ECHR.

Yet there are various pointers in the Lowe judgment referred to earlier in the chapter that ring alarm bells or at least underline a need for caution. There are certainly massive risks in assuming that anything goes as long as we run it under the banner of comment. The judgment also highlights the ways in which the legal waters are muddied further by the growing tendency in UK media, particularly print, not to separate news from comment. This is exemplified by the branding of the Independent as a "viewspaper" not a newspaper.

Both in *Lowe* and *Galloway*, it is clear judges are determined to separate the two. Defamation defences demand it and any defendant seeking to use them must be able to demonstrate the difference.

Lowe had made the distinction more explicit but at the same time quite burdensome, particularly for the wealth of throwaway remarks made in digital as well as mainstream media. The requirements are played through in Case Study Five.

In practice, this created too great a hurdle as exemplified in the legal row between the British Chiropractic Association (BCA) and science journalist Singh which for a period shutdown a highly-significant debate over the efficacy of various medical treatments. Singh wrote a detailed article which accused the BCA of making claims for which there was "not a jot of evidence" and of "happily" promoting "bogus" treatments.

As required for a fair comment defence, he constructed his argument, making the rationale for his opinion very clear. He even wrote: "I can confidently label these treatments as bogus because I have co-authored a book about alternative medicine . . . . . ." His co-author had examined evidence of 70 trials and found no evidence to suggest chiropractors could treat the conditions, such as colic, claimed by the BCA.

The problem was that when, at the behest of the parties, Eady J. ruled on the defamatory meaning of the statements he also classified them as facts, not comment. The BCA, as a limited company, could claim damages.

To restore the freedom for proper debate of scientific arguments, the Court of Appeal had to reach a different interpretation. Lord Chief Justice Lord Judge said at [11] and [12]:

"It is now nearly two years since the publication of the offending article. It seems unlikely that anyone would dare repeat the opinions expressed by Dr Singh for fear of a writ. Accordingly this litgation has almost certainly had a chilling effect on public debate which might otherwise have assisted potential patients to make informed choices about the possible use of chiropractic. . . . . This would be a surprising consequence of laws designed to protect reputation.

By proceedings against Dr Singh, and not the Guardian, and by rejecting the offer made by the Guardian to publish an appropriate article refuting Dr Singh's contentions, or putting them in a proper prospective, the unhappy impression has been created that this is an endeavour by the BCA to silence one of its critics."

Despite the obvious tone of disapproval, he continued: "Again, if that is where the current law of defamation takes us, we must apply it."

Thankfully the Appeal Court was able to construct an interpretation of the case which took the law in a direction more favourable to freedom of expression. It decided that the assertion that there was not "one jot of evidence" for the BCA position was a statement of opinion.

The Court also seemed to prefer the European Court terminology from its art.10 jurisprudence of value judgment, rather than comment. It decided that a scientific debate over whether particular evidence supported a particular conclusion was a matter of opinion, not fact, as Singh argued.

The most erudite analysis at [34] drew on a US judgment by Judge Easterbrook, in *Underwager v Calter Fed. 3d 730* (1994) which stated:

"Plaintiffs cannot, by simply filing suit and crying 'character assassination!', silence those who hold divergent views, no matter how adverse those views may be to plaintiffs' interests. Scientific controversies must be settled by the methods of science rather than the methods of litigation. . . . More papers, more discussion, better data, and more satisfactory models – not larger awards of damages – mark the path towards superior understanding of the world around us."

The judgment was most welcome relief, particular for the growing band of science journalists, such as Ben Goldacre, who set out to question such claims by individual and companies. A supportive ruling in the RSPB case helped to bolster the confidence of those eager to engage in rigorous scientific debate. Science is clearly a sphere where argument and counter-argument must be heard; where information can turn out to be wrong and where the very process of disputation is vital for advance.

Journalists would argue that applies to the whole of society. We need to be able to challenge ideas and behaviours in all spheres if we are to develop our thinking. The focus should remain on attacking the idea, where necessary, rather than the person holding it, but it is not always possible to separate the two.

Singh did shore up the defence of fair comment and paved the way for new formulations of the defence in *Spiller* and in the Defamation Bill. Hopefully not only science journalists will benefit from it. The interpretations of both the Supreme Court and the intended legislation arguably make the defence less onerous. As the judges note, millions of bloggers, as well as mainstream journalists, may need to rely on it to defend their derogatory comments but, with or without statutory codification, it will remain subject to many a semantic argument. Journalists will want to avoid pushing the boundaries of the defence given the reliance on a judge's interpretation of many aspects of the defence, not least whether it can be treated as opinion at all.

v) Offer of amends in practice

The introduction of offer of amends in the 1996 Act has proved a useful avenue either to avoid going to court or to act as a defence to reduce eventual damages.

An offer of amends makes sense where the publisher is not going to contest the libel for whatever reason. Sometimes stories are run which put the author clearly in the wrong, say where a libel has been run by mistake or through failure to spot the risk. It can also be useful where the author is unable to mount a defence because the evidence is weak or unwilling to pursue a defence because of the worst case scenario on costs. Sometimes editors cut their losses.

Certainly, where the defamation was unintentional or due to a mistake—which happens more times than editors would like to admit—it can be worth instigating an offer of amends. There is no point prolonging the agony and seeing costs mount pursuing a lost cause. Drafting an offer of amends which is suitably generous generally puts the publication in a stronger negotiating position than having to respond to an overblown draft from the claimant. Typically, the text first acknowledges that the claim was wrong then apologises for having published it. In print, this is usually taken to be an article of agreed wording headlined "Claimant name: an apology." There will probably also be negotiations over positioning so that reasonable prominence is given relative to the prominence given to the material complained of.

(See Case Study Two: *Henry v BBC (No. 2)* [2005].[107]) Having to bite the bullet and make offers, not just of correction but usually apology too, plus probably some compensation and costs makes this by no means penalty free.

The defence was born out of a desire not just to settle more such matters without recourse to the court but also to avoid the impasse whereby if a libel claim was threatened or even conceivable, the last thing a newspaper would do was run any sort of follow-up which was tantamount to an admission of guilt.

Issuing an offer of amends commensurate with the seriousness of any initial complaint will generally now be seen as working in the defendant's favour although the negotiations will be conducted "without prejudice."

However, reaching an agreement on an offer of amends can be fraught. A potential claimant may demand far more than an editor is comfortable about conceding or paying. In these instances, the court expects some negotiation to take place. The advice from *Henry (No.2)* was that the BBC should not have rejected the claimaint's suggested correction and apology out of hand. The judge said it was incumbent on the BBC to raise objections and try to reach agreement on the wording proposed.

If an offer of amends cannot be negotiated and the matter goes to trial, the defendant will be credited for having attempted to agree an offer of amends and any damages can be discounted by a third or more. The degree of discount will depend on how any such negotiations were handled.

The *Guardian* suffered for being both grudging and tardy in its apology over Abu Ghraib so it was given less credit for what it ran. (See p.128).

If an offer of amends is accepted, the party accepting the offer cannot bring or continue defamation proceedings.

However, as in the *Guardian* case, even where agreement is reached, the parties may end up in court if there is a dispute over the implementation of the offer. Similarly the court may be called upon to settle the appropriate level of compensation, which will be affected by the court's assessment of how reasonably the defendant has behaved over the offer of amends.

If the offer is not accepted, the fact that the offer was made is a defence to defamation. The defence cannot be advanced if the person making the offer knew or had reason to believe that the material referred to the claimant and was both false and defamatory, although that would have to be demonstrated to the court.

The restriction is a warning shot for journalists against running blatant false stories then expecting to limit the damage by claiming to be really sorry.

---

[107] [2005] EWHC 2787 (QB).

If the offer is used as a defence it can be the only defence but whatever the defence pursued the offer can be used to mitigate damages.

The *Guardian*'s response to the judgment against it is illuminating and in true *Guardian* style much of it is on the record. It ran the judgment across eight columns with the headline "British colonel wrongly linked to Iraqi jail abuse awarded damages." The newspaper also records and discusses the judgment against it both on the website and in a column by its then readers' editor, Ian Mayes.

It did seem almost perverse that a national newspaper which pioneered a daily Corrections & Clarifications column should lose out for being slow to resolve a complaint. However as Ian Mayes made clear:

"I do not touch complaints in which lawyers are involved. I do not deal with complaints once the Press Complaints Commission is involved. I never represent the Guardian in disputes. When people come to me without the threat of legal action I deal with their complaints impartially."[108]

In this sense, the readers' editor is the first avenue of recourse for complainants. Often grievances which could have ended up with legal action are resolved by his intervention, promptly and to the satisfaction of the complainant. A few dissatisfied parties subsequently take their complaint to the next stage. But, if complainants make it clear from the outset that they want to by-pass the readers' editor then he doesn't get involved.

Once solicitors' letters start flying, the *Guardian* deals lawyer-to-lawyer, as most newspapers do. Then negotiations take place on a much more formal basis, without prejudice, as both sides explore ways to resolve the dispute. This may account for the time taken which the judge found unacceptable.

The *Guardian* initially contemplated a *Reynolds* defence to the action, probably because the offending article was born out of a series of Parliamentary questions, which themselves were prompted by testimony to the Abu Ghraib inquiry itself.

However it did belatedly run an apology in its Corrections & Clarifications column, which the judge considered inappropriate. Here, the *Guardian* fell victim perhaps to Ian Mayes' renowned ability to make the column immensely readable, embracing as it does sarcasm and the more humorous Homophones. The judge was not amused.

Indeed the *Guardian* has responded to the criticism by accepting such juxtaposition is not appropriate to the more significant corrections required. In the wake of the *Col Campbell-James* ruling, the newspaper made an immediate settlement for a similar amount

---

[108] A costly lesson in libel, *Guardian*, June 4, 2005.

with the second named officer, Col Christopher Terrington. The apology to him appeared as the only item in the corrections column that day.

It is worth noting that, despite the scathing remarks of the judge, damages were still discounted by 35 per cent, less than the ball park 50 per cent, but still enough not to deter parties from contemplating that route which the courts are seeking to encourage.

6. Conciliation

Conciliation is worth mentioning here, not as a defence to defamation but as a way of handling potential actions. It may also become more common if the current Government ends the no-win, no-fee arrangements for civil action. The motivation had been coming from likely defendants and from within the legal system, but if conditional fee arrangements end, conciliation may appeal as a "low-cost" alternative for complainants too.

The aim of conciliation would be to resolve "sticking points" in actions without the parties having to set foot in court. This is often done on a formal basis already—few actual defamation trials are heard. Most rulings involve assessment of points of law, such as meaning of words or whether a defence can run or not. Evaluations could be conducted outside court perhaps with less authority but certainly at less expense.

Key players in the field of defamation representing both newspapers and leading law firms now seem interested in moving in this direction which may prove a useful way of resolving defamation claims relatively cheaply and speedily.

Any restriction on the no-win, no-fee regime could also lead more potential litigants to run their complaint through the relevant regulatory body rather than the courts. (See Ch.8 on Regulation).

DEFAMATION CASE STUDIES

The case studies that follow are chosen to illustrate the pitfalls facing journalists when published material is claimed to be defamatory. They involve a mix of the various defences to defamation outlined earlier in the chapter and applied more or less successfully in court.

These cases help to explain how the requirements of the defences are met or not in practice and how risks could have been mitigated by changing the way journalists investigated and/or published the relevant stories.

One can never predict with certainty the outcome of any proceedings but by drawing attention to journalistic practices that failed to impress the judges and courts of this country we hope your decision making will be better informed and "defamation free".

Case Study One: Galloway v Telegraph Group Ltd [2004] EWHC 2786 (QB)

The Galloway case remains fascinating and relevant for the working journalist. The media, in this case the *Daily Telegraph*, lost the case in which it had hoped to rely on a *Reynolds* (now responsible publication) defence of qualified privilege for its news reports. It also lost a fair comment defence. The judgment makes it very clear why.

MP George Galloway received libel damages of £150,000 over claims he received money from Saddam Hussein's regime in Iraq. Coverage variously talked of:

- him receiving at least £375,000 a year from Saddam;
- "damning" new evidence;
- "bluster" in his responses; and
- him being Saddam's little helper.

One leader column began: "It doesn't get much worse than this." It later said: "There is a word for taking money from enemy regimes: treason." And "The alleged payments did not come from some personal bank account of Saddam's but out of the revenue intended to pay for food and medicines for Iraqi civilians; the very people whom Mr Galloway has been so fond of invoking."

The story was prompted by the contents of documents said to have been found in Iraqi intelligence files after the fall of Baghdad which also referred to Fawaz Abdullah Zureikat, who acted in Iraq for the Mariam Campaign, an appeal launched by Galloway to pay for medical treatment for a particular Iraqi child but also to campaign against the war.

Galloway complained that the coverage, in April 2003, accused him of being in the pay of Saddam; of making profits personally and secretly from the oil-for-food programme; of asking Iraqi intelligence to "up" his payments and of using his Mariam Appeal as a front to obtain money for himself.

The outcome in his favour is certainly further evidence that the *Reynolds* defence is not the panacea some hoped it would be in running stories of public interest where reputations are at stake but where material is not easily susceptible to proof.

The importance of the story is not enough. The judgment made it very clear that a story covering claims about a British MP in a secret service dossier in Iraq would pass the duty/interest or public right to know test. The *Daily Telegraph* lost because it fell down on the "responsible journalism" test in several ways. Its *Reynolds* defence failed because the judge deemed that it had:

- rushed to print;
- not approached obvious third parties for verification;
- not put the "sting" of the libel to Galloway in advance of publication; and
- rubbished his other responses.

In terms of the *Reynolds* ten-point but non-exhaustive list, several key elements were:

Under i: the seriousness of the allegation. The allegation was very serious so if it were wrong, the public would be badly misinformed as well as Galloway being defamed. It's a double-edged sword as a media defence.

Under iv: the steps taken to verify the allegation. These were deemed inadequate, particularly as no approaches were made to third parties. In this case the *Daily Telegraph* journalists were expected to have talked at least to Zureikat who featured prominently in the source documents and was Galloway's representative for the Mariam Campaign in Iraq. It didn't help that, as the court noted, Channel 4 had managed to interview Zureikat on the day the *Daily Telegraph* began its coverage.

Under vi: the urgency of the matter. The judge was not convinced of the urgency of running the story without further investigation. The urgency must extend beyond the desire for a scoop. A quest for competitive advantage is not sufficient.

Under vii: comment from the claimant. Galloway was interviewed, but the judge was particularly dissatisfied with how this element was handled on various levels. Primarily, although the documents were discussed, the "sting" of the libel was not put to him. Galloway was told that the documents claimed money had gone from the oil-for-food programme to the Mariam Campaign but not that the *Daily Telegraph* was going to say he had gained personally; that he was "in the pay" of Saddam. Galloway denied that any money had been paid to the Mariam Campaign. The *Daily Telegraph* later tried to argue that Galloway, having denied that any monies were paid by Iraq, was effectively denying having received any personally, as well as denying any had gone to the campaign. The judge deemed this disingenuous.

Under viii: giving the gist of the claimant's side. The defence fell down here. As well as Galloway not being invited to reply to the "sting" of the libel, what he did say was presented as "bluster". The

transcript of the reporter's conversation with Galloway was pored over
by the court in forensic detail.

This is part of their exchange quoted word for word in the judgment:

> Mr Sparrow said: "Just to recap. You've sort of made this clear before,
> but I just want to be sort of crystal clear on this, because I mean it's
> quite serious. You say the Mariam Campaign sort of never to your
> knowledge sort of received money or solicited money from the Iraq
> regime?"
>
> Mr Galloway said "No" and Mr Sparrow persisted: "Did they
> ever—did they ever sort of try to give you money? It must have been
> very tempting for them."
>
> The judge was not impressed.

How would your notes stand up to such scrutiny?

Under ix: the tone. This applies at every stage in the story; the
investigation, the story content and its presentation. The tone as well
as the substance of the reporter's conversation was commented upon.
There was particular concern that the reporter had invited Galloway to
"explain away" the claims in the documents. The tone of the headlines
was also criticised for presenting Galloway as guilty rather than under
investigation. This even extended to scrutiny of story lists at editorial
conferences—not known for their restrained descriptions of stories.
All this was used as evidence that the *Daily Telegraph* had made its
mind up about the allegations—that it had gone beyond reportage and
"adopted" the allegations.

The choice of words such as "damning" and "bluster" did particular
damage here. Journalists must choose their words carefully during the
investigation as well as the reporting of a story. For instance, don't talk
of "shocking revelations". Tell it to readers straight and let them decide
to be shocked or not. The language required for a *Reynolds* defence may
seem bland but is a smattering of flamboyant adjectives really worth
losing a libel case with damages and say £1 million in costs? Any whiff of
trial by media is particularly offensive to judges who believe questions
of guilt should be established by due process. It is considered acceptable, even in some cases desirable, for the media to reveal matters and to
call for and report on official inquiries into them, but judges, and often
juries too, decide the media is overstepping the mark if it dispenses its
own verdict.

Building a *Reynolds*/public interest defence

So how could the *Daily Telegraph* have run the story in such a way as to
have a defence against defamation?

Some of this should now become obvious in that it needed not to do
those things which cost it a *Reynolds* defence of common law qualified
privilege.

In the *Galloway* case, these related to various aspects of journalistic
procedure and behaviour.

The *Daily Telegraph* tried to argue that readers were told, in the introduction to the first story and at various other times, that these were allegations. This failed to convince the judge. Stating that the defamatory "sting" is based on a claim or allegation is never enough of a defence on its own. Repeating someone else's libellous statement is, in principle, unsafe. Journalists can only escape its restriction where they can demonstrate a high standard, not just of their sources, but of the way in which a story has been handled and projected. Reportage can only help if we have at least two sides of a story and treat all versions "neutrally".

If, as in this case, other elements of the article, and comment on it, go on to discuss the claims as proven fact, journalists will struggle to sustain the defence. Thinking the insertion of "alleged" makes a story safe is a dangerous rule of thumb. Judges require genuine balance not a disingenuous "nod" in the direction of avoiding action.

Put all allegations to Galloway.

What wasn't put to him included what the court deemed to be the "sting" of the libel that monies said to be paid had benefited him personally rather than going to the Mariam Campaign. The judge couldn't understand why the Daily Telegraph had not gone to Galloway in Portugal and showed him the documents. In practice putting allegations to a potential claimant is made more complex when several reporters are working on the same story. The interview with Galloway was based on early notes rather than copy produced with a view to publication. If the story has moved on and the content changed, the subject must be re-interviewed, especially if the claims have become more serious. Otherwise a *Reynolds* defence will not stand up.

Assess reliability of documents.

There is a quandary for the journalist here. A balanced story requires acknowledgment at very least that Galloway claimed the documents must be forged. So if we are alerting readers that there is question mark over the authenticity of the documents or the accuracy of the contents, what are we doing using them as a single source for very serious allegations?

Question third parties.

Galloway's agent Zureikat was an obvious omission but there were many potential sources who could have helped, say about the oil-for-food programme. Security sources, for which the Daily Telegraph is renowned, could have shed some light on authenticity.

Don't go beyond the information in the documents.

The right to know in this case was based on the defence that the public should be told of the claims about a British MP. These documents, whether genuine or forged, accurate or inaccurate, did not say Galloway was receiving money personally.

The courts may have been prepared to live with a little journalistic exaggeration but not reporting which creates new allegations. So where it might not have been fatal to the defence to exaggerate how much money was involved; it was fatal to suggest it had gone to Galloway himself rather than to the Mariam Campaign. The *Daily Telegraph* records and reports treated the Mariam Campaign and Galloway's personal gain as equivalents; a blurring of the situation which weakened its position. The court was not prepared to accept that the two were interchangeable.

Don't revel in the revelation.
The *Daily Telegraph* was criticised for treating the accusations with "relish". This is a particular difficulty for newspapers with a perceived political stance. The *Daily Telegraph*'s pro-establishment tendencies put it on the back foot when trying to claim neutrality in reporting a provocative left-wing figure such as Galloway.

All journalists cross swords with people, politically and/or personally, and the challenge of proving fairness is much greater if you can be accused of initiating and pursuing inquiries "against" someone from a pre-existing hostile position. This leads to another key piece of advice, not just for legal protection. Journalists love to expose wrongdoing but such enthusiasm can cloud one's judgment. The more useful information is to your story; the more it is what you want to hear; the more sceptical you must be of it. Battle-hardened investigative reporters sum up the risk as: "If it sounds too good to be true, it probably is." Beware.

Claiming qualified privilege requires a demonstrable fairness and neutrality. A reporter is not assembling and presenting the case for the prosecution. Balance extends to tone as well as content. Don't present a potential claimant's responses as excuses, or worse, lies.

Keep an open mind and look back over the facts from all sides.
What other explanations could there be? Journalists can right wrongs but need to take tremendous care ethically and legally. It is easy to get caught up in a crusade where you decide who the good and bad guys are in advance and then seek the evidence to prove it. Legally that can lead into high-risk territory. Like a "bent" copper, you decide someone is guilty and warp the evidence to fit. That is not good journalism and, significantly, it will lay you wide open to successful defamation actions. Only journalism of impeccable procedure and approach will be able to claim the protection of the law. Let the facts speak for themselves.

If journalists want to claim protection under a broader responsible publication defence they must employ procedures which demonstrate proficiency as journalists. Whether we like it or not, journalists are now reliant on judges for a broad brush definition of what is expected from us to sustain a *Reynolds* public interest defence and for their individual decisions in any case that goes the distance.

Case Study Two: Henry v BBC (No.2) [2005] EWHC 2787 (QB) & Henry v BBC (No.3) [2006] EWHC 386 (QB)

The claim arose from a report on BBC Points West responding to an inquiry vindicating a whistleblower who had quit her job at a hospital in the region after claiming she was instructed to manipulate waiting lists to meet Government targets. Two earlier inquiries had dismissed her allegations; the third upheld them.

The broadcast named three of the senior managers in the relevant hierarchy including Marion Henry who sued.

The BBC rejected a request to air a retraction which might have served as an offer of amends because it objected to the wording which it said was more emphatic than the findings of the inquiry.

The BBC claimed privilege; both statutory and *Reynolds*. It kept a defence of justification in reserve. Typically, a defence of justification is seen as extremely difficult to sustain. Also, where justification is one of multiple defences, if it is lost, the case as a whole has been considered to be lost. Only if it lost on *Reynolds* privilege, did the BBC wish to countenance the justification defence.

In the privilege hearing, *Henry (No.2)*, the judge accepted that reporting on the executive summary of the inquiry issued by the hospital was covered by statutory privilege as outlined in s.15 of the Defamation Act 1996 but that the item as a whole forfeited that privilege by moving beyond the facts of the report into "editorialising" and into naming Mrs Henry. He ruled that neither statutory privilege nor *Reynolds* common law privilege extended to identifying Mrs Henry. She was not named in the privileged executive summary of the inquiry report nor was it in the public interest to identify her.

He did, however, accept that a press conference called in a car park by the whistleblower constituted a public meeting for the purposes of s.15 of the 1996 Act which could help future reports of relatively informal gatherings.

And he accepted that although the source could be considered to have an axe to grind—she had mixed motives for being a whistleblower—the journalist was entitled to treat her as a credible source. As was the norm in libel cases at the time, the judge dealt with each of the ten points of the *Reynolds* defence, although he did express caution saying they were not definitive criteria and that focusing on them too closely created a danger "of missing the wood for the trees." This further emphasises that mounting a successful *Reynolds* defence required far more than a tick-box exercise.

A further element was considered in this case, namely the claim for greater freedom of expression for the whistleblower because she was replying to attack, having been criticised in press releases relating to earlier inquiries into her claims. However the judge was adamant that any attack on the whistleblower came from the

hospital, not from Mrs Henry, so again it was not reasonable to identify her.

The BBC went on to mount a justification defence in *Henry (No.3)*
which it won. The judge ruled that on the evidence of the whistleblower, reports of conversations and partial email records, the damaging comments of which Mrs Henry complained were substantially true.
A lot hinged on his assessment of the credibility of various witnesses.
Remember in a libel case the standard of proof is that it is more probable than not that the words are true; not that they are proved beyond
reasonable doubt. Also, although he ruled the BBC had not justified
one of the accusations against Mrs Henry, because the criticisms it
had proved were more serious, overall the defence of justification was
sound. The case ended in victory for the story and the BBC certainly felt
vindicated overall. However, few organisations have its persistence and
resources. Many would have settled after the first defeat or even earlier.
There are pointers, particularly from the defeat on privilege, which can
help a journalist make a similar action less likely to be mounted and
certainly easier to defend on either front.

The two judgments contrast sharply, not only because the BBC lost
one and won the other. The journalist and the coverage are central
to the judgment on the privilege defence; whereas the justification
defence focuses on the hospital, the evidence of waiting list manipulation and who was complicit in it. It certainly bears out the earlier
observation that in a *Reynolds* defence the person on trial was the
journalist.

The result in *Henry (No.3)* may cause libel lawyers to re-evaluate
the chances of success as between justification and *Reynolds* privilege.
Justification puts the focus on substance. If a journalist basically gets
the facts right and can prove they are substantially true, the defence
succeeds. In privilege, the journalist can be right but if the judge takes
some exception to the methods or language used, the defence may
fail.

The judgment also included some very interesting commentary on
the nature of the hospital's waiting list manipulation. The judge said it
seemed plain to him that incriminating documents had been deliberately removed, although it was not suggested that Mrs Henry removed
them. He also commented on the behaviour of managers senior to Mrs
Henry by name, including those who had ordered manipulation of the
lists. This was very helpful in establishing what had gone on at the hospital; a matter of considerable public interest.

How to sustain a privilege defence

Who is, or needs to be, identified?
The judge ruled that privilege did not extend beyond the publicly-
available executive summary of the inquiry report into identifying any
individual. It was not safe to be specific about individual responsibility
because the report essentially covered collective responsibility. On first

reading this seems to be at odds with the advice not to blur questions of identity in potential libel cases. Too general a description can lay the journalist open to claims from innocent members of the group and a specific description, which fights shy of naming someone but effectively identifies them, will be liable anyway. However in this case there was a collective rather than individual responsibility.

The Points West piece actually followed up an interview with the whistle-blower in the *Sun* which didn't name names. Technically various senior managers at the hospital could have tried to claim the article defamed them but the *Sun*, by being more in line with the executive summary, could have mounted a stronger privilege defence than the BBC.

Consider exactly what elements of the story can be deemed to be in the public interest.

While the substance of the story—exposure of wrongdoing at the hospital—passed the test as did the executive summary of the official investigation into it, additional elements, such as exactly who might be to blame, were not deemed to be covered particularly as there was the prospect of future and separate disciplinary action against individuals.

Be sure of what you are being told.

Being told that someone "must have known" isn't enough to prove that they did. Being aware of something is not the same as authorising it. Both may be reprehensible depending on circumstances, but indicate very different levels of responsibility for an event or practice. Although the reporter sensibly sought documentary evidence to back up the whistleblower's claims, the judge questioned the inferences drawn from the emails produced and also agreed with the defence that an email being sent is not evidence of an email being read.

Allow those whose reputation is at stake to respond.

The reporter had requested an interview with Mrs Henry through the press office and been refused. This is no substitute for putting allegations directly to the subject and is unlikely to be deemed adequate for a *Reynolds*/public interest defence. Making a general request for an interview via a press office and being fobbed off won't cover it. One option is to put in writing to the subject the exact nature of the allegations under investigation.

Let the facts speak for themselves.

Don't try to dramatise a report by peppering it with loaded adjectives. Don't over-egg it. Exaggeration is not always fatal to a defamation defence, but it will weaken it and is one of the most common reasons a lawyer will advise a publisher to settle. The language used in the waiting lists report led the judge to rule that the BBC had "adopted" the whistleblower's claims which puts it outside the protection of reportage. Statutory privilege attached only to the inquiry report and he said the

Points West broadcast was "far from a detached account" of its findings. He, for instance, objected to the report calling the whistleblower "brave" and the description of what took place as a "scandal". Most journalists wouldn't think twice about using such language but it can fatally undermine a privilege defence. The media's natural instinct to side explicitly with the underdog—in this case a vindicated whistleblower—must be suppressed if a *Reynolds*/public interest defence against any defamatory content involved is to succeed.

Be prepared to negotiate the wording of an offer of amends.

Don't reject a claimaint's suggested correction and apology out of hand. The judge in *Henry (No.2)* said it was incumbent on the BBC to raise objections and try to reach agreement on the wording proposed. A defendant will generally be credited for any attempt to resolve matters without resort to the court. If the case goes to court despite what the judge deems to have been a reasonable offer of amends, any damages can be discounted by around a half.

Cost is a powerful consideration. The process of resolving a defamation complaint can be expensive in itself without going anywhere near court. Offers of amends will also be recommended where defences are weak but also where a publisher isn't prepared to risk the cost of wrangling let alone losing in court.

Case Study Three: Jameel v Wall Street Journal Europe Sprl [2006] UKHL 44

Jameel was about getting the balance right in being able to mount a defence of responsible journalism on matters of public concern in a *Wall Street Journal* article described in Part One of this Chapter.

Lord Hoffmann makes explicit at [38] the new balance sought by the courts.

> "Until very recently, the law of defamation was weighted in favour of claimants and the law of privacy weighted against them. True but trivial intrusions into private life were safe. Reports of investigations by the newspaper into matters of public concern which could be construed as reflecting badly on public figures, domestic or foreign, were risky. "

Campbell v MGN Ltd [2004] redressed the balance in favour of privacy and *Reynolds v Times Newspapers Ltd* [2001] in favour of greater freedom for the press to publish stories of genuine public interest. The value of the *Jameel* judgment was to strengthen and evolve the *Reynolds* defence, which was considered by the media, and possibly by the senior judiciary, not to have made enough difference to this balance. Judges were still clinging to older interpretations of privilege and interpreting *Reynolds* too narrowly, thereby placing an unreasonable restriction on freedom of expression and of public debate. A House of Lords judgment was required to achieve the necessary rebalancing.

A major legal element was whether a company's reputation should be treated differently from an individual's by requiring evidence of actual financial damage to distinguish it from a more personal approach where evidence is not required. Upholding the level of protection for a corporation is annoying for journalists but the reservations expressed within the overall judgment on this issue give some room for optimism that the position, still relying in part on a judgment from 1894, could ultimately be challenged successfully in the light of the ECHR.

The encouragement came from Baroness Hale who favours requiring corporations to produce at least some evidence that financial loss was likely. She said at [157]:

"In my view such a requirement would achieve a proper balance between the right of a company to protect its reputation and the right of the press and public to be critical of it. These days, the dividing line between governmental and non-governmental organisations is increasingly difficult to draw. The power wielded by the major -multinational corporations is enormous and growing. The freedom to criticise them may be at least as important in a democratic society as the freedom to criticise the government."

However we will concentrate here on the implications for a responsible publication defence.

Jameel may not rely on a point-by-point application of the *Reynolds* defence but it very much reinforces the spirit of it: that there is a defamation defence for responsible journalism on a matter of public interest. It also emphasises the divide over the types of story that could claim to be in the public interest, particularly with regard to remarks by Baroness Hale quoted earlier.

The Journal had lost in the Court of Appeal over *Reynolds* considerations of right to reply. The Court of Appeal ruled that the claimant should have been given longer to respond. This was overruled by the House of Lords partly because of the move away from the *Reynolds* "ten-hurdle" approach, but also because of the particular nature of the alleged libel and what might have been achieved by waiting. Let's compare the two.

Under iii) The source of the information.
The Journal claimed five sources for its story from within the American and Saudi establishments but the jury was not convinced, perhaps because the judge directed that in the absence of a plea of justification the jury should assume the fact of the surveillance to be untrue.

Under iv) The steps taken to verify the allegation.
Reporter, James Dorsey, was able to provide very detailed evidence of the processes he and colleagues followed to verify his story. These

included the time of his calls, the questions asked and answers given. There is also a lovely line in his own account of the case which would put many journalists to shame in that he apparently withheld one name because it had been authenticated by only four of his five sources. Not all of the Journal evidence of the process of verification was accepted by the original jury but the thoroughness shown and the meticulous records kept did put Dorsey in a strong position to claim the title of responsible journalist whose work was professional and appropriate under the circumstances.

He had a more sympathetic hearing in the final judgment. Lord Hoffmann was even prepared to accept the kind of horse-trading that goes on between journalists and official sources of the "you might say that, I couldn't possibly comment" variety. The reality of day-to-day dealings is that a code can develop with regular contacts and that, in some cases, the absence of a denial is effectively a confirmation. It also establishes that an off-the-record response can be an official response rather than an unofficial leak. It is perhaps an extreme variant on the principle in libel actions that the meaning of any word is significantly dependent on the context in which it is used.

Under vii) whether comment was sought from the claimant.

He may have information others do not possess or have not disclosed. An approach to the claimant will not always be necessary but failure to make it makes the defence vulnerable. The claimant objected to being included in a list of companies believed to be under surveillance by the Saudi government at the behest of the Americans post 9/11 seeking to track terrorist funds. The company was not in a position to confirm or deny that the surveillance was taking place. Whether it was or was not, the company would not know of the surveillance. All the company could have said would have been to claim that any such surveillance would uncover nothing untoward but the story did not say it would. So the key assertion, unlike the accusation against Galloway, was not something the claimant was in a position to verify or deny. This is particularly helpful in hopefully deterring respondents from thinking that failure to reply can put an effective block on a story.

Lord Hoffmann also challenged the naïvety of the assumption that a denial from the Saudi agency, SAMA, would have killed the story. As he put it in typically succinct manner:

> "There was no way in which SAMA would admit to monitoring the accounts of well-known Saudi businesses at the request of the US Treasury."

Where a delay would not have made any difference, the decision to publish before responses were obtained was not enough to lose the Journal its *Reynolds* privilege, he ruled. This is hinted at in the original point.

The newspaper had also been admonished for publishing information that the US government had agreed not to publish. Thank goodness Lord Hoffmann challenged and rejected this. Any undertaking the US government gave was not binding on a newspaper and was not enough to deprive the matter of designation in the public interest. The US Treasury had not tried to claim that national security or interest was at risk, so it was for the newspaper to decide whether it was right to run or not.

Under ix) the tone can raise queries or call for an investigation but it should not adopt allegations as statement of fact.

The Journal played it straight. It never suggested that wrongdoing by the companies had been found, or indeed that it would be. The whole point of the story was the action of the Saudis; not of the companies mentioned. What was in the public interest was the behaviour of the Saudi government; not the behaviour of the companies about which nothing was claimed. The names of the companies were used to give the story credibility not to lay accusations at their door.

As Lord Bingham of Cornhill said at [35]:

"The subject matter was of great public interest, in the strictest sense. The article was written by an experienced, specialist reporter and approved by senior staff on the newspaper and the Wall Street Journal who themselves sought to verify its contents. The article was unsensational in tone and (apparently) factual in content. The respondents' response was sought, although at a late stage, and the newspaper's inability to obtain a comment recorded. It is very unlikely that a comment, if obtained, would have been revealing, since even if the respondent's accounts were being monitored it was unlikely that they would know.

It might have been thought that this was the sort of neutral, investigative journalism which the Reynolds privilege exists to protect."

Elsewhere in the appeal judgment are various useful pointers of a more general nature.

Lord Hoffmann exhibited some "real world" appreciation of how sources are to be assessed and also understood why a plea of justification could not have been mounted. As he said at [42]:

"In the nature of things, the existence of covert surveillance by the highly secretive Saudi authorities would be impossible to prove by evidence in open court. That does not necessarily mean that it did not happen. Nor, on the other hand, does it follow that even if it did happen, the Jameel group had any connection with terrorism. The US intelligence agencies sometimes get things badly wrong."

Indeed they do. The Journal article was written on that basis and asserted no more, no less than its evidence that the monitoring was taking place.

Lord Hoffmann went on to describe the article as "a serious contribution in a measured tone to a subject of very considerable importance". He also provided support for journalists when it comes to deciding how much detail is reasonable to include to justify the thrust of the story. An argument is often advanced that detail is not necessary, yet Lord Hoffmann here recognises the contribution it makes to lending the story credibility with its audience. He said at [52]:

> "The inclusion of the names of large and respectable Saudi businesses was an important part of the story. It showed that co-operation with the US Treasury's requests was not confined to a few companies on the fringe of Saudi society but extended to companies which were by any test within the heartland of the Saudi business world. To convey this message, inclusion of the names was necessary. Generalisation such as "prominent Saudi companies", which can mean anything or nothing, would not have served the same purpose."

And Baroness Hale said at [148]:

> "This was in effect a pro-Saudi story, but one which, for internal reasons, the Saudi authorities were bound to deny. Without names, its impact would be much reduced."

And she went on at [150]:

> "We need more such serious journalism in this country and our defamation law should encourage rather than discourage it."

Precisely. Providing specific detail is part of what it takes to stand up a story and it needs to be included. And, of the *Reynolds* ten matters, Lord Hoffmann says at [56]:

> "They are not tests which the publication has to pass. In the hands of a judge hostile to the spirit of Reynolds, they can become ten hurdles at any of which the defence may fail. That is how Eady J treated them."

Lord Scott of Foscote pointed out that the only response Jameel could have given was to deny any involvement in terrorist funding and that there was no reason for its accounts to be monitored. The company could have requested, or demanded, publication of such as response in the next edition of the *Wall Street Journal Europe* but never did so. This was raised as part of the opinion that the delay was not enough to demolish the *Reynolds* defence.

So, a judgment designed to draw something of a line in the sand regarding the definition of what constitutes responsible journalism on a matter of public interest, certainly set down a range of markers for the future. The scrutiny of journalists' methods is key but perhaps is assessed more generously than in the early stages of *Jameel*.

What is also clear is that there will be greater focus on editorial decision-making. Evidence of supervision of the reporting process, of extra checks being made further up the hierarchy and of an explicit consideration of what it is reasonable to run in the public interest were all influential in the media's ultimate victory in *Jameel*.

The current concern is that the principles of *Jameel* are challenged by the opposing judgments in the *Flood* case which is set to reach the Supreme Court later this year. The fear is that the weight being given to responsible journalism when freedom of expression impinges on the right to reputation may be diminished. Freedom of expression has lost out to privacy rights because of the narrow interpretation of the public interest in exposure in most cases. It is vital that the Supreme Court attaches due value to the public interest in responsible journalism defences.

But there is nothing in the Defamation Bill to challenge *Jameel*.

Case Study Four: Roberts & Another v Gable & Others [2007] EWCA Civ 721

This case is significant for its development of the concept of "reportage" within the context of the responsible journalism qualified privilege defence. The magazine Searchlight, which reports on the activities of the far right, covered a "feud" within the British National Party in London involving allegations of theft and threats of physical violence. Both claimants stood as candidates in the 2005 general election.

When running a responsible journalism defence, the publisher will normally have to show that reasonable steps were taken to verify the truth and accuracy of what has been published. There is no public interest in receiving misinformation. However, if reportage is relied upon, then there is no need to ensure the accuracy of what has been published.

Ward L.J. even acknowledges the pressures placed on editors when deciding, at short notice, whether to run a story. Reportage equally applies whether there are time constraints or no time pressures.

The full nine considerations for establishing a reportage defence were given at [61]:

"(1) The information must be in the **public interest** (our emphasis).

(2) Since the public cannot have an interest in receiving misinformation which is destructive of the democratic society (see Lord Hobhouse in *Reynolds* at p. 238), the publisher will not normally be protected unless he has taken reasonable steps to verify the truth and accuracy of what is published (see, also in *Reynolds*, Lord Nicholls' factor four at page 205 B, and Lord Cooke at p. 225, and in *Jameel*, Lord Bingham at paragraph 12 and Baroness Hale at paragraph 149). This is where *reportage* parts company with *Reynolds*. **In a true case of**

reportage there is no need to take steps to ensure the accuracy of the published information.

(3) The question which perplexed me is why that important factor can be disregarded. The answer lies in what I see as the defining characteristic of *reportage*. I draw it from the highlighted passages in the judgment of Latham L.J. and the speech of Lord Hoffmann cited in paragraphs 39 and 43 above. **To qualify as** *reportage* **the report, judging the thrust of it as a whole, must have the effect of reporting, not the truth of the statements, but the fact that they were made. . . .** If upon a proper construction of the thrust of the article the defamatory material is attributed to another and is not being put forward as true, then a responsible journalist would not need to take steps to verify its accuracy. He is absolved from that responsibility because he is simply reporting in a neutral fashion the fact that it has been said without adopting the truth.

(4) Since the test is to establish the effect of the article as a whole, it is for the judge to rule upon it in a way analogous to a ruling on meaning. It is not enough for the journalist to assert what his intention was though his evidence may well be material to the decision. The test is objective, not subjective. All the circumstances surrounding the gathering in of the information, the manner of its reporting and the purpose to be served will be material.

(5) **This protection will be lost if the journalist adopts the report and makes it his own or if he fails to report the story in a fair, disinterested and neutral way.** Once that protection is lost, he must then show, if he can, that it was a piece of responsible journalism even though he did not check accuracy of his report.

(6) To justify the attack on the claimant's reputation the publication must always meet the standards of responsible journalism as that concept has developed from *Reynolds*, the burden being on the defendants. In this way the balance between Art. 10 and Art. 8 can be maintained. All the circumstances of the case and the 10 factors listed by Lord Nicholls adjusted as may be necessary for the special nature of *reportage* must be considered in order to reach the necessary conclusion that this was the product of responsible journalism.

(7) The seriousness of the allegation (Lord Nicholls' factor 1) is obviously relevant for the harm it does to reputation if the charges are untrue. Ordinarily it makes verification all the more important. I am not sure Latham L.J. meant to convey any more than that in paragraph 68 of his judgment in *Al Fagih* cited in paragraph 39 above. There is, however, no reason in principle why *reportage* must be confined to scandal-mongering as Mr Tomlinson submits. Here equally serious allegations were being levelled at both sides of this dispute. In line with factor 2, **the criminality of the actions bears upon the public interest which is the critical question: does the public have the right to know the fact that these allegations were being made one against the other?** As Lord Hoffmann said at paragraph 51 in *Jameel*:

"The fact that the material was of public interest does not allow the newspaper to drag in damaging allegations which serve no public purpose. They must be part of the story. And the more serious the allegation, the more important it is that it should make a real contribution to the public interest element in the article."

All the circumstances of the case are brought into play to find the answer but if it is affirmative, then *reportage* must be allowed to protect the journalist who, not having adopted the allegation, takes no steps to verify his story.

(8) **The relevant factors properly applied will embrace the significance of the protagonists in public life and there is no need for insistence as pre-conditions for** *reportage* **on the defendant being a responsible prominent person or the claimant being a public figure as may be required in the USA.**

(9) The urgency is relevant, see factor 5, in the sense that fine editorial judgments taken as the presses are about to roll may command a more sympathetic review than decisions to publish with the luxury of time to reflect and public interest can wane with the passage of time. That is not to say . . . the *reportage* can only flourish where the story unfolds day by day as in *Al Fagih.* Public interest is circumscribed as much by events as by time and every story must be judged on its merits at the moment of publication."

Do note that reportage can easily appear to be at odds with the *repetition* rule which makes the repetition of defamatory remarks made by others still defamatory. As a result, there may be a tendency for judges to seek to interpret reportage in a restrictive way. The public interest in the fact of the dispute has to distinguish reportage from simple repetition of attacks on reputation which would not be covered by such privilege.

Journalists may often be embroiled in such a "spat" and the concept has potential to support genuine reporting in the public interest. Like other elements of the responsible reporting defence, the level of unpredictability means no journalist would seek to have to rely on it but its development can be of assistance.

Although we examine many cases where the responsible journalism defence has not won the day for the reporter, its development and various applications can be used to nip threatened actions in the bud. The *Gable* ruling gives further ammunition for media lawyers to deter potential writs and there is some evidence that the defence overall has been successful in warding off what would otherwise have been costly actions. Clause 2(3) of the Defamation Bill would put reportage into a statutory basis.

How to rely on "reportage"
Be very clear of the public interest element
Be very clear about why the story is in the public interest. Does the public have a right to know? The fact of the dispute must be in the

public interest and the inclusion of defamatory allegations and counter allegations must be necessary to make sense of the story. Keep the focus on the "fact" of the dispute or inquiry rather than the truth/falsity of the allegations.

Do not adopt the allegations of either party

This can be difficult to achieve. Stories can very easily cast one side as the aggressor and the other as a victim. The defence will only succeed if the article is genuinely neutral. The reporting should relate not to "the truth of the statements, but the fact that they were made". There could be a public interest in the fact of a split—the clichéd "war of words"— say in a political party, as here, or within public companies, local councils or other publically-accountable bodies.

Give a balanced version of the story

A defence of reportage within the responsible journalism defence will only be available for certain stories likely to involve a "he said, she said" format. This certainly does not give carte blanche to repeat defamatory statements by others. This defence is not so helpful when the allegations are essentially against one person and the other "side" is essentially a rebuttal. Reportage was ruled out as an element in the responsible journalism defence mounted in the *Flood* case.

Case Study Five: Lowe v Associated Newspapers Ltd [2006] EWHC 320 (QB)

This case centred on an article by celebrity columnist David Mellor. Lowe, then chairman of Southampton FC, sued Associated Newspapers Ltd over the article which contained two accusations: alleging that his company's take-over of the football club in 1997 had been a "repellent piece of financial chicanery". To sustain a fair comment (now honest opinion) defence, journalists could do well to take into account various of the principles outlined here.

Case Study Six: *Spiller* shows how the defence has evolved and, in some respects, become less onerous since this 2006 judgment, but *Lowe* remains the source of much valuable advice, particularly for journalists needing a strong defence for opinionated articles. Meeting the higher standards outlined here would make the defence robust.

Eady J. returned to the five points provided by Lord Nicholls in the Cheng case.

1. The comment must be on a matter of public interest. Public interest is not to be confined within "narrow" limits.

To date, this suggests judges are prepared to accept a public realm wider than formal politics. Commerce, certainly so far as it involves public companies, is also likely to be covered. The running of football clubs appears to be included but fame itself is not enough.

2. The comment must be recognisable as comment as distinct from imputations of fact.

This is a challenging one. The focus is clearly on whether the audience, not the journalist, can differentiate between the two. It will certainly help if a journalist aids that distinction, by clear labelling and separation of news and comment within the publication or programme. However that is not necessarily enough as emerged in *Galloway*, *Singh* and *Flood*. Even where material appears clearly under the banner of opinion, it may not be accepted as such by the court.

Sport coverage relies heavily on comment, often vehemently expressed and that has often been shrugged off as being in the nature of the beast. Eady J. draws no such distinction in his expectation of the calibre of debate required to satisfy a fair comment defence. The widespread use of "celebrity" columnists, again prevalent in sport, may come into play given that the disputed piece was written by former MP-turned-commentator, David Mellor. He may not be such an obvious case, as he has acquired credentials as a pundit that have arguably eclipsed his political career, but this could be another warning shot across sports commentators' bows. The legal expectations of a celebrity columnist are just as high as of any other commentator. The concept of "responsible journalist" may raise interesting questions about such contributors. They may need to argue that their sporting experience makes them better informed and provides a wealth of "facts" to draw upon to justify their opinions.

3. Any comment must be based upon facts which are either true or have the protection of privilege.

No change there. Not all the facts supporting the opinion need to be included in the piece. The defendant does not have to prove every fact mentioned, just sufficient to support the comment to the satisfaction of the jury (para.38). But that does still mean the comment cannot rely on facts that are wrong.

4. The reader or viewer should be able to glean the facts from what has been published.

Defamatory opinion, to be defensible, must not just rely on fact, but those facts must be transparent. There is debate in *Lowe* over the degree to which those facts have to be included in the article defended under fair comment. Eady J. allows that facts on which the opinion is based may range from being used in great detail in the piece to being already of common knowledge, of which more later.

However, a telling point to emerge in these considerations relates to the rigour of argument advanced and that the audience should be able to follow that argument, as well as being presented with the opinion. The significant requirement seems to be that an argument must be advanced. Whether the facts are stated or not, the reason why the facts lead to a particular opinion must be explained. Readers must be able to assess the situation for themselves.

In a successful fair comment defence, the rights of the defamed claimant are sacrificed, not so much to the commentator's freedom of expression but to the reasonable requirement for public debate on matters of public interest. The judgment is spelling out that the pursuit of enlightened public opinion can only be served by the audience being brought into the debate so as to be able to draw conclusions for themselves. There is no right to bombard the audience with opinion in isolation; "bald" opinion may find itself being treated as a statement of fact.

The interpretation of fair comment here clearly put a greater onus on the journalist. Fair comment has always had to be based on fact or privileged information. The facts have always been at issue but here the focus is the "based on" element. The route from the facts to the opinion must be clear, and to the audience not just to the journalist. This again places demands on the journalist and puts their abilities under scrutiny.

5. The comment must be one which an "honest person" could hold, however prejudiced he might be and however exaggerated or obstinate his views.

This is of some assistance, in that the journalist isn't required to come up with the sort of mathematical proof that makes an opinion indisputable. The whole audience does not have to be won over to that view; it just has to be one of many possible opinions capable of being drawn from the facts. Again this supports the principles of healthy public debate in defending a plurality of opinion. However the scope to exaggerate or be obstinate would not remove the requirement to provide a rationale for the view being held, even where it is expressed flamboyantly. Indeed the more emphatic and damaging the opinion, the more important it will be to back it up with a strong, clear argument.

How to sustain an honest opinion defence

Focus on the audience.

Provide enough information and argument for them to make up their own minds on the issue. Provide them with an opinion piece that is coherent, evidence-based and well-argued. Do not fudge the facts or argument. Lack of clarity makes it worse. The article at issue in Lowe written by David Mellor comes in for criticism for its lack of clarity. As Eady J. states in para.3:

"One of the difficulties about the present case is that the article is written in such an obscure way that it is difficult to divine its message or messages."

He goes on to make it clear that such obscurity will not aid a defendant's position. He allows the claim to proceed on the basis of any imputation which the words complained of are capable of bearing.

Be sure of the facts upon which you are basing your opinion and make that obvious to the audience. Eady J.'s nine-point framework goes into considerable detail about the requirements on the commentator before the piece is written. Again, as in the *Reynolds* defence, the argument is not just over what was aired, it places demands on the processes which underpin the formulation that is put in the public domain. So for Mellor it is not just about what he wrote; it is about whether he was in a reasonable position to write what he wrote in terms of what he—and his audience—knew at the time.

There is some acceptance that not every fact relied upon needs to be included in the item, but this does not allow for the kind of cavalier reasoning so often heard in common conversation: "Everybody knew that . . .". Such reasoning will not suffice in a fair comment defence. There not only have to be facts; there have to be "specific" facts.

There is also allowance for fair comment defence to rely on a "general" fact known at the time which is fleshed out later, but the commentator cannot trawl around for supporting evidence after publication.

Eady J. also allows for a fact to be in the back of a commentator's mind rather than in the forefront but it needs have been there somewhere. This, to me, reflects rather well the ways in which a journalist's mind works. Many aspects of a situation are just sort of out there and accepted as "known". Recall may be hazy but some incident or story from long before will be lodged in the memory and feed in to subsequent coverage. (This was queried in *Spiller*.)

There are, however, two major stumbling blocks in attempting to argue such a defence. How is a commentator able to convince a judge as to the extent of any "hazy" background knowledge she did or did not possess to underpin her piece at the time of writing? It is quite a big ask given the onus is on the defendant to establish such matters. Where a defence is required, this allows some chance of justifying how a defamatory opinion was advanced but if we are looking at ways of avoiding claims, the advice would certainly be to avoid having to go down that road in court.

It also still leaves open the question, very likely to be asked by the courts these days, why weren't the facts checked? If expressing an opinion involves the inclusion of potentially defamatory material, it is worth the extra effort required to dredge up those hazy memories and pin them down. If writing a news story which needed to recap on background material, a journalist would not rely on memory. Checks would be made and information verified. That has to be the sensible course when putting together a comment piece too. For comment to be valuable to the audience, and to be sure of attracting the protection of the courts, it clearly needs to be well-informed.

Make a reasoned case for your opinion and make that reasoning clear.

How exactly do those facts justify your opinion? Spell it out and present an argument to establish how the opinion is based on the facts. Colourful language and harsh criticism can still be defended but reason and fairness have also to be in evidence to justify them. A defamatory comment cannot be made carelessly nor as part of an indulgent tirade. Avoid offhand, throwaway remarks or innuendo. Commentary becomes legally risky where a journalist is simply venting spleen.

Make it your opinion based on your facts

It is also crucial to learn the lesson of point 9:

> "It is not permitted to plead fair comment if the commentator was doing no more than regurgitating the opinions of others without any knowledge of the underlying facts—still less if he was simply echoing rumours."

A journalist seeking to rely on a fair comment defence has to build a case for the opinion. An opinion on its own without the supporting facts is likely to be treated as a statement of fact requiring a defence of justification. It is the linking of the opinion to the fact that makes it fair comment. Any journalist who doesn't provide the link may lose the defence.

Case Study Six: Spiller & Anor v Joseph & Ors [2010] UKSC 53

This Supreme Court ruling offers a new interpretation of the evolving defence it dubbed honest comment. It moves the defence on from the high-profile Court of Appeal judgment in *Singh* (which called it honest opinion) but both are potentially overtaken by the new defence of honest opinion envisaged by the Defamation Bill and discussed in Part One of the chapter. For now, it is particularly welcome as it makes the demands of the defence less onerous on the journalist or, in this case, web writer.

Not unusually an authority has been established in a case described as "a storm in a teacup" in which a musical act sued over a posting on its agent's website that suggested the act would not abide by contracts. It is also revealing of current judicial attitudes to online publication.

Part of the posting, quoted at [14] read:

> "1311 Events is no longer able to accept bookings for this artist as the Gillettes c/o Craig Joseph are not professional enough to feature in our portfolio and have not been able to abide by the terms of their contract......"

There had been a difference of opinion on the very distinction between fact and comment as the case worked its way through the lower courts. Eady J., at first instance, said the words complained of were not comment and not in the public interest. The Court of Appeal disagreed, saying the words were comment and were in the public interest.

Eady J. said, quoted here at [26]:

"Also I cannot see that a (one-sided) summary of a private contractual dispute can be said to constitute a matter of public interest."

But in the Court of Appeal[109] Pill L.J. said, quoted here at [28]:

"Those in the business of entertaining the public, a business in which many people are engaged, will be concerned, when serving the public, to know which artists can be relied on to perform their contracts and which cannot. The comment is arguably in the public interest."

That wider definition of the public interest was accepted. Although the Court of Appeal categorised the words as comment, it still rejected the fair comment defence because the facts upon which the comment was said to be based were not sufficiently set out in the words complained of. The case became complex partly because the website content was rather sloppy. An email was misquoted and it wasn't clear which contract or contracts the posting referred to. The defendants relied on the comment being based on the gist of previous experience but their case was a long way from meeting the rigorous nine-point demands of *Lowe*,[110] and even the broader requirements of *Cheng*.[111]

The Supreme Court basically decided that previous hurdles for a fair comment defence had been set too high, particularly for the legions of bloggers whose output can be the source of defamation actions. It returned to the *Cheng* approach, with a softening of the fourth of Lord Nicholls' original five points, removing the sentence: "The reader or hearer should be in a position to judge for himself how far the comment was well-founded." They key point that remained, which was stressed by the Supreme Court, was that the facts on which the comment was based need only be indicated in "general terms". Compare this with the requirements in Case Study Five: *Lowe*.

So a fair comment defence was allowed despite the vagueness of the link between fact and comment. This is welcome for journalists but appears to have been driven mainly by the need of the law to cope with the deluge of potentially defamatory material online.

Lord Phillips at [99] says:

---

[109] [2009]EWCA Civ 1075; [2010] I.C.R. 642.
[110] *Lowe v Associated Newspapers Ltd* [2006] EWHC 320 (QB).
[111] *Tse Wai Chun Paul v Albert Chen 2* [2001] E.M.L.R. 777.

"Today the internet has made it possible for the man in the street to make public comment about others in a manner that did not exist when the principles of the law of fair comment were developed, and millions take advantage of that opportunity. Where the comments that they make are derogatory it will often be impossible for other readers to evaluate them without detailed information about the facts that have given rise to the comments. Frequently these will not be set out. If Lord Nicholls' fourth proposition is to apply the defences of fair comment will be robbed of much of its efficacy."

Lord Walker, in agreeing with the main judgment, stressed the point at [131]:

"The creation of a common base of information shared by those who watch television and use the internet has had an effect which can hardly be overstated. Millions now talk, and thousands comment in electronically transmitted words, about recent events of which they have learned from television of the internet. Many of the events and the comments on them are no doubt trivial and ephemeral, but from time to time (as the present appeal shows) libel law has to engage with them. The test for identifying the factual basis of honest comment must be flexible enough to allow for this type of case in which a passing reference to the previous night's celebrity show would be regarded by most of the public, and may sometimes have to be regarded by the law, as a sufficient factual basis."

The ruling can be seen as a mix of legal principle and pragmatism; a squaring of the circle to help adjust to the realities of the digital age.

As ever the law seems to give with one hand as it takes with another. Fair comment may morph into honest opinion to protect bloggers who undermine reputations. Effectively here freedom of expression is gaining at reputation's expense. Yet the mainstream media is having to fight tooth and nail to protect its freedom of expression while facing much stiffer tests of what is deemed to be in the public interest and higher hurdles to clear to mount a successful responsible journalism defence.

Associated Newspapers, Guardian News and Media and Times Newspapers had been allowed to intervene because a Supreme Court definition was wanted to help clarify the defence. So where does that leave the journalist? Perhaps the media should be grateful for small mercies on honest opinion.

Mounting an honest opinion defence

Honest comment/opinion remains a tricky defence to define. Of the various challenges, one central to many cases is the difficulty of distinguishing between fact and comment/opinion. Whereas most people would think it easy to determine a matter of fact, it is a great deal harder in practice.

Make the comment recognisable as opinion

Bald comment is best avoided legally and journalistically. To say someone is a "hopeless MP" can be taken as a statement of fact unless some evidence is provided to back it up. That will then risk losing the opportunity to mount an honest comment defence. It is also of little value to a reader.

Be sure the comment is on a matter of public interest

The Supreme Court adopted the broader definition, certainly to embrace artistic and commercial considerations

Be sure of the facts/privileged information on which the comment is based

Check out your facts before holding forth on your opinion.

Link the comment to the facts

A commentator is expected to give some grounds for maligning someone. An explicit rather than implicit reference to facts/privileged information on which the comment is based is likely to be easier to defend. "He is a hopeless MP because he has only held four constituency surgeries this year" becomes defensible as comment as long as your facts are right.

The *Spiller* ruling allows for this link to be in "general terms" and journalists may on occasion have to rely on the new less onerous definition. But the original Eady nine points are worth re-reading in *Lowe*. Good analytical journalism will share the "working out" with readers. An article is far more convincing if readers can follow the train of thought—a clear argument in which facts or privileged information are marshalled to arrive at a clear conclusion of opinion. That will make the material not only safer legally but a more valuable contribution to your audience.

CHAPTER SUMMARY: DEFAMATION

Defamation is a massive topic for journalists. Significant changes are in the pipeline in the form of the Defamation Bill, changes to conditional fee arrangements and the Supreme Court ruling on *Flood*. All could take effect by the end of 2011. This underlines the need for every journalist not just to know the law as it stands but to keep up-to-date as it changes.

For now we would suggest you note the following:

- Under the current Defamation Act, a successful action can be brought over material that damages reputation by having a defamatory meaning, identifying the claimant and being published to a third party.

- Reputation: Defamation actions allow claimants, whether individuals or companies, to protect their reputation and seek damages.
- Defamation actions, when viewed within the ambit of the Human Rights Act, balance art.8 rights of the complainant against the art.10 rights of the journalist
- Online: In the digital age, millions of bloggers and social network members now run a risk of being sued for publishing defamatory material. Case law is beginning to reflect the challenges of this deluge of potential actions but the full impact of online publication on media law has yet to be felt.
- **Defences** can be used by those publishing the material to defeat a claim by justifying use of the material and avoid paying damages
  - **Absolute privilege**—a reliable defence for fair, accurate and contemporaneous reports of court proceedings an see s.14 of the Defamation Act 1996 and suggested extensions in the Defamation Bill.
  - **Statutory qualified privilege**—a reliable defence for fair and accurate reports on matters of public interest, published in good faith often subject to rebuttal—see s.15 of the Defamation Act 1996 and suggested extensions in the Defamation Bill.
  - **Responsible publication including reportage**—key cases such as *Reynolds* and *Jameel* have developed a qualified privilege defence of responsible journalism, which also embraces neutral reporting of derogatory allegations. The stress is on the pursuance, and thus the definition, of **public interest**, but also on the degree of rigour and probity required of the journalistic inquiry. The courts decide the investigations and coverage deemed "worthy" of the defence. A risky defence to run.
  - **Truth**—the defence previously known as justification appears in the Defamation Bill much as before. A defendant must prove that the "sting" of a defamatory article is substantially true. The defence is based on a simple concept but in practice is difficult to run. Defences rely on how judges interpret the meaning of the "sting" and on the availability and credibility of witnesses.
  - **Honest opinion**—this defence formerly known as fair comment protects the expression of honest opinion based on fact. The Defamation Bill redefines it as honest opinion; the Supreme Court in *Spiller* made it less onerous under the banner of honest comment partly given the need to protect bloggers.
  - **Offer of amends**—this is a formal process for correcting defamatory mistakes.

CHAPTER 4: CONTEMPT OF COURT

PART ONE: CONTEMPT OF COURT

Article 6 of the European Convention on Human Rights establishes that everyone is entitled to a fair and public hearing within a reasonable time by an independent and impartial tribunal established by law if deemed to have contravened the criminal law. It goes on to state that:

> "Judgment shall be pronounced publicly but the press and public may be excluded from all or part of the trial . . . or to the extent strictly necessary in the opinion of the court in special circumstances where publicity would prejudice the interests of justice."

Open access to our courts has been a long-standing principle. Lord Chief Justice Hewart said in the *R v Sussex Justices* that "justice should not only be done, but should manifestly and undoubtedly be seen to be done."[1]

The Contempt of Court Act 1981, therefore, has a strong legal and principled underpinning. In truth, the Act is something of a ragbag of provisions each well intentioned but by now the Act is beginning to show its age. This is especially true of the provisions designed to deter the media from publishing anything that *"creates a substantial risk that the course of justice in the proceedings in question will be seriously impeded or prejudiced."*[2]

The Act was passed in an era that did not possess the rolling news environment that we have today. Nor did we have the internet. Judges may advise jurors that during the course of a trial they must not access the internet in order to discover information about the defendant such as previous convictions. Yet how is this to be policed? It is somewhat disingenuous to assume that jurors, who are often regarded as the weak link in the criminal justice system, will not succumb to the temptation to trawl the internet in search of information that they would not normally be made aware of during the trial. This was a theme addressed by the Lord Chief justice in November 2010.[3]

---

[1] [1923] All E.R 233, [1924] 1 K.B. 256.
[2] Contempt of Court Act 1981, s.2(2).
[3] Lord Judge: Judicial Studies Board Lecture, Belfast, November 2010.

"There is the problem of the jury consulting the internet . . . so we give clear directions to the jury that they should not consult the internet. Sometimes, I am told they find this difficult to believe. Not least because they are so accustomed to looking at the internet."

The Lord Chief Justice then referred to research undertaken by Professor Cheryl Thomas[4] that suggested that jurors were developing the habit of seeking information about the case they are trying from the internet. Some of course would regard this as normal human behaviour. There is likely to be a correlation between high profile cases and jurors searching for information particularly about the defendant. In the study 12 per cent of those questioned said they actually looked for information rather than simply stumbled across it while, for example, seeking the latest national or regional news.

The consequences of jurors gaining access to information that would otherwise be denied to them can have serious consequences. The most obvious is that a case will collapse and a re-trial ordered at great expense in both time and cost. The Lord Chief Justice did not mince his words:

". . . if the jury system is to survive as a system for a fair trial in which we all believe and support, the misuse of the internet by jurors must stop. And I think we must spell it out to them in yet more clarity. It must be provided in the information received by every potential juror. It must be reflected in the video which jurors see before they start a trial. Judges must continue to direct juries in unequivocal terms from the very outset of the trial . . . the notice in jury rooms which identifies potential contempt of court arising from discussions outside the jury room of their debates (should) be extended to any form of reference to the internet."

The main provisions of the 1981 Act are undoubtedly a restriction on freedom of expression and work against the principle of open justice. Parliament determined that any breach of s.2 (2) is to be regarded as a *strict liability* offence. In practice that means that a publication or series of publications that creates a substantial risk of prejudice to the criminal justice process will breach the section without proof of any intent on the part of the publisher. It is the same approach that results in the speeding motorist being convicted without the need to prove that he intended to break the law or was reckless as to whether the speed limit was breached. The objective of strict liability is to raise standards by conveying the message that dropping below the legal expectations in respect of a particular activity will be certain to result in conviction. In light of the reporting of the Joanna Yeates murder investigation after the arrest of Chris Jefferies, her landlord in Bristol at the end of 2010, the conclusion

---

[4] Are Juries Fair? Ministry of Justice, February 2010.

must be that the principle of strict liability has failed to achieve its objective in leading to responsible reporting.[5]

Therefore, the expectation running through the Act is that the media will be restrained in its pre-trial and in-trial reporting. This will not be a consideration in the overwhelming majority of cases because the media will show little or no interest in an upcoming trial. It does though become important if the trial is deemed to be high profile or notorious because of the identity of the defendant(s) or because of the nature of the offence with which he is charged or both. Two of the "second wave" of London bombers were arrested in late July 2005. The final moments prior to their arrest were captured on videotape by a member of the public who lived in the block of flats where the arrests took place. Within minutes the media had secured the rights to the tape and broadcast the images around the world. The following day the headline in the *Sun* newspaper screamed "Got The Bastards". This type of publicity led to calls for the media to show more restraint and much debate as to whether the actions had indeed contravened the 1981 Act.

The trial commenced at Woolwich Crown Court some 18 months after their arrest. Nevertheless, it would be naïve to assume that at least some members of the jury would not still remember the television footage or the *Sun*'s headline. But the key question is whether or not those memories will influence a jury in its decision-making. Will they be able to decide the case purely by reference to all the evidence they have seen and heard throughout the duration of the trial?

Prior to the commencement of the trials of Ian Huntley and Maxine Carr at the Old Bailey in November 2003, the press were issued with a stark warning by the trial judge, Mr Justice Moses. He told the press:

> "The detection and suppression of crime depends to an important degree on a fair trial with safe verdicts. The press plays its part in that fairness by ensuring balanced and fair reporting. I cannot imagine that any journalist wants to face the families and friends of the victims, whose interests they so loudly seek to defend, and confess that their work, their articles, their stories, their photographs have prevented a trial taking place at all or continuing. In short the important right of the press to report on public trials carries with it a responsibility to protect the fairness of a trial not just for the defendants but for the victims, their families and the community."

It appeared the press were not listening because some six weeks later the judge had to make a postponement order under s.4(2) of the 1981 Act "prohibiting publication of any report revealing or tending to reveal the detail of the evidence against [Huntley and Carr] until such time

---

[5] See Ch.2 for more details.

as proceedings against [them] are concluded." The judge later issued a clarification because the order as written would have prevented the press from reporting the trial.

So the question is: how real is the threat to the criminal justice process from pre-trial and in-trial reporting? Parliament believed in 1981 that certain types of background reporting could produce a substantial risk that a defendant may not receive a fair trial. What is the current view?

The Act has not been amended but judicial thinking would appear to downplay the threat. In *R v Abu Hamza* [2006],[6] Lord Phillips, the Lord Chief Justice, offered the following statement of principle:

> "The fact, however, that adverse publicity may have risked prejudicing a fair trial is no reason for not proceeding with the trial if the judge concludes that, with his assistance, it will be possible to have a fair trial."[7]

In reaching this conclusion, the court took into account the following statements from other relevant cases:

R v West [1996].
"... however lurid the reporting, there can scarcely ever have been a case more calculated to shock the public who were entitled to know the facts. The question raised on behalf of the defence is whether a fair trial could be held after such intensive publicity adverse to the accused. In our view it could. To hold otherwise would mean that if allegations of murder are sufficiently horrendous so as inevitably to shock the nation, the accused cannot be tried. That would be absurd. Moreover, providing the judge effectively warns the jury to act only on the evidence given in the court, there is no reason to suppose that they would do otherwise."[8]

Montgomery v HM Advocate [2003].
"Recent research conducted for the New Zealand Law Commission suggests that the impact of pre-trial publicity and of prejudicial media coverage during the trial, even in high profile cases, is minimal ... The actions of seeing and hearing the witnesses may be expected to have a far greater impact on their minds than such residual recollections as may exist about reports about the case in the media. This impact can be expected to be reinforced on the other hand by such warnings and directions as the trial judge may think appropriate to give them as the trial proceeds, in particular when he delivers his charge before they retire to consider their verdicts."[9]

---

6 [2006] EWCA Crim 2915.
7 [2006] EWCA Crim 2915 at para.93.
8 [1996] 2 Cr.App.R. 374 at pp.385-6.
9 [2003] 1 A.C. 641.

In the Matter of B [2006].
". . . juries up and down the country have a passionate and profound belief in, and a commitment to, the right of a defendant to be given a fair trial. They know that it is integral to their responsibility . . . The integrity of the jury is an essential feature of our trial process . . . Juries follow the directions that the trial judge will give them to focus exclusively on the evidence and to ignore anything they may have heard or read out of court . . . We cannot too strongly emphasise that the jury will follow them [appropriate directions], not only because they will loyally abide by the directions of law which they will be given by the judge, but also because the directions themselves will appeal directly to their own instinctive and fundamental belief in the need for the trial process to be fair."[10]

In the *Abu Hamza* case, the trial judge had rejected an application to stay the proceeding on no fewer than three occasions. The defence submission was that the defendant could not possibly have had a fair trial in light of the general and specific pre-trial reporting. The "general" issue was the media's response to the July 2005 bombings and the judge postponed the trial for some six months in recognition that there would be a fair amount of anti-Muslim feeling generated in the print and broadcast media. The "specific" matters related to the defendant and his regular appearance in UK broadcast news bulletins and the print media because of his association with the discredited Finsbury Park mosque and the Home Secretary's withdrawal of his British citizenship.

It was held by the Court of Appeal that, in light of the admirable summing up by the trial judge to the jury, there was ". . . no reason to believe that the jury were not able to consider and resolve the relevant issues objectively and impartially."[11]

So it would appear that the threat to a fair trial envisaged by Parliament in 1981 is more apparent than real. In the *Huntley and Carr* case, the judge proceeded to trial despite having been told by defence counsel that the pre-trial reporting was the worst in 15 years, because he said the jury would only have a "general recollection" of what had been reported in the media. The murders were perpetrated in August 2002 and the trial did not commence until late 2003. It will also be recalled that an embargo was placed upon the media in June 2003 preventing any reference to any matter pertinent to the defendants up to the date of trial. We can conclude from all of this that trial judges will not wish to stay proceedings unless there is absolutely no prospect of a fair trial being held.

However, the media should take note. The fact that a trial proceeds is not the final determinant of whether the media has breached the provisions of the Contempt of Court Act. As the wording of the legislation has it the media simply has to create a "substantial risk" of impediment

---

[10] [2006] EWCA Crim 2692.
[11] [2006] EWCA Crim 2918 at para.106 per Lord Phillips C.J.

or prejudice to the course of justice. In other words, there can still be both a trial and a prosecution for contempt. The impact of any pre-trial publicity is going to be a factor that the defence will take into account when determining its strategy in respect of any appeal against conviction. In *Her Majesty's Attorney General v Associated Newspapers and Another* [2011][12] the *Daily Mail* had mistakenly published in its online edition a photograph of a defendant at a murder trial holding a pistol with his index finger on the trigger. The photograph should have been cropped to remove the weapon but by mistake wasn't. The newspaper was found guilty of contempt of court emphasising that ". . . since the statute imposes strict liability, notwithstanding that the publication of the image of the accused with a pistol was a mistake, both defendants were guilty of contempt."[13]

In December 2003, the High Court in Northern Ireland found the *Belfast Telegraph Group* and Martin Lindsay, the editor of the *Sunday Life* newspaper, guilty of contempt and fined them a total of £5,000. The defendant, one Sean Toner, was to face trial at Belfast Crown Court on September 22, 2002 on serious drugs charges. One week before the trial the newspaper published an article that repeatedly linked Toner to drugs. The headline was "Fugitive Dealer Busted." Toner was named and was referred to as "A drug dealer," "the fugitive dealer," and the readership was informed that he had "escaped from a drugs raid on his south Belfast home. A more blatant example of contempt would be difficult to find.[14]

Proceedings for contempt under the 1981 Act must be approved by the Attorney General or "on the motion of a court having jurisdiction to deal with it."[15] The strict liability provisions of the 1981 Act apply once proceedings are *active*. The "initial steps" are:

- Arrest without warrant.
- The issue of a warrant for arrest.
- The issue of a summons to appear.
- The service of an indictment or other document specifying a charge.
- Oral charge.

Proceedings cease to be *active*:

- By acquittal or sentence.
- By any other verdict or order putting an end to the proceedings.
- By discontinuance or by operation of law.[16]

---

[12] [2011] EWHC 418 (Admin).
[13] [2011] EWHC 418 (Admin) at para.55 per Moses L.J.
[14] Re an Application by Her Majesty's Attorney General for Northern Ireland [2003]NI Q.B. 73.
[15] S.7.
[16] S.2(3).

In "sensitive" cases, the Attorney General may issue advice notices (legal advisories) to the media informing them to respect the underlying principles of the legislation. This was done in December 2006 when the Attorney General had concerns over the reporting of the murders of five Ipswich prostitutes. Two suspects were arrested and the second, Steven Wright, was subsequently charged with all five murders. In a BBC radio interview the Attorney General said:

> "I think the time has come to ask the media, to urge the media, to exercise restraint in the reporting of these events, though . . . it is for them to take their own legal advice."[17]

He had two major concerns. The first related to reports that the press were interviewing witnesses or potential witnesses. The second that he did not wish to see the possibility of a subsequent trial being aborted because of a high degree of prejudicial reporting. The intensity and volume of media reporting could have a lasting effect upon the minds of potential jurors. Against that there was no certainty that the trial would be held in Ipswich in which case potential jurors, while being aware of the background, might not take such an "intimate" interest in the detail. Local news stations and newspapers would in all probability have a more intense focus on the story than the national media organisations. In the event the trial was held at Ipswich Crown Court which presumably indicates that subsequent reporting prior to the trial was not viewed as potentially prejudicial. Any prejudicial impact of the BBC's reporting would have been regarded as minimal as a year elapsed before the trial began.

It should be stressed that the Attorney General will simply give his opinion. It is for the media to take their own legal advice and make their decisions in light of the strict liability provisions of the 1981 Act. The media will also be aware that despite the criticism surrounding the *Huntley and Carr* reporting no newspaper or broadcasting organisation was ever prosecuted for contempt. The media may feel with some justification that they can push the limits without being overly concerned with the prospect of contempt proceedings following.

The major concern from a police point of view is the collection of evidence and issues of identification. Powerful images in newspapers or on television may play tricks with the memory when, months later, a witness is asked to testify at the trial. Did he or she really see the defendant at that spot at that time or was he recognisable simply because the witness had seen photographs in the newspapers? Identification evidence, and particularly a victim's testimony, can be critical to a successful prosecution. This was never more evident than in the aftermath of the "Premiership Footballers Rape Allegations" in September 2003. A young woman made allegations of rape against a

---

[17] December 21, 2006.

number of Premiership footballers. She claimed to have consented to sex with one of them but not to others who were present in the hotel room. The Attorney General and the Metropolitan Police made numerous requests to the newspapers not to name the players who had been questioned.

The *Daily Star* broke ranks and in its edition of October 23 identified two players. There was also a pixilated photograph of one of them. Both according to the report had answered bail at a London police station in connection with a gang rape. The Attorney General brought contempt proceedings against the newspaper. The court, in *Her Majesty's Attorney General v Express Newspapers* [2004][18] emphasised that the report was the "culmination of a series of media pieces published . . . by newspapers and television, on an almost daily basis, from September 30, 2003 until October 23, 2003."[19] The court went on to emphasise that the newspaper "did not heed the guidelines, requests and advice repeatedly issued in relation to this case from September 30 to October 22."

The guidelines had stated that identification was an issue and requested that the suspects should not be named, nor any photograph or likeness of them published. The newspaper for its part admitted that the guidelines had been "overlooked" and admitted the story should not have been published.

Early the following year, the Crown Prosecution Service decided there was insufficient evidence upon which to proceed to charge the players. We shall probably never know how influential the publication was in the CPS decision not to progress the case to trial.

The Court concluded that the publication had clearly contravened the provisions of the Contempt of Court Act 1981 and fined the newspaper £60,000. In so doing the court identified certain points of law in relation to the application of the strict liability provisions. As Lord Justice Rose said:

"There is no material issue between the parties as to the relevant legal principles to be applied in relation to the statutory test."

They are:

- The risk of impediment or prejudice has to be assessed at the date of publication per Lord Diplock in *Attorney General v English*.[20]
- "Substantial risk" means a risk that is more than remote[21] or "not insubstantial"[22] or "real."
- The risk must be "practical rather than theoretical or illusory."[23]

---

[18] [2004] EWHC 2859 (Admin).
[19] [2004] EWHC 2859 (Admin) para.3 per Lord Justice Rose.
[20] [1982] 2 All E.R. 903 at p.918 (j).
[21] [1982] 2 All E.R. 903 at p.919 (b).
[22] *Attorney General v News Group Newspapers* [1987] Q.B. 1 at p.15C.
[23] *Attorney General v Guardian Newspapers Ltd (No 3)* [1992] 1 W.L.R. 874 at p.881 C.

A key factor in all of this is to assess the degree of likelihood in the publication(s) coming to the attention of potential jurors and critically, if it does so, whether it is likely to remain in their memories. The "fade factor" is the label attached by judges to the length of time between the publication(s) and the date of the trial. It will be obvious that each case will depend on its own particular facts.

So, given the criteria mentioned above, it will be obvious to the media that potentially all but trivial risk will be covered by the adjective "substantial" and the adverb "seriously." Sir John Donaldson, the Master of the Rolls, explained in the News Group case[24] that the tests of "substantial risk" and "serious prejudice" are separate but overlapping concepts. One has to consider the likely impact of the risk upon a trial together with the extent of any impact. Judges are then asked to make value judgments taking into account all the circumstances. What the courts do seem to be clear about is that the facts of other cases are of little value nor will the solution necessarily be provided by the decision in the trial.

The question to pose is whether a publication would have to render a conviction unsafe before there could be a finding of contempt against the media responsible for the publication(s). In *Attorney General v Unger [1998]* Simon Brown L.J. was of the view that before contempt could be established it had to be shown that the "publication materially affects the course of the trial . . . requires directions from a court well beyond those ordinarily required or routinely given to juries . . . or creates at the very least a seriously arguable ground for an appeal on the basis of prejudice."[25] He reiterated that view in *Attorney General v Birmingham Post and Mail* [1999].[26]

He said:

"... one and the same publication may well constitute contempt and yet, not so prejudice the trial as to undermine the safety of any subsequent conviction."

However, a different view was taken by Collins J. in *Attorney General v Guardian Newspapers Ltd* [1999].[27] He said:

"To establish contempt it needs only be shown that there was a substantial risk that serious prejudice, which must in my view mean such prejudice as would justify a stay or appeal against conviction, would result from the publication. That such prejudice does not in the event result is nothing to the point."

What appears to have been a contentious point in the late 1990s does not appear since to have troubled the courts. The judge in the *Belfast*

---

[24] *Attorney General v Guardian Newspapers Ltd* (No 3) [1992] 1 W.L.R. 874 see note 16.
[25] [1998] 1 Cr.App.R. 309.
[26] [1998] 1 Cr.App.R. 309 at pp.318-9.
[27] [1999] 1 W.L.R. 361 at p369H.

Telegraph case did not ". . . find it necessary to choose between these differing positions in order to reach a decision . . ." and the court in the *Express* case had no need to take on board the precedents as there was not to be a trial of the issue. The point remains to be decided but Lord Diplock's view in the only House of Lords case dealing with the strict liability rule was unambiguous:

> "That the risk that was created by the publication when it was actually published does not ultimately affect the outcome of the proceedings is . . . neither here nor there . . . the true course of justice must not at any stage be put at risk."[28]

In light of comments made by the Divisional Court in the *Associated Newspapers case* in 2011 it would appear that this is the prevailing view. It was emphasised that the question in respect of the Contempt of Court Act is whether the publications(s) created a substantial risk of serious impediment or prejudice to the trial. That is not the same question as posited by the Criminal Appeal Act 1968 of whether any conviction should be regarded as unsafe. When considering whether a conviction is unsafe the Court of Appeal takes a retrospective approach. It considers the impact of a publication in the context of the whole trial process including the nature of the evidence and any directions given by the judge. However the Divisional Court is simply assessing future risk.

However much judges speak of the desire of juries to adhere to their constitutional duty of deciding a case on the evidence, a publisher who creates such a risk cannot ". . . always rely upon the steps taken to allay the very risk it has created."[29] Taken to its logical conclusion if juries always did as directed by the judge then there would be no need for the law of contempt because they would not consider anything other than the evidence presented to them in court. We must not though forget that criminal proceedings for contempt are rare.

The overall objective must be to avoid trial by media. Lord Diplock was blunt:

> "The public policy that underlies the strict liability rule in contempt of court is deterrence. Trial by newspaper or, as it should be more comprehensively expressed today, trial by media, is not to be permitted in this country."[30]

So what is the current legal position? The expectation is for the media to be measured in its reporting particularly in high profile cases both before and during the course of the trial. There have been some examples of good practice when the media has arguably *not* said enough to keep the public informed. For example, very little was published in the

---

[28] *Attorney General v English* [1982] 2 All E.R. 903 at pp 918-919.
[29] *Attorney General v Associated Newspapers & Another* [2011] EWHC 418 (Admin) at para.48.
[30] *Attorney General v English* [1982] 2 All E.R. 903 at page 918.

run up to the trial of the alleged "second wave" of London bombers prior to the commencement of their trial at Woolwich Crown Court in early 2007. Yet it is suggested that the combination of the Lord Chief Justice's strong support for the objectivity of juries and the Attorney General's decisions not to prosecute any media organisation for the *Huntley and Carr* reporting leads to the conclusion that the media is on reasonably safe ground.

It is hard to imagine that if the facts of the *Attorney General v BBC & Hat Trick Productions* [1997][31] were to arise today the result would be the same. In a broadcast of the popular programme *Have I Got News for You*, Robert Maxwell's sons were referred to as ". . . heartless, scheming bastards." Six months later, they were due to face trial on fraud charges. The court found the respondents to be in contempt. The words used were, said the judge, ". . . strikingly prejudicial and go to the heart of the case." The broadcast apparently created such a risk that any juror who had seen the programme (and of course was able to recollect what was said) would not approach the matter with an open mind. As a result there was a substantial risk that the trial would be seriously prejudiced.

Compare this decision with that of the Attorney General not to proceed with contempt charges in the *Huntley and Carr* case. Compare the degree and extent of the publicity in that case with this single isolated comment in the *Hat Trick* case. Not even in the same league.

Material that contradicts what the judge has said to the jury when summing up at the conclusion of the trial is also more likely to provoke action. The *Sunday Mirror* was fined £75,000 for contempt in 2001 when a trial at Hull Crown Court collapsed as a result of a story, seen by jurors that informed readers the attack on the victim was racially motivated when the judge had said the exact opposite when summing up to the jury. A retrial was ordered at great expense to the public purse. With the advent of the Courts Act 2003, such "serious misconduct" could escalate that penalty considerably by making the publisher liable for the money wasted on the collapsed trial.

Sometimes very basic principles can be overlooked or ignored. A prime example was the case of *HM Attorney General v ITV Central Ltd* [2008].[32] In October 2007, a trial for murder was due to commence at Leicester Crown Court. One of the defendants had already been convicted on a previous occasion of another murder and was serving a sentence of life imprisonment. That fact was information of which the jury would not have had knowledge as it would have been hard to ignore in the consideration of this particular murder. On the morning of the trial *GMTV* broadcast a news item three times between 6.30am and 8am referring to the impending trial. Unfortunately on each occasion it was stated the defendant had a previous conviction for murder. The issue of contempt was referred to the Attorney General and the trial postponed

[31] [1997] E.M.L.R. 76.
[32] [2008] EWHC 1984 (Admin).

for two weeks. The news broadcasts covered the east Midlands region. Counsel for the company accepted that ". . . there had been a serious breach, as serious as it is basic . . ." Every journalist who reports from the courts should be aware is that previous convictions should not be published or broadcast. The journalist in question was dismissed from his post. ITV also picked up the costs bill of the adjourned trial which amounted to £37,000 and was fined £25,000 in respect of the contempt. All in all, a costly experience for such a basic error.

The most recent contempt case introduces a new dimension to the application of the contempt principles. *HM Attorney General v Associated Newspapers & Another* [2011][33] is the first case in England and Wales to consider whether a publication on the online news websites of two national newspapers amounted to a contempt of court. The issue was a simple one and has been referred to elsewhere—the publication of a photograph of the defendant in a murder trial holding a pistol. At 5pm on the first day of the trial the *Mail Online* website carried the photograph. It was on the site for nearly 5 hours. It will be remembered that the photograph should have been cropped to show just the head and shoulders of the defendant. The photograph also appeared on the *Sun Online* at 01.22. It remained on the site for most of the day, the second day of the trial. The jury members were asked if they had seen the images. All said they hadn't. The judge continued with the trial. The outcome was the court finding that the newspapers were in contempt. Did the publication of these photographs really seriously prejudice the trial? Whether it did or didn't was not really an issue. (See discussion above.) The only question was whether the publication created a serious risk of prejudice and the court held that it did.

Judges will now, as a matter of course, give a strongly worded direction to jurors not to trawl the internet once they have discovered the name of the defendant. The court took the view that such a direction did not amount to a total embargo on using the internet. Many people will gain their daily news quotient from the internet rather than from conventional news sources. In doing so they may inadvertently follow a link to information of the type at the centre of this case. Publishers therefore need to be aware of this fact in respect of their online publications and to take on board the decision in this case.

The Attorney General has expressed the view that the contempt laws apply to the internet.[34] In September 2008 Alun Jones QC wrote to *The Times* newspaper posing the question whether the contempt laws no longer applied to the media as prosecutions were few and far between.[35] Baroness Scotland, the Attorney General at the time, mounted a robust defence of her office's record in bringing contempt proceedings in appropriate circumstances. However it still remains the case that

---

[33] [2011] EWHC 418 (Admin).
[34] *Media Lawyer*, October 12, 2010.
[35] *The Times*, September 10, 2008.

very few actions are commenced and that may indeed reflect a more responsible approach to reporting by the media—until perhaps one thinks of the Chris Jefferies reporting. (See earlier in this chapter, Case Study One and Ch.2).

1. Section 4

This section of the Contempt of Court Act 1981 establishes that fair and accurate reports of legal proceedings held in public and published contemporaneously and in good faith will never result in a finding of contempt under the strict liability provisions.[36] Clearly this provision relates to reporting during the course of the trial. There are a number of points to mention but the section gives rise to very little legal difficulty.

The key words of warning relate to the word *proceedings*. It is possible and from a media perspective occasionally desirable to detail other matters which have been observed while in court, for example the demeanour of the friends or relatives of the victim who are sitting in the public gallery. Any such report would *not* be covered by these provisions even though they are fair, accurate and published in good faith. Who is seated in the public gallery and how they react is no part of criminal justice proceedings. However, what is written or broadcast could in fact influence the jury and the newspaper and the reporter could be found guilty of contempt.

In the *Huntley and Carr* case, an article by Brian Reade, a writer for the *Daily Mirror*, was referred to the Attorney General for possible contempt proceedings. In the article he used emotive and emotional language to describe the pain and suffering etched on the faces of the young victims' parents as the defendants gave evidence. It is not difficult to comprehend that not only critical and openly damaging material could influence a jury.

The words *fair and accurate* echo the words used by Parliament in ss.14 and 15 of the Defamation Act 1996. This public interest defence in the 1996 Act means that the publisher of defamatory material when for example reporting on court proceedings will avoid legal action. The recent case of *Curistan v Times Newspapers Ltd* [2007][37] provides invaluable guidance on the meaning of "fair and accurate" as the words refer to reporting of judicial proceedings albeit, in this case, in the context of the Defamation Act rather than the Contempt of Court Act. Gray J. cited with approval statements contained in *Gatley on Libel and Slander*[38] to the effect that what is required is *"substantial fairness and substantial accuracy."*[39]

---

[36] S.4(1).
[37] [2007] EWHC 926.
[38] 10th edn (London: Sweet & Maxwell, November 2005).
[39] [2007] EWHC 926 at para.48.

Section 4(2) relates to postponement orders. A court has the power under this subsection to order that a report of the proceedings should be postponed for such a period as the judge thinks necessary. This is obviously a restriction on freedom of expression but Parliament must be assumed to have considered this before the Bill became law.

It should be emphasised that the restriction can also be imposed in relation to one trial in order to avoid a ". . . substantial risk of prejudice to the administration of justice in . . . any other proceedings pending or imminent".

There are any number of cases of where s.4(2) orders have been used. One that attracted enormous publicity was the case of Baby P in 2009. The mother and partner were found guilty of causing or permitting the child's death. They were cleared of murdering the child. At the end of the trial the judge imposed a postponement order preventing the media from naming the defendants in order to protect the identities of Baby P's four siblings. In the event there was massive speculation over the internet as to their identities. Anyone intent upon discovering their names could do so with relative ease. Within a few days the order had been rescinded allowing the media to name the parties on the basis that the internet campaign had rendered the postponement order against the conventional media irrelevant.

The mother and her partner's brother then faced a further trial on charges of rape. The massive publicity surrounding the original order led to them standing trial using aliases in an endeavour to ensure that the jury had no inkling that the defendants were linked to the Baby P trial. Defence lawyers had questioned whether the pair could receive a fair trial given the fact that nearly half a million people had signed up to numerous online groups discussing the Baby P case. Their argument was there were so many photographs of the pair on the internet that it would be easy for a juror to stumble across the images while surfing the net. The judge allowed the trial to proceed.

The case does raise the thorny issue of whether internet sites such as Facebook should be made subject to postponement orders in the same way as the conventional media. Court orders are granted for reasons that will ensure a fair trial or for the protection of parties to the pro-ceedings. Those contributing their views on the internet will usually be unaware of these reasons. Justice will not be served in such circum-stances and the established media will be at a disadvantage.

It is rare for many cases to achieve the notoriety of the Baby P case. A s.4(2) order came under scrutiny by the Court of Appeal (Criminal Division) in 2007.[40] In this case the two defendants had been charged under the Official Secrets Act 1989. In the case of the first defendant David Keogh a s.4(2) order had been made ". . . postponing indefinitely any reporting of a question and answer given in open court during evidence in chief." *The Times* and other newspapers appealed the order

---

[40] *Times Newspapers Ltd & Others v R* [2007] EWCA Crim. 1925.

on the basis that the order contravened the open justice principle that court proceedings should take place in public and there should be the freedom to report such proceedings.

The case is instructive because of the analysis undertaken by the Court of Appeal of the circumstances when reporting restrictions are justified in the interest of the administration of justice. The Lord Chief Justice identified three categories:

- In order to ensure the fair trial of the proceedings in which the restriction is sought or subsequent proceedings.
- To protect a person involved in the proceedings such as a rape victim or a victim of blackmail.
- To protect the object of the proceedings such as the protection of an official or trade secrets.[41]

In this case by mistake a question was asked and the answer given in the public part of the trial when it should have been given *in camera*. The trial judge, realising the mistake, made an immediate order under s.4(2) ordering that no report of the information ". . . should be published in any form." The court was heavily influenced by the decision of the Court of Appeal in *R v Horsham Justices ex parte Farquharson* [1982][42] Lord Justice Ackner expressed his view of the object of s.4(2) in these terms:

"First of all, the power to postpone, not to prohibit totally, publication. Secondly, the power may be exercised in relation to only a part of the proceedings. Thirdly, that in order for the jurisdiction to be exercised the court must be satisfied that an order is necessary for avoiding a substantial risk of prejudice to the administration of justice . . . the prejudice to the administration of justice which is envisaged is the reduction in power of the court of doing that which is the end for which it exists-namely to administrator justice duly, impartially and with reference solely to the facts judicially brought before it."[43]

At the close of the trial the judge in *The Times* case had re-issued the order with "indefinite effect." It was therefore concluded that this order made by the trial judge was unnecessary to avoid a substantial risk of prejudice to the administration of justice in the particular proceedings. To repeat the order after the trial had concluded fell outside of the jurisdiction conferred by s.4(2) of the 1981 Act. There is no basis for using this section if the intention of the court is to prohibit the information from ever being published.

The postponement will normally be only for a short period but everything will depend on the circumstances of the particular case or any pending litigation. One of the longest embargos imposed under this

[41] *Times Newspapers Ltd & Others v R* [2007] EWCA Crim. 1925 at para.3.
[42] [1982] 1 Q.B. 762.
[43] [1982] 1 Q.B. 762 at page 806.

section ran from January 2001 until October 2004 as other members of an alleged criminal conspiracy were tried after the alleged mastermind was convicted.[44] In October 2006, the Court of Appeal overturned a postponement order after the convicted terrorist Dhiren Barot was sentenced to 40 years' imprisonment. The judge sought to prevent the press from reporting the severity of the sentence because he believed that it could influence jurors at upcoming terrorist trials involving a number of men with whom Barot had been expected to stand trial. This had not occurred because he changed his plea to guilty. The Appeal Court overturned the order.

The risk with this type of order when it relates to the sentencing hearing is that the media often fear that the order will prevent *any* discussion or analysis of the case on the assumption that such reporting might prejudice the trial of other defendants. The Court accepted that the media could report a "sensational" case without the words "sensational" and "prejudicial" being synonymous.[45] Judges should exercise their discretion very carefully and in light of all the circumstances given that any such order is a restriction on the freedom of the press to report, often, on matters of great public concern and interest.

In a case such as this the judge at the subsequent trial of the other alleged participants in the conspiracy to murder would be well aware of the reporting of the previous sentencing hearing. As such it would be a simple task to bring this to the jury's attention with a warning that whatever happened in the previous case should not be taken into account in assessing the guilt or innocence of these defendants.

Journalists also need to be aware of the fact that case reports may also be subject to s.4(2) restrictions. In *A,B,C and D v R* [2010][46] the case report contains the following warning:

> "This judgment is published in redacted form pursuant to an order of the court made under s.4(2) of the Contempt of Court Act 1981. That order will remain in force until further order of the court. It is a contempt of court to publish any of the redacted details."

An examination of the report shows that details of 5 of the 46 paras have been removed.

2. Discussion of Public Affairs

Section 5 of the 1981 Act provides that it is not a contempt of court for the media to publish, in good faith, material that forms part of a

---

[44] Tim Robinson: see *www.sfo.gov.uk* October 29, 2004.
[45] [2006] EWCA Crim 2692.
[46] [2010] EWCA Crim 1622.

discussion "of public affairs or other matters of general public interest." This is subject to the proviso that the ". . . risk of impediment or
prejudice to *particular* legal proceedings is merely incidental to the
discussion." It would appear that, in light of the Lord Chief Justice's
comments in *Abu Hamza*, this section is unlikely to be called upon by
the media in the way that it was in the case of *Attorney General v English*
[1982].[47] In this case, the *Daily Mail* published an article in support
of a pro-life candidate in local elections in London. The publication
coincided with the highly publicised trial of a well-known paediatri-
cian being held in the East Midlands. The article stated that it was
common practice among paediatricians to let severely handicapped
babies die of starvation. Proceedings against the newspaper were instituted by the Attorney General with the newspaper relying on the s.5
defence. The House of Lords found in the newspaper's favour. There
was no reference in the article to the trial. The reporting of the election address would have been meaningless without reference to such
allegations.

As Lord Diplock said:

"The gagging of bona fide public discussion in the press of controversial matters of general public interest, merely because there are in
existence contemporaneous legal proceedings in which some particular instance of those controversial matters may be in issue, is what s.5
. . . was in my view intended to prevent."[48]

3. Juries

It was stated earlier that the jury is perceived to be the potential weak
link in the criminal justice system in the sense that members could
be influenced by potentially prejudicial reporting. Lord Phillips in his
capacity as Lord Chief Justice stated that whatever pressures might be
placed upon juries as a result of media reporting, members will carry
out their tasks in a professional way and decide the case only on the
basis of the evidence presented in court. In controversial cases judges
will issues warnings to juries about any potentially prejudicial reporting and also in respect of surfing the internet in order to discover details
about the defendant.

Views should then be exchanged in the jury room with members convinced that they can speak openly and with the knowledge that what
is said will remain confidential. Section 8 of the Contempt of Court Act
is designed to support this principle and provides that it will be a contempt of court for the media to:

---

[47] [1982] 2 All E.R. 903.
[48] [1982] 2 All E.R. 903 at p.920.

". . . obtain, disclose or solicit any particular statement made, opinions expressed, arguments advanced or votes cast by members of a jury in the course of their deliberations in any legal proceedings."

Any action for alleged breach of s.8 must be made with the consent of the Attorney General or the court.

It may well be that journalists are approached by members of the jury expressing dissatisfaction at the process by which the decision was reached. While jury members may believe that they are acting in good faith and after all due consideration, the media is still in breach of its s.8 obligations if such concerns are published. In *R v Connor and Mizra* [2004],[49] the House of Lords made it clear that if jurors had concerns about what was occurring once they had retired then they should be brought to the attention of the trial judge at that time not after the trial had been concluded. The principles to be applied in respect of s.8 are to be found in the decision of the House of Lords in *Attorney General v Associated Newspapers* [1994].[50]

In this case, a newspaper revealed information about the jury's deliberations in the aftermath of a much publicised fraud trial. Some members of the jury, believing that they were contributing to a legitimate research exercise, had passed on their views and opinions. The transcripts of the "research" formed the basis of the publication. Jury members had not spoken directly to the newspaper. It was held that the newspaper was in breach of the ". . . plain and unambiguous" wording of s.8. The newspaper, its editor and the journalist concerned were fined a total of £60,000 for the disclosure.

The current position in respect of s.8 liability is to be found in the decision of the Divisional Court in *Attorney General v Seckerson & Times Newspapers* [2009].[51] The article published in *The Times* that attracted the Attorney General's attention concerned the trial of a childminder in whose care the baby had died. The jury convicted her of manslaughter for which she was sentenced to three years imprisonment.

Two jurors later spoke to *The Times* Legal Editor about their concerns that the verdict was wrong and that perhaps the case should never have been brought to trial because of the level of circumstantial evidence.

The article carried a number of disclosures of what occurred in the jury room. For example:

". . . the consensus was taken 3 minutes after the foreman was voted in. It was 10–2 against, all based on the evidence. After that there was no going back."

There was no dispute in this case about whether the Attorney General needed to prove that the defendants had intended to breach the terms

⁴⁹ [2004] UKHL 2.
⁵⁰ [1994] 1 All E.R. 556.
⁵¹ [2009] EWHC 1023 (Admin).

of s.8(1). That was self evident. The court was asked to consider the impact of the Human Rights Act upon the interpretation of s.8(1). Clearly s.8(1) amounted to a restriction on the freedom of the press to report to the public on the administration of justice. There are exceptions to the "dominance" of freedom of expression and Parliament in 1981 had considered that the right to a fair trial included the right for jury members to express themselves freely within the confines of the jury room. In 1994 the European Commission of Human Rights concurred with this view and saw the "unlimited prohibition on disclosure" as being an inevitable protection for jurors and could therefore be regarded as 'necessary' in a society which has determined to retain this mode of trial.

In *Gregory v United Kingdom* [1997][52] the court had stated:

> "The court acknowledges that the rule governing the secrecy of jury deliberations is a crucial and legitimate feature of English trial law which serves to reinforce the jury's role as the ultimate arbiter of fact and to guarantee open and frank deliberations among jurors on the evidence which they have heard."

The disclosure above was found to be a breach of s.8(1) and the newspaper was fined £15,000 and the jury foreman £500. The media of course is not forbidden to speak in general terms with jurors about their experiences. It is simply warned off approaching jurors with a view to discovering what went on in the jury room. There can in practice be a very fine dividing line between what does and does not amount to a breach of the section. This judgment would tend to support the view that journalists should err on the side of caution.

4. Section 11 Orders

Providing that the name of a witness or defendant or other matter has not been mentioned in open court, it is possible for a court to place a permanent embargo upon the media to prevent disclosure. As may be expected the use of s.11 is not widespread because it runs counter to the presumption in favour of freedom of expression and open justice. The section says that if a court has power to withhold a name from the public it:

> ". . . may give such directions prohibiting the publication of that name or matter in connection with the proceedings as appear to the court to be necessary for the purpose for which it was so withheld."

---

[52] [1997] 25 E.H.R.R. 577.

Section 11 orders may be used when members of the security services are called as witnesses if their lives may be put at risk because of public exposure. They may be used to persuade key witnesses to come forward to give evidence in circumstances where they fear for their safety if identified. The Court of Appeal in the *R v Davis* [2006][53] paints a graphic picture of the dangers faced by those who seek to assist the police to bring ruthless criminals to justice. The President of the Queen's Bench Divisional Court quoted from Hughes J. in *R v Bola* [2003][54]:

> "... the experience of police is that after an incident of this kind (fatal shooting) witnesses are frequently content to come confidentially to the investigators to tell them what they know, what they saw, to give them leads and help them about what the background may be and sometimes to name names but that such witnesses are to a very large extent frightened to be identified as co-operating with the police ... they fear similar incidents ..."

Section 11 orders can help to allay such fears but should not be used in such a way as to stifle freedom of expression, without good cause. The terms of any such order should be very specific and be in writing.

In *Harper & Johncox v Aldershot Magistrates Court* [2010][55] the claimants were police officers who attended Aldershot Magistrates Court facing charges of misconduct in public office. The purpose of the hearing was to decide whether to send the case to the Crown Court for trial. An application was made that their home addresses should not be published. They were both high ranking officers and over the years had brought many criminals to justice. To publish their addresses would put them and their families at risk. The court was told that their addresses could be found easily via the internet or electoral register. The principles considered when deciding whether s.4(2) is appropriate apply equally to a decision involving s.11. As Lord Judge said in the *Trinity Mirror* case[56] "... it is impossible to over-emphasise the importance to be attached to the ability of the media to report criminal trials ... and important aspect of the public interest in the administration of criminal justice is that identity of those convicted and sentenced for criminal offences should not be concealed."[57] The application was refused.[58]

Further general guidance on the working of s.11 can be found on the Crown Prosecution Service website at *www.cps.gov.uk*.

[53] [2006] EWCA Crim. 1155.
[54] [2003] Unreported June 18, 2003.
[55] [2010] EWHC 1319 (Admin).
[56] [2008] EWCA Crim. 50.
[57] [2008] EWCA Crim. 50 at para.32.
[58] See also *R v Evesham Justices ex parte McDonagh* [1988] Q.B. 553.

PART TWO: CONTEMPT IN PRACTICE

The Christmas Day 2010 discovery of the body of landscape architect Joanna Yeates near Bristol generated saturation media coverage followed by a frenzy when her landlord Chris Jefferies was arrested by murder detectives. By the time he was released without charge his name had been dragged through the mud both in mainstream, online and mobile media. The stream of pejorative commentary seemed to drive a coach and horses through the provisions of the Act and the principle of avoiding trial by media. (See Case Study One.)

All those publishing potentially prejudicial content were warned off by the Attorney General, who has the power to bring criminal proceedings for breach of the Contempt of Court Act in the most damaging instances. The penalties are imprisonment and/or unlimited fines. Yet prosecutions are rare even where pre-trial reporting points the finger even more explicitly at a suspect as discussed in Part One of this chapter. Despite the wide margin in favour of freedom of expression, the judicial system remains committed to the principle of avoiding trial by media.

The freedom of journalists to put legal proceedings in the public domain relies on the long-standing commitment to open justice and the recognition of its benefits to a democratic society. That said, the core commitment is to the publication of judgments. The public access to, and airing of, any particular proceedings have long been seen as sacrificeable to the broader interests of justice, particularly to protect the jury system itself. The principle is now further circumscribed by the requirement to uphold the art.6 rights of any defendant to a fair trial.

These various limitations on the freedom to provide a public account of legal dealings are mainly outlined in a variety of provisions within the Contempt of Court Act. Contempt under the Act becomes a criminal offence which is daunting for journalists but does require a case to be proven beyond all reasonable doubt as well as meeting the more particular requirements of the Act.

The legal restrictions designed to protect the right to a fair trial have a wide variety of repercussions for journalists and impact on far more than straightforward court reporting.

Day-to-day crime coverage and any stories relating to issues which could end up in court require an understanding by the reporter of the basic principles at stake and of the specific restrictions which apply at each stage. In practical terms a useful distinction can be made between pre-trial and in-trial reporting as outlined in Part One of this chapter.

On paper, the Act provides considerable protection for the defendant and for the process of trial by jury by imposing limits on any reporting which creates a substantial risk of serious prejudice—and those limits kick in very early in the process. This is in stark contrast to the sort of reporting allowed in the United States both before and even during a trial.

Historically journalists had free reign to report on crime, for instance, until a suspect was charged. Now proceedings are active from the point of arrest or the issuing of a warrant. As soon as the finger points at a particular individual, restraint is demanded under strict liability provision.

Avoiding contempt according to the letter of the law imposes considerable restrictions on the manner in which crime is reported. In practice, the absence of enforcement has led to risky material being run routinely. In many cases this custom and practice has merely allowed reasonable latitude for the public right to know about such incidents and suggests the judicial interpretations of "substantial" and "serious" have put the bar high for establishing contempt. Certainly journalists are far less cautious now than they were in the early days of the Act.

The danger for any novice, and indeed for more experienced journalists, is that we are behaving almost as if the law did not exist and that could tempt us to be too cavalier. The process of assessing the risk of being held in contempt must be gone through even where the likelihood of being prosecuted seems remote enough to take that risk.

Journalists should also consider their moral position. Any journalist concerned about being fair to all, high and low, needs to move beyond a simple assessment of the chances of being called to account. We need to examine our responsibilities to the vital principle that any suspect is innocent unless proven guilty. Personally, being responsible for coverage which set the stage for an innocent person to be wrongfully convicted would prey on my conscience far more than falling foul of a privacy complaint from a celebrity with a punctured ego. There is also the risk that, if an action for contempt led to a trial being abandoned, a journalist could be responsible for a "guilty" defendant being freed and the victims forever being denied justice.

5. Pre-trial Contempt in Practice

Where proceedings are active, it is important to recognise the risk attached to different elements of the story. Not all material is deemed equally prejudicial. Journalists covering crime or any sort of pre-trial reporting should run through the following checklist.

Are proceedings active?
Remember the restrictions apply from the time of arrest; the issue of a warrant or summons, the service of an indictment or an oral charge. They also continue to apply until acquittal or sentence.

In practice it can be difficult to establish whether proceedings are active but reporters are expected at least to attempt to find out. Police still talk of people "helping with inquiries" which may, or may not, involve arrest. If someone being questioned is not free to leave, proceedings are definitely active. The same is true if they are released on police bail. However if they are simply released without charge and not bailed, there are no proceedings to be active in relation to them.

Alert newsdesk if proceedings are active—this ensures the risk is weighed by those with the responsibility to assess any legal risks and it covers your back if the worst should happen.

A campaign in the wake of the Yeates coverage to make it illegal to name anyone at arrest stage fell by the wayside. Police tend not to confirm identity until charge but names often emerge locally and the publicity can aid the police inquiry. Coverage can be in the suspect's interest as a police appeal for witnesses can put them in the clear rather than necessarily incriminate them.

Will a report create a substantial risk of serious prejudice?

This is a tough test, with a high threshold, and proceedings for contempt by publication under the Act have to be authorised by the Attorney General. But journalists should not be complacent about creating coverage that could be held in contempt. The barrier for pre-trial coverage has been set high as evidenced in *R v Abu Hamza* discussed earlier, partly because of the credit given to juries to disregard old media reports.

Definitions of "substantial" vary from anything more than trivial through to only that that causes a trial to collapse. The last government's Attorney General Baroness Scotland, when defending herself against accusations of failing to enforce the law, said: "Not every public comment about a particular case, however outspoken, will seriously interfere with the rights of the accused." Evidence that the jury would hear anyway would also not be actionable, she said.

Is the report written as if the person arrested is definitely the person who committed the crime?

The risk of being held in contempt rises considerably if a report is worded so as to leave no doubt that the suspect is guilty. Police cannot have definitely caught the guilty person: that is for the courts to decide. To be safe there needs to be enough wriggle room to allow for the suspect to be innocent. It must at very least be possible for someone other than the suspect to be guilty. This need not prevent a pretty full account of the nature of the crime but it does restrict coverage of who is responsible for it. A report needs to be about the crime and the victim, rather than a whodunnit. This, logically, tends to push reports into focussing on the victim rather than the perpetrator. To cover an incident by the book where proceedings are active, it is best to focus on common ground—a sequence of events which is not disputed, such as who the victim was, how the body was found, the cause of death, items removed by police. The aim is to exclude material that is likely to be disputed at trial. In practice, it is rarely possible to be certain what exactly that includes. But, in the current more lax climate, a reasonable amount of detail could be given on the basis that judges have defended the entitlement of the public to know the facts of major criminal incidents. A degree of care not to incriminate the suspect should be sufficient but reporters should always bear in mind that the risk exists.

Does it place the suspect at the scene?

Problematic cases are where suspects are "caught red-handed", arrested on the spot, after a chase or in a citizen's arrest or other dramatic, newsworthy way. The account of the crime should be separated from the arrest in such a way as to leave open the possibility that the police could have detained the wrong person.

Is identity going to be an issue?

Identity very often is an issue and it will certainly be difficult to rule it out in the immediate aftermath of an incident. The printing of photographs of those accused is particularly frowned upon and is likely to provoke a warning if not full-blown proceedings. The fear is of a kind of auto-suggestion that by running a photograph witnesses may convince themselves they saw the suspect when they didn't. This would particularly taint any identity parade evidence.

However, an exception is made for the publication of photographs of, and other information regarding, suspects "wanted" by the police for serious crimes. This is a typical area of compromise where the public interest is seen to be sufficient to outweigh concerns for the suspect's rights. Usually this is justified on the grounds that a violent suspect poses a threat to the public who may need to protect themselves, as in the case of Derrick Bird who went on a shooting rampage in Cumbria. The issuing of a warrant for the arrest makes proceedings active for contempt and the material aired in appeals is likely to be highly prejudicial. But the then Attorney General assured the media during the Contempt of Court Bill's passage through Parliament that proceedings would not be brought in such cases as long as the press reported the police appeals in reasoned terms. That however only covers the period of the hunt; once the suspect is apprehended the protection ends.

In the case of the footballers, mentioned earlier, even using the names was seen as provoking a risk because where the suspects are celebrities that can be enough to raise a doubt over the reliability of witness evidence because their image may be seen as sufficiently familiar even if not run with the report.

Does the suspect have previous convictions?

If these are known, they should definitely NOT be mentioned at any stage other than as part of a police appeal and even then only for the duration of the hunt for the suspect. The presumption of innocence which is said to be a foundation of the judicial system used to mean that these were never made known to the jury during the trial. Even though they now can be under bad character provisions this is only at the judge's discretion so including them in any pre-trial report would deprive the judge of this power so still be at risk of being deemed in contempt.

How is the suspect described?

Be as neutral as possible. A man was arrested; not the man was arrested. Some reservations about behaviour or personality could be expressed (but note the defamation risk). The more closely these relate to the accusation at issue the riskier they become. Be cautious with any damning quotes from neighbours or colleagues suggesting guilt.

Will any charges be tried by jury?

The vast majority of incidents that attract major coverage will involve an indictable offence, namely one that is likely to end up at jury trial and remember it is primarily the jury process the Act is designed to protect.

If the nature of the crime means it will be tried by magistrates, the risk of contempt is very low as magistrates are not to be swayed by media reports. Given that they decide questions of innocence and guilt in full knowledge of a defendant's previous convictions and that, for instance, other reporting restrictions such as those of the Magistrates' Court Act, do not apply to trial before magistrates, it would be difficult to sustain an argument that they were influenced by media coverage.

The fact that the jury is central to issues of contempt and that the jury is drawn from the area close to the crime means that local newspapers are more likely than the nationals to face action. Their coverage is literally closer to home and can be considered more likely in the first instance to be read by jurors and also to be more meaningful and thereby to persist in their minds. Trials can be moved to a different area to reduce the risk but that could increase the irritation with the author of the local coverage that made the switch necessary and hance make prosecution for contempt more likely.

How long will it take to come to trial?

The public interest in reporting crime helps provide the extra latitude when covering the crime itself and it can easily be 18 months before a major case comes to trial. The fade factor may help with coverage of a crime at the time it comes to light but as the trial date nears there comes a point where there may not be time for memories to lapse. What is not clear is when that point is. Often the bigger the case the longer it takes to get to trial. But is three months long enough? Is three weeks? Certainly the closer to trial the harder it would be to use the fade factor defence and the public interest in disclosure may be harder to argue too. Generally a more cautious approach is usually adopted from the first court appearance before magistrates.

Action was taken to rein in the media six months before the Huntley trial and media lawyers talk of becoming more nervous within three or four months of trial. The last government's Attorney General Baroness Scotland also commented that material such as that published when reporting the crime would not "weigh heavily" in the minds of the jury after a "long gap".

The media's reliance on the fade factor does however depend on the sense of transience. In this regard a newspaper's role as tomorrow's catlit liner worked in its favour and judges have previously deemed broadcast news to be even more forgettable. However the 21st century availability of online archives makes it much harder for the media to rely on fade factor if the material in contempt is still on the website for jurors to see. Earlier coverage of crimes should at very least not be linked to any court reports and it may be safest to make it inaccessible in the archive for the duration of "active" proceedings.

Is it safe to include eyewitness accounts?

Witness accounts in pre-trial reports can easily be seen to risk prejudicing a fair trial. The concern here is that once an eyewitness goes on the record in the media, there could be an argument that the evidence is tainted. If say, the witness or the reporter exaggerates the account, there is a danger the witness may feel obliged to live up to the initial media statement when it comes to giving evidence in court or, even sooner, when giving a statement to police.

The closer the source was to witnessing the crime itself rather than, say, its aftermath, the greater the risk is and nothing should be used which points to the guilt of any particular individual.

However the main threat to the integrity of witnesses was the old habit, previously prevalent among the national mass market tabloids, to "buy up" witnesses for the backgrounder at the end of the trial. Some payments were even conditional on conviction. That made sense for the newspaper as there would nearly always be far more interest in the background of a mass murderer than the ordeal of an acquitted defendant. Yet effectively the payment gave the witness a significant incentive to provide damning evidence. This practice was frowned upon by the judiciary as tending to pervert the course of justice. It was ruled out in the Press Complaints Commission code in the wake of the Rosemary West trial. Care still needs to be taken to make a proper assessment of the witness's reliability.

Is it safe to interview the victim?

It can be with care. Again the focus needs to be on the ordeal with the inclusion of verifiable facts which will not be at issue at trial and which do not point to any particular guilty party.

Is it safe to run a confession?

If someone confesses to a crime, it might be tempting to think it would be safe to run because there would be no trial and therefore no jury to prejudice. However, a confession made to a journalist carries no legal weight, is not binding on the confessor, and is certainly not the equivalent of a guilty plea in court. Also such coverage would certainly provoke the wrath of the judiciary as being in the realms of "trial by media." Confessions can only properly be made through legal channels and otherwise would be inadmissible and could actually make conviction impossible.

It is generally considered safe to report claims of innocence although technically these are potentially prejudicial, especially if the defendant effectively introduces evidence, as again this would stray into trial by media.

Is the risk of prejudicing a trial incidental to discussion of an issue of general public interest?

This defence under s.5 of the Contempt of Court Act 1981 can be useful but journalists can't afford to be disingenuous. A s.5 defence is harder, although not impossible, to sustain if the upcoming trial is what makes debate of the issue timely. The natural tendency for a reporter, and particularly a sub, is to use the trial as the "hook" for the related coverage. A heading along the lines of : "As Joe Bloggs awaits trial for the murder of his son, the *Daily Bugle* talks to a father who defends mercy killing" would clearly not meet the requirements of the defence. To be safe, the article at risk of being in contempt should make absolutely no reference to the trial.

How can I describe the crime?

Technically it is not for a crime reporter to determine the nature of the offence committed, particularly to distinguish between murder and manslaughter. So if someone has been arrested on suspicion of murder, a report should stick to the physical events, at least referring to a stabbing say, or even more cautiously to the victim being found with knife wounds.

Judges are very sensitive to anything that smacks of trial by media so reports in that vein are much more susceptible to action. Coroners have been known to challenge incident reports referring to suicide, arguing that it is for their inquest to reach a verdict as to how a victim came to be found hanging or dead from a drugs overdose. How cautious a newspaper is may depend on how protective a particular coroner is of the procedure. A good rule of thumb in deciding what to include is to ask: will it annoy the judge or coroner? Will it be seen as treading on judge's toes? That may still not absolutely rule it out but the likelihood of action is significantly increased.

One further note of caution is that the sort of report that could provoke action under the Contempt of Court Act is also likely to be defamatory and there could be a serious libel risk if a suspect is identified and subsequently charges are dropped or never even brought. So although the contempt risk may be dismissed, the chances of a libel action need to be considered too.

Case Study One: Arrest of Christopher Jefferies in Joanna Yeates murder investigation, Christmas 2010

Christopher Jefferies was the dead woman's landlord who was arrested but not charged at one stage in the murder inquiry. A massive amount of background information was run about him which could have been seen as generally prejudicial, although little of it related directly to the crime. The media were condemned for character assassination and the Attorney General warned commentators on all platforms to "back off". Jefferies was released, another man was charged and was awaiting trial as we went to press, and the case triggered the calls for a ban on naming suspects at arrest stage. Now the dust has settled contempt actions have been brought against The *Sun* and *Daily Mirror* and Jefferies is suing various media outlets for defamation.

On the contempt front, the mass-circulation newspapers and Twitterati pushed their luck either through taking a calculated risk or through ignorance. In most cases the information given about Jefferies, although potentially defamatory, was a long way from being directly prejudicial and was less damning than in some other cases, such as the terrorist trials discussed earlier.

Were proceedings active? Yes. Jefferies had been arrested.

Will a report create a substantial risk of serious prejudice? Each report would have to be examined. Some may have been direct enough to cause a "substantial" risk which would have necessitated special warnings to the jury to ignore previous reports.

Is the report written as if the person arrested is definitely the person who committed the crime? In the mainstream media it could be argued this was implied but not stated.

Did it place the suspect at the scene? Particularly dangerous material would be any descriptions linking the arrested man to the dumping of the body or, for example, the discovery of the infamous missing sock.

How was the suspect described? Very negatively. Jefferies was described in somewhat menacing tones but the literal content of the descriptions was in some way innocuous. Being eccentric, even if arguably true, does not make anyone more or less likely to be guilty of murder and certainly not of any particular murder.

Was identity going to be an issue? Identity was likely to be an issue as much of the investigation focused on the body which had been dumped. Any eyewitness accounts would be open to challenge as being tainted if previously aired in the media.

How long would it take to come to trial? Had Jefferies been charged, the media would have had to rely heavily on the fade factor. Murder trials typically take months to come to trial so this would have been one of their strongest arguments that proceedings would not be seriously prejudiced. There is no set time for how long it takes for the impact of material to "fade" although more than six months should be enough. In most cases, once the court process begins, coverage becomes much more restrained. The media needs some leeway to be able to report crime in a meaningful way but once a suspect becomes a defendant and makes the first appearance before magistrates, most outlets fall into line, not least with the restrictions of the Magistrates' Court Act.

Trends in Pre-trial Contempt

The discernible trend is of greater risks being taken pre-trial. Perhaps it is reasonable not to wring our hands over this. Even judges and Attorney Generals recognise the fade factor.

Also given the proliferation of material online and the relative difficulty of closing the jury off to outside, and certainly, historical influences, the protection envisaged in the Contempt of Court Act is simply not achievable. Moreover, if we trust the jury to recognise their personal prejudices and put those aside, is it really that unreasonable to require them to ignore any preconceived ideas generated by banner headlines in the media months before?

Where a case has received considerable media attention, the judge can step up the force of the reminder to the jury that they must swayed only by the evidence heard in court.

Judges are reluctant to concede that the jury will not weigh the case on the facts but also that their own powers of persuasion are limited.

Also, despite the caveat that coverage can be contempt without necessitating the abandonment of a trial, the very rarity of prosecutions runs the risk of a future or current trial collapsing if the defence can argue that the expectation on the jury is just too great.

Similarly there are broader reasons why the Attorney General is reluctant to instigate contempt proceedings, preferring the warning shot across the bows.

The role of Attorney General has a political dimension and, whatever UK Governments do behind the scenes, they are ultimately reluctant to be seen to be acting overtly to curb the press.

Politically too, there are few Brownie points to be won with the public by standing up for the rights of suspects to a fair trial, especially where terrorism is allegedly involved. If the case against a defendant collapses as a result, perhaps the Attorney General would end up taking a share of the blame along with the media.

For all these reasons, it would appear the judges and Attorney General would have a lot to lose by clamping down, particularly on pre-trial contempt.

That is further grounds for journalists themselves to pause for thought. Journalists could well celebrate the ineffectiveness of the Contempt of Court Act as a victory for freedom of expression and a sign of a more reasonable balance between the right to record what is going on in the world. It would also suggest the jury system is more robust than the Act presumes.

However, is the Attorney General's reticence good enough reason to report an arrest in such a way as to undermine the chances of a fair trial? Just because we might get away with something does not make it reasonable to do it anyway. In many other contexts, journalists have established a noble tradition of upholding the rights of the individual against oppressive State machinery. Should we really be applauding the use of pre-trial headlines which damn a defendant, especially an "unfashionable" one such as a terror or paedophile suspect?

Perhaps the increased latitude allowed in practice pre-trial has intentionally, or otherwise, developed as a counterbalance to a more draconian system for reporting during the trial.

6. Contempt at Trial

A court report that is not both fair and accurate, or is run with malice, can be held in contempt. Coverage independent of the trial but run during it may also be in contempt.

Information given in the absence of the jury can also not safely be reported during the trial because of the risk of contempt. Common sense dictates that it should not be used at that stage given that the jury is absent only because it is deemed jurors should not be privy to it lest it prejudice their deliberations.

What has made media operators sit up and take notice is the provision of the Courts Act 2003 whereby in cases of "serious misconduct"— effectively where reporting is so prejudicial that it triggers the collapse of a trial — the publisher can be held liable for costs of the trial to date, which can run into millions of pounds.

The Act also firms up the position on reporting of material in the absence of the jury. It had been argued that it was for the court to issue a postponing order to delay use of such information and that in the absence of an order a journalist could go ahead without risk of being held in contempt. However the Act raises the prospect of treating such revelations as "serious misconduct" which could prove even more costly.

Even for organisations driven by financial rather than ethical considerations, this tips the balance firmly towards extra caution during trial. Magistrates and judges are likely to be less reticent than the Attorney General in making the media pay for overstepping the mark.

Case Study Two: *HM Attorney General v Associated Newspapers & Another* [2011]

This case, outlined in Part One of the Chapter, demonstrates the heightened risk of contempt proceedings during a trial. It confirmed that the Contempt of Court Act applies to online material and that removing it some hours later is not adequate remedy. It also demonstrates how costly oversights can be.

The proceedings related to the high-profile murder trial of Ryan Ward, who claimed he killed 39-year-old father Craig Wass in self-defence. Wass had intervened after seeing Ward head-butt a young woman. The self-defence approach demonstrated that identity was not an issue as the physical presence of the defendant at the scene was not in dispute. So a basic headshot would not have been prejudicial and thus safe to run.

Both the *Daily Mail* and *Sun* were supplied with a picture of Ward holding a gun. For the print editions the gun was cropped out but when the image appeared on *Mail Online* and *Sun Online* it was obvious Ward was holding a gun. The version of the *Mail Online* story was handled by a freelancer. When the picture was initially submitted, the picture desk was warned the handgun should not be included in any copy of the photograph because it could prejudice the trial. Similarly on the *Sun* when the picture arrived via an agency, picture desk accepted that the gun needed to be cropped out.

When the Attorney General brought proceedings against both newspaper companies, the judgment was very clear that the image was prejudicial. Being seen brandishing a gun about would seriously undermine Ward's claim to self-defence. There is a "can't win" element here too. Both papers had decided the picture needed to be cropped for the print editions and argued that the appearance of the gun in the online versions was a mistake, so both defendants were effectively acknowledging that they believed the inclusion of the gun to be prejudicial.

As Lord Justice Moses says at [42]: "We were surprised that this point was in issue."

The main argument was over the risk of the jury seeing it. (In practice, all jurors said they had not seen it.)

The judgment does acknowledge that jury members were warned by the judge not to "consult" the internet but to rely solely on evidence given in court. But Lord Justice Moses considered that jurors obeying this instruction not to seek out information on the defendant or background to the case might still think it OK to follow the day-to-day trial coverage online as they might in a newspaper or on television. Indeed they could hardly avoid it entirely.

He was also not impressed by the argument that only users clicking into the story would have seen the picture which was removed in both cases once the mistake was realised; nor by the fact that it was only up on the *Mail* site for about five hours and the *Sun*'s for about 19.

Ultimately the judgment allows the courts to have their cake and eat it in that it falls back on the distinction in *Attorney General v Birmingham Post and Mail Ltd*[59] that there can be contempt and a safe conviction, particularly as in this case no juror had seen the offending material.

This is the distinction between risk and reality. The jury had not seen the image so the trial had not been tainted and could go ahead. But the careless use of the image was deemed most certainly to have created a substantial RISK of serious prejudice as the jury members could have seen it. This allowed contempt proceedings to be brought without collapsing the trial.

That is a mixed blessing for the media. If the trial had collapsed, the *Mail* and *Sun* could have been liable for costs under the Court Act 2003 but the distinction between risk and reality does create more wriggle room for the Attorney General which may diminish the reticence to bring contempt proceedings against the media in cases where the integrity of the trial can be protected.

Also, if we really do trust juries to reach verdicts based solely on the evidence given in court and to obey judges' warnings, the Contempt of Court Act is surely redundant. Despite the fancy footwork required to bring successful proceedings, the system appears to be committed to maintaining it. Those who create a risk to a fair trial are not off the hook. Lord Justice Moses says at [38]:

> "The publisher who has created such a risk cannot always rely upon the steps taken to allay the very risk it has created. Of the courts' recognition of the robustness of juries Simon Brown J said:
>
> > 'If one carries this principle too far, there could be no need for a law of contempt in the first place, and on occasions it is quite unrealistic to expect the jury to disregard extraneous material, in particular when published contemporaneously with the trial'. (Birmingham Post 371B.)"

---

[59] [1999] 1 W.L.R. 36.

There is a further practical cautionary note here. Online editions of many newspapers are still treated as a poor relation to the main print offering. Editorial and legal checks focus on the print edition which may still be the first to receive the material. This ruling underlines the need for as much care to be taken with pictures and captions as with words; and with online offerings as with print editions. Lessons to be learnt include:

- **Formalise and extend communication of legal queries**
  In the past a note to or even just a conversation with news/picture desk would have sufficed. Nowadays with multiple platform publication, repurposing and 24/7 operation, written warnings must be flagged up to ensure everyone handling the material is alerted.
- **Formalise and extend legal responsibilities**
  Everyone handling material and responsible for putting it into the public domain needs to be legally aware. Alarm bells should ring even if detailed legal knowledge is lacking. Online platforms carry the same risk as print for contempt. Do not be more cavalier with one than the other. Freelance as well as permanent staff must know their law and the procedure for seeking legal advice. If you publish 24/7, legal advice must be available 24/7. Or those handling material must hold material back until legal advice can be sought. Subsequent to this mistake *Mail Online* journalists were instructed to submit for legal check all articles relating to crime and courts, including captions and photographs.
- **Examine your procedures for publishing online**
  Is the online team less experienced than your print operation? Are they trained? Are photographs and other material being fed semi-automatically into pre-ordained templates, without much if any regard to the image content? Are pre-publication checks in place? Is information passed properly between shifts and between print and online teams?

Tellingly, the penultimate paragraph of the judgment refers specifically to the challenges of online publication and also of the risk of juries being passed information via Twitter or RSS feeds. Lord Justice Moses says at [54]:

"This case demonstrates the need to recognise that instant news requires instant and effective protection for the integrity of a criminal trial."

Journalists are expected to be on the ball to deal promptly with any legal issues that arise around online material.

7. Contempt Post-trial

Technically proceedings are active for contempt until sentence. For big trials, nationally or locally, the media will want to run a "back-grounder" including angles such as the police inquiry, the feelings of the victim towards the accused and perhaps a profile of the perpetrator. Much of this material would be prejudicial and often blatantly in contempt.

But the Contempt of Court Act is designed to protect the jury from undue influence and once jurors have returned their verdict, their role is over. The judge is the one determining sentence and the received wisdom is that a judge is not susceptible to media influence or, at least, would never admit to being so many backgrounders are now run immediately after verdict rather than waiting until sentence which can be months later.

8. Section 4(2) Postponement Orders in Practice

These orders are proving popular with judges and magistrates and as a consequence they are throwing up difficulties for reporters and giving rise to a growing number of challenges. Reporters in court should be aware of the requirements of the orders and the likely erroneous justifications used in making them, which can be challenged.

Lack of clarity can be an issue. The court should make clear the scope of the order—exactly what information needs to be postponed or withheld. It should also give the grounds for making the order. Reporters should always request this information in writing. This is partly to protect the journalist to ensure compliance with the order; so that neither too much nor too little information is withheld. The mere act of requesting clarification may help to ensure any order receives appropriately detailed consideration and is no broader than it need be. It will also highlight possible grounds to challenge the order, or at least its scope.

Two key judgments that may be employed when considering a s.4 challenge are *Ex p HTV Ltd v Rhuddlan Justices* 1986[60] which established that s.4 orders cannot be used to postpone reports of matters outside the court and *R v Horsham Justices, ex p Farquharson* 1982[61] which reminds

---

[60] [1986] Crim.L.R. p.329.
[61] [1982] Q.B. 762.

judges and juries of the requirement to act according to the evidence put in front of them and not what they read in the papers.

Section 4(2) postponing orders tend to be used where a sequence of related trials is taking place and is again based on the desire not to prejudice a jury by knowing the outcome of these other trials. But there is a growing inconsistency with their application given the general trends to treat juries as more impervious to influence than previously. If we trust juries to come to a verdict based solely on the evidence given, could we not also trust them to ignore the guilt or innocence of another defendant in a different aspect of the overall case.

This aspect came to the fore in the *Barot* case (See p.184) in the judgment of Sir Igor Judge. He said:

> "The freedom of the press to report the proceedings provides one of the essential safeguards against closed justice. In our view, broadcasting authorities and newspaper editors should be trusted to fulfil their responsibilities accurately to inform the public of court proceedings and to exercise sensible judgment about the publication of comment which may interfere with the administration of justice."[62]

This was a victory in the specific case and a welcome reiteration of the "precious principle" of open justice. However, there is, as usual, a caveat. The judgment is not giving carte blanche for the material to be printed; rather it is saying it is not for the court to ban coverage. It puts the onus on the media to make its own decision about what to include/exclude but reminds them of the broader restrictions of common law contempt.

Significantly it was also an "important consideration" that Barot's conviction would be admissible at the forthcoming trial and that the jury would be told details of his activities.

What then is the purpose of contempt which is designed to shield the jury from information they were going to be given? The introduction of the bad character provisions basically calls into question the whole underpinning of the Contempt Act which assumes juries need a great deal of protection from information which could undermine the defendant's chances of a fair trial. If they can have his previous convictions put to them at trial, most other potentially damaging facts pale into insignificance.

---

[62] Cited by Tony Jaffa and Nigel Hanson, of Foot Anstey Solicitors, on *www.holdthefrontpage.co.uk*

9. Juries in Practice

Any journalist who spends time in court will find themselves musing on the minds of the jury—watching their reactions to certain revelations, wondering what they are thinking, guessing what verdict they will reach. But these remain among the unanswered questions of our time.

Juries are the bedrock of our judicial system and we rely on them to decide on guilt or innocence based on the evidence before them. So it should be of some concern that we know so little of how they actually operate. As discussed earlier, the press cannot investigate the workings of juries and very limited research has been sanctioned into their behaviour. Perhaps if appropriate questions could be asked we would all be enormously reassured by the probity and common sense of these panels but the continued censorship of such a debate does raise suspicions that the powers-that-be fear such a reality check would undermine faith in the process.

The restrictions imposed by s.8 of the Contempt of Court Act, outlined in Part One of the chapter, do stand in the way of what could be a very healthy examination of how juries really deal with evidence, such as that of expert witnesses.

Case Study Three: Attorney General v Seckerson & Times Newspapers [2009] EWHC 1023 (Admin)

An article based on comments from two jurors questioning the verdict in a murder trial was pushing the boundaries of the s.8 restrictions of the Contempt of Court Act. Neither juror was identified but there were references to jury room deliberations and a 10/2 split, which matched the eventual majority guilty verdict.

The Times was attempting to examine the use of expert witnesses in achieving conviction—a controversial role which has been at the heart of several miscarriages of justice, particularly regarding the deaths of babies. The public interest in this issue is immense. Some suggestion of the importance of expert testimony can be gleaned from judges' guidance to juries but it is difficult to know exactly what weight it carries in the ultimate verdict without talking to jurors about their behaviour.

Section 8 effectively prevents this by banning disclosure of "statements made, opinions expressed, arguments advanced or votes cast". There is no way to determine the real impact of expert witnesses unless jurors can disclose their decision-making process which is expressly forbidden in s.8.

The Attorney General's position was that jurors were free to discuss their "general" views about the use of expert witnesses but a purely theoretical discussion is of limited value. Unless the reader can understand how the evidence was applied in the process of reaching a verdict, the reality remains obscure. How is a reader supposed to assess if something unreasonable or unjust is taking place without some concrete examples?

Gavin Millar QC, for *The Times*, argued that s.8 needed to be interpreted in a way compatible with art.10 rights. The purpose of s.8 was to prevent disclosures which interfered with the proper administration of justice, which those in the article did not.

But Lord Justice Pill argued at [29] that the stance of protecting deliberations was already ECHR compliant, based on the 1994 Associated Newspapers case, cited earlier in the chapter, among others. The Commission declared inadmissible a challenge by Associated from the national courts on the basis that s.8 could indeed by regarded as "necessary" in a democratic society with our form of jury trial [63] and was within the State's margin of appreciation.

The foreman, in the course of discussing the part played by the expert testimony, also referred to jurors relying on common sense rather than "correct and logical thinking". This was deemed to be in breach because it effectively revealed the opinions of the other jurors. Lord Justice Pill said at [56]:

> "The foreman should not have disclosed the approach to the evidence of other jurors."

So even seemingly broad comments on the "approach" to decision-making, although not specifying particular arguments by particular jurors, were held to be in breach because they constituted disclosure of the deliberations of a particular jury in a particular case.

Earlier Lord Justice Pill says at [8]:

> "Mr Havers *(for the AG)* did not urge the court to take the view that the case constituted the most serious breach of section 8(1). There had, however, been a significant breach of the important principle of the sanctity of the deliberations of a jury. It is important that the principle be strictly observed."

The reference to "sanctity" in this context does convey a quasi-religious attitude to the role of the jury—suggesting it is now an article of faith rather than a demonstrably-effective provider of sound verdicts. Jury-dispensed justice is something we "believe in" while shying away from the healthy degree of scrutiny that would establish whether it exists. Such a position sustained by ignorance must surely be questionable.

But the strict, literal application of s.8 remains despite the proportionality test demanded by the Human Rights Act. Jury room deliberations are off limits to the media.

---

[63] *Attorney General v Associated Newspapers Ltd* [1994] 2 A.C. 238

10. Section 11 in Practice

Section 11 was designed to protect vulnerable witnesses and was seen as a justifiable retreat from openness in the interests of justice so as to encourage witnesses to come forward. However, this is no guarantee that it will be employed to those ends.

There is a tendency for s.11 to be used out of some kind of sympathy for the defendant so reporters should be in a position to remind the court that "it was not enacted for the comfort of defendants and so cannot be used to exclude, for instance, the address".[64] Any perceived misuse should not go unchallenged.

The Judicial Studies Board guidelines advise:

> "Consistent with the general requirement of open justice, the Court's prime consideration should be the administration of justice and whether it is satisfied that failure to make an order would frustrate or impede it (sympathy for the accused or protection of his business interests against economic damage are not good enough)."[65]

But it would appear that sympathy for the defendant's family is being considered by the courts in these hearings as in many others. Various news organisations, as of May 2007, successfully challenge an order by a judge to protect the identity of an alleged paedophile because of the upset coverage would cause to his child. While one can have every sympathy for the innocent relatives of criminals, this is a route the courts can simply not be allowed to go down unchallenged.

The logic would be that any defendant with a family could be protected from being held publicly accountable for his crimes. This would be a massive retreat from the principles of open justice. Moreover, one of the serious issues underlying criminal behaviour is that many people end up in the dock precisely because they have not considered the consequences of their actions, either for themselves or other people. Allowing them to evade them further by granting anonymity would not be fair but would also not do anything to get them to face up to the reality of their offending. (See also discussion of injunctions in Ch.5 on Privacy.)

Any court contemplating a s.11 order is also invited in the guidelines to consider if a lesser order, such as a postponement order under s.4(2) might suffice. Also, in accordance with *R v Arundel Justices ex parte Westminster Press* [1985],[66] a s.11 order cannot make secret a name that has already been spoken in open court or put on the court list.

---

[64] *R v Evesham Justices, exp McAonagh* [1998] Q.B. 553.
[65] Reporting Restrictions in the Magistrates' Court, Judicial Studies Board.
[66] (43) [1985] 2 All E.R., at p.390.

CHAPTER SUMMARY: CONTEMPT

Nearly every section of the Contempt of Court Act has a bearing on journalists and we have covered most of them here. This is the main statute upholding the art.6 rights of defendants to a fair trial, protecting the integrity of jury trials and limiting "trial by media".

- Material that creates **a substantial risk of serious prejudice** to active proceedings can be in contempt.
- The **Attorney General** can prosecute breaches which are punishable by **fine and/or imprisonment.**
- **Contempt in pre-trial reporting**
  - When reporting crime, be aware of when a case is "active" for contempt.
  - While active do NOT make reference to a suspect's **previous convictions** or run **photographs.** Such material can be highly prejudicial and is high risk.
  - Some background or witness material may be run at the time of the crime being committed which although potentially prejudicial can rely on the **"fade factor".** This is medium risk material.
  - General "common ground" information about the crime and the victim which does not point the finger at the suspect is safe.
  - **Police appeals** for wanted suspects, even if including previous convictions and photographs, are safe for the duration of the hunt if run in **reasoned terms.**
- **Contempt at trial**
  - Prejudicial material run during a jury trial, other than a fair and accurate report of the proceedings, is very high risk, particularly pictures and previous convictions but less damaging material too. Do not produce material or link to it in archives for the duration of a trial.
  - If jury exposure to prejudicial reports causes a trial to collapse, the media can be made to pick up the bill for the wasted court time under the Courts Act 2003.
- **Postponement orders Section 4(2)**
  - These orders are designed to protect defendants in linked trials so that material from one does not prejudice the jury in the next.
  - S.4(2) states: "In any such proceedings the court may, where it appears to be necessary for avoiding a substantial risk of prejudice to the administration of justice in those proceedings, or in any other proceedings pending or imminent, order that the publication of any report of the proceedings, or any part of the proceedings, be postponed for such period as the court thinks necessary for that purpose."
  - Orders made for any other reasons should be challenged.
  - Any departures from the principle of open justice under any

sections of the Contempt of Court Act should be limited to the minimum absolutely necessary to achieve the required protection of the administration of justice.

- **Discussion of public affairs Section 5**
  - This clause is designed to allow the free flow of discussion on issues despite the simultaneous progress of various trials related to similar matters. So for instance, a feature on rape in a regional newspaper might unwittingly pose the same questions facing a jury in a local Crown Court trial. The protection is vital to avoid accusations of contempt.
  - S.5 states: "A publication made as or as part of a discussion in good faith of public affairs or other matters of general public interest is not to be treated as a contempt of court under the strict liability rule if the risk of impediment or prejudice to particular legal proceedings is merely incidental to the discussion."
  - S.5 provides a reliable defence as long as its use is not disingenuous.
  - Never link such discussion explicitly to an "active" trial or the defence will be lost.
- **Juries Section 8**
  - The judicial system is very protective of juries and will push for prosecutions for breaches of s.8.
  - S.8 states: "..it is a contempt of court to obtain, disclose or solicit any particulars of **statements made, opinions expressed, arguments advanced or votes cast** by members of a jury in the course of their deliberations in any legal proceedings".
  - Do not approach jurors when covering court.
- **Prohibition orders Section 11**
  - These allow details such as a witnesses name and/or address to be withheld in the interests of justice.
  - They are not designed "for the comfort or protection" of defendants.
  - The requirements are quite onerous and courts have a tendency to overuse at the behest of defence counsel.
  - Be prepared to challenge.

CHAPTER 5: PRIVACY

PART ONE: PRIVACY AND CONFIDENTIALITY

So where does the law currently stand in respect of protecting personal privacy? When does an individual have a "reasonable expectation of privacy?" This latter question is critical because if answered positively then the claimant's art.8 rights are engaged. Article 8 of the European Convention on Human Rights states:

1. Everyone has the right to respect for his private and family life, his home and his correspondence.
2. There shall be no interference by a public authority with the exercise of this right except such as is in accordance with the law and is necessary in a democratic society in the interests of national security, public safety or the economic wellbeing of the country, for the prevention of disorder or crime, for the protection of health or morals, or for the protection of the rights and freedoms of others.

It then becomes obvious that the exercise of any rights under art.8 is inevitably going to result in conflict with the exercise by the press of its art.10 rights to freedom of expression. One is then entering into the realms of "parallel analysis" to decide which right should prevail over the other. One of the key issues from the media's viewpoint is whether there is a public interest justification that will override the claimant's attempt to keep information private. On occasions, the more lurid revelations of a personal nature will go hand in hand with revelations about abuse of position or resources and a conflict of interest.

The most obvious example is when a senior politician is exposed having an affair. David Blunkett, when Home Secretary, was revealed to have had an affair with Kimberly Fortier, a married woman. The press were able to justify bringing the relationship to the public's attention because it was alleged that he had abused his position in helping Ms Fortier to obtain a visa for her nanny and using taxpayers' money on train travel for his mistress. If there is an obvious public interest element then the press is in a strong position.

However, this kind of situation raises the question: Should personal details remain secret and only the "public interest" element be reported? This may appear the obvious solution but of course, the story would be virtually meaningless unless the press could provide the full context. And, of course, it would not sell as many newspapers if the identity of the participants were to be kept secret.

Also of importance is the answer to the question: Is any or all of the information that the press wishes to publish already in the public domain? If so then there will be little or nothing to protect by way of injunction.

Another issue to ponder at this preliminary stage is that, in stark contrast to the failure to recognise a tort of privacy, English law has, since 1849, provided an *equitable* remedy for breach of confidence. It will be obvious that much of any "kiss and tell" content will be derived from a relationship that from the very outset the parties wished to keep secret, usually from their partners. It follows that if a relationship were to break down and one party wished to sell their story to a newspaper the other may resort to an action for breach of confidence in order to prevent intimate details entering the public domain. Therefore art.10 rights of the press may be pitted not only against the claimant's art.8 rights but also against any right to confidence.

1. Background Information

English common law has never recognised a tort of privacy and there has certainly been limited government enthusiasm for putting forward legislation on the topic.

The fact that English law did not recognise a tort of privacy was graphically illustrated when the Court of Appeal failed to identify a "privacy" remedy for Gorden Kaye in his dispute with the Sport Newspaper over being "ambushed" in his hospital bed whilst recovering from a serious accident.[1] Lord Justice Gildwell left no room for doubt as to the current position within this jurisdiction:

"It is well known that in English law there is no right to privacy and accordingly there is no right of action for breach of a person's privacy. The facts of the present case are a graphic illustration of the desirability of Parliament considering whether and in what circumstances statutory provision can be made to protect the privacy of individuals."

Other judges supported this assessment of the law. Bingham L.J. said that the case highlighted the failure of both the common law and statute to "protect in an effective way the personal privacy of individual citizens."

[1] [1991] F.S.R. 62.

In 1991 the Human Rights Act was a long way from the statute book. With its introduction into law in October 2000 a new dimension was introduced into the battle to assist individuals in seeking to protect their "privacy" from unwanted intrusion from the media, particularly the tabloid media. The Act ensured that provisions of the European Convention on Human Rights would be brought under the scrutiny of UK judges for the first time in legal history. This fact has had a profound effect over the past decade in helping to define the protection on offer to claimants who seek injunctions or occasionally damages against the media for what is incorrectly called breach of privacy. The remedies available result from alleged media *misuse of private information.*

The background to this statement of principle is to be found in the leading case of *Campbell v Mirror Group Newspapers Ltd* [2004].[2] The newspaper had surreptitiously taken photographs of supermodel Naomi Campbell leaving a branch of Narcotics Anonymous. She brought a claim for damages against the newspaper alleging wrongful use of private information an action that had to be based upon the only remedy available: breach of confidence. Lord Nicholls who delivered the leading speech summed up the legal position at the time with these words:

> "In this country unlike the United States of America, there is no over-arching, all embracing cause of action for 'invasion of privacy.'. . . the present case concerns one aspect of invasion of privacy: wrongful disclosure of private information."[3]

He goes on to point out the fundamental nature of the clash between two articles of the European Convention, the right to respect for family, home and correspondence (art.8) and the right to freedom of expression (art.10). It will be recalled that in the case of *Reynolds v Times Newspapers* [1999] Lord Nicholls had referred to freedom of expression as a "fundamental right."[4] He points out, and this is still the case, that neither right takes automatic precedence over the other. However important freedom of expression is to a modern democratic state, privacy also ". . . lies at the heart of liberty in a modern state. A proper degree of privacy is essential for the wellbeing and development of an individual. And restraints imposed on government to pry into the lives of the citizen go to the essence of a democratic state."[5]

The action for breach of confidence has its foundations in the improper use of information disclosed by one person to another in confidence. A key question to be answered was whether the information possessed the characteristics of being of a confidential nature. This in turn was based upon whether a legally recognised relationship existed

---

[2] [2004] UKHL 22.
[3] Paras 11 & 12.
[4] [1999] 3 W.L.R. 1010.
[5] per Lord Nicholls at para.12.

between the parties. This was clearly a constraining factor preventing
the development of the law beyond those involved in such relationships. In *Stephens v Avery* [1988][6] the Court of Appeal removed this
restricting factor and emphasised that in future a duty of confidence
would be created whenever the recipient of information knew or ought
to have known what was reasonably to be regarded as confidential.[7]
Lord Nicholls in the Campbell case was adamant that:

> "Information about an individual's private life would not in ordinary
> usage, be called 'confidential.' The more natural description today
> is that such information is private. The essence of the tort is better
> encapsulated now as misuse of private information."[8]

Lord Nicholls' conclusion was that the time had come to recognise
that the values enshrined in arts 8 and 10 were now part of the cause
of action for breach of confidence. This perhaps was the inevitable
conclusion given that the case was presented throughout exclusively
on the basis of breach of confidence. In other words the competing
claims of arts. 8 and 10 were to be assessed as part of an action for
misuse of private information in the context of an action for breach of
confidence.

In any challenge to the media's actions in exposing the private lives
of individuals the label "misuse of private information" is probably
an adequate form of words to describe the nature of the revelations.
However the words are not wide enough to describe other aspects of a
breach of art.8 rights, for example, behaviour that causes humiliation or
distress such as constantly being followed by the paparazzi in search of
that "exclusive" photograph or to use Lord Nicholls' own example taken
from the Wainwright case[9]—being stripsearched.

Lord Nicholls alluded to the possibility that the recognition that an
action for breach of confidence could now incorporate an assessment
of art.8 of the European Convention on Human Rights might not be the
end of the story. Referring to the case of *Hoskins v Runting* [2004][10] he
said that "... protection of various aspects of privacy is a fast developing
area of the law, here and in some other common law jurisdictions ... in
this country development of the law has been spurred by enactment of
the Human Rights Act 1998."

In deciding whether a cause of action for breach of confidence based
upon misuse of private information was to be progressed Lord Nicholls
considered that there should be a preliminary to be decided. He asked
". . . what was the ambit of an individual's private life in particular

---

[6] [1988] 2 All E.R. 477.
[7] See Lord Goff of Chieveley in *Attorney-General v Guardian Newspapers Ltd* (No2) [1990]
1A.C. 109.
[8] per Lord Nicholls at para.14
[9] *Wainwright v Home Office* [2003] 3 W.L.R. 1137.
[10] [2004] NZCA 34.

circumstances . . .?"[11] He answered his own question by declaring that a "threshold test" should be applied and that should involve deciding whether the ". . . *person in question had a reasonable expectation of privacy.*"[12] If the answer to the question is "yes" the case can proceed to trial or settlement out of court. If "no" the case ends at that point. Therefore to take the Campbell facts as an example it was decided that she had a reasonable expectation of privacy when visiting Narcotics Anonymous and was photographed leaving the building. If the photographs had been taken without her knowledge a few minutes later when she was in a public place then the decision would in all likelihood have been different. However such photographs would have been of little value to the newspaper as they would not have proved that she had visited the treatment centre, i.e. supported the print version of the story. The question in the aftermath of the *Campbell* decision was whether there would remain one single cause of action, i.e. breach of confidence or whether as the law developed a second cause of action would be needed reflecting the head-on clash between art.8 and art.10 rights.

This was alluded to by Lord Phillips M.R. in *Douglas & Others v Hello Ltd & Others* [2005].[13] He posed the question: What is the United Kingdom's Convention obligation in respect of privacy? At the heart of the question is whether a state is required under the Convention to provide a private remedy against private actors, as opposed to state interference with a person's private life. The answer for Lord Phillips was provided by the decision of the European Court of Human Rights in the case of *von Hannover v Germany* [2004].[14] As Lord Phillips said:

> "It follows that the ECtHR has recognised an obligation on member states to protect one individual from an unjustified invasion of private life by another individual and an obligation on the courts of a member state to interpret legislation in a way that will achieve that result."[15]

The position in 2005 appears to have been that the cause of action is breach of confidence but that "within" that action the courts should:

> ". . . develop the action for breach of confidence in such a manner as will give effect to both Article 8 and Article 10 rights . . ."[16]

However the Master of the Rolls concluded that it could not be concluded that "we find it satisfactory to be required to shoe-horn within the cause of action of breach of confidence claims for publication of unauthorised photographs of a private occasion." The issue in the

---

[11] at para.21.
[12] at para.21.
[13] [2005] EWCA 595.
[14] [2004] ECHR 294.
[15] [2004] ECHR 294 at para.49.
[16] [2004] ECHR 294 at para.53.

Douglas case was the unauthorised photography at their wedding. The couple had taken the whole of a floor at the Plaza Hotel in New York and had strict security measures in place to ensure that only invited guests were allowed in. As the court implicitly acknowledged if one where pinning a notice at the entrance to the floor it would in all probability read "Private Function" not "Confidential Function."

In *Ash v McKennitt* [2006][17] Buxton L.J. summarised the position in respect of what he called the "taxonomy of the law of privacy and confidentiality."[18] The following are what he considered to be "straight-forward matters":

> "There is no English domestic law tort of invasion of privacy. In developing a right to protect private information, including the implementation in the English courts of articles 8 and 10 the European Convention on Human Rights, the English courts have to proceed through the tort of breach of confidence, into which the jurisprudence of Articles 8 and 10 has to be 'shoe-horned'."

That feeling of discomfort arises from the action for breach of confidence being employed where there was no pre-existing relationship of confidence between the parties, but the "confidence" arose from the defendant having acquired by unlawful or surreptitious means information that he should have known he was not free to use.

At least the verbal difficulty referred to in footnote 3 has been avoided by the rechristening of the tort as misuse of private information.

The complaint here is of what might be called old-fashioned breach of confidence by way of conduct inconsistent with a pre-existing relationship, rather than simply the purloining of private information.[19]

So within the ambit of the action for breach of confidence the courts have "absorbed" the rights which arts 8 and 10 of the Convention seek to protect.[20] It must be remembered that despite the wording of art.8 that suggests the protection offered should be against state intervention into private life European jurisprudence has resulted in the acceptance that individuals can complain about breaches of private and family life committed by individuals and private organisations such as newspapers. Article 8 is deemed to impose not just negative but also positive obligations on the state.[21]

At this point in the chronology the language of the law became a little confused. The cause of action still lay in the action for breach of confidence but the essential approach to determining the issue stems from answering the question "Was there a reasonable expectation of

---

[17] [2006] EWCA Civ 1714.
[18] [2006] EWCA Civ 1714 at para.8.
[19] [2006] EWCA Civ 1714 at para.8.
[20] *Lord Woolf in A v B plc* [2003] Q.B. 194.
[21] See *Marckx v Belgium* (1979) 2 EHRR 330 and Buxton L.J. in *Ash v McKennitt* [2006] EWCA Civ 1714 at para.9.

privacy?" Eady J. put it this way in *Lord Browne of Madingley v Associated Newspapers* [2007]:[22]

"It has long been recognised that intimate personal relationships, including those of a homosexual nature, can in themselves give rise to obligations of confidence (and correspondingly to a "reasonable expectation of privacy") in respect of information gained in the course of them."

In December 2010 Eady J. described a claim in these terms:

"The claim is based upon apprehended infringements of rights of confidence and/or privacy based upon Article 8 of the European Convention on Human Rights and Fundamental Freedoms."[23]

In the Lord Browne case the Court of Appeal[24] acknowledged there had been "considerable" development of the principles applicable to cases of this kind and went on to agree with the analysis conducted stated by Buxton L.J. in the *Ash v McKennitt* case.[25] It will be clear that in many cases such as *Browne* and *McKennitt* a breach of trust is evident.

That was also the case when the Prince of Wales took action against *Associated Newspapers* in 2006 to prevent information in his private diaries from being published.[26] Information from one of his journals related to the time he represented the Queen at the handover of Hong Kong to China and had already been published by the *Mail on Sunday*. The *Mail* had copies of eight other journals written by the Prince and he commenced legal action to obtain an injunction to prevent the material from entering the public domain.

It transpired that copies of the journals had been copied by a secretary in his private office and supplied to the *Mail on Sunday* through an intermediary. As the case report indicates "she had given the usual undertaking of confidentiality . . . and had not been authorised to make typed copies of the journals or to remove photocopies of them from the Private Office."[27] The Prince obtained his injunction despite the robust denial of wrongdoing by the newspaper. It had contended that the information in the Hong Kong journal was not confidential and there was no reasonable expectation that it would be kept from the public. This argument was based on the fact that the contents did not amount to "intimate personal information . . . but information relating to the

[22] [2007] EWHC 202 (QB) at para.11.
[23] per Eady in *CDE & Another v MGN Ltd & Another* [2010] EWHC 3308.
[24] [2007] EWCA Civ 295.
[25] [2006] EWCA Civ 1714 at para.8.
[26] [2006] EWHC 522 (Ch).
[27] [2006] EWHC 522 (Ch) at para.50.

claimant's public life and to a 'zone of his life' which he had previously put in the public domain."[28]

The "trust" factor may be established through the creation and maintenance of a relationship or through a contractual obligation or presumably friendship that has endured for some time. Other factors may impinge and the breach of trust may not necessarily bring the expected results but it is a reasonable "foundation" principle upon which to base an argument that there has been a breach of confidentiality or misuse of private information.

An example of where a breach of trust/confidentiality failed to result in an injunction was the Beckhams' attempt to obtain an 11th hour injunction to prevent the *News of the World* publishing information about the couple's relationship supplied by their former nanny, Abbie Gibson. The *5rb.com* website reported that this was due to the judge accepting that he was not confident that they would ultimately be successful in securing an injunction at trial because of the newspaper's public interest defence and the fact that the Beckhams were not averse to putting information about themselves in the public domain. The public interest defence was widely assumed to relate to their projection of a "false image" as a "golden couple" when according to their nanny in fact their marriage was at breaking point.[29]

According to Duncan Lamont, who was at the time a partner in the Media Group at City legal practice Charles Russell, the advice to journalists who are planning to publish in breach of a confidentiality agreement is: "It is worth . . . having material already in the public domain at their fingertips so that it can be shown to a judge or even read to him or her down a phone line." He goes on to make the point: "The public interest argument can be harder to run, save in the most unusual circumstances, than showing that the material (or the relevant and most important bits of it) are already in the public domain."[30]

It may be opportune at this point to note that judges do pay serious attention to how much or how little claimants have utilised the media to promote self-image. The more this is done the less likely it is that judges will regard the legal action as being a serious attempt to protect privacy rights as opposed for example to protect the value of their image rights or commercial or sponsorship deals. In *X & Y v Person's Unknown* [2006][31] Eady J. suggested there should be a distinction between those who are in the public eye and those who may be classed as *publicity seekers* while recognising that occasionally the two will overlap. Someone in the public eye does not necessarily "waive entitlement to privacy with regard to, say, intimate personal relationships or the conduct of a private life generally." In this case, the judge concluded that X, the

---

[28] [2006] EWHC 522 (Ch) at para.7.
[29] *Daily Telegraph,* April 25, 2005.
[30] Quoted in the Press Gazette, May 13, 2005.
[31] [2006] EWHC 2783 (QB).

model, was not a person who "willingly sets out for self-promotion to live her private life in the public eye."

Eady J. is a most experienced media law judge. He states in *X & Y* that there ought to be a distinction drawn between ". . . *matters which are naturally accessible to outsiders and those which are known only to the protagonists.*" The fact, for example, that the parties are living separate lives or are regarded by friends as "no longer an item" is hardly likely to result in art.8 being engaged in respect of those particular pieces of information.

The information that a claimant wishes to protect should be specifically defined. At this early stage in proceedings, a court will also wish to consider the s.12 (Human Rights Act) issue of whether it is likely that, if the case were to proceed to a full trial, the claimant would be successful. Newspapers for their part will no doubt resort to their electronic archives to "dredge up" everything possible to endeavour to prove to a court that "he or she has indeed become public property." From the claimant's point of view there should be a full and frank disclosure. That is not to say that every possible item discovered in the newspaper archives must be addressed. It is suggested that the claimant's lawyers should engage in a search of the internet as a means of second-guessing what the defendant's lawyers are likely to rely upon. In this way the claimant's lawyers should be able to defeat a claim of non-disclosure by the defendants.

The judge should then decide whether, in light of all the circumstances there has been a "genuine waiver" of privacy on the part of the applicant.

This approach was evident in the *McKennitt* case when the judge accepted evidence that despite having a public profile she closely guarded her private life. So at press conferences it was always made clear that while she was willing to discuss her latest record or her career she would not answer questions about her private life.

A more recent example is the case of John Terry[32] the Chelsea football Club captain who in January 2010 applied for an interim injunction to prevent rumours about his private life being published by the media. An interesting aspect of this case was that no notice had been given to any respondent, the claimant contenting himself with the assertion that any order was likely to be served on media third parties although the *News of the World* was named in the evidence.

It could be argued that a PR rather than a legal response to the rumours that were circulating would have been preferable. The legal action drew the media's attention to the application and the rest, as they say, is history!

In such a situation the defences of any potential newspaper respondent will not be heard. The judge refused the application for an injunction for a number of reasons. First that there was only a "threat" to publish information about the relationship and on the evidence

---

[32] *Terry (Formerly LNS) v Persons Unknown (Rev1)* [2010] EWHC 119 (QB).

available the judge was not satisfied that at a full hearing the applicant would succeed. Secondly it was judged that the application was more to do with protecting the applicant's reputation in particular with sponsors and this brought him within the rule in *Bonnard v Perryman* which precludes the granting of an injunction in favour of damages being an adequate "after the event" remedy.

What of the "relationship" between Terry and a team mate's former partner? The judge was not satisfied that there had been a breach of any duty of confidence owed to Terry nor did he believe that the applicant was likely to succeed in defeating a public interest defence. This would be based on the public domain argument that Terry had attracted publicity over a number of years and much of it was adverse to his image. The *Daily Telegraph* reported that he had "previously faced allegations of womanising, violent conduct, drunkenness and gambling" as well as reporting that before his marriage in 2007 he ". . . faced public allegations of affairs with no less than eight women."[33]

While the case does not create any new legal principles it does illustrate the need for compelling evidence to be presented at any application for an interim injunction. The judge was clearly underwhelmed by the fact there was no respondent in the case. The presence of a respondent will ensure that a judge is able to make an informed decision on the merits of any application. It was commenced on the basis of a "belief" that a newspaper was about to publish information about the applicant's private life. That would suggest that there was insufficient evidence of a real threat to publish and therefore it is likely that any application presented to the court on this basis is doomed to failure.

Lawyers advising clients will also need to determine on the evidence available whether the case is one about protecting reputation as opposed to the intimate or personal details of a person's private life. If the evidence, as in this case, tends towards the protection of reputation because, for example, of existing sponsorship deals then because of the prior restraint rule it will be almost impossible to obtain an injunction. In privacy cases damages are usually the least appealing of remedies available to an applicant. An injunction is the key remedy. In respect of breach of confidence application, the court has to consider the wording of s.12 of the Human Rights Act 1998. Under s.12(3), it has to be determined, in respect of each piece of information that is the subject matter of the application whether, if the case were to go forward to a full trial, the applicant is *likely* to establish that the publication will be allowed.

There is no one legal definition of the word "likely". Lord Nicholls considered the matter in *Cream Holdings v Banerjee* [2004].[34] The word should be given a "flexible" meaning depending on the circumstances. There can be "no single, rigid standard governing all applications for interim restraint orders." The threshold test would appear to be whether the applicant's prospects of success are "sufficiently favourable" to

---

[33] *Daily Telegraph,* January 30, 2010.
[34] [2004] UKHL 44.

justify the order being made. Courts should be "exceedingly slow" to make interim restraint orders if the applicant "has not satisfied the court he will probably (more likely than not) succeed at the trial."

The Court of Appeal in *Browne* suggested the following approach:

1. Is art.8 engaged? In other words is there a reasonable expectation of privacy from the claimant's viewpoint?
2. Is art.10 engaged?
3. Has the applicant satisfied the court that if the case went to trial he is likely to establish that publication should not be allowed?

The decision-making process is far from simple and is fraught with uncertainty. Eady J. put it this way in *CDE & Another v MGN Ltd & Another* [2010]:

"This is a jurisdiction in which the decisions to be made are rarely straightforward . . . Parliament has clearly imposed upon judges, through s.12 (3) of the Human Rights Act 1998, the burden of deter-mining at this preliminary stage, almost always on incomplete and partial evidence, whether an injunction is likely to be granted at trial. Guidance has been given by the House of Lords in *Cream Holdings Ltd v Banerjee* [2005]! AC 253, but that does not make it any easier. There are no hard and fast rules. It is a question of weighing up competing Convention rights and forming a judgment on the unique facts of each case."[35]

So there we have it. Guidance can be given and precedents set but the task on a case-by-case basis in deciding whether to grant an interim injunction is rarely straightforward. One of the most important things from an applicant's viewpoint is having notice that the media outlet is about to publish personal or intimate details. If an injunction is the major weapon in an applicant's armoury then it follows that prior noti-fication should be given. However that is not the current legal position and editors are under no legal obligation to provide "targets" with the information that their activities are about to be spread over the Sunday tabloids. All of which leads us on to Max Mosley.

2. Mosley and Prior Notification

The front page headline in the *News of the World*'s edition of March 30, 2008 blazed: "F1 BOSS HAS SICK NAZI ORGY WITH 5 HOOKERS." The story of which Max Mosley had no prior notice concerned events

---

[35] [2010] EWHC 3308 (QB) at para.2.

that took place at what he claimed was "party" at which the participants engaged in sado-masochistic practices. Never prone to understatement the *News of the World* referred to it as an "orgy."

The newspaper's headline one week later was: "MOSLEY HOOKER TELLS ALL: MY NAZI ORGY WITH F1 BOSS."

Max Mosley is the son of Oswald Mosley who led the fascist movement in the UK in the 1930s. The action brought by Mosley against the *News of the World* was expressed in conventional terms: For breach of confidence and/or the unauthorised disclosure of personal information. In other words, that his rights to privacy protected by art.8 of the European Convention on Human Rights had been infringed. The major arguments on behalf of the claimant were straightforward:

- There was a pre-existing relationship of confidentiality between the participants. They took part in the activities willingly and there was an understanding, presumably unwritten, that none of them would reveal what had taken place.
- The activities took place on private property.
- There was nothing illegal about the activities.
- All the participants were adults who had freely consented to take part. There was no element of exploitation.
- That the female participant (referred to throughout the case as Woman E) had breached trust and given that she was under contract to the *News of the World* to obtain video footage of the activities the journalist who wrote the story must have appreciated that she was breaching trust.
- There was no public interest that would justify publishing the story. The allegation that the participants were engaged in a "Nazi Orgy" was not borne out by the facts. In other words the *News of the World* justification for publishing was a "contrived" rather than "genuine" public interest reason.

Immediately after the publication of the article and the release of an edited version of the video online, Mosley tried to obtain an interim injunction preventing the further dissemination of the online material. This was denied on the basis of the "public domain" argument when it was revealed that in the 24 hours since its release the video had been viewed 1.4 million times. [36]

It was at that point that Mosley decided to bring the action for breach of confidence against the newspaper. The case was decided in July 2008[37] and the court decisively rejected the defendant's arguments that the publication was in the public interest. The court held there was no evidence to show that the role play had been intended to mimic Nazi prison camp behaviour. The activities were labelled "unconventional" by the judge but that did not mean there was any public interest in

---

[36] [2008] EWHC 687 (QB) See below p.225 for discussion on the Public Domain argument.
[37] [2008] EWHC 1777 (QB).

making the recordings and then publishing extracts on the *News of the World* website. Mosley was awarded £60,000 in damages and his costs against the newspaper amounting to some £500,000.

The Mosley case is instructive for a number of reasons particularly as it illustrates the approach to be adopted in "privacy" cases. Eady J. commenced his analysis by referring to "the new methodology." This term has gained credence since the decision of the House of Lords in *Re S (A Child)*.[38]

It was described in the following terms by the President of the Family Division of the High Court in the case of *A Local Authority v W* [2005][39]:

"The exercise to be performed is one of parallel analysis in which the starting point is presumptive parity, in that neither Article has precedence over or 'trumps' the other. The exercise of parallel analysis requires the court to examine the justification for interfering with each right and the issue of proportionality is to be considered in respect of each. It is not a mechanical exercise to be decided upon the basis of rival generalities. An intense focus upon the comparative importance of the specific rights being claimed in the individual case is necessary before the ultimate balancing test in terms of proportionality is carried out."

Eady J. described it in these terms in the Mosley case having accepted that the "first hurdle" of establishing a reasonable expectation of privacy had been overcome:

"... it is now clear that the court is required to carry out the next step of weighing the relevant competing Convention rights in the light of the intense focus upon the individual facts of the case ... It was expressly recognised that no one Convention right takes automatic precedence over another ... In order to determine which should take precedence, in the particular circumstances, it is necessary to examine the facts closely as revealed in the evidence at the trial and to decide whether ... some countervailing consideration of public interest may be said to justify any intrusion which has taken place. This is integral to what has been called 'the new methodology'." [40]

That "intense focus" came down in Mosley's favour. Yet it was something of a pyrrhic victory. Mosley had failed to keep private that which all the participants had regarded as a confidential activity with a number of negative consequences in terms of his marriage and family life. The remedy that most claimants will seek is an injunction to prevent the information entering into the public domain. That has occasionally involved applications for "super injunctions" and most recently the

---

[38] [2004] UKHL 47.
[39] [2005] EWHC 1564 (Fam) at para.53.
[40] [2008] EWHC 1777 at paras 10-11.

request that a claimant's identity should be kept anonymous as well as protecting the information claimed to be personal and therefore private.

Max Mosley in appealing against the decision in *Masley v UK* [2010] ECHR 774, arguing that UK law is deficient in that there is no legal obligation placed on editors to reveal to the person whose private life is to be exposed to the public that publication is imminent. To put the issue in simple terms, it would be for the court to resolve any conflict between art.8 and 10 rights and not an editor of a tabloid newspaper whose motivation, ostensibly in the public interest, may well be purely commercial. So following this logic a court could only reach a conclusion if the "target" had the opportunity to place the issue before the court before any potential damage occured, i.e. before publication.

The media unsurprisingly maintained the right to freedom of expression could be whittled away by judicial decision making if there was a legal obligation for prior notification. One counter argument is that if the media is convinced of the strength of its public interest justification (surely its only defence if a case comes to trial after the event) then it has nothing to fear. The "target's" legal representatives will surely advise that commencing a legal action could well be counter-productive, not to mention expensive, if the evidence available tended to support the newspaper's case. In evidence provided to the House of Commons Culture, Media and Sport Select Committee in 2009 it was conceded by the Chairman of the Press Complaints Commission Editor's Code Committee that prior notice was given in virtually every instance.[41] Why not in the other 1 percent? The reason is obvious because the editor is aware that an interim injunction would in all likelihood be granted with the possible consequence that the story would never be told to a wider audience and a commercial opportunity lost.

In practice it would mean that, consistent with the principles of responsible journalism, the media would have to take all reasonable steps to notify the individual.

Is the media's fear justified that art.10 rights would be diminished as a result of the appeal finding in Mosley's favour? It could be argued that the Human Rights Act already sends a clear message to judges about the importance of freedom of expression through the medium of s.12:

(2) If the person against whom the application for relief is made ("the respondent") is neither present nor represented, no such relief is to be granted unless the court is satisfied—

    a) that the applicant has taken all practicable steps to notify the respondent; or

    b) that there are compelling reasons why the respondent should not be notified.

---

[41] Paul Dacre, "Prior notice given ninety-nine times out of a hundred."

(3) No such relief is to be granted so as to restrain publication before trial unless the court is satisfied that the applicant is likely to establish that publication should not be allowed.

(4) The court must have particular regard to the importance of the Convention right to freedom of expression and, where the proceedings relate to material which the respondent claims, or which appears to the court, to be journalistic, literary or artistic material (or to conduct connected with such material), to—

  (a) the extent to which—
      (i) the material has, or is about to, become available to the public; or
      (ii) it is, or would be, in the public interest for the material to be published;
  (b) any relevant privacy code.

The section applies when a court is considering whether to grant relief that might affect the exercise of art.10 rights. First if action is to be commenced against the newspaper then s.12(2) obliges the applicant to notify the respondent that the action is due to commence. It seems somewhat ironic that there is a legal obligation imposed upon the applicant to notify yet there is no corresponding legal duty on the media to inform a potential applicant that his private life is to be laid bare, possibly for the most flimsy of public interest justifications.

The court has then under s.12(3) to be convinced that the applicant is likely to establish that publication should not be allowed. This could be very difficult given the sometimes 11th hour application to the court. As Lord Nicholls clearly stated in the *Cream Holdings* case:

> "Its principal purpose was to buttress the protection afforded to freedom of speech at the interlocutory stage. It sought to do so by setting a higher threshold for the grant of interlocutory injunctions against the media ..."[42]

So what is the current position and what will an applicant have to establish to obtain an interim restraint order against the media? Lord Nicholls again:

> "Section 12(3) makes the likelihood of success at the trial an essential element in the court's consideration of whether to make an interim order ... There can be no single, rigid standard governing all applications for interim restraint orders ... the court is not to make an interim restraint order unless satisfied the applicant's prospects of success at the trial are sufficiently favourable to justify such an order being made in the particular circumstances of the case."[43]

---

[42] [2004] UKHL 44 at para.15.
[43] [2004] UKHL 44 at para.22.

In assessing the meaning of the words "sufficiently favourable" the general approach should be that courts will be exceedingly slow to make interim restraint orders where the applicant has not satisfied the court he will probably (more likely than not) succeed at the trial.[44] This approach was followed by Mann J. in *BKM Ltd v British Broadcasting Corporation* [2009][45] when the applicant care home company sought an interim injunction preventing the respondents from broadcasting a programme dealing with the regulation of care homes in Wales. Its theme, unsurprisingly, was that regulation was not particularly effective. The producers of the programme wished to illustrate this by reference to the Glyndwr Nursing Home, owned by BKM Ltd, that had received criticism from the inspectorate because of a number of shortcomings in the standard of care offered to residents. In order to gather evidence to support the contention a reporter gained employment at the home and conducted some secret filming.

The judge, after referring to the conflict of arts 8 and 10, dealt with the obligations imposed by s.12(3). He said:

"I therefore have to conduct such an exercise, but with a very firm eye on section 12(3). I have to determine not only how the competition between the rights is to be resolved for present purposes, but also to do so with an eye to determining whether an injunction would be granted to restrain the broadcast at a trial. An injunction should not be granted unless I am satisfied that at a trial it would be likely to be determined (in the sense of more probable than not - see *Cream Holdings v Banerjee*) that the broadcast should not be allowed."[46]

The application failed. The case would seem to support two propositions. Firstly, that the approach to the resolution of an application for an interim injunction is still that established in the *Cream Holdings* case. Secondly, that judges are well aware of their obligations under s.12(3). That may be of some comfort to the mass-market tabloids as they await the decision in the *Mosley* case but even with this awareness the recent cases have rarely gone in the media's favour.[47]

Finally under s.12(4) the court has to have particular regard to the right of freedom of expression and any public interest argument put forward by the respondent or any relevant privacy code. In the case of the print media this is the Press Complaints Commission Code of Practice and in particular cl.3 which states:

"i) Everyone is entitled to respect for his or her private and family life, home, health and correspondence, including digital communications.

---

[44] [2004] UKHL 44 at para 22.
[45] [2009] EWHC 3151 (Ch).
[46] [2009] EWHC 3151 (Ch) at para.23.
[47] See for example *AMM v HXW* [2010] EWHC 2457 at para.17.

ii) Editors will be expected to justify intrusions into any individual's private life without consent. Account will be taken of the complainant's own public disclosures of information.

iii) It is unacceptable to photograph individuals in private places without their consent.

Note: Private places are public or private property where there is a reasonable expectation of privacy."[48]

The applicable principles have been frequently re-iterated in European Human rights case law. In *Armonas v Lithuania* [2008][49] the European Court of Human Rights said that while the objective underpinning art.8 is "essentially that of protecting the individual against arbitrary interference by public authorities, it does not merely compel the State to abstain from such interference . . . there may be *positive* obligations inherent in the effective respect for private and family life. These obligations may involve the *adoption of measures designed to secure their right even in the sphere of the relations between individuals.*"

The duty of the press is seen as to ". . . impart information and ideas on matters of public interest" but recognises that a "fundamental distinction needs to be made between reporting facts—even if controversial—capable of contributing to a debate in a democratic society and making tawdry allegations about an individual's private life . . ."[50]

Even if the European Court of Human Rights allows Mosley's appeal that will be the start not the end of the matter. The government would then be obliged to frame a new law giving effect to the judgment. We are already witnessing some interesting debate about the balance between privacy and free expression and, a vociferous media campaign that questions the fundamentals of the Human Rights Act.

3. The Public Domain Proviso

As alluded to earlier, if a person is in the public eye, then it is more than likely that the media will have a plethora of information, both recent and from the past, stored away for future use. Therefore, if information is in the public domain, the press needs to know exactly what they are not permitted to publish. Any injunction should therefore include what has become known as a Public Domain Proviso. As Eady J. said in *A v B* [2005][51]:

---

[48] Press Complaints Commissions: Editors Code of Practice 2011. Available at *www.pcc. org.uk*
[49] [2008] ECHR 1526 at para.36.
[50] [2008] ECHR 1526 at para.39.
[51] [2005] EWHC 1651 (QB).

"An important consideration when assessing the background . . . is that the claimant has himself made public through the media a great deal of information that might usually be considered as falling within the protection afforded to private or personal information . . ."[52]

From the media's perspective, knowing what is or is not in the public domain is crucial when deciding what to publish without fear of breaching any injunction that may exist.

Hence, a court must make it absolutely clear when including such a proviso in the injunction. That had been one problem stemming from the interim injunction granted on an *ex parte* basis in the *X & Y* case. (See footnote 31.) It may be that certain pieces of information have reached the public domain but the court believes that its confidentiality has not been lost. This may be true when the internet is used as the medium to disseminate information. Given the vast scale and reach of the internet it may be that the particular information has passed relatively unnoticed. In these circumstances, the court should make it clear that the information is not to be included within the proviso.

In the *X & Y* case, the injunction was against persons unknown. It was argued that this was not "sufficiently certain to identify those who are, and those who are not included within the restrictions." However, the court was prepared to follow the reasoning adopted in *Bloomsbury Publishing Group v News Group Newspapers Ltd* [2003][53] to the effect:

"I can see no injustice to anyone if I make the order . . . but considerable potential for injustice to the claimants if I do not."[54]

The facts that led to the case of *Re Stedman* [2009][55] had provoked extensive media coverage when an under-age girl became a mother. It may be thought there is nothing unusual about that fact in modern day Britain but the media picked up on the allegation that the child's father was only 12 when the child was conceived. He was 13 at the time of the birth. The birth had generated a front page article in the *Sun* newspaper and on its website together with photographs and a video of the "parents" with their new daughter. The story attracted national and international media attention and much national soul searching about pregnancy and sex education for those under the age of consent. The media circus that resulted led the local authority to make the children wards of court.

The local authority asked for a reporting restrictions order. This meant that the judge had to consider the amount of information and images that were already in the public domain. The judge made the order and it contained the "usual public domain exception" so that the order did not restrict:

[52] [2005] EWHC 1651 (QB) at para.16.
[53] [2003] EWHC 1205 (Ch).
[54] [2003] EWHC 1205 (Ch) at para.22 per Sir Andrew Morritt VC.
[55] [2009] EWHC 935 (Fam).

"... publishing information which before the service on that person of this order was already in the public domain in England and Wales as a result of publication by another person in any newspaper, magazine, sound or television broadcast or cable or satellite programme service or on the internet website of a media organisation operating within England and Wales."[56]

Privacy in Public places

Do people have a reasonable expectation of privacy when in a public place, for example, walking down Oxford Street in London? Does it make any difference to the legal position if photographs are taken without the subject's consent? English legal principles and European Human Rights law diverge on this point. The conflict arises as a result of the decisions in the *Campbell v MGN Ltd* [2004][57] and *von Hannover v Germany* [2004].[58] In the former case it will be recalled that the super model Naomi Campbell was photographed without her knowledge as she exited a branch of Narcotics Anonymous. The House of Lords decided by a 3:2 majority that her privacy had been breached in the particular circumstances but there was little support for the proposition that people in public places enjoyed a reasonable expectation of privacy. Baroness Hale put it this way:

"We have not so far held that the mere fact of covert photography is sufficient to make the information contained in the photograph confidential. The activity photographed must be private. If this had been, and had been presented as, a picture of Naomi Campbell going about her business in a public street, there could have been no complaint. She makes a substantial part of her living out of being photographed looking stunning in designer clothing. Readers will obviously be interested to see how she looks if and when she pops out to the shops for a bottle of milk. There is nothing essentially private about that information nor can it be expected to damage her private life. It may not be a high order of freedom of speech but there is nothing to justify interfering with it."[59]

Princess Caroline of Monaco, the wife of Prince Ernst von Hannover, had taken exception over a number of years to photographs of her appearing in German "celebrity" magazines. She was not concerned about images of her attending functions and galas at which she expected to be photographed, but drew the line at photographs of her undertaking "everyday" activities with her family and friends. She tried unsuccessfully to rein in the paparazzi's activities by taking action in

---

[56] [2009] EWHC 935 (Fam) at para.9.
[57] [2004] UKHL 22.
[58] [2004] ECHR 294.
[59] [2004] UKHL 22 at para.154.

the German courts. From there her only recourse was to the European Court of Human Rights.

The question for the court was whether German laws provided adequate protection for her art.8 rights to be upheld. The answer was an emphatic no. It should be remembered that Princess Caroline had no "official" status. She did not represent Monaco and did not succeed as Head of State on the death of her father Prince Rainier. The court had no doubt that her art.8 rights were engaged, i.e. she had a reasonable expectation of privacy. It was noted that the taking of such photographs created a climate of "continual harassment leaving a strong sense of intrusion into private life or even a feeling of persecution."

The taking of such photographs did not contribute to "a debate of general interest." In simple terms, there was no public interest reason to justify such intrusion into her private life. The public had no legitimate interest in knowing anything about her lifestyle, which restaurants she frequented or her whereabouts in general. Individuals deserved protection under art.8 as a means of helping to develop every human being's personality. Even well known people had a legitimate expectation that their private lives would be protected from unwarranted media intrusion.

This decision prompted Eady J. in *McKennitt v Ash* to state that a "significant shift" was taking place in favour of citizen's having their private lives protected under art.8 and away from the "trump card" of art.10 rights of the media.

The opposing views were examined in the important case of *Murray v Express Newspapers & Another* [2007][60] and subsequently in the appeal in 2008.[61] In this case JK Rowling the well-known author of the *Harry Potter* novels, together with her husband, were taking David, their small son, for a birthday treat to a MacDonalds restaurant in Edinburgh. Photographs were taken without their knowledge and eventually appeared in the *Sunday Express Magazine*. The child, acting through his parents, claimed that his privacy had been breached. It should be noted that this case was not about the parents' rights to privacy in public places the court was simply concerned with the child's art.8 rights in such circumstances. The trial judge after assessing the merits of both the *Campbell* and *von Hannover* decisions concluded that he was bound by precedent and had to follow the *Campbell* reasoning. He therefore concluded that as this was a public place there was no reasonable expectation of privacy.

On appeal the Master of the Rolls made it clear from the outset that the only issue in this case was whether the child had a reasonable expectation of privacy in these circumstances:

"In our judgment the question in the action is whether there was an infringement of David's rights under Article 8, not whether there was an infringement of the parents' rights under it . . . it seems that David

---

[60] [2007] EWHC 1908 (Ch).
[61] *Murray v Big Pictures (UK) Ltd* [2008] EWCA Civ 446.

may have a reasonable expectation of privacy in circumstances in which his famous mother might not."[62]

It was pointed out that in this case there was no fear or distress caused to the claimant. It is simply a matter of whether a child who is not a public figure in his own right but is a child of one is "entitled to protection from being photographed in a public place even where the photograph shows nothing embarrassing or untoward."[63]

There are a number of subsidiary questions. Firstly, suppose the child has a medical condition and this has become public knowledge. Intrusive press exposure could cause distress to a child who is already vulnerable. Secondly, suppose the celebrity parent has, in enhancing his or her career, deliberately exposed the child to publicity? Does this mean that by the simple expedient of making the child the claimant it can be assumed that the law will recognise that the child has its own personal space? Thirdly, what conclusions, if any, can be drawn from the fact that a picture agency or photographer does not seek the parents' consent to take and to publish photographs of the child? As with the decision not to inform Max Mosley of the impending revelations so to it is reasonable to assume that parents are not asked to give their consent because the media outlet or picture agency well knows that any such request will be met with a refusal.

How is it decided if there is a reasonable expectation of privacy? The Master of the Rolls offered the following analysis in the Murray case having stated that the question is a "broad one" taking into account all the circumstances of the case:

"They include the attributes of the claimant, the nature of the activity in which the claimant was engaged, the place at which it was happening, the nature and purpose of the intrusion, the absence of consent and whether it was known or could be inferred, the effect on the claimant and the circumstances in which and the purposes for which the information came into the hands of the publisher."[64]

In practice this means that the weight to be attached to the various considerations will be a matter of fact and degree. In addition one always has to be mindful that there is large measure of judicial agreement that certain activities that could be classed as trivial, anodyne, innocuous or unremarkable will not garner the protection of the law. For example the shopping trip to Italy mentioned in the *McKennitt* case or the popping out for a pint of milk example in *Campbell*.

In conclusion, the Court of Appeal thought that in all the circumstances there was an arguable case that David had a reasonable

[62] *Murray v Big Pictures (UK) Ltd* [2008] EWCA Civ 446 at para.14.
[63] *Murray v Big Pictures (UK) Ltd* [2008] EWCA Civ 446 at para.15.
[64] *Murray v Big Pictures (UK) Ltd* [2008] EWCA Civ 446 at para.36 per Sir Anthony Clarke M.R.

expectation of privacy. His parents fought hard to protect his privacy and would certainly not have consented to the photographs being taken had they known, let alone consented to them being published. At the time of writing this case had not proceeded to trial and therefore the position in respect of the public place argument seems to be:

   i)   A child could have a reasonable expectation of privacy in respect of both the taking and the publishing of photographs.

   ii) Prima facie adults do not have a reasonable expectation of privacy in public places but with the caveat that everything will depend on the circumstances. Such circumstances might ape those in the von *Hannover* case where a court might be swayed by evidence of harassment and the regularity of the photography.

   iii) English law does not recognise a self-image right but if the activity that forms the basis of the photograph is deemed a private activity then a successful application for an injunction is a distinct possibility.

4. Injunctions, Super-injunctions and Anonymity

There is no doubt that the decision in the *Mosley* case forced the tabloid media to pause for reflection. £60,000 in damages would not be a major cause for concern but the prospect of costs in the region of £500,000 would be a huge deterrent to publishing personal or intimate information with impunity. 2009 was a "quiet" year for privacy cases but that cannot be said about 2010 and into 2011.

The year 2010 started with the John Terry application for an injunction to prevent details of his relationship with a team-mate's former partner being published. The application was lost for a number of reasons not least the fact that the judge did not believe this was an application to protect personal information but an attempt to protect the value of his commercial sponsorships. Once the action which was listed as a "no name" case was lost the judge gave permission for the applicant to be identified.[65]

The "floodgates" opened in September 2010 with the decision of Sharp J. in *DFT v TFD*.[66] At the heart of the matter is the derogation from the principle of open justice if the applicant can secure an injunction not only preventing private information being published but also preventing their identity from being known. In this case a without notice

---

[65] *John Terry (Formerly LNS) v Persons Unknown* [2010] EWHC 119 (QB).
[66] [2010] EWHC 2335 (QB).

application had been made approximately two weeks prior to the trial of the case. Without notice in this particular case meant that neither the intended respondent nor the media was informed. The hearing was conducted in private as the judge was convinced this was necessary with regard to the nature of the application.

In essence this concerned the threat of blackmail. The applicant claimed that the respondent had threatened to "... make public private and confidential information concerning a sexual relationship between them unless she was paid a substantial sum of money." When the applicant had refused it was suspected that the respondent had been in touch with journalists with a view to fulfilling the blackmail threat. The judge had made the order because she felt that the respondent might try to "... avoid service and/or attempt to frustrate any order made before she could be served."[67] The authority for such an approach is to be found in the Court of Appeal decision in *ASG v GSA* [2009].[68] In this case Lord Justice Waller stated:

> "... it seems to me that if the allegation of blackmail is established, it would also be established that there was a serious risk that if given notice of the application of an injunction, the girl would have simply gone to the media and either sought to obtain money for the publication or simply published."[69]

The judge ordered that the parties should remain anonymous and also restricted access to documents on the court file. She acknowledged that the circumstances will determine whether or not there is any justification for taking these steps and that has to be done on a case by case basis. As to the reasons why a "super injunction" should be made the judge referred to a passage in the judgment of Tugendhat J. in the *Terry* case:

> "The reason why, on some occasions, applicants wish for there to be an order restricting reports of the fact that an injunction has been granted is in order to prevent the alleged wrongdoer from being tipped off about the proceedings before the injunction could be applied for, or made against him, or before he can be served."[70]

The judge went on to hold that the injunction should be extended until trial because of the real threat of blackmail but could find no convincing reason why the super injunction element of the order should be renewed. In other words anonymity was necessary because if identified there was a "serious risk that the private information which the order is supposed to protect would emerge and that the purpose of

---

[67] [2010] EWHC 2335 (QB) at para.6.
[68] [2009] EWCA Civ 1574.
[69] [2009] EWCA Civ 1574. at para.3.
[70] [2010] EWHC 119 (QB) at para.138.

the order . . . would therefore be frustrated."[71] However information regarding the subject matter of the proceedings and the identity of the applicant was limited to that contained in the case report, i.e. the bare bones!

It will be obvious from the above case that guidance is needed on when the court should preserve the anonymity of the applicant as well as the private information that is at the heart of any case. That guidance has now been provided by the Master of the Rolls in *JIH v News Group Newspapers* [2011].[72] The principles listed below apply when an anonymity order or "other restraint on publication of details of a case which are normally in the public domain . . ." is being considered:

- "The general rule is that the names of the parties to an action are included in orders and judgments of the court.
- There is no general exception for cases where private matters are in issue.
- An order for anonymity or any other order restraining the publication of the normally reportable details of a case is a derogation from the principle of open justice and an interference with the Article 10 rights of the public at large.
- Where the court is asked to make such an order if should only do so after closely scrutinising the application and considering whether a degree of restraint on publication is necessary, and, if it is, whether there is any less restrictive or more acceptable alternative than that which is sought.
- Where the court is asked to restrain the publication of the names of the parties and/or the subject matter of the claim, on the ground that such restraint is necessary under Article8, the question is whether there is sufficient general, public interest in publishing the report of the proceedings which identifies a party/or the normally reportable details to justify any resulting curtailment of his right and his family's right to respect for their private and family life.
- On any such application, no special treatment should be accorded to public figures or celebrities: in principle, they are entitled to the same protection as others, no more and no less.
- An order for anonymity or for reporting restrictions should not be made simply because the parties consent: parties cannot waive the rights of the public.
- An anonymity order or any other order restraining publication made by a judge at an interlocutory stage . . . must be reviewed at the return date.
- Whether or not an anonymity order or an order restraining publication of normally reportable details is made, then, at least where a judgment is or would normally be given, a publicly available

---

[71] [2010] EWHC 2335 at para.35.
[72] [2011] EWCA Civ 42 at para.21.

judgment should normally be given, and a copy of the consequential court order should also be publicly available, although some editing of the judgment or order may be necessary. In addition notice of any court hearing should also be given to the defendant unless there is a good reason not to do so in which case the court should be told of the absence of notice and the reason for it, and should be satisfied that the reason is a good one."

These principles were applied in the case of *MNB v News Group Newspapers Ltd* [2011].[73] This is an important decision because it deals with the obligations of the media in light of the wording of an interlocutory injunction. The chronology becomes an important factor. In this case a temporary injunction was granted to the claimant on March 1, 2011. The hearing was on short notice and conducted over the telephone and in private. The application for an injunction was contested but at the time of the hearing any public interest justification for publishing details of the claimant's sexual relationship with another person had been abandoned.

The judge ordered that the claimant should not be identified. The order was deemed to be valid until the return date on March 4, 2011. The order prevented the ". . . publication of any information concerning the subject matter of these proceedings . . . and any information concerning the facts or details of any sexual relationship between the applicant and the (other person) . . . ."

However, the order also made it clear that the respondent could publish ". . . any material that before the service of this order was already in or that thereafter comes into the public domain as the result of national media publication (other than as a result of this order or a breach of confidence or privacy."

The issue was whether an article published by a national newspaper on March 3, 2011 and at the date of the hearing (March 9) remained on the newspaper's website contravened the judge's order. The article referred to ". . . the fact that an individual with a particular occupation had 'gagged'" the newspaper. It was claimed that this article had spawned similar articles in other newspapers and on the internet. The concern from the claimant's perspective was not that any one newspaper had breached the terms of the order but that collectively the publications raised the possibility of "jigsaw identification" which would undermine the purpose of the order. It was argued that a core purpose of the order was aimed at preventing this type of identification. In practical terms if as a general rule super injunctions are to be avoided but the claimant's art.8 rights are to be protected the key question is a simple one. How much information can be published by any one newspaper without being in breach of the court order?

---

[73] [2011] EWHC 528 (QB): See also *POI v The Person Known as LINA* [2011] EWHC 234 (QB).

Much, of course, will depend on the clarity of the terms of any order. Should the claimant's occupation be mentioned? Should reference be made to his wealth? Is there any public interest justification for such an article? Are the interests of the claimant's family being appropriately taken into account? Another important point from a claimant's view-point is that a newspaper should not be allowed to rely on information that it has initially published and therefore placed in the public domain because such an action is in itself a breach of the claimant's art.8 rights. In other words the newspaper should not be allowed to benefit from its own "wrongdoing."

The opposite view will be that such an article is written with the terms of the order in mind. That it doesn't contain any private information nor does it name or identify or even *tend* to identify the claimant.

It doesn't, for example, say whether he is married or in a long-term partnership relationship nor does it report views ascertained from people aware of the circumstances or who are friends or associates of the claimant and his family.

Whether or not an order is deemed to have been breached will ulti-mately depend on the circumstances of the case. Clearly newspapers will always bear in mind that to transgress may well amount to a con-tempt of court and that is something which they would wish to avoid. It is instructive to quote the "definition" of jigsaw evidence advanced by Sharp J. in the *MNB* case:

"By its nature, jigsaw identification involves the separate publica-tion by different entities of different items of information which do not identify the claimant when looked at separately, but do so or risk doing so, when they are put together. Such information therefore does not have to actually identify a claimant. Nor need it be private. The conjunction of publicity available information with the report of proceedings may well lead to 'two and two' being put together."[74]

In this case the judge concluded that the need for anonymity had been "reinforced" by the publications which have taken place since the order was made by Henriques J. There was an ongoing need to protect the claimant against the "continuing risk of jigsaw identification." It is also worth pointing out the March 3 "type" of publication may be counter-productive in that it may mean that it reduces what can be said of the facts as part of the public judgment in the case.

At the time of writing there are two Court of Appeal judgments and a number of first instance examples where the issue of claimant anonymity and injunctions have been discussed. The principles to be applied have been clearly established in the *JIH* case. The other Court of Appeal decision is *Ntuli v Donald*.[75] In this case the court could find

---

[74] [2011] EWHC 234 (QB) at para.33.
[75] [2010] EWCA Civ 1276.

no reason why the parties should not be identified provided that the information about which there was a reasonable expectation of privacy was not identifiable from the public judgment. Lord Justice Maurice Kay concluded:

"Provided that publicity is limited to what is contained in this judgment, there is no justification for continued anonymity . . . the material in respect of which Mr Donald has been found to have a reasonable expectation of privacy is not detailed in the judgment."[76]

Hirschfeld v McGrath [2011][77] is also worth considering for the proposition that an anonymity order may be needed more at the interlocutory stage than at a subsequent hearing in order to ensure that at the return date the court could consider all the options. In the event the court determined that an anonymity order was not needed but the details that the defendant had proposed to reveal in a forthcoming book were to remain protected. Reports in cases involving private information usually carry a warning of the type following:

"There is an Order restraining publication of information concerning this case, other than the information contained in this judgment and in the Order of the Court made in this action."

Quoting Maurice Kay L.J. in the *Ntuli* case the judge stated that it was "axiomatic" that any injunction:

"Should be to the highest degree clear and precise so that no publisher would be in any doubt whether he was infringing it or not."[78]

That the courts are taking a robust stance on tabloid or celebrity revelations which cannot be justified as being in the public interest cannot be doubted. In addition, anonymity orders seem to be almost routinely granted in order to complement the protection offered to claimants who wish to protect private information under art.8. The same though cannot be said in the case of super injunctions and there is a marked reluctance to further "gag" the press by preventing any mention of the fact that the case has been heard. The evidence for the above assessment comes from cases such as *AMM v HXW* [2010][79] (possible hint of blackmail) *KJH v HGF* [2010][80] ("high degree of probability that KJH was the victim of blackmail involving the threat of the revelation of stolen private and

---

[76] [2010] EWCA Civ 1276 at para.55.
[77] [2011] EWHC 249 (QB).
[78] [2011] EWHC 249 (QB) at para.15. The quotation comes from Sir Thomas Bingham M.R. in *Times Newspaper Ltd v MGN Ltd* [1993] EMLR 443 at page 447.
[79] [2010] EWHC 2457 (QB).
[80] [2010] EWHC 3064 (QB).

confidential information") and *XJA v News Group Newspapers* [2010][81] (misuse of private information).

Mr Justice Eady opined in December 2009 that "From the coal face, however, it does seem that there are now very few privacy cases being contested."[82] That is still true in respect of contested trials. The battleground is not at this stage but at the interlocutory and return stages as demonstrated by the cases discussed above.

Let us not forget that we are seeking an answer to the question how influential is art.8 when pitted against freedom of expression as defined in art.10. In the years immediately following the Human Rights Act coming into force there was no doubt that other things being equal the "trump card" was art.10. Today it is probably fair to assume that if not yet the trump card art.8 is certainly holding its own against the tabloid newspapers' attempts to exploit their art.10 rights.

We need to ask whether the courts are now accepting what Lord Justice Sedley said in a speech at Oxford University in 2006:

> "Britain has a press which is among the world's leaders in serious investigative journalism . . . It also has a press which is the undisputed world leader in prurience and vulgar abuse. Nothing in my suggestions or in the developing privacy jurisprudence threatens serious investigation of issues of public concern: rather the reverse. If the long field-day of those who live and prosper by unwarranted intrusion into private lives is now drawing to a close, it will not be necessarily be a bad thing, even if it is the end of civilisation as we have come to know it. It will never, one fervently hopes, inhibit the ability of the press to confront us with questions of the kind with which the Daily Express not long ago stunned its readers: Did Diana's driver have bird flu?"[83]

The application of the principles relating to the award of interlocutory injunctions was considered further by the Court of Appeal in *ETK v News Group Newspapers* [2011].[84] The applicant who was simply referred to as "a married man" began a sexual relationship with a female work colleague (X). The relationship had lasted some six months when he admitted his adultery after being confronted with the allegation by his wife. The adulterous relationship ended and the couple began the process of rebuilding their family life together with their two children. The adulterous relationship had been known to their workmates and employer. The couple continued to work together and conducted themselves with "due decorum" for some eight months until their employers

---

[81] [2010] EWHC 3174 (QB).

[82] Eady J.: Privacy and the Press: Where are we now? JUSTICE conference December 2009.

[83] Sex, Libels and Video-Surveillance: Blackstone Lecture, Pembroke College, Oxford: May 2006.

[84] [2011] EWCA Civ 439.

dismissed X. News of these events leaked to the *News of the World*. The newspaper wished to publish a story indicating that X's dismissal was as a result of the affair. The appellant sought an injunction to prevent the story from being published. The application was supported by his wife and X neither of whom wanted publicity.

The court considered a number of the standard principles such as whether the applicant had a reasonable expectation of privacy so as to engage his art.8 rights. If the answer is yes then the second question is whether there is a reasonable expectation of privacy in relation to the particular information. This involves assessing all the circumstances of the case. Thirdly, if the information which the applicant seeks to protect is already in the public domain then the application will fail. It is important to consider the distinction drawn by Sir Anthony Clarke M.R. in *Browne v Associated Newspapers* [2007].[85] He said that there was:

"... potentially an important distinction between information which is made available to a person's circle of friends or work colleagues and information which is widely published in a newspaper."

It would appear from the facts of this case that the information about the affair was known to a limited number of people who worked at the same organisation as the couple. Assuming that the "threshold" test is passed then the second stage is that advocated by Lord Steyn which is usually referred to as the "ultimate balancing test."[86]

This decision is striking because at the second stage the court relies heavily upon European Court of Human Rights jurisprudence in particular reference in the *von Hannover v Germany* [2004] case as to whether when balancing protection of private life against freedom of expression the focus the contribution the article will make to a "debate of general interest."

This approach would appear to go against the stance taken in *Murray v Big Picture Agency* [2008][87] when the court took the view that it was bound to follow the *Campbell* precedent rather than *von Hannover*.

Turning to the facts, the court was clearly impressed by the fact that all parties spoke with one voice rejecting the "offer" of publicity via the *News of the World*. It was stated that art. 8 offers "respect" not just to the applicant but also in this case to his wife and his children and his former lover. It was stated that the fact that the relationship was adulterous did not mean that privacy was lost. The court was adamant that the fact the applicant had children and publicity would in all likelihood have an adverse effect on them should tip the balance in favour of art.8 protection for the applicant.

Quoting from *Neulinger v Switzerland* [2010][88] the court agreed with

---

[85] [2007] EWCA Civ 295 at para.61.
[86] *Re S (A Child)* [2005] 1 A.C. 592 at para.17.
[87] [2008] EWCA Civ 446.
[88] [2010] 28 ECHR 706.

the statement that there was a broad consensus in international law in support of the idea that ". . . in all decisions concerning children their best interests must be paramount." With all respect this case was not one concerning children in the conventional sense that one sees in family law where their interests are paramount. The children in this case were peripheral to the main issue of publicity and freedom of expression. They were not parties to the proceedings in the conventional sense.

The court then analysed whether the public interest (or general interest in *von Hannover* terms) was served by the publication of the information. There was no "political edge" to the publication. The ". . . economic, social and political life of the country so crucial to democracy, is not enhanced by the publication. The intellectual, artistic or personal development of members of society is not stunted by ignorance of the sexual frolics of figures known to the public."

The court concluded that the injunction should be granted. Lord Justice Ward concluded:

". . . the benefits to be achieved by publication in the interests of free speech are wholly outweighed by the harm that would be done through the interference with the rights to privacy of all those affected, especially where the rights of the children are in play."

We are entitled to ponder when the rights of children will come into play in such cases. Does their mere existence mean they will now become a dominant factor if not THE dominant factor in deciding the outcome of such applications?

5. Protection from Harassment

Lawyers representing celebrity clients are increasingly resorting to the Protection from Harassment Act 1997 (as amended by s.125 of the Serious Organised Crime and Police Act 2005) as a means of putting pressure on the media to stop photographers chasing their clients in a hope of getting cash-generating photographs.

The Act was never intended to be used for this purpose rather as a means of offering protection to those at risk from "stalkers."

In order to gain a conviction or injunction, the Act requires evidence of a course of conduct which amounts to harassment of another and which he knows or ought to know amounts to harassment. The test therefore combines both subjective and objective factors. In assessing whether the person ought to have known a reasonable person test will apply bestowing upon the reasonable person the same information as known to the defendant. The remedies available to the applicant are both criminal and civil. In the latter case an injunction can be obtained and in the former a person can be imprisoned for up to five years for breaches of the injunction.

The use by parliament of the words "course of conduct" clearly indicates that a single act will be insufficient to achieve the desired remedy. There must be at least two instances of the behaviour that is the subject of the complaint. The two most obvious examples are the persistent encroachment of photographers into a person's private life and the "doorstepping" techniques much practised by journalists to achieve a meaningful soundbite.

Cases actually initiated against the media are rare. The one notable exception is *Thomas v News Group Newspapers* [2002].[89] It is an important decision because it reminds editors that it would be wrong to "target" particular individuals, for example, as part of a smear campaign, if it was apparent that the individual would be subject to abuse or possibly violence. A clear distinction though must be drawn between this type of journalism and "normal" press criticism. As Lord Phillips M.R. said:

> " In general, press criticism, even if robust, does not constitute unreasonable conduct and does not fall within the natural meaning of harassment . . . It is common ground . . . that before press publications are capable of constituting harassment, they must be attended by some exceptional circumstance which justifies sanctions and the restriction on the freedom of expression that they involve."[90]

The court held that, in three articles, the newspaper had harassed Ms Thomas by "publishing racist criticism of her which was foreseeably likely to stimulate a racist reaction on the part of their readers and cause her distress."

Reference should be made here to the Press Complaints Commission Code of Practice which states

> "Journalists must not engage in intimidation, harassment or persistent pursuit."[91]

We simply pose the question: Has anything really changed in the approach of the paparazzi? Probably not except that it is now more likely that their activities can be controlled on a case-by-case basis as a result of celebrities seeking redress under the 1997 Act. A good example is the agreement reached between Sienna Miller and Big Pictures (UK) Limited and Darryn Lyons in late 2008.[92] The defendants gave an undertaking to the court that they would not pursue a course of conduct that amounted to harassment of Miller contrary to s.1(1) (a) of the 1997 Act.

---

[1] [2001] EWCA Civ 1233.
[0] [2001] EWCA Civ 1233 at para.49.
Cl.4.
[2] November 21, 2008.

These types of agreements are usually very specific. In this particular case the defendants agreed not to:

- Pursue or follow the claimant whether by any means whatsoever.
- Place the claimant under surveillance.
- Take pictures of the claimant:
    - in her home or home of any members of her family or friends or when she is in the garden of the said homes;
    - office blocks or buildings not open to the general public;
    - entering or leaving her home, family and friends' homes or when in the garden of these homes;
    - while she is being followed or pursued by photographers;
    - or otherwise where she has a reasonable expectation of privacy.

The claimant accepted that she did not have a reasonable expectation of privacy when leaving a place of social entertainment such as a bar or nightclub. Nor did she have a reasonable expectation of privacy on a public highway or footpath or when attending an event or similar in an official capacity.

Similar injunctions were obtained by lawyers acting from Amy Winehouse and Lily Allen in 2009.[93]

In all cases action was taken against a picture agency in preference to any individual photographers. In addition to the 1997 Act note should be taken of the Serious Organised Crime and Police Act 2005 amending the Criminal Justice Act 2001. Section 126 of the 2005 Act inserts a new s.42A into the 2001 Act creating an offence of harassment of a person at his home. This offence is aimed at preventing intimidation of people by agitators or protesters such as animal rights group campaigners. Although it is envisaged that this section will rarely be used against the media, in legal terms, it is not outside the bounds of possibility. If the continuing presence of the paparazzi causes distress to celebrity residents to the extent that they are afraid to come out of their house then it is possible an offence has been committed. The inclusion of the word *vicinity* also means that photographers waiting to apprehend a celebrity a few hundred yards away from their residence could also be caught by the provision. A constable in uniform may arrest without warrant any person he reasonably suspects is committing or has committed an offence under s.42A.

Section 127 of the 2005 Act amends s.42 of the 2001 Act and gives the police powers to order that a person may be required to leave the vicinity of any premises in which the "resident" feels harassed and not return for a period not exceeding three months.

It should not be assumed that it is always celebrities or those in the public eye that will be aggrieved by press intrusion. In March 2011 the

---

[93] *Guardian*, March 16, 2009 and May 1, 2009.

Press Complaints Commission upheld a complaint against the *Scottish Daily Mail* on the basis that its journalists had harassed the family of a student who had been photographed at the tuition fees demonstration in London in November 2010 allegedly attempting to remove a police officer's helmet. It was said that reporters and photographers had attended the family home four times in 24 hours. On each occasion the family members had refused to comment and had asked the press representatives to leave. The Code was breached because the family were not at the centre of the story and receiving comments from the student's father had only a "limited" public interest value. (See also Ch.8 on Regulation.)

6. The Need for Privacy Legislation?

The question is often asked but rarely answered in the positive, although that could be changing. In the first edition of this book we pointed out that in 2006 the Irish government had introduced a Privacy Bill which we said had "received a predictably cool response from the media."[94] The accuracy of that comment was soon confirmed when the proposal disappeared into the long grass never to reappear.

The question in respect of this jurisdiction was asked again by the members of the House of Commons Culture, Media and Sports Committee in 2010.[95] In its previous report on this matter in 2003 the Committee had concluded that government should reconsider its position and "bring forward legislative proposals to clarify the protection that individuals can expect from unwarranted intrusion by anyone—not the press alone—into their private lives".[96] The government's response was unsurprising. The courts and not Parliament should weigh the competing rights in individual cases. However Parliament should be prepared to intervene if there were ". . . signs that the courts are systematically striking the wrong balance . . ."[97]

The issue resurfaced in 2007 when the committee examined self-regulation of the press. The conclusion was that a case had not been made for a law of privacy.[98] In its current report the Committee has adopted a wait-and-see approach for the following reasons:

The media industry was not united on the need for privacy legislation. One respondent felt that there hadn't yet been a case that had gone

---

[94] Hadwin & Bloy: *Law and the Media*, 1st edn Sweet & Maxwell (2007) p.139.
[95] Press Standards, Privacy and Libel; Second Report Session 2009–12. February 2010.
[96] Privacy and Media Intrusion. Fifth Report session 2002-3 HC458-l para.111.
[97] Government reply to the 5th Report 2004.
[98] Self regulation of the Press, Seventh report of the Culture Media and Sports Committee session 2006–7.

to trial where ". . . someone has tried to gag a newspaper with a really good public interest defence".[99]

Very few cases claiming misuse of private information actually go to trial. The committee discovered only a couple in the two years prior to the publication of the report in 2010.

The Human Rights Act has only been in force for a decade and therefore the number of judgments involving freedom of expression and privacy is limited. Evidence was given by the Lord Chancellor that the law relating to privacy would become clearer as more cases are decided by the courts particularly the higher courts. A good example of this reasoning is the formulation by the Court of Appeal in the *JIH* case of a number of principles to be considered when deciding whether anonymity should be granted to a claimant.

Even if there was privacy legislation judges would still exercise a wide discretion when deciding cases. Therefore the situation would be little different from today's position.

Summary of the law

It is probably fair to say that people complaining of unwarranted media intrusion into their lives have never been in a stronger legal position. As a result of the recognition by the Court of Appeal that the law on confidence can now provide an effective remedy through which to protect private information, and the statutory provisions centred on the prevention of harassment, the media will have to rethink its strategy about how "kiss and tell" stories and "intimate" revelations are put, if at all, into the public domain. However, a clear public interest justification for publication will invariably override privacy protection. Yet the media would welcome a modern interpretation of what exactly constitutes the definition of *public interest*. It is reasonable to suggest that there will yet be further mileage in the battle to balance privacy rights against those protected by art.10 of the European Convention on Human Rights.

The current "battleground" surrounds the granting of injunctions to protect "private information." In practice many of those injunctions are granted at the 11th hour often by duty judges who have little knowledge of media law. This means that in such circumstances it is more likely than not that the media will be prevented from publishing. The "protection" offered by s.12(3) of the Human Rights Act will only be relevant once the two sides have gone to court and, if this is the case, then the media is at a disadvantage from the outset.

The Court of Appeal has given guidance on how anonymity requests should be resolved. The threshold test of "reasonable expectation of privacy" is well known to all those concerned with the legal process. Guidance as to what amounts to the public interest is to be found in the

---

[99] *Guardian* newspaper editor, Alan Rusbridger.

Press Complaints Commission Code of Practice as well as judicial guidance dating back at least to the judgment of Lord Justice Stephenson in *Lion Laboratories v Evans* in 1984.[100] The public place argument is seemingly resolved in favour of the *Campbell* rather than the *von Hannover* approach.

Children in public places would appear to have a reasonable expectation of privacy. The legal action appears to be for breach of confidence/misuse of private information as we still do not have a recognised tort of privacy in this jurisdiction.

PART TWO: PRIVACY IN PRACTICE

Mosley, Marr and Ferdinand have made privacy headline news. Sex sells and that undoubtedly explains much of the media attention but the controversies in each case have acquainted the British public with at least the gist of the battle being waged between privacy and free speech.

The court decided Max Mosley, then boss of Formula One motor racing, should have been able to keep secret his penchant for paid-for sado-masochistic group sex; BBC journalist Andrew Marr outed himself as the formerly anonymous winner of a super-injunction preventing reporting of his extra-marital affair and Premiership footballer and "family man" reported variously as xxxxx, ***** or CTB[101] was able to secure a gagging order preventing revelations of a six-month affair.

Significantly a married man in the entertainment industry known only as ETK[102] called the privacy rights of his children into play to prevent him being identified as the adulterer in a work affair which led to the woman involved losing her job.

Article 8 does indeed offer respect for private and family life. Yet it is an odd perversion of the right to that respect when any rich and powerful man who cheats on his wife, pays for sex and lies about it can rely on the "sanctity" of family life to protect him from the full consequences of his actions. The threat to his children was created by his own behaviour. If he cared so much for their rights, why risk all for a fling?

Several injunctions have been granted and anonymised because of a blackmail element. Sex workers can potentially extort money from clients by threatening to expose them. So what courts are really protecting is men's rights to pay for sex in secret. There is precious little moral high ground anywhere in these sordid cases.

Some media are determined to justify continuing to run the juicy gossip on celebrities and even the kiss-and-tell exposes of their sex lives by coming up with a public interest justification.

---

[100] [1984] 2 All E.R. 417.
[101] *CTB v News Group Newspapers Ltd & Anr* [2011] EWHC 1232 (QB).
[102] *ETK v News Group Newspapers* [2011] EWCA Civ 439.

Sexual behaviour, per se, whether involving adultery, homosexuality or any other non-criminal activity, is now heavily protected. It is very private on the one hand; yet will rarely qualify as wrongdoing or even "impropriety" in public interest terms. For some time running such material has required the media to identify public interest grounds for the invasion beyond the breach of the marriage vows or payment for sex in itself. Even with Government ministers, revealing the fact of an affair might not be enough, so misuse of public funds and serious impropriety are brought into the equation as referred to in *Blunkett* but also applied when revealing John Prescott's infidelity with a subordinate.

These public interest justifications could be seen as disingenuous and in print used incidentally to the main revelation but it does not always make it wrong to allow it. Just because a popular tabloid and/or its readers may not focus primarily on the public interest element of a story does not mean it is not proper for the courts to recognise it. Indeed it is vital that they do.

More serious investigative journalism relies on these elements to justify exposure. Distaste among the upper echelons of society for the scandal-mongering of the popular tabloids must not provide a justification for stricter controls generally on the media. The danger is there and that is part of the dilemma for supposedly more high-minded journalists. It is not just about reining in the excessive methods of the popular tabloids; it becomes about the courts deciding what matters to the public.

Do we condemn the froth of the popular tabloids because it is goading the powers-that-be into more draconian controls which would affect serious journalism too or do we defend their right, as we defend ours, to decide what to cover and how to cover it with the minimum intervention by the state, as required under art.10? Journalists would certainly not accept that the curbs are "necessary" in a democratic society; indeed they would argue, as Dacre did in Ch.2 on Freedom of Expression, that the elevation of privacy rights is damaging proper discussion of right and wrong.

7. Public Domain in Practice

Media opposition to injunctions often involves the argument that the information to be injuncted is already in the public domain. This used to be a relatively simple concept when access to mass audiences was pretty much limited to mainstream media.

Even then there was the oxymoronic concept of an "open secret". Many people in politics and business knew that Lord Browne was gay; ETK's work colleagues knew of his affair. At what stage does that information become public knowledge? The law is clear that family or workplace circles do not constitute public domain. Quite how large those circles can become before the secret is out, is not specified.

But the real tension these days is between mainstream and online media. Courts are still tending to downplay online availability of information. The 1.4 million hits of the Mosley sex video in 24 hours could hardly be ignored[103] but a great deal of digital material is still dismissed as gossip. Injunctions are granted repeatedly when information is freely available online. The injuncted name of a member of the Royal family was easy to find and it took seconds to work out the identity of CTB. His injunction was stepped up to "contra mundum"[104] so that information cannot legally be shared by me or anyone else with anyone anywhere in the world.

8. Privacy in Public Places in Practice

The notion of privacy in a public place is another oxymoronic concept with which many journalists are uncomfortable. How can anyone walking down a street in public view consider themselves to be in private? If you have sex in a club doorway, is it private if only 50 people see you but not if the image is shared with 500,000 You Tube viewers? The first obvious question is: why on earth have sex in public view if you consider it to be an intrinsically private activity?

But add society's obsession with celebrity to the mix and privacy becomes a stick with which to fend off the paparazzi and other media interest. The paparazzi have a lot to answer for but so have the public who flock to see the pictures. Images, which are treated as more intrusive than the factual information they convey, are at the heart of many landmark privacy cases—*von Hannover*,[105] *Mosley*[106] and *Murray*,[107] to mention but three. And famous names abound—Princess Caroline of Monaco, Naomi Campbell, JK Rowling, Paul McCartney, Elton John.

Celebrity photographs are the battleground where the gulf between what interests the public and what the courts deem to be in the public interest is at its widest.

Under the Press Complaints Commission Code of Practice, it is unacceptable to photograph individuals in private places without their consent. Private places are defined as **public or** private property where there is a "reasonable expectation" of privacy. This began to confront the difficult grey area within privacy which is being played out in adjudication of code complaints as well as in judicial rulings. (See more in Ch.8 on Regulation).

As well as "public" privacy there is also "controlled" privacy. The long *OK!/Hello* spat[108] over pictures of the Douglas wedding is still worth

---

[103] [2008] EWHC 687 (QB).
[104] *OPQ v BJM* [2011] EWHC.
[105] *von Hannover v Germany* [2004] ECHR 294.
[106] [2008] EWHC 1777 (QB).
[107] *Murray v Big Pictures (UK) Ltd* [2008] EWCA Civ 446.
[108] *Douglas & Others v Hello Ltd & Others* [2005] EWCA Civ 595.

examining from a privacy perspective even though at heart it is a classic breach of confidence action. The response of leading media commentator Simon Jenkins can stand as a journalist's "take" on the whole saga. He said:

> "Nobody can stage a wedding, sell the publicity rights for £1m and then claim that they were trying to remain private. Managed publicity is not privacy. As for the 'obligations of confidence' on newspapers not to scoop rivals who have paid for so-called exclusives, this is censorship born of madness. Newspapers must guard their exclusives as best they can, not call on law lords to act as their bouncers and heavies. Either way, this is a blatant case of one law for the rich and one for the poor."[109]

9. Injunctions, Super-injunctions and Anonymity in Practice

Judgments from *von Hannover* to *Mosley* made it clear the media could expect many more battles between art.8 and art.10 rights and that these were very likely to involve applications for injunctions.

They were also likely to involve the media losing unless really strong public interest grounds could be argued for the intrusion.

Any attempt to keep secrets is going to involve issues of prior restraint. Damages may be sought after publication but a breach of privacy cannot be rectified after the event in the same way as a defamatory statement can be retracted. The secret is already out.

So the media need to be prepared to have to fight it out over injunctions. The threat of injunction makes it tempting not to approach the subject of the story at all, or only immediately prior to publication when it would be difficult to trigger legal action in time. However the courts tend to take a dim view of this practice. An approach may not be as crucial as it is in defamation actions, but it would still be expected of journalism wanting to claim the protection of the law to assert its freedom of expression over another's privacy. Arguably, it is also potentially cheaper to fight it out at injunction stage. If there is going to be a dispute, better to know before publication. The hurdles for achieving an injunction are still fairly high. The onus will tend to be on the complainant to justify the use of prior restraint, which does retain a vestige of special pleading for freedom of expression within the Human Rights Act. If the case is not clear cut and deemed not likely to succeed at trial, the newspaper may still be allowed to run at least part of its story, as it

---

[109] Quoted by Peter Preston, *Observer*, May 6, 2007.

did in *Browne*. But there is nevertheless strong resistance in the media to Mosley's bid to make a prior approach a legal requirement in such cases. That would allow those rich enough to pursue injunctions to tie the media up in knots and effectively allow them to "vet" content. Prior approach smacks too much of the habit of some celebrity magazines of offering copy approval. Celebrities would just love to be able to control everything ever said about them.

The Court of Appeal decision in *McKennitt* weakened the limits of prior restraint by deciding that information can be deemed private, without having to decide if it is true or not. Previously disputes over the truth or otherwise of allegations were in the realm of defamation. Privacy issues were used where information was true but secret. Significantly for the media, under *Bonnard v Perryman*,[110] an injunction cannot be granted on publication of material claimed to be defamatory if the defendant intends to plead justification. So, where a claimant seeks to prevent false information being run, a privacy route and thereby most likely an injunction could be pursued to circumvent *Bonnard*.

Even that protection is challenged by the recent granting of injunctions in libel cases. What is thought to be the first anonymised interim libel injunction was granted in *ZAM v CFW & TFW*[111] which relied on a harassment element to justify prior restraint in a potential defamation action within a dispute over family trusts. Tugendhat J. granted an anonymity order and what he described as a "rare" interim libel injunction despite it coming just six months after a gagging order in *Farrall v Kordowski*.[112] In that case, the claimant had been defamed on the "*solicitorsfromhell.co.uk*" website. The publisher had not put forward anything to the effect that he had a libel defence, so the judge granted an interim gagging order.

In the more significant Trafigura[113] super-injunction, a combination of Twitter and the threat to limit coverage of Parliamentary discussion of the topic proved bridges too far and the information found its way into the public domain. The oil-trading firm was trying to stop the *Guardian* publishing a story based on a draft scientific report about the alleged dumping of toxic waste in west Africa. The banned Minton report was also hosted on Wikileaks.

The super-injunction clause reads at [5]:

"Upon it appearing to the Court i) that the action is one likely to attract publicity, (ii) that publicity revealing the identity of the Applicants is likely unfairly to damage the interests of the Applicants and (iii) that accordingly publication of details revealing the Applicant's identity ought to be prohibited . . . a) The application hearing to which this Order relates was held in private and **the publication of all informa-**

---

[110] *Bonnard v Perryman* [1891] 2 Ch 269.
[111] *ZAM v CFW and another* [2011] EWHC 476 (QB).
[112] [2010] EWHC 2436 (QB).
[113] *RJW & SJW v Guardian News and Media Ltd & persons unknown*, [2009] QB HQ09.

tion relating to these proceedings or of information describing them or the intended claim is expressly prohibited." (Our emphasis)

Guardian editor, Alan Rusbridger, later produced an annotated analysis of the injunction which makes fascinating reading.[114]

Trafigura was eventually fined one million Euro for dumping toxic waste in Ivory Coast. We are left wondering how any damage to its interests caused by the reporting was considered to be "unfair". Indeed the paucity of information about the substance of super-injunctions is one of their many drawbacks. Access to supporting documentation is often limited as it was here so it becomes nigh on impossible to tell if the injunction and its conditions were reasonable.

Injunctions require speedy responses. The initial injunction here was granted on September 11, 2009, a Friday, to last one week. Any evidence to be heard at the subsequent hearing on September 18 was to be submitted by 4pm on the Monday with a skeleton argument by the Tuesday lunchtime. Often the defence has to turn round arguments even faster in phone calls to duty judges.

This underlines the need for journalists to be very sure of the basis on which privacy is being invaded. Public domain and/or public interest arguments, supported by evidence, may have to be marshalled at very short notice if injunctions are to be fought successfully. It also supports the suggestion that when it comes to establishing "limiting factors", journalists often have more chance of convincing a judge, on the basis of other media coverage, that the gist of the secret is already in the public domain than of persuading them of a public interest in the revelation.

The case also raised debated about whether court gagging orders extended to Parliament. Getting an MP to raise a question about a contentious claim has always been a fall-back position where the media is constrained, in the past more often by the threat of defamation action.

In October 2009 Paul Farrelly MP tabled a parliamentary question about the report which was subject to the injunction. The question was printed on the House of Commons order paper and up on the parliament's website. But Trafigura, through its lawyers Carter-Ruck, argued that the injunction barred the *Guardian* from publishing the contents of Farrelly's question. There was outcry from MPs and the Twitterati and Trafigura backed down.

Lord Chief Justice Sir Igor Judge told editors later that year:

"What I find astonishing is this. I have never understood and still do not understand that anybody could possibly believe that a judge sitting in the High Court in London, giving such an injunction, would ever have it cross his mind that he was making an order that Parliament could not debate if Parliament wished to do so. This is what the Bill of Rights was all about. One of the fundamental

---

[114] *http://www.guardian.co.uk/media/2009/oct/20/trafigura-anatomy-super-injunction* [Accessed April 2011].

principles of our constitution is that members of Parliament can discuss anything they like. No judge in my view has ever thought he was making an order that could in any way diminish the ability of Parliament to discuss anything."[115]

Above all, this case demonstrates that concerns about the spread of injunctions cannot be waived away on the basis that all we lose is news of footballers' sexual indiscretions. Rich and powerful companies can use the law too to thwart the media. Even though the *Guardian* wore Trafigura down, such legal actions are expensive in time and money. The threat of privacy actions does represent a new "chilling effect" which can jeopardise serious as well as celebrity reporting.

10. Children

Determining cases by balancing one right against another when they are in conflict only works if there are no automatic trump cards. Yet there is growing reference to the "primacy" of the interests of children in both civil and criminal cases to which they are not even party. This seemingly-worthy focus on the rights of children has profound repercussions which allow parents to avoid facing up to the consequences of their actions. It does not feel right for a philandering father to protect himself via an appeal to his children's privacy rights. The principle of human rights is warped when it allows adults to hide behind their children in this way when the children's rights are only in play because of the parent's breach of marital trust, say, or criminal behaviour. Parents are traditionally required to be responsible for their children—to honour commitments to them—not benefit from the trauma their own actions have caused them.

Having children would effectively grant parents greater licence for wrongdoing than other adults who can't wring their hands over the agony they have caused their offspring. That does seem to be the wrong way round.

The courts used to be much less sensitive to the embarrassments caused to children by their errant parents. In *Re X (a minor)* in 1974[116] Lord Denning M.R. threw out an application to prevent publication of references in a book to a man's lurid sex life on the grounds that it would disillusion and distress his highly-strung daughter (X) who was ignorant of her deceased father's true lifestyle. Lord Denning said:

[115] Keynote speech to Society of Editors conference, Stansted 2009—*http://www.society-ofeditors.co.uk/page-view.php?pagename=KeynoteAddress2009* [Accessed April 2011].

[116] *Re X (a minor)* [1975] 1 All E.R. 697 at p.703.

> "On the one hand there is the freedom of the press to consider; on the other hand, the protection of a young child from harm."

He did not think it right to prevent publication of true information, even though it wasn't about a matter of public interest.

> "The reason why in these cases the law gives no remedy is because of the importance it attaches to the freedom of the press; or, better put, the importance in a free society of the circulation of true information."

Allowing publication he said:

> "The relatives of the child must do their best to protect her by doing all they can to see that the book does not come into her hands. It is a better way of protection than the court can give. In my opinion it would be . . . infringing too much on the freedom of the press for us to grant an injunction in this case."

The decision in ETK shows how far we have moved in favour of privacy.

11. Privacy is the New Libel

Privacy is an uncomfortable subject for a journalist. Editors used to rail about libel actions—now we have privacy to contend with. For most people privacy is considered a "good". The expression "a right to privacy" is bandied about despite the fact that breach of privacy does not exist as a tort in its own right (although arguably it may as well do given the way judgments are going).

For a journalist there is something unhealthy about the concept. That may be difficult for some to understand. But consider one of the most famous definitions of news (Randolph Hearst's actually):

> "News is something someone, somewhere doesn't want to see published."

Privacy plays into the hands of those with something to hide. And the more they have to hide the harder they will work to keep facts hidden and the more expensive they will make it for a journalist to expose them. The richer and more powerful they are, the more they have to lose and the more easily they can afford to block media disclosure.

The starting point for journalists is that everything should be out in the open. The public right to know demands it. It is then up to a society to determine what the exceptions should be; what information can reasonably be withheld.

A full-blown privacy law as applied in France, say, could make some information sacrosanct; it could effectively sanction not only secrecy but deception too. Statute there is seen by journalists as a major curb on investigative journalism because it is so protective of reputation and confidentiality, being at least as much about image rights as genuine individual privacy.

Yet some UK media players feel statute would be preferable to the creeping limitations of case law. Why do journalists find the threat of privacy legislation worse than other restraints such as libel?

It is because truth is a defence to libel. It is not to claims of privacy invasion. Exposing the truth is an essential part of being a good journalist. Citizens need to know what is really going on. Society is ultimately the healthier for it. We can thank John Stuart Mill for asserting that truth should never be denied a platform.[117]

The majority of cases concern celebrities, and often C-list ones at that. This creates a complacency, and even approval, for courts upholding art.8 rights which threaten to put an end to paparazzi hounding celebrities and to the "tittle-tattle" of kiss and tell.

Apart from the slippery slope argument it is reasonable to ask why so many cases are brought by celebrities. It is not just because they make the headlines while Jo Bloggs' plight is ignored; it is not just because newspapers consider them fair game; and it is not just because the popular tabloids have moved to a celeb-driven agenda.

It is because maintaining privacy can be worth a fortune to celebrities desperate to protect their image; even where that image is false. What media commentators so often fail to acknowledge in the rush of sympathy for the claimant—and recently for their children—is that, for some, this is business.

Lucrative endorsements depend on maintaining the squeaky clean public image which makes it well worth taking even costly action to maintain it. Too many celebrities rely on being phoney and have a great deal to lose from exposure of the truth about them.

When this motivation becomes too obvious to ignore, even the courts see through the privacy claims as they did in the *Terry* case.[118] The victory for the media in *Terry* led to a brief run of kiss-and-tells, notably regarding Wayne Rooney, who lost valuable sponsorship deals as a result, and Ashley Cole. But claimants soon learnt not be so carelessly transparent about their financial interests which are now just one more aspect of the cases they will strive to keep hidden.

Surely, it cannot be wrong for a newspaper to reveal the truth about someone who is peddling a lie, even if that lie concerns their private life. The more significant that lie is, the more the liar has resting on it, the more public reputation rests on perpetuating the lie—the more important it is for it to be exposed AND the greater the lengths to which the mythmaker will go to keep it secret.

The tension is there.

---

[117] Mill, JS, *On Liberty*.
[118] *Terry (Formerly LNS) v Persons Unknown* (Rev 1) [2010] EWHC 119 (QB).

Take the thorny issue of an elected politician's sexuality. Is it private or not?

A voter may not care what her MP's sexual orientation is—but it would concern her if he/she were lying about it. It is the pretence and potential hypocrisy that matters. In a representative democracy it is vital to trust those we elect. They should be who they appear to be. Any legislation which makes it easier for them to act covertly has to be a retrograde step in an elected democracy.

There is a balance to be struck. In the ECHR, now incorporated into our Human Rights Act, it emerges as art.8 v art.10.

The Press Complaints Commission Code of Practice also upholds privacy entitlements but these are, if not exactly trumped, at least more explicitly circumscribed when the public interest is at stake. Editors will be expected to justify intrusion into any individual's private life without consent but the door is opened to such arguments.

However, at least within the PCC code, the public interest exemption challenges the privacy entitlement by including the justification of *preventing the public from being misled by an action of statement of an individual or organisation.*[119]

Outing the phoney is OK in Code terms and no distinction is made between different categories of individual or organisation. Certainly the more significant a role someone plays in public life the more likely it is to matter if they are misleading the public, but anyone could fall within the definition.

Elected politicians and public servants should not be allowed to mislead the public, even where otherwise private information has to be revealed to prevent it. But what about other public figures, such as TV personalities? There the PCC is working hard to strike an appropriate balance. Celebrities who court press coverage to promote their careers do not lose all protection but they do become in a sense public property. And they should not have a right to mislead.

And too often newspapers play along. Society should censure newspapers for perpetuating myths not for debunking them. Far too many titles collude in celebrity pretences where it suits agents to raise the profile of their clients and newspapers to sell copies. The deals struck there are far more unethical than occasional intrusive photographs. Journalists and editors who knowingly present false information to the public are the real villains of the piece.

Deciding whether or not to print a controversial—and potentially actionable—story is complex. Different editors will consider different elements in the equation—and lend very different weight to them. Watching the popular tabloids, there can appear still to be a cavalier attitude. Who cares about falling foul of the law as long as the money from extra sales outweighs any penalty?

Apart from the fact that a reliable calculation is hard to come by,

---

[119] PCC Code of Conduct, available at *www.pcc.org.uk*

few editors are actually that unsophisticated. Newspapers want to be right—for their reputation, for their readers, for their professional pride but a journalist wouldn't necessarily feel that bad about invading the privacy of the great and the good—when it involves revealing that they are neither as great nor as good as they would have us believe. Because truth is no defence to an invasion of privacy it would not necessarily be damaging to an editor's reputation to lose a privacy case. Editors might therefore still be inclined to push the boundaries, dare I say it, on a point of principle.

Would it were otherwise, but that leads us back to celebrities. The fabrication that surrounds many celebrities leaves them wide open to a media-delivered reality check. Many celebrities want a legal remedy to compensate them for the possible damage done to their earning power. In those cases our existing laws of confidentiality—borne from a business model—seem much more appropriate and adequate.

Genuine cases of infringement of privacy where a real personal hurt has been caused can be dealt with appropriately by the PCC. (See Ch.8 on Regulation.)

The privacy debate has thrown up some broader and questionable assumptions.

One is that the media is more intrusive now than previously. The reality is more complex. The language used to discuss more intimate issues has become more explicit, coarser too. Yet the average journalists' behaviour is, if anything, more restrained as media commentator Roy Greenslade outlined in a memorandum to the Commons Select Committee on Culture, Media and Sport.[120]

There are also changes in what is deemed the public sphere. People live their lives behind closed doors far more than they used to. They shrink from the real world while simultaneously baring their souls—and more—on social networking sites and personal blogs. This is a really unhealthy dichotomy.

Take the matter of funerals. In local and national papers, funerals used to be a regular source of lengthy stories, complete with lists of mourners. A reporter would stand at the gate taking all the names. The longer the report and list of mourners the more important the person clearly had been. Attendance by the newspaper was a mark of respect. Suggest attending a funeral now and many people are highly offended. Funerals are seen as private events. In the spirit of the PCC code journalists would seek permission, especially for photographs, and would often be denied.

The public realm is shrinking and in sociological terms this increasing paranoia over privacy is alarming. Human Rights legislation was supposed to be about protecting individuals from the excesses of public authorities. The use of those safeguards against the media is part of a broader withdrawal from society driven by the fear that participation in

---

[120] Commons Select Committee on Culture, Media and Sport, 5th report, June 2003.

the public sphere makes one vulnerable; that other people are a threat. That raises issues far wider than whether or not a newspaper gets to run a photograph of a drunken prince.

The judges who wanted to strike a new balance of less draconian libel restraints but more restrictive privacy protection have certainly succeeded in the latter endeavour. (The former is far from secure.)

We need to think long and hard about the implications this has not just for the media, but for society as a whole.

Why do people guard their privacy so jealously? For many celebrities, it is more about controlling image for commercial purposes. For those suddenly not enjoying their 15 minutes of fame, the fear of disclosure seems disproportionate. Each of us should have a degree of choice as to how much of our lives we share with the public but it is not necessarily a bad thing. The public did not have a right to know Lord Browne's sexual orientation but surely one of the big questions we should be asking ourselves is why, in this day and age, was he so bothered about people finding out?

The supposed trade-off between more relaxed libel laws and more restrictive privacy doesn't in practice deliver much of a benefit to meaningful journalism; it just changes the line of attack for those who want to keep things quiet. Where a claimant has a grievance against the media, instead of bringing a defamation action, the option will be taken to couch the complaint in terms of invasion of privacy, which now includes the protection of false private information, and grants much greater injunctive powers as the events of 2011 have demonstrated.

How exactly have the public right to know and freedom of expression been protected here?

12. Privacy Checklist

In the light of recent privacy case law, and particularly the controversial run of injunctions, it is worth looking at how journalists can develop a privacy checklist which can be applied to other key cases and to potential legal challenges arising from future investigations. These questions can then be applied to a series of Case Studies representing developments in the emerging rights to challenge "misuse" of private information. First we establish if the claimant has a reasonable expectation of privacy—if art.8 rights are engaged? Then we look for "limiting" factors which weigh against protection of that right. Is the information already in the public domain? Is its revelation in the public interest?

Does the claimant have a reasonable expectation of privacy?

This will depend on the nature of the information and the circumstances in which it has been imparted or obtained. Hoffmann in *Campbell v MGN* [2004][121] said at [21]:

> "Essentially the touchstone of private life is whether in respect of the disclosed facts the person in question had a reasonable expectation of privacy."

Judicial interpretation has broadened considerably since *von Hannover*, and *Peck*[122] influences the definition too. Court battles have frequently boiled down to issues of the images used alongside stories. In various cases, such as *Campbell*, the facts in the story have been allowed; it was the accompanying image that offended.

The old PCC rule of thumb was that if someone was clearly visible in a public place, permission was not needed to take and use a photograph of them, whether they were aware of the photograph being snapped or not. There were issues over use of long lens but they now seem almost out-of-date. Even where someone is in clear public view, without any suggestion of the need for a long lens, they can be deemed to enjoy a "reasonable expectation of privacy". The photographer should certainly not be hiding but even if they, and the subject, are fully visible, an intrusion of privacy may be claimed.

All is not lost. It will depend what they are doing when the photograph is taken. If what they are doing has a private or embarrassing quality to it, such as attending Narcotics Anonymous, judges may consider this a private matter.

However, even in *von Hannover* which is considered as setting a draconian benchmark in press terms, there were extra requirements established to claim a reasonable expectation of privacy in a public place. The *von Hannover* ruling was influenced by the fact that the whole catalogue of images involved in the action were held to be part of a campaign of harassment of Princess Caroline as she went about her daily life and that she was entitled at times to be considered "off-duty".

This is the kind of principle behind the deals brokered by our British royal family, say when they go ski-ing. Prince Charles and his sons, for example, agreed to a formal, official photocall in return for being left alone in an otherwise public place to have some time to themselves. This was the kind of relief from permanent paparazzi presence that the *von Hannover* ruling was designed to provide.

There was also mention of one photograph of her tripping up which

---

[121] [2004] UKHL 22.
[122] *Peck v United Kingdom* [2003] ECHR 44.

also suggested that any embarrassing shots of the subject off-guard would earn more protection than those of her looking good.

The court also took into account the massive audience reach of paparazzi shots so that behaviour that, although in public, might be witnessed only by a handful of people could end up being shared with millions. The same reasoning arises in *Murray*[123]—see Case Study Three.

The conclusion of the judgment is worryingly emphatic about the lack of public interest in Princess Caroline of Monaco and the extent of her right to privacy, but in the arguments which precede it, there is more recognition of the special circumstances involved and the sense that the court, put simply, believed she deserved a break.

Baroness Hale in *Campbell*[124] made a useful distinction to help define "reasonable expectation of privacy" in a public place. She says in para.154:

> "We have not so far held that the mere fact of covert photography is sufficient to make the information contained in the photograph confidential. The activity photographed must be private. If this had been, and had been presented as, a picture of Naomi Campbell going about her business in a public street, there could have been no complaint. She makes a substantial part of her living out of being photographed looking stunning in designer clothing. Readers will obviously be interested to see how she looks if and when she pops out to the shops for a bottle of milk. There is nothing essentially private about that information not can it be expected to damage her private life. It may not be a high order of freedom of speech but there is nothing to justify interfering with it."

Based on this line of reasoning, Elton John failed to secure an injunction to prevent publication of photographs of him in the driveway of his home.

It is no coincidence that photographs have been at the centre of so many privacy disputes. In part this emphasises how often the real issue at stake is more about image rights than personal concerns of privacy. But it is also because photographs are seen as more damning and intrusive than words to the same effect. Photographs can be more memorable, less easy for readers to brush off, less transient, but that is why newspapers want to run them, to stand the story up and give it credibility with the reader. The photograph is the evidence. The suggestion now is that journalists should take the photographs to back up a story but not necessarily seek to run them.

Historically, the more visual broadcast media tended to be seen as more transient and forgettable compared with the printed word in defamation terms. But for privacy, images loom large.

---

[123] *Murray v Big Pictures (UK) Ltd* [2008] EWCA Civ 446.
[124] *Campbell v MGN Ltd* [2004] UKHL 22.

What were the expectations of any pre-existing relationship?

This is still a relevant question within the overall ambit of what constitutes a "reasonable expectation of privacy". Where a formal contractual relationship exists, the claim is much stronger and becomes akin to the original breach of confidence actions. But any former "confidential" relationship necessitates an assessment of whether the party disclosing the information had reason to believe it was to be kept secret. This is a complex matter relating to states of mind. The closer, especially sexually, the relationship was the easier it is to argue an expectation of privacy and the harder it is to justify infringement of privacy rights of any parties, even if one wants to tell her story.

The public interest in protecting confidential relationships is weighed by the court. There is a value in upholding the expectations of trust in commercial and personal relationships.

In freedom of expression terms, those wanting to exercise art.10 rights but "guilty" of breach of trust will lose out. Article 10 rights can be overridden by the need to protect confidential arrangements as in a marriage. In the eyes of the law, someone who has breached a trust has generally done wrong. Yet, the gross breach of trust involved in adultery is no longer treated as wrongdoing or a serious impropriety when it comes to establishing a public interest in divulging private information about that breach.

The expectation of privacy surrounding group sex makes the breach of trust that would be involved a reason for it not to be revealed; yet protecting one confidence allows the breach of another, namely the infidelity involved, to be kept secret.

If it is private, how serious an invasion is it?

Think like a judge, not a journalist. As well as establishing if art.8 rights are engaged, the courts consider the seriousness of the invasion. Sex is very private; medical treatment and health concerns are private and, as in *McKennitt*,[125] "home" is sacrosanct. So the subject matter will influence the strength of the art.8 claim for privacy and thus the strength of the argument required to justify revelation.

Once it is established that a claimant's art.8 rights are engaged and to what degree, the courts look for limiting factors. The information for which protection is sought can be dismissed as useless or trivial, but the two main arguments are either the secret is already out or that the public has a right to know.

---

[125] *Niema Ash and others v Loreena McKennitt and others* [2006] EWCA Civ 1714.

Is the information already in the public domain?

This may seem obvious but judgments in *Browne*,[126] *Prince Charles*[127] and others make it difficult to determine how many people need to know a "secret" before it is considered secret no more. The "amalgam" of considerations come into play relating to how the information was gleaned, in what circles it has been disseminated previously and in what form.

Courts tend to focus on the specific information and are becoming generous about the number and range of people who may already be privy to the "private" information before it is considered to be in the public domain. In the realm of "open secrets" a journalist would say the "open" is the clue that the privacy has already been breached whereas the courts are treating the information as remaining "secret". Even inclusion on websites is not enough to put material in the public domain, so here again proportionality goes against the mainstream media players. A complainant would struggle to gain redress against a website read by a few hundred people; but can claim against or injunct operators with larger audiences. By happy coincidence for the claimants, they also tend to be the defendants with assets to claim against.

What is the claimant's history of prior revelations?

Has material on a par with the story in question been placed in the public domain previously with the claimant's full consent or indeed at their behest? Have they sought publicity and what level of intrusion have they allowed? A celebrity may have effectively put most of their "private" life on show. Can those who have bared all literally and figuratively then decide to cover up? They may not only have put specific information in to the public eye; they have put every sordid detail of their lives out there. This gives some room for manoeuvre but is not a reliable protection.

The general stance is that previous behaviour does not prevent the new material being considered private but it can have a bearing on proportionality. Yes, the more exposed a celebrity has been previously, the harder it will be to justify secrecy further down the line but, as ever, it depends. If the intrusion is great enough, previous exposure, even of similar sorts of information, may still mean judges uphold art.8 rights over art.10.

Are there public interest grounds to warrant the intrusion?

Journalists wanting to run a story which breaches privacy rights need to be very clear about their justification for the intrusion. They need to be

---

[126] *Lord Browne of Madingley Asssociated Newspapers Limited* [2007] EWCA Civ 295.
[127] *Associated Newspapers Ltd v Prince of Wales* [2006] EWCA Civ 1776.

able to define for editors, lawyers and judges, exactly where the public interest lies. As *Mosley*[128], for example, shows, a possible public interest in principle is not sufficient. The intrusion, such as clandestine reporting, must be proportionate to the degree of public interest reasonably expected in the discovery.

The Press Complaints Commission Code definition[129] of public interest may be of some help here. It says the public interest includes, but is not confined to:

- detecting or exposing crime or serious impropriety;
- protecting public health and safety; and
- preventing the public from being misled by an action or statement of an individual or organisation.

Technically, according to s.12(4) of the Human Rights Act, the courts should consider the relevant privacy codes when deciding whether to grant an injunction. The PCC Code's clause on privacy does tend to be mentioned but there is less discussion of its inbuilt public interest exemption based on the definition above which the media have interpreted much more broadly than the courts have.

Serious impropriety can be called upon where there is alleged misuse of public or corporate resources but is no longer deemed, by the courts, to include sexual indiscretion or adultery.

The third element has been much to the fore in say *Campbell*[130] where the *Mirror*'s justification was to "put the record" straight over Campbell's drug involvement. Campbell was accepted as a role model so it was reasonable for the public to know they were being misled. Putting the record straight has on occasion relied on provoking a celebrity into denial then revealing their lie, as in *Campbell*. Such behaviour, if blatant, is likely to be off-putting to judges.

The courts are tending to a view that it doesn't matter whether a celebrity is telling the truth about their private life or not. There is also a pecking order as established by Baroness Hale on which most "celebrities" are in danger of dropping off the bottom such that the answer to whether the image they present to the public is real or not is none of our business.

Eady J. in *Mosley* also suggests applying the responsible journalism test where public interest is relied upon as a limiting factor such that not only would the story need to be of public significance but it would need to have been gathered and processed rigorously.

Who is it about?

The assessment of public interest will depend on the target; their position held in society as well as the prior approach to publicity. An

---

[128] *Mosley v News Group Newspapers Ltd No 3* [2008] EWHC 1777 (QB).
[129] PCC Code of Conduct available a *www.pcc.org.uk*.
[130] *Campbell v MGN Ltd* [2004] UKHL 22.

adulterous MP would do it but only if he had previously overtly promoted family values. Think about who the subject is accountable to.

What rights can be claimed under art.10?

The focus tends to be on whether art.8 rights are involved and whether the infringement of them can be justified. But technically the parallel weighting must also take place. The claimant is requesting an infringement of the journalist's art.10 rights and the "damage" caused in so doing must be considered by the court. So it is important that journalists can argue what is being lost for them and more particularly the public by the infringement. How serious are the consequences of the public remaining in ignorance? This tends to be less emotive than the damage claimed of an art.8 infringement so it is important to ensure it is not overlooked or discounted during the "proportionality" test.

> ## Case Study One: Lord Browne of Madingley v Associated Newspapers Limited [2007] EWCA Civ 295

The Browne case provoked mixed reaction in the media itself. It was derided in some quarters as primarily concerned with cheap revelations driven by his sexuality, for which the alleged abuse of his position within a public corporation provided a public interest justification for avoiding part of the injunction.

However, it can be argued that there was a proper story to be run about revealing the allegations of abuse of position for which identification of the source and how he came by the information underpinning the accusation was required to lend authenticity to the claims. This ultimately was the argument the courts recognised.

The manner in which the combination of information is revealed is not for the judges to determine as a concession to free speech and the need for plurality, especially where those creating the climate of public discourse are partisan. So the prominence given by the media to the different elements could not be controlled by the courts.

We should ask ourselves why Lord Browne resigned as head of BP. It wasn't because of revelations of his homosexuality; it doesn't appear even to have been about whether the accusations of misuses of company resources were true or not; it was because in the process of trying to stop the matters being aired he lied to the court.

The lie to the court is arguably also why the partial lifting of the injunction was granted—enough to do the damage and enough to reveal the lie. Yes, he could decline to answer media questions about his private life but he could not lie to a court about them and expect sympathetic treatment. There was, of course, also a legal justification for this lack of sympathy in that, by undermining his own credibility, he lessened the chances of success in a subsequent legal claim to a level where success could be deemed not "likely" and therefore the injunction could be lifted. We can only speculate whether, in the absence of the lie, the public interest in the accusations would have been sufficient to lift the injunction.

The newspaper cannot entirely claim victory as various elements of its story from his ex-lover Jeff Chevalier remained subject to injunction.

The Court of Appeal judgment in the case pulls together strands from various cases outlined earlier in the chapter and provides a useful summary in itself of where the law stands. Setting aside the particular requirements of an injunction, the questions the court considers are whether art.8 rights are engaged and whether art.10 rights are engaged.

The art.8 consideration centres on the question: Is there a reasonable expectation of privacy from the claimant's viewpoint?

Chevalier had a pre-existing relationship of confidence which gave Browne a reasonable expectation of privacy for much of what passed between them. However the court accepted that a previous contractual or intimate relationship does not create a reasonable expectation of privacy in relation to all information learned or activities witnessed during the relationship. (The exemptions granted were enough to give the *Mail on Sunday* its story.)

More generally, what guidance does the judgment provide for journalists regarding the nature of private information?

There are some worrying definitions cited. Lord Phillips C.J. in *Douglas v Hello!* (No 3) [2005] EWCA Civ 595 [2006] Q.B. 125 at [83] answered the question thus:

"It seems to us that it must include information that is personal to the person who possesses it and that he does not intend shall be imparted to the general public. The nature of the information, or the form in which it is kept, may suffice to make it plain that the information satisfies these criteria."

The definition is of little help to defendants in that any claimant attempting to keep secrets clearly does not intend them to be imparted to the general public so would effectively be calling the shots over the definition. Information is private if the claimant wants it to be.

Also the use of the words general public would seem to allow for a pretty wide circle of people to be "in the know" as so many were about Browne's homosexuality, before it will be considered to be already in the public domain.

The Court of Appeal challenged the original acceptance that the relationship between Browne and Chevalier was already in the public domain. Although it didn't affect the outcome, there was an ominous statement in [61]:

"It appears to us that there is potentially an important distinction between information which is made available to a person's circle of friend or work colleagues and information which is widely published in a newspaper."

So large sections of the establishment and the oil industry can know of a relationship, and the couple can dine with the Prime Minister, but that still does not put the relationship in the public domain.

Call something a diary or journal and it is "obviously" private even if, as in the case of Prince Charles', it is copied and circulated by civil servants to a range of people including journalists rather than hidden under the bed.

Looking at Lord Browne, and other recent privacy rulings, it would appear likely that journalists will be forced to rely on public interest justification rather than trying to argue that the information is not private, although it worked to a limited extent in *Browne*.

Where there is a pre-existing relationship even trivial information may be regarded as subject to an expectation of privacy. So the relationship does raise the barrier. The expectations can be higher. The law seeks to uphold confidential relationships so the onus will be on the defendant to demonstrate how breaches of that trust would be justified. On the other hand that does not mean that anything said within a confidential relationship is private.

In *McKennitt v Ash* seemingly trivial matters were not allowed partly because they related to the home but also because there had been a relationship which created a general expectation of privacy. Not everything that happened during the course of it would be deemed private but where the relationship exists it seems the onus is on the party wanting to exercise freedom of expression to demonstrate that the facts to be disclosed can be exempted from that general expectation.

When it comes to sex, the issue is pretty clear cut. Personal sexuality is considered "extremely intimate" by the courts and the more intimate the aspect of private life that is being interfered with, the more serious must be the reasons for interference before the disclosure can be legitimate. Which explains why the *Mail on Sunday* did not seek to go into detail, of which more later.

Business dealings
Also in *Browne*, it was not accepted that business information necessarily fell outside the definition of private. Sir Anthony Clarke said at [34]:

> "It seems to us that business information passed by a company direc-
> tor to his sexual partner could readily be held to be information which
> the latter knew or ought reasonably to have known was fairly and
> reasonably to be regarded as confidential or private and in respect of
> which the former had a reasonable expectation of privacy."

A section of the disclosures was allowed not only because it related to misuse of BP assets; the matters also related to Lord Browne's actions, mainly in the outside world, taken as a result of the relationship rather than "secrets" passed on in the course of the relationship. Although the Court of Appeal questioned this distinction it did endorse the reasoning outlined by Eady J. at [43]:

"One may ask whether there can be a reasonable expectation that the law will protect the privacy of a senior executive, in relation to the use of corporate information and resources, when the effect would be to keep such allegations from those who might ordinarily be expected to make the relevant judgments or exercise supervision; that is to say, shareholders and colleagues on the board of directors."

He also said it was for the company not the judiciary to assess the extent and gravity of any such behaviour and it was not for a judge to keep the relevant information from them.

The Court of Appeal judged that art.8 was engaged. The question was whether interference with those rights could be justified under art.8(2) which in cases of protecting private information would usually be found in the rights and freedoms created by art.10. Similarly where art.10 rights are engaged the court has to consider whether interference with those rights can be justified under art.10(2) to prevent the disclosure of information received in confidence.

Then, at trial, it is a question of proportionality. Where rights clash, something has to give and the court will consider the nature and degree of sacrifice involved on either side.

Supporting detail

There is further good news in the *Browne* judgment over the revelation of the relationship. The motives of the *Mail on Sunday* for wanting to reveal it can be questioned but in practice it does reinforce a key consideration for journalists in terms of the need to provide supporting evidence for a story as was allowed, under different circumstances, in *Jameel*. Various elements of helpful definition emerged.

The newspaper did not seek to publish "intimate details of the relationship such as sexual matters or minutiae of domestic life" (and wouldn't have been allowed to) but sought to refer just to the fact that the relationship took place "not least because it may be important background in authenticating in readers' minds the other allegations they wish to publish. That is, of course, a legitimate consideration," Eady J. said.

The Court of Appeal endorsed that view in [59]:

"In our judgment, that is sufficient reason to permit publication of the bare fact of the relationship. Publication of the information in categories b) and d) would make no sense without publication of the nature of the relationship between the claimant and JC."

Mary Riddell, commentating in the *Observer*, concluded:

"Today, readers of the Mail on Sunday may learn more than most people could wish to know about Browne. The squeamish may recoil from the account of his remaindered 'rent boy' but, in the end, this is all about freedom and liberties. Without the freedom of the muck-raking and imperfect British media, we should know nothing of the liberties Lord Browne has taken with truth and justice."[131]

It should be remembered that some material was injuncted and that reportedly included accounts of dinners with Blair and Mandelson. Here there would at least be an argument that, if the views expressed privately differed markedly from their public utterances, a public interest exists in voters have a fuller account of their position to weigh against their reasonable expectation of privacy at a private dinner. Evidently this was weighed and the freedom of expression case found wanting.

Case Study Two: Mosley v News Group Newspapers Ltd No 3 [2008] EWHC 1777 (QB)

Before considering the main judgment of Mosley's action for abuse of private information, it is worth examining Eady J.'s ruling in the original attempt to injunct the video in *Max Mosley v News Group Newspapers Ltd* [2008] EWHC 687 (QB).

With Eady-esque restraint and attention to detail he refers to his viewing of the edited video at [4]:

> "It is very brief, containing shots of Mr Mosley taking part in sexual activities with five prostitutes, and it also covers the tea break."

Eady J. argued that the nature of the activity meant that Mosley certainly had a reasonable expectation of privacy and went on to consider whether there were 'limiting factors'.

Because the injunction referred to the video, Eady J. considers the status of the online imagery as distinct from the print edition. He cites Hoffmann in *Campbell* referring to a hypothetical case in which there would be "a public interest in the disclosure of the existence of a sexual relationship (e.g. because of corrupt favours) but where the addition of salacious details or intimate photographs would be disproportionate to any legitimate purpose and unacceptable".

He notes that the courts have also separated the publication of a photograph from the publication of the information it conveys. At [24] he cites Waller L.J. in *D v L* [2004] E.M.L.R. 1:

> "A court may restrain the publication of an improperly obtained photograph even if the taker is free to describe the information which the photograph provides or even if the information revealed by the photograph is in the public domain. It is no answer to the claim to restrain the publication of an improperly obtained photograph that

---

[131] *Observer*, May 6, 2007.

the information portrayed by the photograph is already available in the public domain."

The distinction between the original print publication and the linked online video footage was referred to again as Eady J. ponders the existence of any grounds for the intrusion of privacy at [30]:

"It is also appropriate to ask whether any of what Lord Goff described, in *Attorney General v Guardian Newspapers Limited* (No 2) [1990] 1 AC 109, at 282C-F, as the "limiting factors" come into play. A relevant consideration here is whether there is a public interest in revealing the material which is powerful enough to override Mr Mosley's prima facie right to be protected in respect of the intrusive and demeaning nature of the photographs. I have little difficulty in answering that question in the negative. The only reason why these pictures are of interest is because they are mildly salacious and provide an opportunity to have a snigger at the expense of the participants. Insofar as the public was ever entitled to know about Mr Mosley's sexual tastes at all, the matter has already been done to death since the original coverage in the News of the World. There is no legitimate element of public interest which would be served by the additional disclosure of the edited footage, at this stage, on the Respondent's website."

Mosley, as head of F1, had spoken publicly on the question of racism in the sport. The implication of anti-Semitism was an embarrassment in terms of his job. The *News of the World* also tried to suggest hypocrisy over his views on his fascist father Oswald Mosley. One line read: "In public he rejects his father's evil past, but secretly he plays Nazi sex games."

Eady J. acknowledged the PCC Code reference to preventing the public from being misled but said at [32] that, even if Mosley had misled the public, putting the record straight could be achieved "without displaying the edited footage of bottoms being spanked".

Also, the judgment alerts journalists to the dangers that arguing a need to put the record straight can be defamatory of the claimant as Eady J. says it was here. An injunction on defamation would have been harder as the "facts" at that stage were in doubt but that has not stopped Mosley pursuing a defamation claim too.

The main question was whether the video was already in the public domain which Eady J. somewhat reluctantly, conceded was the case. The *News of the World* took the material down following the complaint but it had already spread to many other sites. The court noted that the linking and "embedding" into other sites limits the effectiveness of any bar on access even if the original source is removed. Eady J. said at [34]:

"The Court should guard against slipping into the role of King Canute. Even though an order may be desirable for the protection of privacy, and may be made in accordance with the principles currently being applied by the courts, there may come a point where it would simply serve no useful purpose and would merely be characterised, in the traditional terminology, as a brutum fulmen. It is inappropriate for the Court to make vain gestures."

The question of whether the original print material might be in the public interest was left open at this stage but equally emphatically ruled out when the issue came to trial.

The main Eady J. ruling *Mosley v News Group Newspapers Ltd No 3* [2008] EWHC 1777 (QB) is a worthwhile read. The linguistic contrast between *News of the World* copy and case law precedents is stark and it seems surreal for a group sex game to be subject to such precise legal scrutiny. Which "ism" was this precisely? Nazism or just your average sado-masochism? Is it normal for a dominatrix to speak in guttural German? On the answers to such questions the judgment turned.

Was the information private?

Eady J. established emphatically that Mosley's art. 8 rights were engaged not only because of the sexual nature of the coverage but because of the use of covert filming by Woman E, although this was not relied on by the claimant. Eady J. said at [104]:

".. it becomes fairly obvious that the clandestine recording of sexual activity on private property must be taken to engage Article 8. What requires closer examination is the extent to which such intrusive behaviour could be justified by reference to a countervailing public interest; that is to say, at the stage of carrying out the ultimate balancing test."

What were the expectations of any pre-existing relationship?

Eady J. accepted that those engaged in the sessions expected discretion, whether the activity was paid or not. He said at [107] and [108]:

"It is true that the Claimant on this occasion paid the women participants, although he has not always done so in the past, but this does not mean that it was a purely commercial transaction. Even if it was, that would naturally not preclude an obligation of confidence, but it is quite clear from the evidence that there was a large element of friendship involved, not only as between the women but also between them and the Claimant. For example, had it not been for the intervention of the *News of the World* there was a plan to offer him a (free) session for his birthday (which falls in April).

"In any event, irrespective of payment, I would be prepared to hold that Woman E had committed an 'old fashioned breach of confidence' as well as a violation of the Article 8 rights of all those involved. This may have been at the instigation of her husband, who saw the opportunity of making £25,000 out of the *News of the World* and who made the first approach."

If it is private, how serious an invasion is it?

Eady J. addressed this mainly in terms of the level of damages to be awarded but sexual activity is high on the list of what constitutes confidential information so that creates a heavy presumption in favour of art.8 rights being upheld once it is established that they are engaged. The arguments for revelation have to be that much stronger as a consequence.

Is the information already in the public domain?

The fact that the video had gone viral had removed grounds for an injunction but in terms of this hearing the material in the story, the newspaper photographs and online video footage had not previously been in the public domain, nor had any similar material about Mosley. It was not known to his wife and family.

What is the claimant's history of prior revelations?

Mosley, as president of the FIA, was not as high-profile in motor racing as Bernie Ecclestone, say, but he did speak for the sport on a range of issues, including F1's position on racism.

What exactly is the public interest in the revelations?

Eady J. did accept that if the Nazi theme had been established, that would have created a public interest argument at least. Whether it would have been sufficient to outweigh Mosley's art.8 rights we don't know because the *News of the World* was unable to substantiate the claim which it argued was "obvious" from the video footage. Crucial witness evidence went by the wayside and Eady J. pulled apart the handling of the supposed public interest motivation for the story, saying, for instance, that the clandestine filming was set up before any suggestion of a Nazi theme. He said at [122] and [123]:

"I have come to the conclusion (although others might disagree) that if it really were the case, as the newspaper alleged, that the Claimant had for entertainment and sexual gratification been "mocking the humiliating way the Jews were treated", or "parodying Holocaust horrors", there could be a public interest in that being revealed at least to those in the FIA to whom he is accountable. He has to deal with many people of all races and religions, and has spoken out against racism in the sport. If he really were behaving in the way I have just described, that would, for many people, call seriously into question his suitability for his FIA role. It would be information which people arguably should have the opportunity to know and evaluate. It is probably right to acknowledge that private fantasies should not in themselves be subjected to legal scrutiny by the courts, but when they are acted out that is not necessarily so.

"On the other hand, since I have concluded that there was no such mocking behaviour and not even, on the material I have viewed, any evidence of imitating, adopting or approving Nazi behaviour, I am

unable to identify any legitimate public interest to justify either the
intrusion of secret filming or the subsequent publication."

Attempts to define the sex games as either illegal activity or serious
impropriety as the basis of a public interest justification, were also
ruled out. Even if a technical assault had taken place, Eady J. considered
that, as the CPS would not deem it in the public interest to prosecute
in such consensual situations, the *News of the World* could hardly claim
a public interest defence in revealing the "crime". Eady J. also stressed
that it was not for judges to make moral judgments about the nature
of sexual activity. These were the comments that particularly sparked
the row with *Daily Mail* editor-in-chief Paul Dacre discussed in Ch.2 on
Freedom of Expression.

Eady J. went on to suggest developing the definition of public interest in privacy cases by drawing on the concept of responsible journalism used in defamation. The two types of action, although distinct, are
now both bracketed under art.8. He applied, for the sake of argument,
the expectations of responsible journalism to the *News of the World*'s
behaviour in this case, notably that of its bylined chief reporter Neville
Thurlbeck, whose name is mentioned more than 70 times in the judgment. (Shades of the person on trial is the journalist?.)

Who is it about?
Mosley was the publicly-elected President of the Federation
Internationale de l'Automobile. Note above Eady's remarks about the
duty owed by Mosley to the FIA "to whom he is accountable". But in
the event this did not help as he was not deemed to have done anything
worthy of public interest.

General implications of the case
Images intrude more than words
Eady J. did treat the story, the print photographs and video separately
throughout and that distinction can be helpful as it sets the barriers at
different heights for different elements of the coverage. Words alone
may still attract a public interest defence, as they did in *Campbell*. He
said at [134]:

> "In the light of the strict criteria I am required to apply, in the modern
> climate, I could not hold that any of the visual images, whether pub-
> lished in the newspaper or on the website, can be justified in the
> public interest. Nor can it be said in this case that even the informa-
> tion conveyed in the verbal descriptions would qualify."

The Human Rights Act is Parliament-made law
There was also a reference pertinent to the current injunctions contro-
versy complaining of law being made by judges rather than Parliament.
Eady J. at [7] said:

"The law now affords protection to information in respect of which there is a reasonable expectation of privacy, even in circumstances where there is no pre-existing relationship giving rise of itself to an enforceable duty of confidence. That is because the law is concerned to prevent the violation of a citizen's autonomy, dignity and self-esteem. **It is not simply a matter of "unaccountable" judges running amok. Parliament enacted the 1998 statute which** *requires* **these values to be acknowledged and enforced by the courts.** (Our emphasis.) In any event, the courts had been increasingly taking them into account because of the need to interpret domestic law consistently with the United Kingdom's international obligations. It will be recalled that the United Kingdom government signed up to the Convention more than 50 years ago."

Payment to sources

The debacle over the role of Woman E who made the video and ultimately failed to give evidence included the following observation at [45]:

"It would probably have been wise for me to focus in any event on the footage itself, as containing the "proof of the pudding", rather than upon the evidence of Woman E, **whose credibility would naturally be suspect in view of her willingness to betray a trust for money.** (Our emphasis.) Moreover, if she had been telling Mr Thurlbeck the truth, one would certainly expect to see the allegation borne out on film. I was now asked to draw the inference that there was in fact a Nazi theme on 28 March from, and only from, the content of the hours of recorded material."

The courts consider that the credibility of a witness is lost if she betrays a trust for money not because she was being paid for sex. But the claimant does not lose credibility for paying for sex and betraying the trust of his wife.

Claimant responsibility

When setting the level of damages, Eady J. said at [225] and [226]:

"To what extent is he the author of his own misfortune? Many would think that if a prominent man puts himself, year after year, into the hands (literally and metaphorically) of prostitutes (or even professional dominatrices) he is gambling in placing so much trust in them. There is a risk of exposure or blackmail inherent in such a course of conduct. In this particular case, the evidence is that the Claimant had received a warning from Lord Stevens that he was being watched by some unidentified group of people hostile to him. This was at the end of February. He had also received a similar tip from Mr Bernie Ecclestone in January. He had taken the matter sufficiently seriously to arrange instruction for himself in spotting or avoiding surveillance.

Yet he continued to arrange parties, such as those on 8 and 28 March, knowing of the heightened risk.

"To a casual observer, therefore, and especially with the benefit of hindsight, it might seem that the Claimant's behaviour was reckless and almost self-destructive. This does not excuse the intrusion into his privacy but it might be a relevant factor to take into account when assessing causal responsibility for what happened. It could be thought unreasonable to absolve him of all responsibility for placing himself and his family in the predicament in which they now find themselves. It is part and parcel of human dignity that one must take at least some responsibility for one's own actions. On the other hand, I have no evidence to suggest that the surveillance he was warned against had any connection with Woman E or the *News of the World*."

The £60,000 was a record figure for damages for invasion of privacy but the court rejected the extension of exemplary damages into the privacy field

Public interest and responsible journalism
The judgment did not ultimately hang on this but its application is no coincidence. Eady J. found the journalistic processes involved here sadly lacking in many aspects. These included:

- Covert filming was authorised before any suggestion of a Nazi theme was introduced which might have constituted a public interest.
- The Nazi theme of the sex game was said to be "obvious" to the editorial team but Eady J. was not convinced. The interpretation put on it was the one the *News of the World* wanted to be there for the sake of the story and their public interest grounds for running it. That was not the interpretation accepted by the court.
- Reporter's notes were not available.
- Thurlbeck tried to persuade other women in the sex game to tell their story. If they agreed, he offered to pay them and not identify them in the paper. If they refused, the paper would print their pictures without masking their faces. Thurlbeck called it a choice; the court saw it as a threat.

To Eady J. there is an "obvious analogy" with the concept of responsible journalism required for a public interest defence in defamation cases which would make it logical to bring the definitions into line and in a way which imposes even greater demands on journalistic endeavour. This approach would need support from higher authorities but it delivers a heavy hint to journalists. Employ the elements of responsible journalism and a public interest "limiting factor" in privacy cases is much more likely to succeed. Otherwise, it probably won't.

Case Study Three: Murray v Big Pictures (UK) Ltd [2008] EWCA Civ 446

This case is one of many triggered by photographs taken in a public place but claimed to be private. Unusually the proceedings were brought in the name of David Murray, the son of Dr Neil Murray and Mrs Joanne Murray, better known as Harry Potter author JK Rowling.

There are many similarities with *von Hannover* in that the family group were in a city street, in this case Edinburgh, with the then 19-month-old David in a buggy. The disputed photographs, taken with a long-range lens, showed David clearly as well as his mother.

Did David have a reasonable expectation of privacy?

The activity being photographed wasn't in itself private or embarrassing and no distress was caused to him at the time. At appeal a clear distinction was made between the child's expectation of privacy and his mother's.

The judgment noted the PCC Code of Practice statement under Children:

> v) Editors must not use the fame, notoriety or position of the parent or guardian as sole justification for publishing details of a child's private life.

But the Codebook also says that mere publication of a child's image taken in a public place and unaccompanied by anything to embarrass or inconvenience the child would not breach the Code.

Clarke M.R. stressed that the only interest in David was as 'JK Rowling's' son and said in [57]:

> "Subject to the facts of the particular case, the law should indeed protect children from intrusive media attention, at any rate to the extent of holding that a child has a reasonable expectation that he or she will not be targeted in order to obtain photographs in a public place for publication which the person who took or procured the taking of the photographs knew would be objected to on behalf of the child."

What is the claimant's history of prior revelations?

This was of some significance. As JK Rowling, Mrs Murray accepted a degree of legitimate interest in her activities and appearance, but she stressed that she had '"repeatedly and consistently" taken steps to secure and maintain her children's privacy. She had, for instance, never discussed details of her family life in any interview. Publication of an earlier photograph of her daughter Jessica had resulted in a complaint upheld by the Press Complaints Commission. This strengthened the judges' position that the photographic agency knew that permission would not be granted.

What rights can be claimed under art.10?

The judgment doesn't suggest any arguments in favour of freedom of expression and asserts that once it has ruled that David has a reasonable expectation of privacy "it seems to us more likely than not that, on the assumed facts, it (the ECtHR) would hold that the article 8/10 balance would come down in favour of David."[132]

Technically the matter has not been taken to trial as this was an appeal against an earlier striking out of the claim but it establishes pretty effectively that the children of famous people are "off limits". So for children, the *von Hannover* principles are clearly in force. Perhaps we should be relieved that a distinction was made between children and adults as the judgment suggests that where David's art.8 rights were engaged, his parents most likely were not. But blame this ruling for the now-routine the pixelation of the faces of the children of celebrities in mainstream publications.

CHAPTER SUMMARY: PRIVACY

Article 8 of the European Convention of Human Rights states:

"Everyone has the right to respect for his private and family life, his home and his correspondence."

This allows actions to be brought for misuse of private information. Journalists can be prevented from revealing private information unless they can establish either that the secret is already out in the public domain or that there is a public interest in revealing it which outweighs the claimant's art.8 rights. A journalist contemplating exposure of private information needs to anticipate a claim by asking the following questions of the intended article.

- **Are the subject's art.8 rights engaged?**
  - Does the claimant have a **reasonable expectation of privacy?**
  - Is the information being revealed private?
  - Is the claimant genuinely trying to protect his/her privacy or is the driver commercial concern for image or earnings?
- **Are there limiting factors?**
  - Is it, or equivalent information, already in the public domain?

---

[132] Para.60.

Try to find widely-accessed material regarding the behaviour of the subject, such as previous similar misdemeanours. The threshold is high though—family and workmates aren't enough; nor is an obscure blog.

- Is there a public interest in the revelation? Does it involve crime, serious impropriety, a threat to public health and safety or hypocrisy? Has the claimant been misleading the public? Does it contribute to a debate of general interest? Is the subject accountable to the public in some way ideally through elected or public office?

- Stories most likely to defeat a privacy claim or injunction:
  - Reveal abuse of power/position by a politician, public official or senior manager with responsibilities to shareholders.
  - Target criminal rather than "immoral" behaviour.
  - Focus on information deemed crucial to the public interest dimension of the story. This may well exclude photographs.
  - Report soberly particularly about sexual elements and meet the requirements of "responsible" journalism.

- Stories highly likely to be thwarted by injunctions involve:
  - **Children**, particularly of celebrities, particularly if photographed or even if not directly involved.
  - Images per se which are seen as more intrusive than text.
  - Photographs and/or stories of litigious "low-profile" celebrities.
  - Subjects with a lot to lose financially from disclosure—unless very blatant about their commercial motives.
  - Rich and powerful people who can afford the injunction and those who have most to hide.
  - Adultery, sado-masochism or any other sexual activity.
  - Medical records.
  - Home and family life.
  - Disingenuous/contrived public interest elements.
  - Payments to sources.
  - Revelling in tawdry, particularly sexual elements.
  - Journalists not ready with arguments to challenge them.

CHAPTER 6: JOURNALISTS' SOURCES

PART ONE: THE LAW ON SOURCES

The Press Complaints Commission Code of Practice is unambiguous. Journalists have a *moral* duty to protect their confidential sources.[1] But what is the legal position? Section 10 of the Contempt of Court Act 1981:

> "No court may require a person to disclose, nor is any person guilty of contempt of court for refusing to disclose, the source of information contained in a publication for which he is responsible, unless it is established to the satisfaction of the court that disclosure is necessary in the interests of justice or national security or for the prevention of disorder or crime."

The PCC Code acknowledges, albeit by implication, that no journalist is above the law. This position is not unique to England and Wales. The Canadian Supreme Court in an important decision in May 2010 declared that a journalist's privilege to keep a source's identity secret was not an absolute right under the Canadian Constitution. Each case will be decided on its own particular facts.[2] There is no absolute legal protection for journalists who have given a guarantee of confidentiality to a source. Yet the journalist who endeavours to adhere to his or her professional code of practice is set upon an immediate collision course with the courts should action be commenced to seek a disclosure order.

If journalists comply with court orders to disclose sources then their professional credibility will immediately disappear. How many sources are likely to provide information in return for a guarantee of confidentiality once it is known that the particular journalist cannot be relied upon to adhere to the commitment?

In discussing the legal interpretation of s.10, it should be considered whether litigation in this area of law is really worth the effort, not to mention the cost. In July 2007, the House of Lords refused Mersey Care NHS Trust leave to appeal the decision of the Court of Appeal in its action against Robin Ackroyd.[3] This finally put an end to attempts to obtain the name of the person who revealed the Moors murderer, Ian

---

[1] Cl.14 of the Press Complaints Commission Code of Practice.
[2] *R v National Post* [2010] S.C.C. 16.
[3] *Mersey Care NHS Trust v Ackroyd* [2007] EWCA Civ 220.

Brady's, medical records to a journalist who forwarded them to the *Daily Mirror* for publication. The litigation commenced in late 1999.

Reference will also be made to the *Interbrew*[4] litigation that ended in 2002. On the face of it, Interbrew was successful in that it persuaded the High Court and Court of Appeal to order disclosure but in the end "threw in the towel" when the newspapers involved indicated they were likely to take the case on a point of principle, to the European Court of Human Rights. They were as good as their word but the decision from the court only came in December 2009.[5] Two very important cases and in each case the duration was the litigation was the best part of a decade. The key question to ask in each case was what exactly was achieved?

The European Court of Human Rights has been far from silent in supporting journalists in their endeavours to resist compliance with orders made under s.10. In the well-known case of *Goodwin v United Kingdom* [1996][6] the Court went on record to say:

> "Protection of sources is one of the basic conditions for press freedom . . . without such protection, sources may be deterred from assisting the press in informing the public on matters of public interest. As a result the vital public watchdog role of the press may be undermined and the ability of the press to provide accurate and reliable information may be adversely affected. Having regard to the importance of the protection of journalistic sources for press freedom in a democratic society and the potentially chilling effect an order of source disclosure has on the exercise of that freedom, such a measure cannot be compatible with Article 10 of the Convention unless it is justified by an overriding requirement in the public interest."[7]

The case became something of a cause celebre in light of the fact that the European Court found that the order for Goodwin to release his notes of a telephone conversation with his source breached art.10 of the European Convention on Human Rights. The report of the English decision is to be found at *X v Morgan Grampian* [1990].[8] A company had prepared a business plan based upon which it intended to apply for a substantial loan. A copy was stolen from its premises and details were then telephoned to a magazine. The journalist was William Goodwin and his contact with the firm to verify the story resulted in an application to the High Court for a disclosure order. The claimant believed the identity of the source could probably be gleaned from the notes of the telephone conversation between the source and Goodwin. As a general principle, there is a public interest in preserving commercial confidentiality. It was accepted by the court that releasing this information into the

---

[4] *Financial Times & Others v Interbrew SA* [2002] EWCA Civ 274.
[5] *Financial Times & Others v United Kingdom* [2009] ECHR 2065.
[6] [1996] ECHR 16.
[7] [1996] ECHR 16 at para.39.
[8] [1990] 2 All E.R. 1.

public domain would be likely to cause severe damage to the company's business and could even have resulted in job losses. The House of Lords ordered the documents to be released.

The reasons are as follows:

1. The information had been obtained through unlawful means and there was clearly a breach of confidence. The publishers had "received" this information and wished to publish an article based upon it. In so doing, they were "mixed up in the tortuous acts of the source from the moment they received the confidential information."[9] Consequently the publishers were under a duty to assist the company in its attempt to redress the wrong perpetrated against it.[10] An injunction against the company prevented the dissemination of the story but that did not prevent a court from ordering discovery in such circumstances.

2. Having established the preliminary point the House then considered the matter in light of s.10 of the 1981 Act. The House acknowledged that the protection of the identity of a source was a matter of "high necessity" and "nothing less than necessity would suffice to override it."[11]

The reference in s.10 to the interests of justice did not merely encompass the administration of justice through court proceedings but also in the broader sense of allowing people to exercise important legal rights. Equally, they should be able to protect themselves against serious legal wrongs. The House could find no legitimate public interest that the publication was "calculated to serve." In fact, just the opposite would be true as failure to obtain increased working capital might mean the closure of the company and in consequence significant unemployment. The appeals of the publisher and the journalist were dismissed.

What is interesting about the two judgments is that the principle of upholding press freedom through protecting sources was acknowledged by each court. The difference was in the conclusion. This suggests that everything will ultimately depend on the facts of each case. Judges are expected to engage in a "balancing exercise" starting with the assumption that nothing less than necessity will override the protection offered to journalists by Parliament through the medium of s.10. So what factors will tip the balance one way or the other? Lord Bridge offered the following while at the same time emphasising that they did not amount to "comprehensive" guidance:

1. Does the claimant's livelihood depend upon disclosure?
2. Is the claimant seeking only to protect a "minor interest"?

[9] [1990] 2 All E.R. 1 at p.2.

[10] The dictum of Lord Reid in *Norwich Pharmacal Co. Customs and Excise Commissioners* [1973] 2 All E.R. 943 at p.948 applied.

[11] [1973] 2 All E.R.943 at p.2 (j).

3　The greater the public interest in the nature of the information the greater the need to protect the source.

4　How was the information obtained? If it was obtained legitimately then that will "enhance the importance of protecting the source."

5　If the information is obtained illegally this will "diminish the importance of protecting the source" unless there is a clear public interest in the information being revealed.[12]

The judicial approach would appear to be supportive of the right to protection of sources and lawyers may wonder why journalists such as Goodwin are prepared to risk fines and imprisonment for failing to comply with a court order. As Lord Bridge said:

"**I** have not heard of any campaign in the media suggesting that the law itself is unjust or that the exceptions to the protections are too widely drawn. But if there were such a campaign, it should be fought in a democratic society by persuasion, not by disobedience to the law . . . The journalist cannot be left to be a judge in his own cause and decide whether or not to make disclosure. This would be an abdication of the role of Parliament and the courts in the matter and in practice would be tantamount to conferring an absolute privilege."[13]

There we have the nub of the problem. However reasonable that interpretation may be as a vindication of parliamentary supremacy and the rule of law, individual journalists are most unlikely ever to comply with a disclosure order. The critical period for the journalist is when it is being decided whether to offer a guarantee to the source. If the journalist has doubts about the veracity of the source or the quality of the information or whether the source is seeking to manipulate the journalist then a guarantee should *not* be given. Only when satisfied that the source and the information to be imparted are credible should a commitment to anonymity be agreed. Once that is one the journalist is on a road of no return.[14]

The legal position in this country is no different to other democratic nations. For example in the Australian case of *Harvey v County Court of Victoria* [2006],[15] Hollingworth J. said:

"Although the journalists' code of ethics may preclude them from naming a source, that code has no legal status. The law does not currently recognise any "journalists' privilege." If a journalist chooses

---

[12] [1973] 2 All E.R.943 at p.9(h)-10(h) per Lord Bridge.
[13] [1973] 2 All E.R.943 at p.13 (c) per Lord Bridge.
[14] See the experience of Nick Martin-Clark: When a Journalist Must Tell: British Journalism Review (2003) Vol 14 pp 35-39.
[15] [2006] VSC 293.

not to reveal a source and thereby to commit an act of contempt that is a matter of personal choice."[16]

The fact that a journalist is unlikely to divulge the identity of a source is not a factor that the court should take into account in carrying out the balancing exercise. To do so would mean only one conclusion that self-determination would be invoked on each and every occasion. Citizens cannot select which laws are to apply to them without being aware of the legal consequences of such actions.

There is however no reason why journalists should not be given greater protection in the form of a genuine public interest defence akin to that of *Reynolds/Jameel* defence in respect of the law on defamation rather than the protection being offered through the medium of the contempt laws.

The Canadian Supreme Court decision in *R v National Post* [2010] emphasised that the courts should ". . . seek to strive to uphold the special position of the media and protect the media's secret sources where such protection is in the public interest . . ."[17] In essence the approach in this case as it is in the UK and Australia is to weigh one public interest against another. In the Canadian case it was the suppression of crime against the free flow of accurate and pertinent information. In the *Interbrew* case it was the protection of commercially sensitive information against the right to publish.

Claimants, when considering legal action for disclosure, must take detailed legal advice on the prospects of achieving their objectives. Such proceedings are invariably going to be defended. The time spent, effort expended and the costs accumulated are likely to weigh heavily when making that assessment.

Let us now consider two major pieces of litigation while bearing in mind the question "What has been achieved? Does it justify the time and cost of such litigation?

Case study One: Ashworth Security Hospital Authority v MGN Ltd/Mersey Care NHS Trust v Ackroyd [2000-2007][18]

This litigation commenced in January 2000. Ian Brady, was, and still is, incarcerated in a secure mental hospital in the North West of England. His notoriety stemmed from the "Moors Murders" that he and Myra Hindley committed in the mid 1960s. Hindley died in 2002. Details of his medical records from Ashworth High Security Hospital were published by the *Daily Mirror*. The hospital responded by publishing a statement

---

[16] [2006] VSC at para.90.
[17] [2010] S.C.C. 16 at para.3.
[18] House of Lords decision at [2002] UKHL 29. Final Court of Appeal decision at [2007] EWCA Civ 101.

to the effect that the *Mirror*'s story was a flagrant breach of patient confidentiality. The question for the authorities at Ashworth was: Who was responsible for the leak of Brady's medical records?

It proved to be, as the Court of Appeal said in early 2007 ". . . a most unusual case."[19] The hospital was successful in obtaining a disclosure order from the trial judge in April 2000. Subsequently, MGN appealed and the Court of Appeal and then the House of Lords dismissed the newspaper's appeals. These two courts, unlike the High Court, took into account that the Human Rights Act had come into force. In coming to their decisions, the courts adopted the established view that s.10 of the 1981 Act and art.10 of the Convention had a "common purpose" in seeking to enhance "the freedom of the press by protecting journalistic sources." Lord Woolf said in the House of Lords:

> "The important protections which both section 10 and article 10 provide for freedom of expression is that they require the court stringently to scrutinise any request for relief which will result in the court interfering with freedom of expression including ordering the disclosure of journalists' sources. Both section 10 and article10 are one in making it clear that the court has to be sure that a sufficiently strong positive case has been made out in favour of disclosure before disclosure will be ordered."[20]

The consequence of applying art.10, said Lord Woolf, was that any disclosure order had to be not only *necessary* but also proportionate to achieving the aim in question, i.e. which of the two public interest arguments should prevail? The ". . . necessity for any restriction of freedom of expression must be convincingly established." Adopting the terminology of art.10, the jurisdiction should only be exercised if there was a "pressing social need" and that any restriction upon freedom of expression should be *proportionate* to the "legitimate aim being pursued."[21]

In summing up the "new" post-Human Rights Act approach one can do no better than quote from Lord Justice Laws' judgment in *Ashworth v MGN* in the Court of Appeal. He said:

> ". . . in any given case the debate which follows will be conducted upon the question whether there is an overriding public interest, amounting to a pressing social need, to which the need to keep press sources confidential should give way. That debate will arise under section 10 in the municipal legislation; it will arise more broadly by reference to Article 10 of the Convention, and in the light of the Strasburg jurisprudence on article 10."[22]

---

[19] [2007] EWCA Civ 101 at para.1
[20] [2002] UKHL 29 at para.49.
[21] [2002] UKHL 29 at paras 61-62.
[22] [2000] EWCA Civ 334 at para.101.

However, there was a "curious feature" to this series of cases. *Mirror Group Newspapers* was not aware of the identity of the primary source of the information. The medical information had been passed to a local journalist Robin Ackroyd who in turn passed the information to the *Daily Mirror*. It appears that no one ever thought to ask over the two years of litigation whether MGN knew the name of the original source. As the Court of Appeal said in its most recent judgment "That Rougier J, this court and the House of Lords should consider the matter on the basis of a false assumption is disturbing."[23] Some might argue that it was more than just disturbing; it was an utter waste of time and money.

Mersey Care NHS Trust had by then assumed managerial responsibility for Ashworth. It had a decision to take: to continue the quest for a name by embarking upon further litigation or to throw in the towel. After all there had been no further leaks of information from the hospital and the number of staff having access to the medical records had been dramatically reduced. Unsurprisingly, Ackroyd refused the hospital's request to reveal the source of his information. Proceedings were then issued against him. Gray J. granted summary judgment to the Trust based upon the decision of the House of Lords in the Trust's favour. Ackroyd appealed that decision and the court accepted that there were potentially important differences between the *MGN* issues and the issues in this case. There should be a trial.

That trial commenced in January 2006 and judgment was lodged in Ackroyd's favour in February 2006.[24] In his judgment, Mr Justice Tugendhat acknowledged the importance of European jurisprudence and not only in the context of art.10. Confidential medical records fall within the ambit and protection of art.8 of the Convention as determined by Lord Woolf in the House of Lords. Personal data including medical information was deemed ". . . of fundamental importance to a person's enjoyment of his or her right to respect for private and family life as guaranteed by article 8 of the Convention."[25]

None of this should come as a surprise. Many employees will find that their contracts contain a clause against revealing sensitive or confidential information. That was certainly the case at Ashworth.

The judge went on to consider the approach to resolving conflicting rights based upon the well-known speech of Lord Steyn in *Re S (A child) (Identification: Restrictions on Publication)* [2004].[26] He identified four important points of principle:

1. Neither article had precedence over the other.
2. There must be a detailed examination of the "comparative importance of the specific rights being claimed."

[23] [2007] EWCA Civ 101 at para.87.
[24] [2006] EWHC 107 (QB).
[25] [2002] UKHL 29 at para.95.
[26] [2004] UKHL 47.

3   Judges should identify the reasons for interfering with or restricting each right.

4   The ultimate balancing test was determined by reference to
proportionality.

In reaching his decision not to order disclosure the judge first considered the value of freedom of expression. The court acknowledged
that not all types of speech have equal value. The public interest elements must then be considered. Was it in the public interest to disclose
Brady's medical records? Certainly one can envisage occasions when
it may be in the public interest to divulge some or all of a person's
medical history although that must be kept within very narrow limits
and therefore would be a rare occurrence. X v Y [1988][27] concluded
that the public interest in preserving confidentiality of hospital records
identifying Aids victims "outweighed the public interest in the freedom
of the press to publish such information." The reasoning was that such
publicity would act as a potential deterrent to those with the disease
from seeking appropriate medical treatment.[28] However, in this case,
the court refused to order disclosure of the source that had provided the
newspaper with information about two doctors who were alleged to be
suffering from Aids.

A court has then to consider whether there has been "wrongdoing"
by the source, his duty towards his employer and whether there was any
justification for doing what he did. There had been a number of concerns about the way the security hospital was being managed. Serious
allegations had surfaced giving real cause for concern. Brady, for
instance, had been on hunger strike for a month over plans to move him
from one ward to another and other issues connected with his personal
safety. Ackroyd had taken a particular journalistic interest in the issue
and, given the number of dangerous patients incarcerated it was clearly
a public interest matter to know what was going on inside the hospital.

The judge went on to find that the source was probably someone
working at the hospital but he could not determine from the evidence
available whether the person was actually still employed at the hospital. As such, the judge found that the source, irrespective of whether he
or she was still employed there, owed a duty of confidentiality to both
Brady and the hospital.

Was there any justification for the disclosure? It was accepted that the
source did not receive payment for the information that was provided.
Ian Brady may well have encouraged the leak because he was in dispute
with the hospital authorities and possibly felt this would draw the public's attention to his grievances. No harm may have accrued to Brady,
but a wrong had been perpetrated against the hospital because of the
breach of confidence.

[27] [1988] 2 All E.R. 648.
[28] [1988] 2 All E.R. at p.648 (j).

The next question to consider was whether there was a public interest defence available to the source. Brady had claimed to have been assaulted and mistreated by nurses. That was a matter of general public interest that warranted investigation. However, the judge found that on the balance of probabilities there was no public interest justification for revealing Brady's medical records. The information contained in the records would be of little value when investigating the wider claims of mistreatment and mismanagement at the hospital. A wrong therefore had been perpetrated against the hospital for which there was no public interest defence. The "threshold" test for disclosure based upon the Norwich Pharmacal case (see footnote 10) had been passed.

Having taken the above matters into account the judge decided there was no pressing social need to make a disclosure order. This was clearly at odds with the decision in the *MGN* case but that was justified on the basis that the facts were somewhat different from those in the previous case. The judgment appears to be entirely pragmatic and all the better for it. Six years had passed since the records were released to Ackroyd. If the Health Authority were to discover the identity of the source, what action could it take? The first huge assumption is that the source was still employed by the hospital. In fact, he may never have been an employee. The court was told that over 50 per cent of the hospital employees had left since 1999. The individual could be dead. In each situation, the health authority would have no remedy against the individual.

The court accepted that the numbers having access to medical records had been substantially reduced. If a leak were to occur now it would be much easier to identify potential culprits. There had been no further leaks from the hospital in the intervening period. Thus taking into account the *proportionality* argument for interfering with the concept of freedom of expression, it was clear that the hospital had little to gain from discovering the source of the leak. Even if the person were still an employee, all that the Authority could do would be to discipline the person or dismiss him. All other effective remedies to ensure the confidentiality of medical records had been instigated without the identity of the source being known. Practical and effective remedies to prevent breaches of confidence can be put in place without the necessity of costly litigation. Perhaps the best example of that is the advice given by the Court of Appeal in the case of *John v Express Newspapers* [2000].[29]

Draft documents had been taken from a barrister's chambers. It was assumed someone working for outside cleaning contractors had removed the documents relating to the financial affairs of Sir Elton John. The information found its way to *Express Newspapers*. Legal action was instigated in an attempt to discover the source of the leaked information. The High Court made a disclosure order on the basis that support needed to be given to ensure that the lawyer/client relationship remained as confidential as possible. The Court of Appeal saw this as

[29] [2000] EWCA Civ 135.

an over-reaction. The most efficacious way of ensuring confidentiality in such circumstances thought the Master of the Rolls, was to invest in a shredding machine and to make staff more security conscious rather than engaging in expensive litigation! By that simple expedient, the right to freedom of expression need not be challenged.

The court spoke of the devastating consequences to journalists' careers if they get involved in such litigation. After the Court of Appeal's decision in 2007 Robin Ackroyd "confessed" that the past decade had not been the most auspicious in his life. His career was essentially placed on hold as the litigation continued to roll.

The High Court, and subsequently the Court of Appeal, emphasised that nothing in the judgments should be taken "as providing any encouragement to those who would disclose medical records."[30] All the judges associated themselves with the remarks of the House of Lords in the *MGN* case.

The judge also paid tribute to Robin Ackroyd concluding that he was "a responsible journalist whose purpose was to act in the public interest." It should however be noted that whether the actions taken by a journalist are deemed legally to be in the public interest will be determined *objectively* not *subjectively*.

It is respectfully submitted that the approach of the courts in *Ackroyd* has been the correct one. There has to be a realistic possibility at the outset of litigation that the claimant's objective is attainable. The objective surely is not simply to obtain a court order but to obtain a court order safe in the knowledge that there will be compliance with the order. The initial litigation could *never* have led to the naming of the source. The Court of Appeal said in 2007 that it is:

> "... almost inconceivable that this court or the House of Lords would have given permission to appeal the decision of Rougier J. had it been appreciated that far from disclosing the ultimate source, all that would be disclosed was the journalist who provided the story and who would have had his own right to maintain the confidence of his source ..."[31]

The Court of Appeal also referred to the:

> "... enormous amount of money and, perhaps more significantly, energy on the part of the hospital (that) would have been saved and better directed to other activities."[32]

How might the problem be solved in the future? The Court of Appeal offered two solutions:

---

[30] [2006] EWHC 107 at para.196 and [2007] EWCA Civ 101 at para.86.
[31] [2007] EWCA Civ 101 at para.88.
[32] [2007] EWCA Civ 101 at para.88.

1️⃣ That the "underlying principles are now reasonably clear, so it should not be necessary for cases of this kind to come to this court or go to the House of Lords in the future. It should be possible for any dispute to be resolved by the judge carrying out the balancing exercise."

2️⃣ To ask the editor to confirm that the source of an article or programme is not a journalist "whose own art.10 and s.10 rights would fall to be considered if his or her identity were disclosed." If the editor failed to disclose that information then there should be request for summary disposal of the application.

Disputes of this sort should be "resolved as soon as possible after the relevant incident has occurred." Having said all that it still does not answer the question of whether it is even remotely possible that a journalist will comply with a court order. That of course is not a matter for a court but for "individual" conscience, but what we are dealing with here is a "collective" conscience as hinted at by cl.14 of the PCC Code. In other words the outcome will be known in advance. It is worth noting that no cases dealing with the conflict between source protection and disclosure have been tried by the High Court since the Ackroyd decision in 2007.

Case Study Two: Financial Times v Interbrew SA [2002][33]

Interbrew SA, the largest brewing group in Europe, was considering making a bid for South African Breweries. It was receiving confidential advice from its merchant bankers. The *Financial Times* and a number of other prestigious newspapers received copies of a leaked and (as it turned out) partially forged document containing details of the contemplated takeover. The newspapers ran with the story causing an immediate negative impact on Interbrew's share price. Interbrew commenced litigation against the newspapers seeking a disclosure order in an attempt to identify the source of the "leak" from the document they each had received.

The issue was succinctly described by the High Court in these terms:

"The essential issue on this application is whether the Claimant's interest in obtaining the Documents and its (and I would add the public) interest in identifying the Source is sufficiently compelling to override the defendant's and the public interest in protecting the media's sources of information."[34]

[33] [2002] EWCA Civ 274.
[34] *Interbrew SA v Financial Times* [2001] EWHC 480 (Chan) at para.4.

The major discursive points can be summarised as follows:

- Has crime been committed? Was the document stolen?
- Has a civil wrong been perpetrated against the company?
    - Has there been a breach of confidence?
    - Is the entitlement to disclosure blocked by s.10 of the Contempt of Court Act?
    - If the "shield" of s.10 is to be removed then the "interests of justice" ground would appear to be the most appropriate. This could include the right to bring legal action against the miscreant, the detection of crime and the exercise of any civil rights the company has against the source.
    - In determining whether disclosure is *necessary* there is a "... close regard to be had to the relationship between the mischief and the measure. If the mischief is a civil wrong, the measure which needs to be justified as relevant and proportionate is one which will right the wrong."
    - The source's motive and purpose in revealing the information.
    - Is the court exercising discretion when considering s.10? The Court of Appeal was emphatic in answering that in the negative. It was said Lord Justice Sedley "... a matter of hard-edged judgment, albeit one of both fact and law, and one the less so for having to respect the principles of proportionality."[35]

The Court of Appeal concluded "though not without misgiving" that the order for disclosure should stand. Such evidence as the newspapers held could be vital in identifying the source and permitting the company to bring an action for breach of confidence against the source. The court thought that the right to free expression is not negated only limited, on prescribed grounds and in a particular situation:

"Whether production is then a proportionate response is a value judgement which further analysis cannot assist. It requires a synthesis of what has been established as legally relevant in fact and law."[36]

A determining factor seemed to be the source's evident purpose described by the judge as "... a maleficent one calculated to do harm ..." Sedley L.J. went on:

"The public interest in protecting the source of such a leak is in my judgment not sufficient to withstand the countervailing public interest in letting Interbrew seek justice in the courts against the source."[37]

---

[35] *Financial Times v Interbrew SA* [2002] EWCA Civ 274 at para.45.
[36] [2002] EWCA Civ 274 at para.53.
[37] [2002] EWCA Civ 274 at para.55.

So, armed with victories in the High Court and Court of Appeal, one would have assumed Interbrew would have made sure the story ended there once the documents were handed over. The assumption may have been correct; the reality though was somewhat different.

In July 2002, the editors of the four newspapers and the head of Reuters news agency refused to comply with the court order claiming that there were fundamental issues of press freedom at stake. The five organisations were refused leave to appeal by the House of Lords against the Court of Appeal judgment. There was an indication that, with no further legal avenue open to the five, they would be prepared to take an action to the European Court of Human Rights in Strasbourg.

Of major concern was the relationship between financial journalists and their sources. A key role of the press is to bring to the public's attention any hint of corporate fraud or wrongdoing. This task would be made all the harder as a result of this decision because potential whistleblowers would think twice about revealing information unless there was an absolute guarantee against disclosure. In the light of Enron, the biggest scandal in US corporate history in December 2001, one can easily understand the position adopted by the organisations in response to the *Interbrew* decision. The stakes were raised when Interbrew applied to the High Court for an order to seize the *Guardian*'s assets on the basis that the newspaper was in contempt for failing to comply with the court order.

Fortunately, reason prevailed and Interbrew handed the whole matter over to the Financial Services Authority to carry out an investigation. The FSA has search and seizure powers, yet a nine-month investigation came to nothing. In September 2003, the FSA terminated the investigation. The source was never identified. However the legal spotlight now focused on the European Court of Human Rights as the newspapers fulfilled the threat to move the case to Strasbourg.

The issue for the European Court of Human Rights was very straightforward. Was the order to the newspapers to deliver up the documents they had received from the anonymous source an unjustified interference with the media's art.10 rights because it could lead to the source(s) being identified? The court delivered its judgment in December 2009 and unsurprisingly, given its support generally for the media's art.10 rights, concluded there had been a breach.[38] The case is important because it builds upon the guidance given in the *Goodwin* case.[39]

The court repeated the well known mantra that given the importance to press freedom of protecting journalistic sources any order incompatible with art.10 rights will only be justified ". . . by (the) overriding requirement of the public interest . . . the 'necessity' of any interference with freedom of expression must be convincingly established."[40]

---

[38] *Financial Times & Others v United Kingdom* [2009] ECHR 2065.
[39] *Goodwin v United Kingdom* [1996] ECHR 16.
[40] *Financial Times & Others v United Kingdom* [2009] ECHR 2065 at paras 59–60.

It had been argued that three very important issues were at stake from the company viewpoint. First to protect the rights of others, secondly the prevention of crime and thirdly to prevent the disclosure of information received in confidence. It was also pointed out that the source had acted in a hurtful or criminal way.

The court was not convinced that collectively these arguments outweighed the importance of protecting the media's art.10 rights. The court emphasised that it would be rare for any one factor to be decisive when carrying out the balancing exercise to determine whether an "exception" under art.10(2) should apply. The court would also look at the actions of the journalists in order to determine whether they had acted professionally in their approach to the story. In trying to balance the various factors the court had to determine whether the reasons adduced by the national authorities to justify an interference with art.10 were "relevant and sufficient."[41]

In this case the disclosure of the documents in the possession of the newspapers would not necessarily lead to the identity of the source being revealed and an action for breach of confidence brought. In other cases the name of the source may well be on the document and legal proceedings against the source a certainty. That distinction did not commend itself to the court. Certainly it could be one factor of many but it would not be crucial.

The court concluded that the reasons advanced by the company were insufficient to outweigh the public interest in supporting the "special nature" of the principle of source protection.[42] As was mentioned earlier in the chapter when discussing the *Elton John* case, the company could have taken other actions in an endeavour to protect confidential information which did not interfere with the principle of source protection. An example could be an application for an injunction to prevent the publication of information on the grounds of breach of confidentiality.

1. Sources in the 21st Century

So the first decade of the millennium was a reasonably good one for the media. The Irish Supreme Court also supported the editor and a journalist from the *Irish Times* in resisting demands from the Mahon Tribunal to disclose the source of a story that the tribunal was investigating alleged improper payments to a former senior politician.[43]

They refused to appear before the Tribunal to answer questions. The tribunal successfully applied to the High Court for an order compelling them to appear. They appealed successfully to the Supreme Court. The

---

[41] [2009] ECHR 2065 at para.61.
[42] [2009] ECHR 2065 at para.67.
[43] *Mahon Tribunal v Keena & Another* [2009] IESC 64.

court's reasoning reflected that of the European Court of Human Rights in supporting the art.10 rights of journalists to protect their sources. The court used the same wording found five months later in the *Financial Times* judgment. If there was to be a restriction placed upon freedom of expression then it must be justified by an "overriding requirement in the public interest."

The High Court had been overly influenced by the fact the newspaper had destroyed the documents upon which the story was based. Whether the journalists' conduct had been reprehensible or not was not a major factor. The issue is whether taking account of all the circumstances the public interest was best served by supporting the art.10 rights of the media to protect their sources.

There was however a very nasty "sting in the tail" for the *Irish Times*. The usual practice on costs is that the loser pays. In this case the Supreme Court decided that the newspaper should pay all the costs which exceeded £500,000. The reason was because the newspaper had destroyed the documents and this had resulted in the Tribunal being effectively deprived of the ability to carry out an inquiry. If this decision were to be challenged in the European Court of Human Rights the imposition of such a "fine" may well be deemed to be an unfair attack upon the newspaper's art.10 rights.

We are unlikely ever to see again a litigation saga to parallel the Ashworth case. The legal principles we are told by the Court of Appeal are reasonably clear. The courts in *Ackroyd* have taken a pragmatic approach that doesn't challenge the right of free expression. The European Court of Human Rights had made its position clear in supporting the principle of source protection. The test for the future though is likely to occur when the claimant is the government and the ground relied upon is national security. It is hoped that the reasoning adopted by the House of Lords in *Secretary of State for Defence v Guardian Newspapers* [1984][44] will be consigned to the dustbin of history and civil servant whistleblowers will feel they can reveal information to the media which has a clear public interest imperative, without threat of exposure.

2. Access to Journalistic Material

In the normal course of business, media organisations accumulate a tremendous amount of material. It may be that the media is invited to assist the police and, as part of an investigation, there may be potentially helpful material held by a newspaper or broadcasting organisation. In many situations, the media will take on the role of "good

---

[44] [1984] 3 All E.R. 601. The *Guardian* complied with the disclosure order and the source Sarah Tisdall was prosecuted and sentenced to six months imprisonment.

citizen" and hand over material to the police for analysis. However, a media organisation that *appears* to be working too closely with the authorities may well lose its credibility and to some extent its objectivity. If handing material to the police becomes a regular occurrence then reporters and particularly photographers may be at risk when covering stories. That in turn may have a potentially negative effect on the free flow of information and the withdrawal of co-operation from sources.

We again find that a balancing act is required between two competing public interest issues. The first is helping the police with their inquiries, and the second, freedom of expression.

That fact was recognised by Parliament in the Police and Criminal Evidence Act 1984. As Bingham L.J. said in *R. v Crown Court at Lewes, Ex Parte Hill* (1991)[45]:

> "The Police and Criminal Evidence Act governs a field in which there are two very obvious public interests. There is, first of all, a public interest in the effective investigation and prosecution of crime. Secondly, there is the public interest in protecting the personal and property rights of citizens against infringement and invasion. There is an obvious tension between these two public interests because crime could be more effectively investigated and prosecuted if the personal and property rights of citizens could be freely overridden and total protection of the personal and property rights of citizens would make the investigation and prosecution of crime impossible or virtually so."

Police intent upon obtaining a production order will have to satisfy the relevant provisions of the Police and Criminal Evidence Act. Material held by media organisations falls into one of two categories—Excluded Material or Special Procedure Material. The former is journalistic material consisting of "documents or of records other than documents"[46] which are held in confidence. "Journalistic Material" is defined as "material acquired or created for the purposes of journalism" and is held in confidence if:

(a) he holds it subject to such an undertaking, restriction or obligation; and
(b) it has been continuously held (by one or more persons) subject to such an undertaking, restriction or obligation since it was first *acquired or created for the purposes of journalism.*[47]

This means all journalistic material that does not comply with the above definition becomes subject to the Special Procedure. This material can

[45] (1991) 93 Cr.App. R. 60 at pp.65-66.
[46] Police and Criminal Evidence Act 1984 s.11 (1) (c).
[47] Police and Criminal Evidence Act 1984 s.11(3) and 13(1).

be accessed by the police but only after convincing a circuit judge that the relevant provisions of the Act have been fulfilled. As Mr Justice Maurice Kay put it in *R. v Bright, Alton and Rusbridger* [2000][48]:

"Journalistic material was either special procedure material or excluded material and, in either case, was beyond the reach of the police under the general provisions relating to search warrants to search and enter premises."

The legislation refers to the "access" provisions that have to be satisfied. A judge has to be convinced that a serious offence has been committed and if so the following criteria proved:

- The journalistic material is likely to have substantial value to the investigation.
- That the material is likely to constitute relevant evidence at any subsequent trial.
- That other methods of obtaining the "evidence" have been tried without success or that the police have not even tried to because there was no realistic prospect of success.
- It is in the public interest that the material should be handed over.[49]

The legislation may be perceived as supporting the concept of freedom of expression and the approach adopted by Parliament is consistent with art.10(2) of the European Convention on Human Rights.

The public interest in respect of special procedure material was identified in *R v Bristol Crown Court Ex p. Bristol Press and Picture Agency Ltd* (1987)[50] as :

". . . The balancing exercise which has to be carried out is between the public interest in the investigation and the prevention of crime and the public interest in the press being able to report and to photograph as much as they can of what is going on in our great cities . . . there is also public interest in the press being able to go about that activity in safety."

In June 2009 police in Northern Ireland investigating the murder of two soldiers tried to force Suzanne Breen, the northern editor of the *Sunday Tribune*, to handover phone records and notes of an interview with a member of the dissident Real IRA who had claimed responsibility for the killings. The judge had acknowledged that there had been two very strong competing public interest arguments to consider. The first was the public interest in catching the murderers and the second the right to life of the editor because she had been threatened with death by the

---

[48] [2000] EWHC 560 (QB).
[49] Police and Criminal Evidence Act 1984 s.8.
[50] (1987) 85 Cr.App.R. 19.

Real IRA. In addition the court had to take into account the public interest in supporting the media's art.10 rights. The judge refused to issue a
disclosure order.[51]

In November 2008 the unlawful planting of listening devices in a
police officer's car meant that information gathered could not be used
to support the prosecution of the officer for wilful misconduct in public
office. A local newspaper reporter was also charged with aiding and
abetting the offence as he had been accused of passing confidential
information to her. The judge's reasoning was that the listening devices
contravened the couple's right to freedom of expression and in addition
the journalist's right to protect her sources under art.10 of the European
Human Rights Convention had been compromised.[52]

The European Court of Human Rights has been a strong supporter of
source protection and that principle has extended to situations where
the authorities have sought to get access to journalistic material. The
latest decision upholds the trend. *Sanoma Uitgevers BV v The Netherlands*
[2010][53] concerned a Dutch magazine company that was forced to hand
over photographs of illegal car racing that it intended to use in a feature
article on illegal car racing. The race had taken place in January 2002.
The organisers had given the magazine journalists permission to attend
on condition they did not identify those involved. Any photographs
were to be modified to prevent identification of the cars and participants. The police requested the magazine to hand over a CD-ROM of
the photographs but were met with a refusal on the grounds of source
confidentiality. Later the Amsterdam public prosecutor issued the
company with a summons under art.96(a) of the Code of Criminal
Procedure. The editor again refused to comply which led to his arrest.
A judge later ordered the company to release the CD-ROM having
taken the view that the needs of the criminal investigation outweighed
the magazine's journalistic privilege. The magazine complied with the
order.

The company's lawyers then lodged a complaint before the Regional
Court seeking an order for the restitution of the CD-ROM, that any
data copied from it should be destroyed and an injunction preventing the police and prosecuting authorities from relying on information from the CD-ROM. The court ordered only the restitution of the
CD-ROM. This in turn led to the application to the European Court
of Human Rights claiming that the magazine's art.10 rights had been
infringed.

The Grand Chamber of the European Court of Human Rights was
unanimous in its opinion that the Dutch authorities' actions were not
prescribed by law which is a basic requirement of art.10. The court reiterated the view that:

[51] See *Media Lawyer* June 18, 2009.
[52] See *Media Lawyer* November 28, 2008.
[53] [2010] ECHR 1284.

"The court has always subjected the safeguards for respect of freedom of expression in cases under Article 10 to special scrutiny . . ."

It went on to say that an interference with such rights could only be justified "by the overriding requirement in the public interest"[54]. In this case there had been threats to carry out a search of the magazine's offices, the editor had been arrested and a judge had become involved at the prosecutor's request but agreed that he had no jurisdiction to act. Taking all these circumstances into account it was almost inevitable that the court would reach a decision that would favour the magazine and hold that art.10 had been breached. When such an importance principle as protection of sources and access to journalistic material is at stake there should be adequate, independent processes that will determine whether art.10 rights should be held in abeyance. Clearly this independent process had not taken place in the Dutch case.

Other recent precedents from the European Court of Human Rights includes *Voskuil v Netherlands* [2007],[55] *Godlevskiy v Russia* [2008][56] and *Stoll v Switzerland* [2007].[57] Do note however that in the *Stoll* case the court emphasised that it would consider how responsible the journalism creating the material had been and whether it was a piece that could be regarded as in the public interest.

The overall conclusion must be that irrespective of whether one is trying to hide the known identity of a source or prevent access to journalistic material the Court of Human Rights remains consistent in its approach when dealing with alleged breaches of art.10.

3. Official Secrets

The Official Secrets Act 1989 is of importance to the media as potential sources of public interest information will be bound by its provisions. This legislation makes it an offence for those working for the Crown to reveal information relating to national security, defence, international relations and criminal investigations. Therefore, journalists utilising such information will find they are committing a criminal offence under the terms of s.5 of the Act.

However, not all is lost, because the legislation provides a comprehensive defence for the media in such circumstances. The defence centres on the word "damaging." In relation to "sensitive" information identified in ss.1–3 of the Act[58] an offence is committed only if:

---

[54] [2010] ECHR 1284 at para.51.
[55] [2007] ECHR 965.
[56] [2008] ECHR 1169.
[57] [2007] ECHR 1060.
[58] Security and Intelligence (s.1); defence (s.2); international relations (s.3).

a) the disclosure by him is damaging; and
b) he makes it knowing, or having reasonable cause to believe, that
    it would be damaging.

To date no journalist had been prosecuted so the courts have not
had the opportunity to determine the legal meaning of the word
damaging.

For the offence to be established it appears that the prosecution will
have to establish a causal connection between the release of the information into the public domain and a particular consequence such as an
attack on our armed forces or military buildings. Even then a jury may
acquit on the basis that the journalist did not know or have reasonable
cause to believe that it would be damaging.

We saw earlier in this chapter that the government may seek to
recover names, information or documentation that helps to identify
"whistleblowers" inside government. The consequence was that Sarah
Tisdall, a clerk at the Ministry of Defence, received a six-month prison
sentence for breaching the Act. The policy seems to be to "go after" the
person leaking rather than the journalist who is exercising his or her
art.10 rights and publishing the information. In January 2008 Derek
Pasquill, a Foreign Office official, was prosecuted under the Official
Secrets Act for leaking confidential documents to a Sunday newspaper
and a magazine. The leaks related to secret CIA rendition flights. At the
Old Bailey the prosecution dropped the charges on the basis that documents to be disclosed at the trial would actually have undermined its
case.[59]

No prosecutions have been forthcoming from the recent revelations
about Parliamentary expenses. The anonymous source described as a
man from "inside Parliament" has never been identified. The material
was passed to an intermediary, John Wicks, but no legal action has been
taken against him in an endeavour to discover the source of the leaks.
One major factor is likely to have been the overwhelming public interest
nature of the information.[60]

In May 2007, David Keogh, a Whitehall communications officer, was
jailed for six months after disclosing a "highly sensitive" document
which detailed discussion between George Bush and Tony Blair at
the White House in 2004. The document was sent to Leo O'Connor a
researcher for a Member of Parliament. O'Connor was sentenced to
three months in prison. Mr Justice Atkins acknowledged that the disclosure had not resulted in any actual damage.

Nevertheless the judge was of the opinion that his action in releasing the document "could have cost the lives of British citizens." It was,
said the judge, a gross breach of trust. In this case journalists were not
involved in receiving the information. It had been Keogh's intention
that the information be disclosed in Parliament. Would a journalist

[59] *Guardian*, January 9, 2008.
[60] BBC News, May 23, 2009.

have been guilty of an offence under the 1989 Act if he had published the information? In light of the judge's comments that no actual damage was done then it is difficult to see how an offence would have been committed by a journalist.

4. Other Legislation

It is not the purpose of this chapter to engage in a polemic about the growing number of statutes that increase the powers of the authorities to access information and to engage in covert surveillance. Attention should be paid to the Police Act 1997, the Regulation of Investigatory Powers Act 2000 and the Terrorism Acts of 2000 and 2006, and Counter-Terrorism Act 2008. The terrorism legislation places obligations upon all citizens to reveal information about terrorist-related activity including money laundering. There are no statutory exceptions for journalists. This may cause members of the media real difficulties if they acquire such information as a result of their investigations. The Terrorism Act 2000 is clear. The legal obligation is to reveal the information to the police . . . not publish it.

In *Malik v Manchester Crown Court* [2008][61] a production order had been made under the Terrorism Act 2000 against Shiv Malik, a respected journalist who had been gathering information for a book about Al-Qaeda. He had been collaborating with a man named Butt upon whose experiences the book was based. Butt was well known to the police having publicly admitted his past involvement with Al-Qaeda. He also admitted to Malik that he had been involved in killings, terrorist finding activities and recruiting people to proscribed organisations. The police applied for and obtained a production order against Malik under Sch.5 of the Terrorism Act 2000.[62] On appeal to the High Court the findings of the judge were upheld but the ambit of the order was deemed to be too wide. The court stated its conclusions this way:

- There was a potential clash between the interests of the state in ensuring the police could carry out terrorist investigations and the right of a journalist to protect his confidential sources.
- A balance had to be struck between protecting journalistic sources and their material and facilitating effective terrorist investigations.
- It is for the police to satisfy the court that the balance should be struck in favour of making a production order.[63]

---

[61] [2008] EWHC 1362 (Admin).
[62] Sch.5 is entitled Terrorism Investigations: Information.
[63] See footnote 61 per Lord Justice Dyson at para.110.

The conclusion was that given the importance of the material in the journalist's possession in furthering the aims of investigating terrorist activity and additionally the fact its release might help to prevent a miscarriage of justice the order was awful. The reference to "miscarriage of justice" related to the trial of a man who had implicated Butt as the "instigator" in his alleged criminal activities.

However the court found that the production order had been drafted too widely because it included material in Malik's possession from *any* source and not just that received from Butt. The order was amended to cover only material received from Butt.

PART TWO: JOURNALISTS' SOURCES IN PRACTICE

5. Section 10 Contempt of Court Act 1981 in Practice

This classic clause appears to protect journalists but the exemptions pretty much cancel out that protection in practice. Journalists can be made to give up their source in *the interests of justice, national security or for the prevention of disorder or crime*. The protection is likely to disappear if the name is wanted by the courts, the government or the police, and that embraces most of the agents who are going to demand a source be revealed.

The contentious confidential sources themselves are likely to be accused of committing a crime such as breach of the Official Secrets Act or the Data Protection Act so it would be simple to argue an exemption based on prevention of crime.

Given that the interest of justice can also encompass the exercising of rights by others to claim, for example, breach of confidence, there would appear to be few s.10 situations where the exemptions would not apply.

Effectively the only way to protect a source is to be prepared to be held in contempt and accept the penalty, including a jail term if need be. Every time a journalist agrees to protect a source that is the deal being entered into. This needs to be appreciated by every working journalist so the implications of this in practice will be examined later.

The courts are uncomfortable with a stance that effectively means journalists will uphold their right to protect a source, even in defiance of the law. In other respects, journalists and news organisations will fight their corner but ultimately fall in line with a judgment, such as an injunction. So the courts' disquiet is understandable, but journalists have no choice. A journalist who doesn't protect a source will not be a journalist for long. Some things are worth going to jail for.

But first we need to consider whether the Human Rights Act has strengthened the position of journalists in this regard. The ECHR comment in *Goodwin*[64] is encouraging and the judgments in the *Ashworth* and *Ackroyd*[65] litigation would suggest it has.

In terms of the s.10 exemptions, although the action was billed as protecting patient confidentiality, the hospital was acting to protect the confidentiality of its own procedures. The issue at stake was not effectively the protection of Brady's privacy. The medical records were wanted to corroborate Brady's own claims of poor treatment. The wrong weighed against art.10 rights was the wrong done to the hospital, not to Brady, who claimed to have been assaulted and mistreated by nurses. He went on hunger strike and is being force fed.

The judges accepted there was a public interest in investigating the claims but argued that Brady's medical records would be of little value in investigating the allegations. To a journalist, this seems perverse given the nature of the allegations Brady was making. Investigation was most certainly called for and corroboration was needed. Brady and the other patients deserve fair treatment whatever their crimes but Brady's background clearly detracts from his value as a credible single source.

So, in journalistic terms, the judgment is not particularly sympathetic. The public interest defence was not accepted as justifying the wrong to the hospital. The reason for not making a disclosure order was because it would not have helped the hospital put right the wrong.

This mirrors other key 21st-century cases which have hinged on the extent of detail required, or deemed reasonable, to be included by a journalist to corroborate a story for the audience. Judges vary enormously in their approach to this. It is established that there should be discretion for editorial judgment of the news organisation that has obviously come to its own view on proportionality in deciding what to run. Where that involves, say, private material or breach of confidence, the assessment of proportionality is effectively assumed by the judge.

Lord Hoffmann has been one of the more understanding by both allowing editors some leeway to make a different decision from a judge, but also by appreciating that extra evidence, such as confidential material, extra details or a photograph, can be needed to make a story convincing. The broader package is a mark of a job well done and usually demonstrates responsible, rather than prurient, journalism. However, even with the more liberal judges, journalists have to find a more convincing way of making that distinction. This appears to be easier for a journalist from the *Wall Street Journal* than from the *Sunday Mirror*.

One of the most helpful principles for the journalist who steadfastly maintains a right to protect a confidential source is the *Spycatcher*-derived

---

[64] *Goodwin v United Kingdom* [1996] ECHR 16.
[65] *Ashworth Security Hospital Authority v MGN Ltd/Mersey Care NHS Trust v Ackroyd* [2000–2007].

axiom that *a futile measure cannot be a necessary one*. In the other classic case of *Interbrew*, despite the judgment against the media, the source was not revealed. In *Ashworth*, the fact that the case dragged on for so long helped too. The introduction of effectiveness into the proportionality issues is useful when asking the question: What would be gained by ordering a journalist to sacrifice a confidential source? If the answer is not a lot, there is hope that few disclosure orders will be sought, let alone granted.

The effectiveness approach chimes with journalists in that it encourages organisations subject to breaches of confidentiality to focus on improving their management procedures rather than pursuing the person who exploited the gaps in them. Taking that logic one step further, maybe such organisations could also make it a priority to investigate the allegations which were the catalyst for the leak in the first place and ask themselves some tough questions about why someone felt obliged to leak them.

Lord Saville took a similar line over sources relevant to the Bloody Sunday inquiry which is encouraging but the experience of *Interbrew*,[66] and some of the reasoning in *Ashworth*, demonstrate that judges are adamant that journalists are not off the hook.

The question of a "confidential relationship" privilege is interesting in that it might provide a basis for lending more weight to protection of the relationship but the weighing will always be conducted by judges, and journalists will always have to fight hard to demonstrate that the imperative not to reveal a source is worth protecting.

A further thorny question is where this leaves the news organisation as opposed to the individual journalist. The sanction against an individual journalist is likely to be jail; the sanction against a publisher for contempt is seizure of assets. So although individual journalists see it as a moral duty to protect a source come what may, the companies tend ultimately to cave in as they did in the first round of *Ashworth*. Their shareholders may take a dim view of them defying the court and, to avoid the seizure of assets, would demand capitulation.

Using the effectiveness argument and the debacle in *Ashworth*, it could be safest if the company simply does not know the source. There are difficulties here in practice to be discussed later but this would seem to be the rational response to the judgments.

6. Confidential Sources Checklist

The most useful lesson a journalist can learn from this chapter is not to enter into a confidentiality agreement lightly because the ramifications

---

[66] *Financial Times v Interbrew SA* [2002].

can be enormous for reporter and employer. This is a very unforgiving area in which to be found wanting. The 21st-century judgments analysed reinforce some fundamentals of good journalistic practice but they also generate some new advice for those wanting to pursue effective investigations which may involve dealing with confidential sources.

Exercise extreme caution before giving any undertaking to protect the identity of a source

Once an assurance is given it has to be honoured and this may become more uncomfortable and costly than it first appears. The information has to be worth risking a career for and going to jail for. As in other cases, know the legal ramifications of any journalistic activity and enter into it with eyes open.

Define your terms

As soon as a source even hints at a degree of confidentiality, be very explicit about what exactly each of you is committing to. Establish the ground rules at the beginning of an interview even where nothing momentous seems to be at stake.

What is meant by "off the record", "in confidence" or "don't quote me"?

Even journalists don't agree on what these terms mean so it is very easy to get at cross-purposes with sources. The definitions have to be spelt out with each source. There is a fascinating section on sources in the *Jameel*[67] judgment beginning at para.59 particularly the account of exchanges between the Wall Street Journal and the US Treasury which at face value makes no sense but which reflects an established "code" operated by journalists and officials to negotiate this awkward territory of deniability. Clarity is the aim and lack of it can lead to the downfall of journalist and source.

Assess the source

- Are they who they say they are? Have a telephone number at least and establish that it works. A bricks and mortar address is better.
- What are their motives? It will be very difficult to defend your actions or theirs if the motive is money. Do not pay for their information if you want to rely on it in court. They could also be motivated by revenge against say a company that has sacked them which would also call their credibility into question.

---

[67] *Jameel v Wall Street Journal Europe Ltd* [2006] UKHL 44.

- Are they in a position to know what they claim to know?
- Has what they say happened, happened? Those infamous kiss and tell tales involve questioning which pulls no punches about whether two people have really had sex or not.
- Why do they need to be anonymous? Is their caution necessary?
- Would it be obvious the information had come from them?

Critique the information

- What is the public interest in revealing the information they have? Apply your own "proportionality" test. Does it have public interest value in legal terms as well as being a story that will make you look good? Is that public interest sufficient to risk all.
- What other ways might there be of accessing it? Sometimes information that appears to be confidential is actually available openly if a journalist knows where to look which the source might not. Also, a confidential source can often be shielded from the risk of exposure by using their information as a "tip-off"; a steer on what questions to ask of attributable sources so that the eventual story need make no reference to the existence of any confidential information. It may well be possible to frame subsequent questions so as to give the subject no inkling that they were inspired by inside information. This does not prevent future legal pursuit of the confidential source but it does make it less likely.
- Is there physical as well as oral evidence? Is any documentation authentic? How would you go about establishing that it is? Is the information in it reliable?
- Is the information in a form that would lead easily to identification of the source? This may not be obvious but the informant may know. Think what will be required to protect the identity.

Question yourself

- If the story seems too good to be true, it probably is. Take enormous care not to read what you want to read into information.
- What are your motives? Do you want to believe your source because you like what they are telling you? Don't allow your enthusiasm for a good story to blur your judgment. Play devil's advocate with yourself.
- What other explanations could there be?
- What if you are being set up?
- What if the source, even if genuine, is just wrong?
- What makes the story credible?
- Could the story ever be run or are there simply too many legal obstacles?

Pause

- Can you really protect the source's ID? Can your organisation? If the answer to either of those questions is no, you must not agree to try. Be clear that any confidentiality deal means you must not be tempted to say who isn't your source. Ruling people out may allow the source to be identified by process of elimination. If an organisation points the finger at the wrong person, you may be in an awkward position.
- Does the source realise what might happen next? Warn them of the possible outcomes of which they may not be aware. It is tempting not to in case it deters them from co-operating but it is the only fair way. The source may be taking a considerable risk themselves and might face civil or criminal action if you let them down. Sources should be wary because of the threat of action on breach of confidence and under statutes such as the Data Protection Act, Official Secrets Act or Financial Services Act. The cases examined earlier in the chapter demonstrate that the source is more likely to be prosecuted than the journalist. A whistleblower would often also be risking dismissal from the organisation under investigation.

Consult your editor

This may be advisable before any agreement is entered into, depending on the level of authority permitted. An editor's instinct would be to be in the loop so as to be able to assess the source and the information personally and because it could be the editor's head on the block too. But the editor could be better off not knowing the details, especially if her news organisation would obey the law and comply with any disclosure order. It might be prepared to appeal it, but ultimately it would yield. Companies would be even more loath than an editor to defy a court order so, whether on principle or to protect the company from financial penalty, the editor also has to ask: If I join this agreement to protect a source, can I honour it? If the answer is no, the editor will have to trust the journalist and assess the risk based on the extent of that trust.

Decide what to do with any physical evidence

This is tricky. The physical evidence of documentation is important to the process of verification but hanging on to it can increase the risk of being forced to hand it over. The original would be more helpful in putting together, say, a justification defence against defamation but it is also likely to be more helpful in identifying the source. Destroying material could also be held to be in contempt if it were done to thwart the court. The *Irish Times* picked up £500,000 costs as a penalty for destroying documents in the case mentioned earlier. (That could be deemed "disproportionate" as it was when MGN challenged the *Campbell* costs.)[68]

One compromise is to scan a document, retain it stripped back to text only and return the original to the source. That provides the journalist with a working copy of the information and gives some evidence of the document's existence but makes it harder to trace the source from any identifying marks on the original. Some journalists now decide taking any copy is too risky and just view documents instead.

The handling of confidential sources can be challenging for even the best-intentioned and well-briefed reporter. When the relationship breaks down it can have terrible consequences, as it did in the case of Dr David Kelly, the weapons expert who was found dead, having apparently taken his own life after being revealed as the confidential source of a BBC story challenging the basis of the Government's justification for attacking Iraq.

7. Access to Journalistic Material in Practice

Editors are reluctant to come up with definitive answers on whether to hand over material demanded by a public agency. It depends. Like judges, they prefer to deal with the real circumstances of each case before reaching a conclusion. They too need to weigh the pros and cons of releasing material. Releasing footage, say of a riot, may well help to identify and prosecute rioters which the public might be very happy to see the news organisation play a part in. However, what would happen next time that news organisation sent a camera to a civil disturbance? Releasing material does definitely make a target of journalists, especially those with any sort of camera. More broadly, it is vital that a news organisation is not seen as, and certainly does not behave as, another arm of the State. The lesson must be not to hand over material lightly and certainly not to informal requests. The news media need to establish that disclosure is a "big deal" and that may mean insisting that a request is not only official but subject to judicial scrutiny to decide the proper balance of interests. Vital issues are at stake which rebound on journalists' ability to do an effective job. This is about safeguarding the free flow of information generally, not just in the case involved in a disclosure request. Again there is a danger that the importance of upholding freedom of expression rights will be discounted, and sometimes by journalists themselves.

---

[68] *MGN Ltd v UK* [2011] ECHR 66.

8. Other Legislation in Practice

Journalists can find their pursuit of sources and other information blocked on occasion by a whole range of statutes, often only tangentially connected to the media. Organisations such as the Society of Editors[69] and the Newspaper Society try to monitor all upcoming legislation for its potential impact on freedom of expression. Their lobbying, with other media leaders, can secure significant changes and protect journalists from the intended—and unintended—consequences of legislation. This is a massive undertaking. Planned changes to the commissioning of health services, for example, would have a serious impact on the right to know how public money is being spent. If GPs become responsible for how billions of NHS funding is spent, how will journalists be able to hold them to account on behalf of the public? Where will the transparency be? What rights will we have to examine decision-making processes? The media's role and rights of access to information may not appear central to the debate but it is of vital concern to journalists and the public.

Fighting to uphold freedom of expression involves being alert to any hint of changes which affect rights to information and trawling through reams of policy documents to spot the gains and losses.

Some statutes which impose prohibitions on journalistic sources and material were discussed earlier in the chapter. Here we look at a handful of others which are highly significant for aiding or restraining journalistic inquiry.

Case Study Three: Freedom of Information Act 2000

It speaks volumes about the establishment's attitude to the Freedom of Information Act 2000 that, within two years of its 2005 introduction, the Government tried, albeit relatively unsuccessfully, to retreat from it by complaining about the cost of providing information and condemning journalists for being "serial" requesters of information.

Yet any self-respecting journalist should consider this a badge of honour. If journalists are to be condemned it should be for not making enough use of the Act given the massive backlog of information which is routinely released in other countries but rigidly kept under wraps in the UK. Journalists not making regular requests for information are surely failing in their pursuit of the public right to know.

Authorities also dismissed many requests as "trivial". A few perhaps were but the long list of revelations made possible by the Act by both national and regional media, make it obvious that revelations are far

---

[69] Society of Editors—*www.societyofeditors.org*.

from inconsequential and that some significant strides towards openness have been made at many levels. Also, the law is "purpose blind" and the organisation holding the information requested has no right to ask why a requester wants it.

Then we had the determined efforts by MPs to exempt themselves from the scope of the Act. It appears reasonable to a worryingly-large body of MPs that scrutiny should apply to run-of-the-mill public bodies and lower tiers of public officials but not to them, our most senior elected representatives. Worse, they cloaked their arguments for secrecy in fallacious claims about the need to protect private correspondence from their constituents despite the fact that this already falls within the Data Protection Act. Do they not read the legislation they enact?

There are various curbs on freedom of expression and we have focussed so far on those restricting what can be published or aired. One of the most fundamental curbs on freedom of expression is the secrecy that surrounds information so that we can't even access it, let alone air it. In terms of the public right to know, the Freedom of Information Act should be absolutely key to establishing a balance in the UK's previously overly-secret system.

The Act, resisted by governments for 20 years, could really not be avoided any longer once the UK signed up to the European Convention on Human Rights which made many of the arcane blocks on the release of information from public bodies legally indefensible.

The system is not giving up its secrets without a fight. Despite being given a five-year run up from the creation of the Act in 2000 to its application from January 2005, many organisations have been slow to give ground. It evidently takes more than the law of the land to change the habits of a lifetime within the government and other public bodies. The culture of secrecy is alive and well.

Maurice Frankel, whose lobbying with the Campaign for Freedom of Information over decades finally paid off with the passing of the Act, discovered his work was far from over. In his response to the threatened clawback he wrote:

"What the government really wants is a bit more privacy from our prying eyes. FOI is beginning to put ministers under pressure. We are learning more about the costs of contentious policies like identity cards. We now know that the government considered weakening money laundering controls to encourage US style super casinos in the UK. Unwelcome information about ministers' meetings with commercial lobbyists has been disclosed. FOI has revealed that the apparent success of some academy schools, favoured by the government, is due not to better teaching but to the selection of pupils from better off backgrounds.

At local level, the Act has been even more effective. Spending on contracts, consultancies and expenses has come under new scrutiny. FOI requests have revealed the success rates of individual heart surgeons, the failures of some restaurants to meet hygiene standards, the

millions spent by councils employing temporary agency staff instead of full-time employees, the number of taxi drivers with drink-driving or assault convictions, the amounts hospitals make from parking charges and the care centres whose policy was to leave patients in their rooms during a fire, in the mistaken belief that they were fire-resistant."[70]

The important exhortation to journalists is to use the Freedom of Information Act and be prepared to persist in attempts to extend its limits. Frankel's Campaign for Freedom of Information website is a marvellous source of advice and inspiration at *www.cfoi.org.uk*. Heather Brooke has used her experience in the more open American system to prise up a few establishment stones notably over MP's expenses and see what crawled out from beneath them. Her book, *Your Right to Know*, is packed with practical tips, information on sources and sample request letters, and provides a vocal challenge to the UK's obsession with secrecy.[71]

An amalgam of the advice from both includes the following:

- Find out who holds what information. Knowing your way around the system can save a lot of wasted time and energy. Talk to the organisation's information officer in the target organisation to establish what information is held and in what form before framing a request. Many information officers do believe in their role and may be allies in the process of persuading the organisation to be more open. Under s.16 of the Act organisations are obliged to "advise and assist."

  The organisation that generated the information is not necessarily the only, or easiest, target of a request. Consider which other organisations it shares information with which may have a different approach or a different way of storing the information to make it more accessible and more useful. It may be particularly helpful if material is shared with an organisation in the US, for instance, which has more liberal release laws.
- Work out what you need to know. If the information you want is not collated in that format, the information holder can argue that the necessary collation of data from more than one source would tip the request of over the cost cap.
- Be specific. Frame your request with just the right amount of detail so that it cannot easily be evaded and so that the necessary answer can again be provided within the cost cap. The common mistake is asking for too much information over too long a time frame.
- Be prepared to accept raw data rather than nothing and do the analysis yourself. Computer assisted reporting is a growth area and investigative journalists are becoming more astute about finding stories

---

[70] Maurice Frankel, director, Campaign for Freedom of Information, *www.cfoi.org.uk*

[71] Brooke, Heather, *Your Right to Know, How to use the Freedom of Information Act and other access laws*, see Bibliography.

from data which on the face of it is impenetrable and reveals nothing. And, where material is being withheld from within a document, ask for the original so it is at least clear where material has been deleted.

- Use successes in one area to press for equivalent information elsewhere. Many organisations now at least provide easy access to a disclosure log showing what has been released under the Act. Especially if the Information Commissioner has set a precedent, the pressure on organisations to give in becomes that much greater. The jobsworths can conclude that the cost in financial and reputation terms of releasing the information might at last be less than that of withholding it.
- Be persistent. Appeal to the Information Commissioner if blocked unreasonably.

The Freedom of Information Act in practice has not been particularly useful to overcome the reticence of response in the day-to-day whirl of breaking news. The long response times allowed may even have slowed down some replies. However, when reporters examine longer-term, underlying issues and pursue new angles, the Act has proved valuable.

One of the deterrent factors in making use of it is, however, that it does not allow for the protection of a scoop. A journalist can spend months working on an investigative piece, waiting for a key response under the terms of the Act. However, as soon as the agency involved decides to release that information, it is not released exclusively to the person who has inquired. It will often be posted straight onto a disclosure log so journalists, whose organisations have not invested in investigative reporting, gain the same advantage.

Journalists have to be ready to move fast when a response arrives to keep a competitive edge.

There are various tiers of appeals procedure but given the long response times allowed at each stage, few cases have gone the distance so far. Here again it will be important to scrutinise adjudications to see where precedent is established which can be used to bring other organisations into line; or whether we have to concede defeat and try a different tack.

Journalists must not lose the war of attrition with public bodies that have yet to face up to their obligations. Brooke, who finds UK citizens' complacency over secrecy baffling, concludes:

"The public's right to know is not just a noble ideal for an enlightened society; it is thoroughly practical. Freedom of information is the most effective and inexpensive way to stop corruption and waste, and enhance efficiency and good governance."[72]

---

[72] Brooke, Heather, *Your Right to Know, How to Use the Freedom of Information Act and other access laws*, p.243, see Bibliography.

Therefore, whether in pursuit of principle or efficiency, journalists and indeed the general public should be exercising their rights under the Act to the full.

Governments need not resort to the mechanics of the marketplace to make our public bodies efficient. They could simply just try being open, honest and transparent with the public who pay for the services. This would be far more effective and a great deal cheaper. Scrutiny ensures that comparisons are made; that organisations and the individuals within them learn from their mistakes and that best practice is spread more easily.

It is up to journalists to keep pressing for public information to be made public. As *Guardian* editor Alan Rusbridger puts it in the Foreword to Brooke's book:

> "Inhabitants of the United States are much more aware than their British counterparts that the citizens own the government – and not the other way round."[73]

That's probably because the principle is easy to lose sight of in the fog of bureaucracy and secrecy engulfing our seats of power. Any "responsible" journalist needs to be doing their bit to encourage our public authorities to emerge blinking into the light of transparency and openness.

The Freedom of Information Act is one of the statutes now administered by the Information Commissioner's Office which is the UK's independent authority set up to uphold information rights in the public interest, promoting openness by public bodies and data privacy for individuals. Find out more at *www.ico.gov.uk.*

Case Study Four: Gillan & Quinton v UK [2010] ECHR 28

This case was a response to widespread claims of "over-zealous" use of stop and search powers under s.44 of the Terrorism Act 2000. It followed mounting complaints, mainly from photographers, whether tourists or professionals, about being prevented from taking pictures at locations around the UK, and/or having film and cameras seized.

Section 44 allowed police officers in designated areas to stop and search anyone at random for articles which could be used in connection with terrorism.

The action arose after both claimants were detained by police while trying to cover a protest at an arms fair in London's Docklands. Journalist Pennie Quinton, despite showing a press card, was told to stop filming

[73] Brooke, Heather, *Your Right to Know, How to Use the Freedom of Information Act and other access laws*, Foreword, see Bibliography.

and was searched. Nothing incriminating was found. Kevin Gillan, who was on his way to the demonstration, was also searched. They protested that their treatment was in breach of their art.5, 8, 10 and 11 rights.

Their claim failed to convince the UK courts but when it finally reached the European Court of Human Rights, the Commission upheld the complaint of breach of art.8. (It didn't rule on whether their other rights were infringed. Article 8 was enough.) This was an interesting example of privacy rights being applied to an experience which took place in public. As in *Peck*[74], where CCTV footage was made public, the degree of humiliation and embarrassment was taken into account such that the invasion of privacy was greater by taking place in the public gaze.

As the Commission noted in its judgment, Lord Carlile, the independent reviewer of the workings of the Terrorism Act, had become increasingly concerned in his annual reports about the growing use—and arguably misuse—of the s.44 stop and search powers. The judgment at [43] quotes his June 2009 report of the act's operation in 2008:

"Examples of poor or unnecessary use of section 44 abound. I have evidence of cases where the person stopped is so obviously far from any known terrorism profile that, realistically, there is not the slightest possibility of him/her being a terrorist, and no other feature to justify the stop."

He reminded police and parliament of the supposed limitations on the orders and felt "frustration" that the Metropolitan Police had applied the searches to the whole of its force area where searches under the Act were by then running at up to 10,000 a month.

The judgment also notes at [82] that Lord Carlile had no powers to cancel or alter authorisations for stop and search powers "despite the fact that in every report from May 2006 onwards he has expressed the clear view that 'section 44 could be used less and I expect it to be used less'."

Complaints of people being ordered not to take photographs and of material being destroyed came despite the facts, noted in the judgment, that "the Terrorism Act 2000, even where a s.44 designation is in place, does not prevent people from taking photographs. In addition, although film and memory cards may be seized as part of a search, officers do not have a legal power to delete images or destroy film."

The s.44 powers were time limited but many, particularly in London, had become part of a "rolling" programme of renewals, a procedure tightened up under the new provisions.

The success for the photographers led to the scrapping of s.44 which was, in March 2011, replaced by s.47a under an emergency measure which has brought back stop and search. Its application is governed by

[74] *Peck v United Kingdom* [2003] ECHR 44.

a Code of Practice, which the Association of Chief Police Officers argued would ensure the new provisions were proportionate and respected the rights of photographers.

Home Secretary, Theresa May, announced that "given the current threat environment" the powers to stop and search were necessary in the "interests of national security". A senior police officer can allow stop and search in specific areas in which an act of terrorism is expected to take place. Within that area uniformed police will have the power to stop a pedestrian and to search them and anything carried by them.

Campaigner, Marc Vallee, from *I'm a Photographer, not a Terrorist*,[75] told the *British Journal of Photography* when the new proposals were first aired:

"The devil is always in the detail, and after reading the Home Office review it is clear that the coalition government is planning to give the police new stop-and-search powers to get around the European Court of Human Rights' ruling. I do not think for one minute that these new powers will protect photographers from harassment and abuse from the police on the streets of Britain, far from it."

Interviewed on the *BBC Today* programme in April 2011, he remained far from convinced as the new measures came into force.[76] Chief Constable Andy Trotter, of Acpo, predicted[77] "very few" authorisations would be granted and only if absolutely necessary. He urged photographers and others to complain if they felt the new Code of Practice was not being adhered to.

We can only hope Mr Trotter turns out to be right and that the tighter restrictions of the new section and its related Code of Practice are adopted more effectively than their s.44 counterparts. Photographers in particular need to be aware of the requirements of the orders and take up CC Trotter's invitation to complain if stopped and searched unreasonably.

Case study Five: Criminal Law Act 1977 and Regulation of Investigatory Powers Act 2000

Full marks to anyone who recognises these as the acts used to bring the 2007 prosecutions in the *News of the World* phone message hacking case.

It is more than four years since *NoW* royal editor Clive Goodman and investigator Glenn Mulcaire were jailed over the hacking of mobile phone voice messages of the Royal princes, Harry and William. Both pleaded guilty to conspiracy to intercept communications of members

---

[75] http://photographernotaterrorist.org/2011/03/government-brings-in-emergency-terrorism-laws-to-stop-search/. [Accessed April 2011].

[76] http://news.bbc.co.uk/today/hi/today/newsid_9468000/9468082.stm [Accessed April 2011].

[77] http://news.bbc.co.uk/today/hi/today/newsid_9468000/9468082.stm [Accessed April 2011].

of the Royal Household under the Criminal Law Act 1977. Mulcaire also admitted the unlawful interception of communications under the Regulation of Investigatory Powers Act 2000 (RIPA).

The *News of the World* editor, Andy Coulson, although denying being in on the act, resigned. Numerous parliamentary, police and regulatory inquiries followed and the *Guardian* dug away, convinced the practice was more widespread than the prosecutions indicated. As we went to print, The *News of the World* had closed in response to further allegations of phone hacking and payments to police officers.

The nexus of royalty, Murdoch newspapers and the Metropolitan Police was inevitably meat and drink to conspiracy theorists but the gut feeling of many journalists was that we didn't know the full story.

We do know that the use of inquiry agents is widespread. A report by the Information Commissioner in 2006, *What Price Privacy?* included a table of hundreds of transactions between newspapers and private inquiry agents found to be peddling information illegally during the crackdown known as Operation Motorman. The *Daily Mail* was top at 952. Not all dealings would be known to be illicit, and in some cases media outlets may have had a public interest justification, but it was enough for him to accuse journalists, among others, of "driving" the unlawful trade in confidential personal information. At his behest, the Press Complaints Commission developed a response focussed on demanding journalists clean up their act. (See Appendix 7) Not all use of inquiry agents is illegal. Some are employed, like any other provider, for their specialist expertise. But why weren't journalists doing this work for themselves?

We do know that Mulcaire had a massive contacts list which anyone in his position would build up. Contacts are highly valuable and most are acquired entirely legitimately. He had mobile phone numbers and he knew how to hack into mobile phones but we cannot assume how many he hacked into. Having the means and the motive is not sufficient to prove guilt.

We do know it is common for specimen charges to be pursued. This is acknowledged in subsequent correspondence between the House of Commons Select Committee, the Crown Prosecution Service and the Metropolitan Police.

The police have consistently complained of the difficulty of bringing prosecutions over phone hacking. The correspondence between the current Director of Public Prosecutions, Keir Starmer, the Metropolitan Police Service and the House of Commons Culture, Media and Sports select committee is fascinating. There has been tension regarding remarks made at various stages of the saga about the chances of securing a conviction under RIPA. This may sound contrived but such negotiations do take place, not just in such sensitive cases. Case law was cited by the CPS referring to a "narrow" definition of hacking which covered only messages heard by the interceptor **before** the intended recipient. That is technically difficult to prove and although courts could be persuaded to accept a "wider" definition, prosecutors play the odds because the goal is a conviction. Whatever the exact exchange, a question mark was raised over the likely success of charges under RIPA.

The Metropolitan Police Service's response to the Culture, Media and Sports Committee in July 2009 states:[78]

" 8. When Mulcaire's business premises were searched on 8 August (2006), in addition to finding evidence that supported the conspiracy between him and Goodman regarding the Royal Household allegations, the MPS also uncovered further evidence of interception and found a number of invoices. At that stage, it appeared these invoices were for payments that Mulcaire had received from the News of the World newspaper related to research that he had conducted in respect of a number of individuals, none of whom had any connection with the Royal Household. They included politicians, sports personalities and other well known individuals.

9. The prosecution team (CPS and MPS) therefore had to decide how to address this aspect of the case against Mulcaire. At a case conference in August 2006, attended by the reviewing lawyer, the police and leading counsel, decisions were made in this respect and a prosecution approach devised.

10. From a prosecution point of view what was important was that any case brought to court properly reflected the overall criminal conduct of Goodman and Mulcaire. It was the collective view of the prosecution team that to select five or six potential victims would allow the prosecution properly to present the case to the court and in the event of convictions, ensure that the court had adequate sentencing powers.

11. To that end there was a focus on the potential victims where the evidence was strongest, where there was integrity in the data, corroboration was available and where any charges would be representative of the potential pool of victims. The willingness of the victims to give evidence was also taken into account. Any other approach would have made the case unmanageable and potentially much more difficult to prove. This is an approach that is adopted routinely in cases where there are a large number of potential offences.

12. Adopting this approach, five further counts were added to the indictment against Mulcaire alone based on his unlawful interception of voicemail messages left for Max Clifford, Andrew Skylet, Gordon Taylor, Simon Hughes and Elle MacPherson."

Ultimately both pleaded guilty to the conspiracy charge under the Criminal Law Act 1977 and Mulcaire alone to the five further counts under RIPA.

But some celebrities, convinced they had also been victims of

---

[78] http://www.parliament.the-stationeryoffice.co.uk/pa/cm200910/cmselect/ cmcumeds/362/9090213.htm [Accessed April 2011].

phone-hacking by the *News of the World*, brought civil actions for breach of privacy. We do know that it took judges in these civil cases claiming misuse of private information to demand disclosure of documents which brought more evidence to light and increased the pressure on police to consider further prosecutions in this territory. However the difference between some evidence and enough evidence can be crucial. Civil actions are decided on the balance of probabilities; prosecutions have to be proved beyond reasonable doubt.

We do know there are some genuine, plausible arguments for the sequence of events that unfolded but if your telephone number was on an inquiry agent's list would you feel satisfied with the handling of the issue to date?

The PCC did involve itself at the Information Commissioner's behest in trying to stamp out illegal phone hacking and reminded the media of its duties under the code. Clause 10 reads:

"10. Clandestine devices and subterfuge.
  i) The press must not seek to obtain or publish material acquired by using hidden cameras or clandestine listening devices; or by intercepting private or mobile telephone calls, messages or emails; or by the unauthorised removal of documents or photographs; or by accessing digitally-held private information without consent.
  ii) Engaging in misrepresentation or subterfuge, including by agents or intermediaries, can generally be justified only in the public interest and then only when the material cannot be obtained by other means."[79]

But the phone-hacking allegations involve breaches of the criminal law. Media regulators, to be discussed in Ch.8, must accept their shortcomings in this area but this is not primarily a story about regulation. If the practices for which Goodman and Mulcaire were jailed are as widespread as some suspect, that is a matter for the law. Where the pursuit of sources strays into illegality it is the responsibility of the police and CPS to investigate and prosecute where appropriate. Regulators take a back seat whether they like it or not when criminal inquiries are involved.

As the former PCC chairman, Sir Christopher Meyer, tweeted in September 2010: "If the PCC had the power to take sworn statements and levy fines, it would be an arm of the state. How many more journos do I have to tell that crime is for the police not the PCC?"[80]

The use of phone hacking by the *News of the World*, and possibly elsewhere, was reprehensible. It was not in the public interest. There were no grounds for subterfuge and no justification for invasive fishing expeditions for scandal. If the practice continues, or if cases can be

---

[79] Code of Practice, available at *www.pcc.org.uk*.
[80] Quoted in *Guardian*, September 11, 2010, Sir Christopher tweets @SirSocks.

mounted from past activity, those responsible should be prosecuted in the public interest. Criminal sanctions trump regulation and should do.

This is a grubby business. More heads may roll, and not just at News International. More journalists and investigators face prosecution.

Basically if journalists break the law, they pay the penalty. Sometimes the best in the business do it to protect sources or where the public interest is paramount and they take their punishment with pride. Without those justifications, breaking the law is just criminal.

Case Study Six: Copyright, Designs and Patents Act 1988

Journalists need to be aware when sourcing material that they may be in breach of copyright. Copyright, linked more broadly to intellectual property, is a concern mainly because of the difficulty in defending it in a digital age. The flood of material online has posed a massive challenge to the ability of the creators of original work—be it artistic or journalistic—to protect their copyright.

While understandably concerned about defending its own copyright, any reputable mainstream publication or website which breaches the copyright of others may well find itself subject to action because the breach has been seen by a large audience and because the news organisation is easily identified, is a commercial concern and is worth pursuing.

Copyright claims are also a device used historically to curb investigative journalism by seeking to protect, say leaked documents. So journalists should know at least a little of the law regarding their own and others' rights. Inevitably this case study will just scratch the surface of this burgeoning field.

Essentially copyright exists to defend the right to the fruits of the time, skill and/or creativity involved in the work. The statute covering use in the UK is the Copyright, Designs and Patents Act 1988, which came into force on July 31, 1989 and covers work produced since that date.

The date is significant in this area of law as journalists may well find themselves dealing with material created under the previous act which assigned copyright differently. Pictures accompanying local history, nostalgia or obituaries, for instance, may well pre-date 1989 so care is needed.

The copyright status of any material not generated by staff journalists should be clearly determined before use and the necessary permissions received and/or payments made together with an explicit agreement as to the usage permitted.

The burgeoning of user-generated content requires clarity in this area so that contributors to, say a bulletin board, are aware of the terms under which they are submitting material and what other use the news organisation may seek to make of it. Journalists should also check the copyright status of any material taken from publicly-accessible social networking sites.

Who owns copyright?

An employer automatically owns copyright of work produced by its staff; otherwise an originator owns the copyright, even if work has been commissioned, such as from a freelance photographer.

Copyright in work, including photographs, created before the Act came into force belonged to the commissioner. Under the modern Act the photographer or author owns the copyright but the commissioner retains moral rights, notably the right not to have copies made public without permission.

There is no copyright in facts, news, ideas or information themselves. Copyright lies in the form of words used.

Submitted material, such as readers' letters, involves an implied licence to publish only once. The organisations which supply the media with formal schedules, such as TV listings and sporting fixtures, hold the copyright and such material is commonly used under a licence agreement which imposes restrictions on use and may or may not require payment of a fee.

Fair dealing

Journalists who make use of copyright material are often relying on the defence of fair dealing for reporting of events. Reasonable use can be made of any material which has been made available to the public but dishonestly obtained material is not protected. The source of the copyright material should be acknowledged. Limited extracts can be used but only to the extent required for the purpose of informing the public. Particular care must be taken over reproducing sections of creative works, such as poetry. The leeway of fair dealing doesn't extend to photographs except where they are used, with appropriate acknowledgment and where already made public, to illustrate a review of work.

There is a limited public interest defence against breach of copyright but the threshold is considered to be fairly high. The most illuminating case remains *Lion Laboratories v Evans* [1985].

Remedies

The owner of copyright can seek an injunction to prevent publication of work or damages if work is used without consent. Breach of copyright can also lead to a court fine as it is a criminal offence under the 1988 Act.

CHAPTER SUMMARY: JOURNALISTS' SOURCES

- Journalists have a moral obligation to protect confidential sources of information.
- A journalist must go to prison rather than give up a source so don't make whistleblowers or leakers promises you can't keep.
- The Contempt of Court Act s.10 on Sources of information states:

  "No court may require a person to disclose, nor is any person guilty of contempt of court for refusing to disclose, the source of information contained in a publication for which he is responsible, unless it be established to the satisfaction of the court that disclosure is necessary in the **interests of justice or national security or for the prevention of disorder or crime.**"

- The European Court of Human Rights has proved a stalwart defender of journalists' rights not to reveal confidential sources and often accepted both the value of whistleblowing, the danger to the journalist and/or source of disclosure.
- Legislation, particularly motivated by combating terrorism, has given police some powers to seize journalistic material and stop and search photographers.
- Note the restraining impact of the Official Secrets Act, Copyright, the Regulation of Investigatory Powers Act 2000, the Terrorism Acts of 2000 and 2002 and the Counter-Terrorism Act 2008.
- But welcome the potential of the Freedom of Information Act 2000 and be sure to make use of it.

CHAPTER 7: REPORTING RESTRICTIONS

PART ONE: COURT REPORTING RESTRICTIONS

1. Children and Family Proceedings

Reporting restrictions in respect of the criminal courts are reasonably well known and relatively uncontroversial. The same cannot be said for those relating to children and the family justice system. The family justice system has been the subject of sustained criticism from pressure groups such as Fathers 4 Justice and Families Need Fathers for, among other things, its lack of transparency. This may be a simplistic comment, but that lack of transparency may well have its roots in the inability of the system to encompass even a modicum of publicity and standard press reporting. The principle of "open justice" has never really been a feature of the family system. The press may well be the eyes and ears of the public in relation to criminal cases where liberty may be at stake but the "seeing and hearing" process on behalf of the public has been conspicuously absent as far as family courts are concerned.

This is not meant as a criticism of the judges. They have to work within the legislation that imposes such restrictions. However, since the Human Rights Act came into force in October 2000, it is evident that many members of the judiciary would like to see significant changes in the law. Lord Justice Wall, a passionate advocate for change, put it this way in June 2006:

> "I am in favour of giving the media—and in practice this means the press—access to family proceedings, provided there are clear ground rules about what they can and cannot report. In practice this is mainly going to mean the extent to which, if at all, they are at liberty when reporting the proceedings, to identify the parties, and, in particular, the children concerned."[1]

---

[1] Sir Nicholas Wall: opening Up the Family Courts: An open or closed case. October 30, 2006. Speech available on *www.judiciary.gov.uk*

He went on to say that ". . . the judiciary and practitioners should have nothing to fear from public scrutiny: indeed we should welcome it." Another judge who has campaigned for change is Mr Justice Munby. In giving evidence to Parliament's Constitutional Affairs Committee in 2006 he said:

> "I have come over the years . . . firmly to the view that the balance which is currently held between the confidentiality and privacy interests of the parties and the public interest in open justice is badly skewed, in the sense that the arguments in favour of confidentiality and privacy have left what I believe to be a very serious diminution of public confidence in the system. Any advantages which currently can be gained in terms of confidentiality and privacy proceedings are out-weighed, and I believe fairly heavily outweighed, by the constantly eroding damage to public confidence in the system."[2]

Since the first edition of this book the government has responded to these and other comments and has tried at tackle the problem albeit with a limited degree of success. The reasons why there have been restrictions imposed upon the reporting of the family courts are not hard to find. There have been two underlying assumptions. The first is that it is not in the best interests of children to receive press publicity. As the European Court of Human Rights said in *B and P* [2001][3]:

> "The Court considers that such proceedings are prime examples of cases where the exclusion of the press and public may be justified in order to protect the privacy of the child and parties and to avoid prejudicing the interests of justice. To enable the deciding judge to gain as full and accurate a picture as possible of the advantages and disadvantages of the various residence and contact options open to the child, it is essential that the parents and other witnesses feel able to express themselves candidly on highly personal issues without fear of public curiosity or comment."[4]

The best interests of children will rarely be served by press publicity of the type seen when the father of a 13-year-old boy decided to inform the media that his son was the father of a baby girl born to a 15-year-old mother. In *Re Stedman* [2009][5] Mrs Justice Eleanor King described what happen next:

> "As a consequence of Dennis Patten's actions, Maisie, Chantelle and Alfie (child, mother and father) became the subject of intense media interest. Photographs and video footage were taken at the hospital

---

[2] 6th Report June 2006. Family Justice: The operation of the family courts revisited.
[3] [2001] ECHR 298.
[4] [2001] ECHR 298 at para.38.
[5] [2009] EWHC 935 (Fam).

. . . and video footage and photographs were taken at the Stedman's family home the following day . . . the child's birth was the subject of a front page article in The Sun. The sensational aspect of the feature was not that the mother was aged 15 but that Alfie, the alleged putative father, had only just turned 13 . . . it is hard to comprehend the amount of publicity the birth of this baby generated. There has been extensive publicity throughout the world . . . the story was carried nationally and internationally in the tabloids and in the broadsheets."

Later DNA tests proved that Alfie was not the father. The judge refused an application that an existing injunction should be widened to prohibit the publication of any further images of the children. Her decision was based largely on the public domain argument that so much information had entered the public domain that it was futile to try to limit it at this stage in the chronology of the baby's life. The record also needed to be put straight that Alfie was not the father of the child.

The second is that proceedings dealing with family matters such as the breakdown of marriage or suspected child abuse should not be carried out in the full glare of publicity unless criminal charges result from the latter.

The first of these assumptions is also reflected in the criminal law. There are automatic reporting restrictions imposed by the Children & Young Persons Act 1933 on defendants appearing in the Youth Court.[6] The theory is that young people should not garner, because of press publicity, a reputation as criminals when in fact there may be time for redemption. There may be restrictions imposed if a child is appearing in an adult court because of s.39 of the same Act. It all boils down to one question. Is the public interest in protecting the child from unwanted publicity greater than the public interest in revealing the information?

The developing law on privacy is a "new" factor that is impinging upon this debate but equally it is true that in some circumstances publicity can be advantageous to the children involved. In child abduction cases for example the press will usually offer maximum support in an endeavour to locate a missing child. Equally, there will be almost total agreement that in some cases publicity cannot possibly be in the best interests of a child. Adoption is the most obvious example. Publicity of a transfer of legal parentage at a very early age will not be likely to affect the child at that time but could quite easily do so over the years as he or she becomes established in the local community.

The media has shown little interest in reporting the "run of the mill" family justice cases because of the inherent legal difficulties in trying to tell a coherent story when the numerous participants in the case cannot be identified. In some cases even the local authority applicant will not be named or the hospital where a child is receiving medical treatment. However, the government has taken action, but before we

---

[6] Children and Young Persons Act 1933 s.49.

consider what has happened it will be necessary to examine the major legal restrictions which potentially inhibit comprehensive reporting of family cases.

Legislation

Let us look at the legislation that is used by the judges to impose restrictions upon the reporting of family cases. The term family proceedings for our purposes will embrace divorce, care proceedings, wardship proceedings, and to use the old terminology "custody" disputes when parents separate or divorce. There are three major pieces of legislation covering the reporting of family courts. The first is the Administration of Justice Act 1960 and in particular s.12. As amended, it states:

> 1. The publication of information relating to proceedings before any court sitting in private shall not of itself be contempt of court except in the following cases, that is to say—(a) where the proceedings—(i) relate to the exercise of the inherent jurisdiction of the High Court with respect to minors; (ii) are brought under the Children Act 1989; or (iii) otherwise relate wholly or mainly to the maintenance or upbringing of the child . . ."

The effect of s.12 said Munby J. in *Webster v Norfolk County Council* [2006][7] is:

> ". . . to prohibit the publication of accounts of what has gone on in front of the judge sitting in private, and also the publication of documents (or extracts or quotations from documents) such as affidavits, witness statements, reports, position statements, skeleton arguments or other documents filed in the proceedings, transcripts or notes of the evidence or submissions, and transcripts or notes of the judgment."[8]

That is what the press cannot do. This, according to Munby J., is what they can report:

- That a child is subject to proceedings under the Children Act 1989 or is a ward of court.
- The dates, times and places of past and future hearings.
- The nature of the dispute in the proceedings.
- Anything seen or heard in the public precincts of the court in which the private hearing is taking place.
- The text or summary of any order made in such proceedings.
- The identity of a child publish photographs of the child, other parties or the witnesses.

---

[7] [2006] EWHC 2733 (Fam).
[8] [2006] EWHC 2733 (Fam) at para.49.

- The party upon whose behalf the witness is giving or has given evidence.

Two things should be emphasised at this point. The first is that the court may impose reporting restrictions and the media will be in contempt if the provisions of any such order are ignored. Since that decision there have been new Family Proceedings Rules published that appear to have the effect of extending what can be disclosed. However r.11.2(2) provides that:

"Nothing in [Part XI) permits the communication to the public at large, or any section of the pubic, of any information relating to the proceedings."

As Munby J. said in *Doctor A & Others v Ward & Another* [2010]:[9]

"The effect . . . is that neither the person communicating any information in circumstances permitted by Part XI nor anyone into whose hands it comes can, without prior judicial sanction, put the information into the public domain. And if they do so they will be guilty of contempt of court for they will not be acting in manner "authorised" by Part XI."

Secondly there is a distinction between proceedings held in *private* and those held *in camera*. Hearings in chambers are regarded as private, but not secret, and elements of the proceedings may be reported subject to the current interpretation of s.12.

Hearings in camera are regarded as secret and therefore normally reporting will not be allowed. Reference should be made to the statement of Lord Woolf M.R. in *Hodgson v Imperial Tobacco Ltd*[10] quoted with approval in *Allan v Clibbery* [2002][11]:

"However, it remains a principle of the greatest importance that, unless there are compelling reasons for doing otherwise . . . there should be public access to hearings in chambers and information available as to what happened at such hearings."

He went on:

"To disclose what occurs in chambers does not constitute a breach of confidence or amount to a contempt as long as any comment which is made does not substantially prejudice the administration of justice. (This) . . . does not apply to the exceptional situations identified in s.12 (1) of the Act of 1960 or where the court, with the power to do so, orders otherwise."

[9] [2010] EWHC 16 (Fam).
[10] [1998] EWCA Civ 224.
[11] [2002] EWCA Civ 45.

In summary therefore, chambers hearings are not secret hearings. Cases are held in chambers for administrative convenience. The press and public can be allowed in except in cases covered by s.12 of the 1960 Act. Yet, as Munby J. has said, that does not prevent certain information about a case involving children reaching the public domain. The current view is that s.12 prevents the press from reporting on matters that are *integral* to the case being heard in chambers of the type referred to above. That is the case if the matter relating to children has been brought before the High Court under the inherent jurisdiction or the Children Act 1989. As Munby J. stated in *Ward v British Broadcasting Corporation* [2007][12] in respect of s.12:

> "Section 12, although it prevents the publication of Judge Plumstead's judgment and imposes restrictions upon discussion of the facts and evidence in the case, does not prevent publication of the names of the parties, the child or witnesses: *Re B (A child) (Disclosure)* [2004] EWHC 411 (Fam)."

So the transcript of the judgment is private to the parties unless the court decides that it is in the interests of justice to make it public. Accordingly the press should not quote from a transcript without the authority of the court. Lord Justice Wall admitted that it had been his practice throughout his time in the family courts to give judgments in open court.

> "Every judgment that I published was routinely made available to the press, which did not, I have to say, appear to be even remotely interested, despite some of the cases, on their facts, being quite extraordinary . . . I have an element of cynicism about the current press campaign for "transparency" in family justice. That cynicism derives from many years of trying, without any success at all, to encourage responsible press interest in the issues which regularly come before family courts."

We are dealing with statutory principles which have become incredibly complex to interpret. These issues are about what the press can report and not about access to the family courts. The second major legal principle centres on the Children Act 1989 and again concerns what the press can report.

Children Act 1989

The second major piece of legislation is s.97 (2) of the Children Act 1989. This section makes it a criminal offence to publish the identity of a child who is involved in the proceedings under the Act:

---

[12] [2007] EWHC 616 (Fam).

2. No person shall publish to the public at large or any section of the public any material which is intended, or likely, to identify—

   a. any child as being involved in any proceedings before the High Court, a county court or a magistrates' court in which any power under this Act or the Adoption and Children Act 2002 may be exercised by the court with respect to that or any other child; or
   b. an address or school as being that of a child being involved in any such proceedings.

This section was the subject of judicial scrutiny by the Court of Appeal in *Clayton v Clayton* [2006].[13] It decided that the prohibition imposed by s.97(2) ends when the particular proceedings are concluded. Interestingly in the *Webster* case Munby J. admits that he, in common with his judicial colleagues, believed exactly the opposite to what was decided:

"The common belief (which I confess I shared) that the statutory prohibition outlasted the existence of the proceedings has now been exploded for what it always was—yet another of the many fallacies and misunderstandings which have tended to bedevil this particular area of law."[14]

In light of this "confession" it is perhaps understandable that:

1. The media shows little inclination to attempt to report family cases by focusing on the issues and not the personalities.
2. The media, perhaps almost subconsciously, believes that the legal restrictions prevent a story being told in a way that would be of interest to the public.

A court should consider, as a matter of good practice, whether the restrictions under s.97(2) should be continued beyond the conclusion of the proceedings. If the court does not make a restraining order then the parties and the media will be free of the restrictions imposed.

In *Clayton* the mother and father had a shared care arrangement after their divorce. The father who was actively involved in the fathers' rights campaign wished to discuss the way the case had proceeded through the family justice system. He wished to do so in a responsible and objective way and to involve the media.

However, at the conclusion of the proceedings the judge ruled that s.97(2) prevented identification of the child until her 18th birthday and made an order preventing him from discussing the case openly because it would identify the child. The Court of Appeal discharged the injunction and held that s.97(2) applied only while the proceedings were "live".

---

[13] [2006] EWCA Civ 878.
[14] [2006] EWHC 2733 at para.52.

However, the court was concerned that the father wished to make a film about the case. One salient feature was that the father had abducted his daughter and this was a fact that meant in light of the new methodology in respect of privacy laws her art.8 rights were engaged. In addition because her upbringing was at issue her welfare was paramount within the terms of s.1 of the Children Act 1989. As a result the court substituted a prohibited steps order under s.1 relating to the making of the film.

The impact of the decision in *Clayton v Clayton* is that once Children Act proceedings have been concluded the restrictions imposed by s.97(2) cease. In December 2008 the Secretary of State for Justice Jack Straw announced that in order to protect the anonymity of children after proceedings have concluded the decision in *Clayton v Clayton* was to be reversed. That has not yet happened.

The two major statutory provisions were referred to by Munby J. in the *Webster* case as "automatic restraints."[15]

There are other statutes that deserve to be mentioned. The Magistrates' Courts Act 1980 sets out the reporting restrictions that automatically apply when reporting family proceedings in the Magistrates' Court. Newspapers, periodicals and broadcasters can only lawfully print, publish or include in programmes the following particulars:

- Names, addresses and occupations of the parties and witnesses.
- Grounds of the application and concise statement of charges, defences and counter-charges in support of which evidence is given.
- Submissions on any point of law arising in the course of the proceedings and decisions of the court on them.
- The decision of the court and any observations made by the court in giving the decision.[16]

It will be apparent from the above that this legislation is aimed at permitting the media to publish a limited amount of information, theoretically enough to convey the gist of the case, but without identifying any children involved in the proceedings. This covers all family proceedings in the Magistrates' Court and not just those under the Children Act.

The Judicial Proceedings (Regulation of Reports) Act 1926 (as amended) restricts among other things reports of judicial proceedings for divorce or dissolution of civil partnerships. Originally introduced to prevent "medical" details of divorcing parties appearing the "1920s equivalent of the Sunday tabloids, the Act is showing its age. The *Guardian* reported in late 2006 "Trial by headline—McCartney divorce turns toxic as Mills documents published." The sub-heading was "Coverage may contravene reporting law."

---

[15] [2006] EWHC 2733 (Fam) at para.53.
[16] See s.71 (1A).

Duncan Lamont, media partner at Charles Russell LLP, was quoted as saying:

"But the floodgates are opening because the family courts have indicated they wish to be seen to be more transparent . . . and injunctions are no longer given to those who have already invaded their own privacy and regarded their relationship(s) as being in the public domain. Financial information remains confidential and there is an implied undertaking to the court by the parties that money matters must only be passed to professional advisers, not journalists . . . To lawyers it is not the allegations made by Heather Mills that are sensational: it is that they are being published at all. The break-up of their marriage has seen the unexpected return of Edwardian style reporting of divorce cases."[17]

In the event Bennett J. took into account the massive publicity generated by the case and ordered that the full report should be published. The media of course was confined to publishing material in the "authorised" transcript.[18]

In April 2009 the Family Proceedings Rules were amended to encourage greater media access to all family proceedings.[19] It is crucial to note that this new found "freedom" did not extend to the *reporting* of proceedings to which the media had been given access. The access provisions apply not only to children proceedings but ancillary relief and applications for orders as a result of domestic violence under the Family Law Act 1996 (Pt IV).

In effect this now means that good grounds have to be shown before the media can be excluded. This proposition is supported by case law but the outcome will not always favour the media being present. In *Spencer v Spencer* [2009],[20] an ancillary relief case, the parties failed to have the media excluded. There had already been much media interest in the divorce of the Earl and Countess Spencer. In *Re Child X (Residence and Contact: Rights of Media Attendance* [2009],[21] dealing with a celebrity couple and their daughter there was evidence that the daughter was distressed at media coverage of the case and if representatives of the press were present she may be too emotionally overawed to give evidence. The administration of justice would then be put at risk.

In the former case the transcript states at the outset:

"*This judgment was delivered in private though in the presence of media representatives. The Judge hereby gives permission - if permission is needed - for it to be published.*"

---

[17] *Guardian*, October 19, 2006.
[18] *McCartney v McCartney* [2008] EWHC 401 (Fam).
[19] See Practice Direction:: Attendance of Media Representatives at Hearings in Family Proceedings—High Court and County Courts. April 20, 2009.
[20] [2009] EWHC 1529.
[21] [2009] EWHC 1728.

The position regarding media attendance at ancillary provision hearings and the imposition of reporting restrictions was considered by the Court of Appeal in *Lykiardopulo v Lykiardopulo* [2010].[22] While providing some useful pointers on how these issues could be resolved the only conclusion that can be reached is that no positive conclusion can be reached on exactly what principles will apply.

This creates uncertainty for the media and for those advising litigants. There are a number of dimensions:

The financial affairs of a family are essentially private matters and there is usually no overriding pubic interest in revealing such information (*McCartney v McCartney* being an exception). That means that information provided by the parties will normally remain confidential. The media may be present but will not normally be permitted to report this confidential information. That principle stems from the *Clibbery v Allan* case in 2002 which was decided before the new attendance rules for the media came into force. Query: should the principle be amended just because the media can now attend the hearing?

The media may be permitted to tell the story but as Burnton L.J. said it has long been the practice in family courts to release judgments in anonymised form. This is recognition of the parties' art.8 privacy rights under European Convention on Human Rights. Where a judgment is not to be anonymised, as the Court of Appeal decided in this case, the "... judgment must be redacted to protect the privacy of the husband and the family wherever that protection can be given without reducing or veiling the scale of their litigation misconduct".[23]

In this case the husband had deliberately misled the court as to his financial standing in the hope of reducing the settlement in favour of his ex-wife. The trial judge had directed that the parties should not be named in order to protect the husband's business and commercial interests. That course of action was overturned by the Court of Appeal.

The media needs clear guidance on two things. The first is access to the family courts and the presumption is in favour of attendance. Secondly there needs to be some clear principles which will help to determine what can be reported. The assumption that the media publication cannot give a true picture of what has occurred can only result in fewer reporters in court. This was a fact alluded to by Lord Justice Munby in July 2010[24]:

"... media attendance during the last 15 months has been virtually non-existent. Why? We do not know, though I suspect that the absence of access to the documents and the continued application of s.12 make the ability to sit and observe less than attractive. Indeed some cynics say that the beauty of the scheme is that the journalists

---

[22] [2010] EWCA Civ 1315.
[23] [2010] EWCA Civ 1315 at para.73.
[24] The Hershman-Levy Memorial Lecture: Lost Opportunities: Law Reform and Transparency in the Family Courts. July 1, 2010 St Philip's Chambers Birmingham.

are allowed to be there but because they cannot, in fact, do anything useful they will not turn up."

The solution must be a thorough review and overhaul of the present legal restrictions on reporting family cases in an attempt to meet the art.10 needs of the media but also recognising the public interest in protecting art.8 rights. The assumption is the more open the reporting of the proceedings the less likely it will be that medical and social work professionals will want to give evidence in such cases.

Strasbourg Compliant?

Despite the changes introduced in 2009 to give greater access to the family courts the picture is one of little media interest in family proceedings. However, the media will never willingly turn down a good story that will sell newspapers. Assuming that the story involves a child or young person then it is likely that the media will attempt to rely upon its art.10 rights in order to publish the young person's story. That right will also go hand in hand with the young person's art.10 rights to tell their own story, in effect giving up any privacy right under art.8. Take the following example that occurred soon after the Human Rights Act 1998 came into force:

A girl becomes pregnant at the age of 12. The putative father (X) is approximately the same age. The date is 1999. She was taken into the care of her English local authority and an injunction granted to protect the identities of the parents. Stories appeared in the Scottish press to the effect that the Catholic Church had paid her not to abort the child. The child (Y) was subsequently made subject to a care order and then placed for adoption. The existence of an injunction did not prevent both a local newspaper and then the *Mail on Sunday* from running the story that a 13-year-old mother was being "forced" to hand over her child for adoption.

The media clearly believed that there were points of public importance that could not be aired because of the "gagging order." In 2002, the mother had returned to her family and the care order was discharged in September 2003. The mother (A) approached the *Mail on Sunday* and agreed to talk about her experiences in the care system and the "consequences of having unprotected sex." The newspaper was willing to publish the story and confirmed that there was no intention to name the father (X) or the child (Y) in the article. It was in effect A's story. The local authority sought an order to protect Y's identity. The mother (A) was described as a "mature and articulate young person."

The case was heard by Munby J. and was one of the first to take the post-Human Rights Act approach to resolving such situations. The judge referred to his own statement, in the case of *Kelly v BBC* [2001][25]

---

[25] [2001] Fam 59 at p.74.

saying that when exercising the courts inherent jurisdiction or wardship jurisdiction in relation to the media there were three situations to consider:

1　The jurisdiction is not exercisable at all.
2　The jurisdiction is exercisable but the court is exercising only its *protective* jurisdiction and therefore the child's welfare is not the paramount consideration.
3　The court is exercising a "custodial" jurisdiction when the child's interests are paramount.

Having made this statement the judge then went on to say that the analysis had to be revisited in light of the Human Rights Act. He had the benefit of the Court of Appeal's decision in *Re S (A child)*[26] to the effect that the ". . . child's rights under Article 8 must be taken into account by the court if it is to comply with its obligations under section 6 of the Act."[27] The other judges took the same view:

Hale L.J.: "Now that the Human Rights Act is in force, the relevance of the jurisdiction may simply be to provide the vehicle which enables the court to conduct the necessary balancing exercise between the competing rights of the child under Article 8 and the media under Article 10."[28]
Lord Phillips M.R.: "It is necessary in the individual case to balance Article 8 rights which are engaged against Article 10 rights [. . . of the media]".[29]

Summarising the position Munby J. concluded:

"The exercise of the jurisdiction now requires the court first to decide whether the child's rights under Article 8 are engaged and, if so then to conduct the necessary balancing exercise between the competing rights under Articles 8 and 10, considering the proportionality of the potential interference with each right considered independently."[30]

After carrying out the balancing exercise, Munby J. ordered that the story could be published providing the father and the daughter were not identified.

This story could be told without the art.8 rights of either being breached. The court also focused on A because her art.10 rights were engaged not just the media's. She wished to tell her story and was mature enough to understand the implications of so doing.

---

[26] [2003] EWCA Civ 963.
[27] [2003] EWCA Civ 963 per Latham L.J. at para.75.
[28] [2003] EWCA Civ 963 at para.40.
[29] [2003] EWCA Civ 963 at para.108.
[30] *Torbay Borough Council v News Group Newspapers* [2003] EWHC 2927.

The *Torbay* case was cited in *The Matter of B Children X Council and B and Others* [2008].[31] The court had concluded care proceedings in respect of the family in 2004 and had not permitted the local authority or the parties to be identified. Three years later the mother and two children, then aged 16 and 10, wanted to voice their opinions about the care system in a magazine article. They wrote to the judge asking for permission to name the local authority and also identify themselves. The judge agreed that the council could be named and also accepted that should these members of the family wish to waive their anonymity they were entitled to do so. The judge pointed out that W was 16 years of age and ". . . should be free to decide for himself whether these are matters he wishes to talk about in public." Apart from mentioning the second child's age the judge did give reasons why he felt that she was mature enough to understand the implications of speaking to the media.

Mr Justice Munby did issue this "warning":

"Once they have waived their anonymity, if that is what they choose to do, Mrs B and J and W will not be able to control the media or use the media make of all the information in the public domain including all matters referred to in the judgement of August 2004."[32]

The House of Lords then delivered judgment in the *re S (A Child)* [2004][33] appeal confirming the approach taken by the Court of Appeal. Munby J. in the *Webster* case[34] asks how this exercise is to be performed when a number of conflicting rights and interests have to be balanced. The answer is provided by the well-known speech of Lord Steyn in the *Re S* case[35] which identifies the four propositions mentioned in Ch.6 on Journalists' Sources.

1. Neither article has precedence.
2. If there is conflict between the two articles there must be the intense focus on the comparative importance of the specific rights being claimed.
3. Justifications for interfering with or restricting each right.
4. The Proportionality test must be applied to each. This is referred to as the "ultimate balancing test."

Finally, let us return to s.97 of the Children Act 1989. We have examined the impact of s.97(2) but have so far ignored the wording of s.97(4). It states:

---

[31] [2008] EWHC 270 (Fam).
[32] [2008] EWHC 270 (Fam) at para.20.
[33] [2004] UKHL 47.
[34] [2004] UKHL 47 at para.54.
[35] See note 33 for reference at para.17.

"The court may, if satisfied that the welfare of the child requires it, by order dispense with the requirements of subsection (2) to such an extent as may be specified in the order."

That section too must be interpreted by reference to Convention rights. Section 97 as a whole must be read in such a way as to comply with the Convention simply because the section constitutes a restriction upon the media's right to report under art.10. So in practice it is not only in circumstances where the welfare of the child requires it that subs.2 should be dispensed with.

As Munby J. put it in the *Webster* case:

"... the statutory phrase 'if ... the welfare of the child requires it' should be read as a non-exhaustive expression of the terms on which the discretion can be exercised, so that the power is exercisable not merely if the welfare of the child requires it but wherever it is required to give effect, as required by the Convention, to the rights of others."[36]

The point is also made in *Ward v BBC* [2007][37]:

"... both the disclosure jurisdiction and the restraint jurisdiction have to be exercised in accordance with the principles explained by Lord Steyn in *Re S (A Child)* ... and by Sir Mark Potter P in *A Local Authority v W*...[38] that is, by a 'parallel analysis' of those of the various rights protected by the European Convention fort the Protection of Human Rights and Fundamental Freedoms which are engaged, leading to the ultimate balancing test reflecting the Convention principle of proportionality."[39]

Conclusion: Children and Family Proceedings

The media now has greater access to family courts than ever before. Prior to the changes in April 2009 judges often sought the media's help to publicise cases that had public interest implications. These were often in wardship proceedings where a court had to decide on matters of life and death. For example the "Baby Charlotte" case received a tremendous amount of media coverage when a hospital trust asked the court whether it was obliged to resuscitate a seriously ill baby.[40] In 2006, the High Court was asked to rule on whether a child suffering from severe spinal muscular atrophy should be ventilated. Holman J. permitted the media to attend and report the court proceedings

---

[36] [2006] EWHC 2733 at para.58.
[37] [2007] EWHC 616.
[38] [2005] EWHC 1564.
[39] [2007] EWHC 616 at para.13.
[40] *Wyatt v Portsmouth Hospitals NHS Trust* [2005] EWCA Civ 1181.

but ruled that the media could not identify the parties.[41] The judge acknowledged this was a case that should be heard in public. He went on to thank the media for the "sensitivity they have shown, at any rate within the courtroom." In 2000 the Court of Appeal had to decide whether conjoined twins should be surgically separated in the full knowledge that the weaker twin would die as she was being kept alive by the heart of the "stronger sister."[42] These cases are examples of good practice where the courts and the media work together in the public interest.

One of the last acts of the outgoing Labour government in 2010 was to rush the Children Schools and Families Act through Parliament. It has not been viewed as a success at least concerning the provisions dealing with family justice. Lord Justice Munby, in his July 2010 Hershman-Levy Memorial Lecture, commented that ". . . the process which led to this legislation was hardly likely to inspire confidence and not best calculated to engender ready acceptance in the outcome on the part of all those affected."

There was a lack of consultation, the family justice provisions where "seemingly tacked on" to a Bill primarily concerned with education and there was very little debate in parliament. Almost a year on the provisions are not yet in force and unlikely to be so in the near future. The position was summed up by Sir Nicholas Wall, the President of the Family Division of the High Court. He said:

> "I think the government is wise not to implement the present Act, which is not popular with the press, it's not popular with the judges and it's not popular, I think with most litigants. He suggested that negotiation with the media rather than legislation should be the way forward when attempting to open up the family justice system to greater press scrutiny. "I think we have to reach an accommodation with the press, we have to reach a protocol with the press. We live in a media age and must adapt and so I tend to issue press releases, I encourage my judges to publish their judgments, albeit anonymising them."[43]

The government is therefore committed to await the outcome of its family justice review before deciding what action to take in respect of the family law provisions in the new Act. An interim report was published on March 31, 2011 with final recommendations expected in the autumn of 2011.[44]

The conclusion is that further reform must wait for the moment. The current position seems to be:

---

[41] *An NHS Trust v MB (A child)* [2006] EWHC 507 Fam.
[42] [2000] EWCA Civ 254.
[43] BBC Radio 4: Law in Action: October 19, 2010.
[44] Family Justice Review Interim Report March 2011. Available on the Ministry of Justice website: *www.justice.gov.uk*

1. Good reasons are needed to exclude the media from access to the family courts.

2. Judges are more willing to publish anonymised reports of cases held in private.

3. That there is uncertainty surrounding just what can be reported in ancillary proceedings.

4. The continued presence on the statute book of s.12 of the Administration of Justice Act 1960 and s.97 of the Children Act means that, depending on the circumstances the media may be refused permission to name parties, witnesses, hospitals, local authorities and individual professionals. It is not meant to be suggested that judges will exercise their powers arbitrarily or in a way that automatically disadvantages the media. Yet, continued use of these provisions will simply mean that the media rarely turns up to report family cases and the public will continue to be concerned about the lack of transparency in the system.

2. Reporting the Criminal Courts

There are a number of restrictions imposed upon the media in its reporting of the criminal courts of this country. The open justice principle and the media's art.10 rights go hand in hand in this process. Any restrictions though will clash with art.10 (1) rights and, therefore, must be justified within the context of art.10 (2).

The Open Justice Principle has recently been described in the following terms:

- A general rule is that the administration of justice must be done in public. The pubic and the media have the right to attend all court hearings and the media are able to report those proceedings fully and contemporaneously.
- Any restriction on these usual rules will be exceptional. It must be based on necessity.
- The need for any reporting restriction must be convincingly established and the terms of any order must be proportionate-going no further than is necessary to meet the relevant objective.[45]

Lord Hope of Craighead in *Attorney General's Reference No.3 of 1999* [2009][46] said: "The principle of open justice which lies at the heart of public confidence in the criminal justice system permits the free report-

---

[45] Extract from Judicial Studies Board Guidelines: Reporting the Criminal Courts 2009 at p.6 available online at *www.jsboard.co.uk*
[46] [2009] UKHL 34.

ing of criminal trials and the proper identification of those who have been convicted and sentenced. It permits the proper identification of those who have been acquitted too."[47]

Youth Court

Section 49 of the Children & Young Persons Act 1933 prevents the press from reporting anything that will lead to the identity of a young person appearing before the court being disclosed. There it is an offence to publish or broadcast:

a. the name, address or school or any particular leading to the identification of any child or young person involved in the proceedings as a defendant or a witness;
b. any photograph of or including, any such person.

Anonymity though can be lifted if there is a good public interest reason for so doing. The reasons are listed at s.49 (4A):

* To avoid injustice to the juvenile.
* The public interest requires that anonymity be lifted.
* If the authorities need to trace a juvenile in connection with a serious offence.

Section 44 of the 1933 Act reminds us that every court in dealing with a child or young person . . . shall have regard to the welfare of the child.

There are three important cases to consider in respect of s.49.

The first is *McKerry v Teesdale and Wear Valley Justices* [2000].[48] The Divisional Court thought that it would be a relatively rare event for the anonymity ban to be lifted. Great care should be exercised before doing so. The court was adamant that lifting the ban in order to name and shame the youth was not part of the exercise. Nor should it be seen as imposing an additional punishment upon the individual.[49] From the media's point of view the court should invite any reporters who are present to make representations. (There are unlikely to be many because a story without a name hardly constitutes a basis for catching the public's attention in order to persuade them to buy a newspaper.) The balancing of art.8 and 10 rights will come into the equation. One public interest reason for lifting a ban is protection of the public. The court may deem it important that a community is aware that this particular young person is in their midst especially if the appearance in the youth court is not his first and presumably not expected to be his last.

---

[47] [2009] UKHL 34 at para.6.
[48] [2001] E.M.L.R. 127.
[49] [2001] E.M.L.R. 127 per Bingham C.J. at para.17.

This seemed to be the reasoning for the decision in *Pearl v Kings Lynn Justices*[2005].[50] The defendant was 17 when he appeared at the Youth Court. Lord Justice Maurice described his actions as "dreadful". He had driven the wrong way and at high speed down a dual carriageway causing an accident that led to three people being injured and the passenger in the oncoming car who was six–months pregnant to lose her baby. The media interest in the case led to a request for the court to lift the anonymity requirements. The court acceded to the request finding that it was in the public interest to allow publication of the applicant's name, address and photograph. The reasoning was that he was likely to drive again whilst disqualified and the public needed to know his identity so that he could be reported. The applicant applied for judicial review of that decision. The court upheld the decision on the basis that the correct procedures had been followed.

The third case is *T v Director of Public Prosecutions & North East Press* [2003].[51] In this case the defendant reached the age of 18 during the course of the proceedings. As the anonymity rules applied only to those under 18 the press sought clarification as to whether they could report his identity. Sullivan J. held that his identity could be revealed. The case also confirmed that the purpose of the s.49 restriction was to prevent the defendant from the "adverse consequences of publicity" without being explicit as to what those might be.

Anti-Social Behaviour Orders (Asbos)

The Crime and Disorder Act 1998 introduced anti-social behaviour orders into the judicial lexicon. These are civil and not criminal proceedings and therefore there is no automatic ban on persons under 18 being identified. The media though still needs to exercise caution because it is possible for a court to impose an order under s.39 of the Children & Young Persons Act 1933 preventing identification from taking place.

The general consensus is that publicity is necessary to assist with the enforcement of the order. If the local community is unaware that an order has been made it will be impossible to help with the enforcement. As with the Youth Court, identifying a person subject to an Asbo is not meant to be an exercise in naming and shaming. As Lord Justice Kennedy said in *Stanley v London Borough of Brent* [2004][52]:

> "It is clear to me that, whether publicity is intended to inform, to reassure, to assist in enforcing the existing orders by policing, to inhibit the behaviour of those against whom the orders have been made, or to deter others, it is unlikely to be effective unless it includes photographs, names and at least partial addresses. Not only do the readers

[50] [2005] EWHC 3410 (Admin).
[51] [2003]EWHC 2408.
[52] [2004] EWHC 2229.

need to know against whom orders have been made, but those responsible for publicity must leave no room for misidentification."

The current position is neatly summarised in the Home Office Guide to Anti-Social Behaviour Orders.[53] The following are the major points for the media to note:

- An order made against a child or young person is usually made in open court and not subject to reporting restrictions.
- The information is in the public domain and newspapers are entitled to publish it.
- If the young person made subject to an Asbo has previous convictions for example from the Youth Court, and reporting restrictions were not lifted in that court, no mention of those convictions should be made in the report of the Asbo proceedings.
- On imposing an Asbo it is possible to refer to the behaviour for which he has previous convictions—but not the convictions themselves.
- The court making the Asbo may impose a s.39 order.
- A court must have a good reason for making a s.39 order as the restriction on publicity may render the order less effective than it would have been if the community was aware of its existence.
- Age alone is insufficient to justify reporting restrictions.
- Section 141 of the Serious Organised Crime and Police Act 2005 permits reporting of a hearing for the breach of an Asbo. Prior to July 1, 2005, as the hearing was conducted in the Youth Court, the proceedings were covered by s.49 of the 1933 Act. That is no longer the case.
- However if reporting restrictions applied at the original Asbo hearing they will still be effective at the breach hearing unless lifted by the court.
- The working assumption is that unless the circumstances have changed dramatically in the intervening period then the restrictions will remain in place.
- Recent photographs of the subject of the Asbo may be published in order to assist with the enforcement of the order. A dated photograph will be of little use to the community.[54]

Section 39 Orders

Adult defendants in both the Magistrates' and Crown Court do not enjoy any form of anonymity from reporting. But if children appear in the adult courts for example on a serious charge such as murder or manslaughter lawyers acting for the defendant may ask the court to issue a s.39 order under the Children and Young Persons Act 1933. It must be

---

[53] Youth Justice Board, August 2006.
[54] Home Office Guide to ASBOs, August 2006, s.15 p.55.

stressed that the making of such an order is at the *discretion* of the judge taking account of all the relevant circumstances. Section 39 reads:

> "In relation to any proceedings in any court the court may direct that—
> a. no newspaper report of the proceedings shall reveal the name, address or school, or include any particulars calculated to lead to the identification, of any child or young person concerned in the proceedings (as either defendant or witness)
> b. no picture shall be published in any newspaper as being or including a picture of any child or young person so concerned in the proceedings except insofar as permitted by the court . . ."

Section 39 orders may also be used in Asbo proceedings. It should be noted that this provision applies only to those who are *"concerned in the proceedings."* So, a s.39 order would not be appropriate to prevent identification of a child of the family from the consequences of potentially adverse publicity about his or her father. This was the issue in the very important case of *Trinity Mirror & Others v Croydon Crown Court* [2008].[55] Raymond Cortis pleaded guilty to downloading indecent images of children. He had two daughters aged four and six at the time of the case. At the sentencing hearing the judge sought to restrict the media from reporting the defendant's name even though it had been used throughout the proceedings. His reasoning was that the publicity would have an adverse effect on the two young girls. The media appealed the decision under s.159 of the Criminal Justice Act 1988.

The order had been made first under s.4 (2) and then under s.11 of the Contempt of Court Act. It will be obvious that a s.39 order was inappropriate because neither of the children were parties to the proceedings. This point was confirmed by the Court of Appeal. It will be apparent that if the children had in some way been parties to the proceedings, for example as witnesses, then the order could and probably would have been made.

Judges prevented from this course of action under the terms of s.39 may resort to other legislation for a remedy most notably s.11 of the Contempt of Court Act. It would appear however; that once a defendant has been identified in court then s.11 is inappropriate, as the key information will be in the public domain. This point again is confirmed by the decision of the Court of Appeal in the *Trinity Mirror* case. It transpired that previously an order had been made under s.4 (2) of the Contempt of Court Act 1981 which of course can only postpone publication not prohibit it altogether. The s.11 order was an attempt to achieve what s.4 (2) was never designed to do. The media challenge was successful and a Court of Appeal of five judges strongly endorsed the open justice principle in respect of reporting criminal law cases.

---

[55] [2008] EWCA Crim. 50.

There is a feeling among newspaper editors that circuit judges are too ready to impose s.39 orders with the effect that the orders are becoming somewhat "routine" if a person under 18 is appearing in the Crown Court. The order is *discretionary* and both the statute and case law emphasises that the judges are meant to consider the impact of publicity on the welfare of the child before reaching a decision to restrict the reporting of the young person's identity. If a child of the family is a victim then it is becoming increasingly common for judges to impose s.39 orders preventing the press from identifying the parents who are often facing serious child cruelty charges. In January 2011, *Media Lawyer* reported that Judge Stephen Hopkins had made an order under s.39 at Cardiff Crown Court which banned the identification of the 18-month-old alleged victim and also specified that the defendants could not be named.

The South Wales Argus challenged the order on the grounds that s.39 orders could not be used to give anonymity to adults and pointing out that the judicial Studies Board Guidelines (2009) pointed out that very young children could not be damaged by publicity of which they were unaware and could not read. The order was amended to remove the ban on identifying the defendants. However it was reported that the judge informed the media that naming the defendants would automatically identify the child and therefore the order would be breached.

Media Lawyer reported on April 12, 2011 that a judge at Preston Crown Court had lifted a ban on naming parents who had left their five children aged three to seven home alone while they went to the pub. The judge accepted that open justice demanded that the parents be named although he ordered the media not to name the children or publish their current addresses.

Gerry Keighley, the editor of the *South Wales Argus*, was quoted as saying that he was fed up with "pleading with different judges over the years and quoting the same old precedents. I recognise the judges have a discretion in their own courts but there is little consistency."[56]

The key issue for the media is when, and in what circumstances, should a s.39 order be imposed? Guidance may be obtained from the decisions of the Court of Appeal Criminal Division. Watkins L.J. said in *R v Crown Court at Leicester Ex p.S* [1992][57] that the "mere fact" that a child or young person was before the court would:

> "... normally be a good reason for restricting reports of the proceedings ... it will only be in rare and exceptional circumstances that directions under s.39 will not be given or having been given will be discharged."

That statement was immediately doubted by the Court of Appeal in *R v Lee* [1993] on the basis that it blurred the distinction between

[56] *Media Lawyer*, January 13, 2011.
[57] [1992] 2 All E.R. 659 at p.662 (j).

proceedings in the Youth Court and those in the Crown Court ". . . a distinction that Parliament clearly intended to preserve."[58]

Perhaps the most important decision is that of Simon Brown L.J. sitting in the Queen's Bench Divisional Court *in R. v Winchester Crown Court ex p.B* [2000].[59] He set out a number of principles that are relevant to the question of whether a s.39 order should be imposed on a Crown Court defendant under the age of 18. They are:

1 Are there good reasons for naming the defendant?
2 Considerable weight must be given to the age of the offender and the potential damage to any young person of public identification as a criminal before the offender has the benefit or burden of adulthood.
3 Regard must be had to the welfare of the child (s.44).
4 The court should consider the deterrent effect on others of any publicity as a legitimate objective to be achieved.
5 There is strong public interest in knowing what has occurred in court and that includes the identity of the defendant.
6 The weight attributed to these factors may vary at different stages in the proceedings. After a guilty plea or a finding of guilt the public interest in knowing the identity of the criminal may be the determining factor particularly if the crime is "serious or detestable."
7 There may be notice of an appeal. That may be a material factor in deciding to impose a s.39 order.

After considering all the factors relevant to the case, the court must *indicate the reasons* why an order is imposed or lifted. The above factors were included in the report and approved by the court in the case of *The Queen on the Application of T v St Albans Crown Court* [2002].[60]

The first thing for the judge to decide is whether to make a s.39 order. Once the decision has been taken, the focus of attention switches to its content. The leading authority is *R.v Southwark Crown Court Ex p. Godwin* [1992].[61] Glidewell L.J. said:

> "In our view s.39 as a matter of law does not empower a court to order in terms that the names of the defendants be not published . . . the order itself must be restricted to the terms of section 39 either specifically using those terms or using words to the like effect and no more."[62]

The court is sending out a clear message that it is not up to the judge to determine whether an adult defendant should not be named. It is

---

[58] [1993] 2 All E.R. 170 at p.176(b).
[59] [2000] 1 Cr. App. Rep. 11.
[60] [2002] EWHC 1129 (Admin) at para.20 per Elias J.
[61] [1992] 1 Q.B. 190.
[62] [1992] 1 Q.B. 190 pp. 196H-197B.

an editorial decision to decide how to describe the defendant without revealing the identity of any children made subject of a s.39 order.

In that respect the decision of the Court of Appeal (Criminal Division) in *R. v Teesside Crown Court Ex p. Gazette Media Company Ltd* [2005][63] is instructive. In this case the father (S) of an 11-year-old girl had sent indecent photographs of his daughter to another man (L). The two men shared an interest in indecent photographs of children. At a later stage, the father offered to facilitate sexual relations between L and his daughter.

The men were charged with conspiracy to rape and offences contrary to the Protection of Children Act 1978. The trial judge made an order under s.39 even though the girl was not a party to the proceedings. It purported to prevent:

> "... reporting of any proceedings in respect of Regina v S and L. No identification of the defendant S by name or otherwise the nature of the case against him, the identification of the alleged victim (S's daughter) her age, place of abode or any circumstances that may lead to her identification in connection with these proceedings."[64]

The press was unhappy at the wording of the order and when the judge refused to amend it, appealed to the Court of Appeal pursuant to s.159 of the Criminal Justice Act 1988. The Court of Appeal accepted that the wording went beyond that which is permissible under s.39 and in so doing relied upon the *Godwin* case for authority. It was argued that the effect of *Godwin* should be limited as a result of the Human Rights Act coming into force and in particular account should be taken of the daughter's art.8 rights.

The court would have been more sympathetic to the argument if art.8 was the only provision from the Convention to be relevant. Article 10 had also to be taken into account. Lord Steyn in *Re S (A Child)* [2005] had been careful to point out that the "new methodology" should not be used to create "further exceptions to the general principle of open justice."[65]

Were there other options available rather than to quash the original order and institute a new s.39 order that was *Godwin*-compliant? The daughter's identity was protected by s.1(2) of the Sexual Offences Amendment Act 1992. The offence of conspiracy to rape is covered by this provision and therefore the daughter, as the intended victim, is guaranteed anonymity for life. Unfortunately, there are two offences to be reported in this case. While the daughter's identity must not be revealed by the media in respect of the conspiracy charge, the 1992 Act does not apply to offences under the Protection of Children Act 1978. Therefore, the only option was to "cover" the latter case with the new s.39 order

[63] [2005] EWCA Crim. 1983.
[64] [2005] EWCA Crim. 1983 at para.3.
[65] [2005] UKHL 47 at para.20.

and the conspiracy case with s.1(2) of the 1992 Act. The judges went on to issue a warning that to name the father and simply refer to the intended victim as an "11-year-old schoolgirl" would breach both orders. The reason being that if it is known that the defendant has an 11-year-old daughter it will be reasonable for the public to conclude she was indeed the intended victim. It should also be noted that the Court expressed dissatisfaction with the *Godwin* case but did not seek to distinguish it. Lord Justice Maurice Kay delivering the judgment of the court said:

> "We make no secret of the fact that, if it were not for *Godwin*, we would have construed section 39 as enabling an express restriction of the naming of S and we would have included such an express restriction in the order . . . all this disposes us to the view that we regret the limitation which *Godwin* places on the drafting of orders . . ."[66]

It should be noted that s.39 may at some stage be replaced by s.45 of the Youth Justice and Criminal Evidence Act 1999. Section 45(3) states:

> "The court may direct that no matter relating to any person concerned in the proceedings shall, while he is under the age of 18, be included in any publication if it is likely to lead members of the public to identify him as a person concerned in the proceedings."

Attention should also be focused on s.44 of the 1999 Act. This provides that once a criminal investigation has begun nothing is to be published about a person under 18 if it is likely to identify him as being a person involved in the offence.

Taken together, ss.44 and 45 offer a major challenge to the "open justice" remit of the media. It remains to be seen whether they will be brought into force or whether the government will use them as Swords of Damocles to urge more responsible media reporting in sensitive cases involving children.

Sexual Offences

The Sexual Offences Act 2003 lists numerous offences of a sexual nature, some involving sexual contact others not, for example the crime of voyeurism.[67] The Sexual Offences (Amendment) Act 1992 as amended[68] provides anonymity for the complainant/victim of any of these offences. Once an *allegation* has been made but before an arrest:

> "No matter relating to that person shall during that person's lifetime be included in any publication if it is likely to lead members of the public to identify that person as the person against whom the offence is alleged to have been committed."

[66] [2005] EWCA Crim. 1983 at para.19.
[67] S.67.
[68] By s.48 and Sch.2 of the Youth Justice and Criminal Evidence Act 1999.

Once a person has been *accused* of an offence (in practice this means charged):

> "No matter likely to lead members of the public to identify a person as the person against whom the offence is alleged to have been committed shall during the complainant's lifetime be included in any publication."

A new subs.(3A) was inserted into the 1992 Act as a result of Sch.2 of the 1999 Act. It identifies matters that must be specifically excluded:

* Person's name.
* Person's address.
* Identity of any school or other educational establishment attended by the person.
* Identity of any place of work.
* Any still or moving picture of the person.

These changes became effective in October 2004.

The media by and large adhere to the rules but there are occasional lapses. In February 2006 the *Daily Express* and the *Daily Telegraph* were ordered to pay a total of £15,000 compensation and fined £4,700 after publishing photographs of the victim of an alleged sexual assault. The photographs had been taken from behind. The woman was a member of the military and in uniform when attending court and it was held that she could easily be recognised. Care needs to be taken with such photographs and it may be advisable for photographs to be modified to prevent identification taking place. For example, the colour of hair could be changed or height could be manipulated.

In December 2006, the *Sunderland Echo* was fined and had to pay compensation after a rape victim was identified from a description published by the newspaper. Newspapers need to be on their guard. With the availability of the vast resources of the internet it would not require too much effort on behalf of third parties to research information appearing in newspapers and make an informed judgment as to the identity of a victim.

The Defendant

While the victim of a sexual offence receives anonymity for life the defendant can be named throughout the process from investigation to conviction or acquittal. Soon after the coalition government came into power in May 2010 it floated the idea of giving anonymity to defendants in rape cases. This is not something new as this protection had been introduced by the Sexual Offences Amendment Act 1976 and was repealed in 1988. Since then there has been no anonymity protection for defendants in sexual offences cases.

The government's plans were abandoned in late 2010. Critics had argued that there was no logical reason for singling out one particular crime. The current position is likely to remain for the foreseeable future. Complainants who falsely accuse defendants of rape are likely to be prosecuted for perverting the course of justice and or perjury should the case come to trial in which case the defendant (former complainant) can be identified.

Preliminary Hearings

The Magistrates' Court Act 1980 (s.8) lists the ten matters that *can* be published when reporting on preliminary proceedings as long as there is prospect of a jury trial. They are:

- Identity of the court.
- Names of magistrates.
- Names, address, occupation of the parties and witnesses and the ages of the accused and witnesses.
- Offence or a summary of the offences.
- Names of legal representatives.
- Decision of the court.
- Charges on which the accused is sent for trial.
- If committal proceedings are adjourned, the date and place to which they are adjourned.
- Arrangement for bail if granted.
- Legal aid arrangements.

These have a fundamental impact on reporting of Magistrates' Courts and their practical application will be discussed later in the chapter.

Pre-trial hearings

A pre-trial hearing can take place after the accused has been sent for trial or after proceedings for the trial have been transferred to the Crown Court and before the start of the trial.[69] There are automatic restrictions upon reporting these hearings and in particular rulings made as part of these hearings.[70] These restrictions will apply until the trial has concluded.

Preparatory hearings

In respect of such hearings that may take place where cases are expected to be complex or relatively lengthy reporting is restricted to the following matters[71]:

---

[69] Criminal Proceedings and Investigations Act 1996 s.39.
[70] Criminal Proceedings and Investigations Act 1996 s.41.
[71] Criminal Proceedings and Investigations Act 1996 s.37(9).

- Identity of the court.
- Name of the judge.
- Names, ages, home addresses and occupations of the accused and witnesses.
- Offences charged.
- Names of counsel and solicitors.
- If proceedings are adjourned, the date and place to which they are adjourned.
- Bail arrangements if any.
- Legal aid arrangements.

PART TWO: COURT REPORTING RESTRICTIONS IN PRACTICE

Journalists face a whole raft of restrictions embodied in various statutes, some specifically geared to reporting, others where the impact on media is incidental to the main thrust of the legislation.

The Acts generate relatively few challenges which reach the higher courts but the restrictions embodied in them do apply day in, day out to journalists particularly when covering court. Every working journalist should have at least a basic knowledge of what the restrictions are so as not to fall foul of them inadvertently. An even more detailed knowledge is needed to understand their limits and how to avoid allowing them to hinder reporting more than need be.

That requires an appreciation of the purpose of legislation but also how it is actually framed and how it may now require realignment to satisfy the broad requirements of the Human Rights Act.

Journalists need to keep pushing and testing those limits. Orders made under the various statutes are challenged more frequently, and often successfully, by journalists. It is hard to say whether this is because more poor orders are being made or whether journalists are becoming more adept and confident in challenging them.

An invaluable record and interpretation of the restrictions is provided in the Judicial Studies Board guidelines on reporting restrictions in the criminal courts produced by Lord Chief Justice Sir Igor Judge, with the Society of Editors and the Newspaper Society, which represent newspaper publishers. The guidelines, revised in 2009 and available online, are most helpful in outlining and explaining the restrictions, but also in establishing a best practice expectation and so can be used persuasively with court officials.

As Sir Igor said of the guidelines

". . . there are occasions when the ability to report cases is restricted. The purpose of the guide is to ensure that the representatives of the media can make submissions directly to the court, without the need to instruct lawyers, to point out either that the law does not permit the exclusion of the media or that there is no power or ground to prevent them from reporting, and if it does prevent it, whether the court ought to exclude the media or prevent the reporting with reasons why it should not. The guide can be used for this purpose."[72]

The guide also provides advice to courts when considering an order, including the following:

"Whenever a court is considering excluding the public or the media, or imposing reporting restrictions, or hearing an application to vary existing restrictions, it should hear representations from the media. Likewise, the court should hear any representations made by the media for the variation or lifting of an order in order to facilitate contemporaneous reporting."[73]

The advice can be turned into a useful checklist for reporters. If confronted with any unusual restriction, always aim to establish:

- the statute being employed to impose the ban;
- the grounds for making the ban;
- the precise extent of the ban; and
- how it serves the interests of justice.

Ask the court to make a submission to query or challenge the ban. A well-run court will invite submissions, so every reporter in court should have a sense of whether a ban is both lawful and appropriate in the particular circumstances and be ready to challenge it, at least in outline. There is no harm in respectful haggling to limit the encroachment on meaningful reporting of the case.

3. Reporting Children and Family Proceedings in Practice

Attempts to date to open up the family courts to greater media scrutiny have had very limited success. In some cases, journalists may be allowed to be present but can rarely report enough of what takes place to make

---

[72] Address to Society of Editors, Stansted, 2009 *http://www.societyofeditors.co.uk/page-view. php?pagename=KeynoteAddress2009* [Accessed April 2011].
[73] *Reporting Restrictions in the Criminal Courts.* October 2009. Joint publication by the Judicial Studies Board, Newspaper Society, Society of Editors and *Times Newspapers Ltd.* Available at *www.judiciary.gov.uk* [Accessed May 2011].

a meaningful report to the general public. Blanket bans on access and reporting, which were not Convention compliant, have been replaced by piecemeal but the same Convention's concern for the privacy of children has led to little new light being shed on these proceedings.

In practice, it is rarely worth a journalist attempting to cover family proceedings. Many courts routinely exercise their discretion to sit in private and, even where a journalist is allowed in, the restrictions make it generally an unrewarding experience. Anonymity for the child is understandable but the standard bars on naming other parties, such as local authorities, makes it virtually impossible to find a worthwhile angle which really explains what is at stake.

With rare exceptions, the powers-that-be in the UK consistently struggle to grasp why identity is important to journalists. At best, they understand it purely in commercial or self-interest terms as part of a desire to sell more papers—which is clearly not considered a valid justification. Or they see the thirst for names as part of an obsession with "human interest" (dismissed as trivia) and a lack of engagement with the issues.

What they fail to realise is that the only way most ordinary people connect to issues through the experience of real people with whom they can identify. Abstract concepts presented in "disembodied" form will not capture the audience's attention. Coverage written in the language of an argument over finer points of law will largely go unread and unnoticed, which rather defeats the purpose of opening up some hearings in the first place.

Also, part of the benefit of scrutiny is greater accountability and added pressure on all parties to provide reliable evidence. Without identities being revealed, the level of submission to any kind of "reality check" is limited.

As for "accrediting" journalists, this smacks of vetting and licensing which has to be unhealthy in a democracy. Credentials could be sought as in the Youth Court permission for "bona fide" journalists but there is no sense of having to seek approval, just that a journalist seeking entry should be able to demonstrate who they are and who they represent. The implication is evident that such accreditation could be withdrawn.

The decision in *Clayton* is an interesting one as it allows the identity restrictions to end when the proceedings end which seems remarkably generous in light of the concerns raised during the recent consultation. However in practice courts can elect to impose restrictions beyond the end of proceedings and can fairly easily go through the motions of considering each case individually, despite the expectation of an "intense focus" on competing article rights.

The culture of the family courts, which are even more secretive in practice than they are required to be by statute or case law, would have to relax considerably before any significant level of meaningful media coverage could be achieved.

The remarks by the then Constitutional Affairs Secretary, Lord Falconer, in the Lord Williams of Mostyn Memorial Lecture at Gray's

Inn in March 2007, about the latest round of consultation demonstrated the reluctance to open up. He said:

> "Over the course of the consultation well over 200 children gave their views. Overwhelmingly they rejected the idea—with clear support of key third-party organisations speaking up for the interests of children.
>
> They are clear, crystal clear, that they do not want the family court filled with people who have no involvement in the proceedings. They do not want people in the court hearing private details of their lives. They are worried about themselves or their families being identified by people whom they do not trust to report responsibly."[74]

He continued:

> "There are concerns about a lack of openness yet we know we have a requirement to maintain confidentiality. We need to ensure that people know more about what goes on in the court room; for example the reasons conclusions are reached.
>
> We also need to be clear that families and children know what they rightly regard as private information, rightly remains private. That may well involve allowing the press or the public in only where the judge expressly agreed as an exception."[75]

It was a long way from Munby J.'s rousing evidence to the Commons Constitutional Affairs Committee in May 2006 where he said of care proceedings:

> "They are proceedings where the state is seeking to take away somebody's child. In many care proceedings the outcome is an adoption order, so the stakes in many care cases are higher, I would like to think, than even in many very serious Crown Court cases.
>
> I have to say it seems quite indefensible that there should be no access by the media and no access by the public to what is going on in the courts where judges are day-by-day taking people's children away."[76]

Given the intensely private nature of the matters at stake and the central involvement of children, how often will judges really stand up for art.10 rights over art.8?

One small chink of light has emerged from another arena where justice is dispensed behind closed doors, namely the Court of Protection,

---

[74] Lord Williams of Mostyn Memorial Lecture at Gray's Inn, March 2007, reported in *Media Lawyer*.
[75] Lord Williams of Mostyn Memorial Lecture at Gray's Inn, March 2007, reported in *Media Lawyer*.
[76] Commons Constitutional Affairs Committee, May 2006, reported in *Media Lawyer*.

which deals with vulnerable people deemed unable to make their own decisions. The protective approach to the subjects of the cases resulted in very limited public scrutiny of its work which involves taking control of individual's assets. The *Independent* newspaper has spearheaded a long campaign to increase access to the court and freedom to report some of its cases. It celebrated, in March 2011, a ruling allowing it to identify a father fighting to be allowed to care for his autistic son and to identify the council whose decision he seeks to overturn.[77]

This piecemeal approach does allow some stories to be told in a way that makes sense to the public but these individual battles are expensive to pursue and not every family seeking open justice is fortunate enough to find media outlets or lawyers prepared to take up their cause.

The potential for abuse of power and miscarriages of justice remains worryingly high in the work of these and the family courts which, often driven by genuine concern for the most vulnerable parties involved, remain significant exceptions to our principles of open justice.

Some courtroom doors previously slammed shut are now ajar but the competing interests involved in these sensitive areas have so far defeated attempts for any really meaningful or general opening up.

4. Reporting the criminal courts in practice

Children in Criminal Cases: Youth Court and Anti-Social Behaviour Orders

Children have for decades enjoyed special protection in the courts, particularly the Youth Court, although general assumptions of anonymity have been through a state of flux since the introduction of Anti-Social Behaviour Orders. These were designed to be less serious than full-blown criminal convictions and it was hoped they would nip bad behaviour in the bud among those subject to them. In those circumstances youngsters made subject to Asbos could arguably deserve anonymity more than Youth Court defendants accused of more serious crimes. However, as the media logically argued, given that an Asbo is designed as a warning to the public as well as to its subject, it cannot be properly effective unless the general public are aware of exactly who is subject to it.

For some tearaways the macho culture in which they operate means an Asbo marks a kind of coming of age and in their circles may be viewed as a badge of honour. The cockiness often belies a much deeper

---

[77] "A father and son reunited", The *Independent*, March 1, 2011 p.1.

vulnerability which is worth considering in so far as journalists get caught up in the contradictions of trying to be seen to be punishing young louts while also protecting their chances of turning over a new leaf.

In Magistrates' Court, one of the biggest challenges for a journalist is to keep track of the status of proceedings and the position of a juvenile within them. Watch out for the exceptional circumstances of Asbo hearings. This is an area where challenges have resulted in a great deal of freeing up over the issue of identity.

Is the court sitting as an adult court or youth court? Is an Asbo, or a breach of Asbo, involved where anonymity is not automatic? Has a s.39 (or s.45 order for the Asbo breach) been made to "restore" anonymity? Are there grounds to challenge it? (See p.334 for a reminder of the permutations.)

If a juvenile is found guilty in youth court of criminal damage for spraying graffiti, there is an automatic ban on identifying him. The police then make an application for an Asbo. The magistrates then become civil rather than criminal and the press can name and give details of why the Asbo is being granted, but can't identify him as someone who has just been fined for criminal damage. Also, the magistrates may impose a s.39 order on the Asbo hearing. So one minute a journalist will be taking special care not to print anything which could lead to identification of a juvenile. The next minute the same journalist will be considering grounds for challenging the s.39 order so the juvenile can be named.

Challenging the presumption of anonymity in Youth Court is harder but it can be done. If the defendant is guilty, anonymity can be withdrawn if the offending was persistent, or serious, or had an impact on a number of people or where alerting the public would prevent further offences.

Remember the sections of the Youth Justice and Criminal Evidence Act 1999 that give anonymity to children as soon as a crime is reported are not enforcible yet. A child only gets automatic anonymity when appearing in youth court as a defendant or witness. The PCC Code urges a protective approach to the reporting of children to help the case for continuing to keep the provision in abeyance.

Note that the coalition Government has suggested scrapping Asbos but it is not yet clear what, if anything, would replace them.

Section 39 Children and Young Persons Act 1933 in Practice

Journalists will not spend long in court before being placed under the obligations of a s.39 order requiring anonymity for a child involved in criminal proceedings in an adult court.

Journalists should remember that s.39 orders cannot be made just because the defendant, victim or witness is a child. The court has to justify the protection. Section 39 orders are much used and abused, and are subject to frequent challenge by journalists, sometimes successfully.

The Judicial Studies Board guidelines provide in-depth discussion of these and other discretionary orders. Courts are now encouraged to hear reporters in person and many have formally reconsidered orders or other reporting restrictions after media representations on the spot in court, by letter or discussion with the magistrates' legal adviser. If the courts do not follow these guidelines, an order can be challenged. (See the Case Study later in this chapter.)

Reporting Sexual Offences in Practice

The main controversy in this area of media law is over the right of anonymity for alleged victims in sexual offences, most particularly rape. This has arisen from a handful of high-profile cases where allegations have received a great deal of publicity and not resulted in a guilty verdict. The vast majority of rape cases fail to end in conviction because the case is not proved beyond reasonable doubt. However, in the case that brought the issue back to prominence, the complainant was shown to have made false allegations and to have a history of it. The controversy was all the greater because it arose from the woman being named in 2006 in the House of Lords which provoked debate not just about anonymity for women who claim to have been raped but over the extent of protection of parliamentary privilege whether for a Lord or the media, to breach the anonymity requirement imposed by the Sexual Offences (Amendment) Act 1992.

There has always been disquiet in some quarters over the imbalance created by the anonymity for the complainant in a rape case whereby the woman (or man) claiming to have been raped is anonymous throughout, indeed for life, whereas the accused is identified in the normal way as a defendant in court proceedings and is thus identified whether found guilty or acquitted.

Many men accused of rape are acquitted. It has one of the lowest conviction rates of any category of prosecution. But an acquittal does not mean the complainant was lying; just that the case was not proven beyond reasonable doubt. There are extreme cases such as those raised by Lord Campbell-Savours where the trial exposes blatant manufacturing of an accusation. But the alleged victim could be prosecuted for perjury at which point anonymity could be lifted. The trial judge has the powers already to lift anonymity either to induce evidence to come forward or where it is in the public interest, but not just because there is an acquittal.

The protection of anonymity is crucial for many rape victims who would not otherwise come forward at all. The case raised does not justify any attempt to remove that protection as a remedy already exists to cover such extremes. To remove all anonymity would be taking a sledgehammer to crack a nut. Not for the first time, an outraged Lord is lobbying for changes to legislation to cure a problem which already has a solution. The answer is to call for effective use of the powers that exist rather than demand new ones.

The second question raised by the naming concerned the extent of privilege if the media repeated the name outside Parliament. Any privilege in parliamentary reporting for journalists would provide protection against actions for defamation. It does not provide immunity from prosecution under other statutes. The legal advice, which most news organisations followed, was that it did not protect the media from the sanctions of the Sexual Offences (Amendment) Act so the woman's name should not have been reported. The Attorney General also advised at the time that full blown privilege from any prosecution only attaches to the official record in Hansard or on the Parliament channel; not to a journalist's note.

The Crown Prosecution Service regularly reviews its handling of rape allegations. The Director of Public Prosecutions, Keir Starmer, announced in December 2010 measures designed to strengthen rape prosecutions. He said:

> "Prosecuting rape is very challenging. Public expectations are high and sometimes unrealistic. By their very nature, many cases turn on the word of one individual against another. Rape often occurs in private with the victim the only witness. Unless the defendant pleads guilty, usually the victim has to give evidence in court to establish the basis for a prosecution and the prosecution case must always be proved beyond reasonable doubt.
>
> "As prosecutors we need to reinforce the so-called merits-based approach to rape cases. Cases should be judged entirely on the merits of the evidence: myths and stereotypes have no place in a criminal justice system underpinned by basic human rights."[78]

The changes also dealt with concerns over the threat to men from anonymous, but in some cases, malicious rape allegations. Mr Starmer said:

> "While we must be robust in prosecuting those who seek to pervert the course of justice, cases where someone has reported a rape but then retracts the allegation must be treated very carefully and we must explore the issues behind the retraction, particularly if the victim is under pressure or frightened. We are keen to know the views of all parties, including charities and special interest groups with expertise in this area. This will ensure our new guidance deals properly and sensitively with these, often complex, situations."

Any prosecutor across England and Wales who considers charging a person who has retracted an allegation of rape with an offence of perverting the course of justice now needs the DPP's approval before they can proceed.

---

[78] *http://www.cps.gov.uk/news/press_releases/146-10/index.html* [Accessed May 2011].

Protecting Anonymity in Practice

A requirement to protect anonymity is imposed under various of the acts which restrict reporting, most commonly for children and complainants in sexual offences cases.

Protecting anonymity requires a great deal more than removing a name or even the other specific elements listed in s.49 of the Children and Young Persons Act 1933.

Any combination of detail used needs to be considered in the context of each particular case. The audience must not be able to use the coverage to put two and two together and work out the identity of the anonymous party. How the person is described is the first hurdle. For example, a 13-year-old can be said to be from a large city but not from a tiny village.

Then there is the evidence to consider, including where the offence took place. Is it safe to describe an occupation, a hobby, a pub visited regularly? If the person protected has a close link to the defendant, it can become nigh on impossible to outline the evidence as the relationship would become obvious. This is particularly problematic when protecting the alleged victims of sexual crimes which may have taken place over a number of years while the victim was in the care of the abuser.

Great attention must be paid to how anonymity is protected given the particulars of each case and rigorous processes must be in place for careful checking of such copy by staff sufficiently experienced to be alert to the pitfalls.

In the *Teesside* case,[79] discussed in Part One of this chapter, the judges regretted not being able to order restriction on reporting the name of the defendant.

Yet identifying the defendant is central to operating within the spirit of open justice. We cannot have anonymous people being jailed and we cannot have them evading news of their crime being placed in the public domain. Anonymity for a defendant must surely be an absolute last resort. There are genuine dilemmas, although the court's stance and conclusion was unduly harsh. At para.19 they say:

> "Offences of the kind established in this case of S and L are frequently committed by fathers and stepfathers. The history of photography and the planning of further offences are indicative of a close relationship between the offender and the victim. If the offender is named and the victim is described as 'an 11-year-old schoolgirl' in circumstances in which the offender has an 11-year-old daughter, it is at least arguable that the composite picture presented embraces 'particulars calculated to lead to the identification' of the victim."

They considered, but for *Godwin*, that the solution would have been to withhold the identity of the defendant. The alternative, and for

---

[79] *R v Teesside Crown Court Ex p Gazette Media Company Ltd* [2005] EWCA Crim. 1983.

journalists preferable, conclusion is that greater care was needed in the degree of detail given from the proceedings. Because the public is now more aware that abuse takes place most often in the home, description of the offences and recording of the evidence has to be quite seriously curtailed.

Certainly it is established practice to avoid being precise about ages or, where offences come to light many years later, as to the exact timing of the offences, so that, as the judges say, the audience cannot follow the trail to the children. The victim cannot be shown to be in the care of the defendant and a string of offences over time makes this difficult to achieve. For further discussion see Chapter 8 on Regulation.

The approach settled upon by the PCC is not to be derided. A commitment to naming the defendant and withholding details of relationship and more tends to deprive the media of the newsiest angle and is actually indicative of restraint in the interests of justice being seen to be done. It would be nice if the media were just occasionally given some credit in the courts for trying to operate in something other than naked self-interest.

Jigsaw Identification

Where more than one media organisation is going to run a case requiring anonymity, it is vital they take a consistent line on broadly what to include and what to omit so as to satisfy that requirement. The most crucial is for everyone to name the defendant but omit any relationship to the ananymous party. Until very recently there was a great risk of a member of the public piecing identity together from multiple sources. Local newspapers have tended to identify the defendant on the ground of public accountability, but nationals were more likely to go for the storyline even if that meant sacrificing all identities. Eventually the Press Complaints Commission brought everyone in line.

The PCC code provides the guidance to ensure a consistent approach although, locally, it is always worth confirming that other media representatives are taking the same approach.

1   The press must not, even if legally free to do so, identify children under 16 who are victims or witnesses in cases involving sex offences.
2   In any press report of a case involving a sexual offence against a child:
    i.   The child must not be identified.
    ii. The adult may be identified.
    iii. The word "incest" must not be used where a child victim might be identified.
    iv   Care must be taken that nothing in the report implies the relationship between the accused and the child.

Any reporter covering such a case needs to appreciate that this is one instance where collaboration with the competition is required. The court may well remind the press bench of the demands of anonymity. Reporters need to bear in mind the Code but also discuss, given the particular circumstances of the case, what can safely be included and what cannot so nobody subsequently goes beyond the agreed limits. Newsdesks should be aware of this and further discussion may be required between news organisations before publication.

Preliminary Hearings in Practice

Numerous different reporting restrictions can apply to coverage of adult criminal courts. The ten points of s.8 Magistrates' Court Act 1980 are the most frequently invoked and are worth remembering by rote together with the detail of the occasions when they do and do not apply.

The important guide to their application is to keep in mind their purpose. The restrictions on the various hearings in court in the run up to the trial are motivated by the same desires as the Contempt of Court Act. They are there to protect a defendant's art.6 rights by safeguarding the integrity of the trial, most notably the role of the jury.

So the aim of the limits is to allow the public to know the basic details of who is in court, what they are accused of doing, where and when, and what is happening to them within the legal process. They specifically prevent use of any evidence at that stage which would suggest whether the defendant is guilty or innocent.

As long as there is a chance of a case ending up at jury trial, the restrictions will apply. So if a defendant enters a formal guilty plea or is acquitted, they do not apply. If a case is being tried before magistrates they do not apply (with the exception of preliminary hearings to determine admissibility of evidence at trial by magistrates).

To be completely safe, reports of preliminary hearings should be restricted to the ten points.

In practice, the restrictions are breached daily by court reporters embellishing their reports with extra detail beyond the ten points despite it being a criminal offence. The classic additions are uncontentious points such as what the defendant is wearing. There is also room to include a fair amount of information within the scope of "details of the charge" but anything that is presented as evidence or has a bearing on guilt is dangerous. Technically even a protestation of innocence is beyond the ten points but prosecution would be impossible to sustain given that the system assumes any defendant is innocent unless proven guilty.

However, a journalist reading these extended reports might be lulled into a false sense of security. Journalists need to be aware that, although prosecutions under the section are rare, any breach of the ten points is technically an offence. There is no requirement on the prosecution to prove that a trial was affected or that the journalist had any intent to prejudice proceedings. As ever, know your law and only ever take a calculated risk.

Case Study One: Challenging orders under s39 orders of the Children and Young Persons' Act 1933

These are the discretionary orders most often challenged, and challenged successfully, by individual journalists. In many cases, courts accept the media arguments and the orders can be amended or withdrawn on the spot. At the other extreme, some cases have gone to appeal in an attempt to achieve more general clarity and create a convincing authority which should in theory staunch the flow of inappropriately-made orders. In practice it hasn't, as the examples given in this chapter indicate. So what does make an order improper and provide grounds for challenge?

The first order concerns are that the child or young person made subject(s) of the order must be:

1 **Under the age of 18.**
   The upper age limit is clear but the lower age limit is muddier—see below. The age relates to when the case is heard not to when any alleged crime took place.

AND

2 **Concerned in the criminal proceedings as a victim, defendant or witness in the case.**
   Many of the orders challenged successfully related to children who were not party to proceedings. Defence solicitors should not be able to use general concern for the children of a defendant to secure a s.39 order, particular where the explicit/implicit consequence is anonymity for said defendant.

AND

3 **Still alive.**

Many disputes arise over the scope of the orders. A s.39 order:

> "permits a criminal court to prohibit publication by the media of the name, address, school or any information calculated to lead to the identification of any child or young person concerned in criminal proceedings before that court. The power to prohibit publication also extends to pictures of the child or young person. The order only applies to the proceedings in the court by which it was made."

It is not for the court to go beyond these standard prohibitions by detailing specific other detail that cannot be included in a press report of the case. They certainly cannot directly prohibit the publication of the names of adults involved in the proceedings or other children or young persons not involved in the proceedings as witnesses, defendants or victims.

Magistrates and judges will still attempt to do this despite the clear advice offered within the legal system itself. Some, knowing the limitations of the s.39 orders, will artfully offer advice on how the anonymity may be achieved. That can be very useful for a reporter and needs to be weighed carefully but does not carry the authority of a court order. Maintaining anonymity can be challenging, as discussed earlier in the Chapter, but withholding the name of a defendant should be the last resort. Media codes offer further advice on how to deal with including such difficulties with reminders of the need for multiple outlets to avoid jigsaw identification.

Further requirements often flouted which can give rise to a successful challenge include, as the guidelines[80] state:

- Under s.39 the onus lies on the party contending for the order to satisfy the court that there is a good reason to impose it.
  In deciding whether to impose an order under s39 the judge must balance the interests of the public in the full reporting of criminal proceedings against the desirability of not causing harm to a child concerned in the proceedings.
  Orders cannot be made automatically just because the party to the case is under-18.
- Age alone is not sufficient to justify imposing an order as very young children cannot be harmed by publicity of which they will be unaware and s.39 orders are therefore unnecessary.
  Some ambiguity remains regarding this lower age limit. Clearly a babe in arms cannot be aware of publicity and references have also been made variously to children under reading age and/ or pre-school children being too young to be subject of a s.39. Orders for any children under the age of four are well worth scrutinising on these grounds.
- Any order made must comply with art.10 ECHR—it must be necessary, proportionate and there must be a pressing social need for it.
- If a reporting restriction is imposed, the judge must make it clear in court that a formal order has been made. The order should use the words of s.39 and identify the child or children involved with clarity. A written copy should be drawn up as soon as possible after the order has been made orally. Copies must be available for inspection and communicated to those not present when the

---

[80] *Reporting Restrictions in the Criminal Courts.* October 2009. Joint publication by the Judicial Studies Board, Newspaper Society, Society of Editors and Times Newspapers Ltd.

**order was made (e.g. by inclusion in the daily list). Court staff
should assist media inquiries in relation to the order.**

Here we have the now classic balancing of rights. How much interference is justified with the public right to know what happens in
court?

As soon as the prospect of a s.39 order is raised—usually by the
defence—a journalist should consider whether it is appropriate. Some
courts will seek a response from the press bench but, if not, a journalist
doubting the validity of an order should pass a note to the bench indicating a challenge which may be heard on the spot. So be prepared to
point out what appear to be any failures to meet the basic requirements
of the order. If that fails, be sure to secure a written copy of the order
and consider a formal challenge at a later session or through lawyers.
Each order and each court behaves slightly differently. The guidelines
encourage courts to accept challenges and to take representations direct
from journalists so as to save the time and cost of full legal representation. This has shown itself to be hugely beneficial as even trainee journalists have successfully challenged orders made in the lower courts.
But it can be daunting and demands court reporters are alert to the possible shortcomings or excesses of orders and confident enough to mount
a challenge to them.

The guidelines also urge the courts to be prepared to reconsider an
order, say if a youth is convicted of a serious crime. The balance of interests may arguably have changed if the youth is guilty.

4. Reporting Employment Tribunals

Employment tribunals have the ability to issue Restricted Reporting
Orders.[81] Cases often revolve around issues of sexual discrimination or
harassment for which employment tribunals have their own provision.
However allegations could stray into the realm of sexual offences in
which case usual restrictions would apply as discussed in Ch.1 on the
Legal System. Otherwise, the tribunal can impose its own restrictions
whereby both sides in a sexual case could be granted anonymity until
the tribunal promulgates its decision. There may also be restrictions in
certain cases of claimed discrimination related to the Disability Rights
Act.

Reporters had found it difficult to challenge or even get details of the
reporting restrictions in some instances. But media law specialists at
Foot Anstey, who contribute regular updates to the journalists' website

---

[81] Sch.1 r.50: Employment Tribunals (Constitution and Rules of Procedure) Regulations
2004.

Holdthefrontpage, alerted reporters to a possible means of challenging such restrictions:

> "A freelance journalist has secured a helpful court ruling about challenging reporting restrictions in employment tribunals, albeit that she ultimately lost her appeal on a separate issue. When a claim involving alleged sexual misconduct was settled out of court after a reporting restriction order (RRO) had been imposed, reporter Fiona Davidson persuaded the tribunal to lift the restriction.
>
> The point was appealed to the Employment Appeal Tribunal, which ruled that under the procedural rules that govern all such cases (i.e. the Employment Tribunal (Constitution and Rules of Procedure) Regulations 2004) the journalist had actually had no right to be heard before the employment tribunal.
>
> However, Ms Davidson herself then appealed and won on the question whether reporters are entitled to make representations to employment tribunals about RROs.
>
> The appeal court said it was 'common sense' that the employment tribunal allowed Ms Davidson to make representations to lift the restriction."

The senior judge added:

> "It would, we cannot help adding, assist greatly if the matter were put beyond argument by the introduction of an express provision . . . in the 2004 Rules, enabling a person such as the appellant to apply to the Employment Judge or tribunal to have a right to make representations about the variation or revocation of a restricted reported order.
>
> A party who seeks to keep a full RRO in force, and thus to restrict the freedom of the press to publish reports of the proceedings fully and contemporaneously, can hardly complain if a journalist, who is able to demonstrate a legitimate interest in whether or not the order is varied or revoked, seeks to make representations.

This was a Scottish case but the same 2004 Rules apply in England and Wales, and the appellate guidance is a useful addition to all reporters' armoury."[82]

---

[82] Media law bulletin by Nigel Hanson, Foot Anstey *http://www.holdthefrontpage.co.uk/2009/news/very-few-privacy-cases-being-contested/*[Accessed April 2011].

CHAPTER SUMMARY: COURT REPORTING RESTRICTIONS

The protection of children is at the heart of many reporting restrictions. Courts have, understandably, concern for children caught up in legal proceedings. But every restriction is a departure from the principle of open justice and needs to be justified.

- **Children and Family proceedings.** The last Government tried to open up these very closed proceedings but fundamental tensions remain which are difficult, if not impossible, to reconcile between the art.8 rights of the parties, particularly the children, the art.10 rights of the journalists and public and the commitment to open justice. Note particularly the Children Act 1989 and the impact of the European Court of Human Rights.
- **Children in criminal courts.** Children are given some protection in criminal courts too. Anonymity is automatic for under-18s in criminal proceedings in youth courts and discretionary orders are available under s.39 of the Children and Young Persons Act 1933 when a child is party to a case in adult court.
- **Asbos.** Be aware of the special arrangements for reporting Anti-Social Behaviour Orders on children. (Adults are subject to them too.)
- **Sexual offences.** Alleged victims are granted lifetime anonymity from the point of allegation for rape and a range of sexual offences under various Acts and including non-contact sexual crimes such as voyeurism. Be aware of the challenges of maintaining anonymity and of the risk of **jigsaw identification** where multiple media outlets are involved.
- **Preliminary hearings.** Under the Magistrates' Court Act 1980, reports of a variety of hearings and committals prior to Crown Court trial are limited to ten points. Evidence has to be withheld to protect the integrity of the jury trial. Learn the list of what can be reported at these early stages, together with when the restrictions apply and when they don't. Similar restrictions apply to preparatory hearings at Crown Court before the jury trial.
- **Employment tribunals.** Be aware of the different regime of reporting restrictions, particularly in cases claiming sexual misconduct.
- **Know the relevant law and keep up to date with changes in legislation and case law affecting the media.** Some court reporting restrictions are mandatory, such as anonymity for victims of sexual offences; others are discretionary, such as s.39 orders on children in adult courts. Know when and why they apply so you can in the first instance comply with them; and in the second also challenge them if need be.

Read the Judicial Studies Board Guidelines on Reporting Restrictions in the Criminal Courts. Other invaluable sources include *Media Lawyer* (by subscription), *5rb*, *Holdthefrontpage*, *Media Guardian*. See the Bibliography.

CHAPTER 8: MEDIA REGULATION

PART ONE: REGULATORY BODIES

Various bodies have regulatory powers over the media. In this chapter we consider the regulation primarily of journalistic material which has historically been platform-dependent with different regimes for print and broadcast.

The media is one of many industries subject to regulation and the mix of regulatory bodies is quite normal. Journalists, in common with any employees, find their conduct controlled by a combination of criminal statute; codes of conduct established by either a formal statutory regulator, a professional body or a self-regulatory organisation; and internal management systems and personal ethics.

The real value of regulation is to handle the relationship between journalists and the public—to set expectations of that relationship and allow the journalist as "service provider" to be called to account if those standards are not met. It works particularly well when the transgression does not involve anything illegal but nonetheless leaves an individual or the audience in general feeling short-changed. Regulators can mediate relatively informally but hopefully effectively to resolve complaints and improve performance.

Regulation in any sphere reflects a mix of economic, political and cultural concerns and approaches. The UK in recent decades has tended towards the US free market model; the "light-touch" approach whereby the government makes the minimum intervention required to protect the public. Generally competition is seen as delivering the best deal for consumers. The banking collapse, blamed on inadequate regulation, does not seem to have reversed the general trend.

In media terms, the current government would be expected to lean towards self-regulation and indeed there has been some freeing up of media competition rules.

But for journalists, the political aspects of regulation are a strong part of the mix. Politicians find it very difficult to resist attempting to control the media and, arguably, where they can they do. This helps to explain the more rigid controls on broadcast than print. Broadcasters have historically needed access to limited airwaves, so the State has been able to licence channels in return for much stricter regulation of their behaviour. Airwaves are relatively easy to regulate so the advantage is seized to impose more demanding regulation. Also, given the mass reach of radio, television and now online, regulation in this sphere can control their potentially powerful influence over large swathes of audience.

However much the BBC deserves its worldwide reputation for excellent journalism, it always faces the challenge of fending off interference from Governments which ultimately control its revenue through the setting of the licence fee and its operation through the Charter. The relationship is a long way from the overt control of state broadcasters in many parts of the world but the public subsidy that enables the BBC to do such a fine job also puts a question mark over its real independence.

The cultural battleground is where society works out what balance it wants to strike between the various competing rights involved in the public sphere. A free independent media is vital in a democracy and must resist pressure to rein it in. Attempts will always be made to curb freedom of expression; some society will deem fair and reasonable, others will hopefully be dismissed as inimical to public interest.

Media regulation in the UK is a patchwork of all the models; a result of our long press history, social attitudes to the media; the balance of power in society; and the noble art of compromise.

Regulators tend to have a relatively low profile compared with the courts but far more issues and complaints are resolved through regulation than through the courts and the regulatory framework aims to create channels for conflict resolution which are faster, cheaper and more accessible than those of the legal system. An economic approach driven by a desire to reduce public spending may well see this tendency reinforced.

Regulation may be anathema to the fine *Millian* principles of free speech but it does have a role in helping society to strike the balance between journalists' rights and those of the citizens they serve. A free media is both too important to regulate; yet too important not to regulate.

The regulatory bodies through which the public can hold the media to account sit broadly between the individual editorial source and the courts. So a person aggrieved by press coverage, for instance, might turn first to the "offending" newspaper; if not satisfied, the complaint can go to the next tier in the form of a regulatory body; and if not resolved there, can go to the courts for remedy. Although the hierarchy exists, a complainant need not follow it and can, for instance, proceed straight to law.

The main regulatory bodies we focus on here are the Press Complaints Commission (PCC), which covers newspapers and magazines and crops up most frequently in media law judgments, and the Office of Communications (Ofcom) for broadcast. In terms of standard-setting it is also important to consider the BBC's own Editorial Guidelines and complaint-handling procedure. Some media organisations, notably the *Guardian*, have their own readers' editor or Ombudsman to deal with complaints at one remove from the editorial team.

One key distinction between Ofcom and the PCC is that the former is statutory while the latter is not. In practice, the main difference is in the realm of sanction. Ofcom can impose fines on a broadcaster and, in worst cases, withdraw a licence to broadcast. The PCC relies on public reprimand, the ignominy of having to print hostile adjudications and the threat that being found against constitutes breach of contract for many working journalists and can lead to dismissal.

1. Office of Communication (Ofcom)

The regulatory body for the broadcasting industry is the Office of Communication (Ofcom) established under the Communications Act 2003. Prior to that broadcasting was "policed" by various bodies such as the Broadcasting Standards Commission and the Radio Authority. The current regulations are contained in the Broadcasting Code last updated in February 2011 to take account of the changes regarding product placement.

Ofcom works across the communications industries, dealing with mobile telephony and online provision as well as the broadcast, but not print, media. It also deals with issues such as industrial strategy, physical network provision and competition. This makes it a highly influential body across a wide field but determines that most of its work does not concern journalistic output directly.

Notably Ofcom has *overall* supervision of the BBC but the BBC operates its own editorial guidelines and Ofcom's role is limited. Ofcom handles BBC issues directly in four areas:

- Broadcasting Content Regulation: Tier 1 (negative minimum content regulation).
- Broadcasting Content Regulation: Tier 2 (Quotas for elements of television programme services).
- Compliance with Ofcom's Code on Television Access Services i.e. subtitling, sign language and audio description.
- Competition functions.

Ofcom does not regulate in these areas:

- Broadcasting Content: Tier 1: Programme *Standards* relating to impartiality, accuracy in news and commercial products within programmes.
- Broadcasting Content: Tier 2: Obligations for party political, election and referendum broadcasts.
- Broadcasting Content: Tier 3: Qualitative Public Service remit (PSB) BBC only to "consider" anything of relevance in Ofcom guidance to commercial broadcasters.

Anyone seeking to complain about accuracy or bias in BBC programming needs to complain to the BBC, not to Ofcom. Complainants about any broadcasters are anyway encouraged to follow the broadcaster's own complaints procedure first before making a complaint to Ofcom. If a complainant is not satisfied with the broadcaster's response to their complaint, the complaint can then be submitted to Ofcom. Complaints can also be made directly to Ofcom in the first instance, subject to the BBC exceptions.

Much of Ofcom's work is tied up in the practicalities of keeping the stations on air and with commercial aspects, such as the duration of advertising slots and the boundaries of sexual material. The abuse of premium rate telephone quiz lines hit the headlines and several complaints were upheld against the way competitions were run, extending even to children's favourite Blue Peter.

Ofcom has considerable powers and represents the sort of model some politicians, lawyers and judges would like to see applied to the printed media. Ofcom cannot exercise prior restraint, but it can fine the operator, suspend or even revoke its licence to broadcast.

Examples of its requirements include:

- Rule 2.2: "Factual programmes or items or portrayals of factual matter must not materially mislead the audience."
- Rule 2.3: "In applying generally accepted standards, broadcasters must ensure that material which may cause offence is justified by the context. Such material may include, but is not limited to . . . discriminatory treatment or language (for example on the grounds of . . . religion)."
- Rule 3.1: "Material likely to encourage or incite the commission of crime or to lead to disorder must not be included in television or radio services."
- Rule 5.5: "Due impartiality on matters of political or industrial controversy and matters relating to current public policy must be preserved on the part of any person providing a service."

Ofcom has a board with a chairman and both executive and non-executive members. Together they provide its strategic direction. It describes itself as the main statutory instrument of regulation with a fundamental role in the effective implementation of the Communications Act 2003.[1]

Complaints

Public complaints about journalistic broadcast material are likely to fall within Ofcom's brief to uphold fairness and privacy. Ofcom expects the complaint to come from the "person affected" rather than a third party but can initiate its own complaints. It assesses the complaint to decide if it is going to "entertain" it; seeks a copy of the material and sets about

---

[1] Available at *www.Ofcom.org.uk*.

trying to broker an appropriate resolution. This can include the editing of a programme where it is to be repeated; an undertaking not to repeat the programme; an apology or correction in writing and/or broadcast.

If the complainant accepts the resolution, that is the end of the matter. If the suggested redress is not accepted, Ofcom will proceed with consideration of the complaint. After appropriate submissions, there will be a hearing and the adjudication will normally be posted on the Ofcom website.

Where a complaint is upheld or partly upheld, the offending broadcaster may be required to broadcast a summary of the adjudication. We have probably all heard at least one but they are sporadic.

If the adjudication justifies consideration of statutory sanction, the complaint is referred back to the case leader to apply the published criteria for considering sanctions. In an extreme case, particularly of repeated breaches of the Code, Ofcom can withdraw a licence. A string of complaints about the sexual material broadcast on channels run by Bang Media (London) Ltd and Bang Channels Ltd had been upheld, followed by a fine of £157,250 in July 2010 and final revocation of licences in November 2010.

There is frequent reference to the Human Rights Act 1998 throughout the guidelines for complainants to make clear that the process is convention-compliant.

Appeals

A complainant unhappy with the outcome can seek a review which, if agreed, is undertaken by Ofcom but by someone not previously involved in the case. It is possible to seek judicial review of an Ofcom ruling but the courts are reluctant to intervene given both Ofcom's expertise and that the legislation creating Ofcom did not include an appeals process on fact or law.

2. BBC Editorial Guidelines

The BBC Editorial Guidelines[2] provide copious advice on how standards set out in the BCC Charter can be upheld in practice. All guidelines are publicly available online at *www.bbc.co.uk/editorialguidelines*.

The introduction states:

"Audiences are at the heart of everything we do. We are committed to giving them high-quality, original and at times challenging output. Creativity is the lifeblood of our organisation. Equally, we must give

---

[2] *BBC Editorial Guidelines*, available to journalists and the public, *www.bbc.co.uk/editorial guidelines*.

our audiences content made to the highest editorial and ethical standards. Their trust depends on it.

We must therefore balance our presumption of freedom of expression with our responsibilities, for example to respect privacy, to be
fair, to avoid unjustifiable offence and to provide appropriate protection for our audiences from harm.

(Note: The Human Rights Act 1998 recognises the right to freedom
of expression, which includes the audience's right to receive creative material, information and ideas without interference, subject to
restrictions in law. It also recognises the right to private and family
life and to freedom of thought, conscience and religion.)

We seek to uphold the BBC's Editorial Values in all we do. They
embody our freedoms and responsibilities and, like the Editorial
Guidelines, apply to all our content, whether it is made by the BBC
itself or by an independent company working for the BBC, and
whether it is made for radio, television, online, mobile devices, inter-
active services or the printed word. What follows are challenging
requirements, but they are essential to everything we do."

So BBC journalists are also explicitly operating within the framework of
the Human Rights Act and its intrinsic weighing of freedom of expression with other rights. Note the stress within art.10 on the audience's
right to receive material.

Complaints

The Editorial Complaints Unit deals with serious complaints
about breaches of the BBC's editorial standards in connection with
specific programmes or items of content. It deals with complaints
about any BBC service or product where the BBC has editorial
responsibility.

The Editorial Standards Committee of the BBC Trust (ESC) may
consider any matter which raises questions of a potential breach of
the BBC's editorial standards, set out in its Guidelines, including
appeals against decisions and actions of the Editorial Complaints
Unit and divisional directors in dealing with editorial complaints. All
the ESC's findings are normally published on the BBC complaints
website. It may direct the BBC to broadcast an apology or a summary
of its finding.

Responses to issues of wide audience concern, either because they
generate a significant number of complaints or involve a significant
issue, are published on the website. If appropriate they include any
clarification, correction, apology or action taken as a result.

The BBC's Complaints Management Board of senior executives
meets monthly to see if further response is needed via editorial and
managerial processes. The BBC Trust monitors the effectiveness of
complaints-handling across the BBC, and reports on this in the BBC
Annual Report.

The demands of impartiality are among the extra challenges facing the broadcast journalist but the main issues of regulation reflecting the need for accuracy and compliance with ethical and legal standards in areas such as defamation, privacy and contempt are common to journalists working on any platform or indeed across platforms.

Appeals

If complainants are not satisfied by the Editorial Complaints Unit finding, they can appeal to the Editorial Standards Committee. When the Editorial Complaints Unit identifies a serious breach of the standards in these Guidelines, its finding will normally be published on the BBC complaints website. It may also direct the BBC to broadcast an apology or correction. In rare circumstances, BBC decisions can be subject to judicial review.

3. Press Complaints Commission

The Press Complaints Commission (PCC), created in 1991 to replace the Press Council, is a self-regulatory body covering the print industry, both newspapers and magazines. It operates a Code of Practice[3] to guide both journalistic output and methods of investigation. Editors of print titles are held accountable for maintaining Code standards. The subject of any story who feels a journalist has breached the Code can complain to the PCC.

The Code of Practice was created and is maintained by the Editor's Code of Practice Committee comprising 14 editors from national and regional newspapers and magazines. Funding is channelled through the Press Standards Board of Finance, representing the publishers. The code covers a wide range of issues, notably accuracy, privacy, children and subterfuge. It explicitly embraces the same sort of balancing act faced in the courts in weighing competing articles of the ECHR, attempting to protect both the rights of the individual and the public's right to know.

The PCC cannot fine an editor or shutdown a publication, even if a persistent offender. But Code compliance is written into many journalists' contracts and breach can be grounds for dismissal.

It has no formal powers of prior restraint but it will advise editors, out-of-hours if necessary, on whether certain stories or approaches would be Code-compliant or not. It can also now initiate its own complaints which can be tracked on its website alongside those directly from the public.

---

[3] PCC Code of Practice *http://www.pcc.org.uk/cop/practice.html* [Accessed May 2011].

Complaints

The Press Complaints Commission secretariat processes complaints and pursues resolution, by mutual agreement wherever possible. The PCC itself has 17 members, with seven editors and ten lay members from outside the industry, including the chairman. The Commission oversees the system and adjudicates on complaints. Panels ruling on complaints always comprise a majority of lay members.

The target is to resolve complaints within 35 days. If the PCC regards the complaint as raising a possible issue under the Code, the editor has seven days to provide an initial response. The editor always represents the publication in the process. The PCC secretariat will assess the possibilities for conciliation, act as a go-between and attempt to secure a remedy acceptable to both parties. If conciliation fails, or is inappropriate, or if the case involves a major policy issue, the Commission will adjudicate. Where a complaint is upheld the publication must publish the adverse finding. No editor has ever failed to comply with that condition.

The PCC now carries extensive general guidance on its website and has produced an editors' codebook[4] to provide further guidance on its operation. This includes a useful checklist of its various means of resolving complaints without adjudication, which is predominantly the aim. These are:

- Clarification. A clarification might be appropriate where something has been omitted from the original article or if it is ambiguous or arguably misleading. It stops short of an admission by the editor that the article was wrong.
- Corrections and apologies. Straightforward factual errors are usually dealt with most cleanly and simply by the publication of a correction. In the case of serious errors, this might include an apology. The Code states that an apology should be published where appropriate.
- Letter for publication. This is particularly appropriate where the complainant is taking issue on a matter of opinion rather than fact.
- Follow-up article. An editor might offer to publish an interview with, or article by, a complainant, grudgingly although sometimes enthusiastically. A complainant may assume the newspaper is not amenable to challenging new material and complain direct to the PCC rather than approaching the editor. Just occasionally the complaint actually alerts the newspaper to interesting story developments which it is more than happy to cover.
- Tagging newspaper records. This is an increasingly popular way of resolving complaints, either alone or as part of a package of remedies. The publication's electronic database and cuttings library are tagged with the complainant's objection to ensure the mistake is not repeated.

---

[4] Beales Ian, The Editors' Codebook (2009). See Bibliography.

- Private letter of apology. Further publicity is often not an attractive option for the complainant, particularly in privacy cases or intrusion into grief.
- Private undertaking. Similarly, undertakings by the editor about the future conduct of the newspaper and its staff might also give a complainant some peace of mind.

Appeals

Under its predecessor body the Press Council, complainants had to grant a legal waiver—if their complaint was not upheld they could not go on to sue. That protection was removed when the PCC was created so dissatisfied complainants can, and do, take the same complaint to the courts.

Within the PCC, there is now an Independent Reviewer who handles complaints about the workings of the PCC but he safeguards procedural probity rather than challenging the substance of the adjudications. Attempts have very occasionally been made to subject PCC adjudications to judicial review, notably in 1996 by Moors murderer, Ian Brady, who lost his claim. Newsreader, Anna Ford, who complained over pictures of her in a bikini on a public beach, was in 2001 denied judicial review of the PCC decision that this was not an unwarranted invasion of her privacy.

4. Readers' Editors

Guardian readers, in particular, will be familiar with the role of Readers' Editor as a first tier of recourse for complaints about anything it publishes in print or online. Many regional newspapers take a similar approach but the *Guardian* has the most high-profile internal complaints-resolution procedure. This was a conscious policy to bolster the principle of self-regulation and provide evidence of accountability to readers. A reader's editor, or public editor as they are known in the US, is employed by the media organisation but the role is avowedly more independent, working at one remove from the main editorial team.

The first *Guardian* readers' editor was Ian Mayes whose logic and dry wit made the Corrections and Clarifications column a must-read. The contributions were even collected and published in a book.[5]

However as he made clear:

"I do not touch complaints in which lawyers are involved. I do not deal with complaints once the Press Complaints Commission is involved. I never represent the Guardian in disputes. When people

---

[5] Mayes, Ian, The Guardian Corrections and Clarifications (2000). See Bibliography.

come to me without the threat of legal action I deal with their complaints impartially."[6]

A difficulty arose when his normal observations were combined with a more formal apology made under offer of amends, designed to help resolve a defamation complaint.[7]

But often the readers' editor can resolve grievances which could have ended up with legal action and it is interesting to note that when Mayes retired in 2007, he was replaced as Readers' Editor by a media lawyer, Siobhain Butterworth, who held the post until 2010.

All organisations covered by media regulation will have some process in place for handling complaints but this tends to be managed by someone within the hierarchy, such as a managing or assistant editor.

5. Individual Ethical Codes

The law and regulatory Codes are huge influences on how journalists investigate stories and what they go on to share with the public. But the most significant concern for any journalist must be individual conscience. We all have to draw our own lines in the sand. When are we championing freedom of expression? When are we properly challenging the rights of others and when are we just trampling all over them?

A moral code is key to the credibility of every individual journalist as well as their titles and organisations. Hopefully a personal ethical code is also an essential element of what sets a journalist apart from an individual blogger, bystander or commentator

The National Union of Journalists picks this up in its Code of Conduct.[8] Its "conscience clause" states that journalist members have a right to refuse work that would break the letter or spirit of the code. A similar stance is taken by the US Committee of Concerned Journalists[9] whose members are committed to providing citizens with "accurate and reliable information they need to function in a free society". The core principles are:

- Journalism's first obligation is to the truth.
- Its first loyalty is to citizens.
- Its essence is a discipline of verification.
- Its practitioners must maintain an independence from those they cover.

[6] A costly lesson in libel, *Guardian*, June 4, 2005.
[7] *Campbell-James v Guardian Media Group* [2005] EWHC 893.
[8] NUJ Code of Conduct *http://www.nuj.org.uk/innerPagenuj.html?docid=174* [Accessed May 2011].
[9] *www.concernedjournalists.org.*

- It must serve as an independent monitor of power.
- It must provide a forum for public criticism and compromise.
- It must strive to make the significant interesting and relevant.
- It must keep the news comprehensive and proportional.
- Its practitioners must be allowed to exercise their personal conscience.

The committee is dismissed as too high-brow in some quarters but these are worthy aims which even Eady J. might applaud.

6. Regulation of Privacy

Privacy issues are of growing concern in the courts which might suggest that complainants are unhappy with the remedies available from regulators. But, as we discussed in Ch.5 on Privacy, the nature of a demand for privacy puts the issue firmly into the realm of prior restraint. Not even Ofcom involves itself before programmes are aired and the PCC has no formal powers to prevent publication. Those with secrets to keep will look to the courts.

However the regulators across print and broadcast media have combined to promote a hotline operated by the PCC to help citizens caught in the media spotlight to avoid unwanted intrusion, particularly when it reaches the level of harassment.

The Ofcom website tells users:

"The broadcasters and the broadcasting news organisations have agreed with the Press Complaints Commission that in a situation where an individual feels harassed because large numbers of print and broadcast journalists have congregated to cover a news story, the following emergency number: 07659 152 656 (which operates 24 hours a day) can be used by a person affected to notify the relevant organisations of their concern. Whether the journalists are withdrawn is then a decision for the relevant organisations."

In cases of harassment desist notices can be, and are, issued. Despite the Ofcom caveat, they have been effective in some cases. Members of the public don't have to wait to be harassed to call. Families can tell the PCC in advance that media approaches will not be welcome and the PCC will pass that on to editors. The hotline outcomes reported by the PCC include:

- In 2007, the PCC worked with Cheshire Police to assist the family of Garry Newlove, who had been murdered outside his home in Warrington. The family was concerned about media attention in the run up to the trial of five youths accused of his murder, and went to the PCC for help. The PCC circulated a statement from the family to editors, managing editors and lawyers, which asked the media not to contact them in any way, either in the run-up to the trial or during it, or afterwards. The family explained that previous contact from journalists had been intrusive and made them feel harassed. As a result of the PCC's work, the family did not experience any contact, or indeed harassment, from the press.

- The PCC was contacted by the family of a man who had taken his own life. The family was concerned that the forthcoming inquest into the death would prompt contact from journalists at a time when they were still grieving and did not wish to speak. The PCC disseminated a message from the man's mother to relevant editors not to contact the family. The request was respected.

- Chris Tarrant's manager sought help to minimise the heavy media attention on Mr. Tarrant's wife following their separation. She was feeling harassed by the large number of journalists who had set up outside her house. The PCC sent out a desist message on her behalf explaining that she did not wish to speak. Very shortly afterwards, the media began to disperse.

Other cases do arise before and after the event which prompt privacy complaints to the regulators. A brief look at the handling of privacy complaints by the PCC and the BBC demonstrates the parallels with legal principles.

Privacy and the PCC
Genuine cases of infringement of privacy where a real personal hurt has been caused can be dealt with appropriately by the PCC and it has issued general guidance in this area as well as upholding various complaints. They remain a small proportion of the total, which are predominantly about challenging accuracy, but in 2009 were the basis of more than half the complaints upheld. The PCC 2009 annual report stated[10]:

"Statistically, there are two key causes of complaint – inaccuracy and intrusion into privacy. Of complaints that warranted investigation, over 85% made claims about breaches of Clause 1 (Accuracy) of the Code.

Privacy remained the area that often caused most controversy, with the Commission having to balance the competing rights of individual privacy and freedom of expression. 21% of all investigated complaints had a privacy angle to them. And when it came to published rulings, over 50% dealt with concerns about privacy. That figure rose to over 55% in cases where the editor was censured, which may reflect the seriousness with which the PCC views an unwarranted invasion of privacy."

[10] http://www.pcc.org.uk/annualreports/annualreview.html [Accessed May 2011].

The PCC is driven by the same kinds of considerations as the courts in these issues. Its majority of lay members may weigh the "proportionality" issues slightly differently but the difference is not that great; the PCC could not afford for it to be otherwise the pressures to sacrifice self-regulation would become even greater.

Among its guiding principles on privacy, as quoted in The Editors' Codebook,[11] are:

- Privacy is not an absolute right—it can be compromised by conduct or consent.
- Privacy is not a commodity which can be sold on one person's terms—the Code is not designed to protect commercial deals.
- Privacy does not mean invisibility—pictures taken in genuinely public places and information already in the public domain can be legitimate.
- Privacy may be against the public interest—such as when used to keep secret conduct that might reflect on a public figure or role model.[12]

The language and emphasis is different but there is clear recognition of issues surround art.8 and art.10 rights. The PCC even uses much of the same jargon as the court by referring to its "case law" as effectively setting boundaries in areas such as privacy. In this sense the Editors' Codebook as a whole provides a most useful summary of these precedents and indicates what implications they have for future coverage. Adjudications make it obvious that if another publication investigates or runs a story in a similar fashion its editor can expect to fall foul of the Code.

There are, however, several notorious cases in this area and certainly there are plenty of public figures who have dismissed the PCC, either due to dissatisfaction with its handling of a complaint or by going straight to law. But these cases are not always as straightforward as they seem. The naked honeymoon photographs of DJ Sara Cox and her husband, which were an infringement of privacy, cost the *People* newspaper around £50,000 plus costs of more than twice that. Cox was portrayed as having been forced to court by the inadequacy of the PCC. But as the PCC's then director, Guy Black, pointed out, she accepted an apology brokered by the PCC. The issue never went to adjudication. If it had, the PCC may well have upheld the complaint. And when she sought a legal remedy, the case was settled out of court. No legal precedent was established.

Government Minister, Ruth Kelly, complained to the PCC when the *Daily Mirror* ran the news that she was sending one of her children to a private school for pupils with learning difficulties. Her complaint was not upheld but the adjudication was illuminating. It referred to

---

[11] Beales Ian, *The Editors' Codebook* (2009). See Bibliography.
[12] Beales Ian, *The Editors' Codebook* (2009) at p.24. See Bibliography.

the balance between the child's privacy and the public interest in the actions of her mother and there is clear proportionality at play. It said:

> "While there was unquestionably an intrusion felt by the complainant and her child, it was clear that the newspaper had taken steps to limit the nature of that intrusion in omitting the name of the child, his school and precise details of his condition.
>
> Had further details been included, the Commission may well have considered the intrusion to be unnecessary.
>
> It judged that the naming of the complainant herself—even though it carried with it an implicit identification of her child—was necessary in the context of the story and enabled a fuller, legitimate discussion of the issues at stake, including whether the State in general and Tower Hamlets Council in particular was able to offer appropriate schooling for children with special needs."[13]

The PCC is not a court, but it sounds very much like one. Primacy was given to the public interest in a Minister, particularly a former Education Minister, finding the state provision wanting when it came to her own child. How readers responded to her resolution of the dilemma was up to them. The story made an important contribution to the controversies around public/private education provision and it was run responsibly so as to keep the focus as much as possible on the issue and the Minister rather than the child. The editor may even have discussed it with the PCC beforehand.

In May 2007, the PCC upheld a complaint against the *Sun* for intruding into singer Charlotte Church's privacy in its reporting of her pregnancy. To say merely that the pregnancy was "rumoured" was not enough to evade its Code obligations. The adjudication was printed on p.2 of the newspaper, hardly hidden away.

The PCC is also mirroring court judgments by upholding complaints where the degree of sexual detail provided is not proportionate in the weighing of art.8 and art.10 rights. A complaint over a story about a "Lady Chatterley" affair, published in two national newspapers, was not upheld against one but upheld against the other because it included lurid sexual detail. The adjudication in one said:

> "The amount of information in the article was sufficient to enable the man's girlfriend to tell her story—as she was entitled to do—without including humiliating and gratuitously intrusive detail."

The other said:

> "When reporting one party's account of a relationship, newspapers must also have regard to the other person's private life. The complainant had not courted publicity and any limited public interest inherent

---

[13] Adjudications at *www.pcc.org.uk*

in exposing adultery committed by someone who was married into an aristocratic family was insufficient to justify the level of detail in the piece."[14]

In an adjudication involving the daughter of motor racing magnate, Bernie Ecclestone, the PCC rejected complaints regarding some elements of the story based on an interview with the daughter's former boyfriend but upheld one saying:

"While it is noted that Miss Ecclestone has received publicity in the past on account of her lifestyle as the daughter of a very wealthy man, the commission made clear—as it always has done—that the previous publication of matters into the public domain dealing with a person's private life does not necessarily disentitle that person to any right of privacy."[15]

The extent of intimate detail, of a sexual nature, was not warranted. Sounds familiar.

Privacy and the BCC Guidelines
The PCC has extended the range and detail of information available but the BBC tends to outstrip others when it comes to sharing very detailed explanations of its position. The BBC Editorial Guidelines on Privacy state:

"The BBC respects privacy and does not infringe it without good reason, wherever in the world it is operating. The Human Rights Act 1998 gives protection to the privacy of individuals, and private information about them, but balances that with a broadcaster's right to freedom of expression. . . .
An infringement is considered in two stages, requiring justifications for both the gathering and the broadcasting of material where there is a legitimate expectation of privacy.

Legitimate Expectations of Privacy
An individual's legitimate expectation of privacy is qualified by location and the nature of the information and behaviour, and the extent to which the information is already in the public domain. People in the public eye may, in some circumstances, have a lower legitimate expectation of privacy.
Location: People in public places or in semi-public places cannot expect the same degree of privacy as in their own homes or other sensitive locations. (A semi-public place is somewhere which, though private property, gives the public general access, such as an airport, station or shopping mall.)

[14] Adjudications at *www.pcc.org.uk*
[15] Adjudications at *www.pcc.org.uk*

However, location must be considered in conjunction with the activity. There may be circumstances where people can reasonably expect privacy even in a public or semi-public space, particularly when the activity or information being revealed is inherently private. For example, there may be a greater expectation of privacy when someone is in a public or semi-public place but receiving medical treatment.

Behaviour: There is less entitlement to privacy where an individual's behaviour is criminal or seriously anti-social.

The Public Interest

Private behaviour, information, correspondence and conversation should not be brought into the public domain unless there is a public interest that outweighs the expectation of privacy. There is no single definition of public interest. It includes but is not confined to:

- exposing or detecting crime
- exposing significantly anti-social behaviour
- exposing corruption or injustice
- disclosing significant incompetence or negligence
- protecting people's health and safety
- preventing people from being misled by some statement or action of an individual or organisation
- disclosing information that assists people to better comprehend or make decisions on matters of public importance.

There is also a public interest in freedom of expression itself.

When considering what is in the public interest we also need to take account of information already in the public domain or about to become available to the public.

When using the public interest to justify an intrusion, consideration should be given to proportionality; the greater the intrusion, the greater the public interest required to justify it."

Again the guidelines mirror legal advice. The definition of public interest is very similar to, albeit more complex than, the PCC's.

PART TWO: REGULATION IN PRACTICE

The work of regulatory bodies outlined in Part One impacts every day in every newsroom. When combined with the emergence of the legal concept of responsible publication, journalists' behaviour is more firmly in the spotlight than ever. It is not enough that our stories are in the public interest; we must have pursued them and run them responsibly.

Cases such as *Moldova*[16], discussed in Ch.2 on Freedom of Expression, stress that a journalist seeking to uphold art.10 rights must be able to demonstrate not just the reasonable accuracy of what was run but that it was the product of thorough processes of verification with an ethical underpinning. In the UK, the judges have looked to the codes of our various regulatory bodies to provide the "ethics" test.

Lord Hoffmann, in *Jameel*[17] at para.55, raises the issue specifically in terms of how to move to a definition of "responsible journalism" within a *Reynolds* public interest defence against defamation. He said:

"The standard of responsible journalism is as objective and no more vague than standards such as 'reasonable care' which are regularly used in other branches of the law. Greater certainty in its application is achieved in two ways. First, as Lord Nicholls said, a body of illustrative case law builds up. Secondly, just as the standard of reasonable care in particular areas, such as driving a vehicle, is made more concrete by extra-statutory codes of behaviour like the Highway Code, so the standard of responsible journalism is made more specific by the Code of Practice which has been adopted by the newspapers and ratified by the Press Complaints Commission. This too, while not binding upon the courts, can provide valuable guidance."

How does regulation impact on working journalists? Mechanisms vary between platforms but the principles are similar. BBC editorial staff have extra demands regarding impartiality which makes their output very different from some print material which can be more opinionated. Sanctions regimes are clearly different too but, for the individual journalist, reputation and career are on the line in much the same way.

Not surprisingly, much of the establishment would like to see print publications falling under the remit of Ofcom, or an organisation very much like it. The rich and powerful tend to dislike the media more than most and are often prepared to use their position to restrict its power. Somehow, this is portrayed by Parliament and the courts as motivated by pure public interest, whereas news organisations, and the journalists within them, are generally assumed to be driven entirely by self-interest. No-one—whether politician, celebrity or journalist—can claim to monopolise the moral high ground. At least let us accept that all sides are driven by a mix of pure and baser motives.

Generally, those calling for the PCC to be able to impose fines on news organisations are working on the basis that the only penalty that counts with newspapers is a financial one. Hit the watchdog where it hurts and it will come to heel. A journalist's view is that it would be a massively retrograde step in terms of pursuing pluralism and an

---

16 *Kommersant Moldovy v Moldova* [2007] ECHR 9.
17 *Jameel v Wall Street Journal Europe Ltd* [2006] UKHL 44.

appalling curb on freedom of expression if all media fell under such strict regulation whereby a statutory agent of Government could hold a newspaper hostage and remove its right to print. It would also make the PCC more like a court and restrict the flexibility it has as a conciliator and trusted adviser.

Also if we accept that money can be a motivator for the media, we must also accept that money can be a motivator for complainants. Famous people have agents and clipping services scouring the media for possible actionable material. How disappointing for them to have a press complaints commission that focuses on putting the record straight and upholding standards of conduct. They don't just want fines; they want damages.

The prime ethical base for print journalism is the Press Complaints Commission Code of Practice with which any journalist in the dock is expected to have an intimate working relationship—another good reason for a journalist routinely to carry one of the creditcard-sized copies of it in purse or wallet.

All journalists now have ready access, as do the public, to online copies of the Codes with detailed adjudications and further advice on compliance for print and broadcast output.

The Office of Communication (Ofcom) in practice

Ofcom makes a great deal of information about its operations available to the public. Most of its standard setting and complaint handling is not directly relevant to journalists because of the breadth of its remit. Other elements of its work, such as controlling mobile telephony, often generate media coverage, and much of its in-depth research into audience is fascinating whatever platform speciality a journalist has. But the complaint handling over the content of individual programmes is where it is most likely to cut across the work of journalists—to challenge accuracy or impartiality in particular.

Complaints can be made to Ofcom by any person or body who considers that a broadcaster has failed to comply with a relevant requirement. Complaints can, for example, be made about:

- harmful or offensive material;
- material which is inaccurate or partial;
- material which encourages or incites crime or disorder;
- the protection of those aged under 18;
- radio stations failing to deliver "the proposition" agreed;
- subtitling, signing or audio description; or
- sponsorship and product placement.

In common with areas of media law, the regulator finds itself frequently dealing with issues concerning children. Again, most do not involve journalistic output directly but are concerned with protecting children in various ways, particularly from explicit material as indicated in the list.

Journalists involved in a complaint about their output will find themselves called upon to demonstrate rigour in both information gathering and reporting. Accuracy, reliable record-keeping and precise use of language will all help to avoid a complaint in the first place as well as generating the necessary explanations when challenged. Ofcom adjudications are detailed, legal-style documents based on a welter of fine detail which journalists must be able to provide, even some time after the event. See Case Study One.

BBC Guidelines in practice

For BBC journalists, the BBC's own guidelines are the significant ones in that they regulate editorial content. Broadcast journalists working outside the BBC come under Ofcom's surveillance. In the wake of the David Kelly[18] affair, the BBC has placed greater stress on training and best journalistic practice across the board. One of the massively valuable outcomes of this has been the creation of the BBC's College of Journalism which is a primarily virtual learning environment, open in large part to the public.[19]

The BBC Editorial guidelines, which lie at the heart of its advice, are detailed in themselves but further guidance is provided in their support, both online and in the course of programme-making. So, for instance, on privacy, there is specific guidance on the considerations applying to requests to run appeals for missing people. Guidance may vary according to the type of programme, whether editorially or entertainment-led. So for instance, journalists are told:

"**Doorstepping for News and Factual Programmes With Prior Approach**
    Any proposal to doorstep, whether in person or on the phone, where we have tried to make an appointment for an interview with the individual or organisation concerned must be approved by a senior editorial figure or, for independents, by the commissioning editor.
    Approval will normally only be given when there is evidence of crime or significant wrongdoing and for one, or more, of the following reasons:
    • the subject of a doorstep has failed to respond to repeated requests for interview in connection with the wrongdoing alleged
    • a request for an interview has been repeatedly refused without

---

[18] David Kelly profile, *http://news.bbc.co.uk/1/hi/uk_politics/3076869.stm* [Accessed May 2011].
[19] *www.bbc.co.uk/journalism*

good reason and substantial allegations of wrongdoing have
been avoided

- there is a history of failure to respond to interview requests or
refusal to be interviewed.

Proposals for doorstepping should be proportionate to any wrongdoing. Consideration should be given to the safety of production staff
and the risk of infringing the privacy of third parties who are insuf-
ficiently responsible for any wrongdoing, such as family members or
junior employees."

Again we see the Human Rights Act influence in the reference to the
intrusion needing to be "proportionate" to the wrongdoing being investigated. See Case Study Two.

Press Complaints Commission in practice

As debate raged over privacy, David Cameron, who had previously
appeared open to the prospect of legislation in that area, told the BBC
Radio 4 *Today* programme in May 2011 :

"I sense that there's still more to be done to recognise that actually
the Press Complaints Commission has come on a lot in recent years,
and we should be working with that organisation to make sure that
people get the sort of protection they need . . . while still having a free
and vibrant press.
We don't want statutory regulation of the press."

And, pushed further on the whether there was a need for a specific
privacy law, he reiterated his support for the PCC.

The Press Complaints Commission does not always receive such a
warm endorsement of its work from politicians. Expectations tend to
be very high and the PCC is at times written off simply because it does
not prevent all unethical print journalism. But that would be like saying
that all police services should be scrapped because crimes are still
committed. The powers of the PCC are intentionally limited, so as to
provide the necessary balancing of rights in a democratic society within
a pluralist media. Much as many print journalists admire the BBC and
other broadcasters, they do not appreciate their regulatory regime. The
requirement for impartiality can easily stifle debate and putting all
media under one regulatory umbrella, particularly one that could close
down outlets, would concentrate power in a most alarming way.

The PCC has to muddle through as any regulator must but we should
acknowledge the perceived weaknesses of this self-regulatory regime.
Its critics say:

- The PCC is industry financed and its Code Committee is made
up entirely of editors which means it may not be perceived to be
independent.

- Neither individual journalists, editors nor news organisations can be fined nor is it possible to close down a title, even for flagrant and frequent Code breaches.
- Successful complainants cannot receive financial compensation (although they can't from other regulators either).
- It is difficult to obtain judicial review to examine the process of decision making (again as with other regulators).

The Press Complaints Commission is not noticeably kind to editors. The majority of adjudicators are lay members and the journalist members are not tolerant of other editors letting the side down. Also, given the highly-competitive nature of the media, especially at a national level, rival editors are not renowned for "cosying up", rather they can relish the discomfort of a competitor being shown up in breach of the code.

For an editor, it is humiliating to have to print an adjudication which spells out exactly how her newspaper has fallen foul of the code. And in reaching settlement without adjudication, editors are often pressed into more fulsome apologies certainly than they would have chosen to run. Working editors don't want a complaint even to get as far as adjudication let alone be upheld.

Dealing with a complaint pursued by the PCC:

- Takes time and the editor, or a senior colleague, is expected to handle it promptly.
- May require legal advice on remedies which is more time and expense.
- Often reveals that the publication's checking system and/or remedy procedures haven't worked and will need to be overhauled, with a commitment to complainant and PCC to do the overhauling.
- Means an editor may have to agree a remedy which isn't comfortable.
- Means an editor may be found against.
- Means the publication has to print the hostile adjudication.
- Means the editor and/or reporter may be sacked.

In agreeing to publish any PCC adjudication of censure, an editor is ceding power over content in a way which she would not for a proprietor, managing director or advertiser. This is a major concession. The PCC is not a minor irritant. Newspapers cannot just pay lip service to it even if some used to be inclined to.

An example of a resolved PCC complaint on accuracy was *Lord Prescott v The Sun* in April 2011. Lord Prescott complained that an article about his House of Lords expenses was inaccurate and misleading. The complaint was resolved when the PCC negotiated the publication of the following correction in the newspaper and online, in addition to the removal of the original online article:

"An article on March 4 stated Lord Prescott claimed £10,016 in House of Lords expenses between July and September. In fact, he claimed £9,312, which includes £4,940 for office costs paid for the full period, rather than the 13 days he attended the House. As a result, Lord Prescott did not claim nearly £800 a day. We regret the error and are happy to set the record straight."[20]

Note that the erroneous article was removed from the online archive.

The PCC has become more flexible about who can complain. Where a story concerns an individual, it is still up to that individual to pursue the matter but it is possible for the PCC to invite a complaint if its attention is drawn to a grievance. Where the coverage complained of is more general the PCC may accept a complaint from someone not directly referred to in the piece, say on a claim of inaccuracy. This stance allows for more errors to be corrected without opening the PCC up wholesale to lobbyists.

The sheer volume of material now available on its website and the ease with which someone can complain (without the need of lawyers) has changed the profile of the organisation and made its workings far more transparent than in the past.

The PCC has followed a reactive, rather than pro-active, remit in the past but it now takes far more initiative in making public or private statements regarding required standards. It can also now instigate complaints against titles in its own name as it did regarding payments to a potential witness to an incident relating to the death of Ian Tomlinson at the G8 protest. The PCC can also pre-empt complaints where sources indicate concern over potential publication. There is considerable sensitivity in this area as the PCC wants to be seen as responsive to the public yet does not want its work construed as akin to exercising prior restraint on publication. (See the discussion in Part One on Regulation of Privacy.)

The PCC can help to resolve issues with a story that might arise prior to it being published. Its website states:

"In many cases, stories do not appear thanks to these discussions. Just a few examples of where stories have been published, or have been handled in a different way thanks to the PCC's intervention, include:

• A national newspaper intended to publish a story about a practising dentist who was infected with HIV and Hepatitis C. The individual made clear that he was following established protocol as to how such a situation should be handled, and that there was no public interest in the wider dissemination of details of his illness.

[20] *http://www.pcc.org.uk/news/index.html?article=NzA4OA==* [Accessed April 2011] and the online correction at *http://www.thesun.co.uk/sol/homepage/news/3504644/Lord-Prescott-John-Prescott.html.*

- A soap star was pregnant, and did not wish this to be made public before her 12-week scan. Following the circulation of a desist notice to editors by the PCC, this information did not make it into print.
- A political figure contacted the PCC with concerns about allegations relating to his behaviour before he took up a new role. Through the PCC, he highlighted the inaccuracies in the proposed story. While the newspaper did publish a story, it was notable that it did not include some of the allegations that he had denied."[21]

There is still arguably a contrast between the behaviour of regional and national newspapers although numerically there are more complaints against regional and local newspapers because there are more titles and they are read by so many people. As usual, most of the media debate focuses on a handful of popular tabloids or at best national newspapers as a whole. For the general public, local papers have at least as much, if not more, bearing on their lives. Regional papers work hard to honour the code in the way they gather and present news, and by responding to complaints—and from ordinary readers rather than celebrities. Local readers tend to be very ready to apply a "reality check" through the PCC if the newspaper is at all reticent in dealing with complaints about coverage within their community. For some of the nationals, the highly competitive tabloid market tempts them into excess but they are coming round to compliance with the Code. It was a chasm but it has narrowed.

The PCC is not a draconian body; nor is it a professional body, such as the British Medical Council, because journalism is not a profession. That is one of the key features of journalism which makes the lighter touch of self-regulation appropriate and indeed vital. Freedom of expression and the need for plurality in a democracy means a journalist, unlike a dentist or lawyer, cannot be "struck off" and prevented from practising. This setting apart of journalists from many of the normal strictures of working life rankles in many quarters and the argument is often dismissed as being born out of the arrogance of journalists. But journalists are different; their role in society is different and in ways which the checks and balances of democratic society must recognise and learn to live with.

Case Study One: Ofcom: Complaint by the Free Gaza Movement made on its behalf by Alex Harrison

An edition of *Panorama*, Death in the Med, aired on BBC1 on August 16, 2010, provoked this complaint. The adjudication runs to 9,000 words with even the decision taking more than 3,000. This is easily on a par with the length and complexity of a judge's ruling. It said:

---

[21] *http://www.pcc.org.uk/aboutthepcc/examplesofsuccessful.html*

"Ofcom has not upheld this complaint of unfair treatment made by Ms Alex Harrison on behalf of the Free Gaza Movement.

An edition of Panorama looked at the boarding in May 2010 by Israeli soldiers of the Mavi Marmara, one of the ships in the Gaza Freedom Flotilla, which was attempting to take aid to Gaza. The flotilla was organised by the Free Gaza Movement ("Free Gaza") and the programme referred to the flotilla as "sailing under the banner of the Free Gaza Movement".

In summary Ofcom found the following:

- The programme did not portray Free Gaza unfairly, as a result of the misrepresentation or omission of material.
- The programme did not include any allegations to which Free Gaza should have been given an opportunity to respond.**"**

The complainant from Free Gaza essentially felt the accusations made of one group aboard one boat, the Mavi Marmara, were effectively being levelled at the whole flotilla which was described at times under the banner of Free Gaza.

The complaint was not upheld because Ofcom ruled that the accusations were clearly levelled at the Turkish activists IHH on the one boat, Free Gaza was not implicated and therefore there was no requirement to offer an opportunity to Free Gaza to respond to central claims.

Ofcom is obliged to protect the audience from "unfair treatment" but much of this reads as a judgment on whether this edition of Panorama met the demands of "responsible journalism" particularly as regards any requirement of a response from the complainant's organisation.

The judgment meticulously gives both sides of the story, point by point, and then records its decision, dealing with each challenge in turn. Although the complaint was not upheld, the adjudication does take the programme makers to task over the varying descriptions of the flotilla which "had the potential to cause confusion in the minds of viewers as to the extent to which overall responsibility for the peace activists' role in the events being investigated by the programme was being attributed to the members of the IHH on board the Mavi Marmara and the extent to which it was being attributed more generally to the entire flotilla and Free Gaza." Given that was the nub of the complaint it makes for a rather odd ruling.

- Free Gaza complained that the Israeli version of events was treated as fact and their version as claims but Ofcom felt various references to reporting "both sides" of the story and other interviews, including one from Free Gaza, had provided balance.
- Free Gaza complained that when the reporter questioned the "real agenda" of some of those people who called themselves peace activists she referred to the Free Gaza Flotilla and portrayed them as a violent Islamic activist mission seeking confrontation with Israel. Ofcom said the programme made clear that the violence and

confrontation took place on the Mavi Marmara and only involved activists from IHH and Israeli commandoes. The word "some" definitely helped the reporter there as well as the later focus on IHH.

- Free Gaza complained that the programme referred to the Israeli commandoes as having to "fight for their lives", but Ms Harrison said that the members of Free Gaza were not the aggressors and that nine of them were killed and another 50 injured. Ofcom said the casualty information was given. Viewers would have understood that some of the peace activists also had to fight for their lives and that the Free Gaza protestors were not the aggressors.

Note here the concept throughout of what a "reasonable" viewer would have deduced from the programme.

- Free Gaza complained that the programme included video filmed by them which they said was stolen by Israeli commandoes who passed on selected footage. Ofcom, which didn't enter into the dispute over video ownership, said the selection of shots was a matter of editorial judgment and was not unfair to Free Gaza because it did not portray them as the aggressors.
- Free Gaza complained about use of an offensive audio tape in which a voice was heard to say "Shut up, go back to Auschwitz" and "We're helping Arabs go against the US. Don't forget 9/11, guys" and alleged that it was made by Free Gaza. Ms Harrison said it was known within days that the tape had been doctored. Ofcom considered that the programme made it clear that the recording was disputed and attributed it to the "flotilla" rather than to Free Gaza directly. Any link to Free Gaza was only via the general confusion over references elsewhere in the programme to the Free Gaza flotilla.
- Free Gaza also objected to the programme's claim that "the question of who shot first remains disputed", despite the fact that Free Gaza did not carry any weapons. Ofcom noted that the question came after a sequence in the programme that showed how the group of IHH activists took control of the Mavi Marmara. Viewers would have understood that the question was whether the Israeli commandoes or the IHH activists, rather than the members of the flotilla generally or Free Gaza, had shot first.
- Free Gaza also said it was false to claim that two thirds of the medicines carried on the flotilla were out of date. Again, the crucial point for Ofcom was that having used a vague reference to the flotilla in the opening, the programme went on to be more specific. The adjudication says:

> "As stated at the beginning of the decision, Ofcom considered that the programme's references to "the flotilla" and "the Free Gaza flotilla" had the potential to cause confusion. In Ofcom's view, it was not clear at the beginning of the programme who was being referred to in the context of the aid. However, by the point in the programme when the reporter was looking at the

aid that had arrived in Gaza, it was clear that the medicines she was referring to as "out of date and useless" were provided by the IHH."

- Free Gaza said it was portrayed unfairly as a result of the omission of material facts. More than 30 British passengers on the flotilla, several of whom, including Ms Harrison, had been interviewed at length by the programme makers but only one of the Free Gaza interviews was used. Ofcom again stressed that, because the accusations were directed at IHH, this was not unfair to Free Gaza. The specific selection of clips, as long as it balanced the accusations, was a matter of editorial discretion.
- Free Gaza complained that it was not given a proper opportunity to respond but Ofcom said the programme did not make any significant allegations about Free Gaza so it was not incumbent on the programme makers to give Free Gaza an appropriate and timely opportunity to respond.

The complaint against the BBC was not upheld and the reasoning is clear under the terms of the Ofcom Code. But the way the flotilla was described left room for confusion. That's a different criticism but a valid one none the less. Where the aggression was confined to one boat, it was even more important to take great care when talking about the flotilla more broadly. The mixing of the general and the specific was clearly why Free Gaza felt badly done by. Precise use of language is crucial to clarity. The confusion here fell short of causing unfairness but it was a complaint that could so easily have been avoided by more careful wording of the script.

Case Study Two: BBC Editorial Complaints Unit ruling on claims that aid intended for famine relief in Ethiopia had been diverted to buy arms[22]

"Last March, in reports about aid money donated to Ethiopia in the mid-1980s, a number of BBC programmes and online items implied or stated that large amounts of money raised by Band Aid and Live Aid for famine relief in Ethiopia had been diverted by a rebel group to buy weapons. Following a complaint from the Band Aid Trust the BBC has investigated these statements and concluded that there was no evidence for them, and they should not have been broadcast. The BBC wishes to apologise unreservedly to the Band Aid Trust for the misleading and unfair impression which was created."

---

[22] Publication date: November 17, 2010. *http://www.bbc.co.uk/complaints/content/ecu/ecu_bandaidmoneydonatedethiopia* [Accessed April 2011].

The story ran at varying lengths on several different BBC programmes across radio and television. Each specific item was addressed in turn. Here again the adjudication reads very much like a court judgment.

The reports were based on claims that aid intended for famine relief in Tigray during the Ethiopian famine of 1984-5 had been subject to large-scale and systematic diversion by the Tigrayan People's Liberation Front (TPLF) and its relief agency REST, to buy arms and for other political purposes. The Band Aid Trust ("the Trust") complained that the programme and coverage generated by it had given the inaccurate and unfair impression that much or most of the money raised under the Band Aid banner had been diverted, whereas Band Aid was noted for the effectiveness of its monitoring of funds, and there was no evidence that funds raised by Band Aid had in fact been used to buy arms.

The BBC dealt with each report and each of Band Aid's complaints in turn. Some were rejected, some upheld and others upheld in part.

"Assignment
The programme gave the impression that the claims of diversion related, inter alia, to Band Aid/Live Aid money (and the programme-makers acknowledge that such an impression, though unintended, might have been formed by a fair-minded listener). However, the programme's evidence did not relate to Band Aid/Live Aid money, and the impression given by the programme in this respect was therefore unfair to the Trust.

There was no evidence that the programme's allusions to Band Aid were motivated by a desire to sensationalise the story.

In the section of the programme dealing with the alleged swindling of an agent of Christian Aid, it was made clear that the allegation concerned Christian Aid money, and it was not suggested that Band Aid money might have been involved.

The programme was not clear about the extent to which the evidence of Aregawi Behre (who was the source of the claim that REST had, at a certain point, decided to divert 95% of aid money to the purchase of arms and other political purposes) was open to question.

The evidence of Gebremehdin Araya (who claimed to have swindled the Christian Aid agent) rested on a somewhat different basis, and the programme had not placed undue reliance on it.

The inclusion of evidence from a CIA report and from Robert Houdek contributed to the impression that the programme's allegations of diversion included Band Aid money, whereas those items of evidence did not apply directly to Band Aid (and, in the case of the CIA report, could not have applied to Band Aid).

As the allegations were not deployed in the programme as criticism of Band Aid, there was no requirement under the BBC's Editorial Guidelines to offer the Trust a "right of reply". There were, however, strong editorial reasons for seeking comments from the Trust, and the programme-makers' requests for an interview with Bob Geldof or another representative of the Trust did not give enough information about the gravity of the allegation of diversion of funds to enable an informed decision about whether to provide a speaker to be made.

The programme made clear that the allegations of diversion applied to aid reaching Tigray, not to the Ethiopian relief effort as a whole, and that much aid had served its intended purpose.
Partly upheld"

Again, there are echoes of the legal processes in the form and language used, such as reference to the "fair-minded" listener. There are shades of the demands of "responsible journalism" too in the observation that the request for a response from BandAid did not put the full allegations to the source. The adjudication went on:

"Ethiopian Famine Aid 'Spent On Weapons', bbc.co.uk
The sentence *"One rebel leader estimated $95m (£63 m) - from western governments and charities including Band Aid - was channelled into the rebel fight"* was inaccurate in suggesting that the witness in question (Aregawi Behre) had referred to Band Aid, and there was no evidence for associating this claim with Band Aid funds.
Upheld

BBC News (6pm), BBC One, 3 March 2010
Though the body of the report was fair and accurate, the suggestion in the studio introduction that millions of pounds of Band Aid money had been *"siphoned off by rebel groups to buy weapons"* was inaccurate and unfair.
Upheld

Bob, Band Aid and how the rebels bought their arms, The Editors, bbc.co.uk
The article gave a misleading impression that there was evidence of large-scale diversion of Band Aid money. The article was not clear about the extent to which the credibility of the claim of 95% diversion of aid by REST was open to question.
Upheld

Further action
Apologies to the Band Aid Trust will be broadcast on BBC One, the News Channel, Radio 4 and World Service. Appropriate steps will be taken to guard against visitors to any relevant BBC online items being given the impression that the evidence of diversion applied to Band Aid money."

There clearly was a story worth running here but the BBC fell into the trap of equating aid to Ethiopia with Band Aid. Obviously the Band Aid angle provided familiarity and was of concern to a British audience but the connections were just not as strong as suggested, even if the original sources are treated as fully reliable.

The in-depth reports generally managed to provide more balance and perspective. The main problems were with the "soundbites" which over-sold the story but which sadly will have stuck in the audience's consciousness.

Case Study Three: PCC adjudication Two women v Courier and Advertiser (Dundee)[23]

Two women complained that an article published in the Courier and Advertiser (Dundee) in January 2011 contained material that had identified their daughters as victims of sexual assault in breach of cl.3 (Privacy), cl.7 (Children in sex cases) and cl.11 (Victims of sexual assault) of the Editors' Code.

The article reported a court hearing in which a man had admitted sexual offences against two girls, both of whom were under the age of 16 at the time the crimes occurred. The report made reference to the locations where the offences had taken place, including the names of the streets—two of which were the streets on which the victims lived. The article also stated the ages of the girls at the time of the offences.

The complainants both said their daughters' right to anonymity had been compromised by the inclusion of this information. Complainant A said that she and her daughter lived in a rural area with only twelve houses on their street. It was easy for neighbours and others in the local community to identify her daughter as a result of the article. Complainant A added that the level of detail included about the offences was unnecessary.

Complainant B said her daughter was the only female child of the reported age who lived on the other named street. Neighbours, classmates and other acquaintances had, as a consequence, been made aware of her identity and the graphic nature of the offences to which she was subjected. This in turn had led to the girl being extremely distressed.

The newspaper removed the partial addresses from its electronic archive and excluded similar references in a subsequent report about sentencing. The complaint was upheld.

"Adjudication:
    The terms of Clause 7 (Children in sex cases) of the Editors' Code are very clear: "the press must not . . . identify children under 16 who are victims in cases involving sex offences". Clause 11 (Victims of sexual assault) adds that the press "must not publish material likely to contribute to [the] identification" of victims of sexual assault. If in doubt, newspapers should always err on the side of caution when

[23] *http://www.pcc.org.uk/cases/adjudicated.html?article=NzA4NQ==* [Accessed April 2011].

considering what details to publish in relation to such cases. In this instance, the inclusion of the girls' ages and of their partial addresses clearly had the potential to contribute to their identification. Indeed, given the relatively small number of houses on the streets in question, identification was always going to be a strong possibility.

This was a bad mistake by the newspaper, which had acknowledged that its practice of publishing only outline details of cases such as these had not been followed. The Code affords particular protection to those who are vulnerable - and it is hard to imagine anyone more vulnerable than a child victim of sexual crimes. The failure of the newspaper properly to consider the likely consequences of publishing the information in the report, especially the references to the girls' partial addresses, was a serious one."

Regulation and illegal trade in private information

The continuing criminal and civil actions over phone-hacking have had various impacts upon regulators, particular the Press Complaints Commission. The controversy has run in tandem with investigations by the Information Commissioner into the illegal trade in private information. (See also the discussion in Ch.6 on Journalists' Sources.)

Section 55 of the Data Protection Act makes it an offence "to obtain, disclose or procure the disclosure of personal information knowingly or recklessly without the consent of the organisation holding the information." Fines for breach are technically unlimited but most cases have been dealt with by magistrates limited to fines of up to £5,000. Journalists have a defence under s.55 of the Act where they can demonstrate a public interest. This is in line with the PCC's own Code regarding use of subterfuge. Clause 10 of the PCC Code states:

"Clandestine devices and subterfuge

  i) The press must not seek to obtain or publish material acquired by using hidden cameras of clandestine listening devices; or by intercepting private or mobile telephone calls, messages or emails; or by the unauthorised removal of documents or photographs; or by accessing digitally-held private information without consent.
 ii) Engaging in misrepresentation or subterfuge, including by agents or intermediaries, can generally by justified only in the public interest and then only when the material cannot be obtained by other means."

The police's Operation Motorman inquiry revealed widespread breaches of s.55 which lead to the Information Commissioner's What Price Privacy? report in May 2006 calling for stronger sanctions for breach of the Act. The then commissioner Richard Thomas argued that the level of criminality meant a greater deterrent was needed in the form of higher fines and the possibility of prison sentences of up to two years. The media, despite its public interest defence, objected to the threat of imprisonment. The Information Commissioner pushed for a strengthening of the Code in this area which was not forthcoming.

His follow-up report, What Price Privacy Now?, six months later revealed a league table of publications making use of the inquiry agents investigated by police. The context was explained as follows:

> "'What price privacy?' reported that 305 journalists had been iden-
> tified during Operation Motorman as customers driving the illegal
> trade in confidential personal information. Following the report the
> Information Commissioner received a request under the Freedom of
> Information Act 2000 for further information about the publications
> that the 305 journalists were employed by and a breakdown of their
> activity. After considering the relevant exemptions information which
> did not identify the journalists or the publications was provided to the
> requester.
>
> Having considered the matter further the Information
> Commissioner has decided that a further disclosure is in the public
> interest and in the context of a special report to Parliament is con-
> sistent with the discharge of his functions under the Data Protection
> Act 1998. The following table shows the publications identified from
> documentation seized during the Operation Motorman investigation,
> how many transactions each publication was positively identified as
> being involved in and how many of their journalists (or clients acting
> on their behalf) were using these services.
>
> It should be noted that while the table is dominated by tabloid
> publications they are far from being alone. Certain magazines
> feature prominently and some broadsheets are also represented. The
> Commissioner recognises that some of these cases may have raised
> public interest or similar issues, but also notes that no such defences
> were raised by any of those interviewed and prosecuted in Operation
> Motorman."

The *Daily Mail* topped the list at 953, followed by the *Sunday People*, the *Daily Mirror*, the *Mail on Sunday* and the *News of the World*. More than 30 publications were listed, including the *Observer* and the *Sunday Times*. As even the Information Commissioner acknowledged, not all of these involved illegality but it was enough to put pressure on the media to rein back its use of such inquiry agents and to ensure that any remaining use was entirely above board.

The PCC was one of many regulatory bodies challenged to respond with action. Although the focus was on the private investigators at the supply end of the bribery and/or blagging of information, Mr Thomas also wanted to ensure that demand for their services dried up.

The PCC did step up its consciousness-raising with editors and data protection responsibilities are included in the Code handbook. Mr

Thomas' successor as Information Commissioner, Christopher Graham, addressing the Society of Editors in 2009, said:

> "There needs to be public trust in the handling of data by government and others. The existing paltry fines are not enough to deter people from engaging in this illegal activity. The threat of jail will be a greater deterrent."[24]

But, on a more conciliatory note, he stressed that journalists working in the public interest were not his target. He said the purpose of strengthening enforcement was about closing down the "sleazy trade" in personal data. "This is so not about you," he told the assembled editors. At that point, given the absence of any post-2007 complaints about press commissioning of illegal data, he felt self-regulation was working.

The PCC was also caught up simultaneously in the fall-out of from the jailing of the *News of the World* royal editor, Clive Goodman, for intercepting mobile phone messages and in May 2007 published new guidance for news organisations of Subterfuge and Newsgathering,[25] stressing its commitment to taking "the severest view" of any publication using inquiry agents in ways that breach the Code. (See Appendix 7).

The PCC has been criticised for being too supine in accepting police decisions not to investigate further at the time but in matters of potential criminality regulatory bodies would be expected to take a back seat to the police and CPS. That said, the PCC has some way to go before sections of the public are convinced that it can exert adequate influence over regulatory "errant" publications. Hints can be dropped, pressure applied and complaints upheld but the PCC can only go so far. In the most serious cases, where illegality is involved, journalists are still accountable to the law and it is up to the police and CPS to act.

Regulation of converged media in practice

The explosion of material in the public domain on digital platforms has challenged regulators as it has the courts. The anarchic, fluid and viral nature of online operations presents logistical difficulties to regulatory mechanisms set up to deal with a limited number of outlets. This made both carrot and stick easier to apply. Compliance could be incentivised particularly in the broadcast sphere. Scarce spectrum and its profit-generating potential could be traded in return for adherence to strict output controls. Online TV, let alone the proliferation of mainstream channels, destroys the equation.

So what about the stick? Big corporate media companies with physical assets are sitting ducks if they don't comply. Bloggers are a lot more difficult and less lucrative to pin down.

---

[24] Society of Editors conference, Stansted, 2009.
[25] PCC report on Subterfuge and Newsgathering, *www.pcc.org.uk*

The potential of digital sources to evade regulation puts them beyond reach; but it also creates an uneven playing field for mainstream media still expected to comply. The imbalance threatens the hold of regulatory bodies in both broadcast and print platforms. Content creators must be asking themselves if submission to regulation is worth it. Why bother if it is all cost and no benefit?

In practice, regulatory regimes have followed their targets down the digital path. The PCC has assumed responsibility for the web presence of all UK newspaper and magazine titles, including associated audio and video. The BBC guidelines apply to its online material on its huge website. But it is difficult to see how the division between print and broadcast in terms of regulatory frameworks can be sustained in an era of growing convergence.

The PCC has also had to apply its code where websites are used as a source of information for mainstream media. Is everything on a website or on mobile platforms such as Twitter in the public domain if it can be accessed without subterfuge? Or do we extend the concept of an expectation of privacy in a public place, and impose limits on what can be lifted, say from a dead person's social networking site?

The Press Complaints Commission has built up its own case law in these areas. The adjudication in *Rundle v Sunday Times*, for instance, said:

> "The Commission wished to point out that newspapers still remained entitled, when reporting the death of an individual, to make use of publicly available material obtained from social networking sites. However, editors should always consider the impact on grieving families when taking such information (which may have been posted in a jocular or carefree fashion) from its original context and using it within a tragic story about that person's death."[26]

The law may be platform-blind, but in reality there are websites galore breaching every kind of law and ethical code all the time. Unless their authors belong to a mainstream media organisation they have generally evaded legal action and often even regulatory control. Just as there are levels of accountability for public figures, it appears there are for individual news providers. The BBC and nearly all major newspaper groups live up to the highest standards of ethical and legal probity. For much of the rest, just about anything goes.

Perhaps soon, newsgathering operations will be regulated either as a condition of funding support or, in the case of newspapers, as a seal of quality and accountability to bolster credibility with the audience (and potentially with the courts). The PCC could be used like a Fairtrade mark seal of approval, guaranteeing certain standards have been upheld in the production and content of the news provided.

[26] PCC Complaint: *Rundle v Sunday Times*, January 2010 *http://www.pcc.org.uk/news/index. html?article=NjE1NQ==* [Accessed April 2011].

The PCC is consulting on whether its remit should be extended to cover all editorial content on websites in the hope that self-regulation will be preferred to statutory. That makes it even more likely that an opt-in system will emerge with Code compliance being used a quality mark.

Certainly the system needs to find a way of rewarding those organisations which have a commitment to credible, reliable news output and are prepared to answer to their responsibilities rather than penalising them for being so obviously in the firing line. Compliance is costing the mainstream a fortune, whether in cash or restraint terms, while guerrilla publishers escape any effective control of standards or legality.

CHAPTER SUMMARY: MEDIA REGULATION

Media organisations in the UK are monitored by a mix of statutory and self-regulatory bodies, which were historically platform-specific. Each works to one or more Codes for journalists determining ethical ways of working and the standards of output expected. They adjudicate on complaints from the public and censure output in breach of the Codes. Standards of accuracy, fairness and privacy are among the key elements of the Codes, with impartiality a further requirement on broadcasters.

- **Office of Communications** (Ofcom) is a statutory body regulating communications, including telephone and online provision as well as radio and television. It can fine broadcasters in breach of its Codes and withdraw their licence to operate.
- **The BBC** has its own Editorial and other Guidelines to regulate the work of its journalists. The BBC Trust monitors the working of its internal complaints system.
- **Press Complaints Commission** (PCC). The PCC delivers a self-regulatory standards regime for newspapers and magazines, plus their associated websites. Editors of offending material must publish any adjudications against them. Journalists and editors can be sacked for breach of the Code.
- **Readers' Editors** are a feature of some UK titles, notably the *Guardian*. These editors, either journalists or lawyers, work at arm's length from the newsroom offering an internal but independent complaint resolution service.
- **Individual ethics** cannot be ignored. Every journalist needs a "moral compass". Regulators encourage best practice and penalise unethical behaviour but the individual journalist has to take personal responsibility too. A "thinking" journalist will fight for

freedom of expression but also be respectful of the rights of others and proportionate if intruding upon them.

Regulatory regimes have stretched themselves to accommodate multi-platform media but convergence has taken us all into new territory where the old rules are not necessarily appropriate and certainly not easy to enforce. Trying to regulate pockets of the media in isolation from each other does not appear to be logically or practically sustainable. But will that mean more regulation or less? The prospects for regulation as a whole will be discussed in our next section: The Future.

Stop Press

Britain's largest-selling Sunday newspaper, News International's *News of the World*, closed abruptly in July 2011 after being sullied by fresh allegations of phone-hacking — variously into the messages of murdered teenager Milly Dowler and relatives of the 7/7 bombing victims, soldiers killed in Iraq and the murdered Soham schoolgirls.

The scandal, still unfolding as we went to press, involves many allegations, not just of phone-hacking but of other aspects of illegal trade in private information, including the very highest in the land — the Queen and the then Prime Minister Gordon Brown. Arrests had also been made in connection with accusations of corrupt payments to police.

New questions were raised over whether the *News of the World's* parent company Murdoch-owned News Corp could be declared under Ofcom guidelines to be a 'fit and proper' owner to take control of the whole of the country's biggest satellite broadcaster BSkyB.

Prime Minister David Cameron talked of scrapping the Press Complaints Commission, which surely faces at the very least major reform, potentially along the lines of the recommendations of the Select Committee. (See Appendix 8.)

But the prime responsibility for the inadequate investigation of criminal accusations lies with the Crown Prosecution Service and police who were under intense pressure in the wake of the closure to explain the limited response to allegations regarding News International dating back to 2003.

The allegations as we go to press all relate to activity prior to the jailing of Clive Goodman and Glen Mulcaire in 2007. It is not known whether the prison sentences and the revelations of the Information Commissioner brought to an end to what is emerging as an inglorious phase for much of the popular press in the UK.

The institutional response to News Corp and other possible media miscreants appears to have been remarkably restrained at every turn and the tough questions awaiting satisfactory answers go way beyond the PCC to the highest echelons of the British establishment.

CONCLUSION: THE FUTURE OF MEDIA LAW

The classic image of the scales of justice has never been as apt as in the 21st century when, guided by the European Convention on Human Rights, our judges must weigh competing claims to fundamental freedoms.

The Human Rights Act, which adopts the convention into law, has taken the ten years since it was enacted really to enter the consciousness of politicians, journalists and now the public.

Behind the latest banner headlines about the secret adultery of footballers we often cannot identify, lies a legal battle between media freedom of expression and celebrity rights to privacy.

Anonymised (and super-) injunctions are the latest manifestation of a tussle the media fears it is losing in the face of determined efforts by individuals to use the Human Rights Act to stop publication of private information. Courts say the injunctions protect family life; the mass circulation newspapers say they shield the adulterers and others who undermine it. And the penalties can be high: Max Mosley was awarded £60,000; Sienna Miller has just settled with the News of the World for £100,000. For some journalists and politicians, it is the judges who have been weighed in the balance and found wanting.

But the reputation of politicians and journalists is even more tarnished courtesy of the MPs' expenses scandal and the slow-burn criminal and civil actions against phone-hacking which highlighted the questionable use of inquiry agents by a host of national newspapers and led to the closure of the *News of the World*.

The impact of the Human Rights Act has been cumulative. It demands case-by-case balancing of rights which creates uncertainty along the way but also means it takes quite some time for patterns to emerge. Concepts gradually evolve to try to codify the law, such as the way fair comment has morphed into honest opinion as a defamation defence.

Statutes do offer some clarity (although they can be too rigid) but it is fanciful to argue that they bring certainty. Try telling that to a journalist running a "responsible journalism" defence in a libel case. The Defamation Act 1996 did not remove all the grey areas and the next one won't either. A Privacy Act could set down markers for how to strike the balance in this controversial area but would politicians really value freedom of expression more highly than judges?

Several key themes have crystallised in the past few frantic months of media law cases. Children, privacy and the public interest are three we highlight here.

The rights of **children** are gaining weight whether in terms of the expectation of privacy of offspring of the famous or as a justification for keeping their father's affairs secret. European law is at the heart of it and even UN doctrines are cited with the word "paramount" featuring. In an age when all rights are equal, are children's more equal than others?

Attempts to protect children are also central to repeated clashes over the use of s.39 of the Children and Young Persons Act 1933 in criminal cases. Judges can overstep the boundaries leading to trials not being covered or adult paedophiles gaining anonymity sometimes by direct (misapplied) s.39 order.

However worthy the motive, the effect is all too often to protect the identity of an adult who has harmed, or is a threat to, children. Anonymity for the perpetrators of abuse against children is a high price to pay for well-meaning concern. It allows those guilty of awful physical and sexual abuse to hide behind the anonymity of their children. It's bad enough when adulterers do it, but when child rapists escape being identified, it sticks in the craw for many journalists. And how long will it be before childless adults claim to be discriminated against?

When it comes to men behaving badly, the string of injunctions granted mainly to male celebrities offers the high-profile evidence that the right to **privacy** for adults too is gaining ground. Judges are paying little heed to the countervailing claims that publication is in the **public interest** if all that is at stake is a sexual indiscretion. Only targets and topics deemed "worthy" by the courts are benefiting from the full regard for freedom of expression. Eady J. has even contemplated a merging of responsible journalism into any public interest justification. Being able to demonstrate a public interest in the secret material—abuse of office or the like—would not be enough. The investigation involved would also have to meet the demands of responsible journalism.

This tipping of the balance towards individual privacy was already emerging at the time of our first edition; but it coincided with countervailing developments such as *Jameel* which seemed to offer greater protection for responsible journalism against defamation claims. If applying the Human Rights Act meant that serious investigative journalism was safe and only kiss-and-tell would be lost, surely there was not too much for the media to worry about?

Four years later the parallel analysis of human rights-based law is blurring the distinction between the right to privacy and the protection of reputation. Journalists tend to fear the worst; that defamation cases will become as hard to defend as privacy ones rather than vice versa. Considering defamation within the ambit of art.8 is a concern. It also seems reasonable to predict that the hurdles of meeting the "responsible journalism" and/or "public interest" tests will continue to be raised. The Supreme Court, in the case of *Flood* later this year, has an opportunity to establish some general principles regarding the nature of responsible journalism. It is devoutly to be wished in a democratic country that journalists retain some expectation that freedom of expression can be upheld in matters in the public interest pursued and published responsibly.

Certainly the definition of the "public interest" warrants a wider debate. A gulf is opening up between the judges' interpretation and that in the Press Complaints Commission Editors' Code of Practice. Opening this discussion up has to be encouraged to inform our approach to balancing competing rights.

Yet, while the acceptable justifications for mainstream publishing narrow; digital media and micro-blogging in particular appear to be making nonsense of these legal restraints.

As the *Guardian* faced a super-injunction on Trafigura, the banned material was available on Wikileaks; the names of most of the celebrities granted injunctions anonymously have been Tweeted around the globe although not necessarily accurately. How are the courts going to square this circle?

An easing of the demands of the old-style fair comment defence in defamation is one example of moves to accommodate the blogosphere where judges have combined legal principle with a healthy dose of pragmatism.

The Press Complaints Commission is likely to extend its remit to any micro-blogging sites run under the aegis of its member publications to try to make its standards platform neutral.

But even with moves to reduce libel tourism, the anomalies of trying to apply the laws of England and Wales to global digital publication will continue to be evident.

For those of us who cannot evade the law, the Human Rights Act remains central to media judgments. Replacing it with a Bill of Rights, as the Government has contemplated, might provide an extra margin of appreciation but we cannot escape the European Convention of Human Rights even if we wanted to as long as Britain is part of the EU.

The journalists among us need to fly the flag to make sure that whenever rights are weighed in the balance—be it in statute or case law; in the UK or the EU; by statutory or self regulators—the greatest possible appreciation is given to freedom of expression.

Our human rights are fundamental but upholding them is a messy business. The desire to protect any one right of any one individual against the over-weaning power of the State inspired the ECHR. But in practice, many claims have been brought against the media and other bodies. When one journalist's right to freedom of expression limits another individual's right to privacy, reputation, fair trial or anything else, a balance has to be struck. Statute, common law and social custom all play a part in how these "fundamentals" are interpreted. The proper limits on freedom of expression are part of a debate that affects us all but journalists more than most need to join an argument on where the line is drawn.

As we say in the business, this one will run and run.

APPENDIX 1

HUMAN RIGHTS ACT 1998

1998 CHAPTER 42

An Act to give further effect to rights and freedoms guaranteed under the European Convention on Human Rights; to make provision with respect to holders of certain judicial offices who become judges of the European Court of Human Rights; and for connected purposes.

[9th November 1998]

BE IT ENACTED by the Queen's most Excellent Majesty, by and with the advice and consent of the Lords Spiritual and Temporal, and Commons, in this present Parliament assembled, and by the authority of the same, as follows:—

Introduction

1.— The Convention Rights.

1 In this Act "the Convention rights" means the rights and fundamental freedoms set out in—
a Articles 2 to 12 and 14 of the Convention,
b Articles 1 to 3 of the First Protocol, and
c [Article 1 of the Thirteenth Protocol][1],
as read with Articles 16 to 18 of the Convention.
2 Those Articles are to have effect for the purposes of this Act subject to any designated derogation or reservation (as to which see sections 14 and 15).
3 The Articles are set out in Schedule 1.
4 The Secretary of State may by order make such amendments to this Act as he considers appropriate to reflect the effect, in relation to the United Kingdom, of a protocol.
5 In subsection (4) "protocol" means a protocol to the Convention—
a which the United Kingdom has ratified; or
b which the United Kingdom has signed with a view to ratification.
6 No amendment may be made by an order under subsection (4) so as to come into force before the protocol concerned is in force in relation to the United Kingdom.

2.— Interpretation of Convention rights.

1 A court or tribunal determining a question which has arisen in connection with a Convention right must take into account any—
a judgment, decision, declaration or advisory opinion of the European Court of Human Rights,
b opinion of the Commission given in a report adopted under Article 31 of the Convention,
c decision of the Commission in connection with Article 26 or 27(2) of the Convention, or
d decision of the Committee of Ministers taken under Article 46 of the Convention,

[1] words substituted by Human Rights Act 1998 (Amendment) Order 2004/1574 art. 2(1)

whenever made or given, so far as, in the opinion of the court or tribunal, it is relevant to the proceedings in which that question has arisen.

2 Evidence of any judgment, decision, declaration or opinion of which account may have to be taken under this section is to be given in proceedings before any court or tribunal in such manner as may be provided by rules.

In this section "rules" means rules of court or, in the case of proceedings before a tribunal, rules made for the purposes of this section—

a by [the Lord Chancellor or]² the Secretary of State, in relation to any proceedings outside Scotland;

b by the Secretary of State, in relation to proceedings in Scotland; or

c by a Northern Ireland department, in relation to proceedings before a tribunal in Northern Ireland—

   i. which deals with transferred matters; and

   ii. for which no rules made under paragraph (a) are in force.

Legislation

3.— Interpretation of legislation.

1 So far as it is possible to do so, primary legislation and subordinate legislation must be read and given effect in a way which is compatible with the Convention rights.

2 This section—

a applies to primary legislation and subordinate legislation whenever enacted;

b does not affect the validity, continuing operation or enforcement of any incompatible primary legislation; and

c does not affect the validity, continuing operation or enforcement of any incompatible subordinate legislation if (disregarding any possibility of revocation) primary legislation prevents removal of the incompatibility.

4.— Declaration of incompatibility.

1 Subsection (2) applies in any proceedings in which a court determines whether a provision of primary legislation is compatible with a Convention right.

2 If the court is satisfied that the provision is incompatible with a Convention right, it may make a declaration of that incompatibility.

3 Subsection (4) applies in any proceedings in which a court determines whether a provision of subordinate legislation, made in the exercise of a power conferred by primary legislation, is compatible with a Convention right.

4 If the court is satisfied—

a that the provision is incompatible with a Convention right, and

b that (disregarding any possibility of revocation) the primary legislation concerned prevents removal of the incompatibility,

it may make a declaration of that incompatibility.

5 In this section "court" means—

a the House of Lords;

b the Judicial Committee of the Privy Council;

c the Courts-Martial Appeal Court;

d in Scotland, the High Court of Justiciary sitting otherwise than as a trial court or the Court of Session;

e in England and Wales or Northern Ireland, the High Court or the Court of Appeal.

6 A declaration under this section ("a declaration of incompatibility")—

a does not affect the validity, continuing operation or enforcement of the provision in respect of which it is given; and

b is not binding on the parties to the proceedings in which it is made.

---

² words inserted by Transfer of Functions (Lord Chancellor and Secretary of State) Order 2005/3429 Sch. 1 para. 3

5.— Right of Crown to intervene.

1 Where a court is considering whether to make a declaration of incompatibility, the Crown is entitled to notice in accordance with rules of court.

2 In any case to which subsection (1) applies—

a a Minister of the Crown (or a person nominated by him),

b a member of the Scottish Executive,

c a Northern Ireland Minister,

d a Northern Ireland department,

is entitled, on giving notice in accordance with rules of court, to be joined as a party to the proceedings.

3 Notice under subsection (2) may be given at any time during the proceedings.

4 A person who has been made a party to criminal proceedings (other than in Scotland) as the result of a notice under subsection (2) may, with leave, appeal to the House of Lords against any declaration of incompatibility made in the proceedings.

5 In subsection (4)—

"criminal proceedings" includes all proceedings before the Courts-Martial Appeal Court; and

"leave" means leave granted by the court making the declaration of incompatibility or by the House of Lords.

Public authorities

6.— Acts of public authorities.

1 It is unlawful for a public authority to act in a way which is incompatible with a Convention right.

2 Subsection (1) does not apply to an act if—

a as the result of one or more provisions of primary legislation, the authority could not have acted differently; or

b in the case of one or more provisions of, or made under, primary legislation which cannot be read or given effect in a way which is compatible with the Convention rights, the authority was acting so as to give effect to or enforce those provisions.

3 In this section "public authority" includes—

a a court or tribunal, and

b any person certain of whose functions are functions of a public nature,

but does not include either House of Parliament or a person exercising functions in connection with proceedings in Parliament.

4 In subsection (3) "Parliament" does not include the House of Lords in its judicial capacity.

5 In relation to a particular act, a person is not a public authority by virtue only of subsection (3)(b) if the nature of the act is private.

6 "An act" includes a failure to act but does not include a failure to—

a introduce in, or lay before, Parliament a proposal for legislation; or

b make any primary legislation or remedial order.

7.— Proceedings.

1 A person who claims that a public authority has acted (or proposes to act) in a way which is made unlawful by section 6(1) may—

a bring proceedings against the authority under this Act in the appropriate court or tribunal, or

b rely on the Convention right or rights concerned in any legal proceedings,

but only if he is (or would be) a victim of the unlawful act.

2 In subsection (1)(a) "appropriate court or tribunal" means such court or tribunal as may be determined in accordance with rules; and proceedings against an authority include a counterclaim or similar proceedings.

3 If the proceedings are brought on an application for judicial review, the applicant is to be taken to have a sufficient interest in relation to the unlawful act only if he is, or would be, a victim of that act.

4 If the proceedings are made by way of a petition for judicial review in Scotland, the applicant shall be taken to have title and interest to sue in relation to the unlawful act only if he is, or would be, a victim of that act.

5 Proceedings under subsection (1)(a) must be brought before the end of—
a the period of one year beginning with the date on which the act complained of took place; or
b such longer period as the court or tribunal considers equitable having regard to all the circumstances,
but that is subject to any rule imposing a stricter time limit in relation to the procedure in question.

6 In subsection (1)(b) "legal proceedings" includes—
a proceedings brought by or at the instigation of a public authority; and
b an appeal against the decision of a court or tribunal.

7 For the purposes of this section, a person is a victim of an unlawful act only if he would be a victim for the purposes of Article 34 of the Convention if proceedings were brought in the European Court of Human Rights in respect of that act.

8 Nothing in this Act creates a criminal offence.

9 In this section "rules" means—
a in relation to proceedings before a court or tribunal outside Scotland, rules made by the [the Lord Chancellor or]³ Secretary of State for the purposes of this section or rules of court,
b in relation to proceedings before a court or tribunal in Scotland, rules made by the Secretary of State for those purposes,
c in relation to proceedings before a tribunal in Northern Ireland—
  i. which deals with transferred matters; and
  ii. for which no rules made under paragraph (a) are in force,
  rules made by a Northern Ireland department for those purposes,
and includes provision made by order under section 1 of the Courts and Legal Services Act 1990.

10 In making rules, regard must be had to section 9.

11 The Minister who has power to make rules in relation to a particular tribunal may, to the extent he considers it necessary to ensure that the tribunal can provide an appropriate remedy in relation to an act (or proposed act) of a public authority which is (or would be) unlawful as a result of section 6(1), by order add to—
a the relief or remedies which the tribunal may grant; or
b the grounds on which it may grant any of them.

12 An order made under subsection (11) may contain such incidental, supplemental, consequential or transitional provision as the Minister making it considers appropriate.

13 "The Minister" includes the Northern Ireland department concerned.

8.— Judicial remedies.

1 In relation to any act (or proposed act) of a public authority which the court finds is (or would be) unlawful, it may grant such relief or remedy, or make such order, within its powers as it considers just and appropriate.

2 But damages may be awarded only by a court which has power to award damages, or to order the payment of compensation, in civil proceedings.

3 No award of damages is to be made unless, taking account of all the circumstances of the case, including—
a any other relief or remedy granted, or order made, in relation to the act in question (by that or any other court), and

---

³ words inserted by Transfer of Functions (Lord Chancellor and Secretary of State) Order 2005/3429 Sch. 1 para.3

b the consequences of any decision (of that or any other court) in respect of that act, the court is satisfied that the award is necessary to afford just satisfaction to the person in whose favour it is made.

4 In determining—

a whether to award damages, or

b the amount of an award,

the court must take into account the principles applied by the European Court of Human Rights in relation to the award of compensation under Article 41 of the Convention.

5 A public authority against which damages are awarded is to be treated—

a in Scotland, for the purposes of section 3 of the Law Reform (Miscellaneous Provisions) (Scotland) Act 1940 as if the award were made in an action of damages in which the authority has been found liable in respect of loss or damage to the person to whom the award is made;

b for the purposes of the Civil Liability (Contribution) Act 1978 as liable in respect of damage suffered by the person to whom the award is made.

6 In this section—

"court" includes a tribunal;

"damages" means damages for an unlawful act of a public authority; and

"unlawful" means unlawful under section 6(1).

9.— Judicial acts.

1 Proceedings under section 7(1)(a) in respect of a judicial act may be brought only—

a by exercising a right of appeal;

b on an application (in Scotland a petition) for judicial review; or

c in such other forum as may be prescribed by rules.

2 That does not affect any rule of law which prevents a court from being the subject of judicial review.

3 In proceedings under this Act in respect of a judicial act done in good faith, damages may not be awarded otherwise than to compensate a person to the extent required by Article 5(5) of the Convention.

4 An award of damages permitted by subsection (3) is to be made against the Crown; but no award may be made unless the appropriate person, if not a party to the proceedings, is joined.

5 In this section—

"appropriate person" means the Minister responsible for the court concerned, or a person or government department nominated by him;

"court" includes a tribunal;

"judge" includes a member of a tribunal, a justice of the peace and a clerk or other officer entitled to exercise the jurisdiction of a court;

"judicial act" means a judicial act of a court and includes an act done on the instructions, or on behalf, of a judge; and

"rules" has the same meaning as in section 7(9).

Remedial action

10.— Power to take remedial action.

1 This section applies if—

a a provision of legislation has been declared under section 4 to be incompatible with a Convention right and, if an appeal lies—

i. all persons who may appeal have stated in writing that they do not intend to do so;

ii. the time for bringing an appeal has expired and no appeal has been brought within that time; or

iii. an appeal brought within that time has been determined or abandoned; or

b it appears to a Minister of the Crown or Her Majesty in Council that, having regard to a finding of the European Court of Human Rights made after the coming into force of this section in proceedings against the United Kingdom, a provision of legislation is incompatible with an obligation of the United Kingdom arising from the Convention.

2 If a Minister of the Crown considers that there are compelling reasons for proceeding under this section, he may by order make such amendments to the legislation as he considers necessary to remove the incompatibility.

3 If, in the case of subordinate legislation, a Minister of the Crown considers—
a that it is necessary to amend the primary legislation under which the subordinate legislation in question was made, in order to enable the incompatibility to be removed, and
b that there are compelling reasons for proceeding under this section,
he may by order make such amendments to the primary legislation as he considers necessary.

4 This section also applies where the provision in question is in subordinate legislation and has been quashed, or declared invalid, by reason of incompatibility with a Convention right and the Minister proposes to proceed under paragraph 2(b) of Schedule 2.

5 If the legislation is an Order in Council, the power conferred by subsection (2) or (3) is exercisable by Her Majesty in Council.

6 In this section "legislation" does not include a Measure of the Church Assembly or of the General Synod of the Church of England.

7 Schedule 2 makes further provision about remedial orders.

Other rights and proceedings

11. Safeguard for existing human rights.
A person's reliance on a Convention right does not restrict—
a any other right or freedom conferred on him by or under any law having effect in any part of the United Kingdom; or
b his right to make any claim or bring any proceedings which he could make or bring apart from sections 7 to 9.

12.— Freedom of expression.

1 This section applies if a court is considering whether to grant any relief which, if granted, might affect the exercise of the Convention right to freedom of expression.

2 If the person against whom the application for relief is made ("the respondent") is neither present nor represented, no such relief is to be granted unless the court is satisfied—
a that the applicant has taken all practicable steps to notify the respondent; or
b that there are compelling reasons why the respondent should not be notified.

3 No such relief is to be granted so as to restrain publication before trial unless the court is satisfied that the applicant is likely to establish that publication should not be allowed.

4 The court must have particular regard to the importance of the Convention right to freedom of expression and, where the proceedings relate to material which the respondent claims, or which appears to the court, to be journalistic, literary or artistic material (or to conduct connected with such material), to—
a the extent to which—
  i. the material has, or is about to, become available to the public; or
  ii. it is, or would be, in the public interest for the material to be published;
b any relevant privacy code.

5 In this section—
"court" includes a tribunal; and
"relief" includes any remedy or order (other than in criminal proceedings).

13.— Freedom of thought, conscience and religion.

1 If a court's determination of any question arising under this Act might affect the exercise by a religious organisation (itself or its members collectively) of the Convention right to freedom of thought, conscience and religion, it must have particular regard to the importance of that right.

2 In this section "court" includes a tribunal.

Derogations and reservations

14.— Derogations.

1 In this Act "designated derogation" means any derogation by the United Kingdom from an Article of the Convention, or of any protocol to the Convention, which is designated for the purposes of this Act in an order made by the [Secretary of State][4].

2 If a designated derogation is amended or replaced it ceases to be a designated derogation.

3 But subsection (3) does not prevent the [Secretary of State][5] from exercising his power under subsection (1) to make a fresh designation order in respect of the Article concerned.

4 The [Secretary of State][6] must by order make such amendments to Schedule 3 as he considers appropriate to reflect—
a any designation order; or
b the effect of subsection (3).

5 A designation order may be made in anticipation of the making by the United Kingdom of a proposed derogation.

15.— Reservations.

1 In this Act "designated reservation" means—
a the United Kingdom's reservation to Article 2 of the First Protocol to the Convention; and
b any other reservation by the United Kingdom to an Article of the Convention, or of any protocol to the Convention, which is designated for the purposes of this Act in an order made by the [Secretary of State][7].

2 The text of the reservation referred to in subsection (1)(a) is set out in Part II of Schedule 3.

3 If a designated reservation is withdrawn wholly or in part it ceases to be a designated reservation.

4 But subsection (3) does not prevent the [Secretary of State][8] from exercising his power under subsection (1)(b) to make a fresh designation order in respect of the Article concerned.

5 The [Secretary of State][9] must by order make such amendments to this Act as he considers appropriate to reflect—
a any designation order; or
b the effect of subsection (3).

---

[4] words substituted by Secretary of State for Constitutional Affairs Order 2003/1887 Sch. 2 para. 10(1)

[5] words substituted by Secretary of State for Constitutional Affairs Order 2003/1887 Sch. 2 para. 10(1)

[6] words substituted by Secretary of State for Constitutional Affairs Order 2003/1887 Sch. 2 para. 10(1)

[7] words substituted by Secretary of State for Constitutional Affairs Order 2003/1887 Sch. 2 para. 10(1)

[8] words substituted by Secretary of State for Constitutional Affairs Order 2003/1887 Sch. 2 para. 10(1)

[9] words substituted by Secretary of State for Constitutional Affairs Order 2003/1887 Sch. 2 para. 10(1)

16.— Period for which designated derogations have effect.

1 If it has not already been withdrawn by the United Kingdom, a designated derogation ceases to have effect for the purposes of this Act, at the end of the period of five
years beginning with the date on which the order designating it was made.

2 At any time before the period—
a fixed by subsection (1), or
b extended by an order under this subsection,
comes to an end, the [Secretary of State][10] may by order extend it by a further
period of five years.

3 An order under section 14(1) ceases to have effect at the end of the period for consideration, unless a resolution has been passed by each House approving the order.

4 Subsection (3) does not affect—
a anything done in reliance on the order; or
b the power to make a fresh order under section 14(1).

5 In subsection (3) "period for consideration" means the period of forty days beginning with the day on which the order was made.

6 In calculating the period for consideration, no account is to be taken of any time
during which—
a Parliament is dissolved or prorogued; or
b both Houses are adjourned for more than four days.

7 If a designated derogation is withdrawn by the United Kingdom, the [Secretary
of State][11] must by order make such amendments to this Act as he considers are
required to reflect that withdrawal.

17.— Periodic review of designated reservations.

1 The appropriate Minister must review the designated reservation referred to in
section 15(1)(a)—
a before the end of the period of five years beginning with the date on which
section 1(2) came into force; and
b if that designation is still in force, before the end of the period of five years beginning with the date on which the last report relating to it was laid under subsection
(3).

2 The appropriate Minister must review each of the other designated reservations (if
any)—
a before the end of the period of five years beginning with the date on which the
order designating the reservation first came into force; and
b if the designation is still in force, before the end of the period of five years beginning with the date on which the last report relating to it was laid under subsection
(3).

3 The Minister conducting a review under this section must prepare a report on the
result of the review and lay a copy of it before each House of Parliament.

Judges of the European Court of Human Rights

18.— Appointment to European Court of Human Rights.

1 In this section "judicial office" means the office of—
a Lord Justice of Appeal, Justice of the High Court or Circuit judge, in England
and Wales;

[10] words substituted by Secretary of State for Constitutional Affairs Order 2003/1887
Sch. 2 para. 10(1)
[11] words substituted by Secretary of State for Constitutional Affairs Order 2003/1887
Sch. 2 para. 10(1)

b judge of the Court of Session or sheriff, in Scotland;

c Lord Justice of Appeal, judge of the High Court or county court judge, in Northern Ireland.

2 The holder of a judicial office may become a judge of the European Court of Human Rights ("the Court") without being required to relinquish his office.

3 But he is not required to perform the duties of his judicial office while he is a judge of the Court.

4 In respect of any period during which he is a judge of the Court—

a a Lord Justice of Appeal or Justice of the High Court is not to count as a judge of the relevant court for the purposes of section 2(1) or 4(1) of the Supreme Court Act 1981 (maximum number of judges) nor as a judge of the Supreme Court for the purposes of section 12(1) to (6) of that Act (salaries etc.);

b a judge of the Court of Session is not to count as a judge of that court for the purposes of section 1(1) of the Court of Session Act 1988 (maximum number of judges) or of section 9(1)(c) of the Administration of Justice Act 1973 ("the 1973 Act") (salaries etc.);

c a Lord Justice of Appeal or judge of the High Court in Northern Ireland is not to count as a judge of the relevant court for the purposes of section 2(1) or 3(1) of the Judicature (Northern Ireland) Act 1978 (maximum number of judges) nor as a judge of the Supreme Court of Northern Ireland for the purposes of section 9(1)(d) of the 1973 Act (salaries etc.);

d a Circuit judge is not to count as such for the purposes of section 18 of the Courts Act 1971 (salaries etc.);

e a sheriff is not to count as such for the purposes of section 14 of the Sheriff Courts (Scotland) Act 1907 (salaries etc.);

f a county court judge of Northern Ireland is not to count as such for the purposes of section 106 of the County Courts Act (Northern Ireland) 1959 (salaries etc.).

5 If a sheriff principal is appointed a judge of the Court, section 11(1) of the Sheriff Courts (Scotland) Act 1971 (temporary appointment of sheriff principal) applies, while he holds that appointment, as if his office is vacant.

6 Schedule 4 makes provision about judicial pensions in relation to the holder of a judicial office who serves as a judge of the Court.

7 The Lord Chancellor or the Secretary of State may by order make such transitional provision (including, in particular, provision for a temporary increase in the maximum number of judges) as he considers appropriate in relation to any holder of a judicial office who has completed his service as a judge of the Court.

7A The following paragraphs apply to the making of an order under subsection (7) in relation to any holder of a judicial office listed in subsection (1)(a)–

a before deciding what transitional provision it is appropriate to make, the person making the order must consult the Lord Chief Justice of England and Wales;

b before making the order, that person must consult the Lord Chief Justice of England and Wales..

7B The following paragraphs apply to the making of an order under subsection (7) in relation to any holder of a judicial office listed in subsection (1)(c)—

a before deciding what transitional provision it is appropriate to make, the person making the order must consult the Lord Chief Justice of Northern Ireland;

a before making the order, that person must consult the Lord Chief Justice of Northern Ireland.

7C The Lord Chief Justice of England and Wales may nominate a judicial office holder (within the meaning of section 109(4) of the Constitutional Reform Act 2005) to exercise his functions under this section.

7D The Lord Chief Justice of Northern Ireland may nominate any of the following to exercise his functions under this section—

a the holder of one of the offices listed in Schedule 1 to the Justice (Northern Ireland) Act 2002;

b a Lord Justice of Appeal (as defined in section 88 of that Act).

]^{12}

Parliamentary procedure

19.— **Statements of compatibility.**

1 A Minister of the Crown in charge of a Bill in either House of Parliament must, before Second Reading of the Bill—
a make a statement to the effect that in his view the provisions of the Bill are compatible with the Convention rights ("a statement of compatibility"); or
b make a statement to the effect that although he is unable to make a statement of compatibility the government nevertheless wishes the House to proceed with the Bill.

2 The statement must be in writing and be published in such manner as the Minister making it considers appropriate.

Supplemental

20.— **Orders etc. under this Act.**

1 Any power of a Minister of the Crown to make an order under this Act is exercisable by statutory instrument.

2 The power of the Lord Chancellor or the Secretary of State to make rules (other than rules of court) under section 2(3) or 7(9) is exercisable by statutory instrument.

3 Any statutory instrument made under section 14, 15 or 16(7) must be laid before Parliament.

4 No order may be made by [the Lord Chancellor or]^{13} the Secretary of State under section 1(4), 7(11) or 16(2) unless a draft of the order has been laid before, and approved by, each House of Parliament.

5 Any statutory instrument made under section 18(7) or Schedule 4, or to which subsection (2) applies, shall be subject to annulment in pursuance of a resolution of either House of Parliament.

6 The power of a Northern Ireland department to make—
a rules under section 2(3)(c) or 7(9)(c), or
b an order under section 7(11),
is exercisable by statutory rule for the purposes of the Statutory Rules (Northern Ireland) Order 1979.

7 Any rules made under section 2(3)(c) or 7(9)(c) shall be subject to negative resolution; and section 41(6) of the Interpretation Act (Northern Ireland) 1954 (meaning of "subject to negative resolution") shall apply as if the power to make the rules were conferred by an Act of the Northern Ireland Assembly.

8 No order may be made by a Northern Ireland department under section 7(11) unless a draft of the order has been laid before, and approved by, the Northern Ireland Assembly.

21.— **Interpretation, etc.**

1 In this Act—
"amend" includes repeal and apply (with or without modifications);
"the appropriate Minister" means the Minister of the Crown having charge of the appropriate authorised government department (within the meaning of the Crown Proceedings Act 1947);
"the Commission" means the European Commission of Human Rights;
"the Convention" means the Convention for the Protection of Human Rights

---

^{12} added by Constitutional Reform Act 2005 c. 4 Sch. 4(1) para. 278
^{13} words inserted by Transfer of Functions (Lord Chancellor and Secretary of State) Order 2005/3429 Sch. 1 para. 3

and Fundamental Freedoms, agreed by the Council of Europe at Rome on 4th November 1950 as it has effect for the time being in relation to the United Kingdom;
"declaration of incompatibility" means a declaration under section 4;
"Minister of the Crown" has the same meaning as in the Ministers of the Crown Act 1975;
"Northern Ireland Minister" includes the First Minister and the deputy First Minister in Northern Ireland;
"primary legislation" means any—
a public general Act;
b local and personal Act;
c private Act;
d Measure of the Church Assembly;
e Measure of the General Synod of the Church of England;
f Order in Council—
    i. made in exercise of Her Majesty's Royal Prerogative;
    ii. made under section 38(1)(a) of the Northern Ireland Constitution Act 1973 or the corresponding provision of the Northern Ireland Act 1998; or
    iii. amending an Act of a kind mentioned in paragraph (a), (b) or (c);
and includes an order or other instrument made under primary legislation (otherwise than by the Welsh Ministers, the First Minister for Wales, the Counsel General to the Welsh Assembly Government, a member of the Scottish Executive, a Northern Ireland Minister or a Northern Ireland department) to the extent to which it operates to bring one or more provisions of that legislation into force or amends any primary legislation;
"the First Protocol" means the protocol to the Convention agreed at Paris on 20th March 1952;
"the Eleventh Protocol" means the protocol to the Convention (restructuring the control machinery established by the Convention) agreed at Strasbourg on 11th May 1994;
"the Thirteenth Protocol" means the protocol to the Convention (concerning the abolition of the death penalty in all circumstances) agreed at Vilnius on 3rd May 2002;
"remedial order" means an order under section 10;
"subordinate legislation" means any—
a Order in Council other than one—
    i. made in exercise of Her Majesty's Royal Prerogative;
    ii. made under section 38(1)(a) of the Northern Ireland Constitution Act 1973 or the corresponding provision of the Northern Ireland Act 1998; or
    iii. amending an Act of a kind mentioned in the definition of primary legislation;
b Act of the Scottish Parliament;
(ba) Measure of the National Assembly for Wales; (bb) Act of the National Assembly for Wales;
c Act of the Parliament of Northern Ireland;
d Measure of the Assembly established under section 1 of the Northern Ireland Assembly Act 1973;
e Act of the Northern Ireland Assembly;
f order, rules, regulations, scheme, warrant, byelaw or other instrument made under primary legislation (except to the extent to which it operates to bring one or more provisions of that legislation into force or amends any primary legislation);
g order, rules, regulations, scheme, warrant, byelaw or other instrument made under legislation mentioned in paragraph (b), (c), (d) or (e) or made under an Order in Council applying only to Northern Ireland;
h order, rules, regulations, scheme, warrant, byelaw or other instrument made by a member of the Scottish Executive,[Welsh Ministers, the First Minister for Wales, the Counsel General to the Welsh Assembly Government,][14] a Northern Ireland Minister or a Northern Ireland department in exercise of prerogative or

---

[14] words inserted by Government of Wales Act 2006 c. 32 Sch. 10 para. 56(4)

other executive functions of Her Majesty which are exercisable by such a person on behalf of Her Majesty;

"transferred matters" has the same meaning as in the Northern Ireland Act 1998; and

"tribunal" means any tribunal in which legal proceedings may be brought.

2 The references in paragraphs (b) and (c) of section 2(1) to Articles are to Articles of the Convention as they had effect immediately before the coming into force of the Eleventh Protocol.

3 The reference in paragraph (d) of section 2(1) to Article 46 includes a reference to Articles 32 and 54 of the Convention as they had effect immediately before the coming into force of the Eleventh Protocol.

4 The references in section 2(1) to a report or decision of the Commission or a decision of the Committee of Ministers include references to a report or decision made as provided by paragraphs 3, 4 and 6 of Article 5 of the Eleventh Protocol (transitional provisions).

5 Any liability under the Army Act 1955, the Air Force Act 1955 or the Naval Discipline Act 1957 to suffer death for an offence is replaced by a liability to imprisonment for life or any less punishment authorised by those Acts; and those Acts shall accordingly have effect with the necessary modifications.

22.— **Short title, commencement, application and extent.**

1 This Act may be cited as the Human Rights Act 1998.

2 Sections 18, 20 and 21(5) and this section come into force on the passing of this Act.

3 The other provisions of this Act come into force on such days as the Secretary of State may by order appoint; and different days may be appointed for different purposes.

4 Paragraph (b) of subsection (1) of section 7 applies to proceedings brought by or at the instigation of a public authority whenever the act in question took place; but otherwise that subsection does not apply to an act taking place before the coming into force of that section.

5 This Act binds the Crown.

6 This Act extends to Northern Ireland.

7 Section 21(5), so far as it relates to any provision contained in the Army Act 1955, the Air Force Act 1955 or the Naval Discipline Act 1957, extends to any place to which that provision extends.

SCHEDULE 1

THE ARTICLES

Section 1(3)

PART I

THE CONVENTION

RIGHTS AND FREEDOMS

Right to life

Article 2

1. Everyone's right to life shall be protected by law. No one shall be deprived of his life intentionally save in the execution of a sentence of a court following his conviction of a crime for which this penalty is provided by law.
2. Deprivation of life shall not be regarded as inflicted in contravention of this Article when it results from the use of force which is no more than absolutely necessary:
a in defence of any person from unlawful violence;
b in order to effect a lawful arrest or to prevent the escape of a person lawfully detained;
c in action lawfully taken for the purpose of quelling a riot or insurrection.

Prohibition of torture

Article 3
No one shall be subjected to torture or to inhuman or degrading treatment or punishment.

Prohibition of slavery and forced labour

Article 4

1. No one shall be held in slavery or servitude.
2. No one shall be required to perform forced or compulsory labour.
3. For the purpose of this Article the term "forced or compulsory labour" shall not include:
a any work required to be done in the ordinary course of detention imposed according to the provisions of Article 5 of this Convention or during conditional release from such detention;
b any service of a military character or, in case of conscientious objectors in countries where they are recognised, service exacted instead of compulsory military service;
c any service exacted in case of an emergency or calamity threatening the life or well-being of the community;
d any work or service which forms part of normal civic obligations.

Right to liberty and security

Article 5

1. Everyone has the right to liberty and security of a person. No one shall be deprived of his liberty save in the following cases and in accordance with a procedure prescribed by law:

a the lawful detention of a person after conviction by a competent court;

b the lawful arrest or detention of a person for non-compliance with the lawful order of a court or in order to secure the fulfilment of any obligation prescribed by law;

c the lawful arrest or detention of a person effected for the purpose of bringing him before the competent legal authority on reasonable suspicion of having committed an offence or when it is reasonably considered necessary to prevent his committing an offence or fleeing after having done so;

d the detention of a minor by lawful order for the purpose of educational supervision or his lawful detention for the purpose of bringing him before the competent legal authority;

e the lawful detention of persons for the prevention of the spreading of infectious diseases, of persons of unsound mind, alcoholics or drug addicts or vagrants;

f the lawful arrest or detention of a person to prevent his effecting an unauthorised entry into the country or of a person against whom action is being taken with a view to deportation or extradition.

2 Everyone who is arrested shall be informed promptly, in a language which he understands, of the reasons for his arrest and of any charge against him.

3 Everyone arrested or detained in accordance with the provisions of paragraph 1(c) of this Article shall be brought promptly before a judge or other officer authorised by law to exercise judicial power and shall be entitled to trial within a reasonable time or to release pending trial. Release may be conditioned by guarantees to appear for trial.

4 Everyone who is deprived of his liberty by arrest or detention shall be entitled to take proceedings by which the lawfulness of his detention shall be decided speedily by a court and his release ordered if the detention is not lawful.

5 Everyone who has been the victim of arrest or detention in contravention of the provisions of this Article shall have an enforceable right to compensation.

Right to a fair trial

Article 6

1 In the determination of his civil rights and obligations or of any criminal charge against him, everyone is entitled to a fair and public hearing within a reasonable time by an independent and impartial tribunal established by law. Judgment shall be pronounced publicly but the press and public may be excluded from all or part of the trial in the interest of morals, public order or national security in a democratic society, where the interests of juveniles or the protection of the private life of the parties so require, or to the extent strictly necessary in the opinion of the court in special circumstances where publicity would prejudice the interests of justice.

2 Everyone charged with a criminal offence shall be presumed innocent until proved guilty according to law.

3 Everyone charged with a criminal offence has the following minimum rights:

a to be informed promptly, in a language which he understands and in detail, of the nature and cause of the accusation against him;

b to have adequate time and facilities for the preparation of his defence;

c to defend himself in person or through legal assistance of his own choosing or, if he has not sufficient means to pay for legal assistance, to be given it free when the interests of justice so require;

d to examine or have examined witnesses against him and to obtain the attendance and examination of witnesses on his behalf under the same conditions as witnesses against him;

e to have the free assistance of an interpreter if he cannot understand or speak the language used in court.

No punishment without law

Article 7

1 No one shall be held guilty of any criminal offence on account of any act or omission which did not constitute a criminal offence under national or international law at the time when it was committed. Nor shall a heavier penalty be imposed than the one that was applicable at the time the criminal offence was committed.

2 This Article shall not prejudice the trial and punishment of any person for any act or omission which, at the time when it was committed, was criminal according to the general principles of law recognised by civilised nations.

Right to respect for private and family life

Article 8

1 Everyone has the right to respect for his private and family life, his home and his correspondence.

2 There shall be no interference by a public authority with the exercise of this right except such as is in accordance with the law and is necessary in a democratic society in the interests of national security, public safety or the economic well-being of the country, for the prevention of disorder or crime, for the protection of health or morals, or for the protection of the rights and freedoms of others.

Freedom of thought, conscience and religion

Article 9

1 Everyone has the right to freedom of thought, conscience and religion, this right includes freedom to change his religion or belief and freedom, either alone or in community with others and in public or private, to manifest his religion or belief, in worship, teaching, practice and observance.

2 Freedom to manifest one's religion or beliefs shall be subject only to such limitation as are prescribed by law and are necessary in a democratic society in the interests of public safety, for the protection of public order, health or morals, or for the protection of the rights and freedoms of others.

Freedom of expression

Article 10

1 Everyone has the right to freedom of expression. This right shall include freedom to hold opinions and to receive and impart information and ideas without interference by public authority and regardless of frontiers. This Article shall not prevent States from requiring the licensing of broadcasting, television or cinema enterprises.

2 The exercise of these freedoms, since it carries with it duties and responsibilities, may be subject to such formalities, conditions, restrictions or penalties as are prescribed by law and are necessary in a democratic society, in the interests of national security, territorial integrity or public safety, for the prevention of disorder or crime, for the protection of health or morals, for the protection of the reputation or rights of others, for preventing the disclosure of information received in confidence, or for maintaining the authority and impartiality of the judiciary.

Freedom of assembly and association

Article 11

1 Everyone has the right to freedom of peaceful assembly and to freedom of association with others, including the right to form and to join trade unions for the protection of his interests.

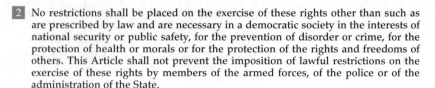 No restrictions shall be placed on the exercise of these rights other than such as are prescribed by law and are necessary in a democratic society in the interests of national security or public safety, for the prevention of disorder or crime, for the protection of health or morals or for the protection of the rights and freedoms of others. This Article shall not prevent the imposition of lawful restrictions on the exercise of these rights by members of the armed forces, of the police or of the administration of the State.

Right to marry

Article 12
Men and women of marriageable age have the right to marry and to found a family, according to the national laws governing the exercise of this right.

Prohibition of discrimination

Article 14
The enjoyment of the rights and freedoms set forth in this Convention shall be secured without discrimination on any ground such as sex, race, colour, language, religion, political or other opinion, national or social origin, association with a national minority, property, birth or other status.

Restrictions on political activity of aliens

Article 16
Nothing in Articles 10, 11 and 14 shall be regarded as preventing the High Contracting Parties from imposing restrictions on the political activity of aliens.

Prohibition of abuse of rights

Article 17
Nothing in this Convention may be interpreted as implying for any State, group or person any right to engage in any activity or perform any act aimed at the destruction of any of the rights and freedoms set forth herein or at their limitation to a greater extent than is provided for in the Convention.

Limitation on use of restrictions on rights

Article 18
The restrictions permitted under this Convention to the said rights and freedoms shall not be applied for any purpose other than those for which they have been prescribed.

PART II

THE FIRST PROTOCOL

Protection of property

Article 1
Every natural or legal person is entitled to the peaceful enjoyment of his possessions. No one shall be deprived of his possessions except in the public interest and subject to the conditions provided for by law and by the general principles of international law.

The preceding provisions shall not, however, in any way impair the right of a State to enforce such laws as it deems necessary to control the use of property in accordance with the general interest or to secure the payment of taxes or other contributions or penalties.

Right to education

Article 2
No person shall be denied the right to education. In the exercise of any functions which it assumes in relation to education and to teaching, the State shall respect the right of parents to ensure such education and teaching in conformity with their own religious and philosophical convictions.

Right to free elections

Article 3
The High Contracting Parties undertake to hold free elections at reasonable intervals by secret ballot, under conditions which will ensure the free expression of the opinion of the people in the choice of the legislature.

PART III

[Abolition of the death penalty
The death penalty shall be abolished. No one shall be condemned to such penalty or executed.][15,16]

---

[15] substituted by Human Rights Act 1998 (Amendment) Order 2004/1574 art. 2(3)

DEFAMATION ACT 1996
1996 Chapter 31

An Act to amend the law of defamation and to amend the law of limitation with respect to actions for defamation or malicious falsehood. (4 July 1996)[1]

Responsibility for publication

1.— Responsibility for publication.

1 In defamation proceedings a person has a defence if he shows that—
a he was not the author, editor or publisher of the statement complained of,
b he took reasonable care in relation to its publication, and
c he did not know, and had no reason to believe, that what he did caused or contributed to the publication of a defamatory statement.

2 For this purpose "author", "editor" and "publisher" have the following meanings, which are further explained in subsection (3)—
"author" means the originator of the statement, but does not include a person who did not intend that his statement be published at all;
"editor" means a person having editorial or equivalent responsibility for the content of the statement or the decision to publish it; and
"publisher" means a commercial publisher, that is, a person whose business is issuing material to the public, or a section of the public, who issues material containing the statement in the course of that business.

3 A person shall not be considered the author, editor or publisher of a statement if he is only involved—
a in printing, producing, distributing or selling printed material containing the statement;
b in processing, making copies of, distributing, exhibiting or selling a film or sound recording (as defined in Part I of the Copyright, Designs and Patents Act 1988) containing the statement;
c in processing, making copies of, distributing or selling any electronic medium in or on which the statement is recorded, or in operating or providing any equipment, system or service by means of which the statement is retrieved, copied, distributed or made available in electronic form;
d as the broadcaster of a live programme containing the statement in circumstances in which he has no effective control over the maker of the statement;
e as the operator of or provider of access to a communications system by means of which the statement is transmitted, or made available, by a person over whom he has no effective control.

In a case not within paragraphs (a) to (e) the court may have regard to those provisions by way of analogy in deciding whether a person is to be considered the author, editor or publisher of a statement.

[1] An Act to amend the law of defamation and to amend the law of limitation with respect to actions for defamation or malicious falsehood. (4 July 1996)

4 Employees or agents of an author, editor or publisher are in the same position as their employer or principal to the extent that they are responsible for the content of the statement or the decision to publish it.

5 In determining for the purposes of this section whether a person took reasonable care, or had reason to believe that what he did caused or contributed to the publication of a defamatory statement, regard shall be had to—
a the extent of his responsibility for the content of the statement or the decision to publish it,
b the nature or circumstances of the publication, and
c the previous conduct or character of the author, editor or publisher.

6 This section does not apply to any cause of action which arose before the section came into force.

Offer to make amends

2.— Offer to make amends.

1 A person who has published a statement alleged to be defamatory of another may offer to make amends under this section.

2 The offer may be in relation to the statement generally or in relation to a specific defamatory meaning which the person making the offer accepts that the statement conveys ("a qualified offer").

3 An offer to make amends—
a must be in writing,
b must be expressed to be an offer to make amends under section 2 of the Defamation Act 1996, and
c must state whether it is a qualified offer and, if so, set out the defamatory meaning in relation to which it is made.

4 An offer to make amends under this section is an offer—
a to make a suitable correction of the statement complained of and a sufficient apology to the aggrieved party,
b to publish the correction and apology in a manner that is reasonable and practicable in the circumstances, and
c to pay to the aggrieved party such compensation (if any), and such costs, as may be agreed or determined to be payable.
The fact that the offer is accompanied by an offer to take specific steps does not affect the fact that an offer to make amends under this section is an offer to do all the things mentioned in paragraphs (a) to (c).

5 An offer to make amends under this section may not be made by a person after serving a defence in defamation proceedings brought against him by the aggrieved party in respect of the publication in question.

6 An offer to make amends under this section may be withdrawn before it is accepted; and a renewal of an offer which has been withdrawn shall be treated as a new offer.

3.— Accepting an offer to make amends.

1 If an offer to make amends under section 2 is accepted by the aggrieved party, the following provisions apply.

2 The party accepting the offer may not bring or continue defamation proceedings in respect of the publication concerned against the person making the offer, but he is entitled to enforce the offer to make amends, as follows.

3 If the parties agree on the steps to be taken in fulfilment of the offer, the aggrieved party may apply to the court for an order that the other party fulfil his offer by taking the steps agreed.

4 If the parties do not agree on the steps to be taken by way of correction, apology and publication, the party who made the offer may take such steps as he thinks appropriate, and may in particular—

a make the correction and apology by a statement in open court in terms approved by the court, and

b give an undertaking to the court as to the manner of their publication.

5 If the parties do not agree on the amount to be paid by way of compensation, it shall be determined by the court on the same principles as damages in defamation proceedings. The court shall take account of any steps taken in fulfilment of the offer and (so far as not agreed between the parties) of the suitability of the correction, the sufficiency of the apology and whether the manner of their publication was reasonable in the circumstances, and may reduce or increase the amount of compensation accordingly.

6 If the parties do not agree on the amount to be paid by way of costs, it shall be determined by the court on the same principles as costs awarded in court proceedings.

7 The acceptance of an offer by one person to make amends does not affect any cause of action against another person in respect of the same publication, subject as follows.

8 In England and Wales or Northern Ireland, for the purposes of the Civil Liability (Contribution) Act 1978—

a the amount of compensation paid under the offer shall be treated as paid in bona fide settlement or compromise of the claim; and

b where another person is liable in respect of the same damage (whether jointly or otherwise), the person whose offer to make amends was accepted is not required to pay by virtue of any contribution under section 1 of that Act a greater amount than the amount of the compensation payable in pursuance of the offer.

9 In Scotland—

a subsection (2) of section 3 of the Law Reform (Miscellaneous Provisions) (Scotland) Act 1940 (right of one joint wrongdoer as respects another to recover contribution towards damages) applies in relation to compensation paid under an offer to make amends as it applies in relation to damages in an action to which that section applies; and

b where another person is liable in respect of the same damage (whether jointly or otherwise), the person whose offer to make amends was accepted is not required to pay by virtue of any contribution under section 3(2) of that Act a greater amount than the amount of compensation payable in pursuance of the offer.

10 Proceedings under this section shall be heard and determined without a jury.

4.— Failure to accept offer to make amends.

1 If an offer to make amends under section 2, duly made and not withdrawn, is not accepted by the aggrieved party, the following provisions apply.

2 The fact that the offer was made is a defence (subject to subsection (3)) to defamation proceedings in respect of the publication in question by that party against the person making the offer. A qualified offer is only a defence in respect of the meaning to which the offer related.

3 There is no such defence if the person by whom the offer was made knew or had reason to believe that the statement complained of—

a referred to the aggrieved party or was likely to be understood as referring to him, and

b was both false and defamatory of that party. but it shall be presumed until the contrary is shown that he did not know and had no reason to believe that was the case.

4 The person who made the offer need not rely on it by way of defence, but if he does he may not rely on any other defence. If the offer was a qualified offer, this applies only in respect of the meaning to which the offer related.

5 The offer may be relied on in mitigation of damages whether or not it was relied on as a defence.

Limitation

5.— Limitation of actions: England and Wales.

1 The Limitation Act 1980 is amended as follows.

2 For section 4A (time limit for action for libel or slander) substitute—

"4A. Time limit for actions for defamation or malicious falsehood.
The time limit under section 2 of this Act shall not apply to an action for—
a libel or slander, or
b slander of title, slander of goods or other malicious falsehood. but no such action shall be brought after the expiration of one year from the date on which the cause of action accrued. ".

3 In section 28 (extension of limitation period in case of disability), for subsection (4A) substitute—

"(4A) If the action is one to which section 4A of this Act applies, subsection (1) above shall have effect—
a in the case of an action for libel or slander, as if for the words from 'at any time' to 'occurred)' there were substituted the words 'by him at any time before the expiration of one year from the date on which he ceased to be under a disability'; and
b in the case of an action for slander of title, slander of goods or other malicious falsehood, as if for the words 'six years' there were substituted the words 'one year'.".

4 For section 32A substitute—
"Discretionary exclusion of time limit for actions for defamation or malicious falsehood

32A.— Discretionary exclusion of time limit for actions for defamation or malicious falsehood.

1 If it appears to the court that it would be equitable to allow an action to proceed having regard to the degree to which—
a the operation of section 4A of this Act prejudices the plaintiff or any person whom he represents, and
b any decision of the court under this subsection would prejudice the defendant or any person whom he represents,
the court may direct that that section shall not apply to the action or shall not apply to any specified cause of, action to which the action relates.

2 In acting under this section the court shall have regard to all the circumstances of the case and in particular to—
a the length of, and the reasons for, the delay on the part of the plaintiff;
b where the reason or one of the reasons for the delay was that all or any of the facts relevant to the cause of action did not become known to the plaintiff until after the end of the period mentioned in section 4A—
i. the date on which any such facts did become known to him, and
ii. the extent to which he acted promptly and reasonably once he knew whether or not the facts in question might be capable of giving rise to an action; and
c the extent to which, having regard to the delay, relevant evidence is likely—
i. to be unavailable, or
ii. to be less cogent than if the action had been brought within the period mentioned in section 4A.

3 In the case of an action for slander of title, slander of goods, or other malicious falsehood brought by a personal representative—
a the references in subsection (2) above to the plaintiff shall be construed as including the deceased person to whom the cause of action accrued and any previous personal representative of that person; and
b nothing in section 28(3) of this Act shall be construed as affecting the court's discretion under this section.

4 In this section"the court" means the court in which the action has been brought.".
5 In section 36(1) (expiry of time limit no bar to equitable relief), for paragraph (aa) substitute—

"(aa) the time limit under section 4A for actions for libel or slander, or for slander of title, slander of goods or other malicious falsehood;".

6 The amendments made by this section apply only to causes of action arising after the section comes into force.

6.— Limitation of actions: Northern Ireland.

1 The Limitation (Northern Ireland) Order 1989 is amended as follows.
2 In Article 6 (time limit: certain actions founded on tort) forparagraph (2) substitute—

"(2) Subject to Article 51, an action for damages for—
a libel or slander, or
b slander of title, slander of goods or other malicious falsehood,
may not be brought after the expiration of one year from the date on which the cause of action accrued.".

3 In Article 48 (extension of time limit), for paragraph (7) substitute—

"7. Where the action is one to which Article 6(2) applies, paragraph (1) has effect—
a in the case of an action for libel and slander, as if for the words from "at any time" to "occurred" there were substituted the words "by him at any time before the expiration of one year from the date on which he ceased to be under a disability"; and
b in the case of an action for slander of title, slander of goods or other malicious falsehood, as if for the words "six years" there were substituted the words "one year".".

4 For Article 51 substitute—

51.—

1 If it appears to the court that it would be equitable to allow an action to proceed having regard to the degree to which—
a the provisions of Article 6(2) prejudice the plaintiff or any person whom he represents; and
b any decision of the court under this paragraph would prejudice the defendant or any person whom he represents,
the court may direct that those provisions are not to apply to the action, or are not to apply to any specified cause of action to which the action relates.
2 In acting under this Article the court is to have regard to all the circumstances of the case and in particular to—
a the length of, and the reasons for, the delay on the part of the plaintiff;
b in a case where the reason, or one of the reasons, for the delay was that all or any of the facts relevant to the cause of action did not become known to the plaintiff until after the expiration of the period mentioned in Article 6(2)—
i. the date on which any such facts did become known to him, and
ii. the extent to which he acted promptly and reasonably once he knew whether or not the facts in question might be capable of giving rise to an action; and
c the extent to which, having regard to the delay, relevant evidence is likely—
i to be unavailable, or
ii to be less cogent than if the action had been brought within the time allowed by Article 6(2).
3 In the case of an action for slander of title, slander of goods or other malicious falsehood brought by a personal representative—
a the references in paragraph (2) to the plaintiff shall be construed as including the deceased person to whom the cause of action accrued and any previous personal representative of that person; and

b nothing in Article 48(3) shall be construed as affecting the court's discretion under this Article.

4 In this Article "the court" means the court in which the action has been brought."

5 The amendments made by this section apply only to causes of action arising after the section comes into force.

The meaning of a statement

7. Ruling on the meaning of a statement.
In defamation proceedings the court shall not be asked to rule whether a statement is arguably capable, as opposed to capable, of bearing a particular meaning or meanings attributed to it.

Summary disposal of claim

8.— Summary disposal of claim.

1 In defamation proceedings the court may dispose summarily of the plaintiff's claim in accordance with the following provisions.

2 The court may dismiss the plaintiff's claim if it appears to the court that it has no realistic prospect of success and there is no reason why it should be tried.

3 The court may give judgment for the plaintiff and grant him summary relief (see section 9) if it appears to the court that there is no defence to the claim which has a realistic prospect of success, and that there is no other reason why the claim should be tried.

Unless the plaintiff asks for summary relief, the court shall not act under this subsection unless it is satisfied that summary relief will adequately compensate him for the wrong he has suffered.

4 In considering whether a claim should be tried the court shall have regard to—

a whether all the persons who are or might be defendants in respect of the publication complained of are before the court;

b whether summary disposal of the claim against another defendant would be inappropriate;

c the extent to which there is a conflict of evidence;

d the seriousness of the alleged wrong (as regards the content of the statement and the extent of publication); and

e whether it is justifiable in the circumstances to proceed to a full trial.

5 Proceedings under this section shall be heard and determined without a jury.

9.— Meaning of summary relief.

1 For the purposes of section 8 (summary disposal of claim) "summary relief" means such of the following as may be appropriate—

a a declaration that the statement was false and defamatory of the plaintiff;

b an order that the defendant publish or cause to be published a suitable correction and apology;

c damages not exceeding £10,000 or such other amount as may be prescribed by order of the Lord Chancellor;

d an order restraining the defendant from publishing or further publishing the matter complained of.

2 The content of any correction and apology, and the time, manner, form and place of publication, shall be for the parties to agree.

If they cannot agree on the content, the court may direct the defendant to publish or cause to be published a summary of the court's judgment agreed by the parties or settled by the court in accordance with rules of court.

If they cannot agree on the time, manner, form or place of publication, the court may direct the defendant to take such reasonable and practicable steps as the court considers appropriate.

[(2A) The Lord Chancellor must consult the Lord Chief Justice of England and Wales before making any order under subsection (1)(c) in relation to England and Wales.
(2B) The Lord Chancellor must consult the Lord Chief Justice of Northern Ireland before making any order under subsection (1)(c) in relation to Northern Ireland.
(2C) The Lord Chief Justice may nominate a judicial office holder (as defined in section 109(4) of the Constitutional Reform Act 2005) to exercise his functions under this section.
(2D) The Lord Chief Justice of Northern Ireland may nominate any of the following to exercise his functions under this section—
a the holder of one of the offices listed in Schedule 1 to the Justice (Northern Ireland) Act 2002;
b a Lord Justice of Appeal (as defined in section 88 of that Act).]²

3   Any order under subsection (1)(c) shall be made by statutory instrument which shall be subject to annulment in pursuance of a resolution of either House of Parliament.

10.— Summary disposal: rules of court.

1   Provision may be made by rules of court as to the summary disposal of the plaintiff's claim in defamation proceedings.

2   Without prejudice to the generality of that power, provision may be made—
a authorising a party to apply for summary disposal at any stage of the proceedings;
b authorising the court at any stage of the proceedings—
    i. to treat any application, pleading or other step in the proceedings as an application for summary disposal, or
    ii. to make an order for summary disposal without any such application;
c as to the time for serving pleadings or taking any other step in the proceedings in a case where there are proceedings for summary disposal;
d requiring the parties to identify any question of law or construction which the court is to be asked to determine in the proceedings;
e as to the nature of any hearing on the question of summary disposal, and in particular—
    i. authorising the court to order affidavits or witness statements to be prepared for use as evidence at the hearing, and
    ii. requiring the leave of the court for the calling of oral evidence, or the introduction of new evidence, at the hearing;
f authorising the court to require a defendant to elect, at or before the hearing, whether or not to make an offer to make amends under section 2.

11. Summary disposal: application to Northern Ireland.
In their application to Northern Ireland the provisions of sections 8 to 10 (summary disposal of claim) apply only to proceedings in the High Court.

Evidence of convictions

12.— Evidence of convictions.

1   In section 13 of the Civil Evidence Act 1968 (conclusiveness of convictions for purposes of defamation actions), in subsections (1) and (2) for "a person" substitute "the plaintiff" and for "that person" substitute "he"; and after subsection (2) insert—

"(2A) In the case of an action for libel or slander in which there is more than one plaintiff—
    a the references in subsections (1) and (2) above to the plaintiff shall be construed as references to any of the plaintiffs, and
    b proof that any of the plaintiffs stands convicted of an offence shall be conclusive evidence that he committed that offence so far as that fact is relevant to any issue arising in relation to his cause of action or that of any other plaintiff.".

---

²   added by Constitutional Reform Act 2005 c. 4 Sch. 4(1) para. 255

The amendments made by this subsection apply only where the trial of the action begins after this section comes into force.

2 In section 12 of the Law Reform (Miscellaneous Provisions) (Scotland) Act 1968 (conclusiveness of convictions for purposes of defamation actions), in subsections (1) and (2) for "a person" substitute "the pursuer" and for "that person" substitute "he"; and after subsection (2) insert—

"(2A) In the case of an action for defamation in which there is more than one pursuer—
a the references in subsections (1) and (2) above to the pursuer shall be construed as references to any of the pursuers, and
b proof that any of the pursuers stands convicted of an offence shall be conclusive evidence that he committed that offence so far as that fact is relevant to any issue arising in relation to his cause of action or that of any other pursuer.".

The amendments made by this subsection apply only for the purposes of an action begun after this section comes into force, whenever the cause of action arose.

3 In section 9 of the Civil Evidence Act (Northern Ireland) 1971 (conclusiveness of convictions for purposes of defamation actions), in subsections (1) and (2) for "a person" substitute "the plaintiff" and for "that person" substitute "he"; and after subsection (2) insert—

"(2A) In the case of an action for libel or slander in which there is more than one plaintiff—
a the references in subsections (1) and (2) to the plaintiff shall be construed as references to any of the plaintiffs, and
b proof that any of the plaintiffs stands convicted of an offence shall be conclusive evidence that he committed that offence so far as that fact is relevant to any issue arising in relation to his cause of action or that of any other plaintiff.".

The amendments made by this subsection apply only where the trial of the action begins after this section comes into force.

Evidence concerning proceedings in Parliament

13.— Evidence concerning proceedings in Parliament.

1 Where the conduct of a person in or in relation to proceedings in Parliament is in issue in defamation proceedings, he may waive for the purposes of those proceedings, so far as concerns him, the protection of any enactment or rule of law which prevents proceedings in Parliament being impeached or questioned in any court or place out of Parliament.

2 Where a person waives that protection—
a any such enactment or rule of law shall not apply to prevent evidence being given, questions being asked or statements, submissions, comments or findings being made about his conduct, and
b none of those things shall be regarded as infringing the privilege of either House of Parliament.

3 The waiver by one person of that protection does not affect its operation in relation to another person who has not waived it.

4 Nothing in this section affects any enactment or rule of law so far as it protects a person (including a person who has waived the protection referred to above) from legal liability for words spoken or things done in the course of, or for the purposes of or incidental to, any proceedings in Parliament.

5 Without prejudice to the generality of subsection (4), that subsection applies to—
a the giving of evidence before either House or a committee;
b the presentation or submission of a document to either House or a committee;
c the preparation of a document for the purposes of or incidental to the transacting of any such business;
d the formulation, making or publication of a document, including a report, by or pursuant to an order to either House or a committee; and

e any communication with the Parliamentary Commissioner for Standards or any person having functions in connection with the registration of members' interests.
In this subsection "a committee" means a committee of either House or a joint committee of both House of Parliament.

Statutory privilege

14.— Reports of court proceedings absolutely privileged.

1 A fair and accurate report of proceedings in public before a court to which this section applies, if published contemporaneously with the proceedings, is absolutely privileged.

2 A report of proceedings which by an order of the court, or as a consequence of any statutory provision, is required to be postponed shall be treated as published contemporaneously if it is published as soon as practicable after publication is permitted.

3 This section applies to—
a any court in the United Kingdom,
b the European Court of Justice or any court attached to that court,
c the European Court of Human Rights, and
d any international criminal tribunal established by the Security Council of the United
Nations or by an international agreement to which the United Kingdom is a party.
In paragraph (a) "court"includes any tribunal or body exercising the judicial power of the State.

4 In section 8(6) of the Rehabilitation of Offenders Act 1974 and in Article 9(6) of the Rehabilitation of Offenders (Northern Ireland) Order 1978 (defamation actions: reports of court proceedings), for "section 3 of the Law of Libel Amendment Act 1888" substitute "section 14 of the Defamation Act 1996".

15.— Reports, &c. protected by qualified privilege.

1 The publication of any report or other statement mentioned in Schedule 1 to this Act is privileged unless the publication is shown to be made with malice, subject as follows.

2 In defamation proceedings in respect of the publication of a report or other statement mentioned in Part II of that Schedule, there is no defence under this section if the plaintiff shows that the defendant—
a was requested by him to publish in a suitable manner a reasonable letter or statement by way of explanation or contradiction, and
b refused or neglected to do so.
For this purpose "in a suitable manner" means in the same manner as the publication complained of or in a manner that is adequate and reasonable in the circumstances.

3 This section does not apply to the publication to the public, or a section of the public, of matter which is not of public concern and the publication of which is not for the public benefit.

4 Nothing in this section shall be construed—
a as protecting the publication of matter the publication of which is prohibited by law, or
b as limiting or abridging any privilege subsisting apart from this section.

Supplementary provisions

16. Repeals.
The enactments specified in Schedule 2 are repealed to the extent specified.

17.— Interpretation.

1 In this Act—

"publication" and "publish", in relation to a statement, have the meaning they have for the purposes of the law of defamation generally, but "publisher" is specially defined for the purposes of section 1;

"statement" means words, pictures, visual images, gestures or any other method of signifying meaning; and "statutory provision" means —

a a provision contained in an Act or in subordinate legislation within the meaning of the Interpretation Act 1978, [. . .]³

[(aa) a provision contained in an Act of the Scottish Parliament or in an instrument made under such an Act, or]⁴

b a statutory provision within the meaning given by section 1(f) of the Interpretation Act (Northern Ireland) 1954.

2 In this Act as it applies to proceedings in Scotland—

"costs" means expenses; and

"plaintiff" and "defendant" mean pursuer and defender

General provisions

18.—

1 The following provisions of this Act extend to England and Extent. Wales—

section 1 (responsibility for publication),

sections 2 to 4 (offer to make amends), except section 3(9),

section 5 (time limit for actions for defamation or malicious falsehood).

section 7 (ruling on the meaning of a statement),

sections 8 to 10 (summary disposal of claim),

section 12(1) (evidence of convictions),

section 13 (evidence concerning proceedings in Parliament),

sections 14 and 15 and Schedule 1 (statutory privilege).

section 16 and Schedule 2 (repeals) so far as relating to enactments extending to England and Wales,

section 17(1) (interpretation),

this subsection,

section 19 (commencement) so far as relating to provisions which extend to England and Wales, and

section 20 (short title and saving).

2 The following provisions of this Act extend to Scotland—

section 1 (responsibility for publication),

sections 2 to 4 (offer to make amends), except section 3(8),

section 12(2) (evidence of convictions),

section 13 (evidence concerning proceedings in Parliament),

section 14 and 15 and Schedule 1 (statutory privilege).

section 16 and Schedule 2 (repeals) so far as relating to enactments extending to Scotland, section 17 (interpretation),

this subsection,

section 19 (commencement) so far as relating to provisions which extend to Scotland, and

section 20 (short title and saving).

3 The following provisions of this Act extend to Northern Ireland—

section 1 (responsibility for publication).

sections 2 to 4 (offer to make amends), except section 3(9),

section 6 (time limit for actions for defamation or malicious falsehood),

section 7 (ruling on the meaning of a statement),

---

³ added by Scotland Act 1998 c. 46 Sch. 8 para. 33(2)

⁴ added by Scotland Act 1998 c. 46 Sch. 8 para. 33(2)

sections 8 to 11 (summary disposal of claim),
section 12(3) (evidence of convictions),
section 13 (evidence concerning proceedings in Parliament),
sections 14 and 15 and Schedule 1 (statutory privilege),
section 16 and Schedule 2 (repeals) so far as relating to enactments extending to Northern Ireland,
section 17(1) (interpretation), this subsection,
section 19 (commencement) so far as relating to provisions which extend to Northern Ireland, and
section 20 (short title and saving).

19.— Commencement.

1. Sections 18 to 20 (extent, commencement and other general provisions) come into force on Royal Assent.
2. The following provisions of this Act come into force at the end of the period of two months beginning with the day on which this Act is passed—
   section 1 (responsibility for publication),
   sections 5 and 6 (time limit for actions for defamation or malicious falsehood),
   section 12 (evidence of convictions),
   section 13 (evidence concerning proceedings in Parliament),
   section 16 and the repeals in Schedule 2, so far as consequential on the above provisions, and
   section 17 (interpretation), so far as relating to the above provisions.
3. The provisions of this Act otherwise come into force on such day as may be appointed—
   a for England and Wales or Northern Ireland, by order of the Lord Chancellor, or
   b for Scotland, by order of the Secretary of State, and different days may be appointed for different purposes.
4. Any such order shall be made by statutory instrument and may contain such transitional provisions as appear to the Lord Chancellor or Secretary of State to be appropriate.

20.— Short title and saving.

1. This Act may be cited as the Defamation Act 1996.
2. Nothing in this Act affects the law relating to criminal libel.

SCHEDULE 1

QUALIFIED PRIVILEGE

Section 15.

PART I

STATEMENTS HAVING QUALIFIED PRIVILEGE WITHOUT EXPLANATION OR CONTRADICTION

1.
A fair and accurate report of proceedings in public of a legislature anywhere in the world.

2.
A fair and accurate report of proceedings in public before a court anywhere in the world.

3.
A fair and accurate report of proceedings in public of a person appointed to hold a public inquiry by a government or legislature anywhere in the world.

4.
A fair and accurate report of proceedings in public anywhere in the world of an international organisation or an international conference.

5.
A fair and accurate copy of or extract from any register or other document required by law to be open to public inspection.

6.
A notice or advertisement published by or on the authority of a court, or of a judge or officer of a court, anywhere in the world.

7.
A fair and accurate copy of or extract from matter published by or on the authority of a government or legislature anywhere in the world.

8.
A fair and accurate copy of or extract from matter published anywhere in the world by an international organisation or an international conference.

PART II

STATEMENTS PRIVILEGED SUBJECT TO EXPLANATION
OR CONTRADICTION

9.—

    1 A fair and accurate copy of or extract from a notice or other matter issued for the information of the public by or on behalf of—
    a a legislature in any member State or the European Parliament;
    b the government of any member State, or any authority performing governmental functions in any member State or part of a member State, or the European Commission;
    c an international organisation or international conference.
    2 In this paragraph "governmental functions" includes police functions,

10.
A fair and accurate copy of or extract from a document made available by a court in any member State or the European Court of Justice (or any court attached to that court), or by a judge or officer of any such court.

11.—

    1 A fair and accurate report of proceedings at any public meeting or sitting in the United Kingdom of—
    a a local authority, local authority committee or in the case of a local authority which are operating executive arrangements the executive of that authority or a committee of that executive;
    b a justice or justices of the peace acting otherwise than as a court exercising judicial authority;
    c a commission, tribunal, committee or person appointed for the purposes of any inquiry by any statutory provision, by Her Majesty or by a Minister of the Crown, a member of the Scottish Executive [, the Welsh Ministers or the Counsel General to the Welsh Assembly Government][5] or a Northern Ireland Department;
    d a person appointed by a local authority to hold a local inquiry in pursuance of any statutory provision;

---

[5] words inserted by Government of Wales Act 2006 c. 32 Sch. 10 para. 40

e any other tribunal, board, committee or body constituted by or under, and exercising functions under, any statutory provision.

(1A) In the case of a local authority which are operating executive arrangements, a fair and accurate record of any decision made by any member of the executive where that record is required to be made and available for public inspection by virtue of section 22 of the Local Government Act 2000 or of any provision in regulations made under that section.

2 In sub-paragraphs (1)(a) and (1A)—

"executive" and "executive arrangements"have the same meaning as in Part II of the Local Government Act 2000;

"local authority" means —

a in relation to England and Wales, a principal council within the meaning of the Local Government Act 1972, any body falling within any paragraph of section 100J(1) of that Act or an authority or body to which the Public Bodies (Admission to Meetings) Act 1960 applies,

b in relation to Scotland, a council constituted under section 2 of the Local Government etc. (Scotland) Act 1994 or an authority or body to which the Public Bodies (Admission to Meetings) Act 1960 applies,

c in relation to Northern Ireland, any authority or body to which sections 23 to 27 of the Local Government Act (Northern Ireland) 1972 apply; and

"local authority committee" means any committee of a local authority or of local authorities, and includes—

a any committee or sub-committee in relation to which sections 100A to 100D of the Local Government Act 1972 apply by virtue of section 100E of that Act (whether or not also by virtue of section 100J of that Act), and

b any committee or sub-committee in relation to which sections 50A to 50D of the Local Government (Scotland) Act 1973 apply by virtue of section 50E of that Act.

3 A fair and accurate report of any corresponding proceedings in any of the Channel Islands or the Isle of Man or in another member State.[6]

12.—

1 A fair and accurate report of proceedings at any public meeting held in a member State.

2 In this paragraph a "public meeting" means a meeting bona fide and lawfully held for a lawful purpose and for the furtherance or discussion of a matter of public concern, whether admission to the meeting is general or restricted.

13.—

1 A fair and accurate report of proceedings at a general meeting of a UK public company.

2 A fair and accurate copy of or extract from any document circulated to members of a UK public company—

a by or with the authority of the board of directors of the company,

b by the auditors of the company, or

c by any member of the company in pursuance of a right conferred by any statutory provision.

3 A fair and accurate copy of or extract from any document circulated to members of a UK public company which relates to the appointment, resignation, retirement or dismissal of directors of the company.

4 In this paragraph "UK public company" means—

a a public company within the meaning of section 1(3) of the Companies Act 1985 or Article 12(3) of the Companies (Northern Ireland) Order 1986 or

b a body corporate incorporated by or registered under any other statutory provision, or by Royal Charter, or formed in pursuance of letters patent.

[6] In relation to England: para. 11 is modified: [See Westlaw UK].

5 A fair and accurate report of proceedings at any corresponding meeting of, or copy of or extract from any corresponding document circulated to members of, a public company formed under the law of any of the Channel Islands or the Isle of Man or of another member State.

14.

A fair and accurate report of any finding or decision of any of the following descriptions of association, formed in the United Kingdom or another member State, or of any committee or governing body of such an association—

a an association formed for the purpose of promoting or encouraging the exercise of or interest in any art, science, religion or learning, and empowered by its constitution to exercise control over or adjudicate on matters of interest or concern to the association, or the actions or conduct of any person subject to such control or adjudication;

b an association formed for the purpose of promoting or safeguarding the interests of any trade, business, industry or profession, or of the persons carrying on or engaged in any trade, business, industry or profession, and empowered by its constitution to exercise control over or adjudicate upon matters connected with that trade, business, industry or profession, or the actions or conduct of those persons;

c an association formed for the purpose of promoting or safeguarding the interests of a game, sport or pastime to the playing or exercise of which members of the public are invited or admitted, and empowered by its constitution to exercise control over or adjudicate upon persons connected with or taking part in the game, sport or pastime;

d an association formed for the purpose of promoting charitable objects or other objects beneficial to the community and empowered by its constitution to exercise control over or to adjudicate on matters of interest or concern to the association, or the actions or conduct of any person subject to such control or adjudication.

15.—

1 A fair and accurate report of, or copy of or extract from, any adjudication, report, statement or notice issued by a body, officer or other person designated for the purposes of this paragraph—

a for England and Wales or Northern Ireland, by order of the Lord Chancellor, and

b for Scotland, by order of the Secretary of State.

2 An order under this paragraph shall be made by statutory instrument which shall be subject to annulment in pursuance of a resolution of either House of Parliament.

PART III

SUPPLEMENTARY PROVISIONS

16.—

1 In this Schedule—

"court"includes any tribunal or body exercising the judicial power of the State;

"international conference" means a conference attended by representatives of two or more governments;

"international organisation" means an organisation of which two or more governments are members, and includes any committee or other subordinate body of such an organisation; and

"legislature"includes a local legislature.

2 References in this Schedule to a member State include any European dependent territory of a member State.

3 In paragraphs 2 and 6"court"includes—

a the European Court of Justice (or any court attached to that court) and the Court of Auditors of the European Communities,

b the European Court of Human Rights,
c any international criminal tribunal established by the Security Council of the
United Nations or by an international agreement to which the United Kingdom is
a party, and
d the International Court of Justice and any other judicial or arbitral tribunal
deciding matters in dispute between States.

4 In paragraphs 1, 3 and 7"legislature"includes the European Parliament.

17.—

1 Provision may be made by order identifying—
a for the purposes of paragraph 11, the corresponding proceedings referred to in
sub-paragraph (3);
b for the purposes of paragraph 13, the corresponding meetings and documents
referred to in sub-paragraph (5).

2 An order under this paragraph may be made—
a for England and Wales or Northern Ireland, by the Lord Chancellor, and
b for Scotland, by the Secretary of State.

3 An order under this paragraph shall be made by statutory instrument which shall
be subject to annulment in pursuance of a resolution of either House of Parliament.

SCHEDULE 2

REPEALS

Section 16

Chapter	Short title	Extent of repeal
1888 c. 64.	Law of Libel Amendment Act 1888.	Section 3.
1952 c. 66.	Defamation Act 1952.	Section 4. Sections 7, 8 and 9(2) and (3). Section 16(2) and (3). The Schedule.
1955 c. 20.	Revision of the Army and Air Force Acts (Transitional Provisions) Act 1955.	In Schedule 2, the entry relating to the Defamation Act 1952.
1955 c. 11 (N.I.).	Defamation Act (Northern Ireland) 1955.	Section 4. Sections 7, 8 and 9(2) and (3). Section 14(2). The Schedule.
1972 c. 9 (N.I.).	Local Government Act (Northern Ireland) 1972.	In Schedule 8, paragraph 12.
1981 c. 49.	Contempt of Court Act 1981.	In section 4(3), the words "and of section 3 of the Law of Libel Amendment Act 1888 (privilege)".
1981 c. 61.	British Nationality Act 1981.	In Schedule 7, the entries relating to the Defamation Act 1952 and the Defamation Act (Northern Ireland) 1955.
1985 c. 43.	Local Government (Access to Information) Act 1985.	In Schedule 2, paragraphs 2 and 3.
1985 c. 61.	Administration of Justice Act 1985.	Section 57.
S.I. 1986/594 (N.I. 3).	Education and Libraries (Northern Ireland) Order 1986.	Article 97(2).
1990 c. 42.	Broadcasting Act 1990.	Section 166(3). In Schedule 20, paragraphs 2 and 3.

APPENDIX 3

DEFAMATION BILL

CONTENTS

A

BILL

TO

Amend the law of defamation

BE IT ENACTED by the Queen's most Excellent Majesty, by and with the advice and consent of the Lords Spiritual and Temporal, and Commons, in this present Parliament assembled, and by the authority of the same, as follows: —

Requirement of substantial harm

1 Substantial harm

A statement is not defamatory unless its publication has caused or is likely to cause substantial harm to the reputation of the claimant.

Defences

2 Responsible publication on matter of public interest

(1) It is a defence to an action for defamation for the defendant to show that—
    (a) the statement complained of is, or forms part of, a statement on a matter of public interest; and
    (b) the defendant acted responsibly in publishing the statement complained of.
(2) In determining whether a defendant acted responsibly in publishing a statement, the matters to which the court may have regard include (amongst other matters) —
    (a) the nature of the publication and its context;
    (b) the seriousness of any imputation about the claimant that is conveyed by the statement;
    (c) the extent to which the subject matter of the statement is of public interest;
    (d) the information the defendant had before publishing the statement and what the defendant knew about the reliability of that information;
    (e) whether the defendant sought the claimant's views on the statement before publishing it and whether the publication included an account of any views the claimant expressed;
    (f) whether the defendant took any other steps to verify the accuracy of the statement;
    (g) the timing of the publication and whether there was reason to think it was in the public interest for the statement to be published urgently;
    (h) the tone of the statement (including whether it draws appropriate distinctions between suspicions, opinions, allegations and proven facts).
(3) A defendant is to be treated as having acted responsibly in publishing a statement if the statement was published as part of an accurate and impartial account of a dispute between the claimant and another person.

3 Truth

(1) It is a defence to an action for defamation for the defendant to show that the imputation conveyed by the statement complained of is substantially true.

(2) Subsection (3) applies in an action for defamation in relation to a statement which conveys two or more distinct imputations.

(3) If one or more of the imputations is not shown to be substantially true, the defence under this section does not fail if, having regard to the imputations which are shown to be substantially true, the imputations which are not shown to be substantially true do not materially injure the claimant's reputation.

(4) The common law defence of justification is abolished and, accordingly, section 5 of the Defamation Act 1952 (justification) is repealed.

(5) In section 8 of the Rehabilitation of Offenders Act 1974 (defamation actions) —
    (a) in subsection (3) for "any defence of justification or" substitute "a defence under section 3 of the Defamation Act 2011 (truth) which is available to him or any defence of";
    (b) in subsection (5) for "the defence of justification" substitute "a defence under section 3 of the Defamation Act 2011 (truth)";
    (c) in subsection (8)(c) for "the defence of justification" substitute "a defence under section 3 of the Defamation Act 2011".

4 Honest opinion

(1) It is a defence to an action for defamation for the defendant to show that Conditions 1, 2 and 3 are met.

(2) Condition 1 is that the statement complained of is a statement of opinion.

(3) Condition 2 is that the opinion is on a matter of public interest.

(4) Condition 3 is that an honest person could have held the opinion on the basis of-
    (a) a fact which existed at the time the statement complained of was published;
    (b) a privileged statement which was published before the statement complained of.

(5) The defence is defeated if the claimant shows that the defendant did not hold the opinion.

(6) Subsection (5) does not apply in a case where the statement complained of was published by the defendant but made by another person ("the author"); and in such a case the defence is defeated if the claimant shows that the defendant knew or ought to have known that the author did not hold the opinion.

(7) The common law defence of fair comment is abolished and, accordingly, section 6 of the Defamation Act 1952 (fair comment) is repealed.

5 Privilege

(1) For subsection (3) of section 14 of the Defamation Act 1996 (reports of court proceedings absolutely privileged) substitute —
    "(3) This section applies to —
        (a) any court in the United Kingdom,
        (b) any court established under the law of a country or territory outside the United Kingdom,
        (c) any international court or tribunal established by the Security Council of the United Nations or by an international agreement; and in paragraphs (a) and (b) "court" includes any tribunal or body exercising the judicial power of the State."

(2) Schedule 1 to that Act (qualified privilege) is amended as follows.

(3) For paragraphs 9 and 10 substitute—
    "9 (1) A fair and accurate copy of, extract from or summary of a notice or other matter issued for the information of the public by or on behalf of-
        (a) a legislature or government anywhere in the world;
        (b) an authority anywhere in the world performing governmental functions;
        (c) an international organisation or international conference.
    (2) In this paragraph "governmental functions" includes police functions.
    10   A fair and accurate copy of, extract from or summary of a document made available by a court anywhere in the world, or by a judge or officer of such a court."

(4) In paragraph 12(1) (report of proceedings at public meetings) for "in a member State" substitute "anywhere in the world".

(5) In paragraph 13 (report of proceedings at meetings of public company) —

    (a) in sub-paragraph (1), for "UK public company" substitute "company which is a quoted company within the meaning of section 385(2) of the Companies Act 2006 (a "quoted company")";

    (b) for sub-paragraphs (2) to (5) substitute—

      "(2) A fair and accurate copy of, extract from or summary of any document circulated to members of a quoted company —

        (a) by or with the authority of the board of directors of the company,

        (b) by the auditors of the company, or

        (c) by any member of the company in pursuance of a right conferred by any statutory provision.

      (3) A fair and accurate copy of, extract from or summary of any document circulated to members of a quoted company which relates to the appointment, resignation, retirement or dismissal of directors of the company."

(6) In paragraph 14 (report of finding or decision of certain kinds of associations) in the words before paragraph (a), for "in the United Kingdom or another member State" substitute "anywhere in the world".

(7) After paragraph 14 insert—

    "14A A fair and accurate —

      (a) report of proceedings of a scientific or academic conference, or

      (b) copy of, extract from or summary of matter published by such a conference."

(8) For paragraph 15 (report of statements etc by a person designated by the Lord Chancellor for the purposes of the paragraph) substitute—

    "15(1) A fair and accurate report or summary of, copy of or extract from, any adjudication, report, statement or notice issued by a body, officer or other person designated for the purposes of this paragraph by order of the Lord Chancellor.

    (2) An order under this paragraph shall be made by statutory instrument which shall be subject to annulment in pursuance of a resolution of either House of Parliament."

(9) For paragraphs 16 and 17 (general provision) substitute—

    "16 In this Schedule —

      "court" includes any tribunal or body exercising the judicial power of the State;

      "international conference" means a conference attended by representatives of two or more governments;

      "international organisation" means an organisation of which two or more governments are members, and includes any committee or other subordinate body of such an organisation;

      "legislature" includes a local legislature; and

      "member State" includes an)/ European dependent territory of a member State."

Single publication rule

6 Single publication rule

(1) This section applies if a person—

    (a) publishes a statement to the public ("the first publication"), and

    (b) subsequently publishes (whether or not to the public) that statement or a statement which is substantially the same.

(2) In subsection (1) "publication to the public" includes publication to a section of the public.

(3) For the purposes of section 4A of the Limitation Act 1980 (time limit for actions for defamation etc) any cause of action against the person for defamation in respect of

the subsequent publication is to be treated as having accrued on the date of the first publication.

(4) This section does not apply in relation to the subsequent publication if the manner of that publication is materially different from the manner of the first publication.

(5) In determining whether the manner of a subsequent publication is materially different from the manner of the first publication, the matters to which the court may have regard include (amongst other matters) —

(a) the level of prominence that a statement is given;
(b) the extent of the subsequent publication.

(6) Where this section applies —

(a) it does not affect the court's discretion under section 32A of the Limitation Act 1980 (discretionary exclusion of time limit for actions for defamation etc), and

(b) the reference in subsection (l)(a) of that section to the operation of section 4A of that Act is a reference to the operation of section 4A together with this section.

Jurisdiction

7 Action against a person not domiciled in the UK or a Member State etc

(1) This section applies to an action for defamation against a person who is not domiciled—

(a) in the United Kingdom;
(b) in another Member State; or
(c) in a state which is for the time being a contracting party to the Lugano Convention.

(2) A court does not have jurisdiction to hear and determine an action to which this section applies unless the court is satisfied that, of all the places in which the statement complained of has been published, England and Wales is clearly the most appropriate place in which to bring an action in respect of the statement.

(3) For the purposes of this section —

(a) a person is domiciled in the United Kingdom or in another Member State if the person is domiciled there for the purposes of the Brussels Regulation;

(b) a person is domiciled in a state which is a contracting party to the Lugano Convention if the person is domiciled in the state for the purposes of that Convention.

(4) In this section—

"the Brussels Regulation" means Council Regulation (EC) No 44/2001 of 22nd December 2000 on jurisdiction and the recognition and enforcement of judgments in civil and commercial matters, as amended from time to time and as applied by the Agreement made on 19th October 2005 between the European Community and the Kingdom of Denmark on jurisdiction and the recognition and enforcement of judgments in civil and commercial matters (OJ No L229 16.11.2005 at p 62);

"the Lugano Convention" means the Convention on judgments and the recognition and enforcement of judgments in civil and commercial matters, between the European Community and the Republic of Ireland, the Kingdom of Norway, the Swiss Confederation and the Kingdom of Denmark signed on behalf of the European Community on 30th October 2007.

Trial by jury

8 Trial to be without a jury unless the court orders otherwise

(1) In section 69(1) of the Senior Courts Act 1981 (certain actions in the Queen's Bench Division to be tried with a jury unless the trial requires prolonged examination of documents etc) in paragraph (b) omit "libel, slander,'.

(2) In section 66(3) of the County Courts Act 1984 (certain actions in the county court to be tried with a jury unless the trial requires prolonged examination of documents etc) in paragraph (b) omit "libel, slander,".

General provisions

9 Meaning of "publish" and "statement"

In this Act-

> "publish" and "publication", in relation to a statement, have the meaning they have for the purposes of the law of defamation generally;
>
> "statement" means words, pictures, visual images, gestures or any other method of signifying meaning.

10 Short title, commencement and extent

(1) This Act may be cited as the Defamation Act 2011.

(2) The provisions of this Act, apart from this section, come into force on such day as the Secretary of State may by order made by statutory instrument appoint.

(3) This Act extends to England and Wales only.

CONTEMPT OF COURT ACT 1981
1981 CHAPTER 49

An Act to amend the law relating to contempt of court and related matters.

[27th July 1981]

Strict liability

1. The strict liability rule.
In this Act "the strict liability rule" means the rule of law whereby conduct may be treated as a contempt of court as tending to interfere with the course of justice in particular legal proceedings regardless of intent to do so.

2.— Limitation of scope of strict liability.

1 The strict liability rule applies only in relation to publications, and for this purpose "publication" includes any speech, writing, [programme included in a cable programme service][1] or other communication in whatever form, which is addressed to the public at large or any section of the public.

2 The strict liability rule applies only to a publication which creates a substantial risk that the course of justice in the proceedings in question will be seriously impeded or prejudiced.

3 The strict liability rule applies to a publication only if the proceedings in question are active within the meaning of this section at the time of the publication.

4 Schedule 1 applies for determining the times at which proceedings are to be treated as active within the meaning of this section.

5 In this section "programme service" has the same meaning as in the Broadcasting Act 1990.][2]

3.— Defence of innocent publication or distribution.

1 A person is not guilty of contempt of court under the strict liability rule as the publisher of any matter to which that rule applies if at the time of publication (having taken all reasonable care) he does not know and has no reason to suspect that relevant proceedings are active.

2 A person is not guilty of contempt of court under the strict liability rule as the distributor of a publication containing any such matter if at the time of distribution (having taken all reasonable care) he does not know that it contains such matter and has no reason to suspect that it is likely to do so.

3 The burden of proof of any fact tending to establish a defence afforded by this section to any person lies upon that person.

4 [...][3]

---

[1]   Words substituted by Broadcasting Act 1990 (c.42), s.203(1), Sch.20 para.31(1)(a).
[2]   Section 2(5) inserted by Broadcasting Act 1990 (c.42), s.203(1), Sch.20, para.31(1)(b).
[3]   Repeals Administration of Justice Act 1960 (c. 65), s.11.

4.— Contemporary reports of proceedings.

> **1** Subject to this section a person is not guilty of contempt of court under the strict liability rule in respect of a fair and accurate report of legal proceedings held in public, published contemporaneously and in good faith.
>
> **2** In any such proceedings the court may, where it appears to be necessary for avoiding a substantial risk of prejudice to the administration of justice in those proceedings, or in any other proceedings pending or imminent, order that the publication of any report of the proceedings, or any part of the proceedings, be postponed for such period as the court thinks necessary for that purpose.
>
> **2A** Where in proceedings for any offence which is an administration of justice offence for the purposes of section 54 of the Criminal Procedure and Investigations Act 1996 (acquittal tainted by an administration of justice offence) it appears to the court that there is a possibility that (by virtue of that section) proceedings may be taken against a person for an offence of which he has been acquitted, subsection (2) of this section shall apply as if those proceedings were pending or imminent.
>
> **3** For the purposes of subsection (1) of this section [...]⁴ a report of proceedings shall be treated as published contemporaneously—
>
> a in the case of a report of which publication is postponed pursuant to an order under subsection (2) of this section, if published as soon as practicable after that order expires;
>
> b in the case of a report of committal proceedings of which publication is permitted by virtue only of subsection (3) of section 8 of the Magistrates' Courts Act 1980, if published as soon as practicable after publication is so permitted.

5. Discussion of public affairs.

A publication made as or as part of a discussion in good faith of public affairs or other matters of general public interest is not to be treated as a contempt of court under the strict liability rule if the risk of impediment or prejudice to particular legal proceedings is merely incidental to the discussion.

6. Savings.

Nothing in the foregoing provisions of this Act—

> a prejudices any defence available at common law to a charge of contempt of court under the strict liability rule;
>
> b implies that any publication is punishable as contempt of court under that rule which would not be so punishable apart from those provisions;
>
> c restricts liability for contempt of court in respect of conduct intended to impede or prejudice the administration of justice.

7. Consent required for institution of proceedings.

Proceedings for a contempt of court under the strict liability rule (other than Scottish proceedings) shall not be instituted except by or with the consent of the Attorney General or on the motion of a court having jurisdiction to deal with it.

Other aspects of law and procedure

8.— Confidentiality of jury's deliberations.

> **1** Subject to subsection (2) below, it is a contempt of court to obtain, disclose or solicit any particulars of statements made, opinions expressed, arguments advanced or votes cast by members of a jury in the course of their deliberations in any legal proceedings.

⁴ Words repealed by Defamation Act 1996 (c.31), Sch.2, para.1.

2 This section does not apply to any disclosure of any particulars—

a in the proceedings in question for the purpose of enabling the jury to arrive at their verdict, or in connection with the delivery of that verdict, or

b in evidence in any subsequent proceedings for an offence alleged to have been committed in relation to the jury in the first mentioned proceedings,

or to the publication of any particulars so disclosed.

3 Proceedings for a contempt of court under this section (other than Scottish proceedings) shall not be instituted except by or with the consent of the Attorney General or on the motion of a court having jurisdiction to deal with it.

9.— Use of tape recorders.

1 Subject to subsection (4) below, it is a contempt of court—

a to use in court, or bring into court for use, any tape recorder or other instrument for recording sound, except with the leave of the court;

b to publish a recording of legal proceedings made by means of any such instrument, or any recording derived directly or indirectly from it, by playing it in the hearing of the public or any section of the public, or to dispose of it or any recording so derived, with a view to such publication;

c to use any such recording in contravention of any conditions of leave granted under paragraph (a).

2 Leave under paragraph (a) of subsection (1) may be granted or refused at the discretion of the court, and if granted may be granted subject to such conditions as the court thinks proper with respect to the use of any recording made pursuant to the leave; and where leave has been granted the court may at the like discretion withdraw or amend it either generally or in relation to any particular part of the proceedings.

3 Without prejudice to any other power to deal with an act of contempt under paragraph (a) of subsection (1), the court may order the instrument, or any recording made with it, or both, to be forfeited; and any object so forfeited shall (unless the court otherwise determines on application by a person appearing to be the owner) be sold or otherwise disposed of in such manner as the court may direct.

4 This section does not apply to the making or use of sound recordings for purposes of official transcripts of proceedings.

10. Sources of information.

No court may require a person to disclose, nor is any person guilty of contempt of court for refusing to disclose, the source of information contained in a publication for which he is responsible, unless it be established to the satisfaction of the court that disclosure is necessary in the interests of justice or national security or for the prevention of disorder or crime.

11. Publication of matters exempted from disclosure in court.

In any case where a court (having power to do so) allows a name or other matter to be withheld from the public in proceedings before the court, the court may give such directions prohibiting the publication of that name or matter in connection with the proceedings as appear to the court to be necessary for the purpose for which it was so withheld.

OFCOM BROADCASTING CODE
SECTION 7: FAIRNESS

(Relevant legislation includes, in particular, sections 3(2)(f) and 326 of the Communications Act 2003 and sections 107(1) and 130 of the Broadcasting Act 1996 (as amended), Article 28 of the Audiovisual Media Services Directive and Article 10 of the European Convention on Human Rights.)

Foreword
This section and the following section on privacy are different from other sections of the Code. They apply to how broadcasters treat the individuals or organizations directly affected by programmes, rather than to what the general public sees and/or hears as viewers and listener s.

As well as containing a principle and a rule this section contains "practices to be followed" by broadcasters when dealing with individuals or organisations participating in or otherwise directly affected by programmes as broadcast. Following these practices will not necessarily avoid a breach of this section of the Code (Rule 7.1).
However, failure to follow these practises will only constitute a breach where it results in unfairness to an individual or organisation in the programme. Importantly, the Code does not and cannot seek to set out all the "practices to be followed" in order to avoid unfair treatment.

The following provisions in the next section on privacy are also relevant to this section:

- the explanation of public interest that appears in the meaning of "warranted" under Rule 8.1 in Section Eight: Privacy;
- the meaning of surreptitious filming or recording that appears under "practices to be followed" 8.13 in Section Eight: Privacy.

Principle
To ensure that broadcasters avoid unjust or unfair treatment of individuals or organisations in programmes.

Rule
7.1 Broadcasters must avoid unjust or unfair treatment of individuals or organisations in programmes.

Practices to be followed (7.2 to 7.14 below)

Dealing fairly with contributors and obtaining informed consent

7.2 Broadcasters and programme makers should normally be fair in their dealings with potential contributors to programmes unless, exceptionally, it is justified to do otherwise.

7.3 Where a person is invited to make a contribution to a programme (except when the subject matter is trivial or their participation minor) they should normally, at an appropriate stage:

- be told the nature and purpose of the programme, what the programme is about and be given a clear explanation of why they were asked to contribute and when (if known) and where it is likely to be first broadcast;

- be told what kind of contribution they are expected to make, for example live, pre-recorded, interview, discussion, edited, unedited, etc.;
- be informed about the areas of questioning and, wherever possible, the nature of other likely contributions;
- be made aware of any significant changes to the programme as it develops which might reasonably affect their original consent to participate, and which might cause material unfairness;
- be told the nature of their contractual rights and obligations and those of the programme maker and broadcaster in relation to their contribution; and
- be given clear information, if offered an opportunity to preview the programme, about whether they will be able to effect any changes to it.

Taking these measures is likely to result in the consent that is given being 'informed consent' (referred to in this section and the rest of the Code as "consent").

It may be fair to withhold all or some of this information where it is justified in the public interest or under other provisions of this section of the Code.

7.4 If a contributor is under sixteen, consent should normally be obtained from a parent or guardian, or other person of eighteen or over in loco parentis. In particular, persons under sixteen should not be asked for views on matters likely to be beyond their capacity to answer properly without such consent.

7.5 In the case of persons over sixteen who are not in a position to give consent, a person of eighteen or over with primary responsibility for their care should normally give it on their behalf. In particular, persons not in a position to give consent should not be asked for views on matters likely to be beyond their capacity to answer properly without such consent.

7.6 When a programme is edited, contributions should be represented fairly.

7.7 Guarantees given to contributors, for example relating to the content of a programme, confidentiality or anonymity, should normally be honoured.

7.8 Broadcasters should ensure that the re-use of material, i.e. use of material originally filmed or recorded for one purpose and then used in a programme for another purpose or used in a later or different programme, does not create unfairness. This applies both to material obtained from others and the broadcaster's own material.

Opportunity to contribute and proper consideration of facts

7.9 Before broadcasting a factual programme, including programmes examining past events, broadcasters should take reasonable care to satisfy themselves that:

- material facts have not been presented, disregarded or omitted in away that is unfair to an individual or organisation; and
- anyone whose omission could be unfair to an individual or organisation has been offered an opportunity to contribute.

7.10 Programmes – such as dramas and factually-based dramas – should not portray facts, events, individuals or organisations in a way which is unfair to an individual or organisation.

7.11 If a programme alleges wrongdoing or incompetence or makes other significant allegations, those concerned should normally be given an appropriate and timely opportunity to respond.

7.12 Where a person approached to contribute to a programme chooses to make no comment or refuses to appear in a broadcast, the broadcast should make clear that the individual concerned has chosen not to appear and should give their explanation if it would be unfair not to do so.

7.13 Where it is appropriate to represent the views of a person or organisation that is not participating in the programme, this must be done in a fair manner.

Deception, set-ups and 'wind-up' calls

7.14 Broadcasters or programme makers should not normally obtain or seek information, audio, pictures or an agreement to contribute through misrepresentation or deception. (Deception includes surreptitious filming or recording.) However:

- it may be warranted to use material obtained through misrepresentation or deception without consent if it is in the public interest and cannot reasonably be obtained by other means;
- where there is no adequate public interest justification, for example some unsolicited wind-up calls or entertainment set-ups, consent should be obtained from the individual and/or organisation concerned before the material is broadcast;
- if the individual and/or organisation is/are not identifiable in the programme then consent for broadcast will not be required;
- material involving celebrities and those in the public eye can be used without consent for broadcast, but it should not be used without a public interest justification if it is likely to result in unjustified public ridicule or personal distress. (Normally, therefore such contributions should be pre-recorded.)

(See "practices to be followed" 8.11 to 8.15 in Section Eight: Privacy.)

OFCOM BROADCASTING
CODE SECTION 8: PRIVACY

(Relevant legislation includes, in particular, sections 3(2)(f) and 326 of the Communications Act 2003, sections 107(1) and 130 of the Broadcasting Act 1996 (as amended), and Articles 8 and 10 of the European Convention on Human Rights.)

Foreword

This section and the preceding section on fairness are different from other sections of the Code. They apply to how broadcasters treat the individuals or organizations directly affected by programmes, rather than to what the general public sees and/or hears as viewers and listeners.

As well as containing a principle and a rule this section contains "practices to be followed" by broadcasters when dealing with individuals or organisations participating or otherwise directly affected by programmes, or in the making of programmes. Following these practices will not necessarily avoid a breach of this section of the Code (Rule 8.1). *However, failure to follow these practises will only constitute a breach where it results in an unwarranted infringement of privacy.* Importantly, the Code does not and cannot seek to set out all the "practices to be followed" in order to avoid an unwarranted infringement of privacy.

The Broadcasting Act 1996 (as amended) requires Ofcom to consider complaints about unwarranted infringement of privacy in a programme or in connection with the obtaining of material included in a programme. This may call for some difficult on-the-spot judgments about whether privacy is unwarrantably infringed by filming or recording, especially when reporting on emergency situations ("practices to be followed" 8.5 to 8.8 and 8.16 to 8.19). We recognise there may be a strong public interest in reporting on an emergency situation as it occurs and we understand there may be pressures on broadcasters at the scene of a disaster or emergency that may make it difficult to judge at the time whether filming or recording is an unwarrantable infringement of privacy. These are factors Ofcom will take into account when adjudicating on complaints.

Where consent is referred to in Section Eight it refers to informed consent.

Please see "practice to be followed" 7.3 in Section Seven: Fairness.

Principle

To ensure that broadcasters avoid any unwarranted infringement of privacy in programmes and in connection with obtaining material included in programmes.

Rule

8.1 Any infringement of privacy in programmes, or in connection with obtaining material included in programmes, must be warranted.

Meaning of "warranted":
In this section "warranted" has a particular meaning. It means that where broadcasters wish to justify an infringement of privacy as warranted, they should be able to demonstrate why in the particular circumstances of the case, it is warranted. If the reason is that it is in the public interest, then the broadcaster should be able to demonstrate that the public interest outweighs the right to privacy. Examples of public interest would include revealing or detecting crime, protecting public health or safety, exposing misleading

claims made by individuals or organisations or disclosing incompetence that affects the public.

Practices to be followed (8.2 to 8.22)
Private lives, public places and legitimate expectation of privacy

Meaning of "legitimate expectation of privacy":
Legitimate expectations of privacy will vary according to the place and nature of the information, activity or condition in question, the extent to which it is in the public domain (if at all) and whether the individual concerned is already in the public eye. There may be circumstances where people can reasonably expect privacy even in a public place. Some activities and conditions may be of such a private nature that filming or recording, even in a public place, could involve an infringement of privacy. People under investigation or in the public eye, and their immediate family and friends, retain the right to a private life, although private behaviour can raise issues of legitimate public interest.

8.2 Information which discloses the location of a person's home or family should not be revealed without permission, unless it is warranted.
8.3 When people are caught up in events which are covered by the news they still have a right to privacy in both the making and the broadcast of a programme, unless it is warranted to infringe it. This applies both to the time when these events are taking place and to any later programmes that revisit those events.
8.4 Broadcasters should ensure that words, images or actions filmed or recorded in, or broadcast from, a public place, are not so private that prior consent is required before broadcast from the individual or organisation concerned, unless broadcasting without their consent is warranted.

Consent

8.5 Any infringement of privacy in the making of a programme should be with the person's and/or organisation's consent or be otherwise warranted.
8.6 If the broadcast of a programme would infringe the privacy of a person or organisation, consent should be obtained before the relevant material is broadcast, unless the infringement of privacy is warranted. (Callers to phone-in shows are deemed to have given consent to the broadcast of their contribution.)
8.7 If an individual or organisation's privacy is being infringed, and they ask that the filming, recording or live broadcast be stopped, the broadcaster should do so, unless it is warranted to continue.
8.8 When filming or recording in institutions, organisations or other agencies, permission should be obtained from the relevant authority or management, unless it is warranted to film or record without permission. Individual consent of employees or others whose appearance is incidental or where they are essentially anonymous members of the general public will not normally be required.

- However, in potentially sensitive places such as ambulances, hospitals, Schools, prisons or police stations, separate consent should normally be obtained before filming or recording and for broadcast from those in sensitive situations (unless not obtaining consent is warranted). If the individual will not be identifiable in the programme then separate consent for broadcast will not be required.

Gathering information, sound or images and the re-use of material

8.9 The means of obtaining material must be proportionate in all the circumstances and in particular to the subject matter of the programme.
8.10 Broadcasters should ensure that the re-use of material, i.e. use of material originally filmed or recorded for one purpose and then used in a programme for another purpose or used in a later or different programme, does not create an unwarranted infringement of privacy. This applies both to material obtained from others and the broadcaster's own material.
8.11 Doorstepping for factual programmes should not take place unless a request for an interview has been refused or it has not been possible to request an interview, or

there is good reason to believe that an investigation will be frustrated if the subject is approached openly, and it is warranted to doorstep. However, normally broadcasters may, without prior warning interview, film or record people in the news when in public places.
(See "practice to be followed" 8.15.)

Meaning of "doorstepping":
Doorstepping is the filming or recording of an interview or attempted interview with someone, or announcing that a call is being filmed or recorded for broadcast purposes, without any prior warning. It does not, however, include vox-pops (sampling the views of random members of the public).

8.12 Broadcasters can record telephone calls between the broadcaster and the other party if they have, from the outset of the call, identified themselves, explained the purpose of the call and that the call is being recorded for possible broadcast (if that is the case) unless it is warranted not to do one or more of these practices. If at a later stage it becomes clear that a call that has been recorded will be broadcast (but this was not explained to the other party at the time of the call) then the broadcaster must obtain consent before broadcast from the other party, unless it is warranted not to do so. (See "practices to be followed" 7.14 and 8.13 to 8.15.)

8.13 Surreptitious filming or recording should only be used where it is warranted. Normally, it will only be warranted if:

• There is *prima facie* evidence of a story in the public interest; and
• There are reasonable grounds to suspect that further material evidence could be obtained; and
• it is necessary to the credibility and authenticity of the programme.
(See "practices to be followed" 7.14, 8.12, 8.14 and 8.15.)

Meaning of "surreptitious filming or recording":
Surreptitious filming or recording includes the use of long lenses or recording devices, as well as leaving an unattended camera or recording device on private property without the full and informed consent of the occupiers or their agent. It may also include recording telephone conversations without the knowledge of the other party, or deliberately continuing a recording when the other party thinks that it has come to an end.

8.14 Material gained by surreptitious filming and recording should only be broadcast when it is warranted. (See also "practices to be followed" 7.14 and 8.12 to 8.13 and 8.15.)

8.15 Surreptitious filming or recording, doorstepping or recorded 'wind-up' calls to obtain material for entertainment purposes may be warranted if it is intrinsic to the entertainment and does not amount to a significant infringement of privacy such as to cause significant annoyance, distress or embarrassment. The resulting material should not be broadcast without the consent of those involved. However if the individual and/or organisation is not identifiable in the programme then consent for broadcast will not be required.
(See "practices to be followed" 7.14 and 8.11 to 8.14.)

Suffering and distress

8.16 Broadcasters should not take or broadcast footage or audio of people caught up in emergencies, victims of accidents or those suffering a personal tragedy, even in a public place, where that results in an infringement of privacy, unless it is warranted or the people concerned have given consent.

8.17 People in a state of distress should not be put under pressure to take part in a programme or provide interviews, unless it is warranted.

8.18 Broadcasters should take care not to reveal the identity of a person who has died or of victims of accidents or violent crimes, unless and until it is clear that the next of kin have been informed of the event or unless it is warranted.

8.19 Broadcasters should try to reduce the potential distress to victims and/or relatives when making or broadcasting programmes intended to examine past events that involve trauma to individuals (including crime) unless it is warranted to do otherwise. This applies to dramatic reconstructions and factual dramas, as well as factual programmes.

- In particular, so far as is reasonably practicable, surviving victims and/or the immediate families of those whose experience is to feature in a programme, should be informed of the plans for the programme and its intended broadcast, even if the events or material to be broadcast have been in the public domain in the past.

People under sixteen and vulnerable people

8.20 Broadcasters should pay particular attention to the privacy of people under sixteen. They do not lose their rights to privacy because, for example, of the fame or notoriety of their parents or because of events in their schools.

8.21 Where a programme features an individual under sixteen or a vulnerable person in a way that infringes privacy, consent must be obtained from:

- A parent, guardian or other person of eighteen or over in loco parentis; and
- wherever possible, the individual concerned;
- unless the subject matter is trivial or uncontroversial and the participation minor, or it is warranted to proceed without consent.

8.22 Persons under sixteen and vulnerable people should not be questioned about private matters without the consent of a parent, guardian or other person of eighteen or over *in loco parentis* (in the case of persons under sixteen), or a person with primary responsibility for their care (in the case of a vulnerable person), unless it is warranted to proceed without consent.

Meaning of "vulnerable people":
This varies, but may include those with learning difficulties, those with mental health problems, the bereaved, people with brain damage or forms of dementia, people who have been traumatised or who are sick or terminally ill.

APPENDIX 6

PRESS COMPLAINTS COMMISSION

Editors' Code of Practice

This is the newspaper and periodical industry's Code of Practice. It is framed and revised by the Editors' Code Committee made up of independent editors of national, regional and local newspapers and magazines. The Press Complaints Commission, which has a majority of lay members, is charged with enforcing the Code, using it to adjudicate complaints. It was ratified by the PCC on the 7 August 2006. Clauses marked* are covered by exceptions relating to the public interest.

The Code

All members of the press have a duty to maintain the highest professional standards. This Code sets the benchmark for those ethical standards, protecting both the rights of the individual and the public's right to know. It is the cornerstone of the system of self-regulation to which the industry has made a binding commitment.

It is essential that an agreed code be honoured not only to the letter but in the full spirit. It should not be interpreted so narrowly as to compromise its commitment to respect the rights of the individual, nor so broadly that it constitutes an unnecessary interference with freedom of expression or prevents publication in the public interest.

It is the responsibility of editors and publishers to implement the Code and they should take care to ensure it is observed rigorously by all editorial staff and external contributors, including non-journalists, in printed and online versions of publications.

Editors should co-operate swiftly with the PCC in the resolution of complaints. Any publication judged to have breached the Code must print the adjudication in full and with due prominence, including headline reference to the PCC.

1 Accuracy

i. The press must take care not to publish inaccurate, misleading or distorted information, including pictures.
ii. A significant inaccuracy, misleading statement or distortion once recognized must be corrected, promptly and with due prominence, and – where appropriate – an apology published.
iii. The press, whilst free to be partisan, must distinguish clearly between comment, conjecture and fact.
iv. A publication must report fairly and accurately the outcome of an action for defamation to which it has been a party, unless an agreed settlement states otherwise, or an agreed statement is published.

2 Opportunity to reply

A fair opportunity for reply to inaccuracies must be given when reasonably called for.

3* Privacy

i. Everyone is entitled to respect for his or her private and family life, home, health and correspondence, including digital communications. Editors will be expected to justify intrusions into any individual's private life without consent.

ii. It is unacceptable to photograph individuals in a private place without their consent.
Note – Private places are public or private property where there is a reasonable expectation of privacy.

4* Harassment

i.   Journalists must not engage in intimidation, harassment or persistent pursuit.
ii. They must not persist in questioning, telephoning, pursuing or photographing individuals once asked to desist; nor remain on their property when asked to leave and must not follow them.
iii. Editors must ensure these principles are observed by those working for them and take care not to use non-compliant material from other sources.

5 Intrusion into grief or shock

i.   In cases involving personal grief or shock, enquiries and approaches must be made with sympathy and discretion and publication handled sensitively. This should not restrict the right to report legal proceedings, such as inquests.
*ii. When reporting suicide, care should be taken to avoid excessive detail about the method used.

6* Children

i.   Young people should be free to complete their time at school without unnecessary intrusion.
ii. A child under 16 must not be interviewed or photographed on issues involving their own or another child's welfare unless a custodial parent or similarly responsible adult consents.
iii. Pupils must not be approached or photographed at school without the permission of the school authorities.
iv. Minors must not be paid for material involving children's welfare, nor parents or guardians for material about their children or wards, unless it is clearly in the child's interest.
v.   Editors must not use the fame, notoriety or position of a parent or guardian as sole justification for publishing details of a child's private life.

7* Children in sex cases

1   The press must not, even if legally free to do so, identify children under 16 who are victims or witnesses in cases involving sex offences.
2   In any press report of a case involving a sexual offence against a child—
    i.   The child must not be identified.
    ii. The adult may be identified.
    iii. The word "incest" must not be used where a child victim might be identified.
    iv. Care must be taken that nothing in the report implies the relationship between the accused and the child.

8* Hospitals

i   Journalists must identify themselves and obtain permission from a responsible executive before entering non-public areas of hospitals or similar institutions to pursue enquiries.
ii   The restrictions on intruding into privacy are particularly relevant to enquiries about individuals in hospitals or similar institutions.

9* Reporting of Crime

    i   Relatives or friends of persons convicted or accused of crime should not generally be identified without their consent, unless they are genuinely relevant to the story.

    ii   Particular regard should be paid to the potentially vulnerable position of children who witness, or are victims of, crime. This should not restrict the right to report legal proceedings.

10* Clandestine devices and subterfuge

    i   The press must not seek to obtain or publish material acquired by using hidden cameras or clandestine listening devices; or by intercepting private or mobile telephone calls, messages or emails; or by the unauthorized removal of documents or photographs.

    ii   Engaging in misrepresentation or subterfuge can generally be justified only in the public interest and then only when the material cannot be obtained by other means.

11 Victims of sexual assault

The press must not identify victims of sexual assault or publish material likely to contribute to such identification unless there is adequate justification and they are legally free to do so.

12 Discrimination

    i   The press must avoid prejudicial or pejorative reference to an individual's race, colour, religion, gender, sexual orientation or to any physical or mental illness or disability.

    ii   Details of an individual's race, colour, religion, sexual orientation, physical or mental illness or disability must be avoided unless genuinely relevant to the story.

13 Financial journalism

    i.   Even where the law does not prohibit it, journalists must not use for their own profit financial information they receive in advance of its general publication, nor should they pass such information to others.

    ii.   They must not write about shares or securities in whose performance they know that they or their close families have a significant financial interest without disclosing the interest to the editor or financial editor.

    iii. They must not buy or sell, either directly or through nominees or agents, shares or securities about which they have written recently or about which they intend to write in the near future.

14 Confidential sources

Journalists have a moral obligation to protect confidential sources of information.

15 Witness payments in criminal trials

    i.   No payment or offer of payment to a witness—or any person who may reasonably be expected to be called as a witness—should be made in any case once proceedings are active as defined by the Contempt of Court Act 1981. This prohibition lasts until the suspect has been freed unconditionally by police without charge or bail or the proceedings are otherwise discontinued; or has entered a guilty plea to the court; or, in the event of a not guilty plea, the court has announced its verdict.

  *ii.   Where proceedings are not yet active but are likely and foreseeable, offer payment to any person who may reasonably be expected to be called as a witness, unless the information concerned ought demonstrably to be published in the public interest and there is an over-riding need to make or promise payment for this to be done; and all reasonable steps have been taken to ensure no financial dealings influence the evidence those witnesses give. In no circumstances should such payment be conditional on the outcome of a trial.

*iii. Any payment or offer of payment made to a person later cited to give evidence in proceedings must be disclosed to the prosecution and defence. The witness must be advised of this requirement.

16* Payment to criminals

i. Payment or offers of payment for stories, pictures or information, which seek to exploit a particular crime or to glorify or glamorise crime in general, must not be made directly or via agents to convicted or confessed criminals or to their associates—who may include family, friends and colleagues.

ii. Editors invoking the public interest to justify payment or offers would need to demonstrate that there was good reason to believe the public interest would be served. If, despite payment, no public interest emerged, then the material should not be published.

The public interest
There may be exceptions to the clauses marked * where they can be demonstrated to be in the public interest.

1 The public interest includes, but is not confined to:
　i Detecting or exposing crime or serious impropriety.
　ii Protecting public health and safety.
　iii Preventing the public from being misled by an action or statement of an individual or organisation.

2 There is a public interest in freedom of expression itself.
3 Whenever the public interest is invoked, the PCC will require editors to demonstrate fully how the public interest was served.
4 The PCC will consider the extent to which material is already in the public domain, or will become so.
5 In cases involving children under 16, editors must demonstrate an exceptional public interest to over-ride the normally paramount interest of the child.

PCC Guidance Notes

Court Reporting (1994)
Reporting of international sporting events (1998)
Prince William and privacy (1999)
On the reporting cases involving paedophiles (2000)
The Judiciary and harassment (2003)
Refugees and Asylum Seekers (2003)
Lottery Guidance Note (2004)
On the reporting of people accused of crime (2004)
Data Protection Act, Journalism and the PCC Code (2005)
Editorial co-operation (2005)
Financial Journalism: Best Practice Note (2005)
On the reporting of mental health issues (2006)
Copies of the above can be obtained online at **www.pcc.org.uk**
Press Complaints Commission
Halton House, 20/23 Holborn, London EC1N 2JD
Telephone: 020 7831 0022 Fax: 020 7831 0025
Textphone: 020 7831 0123 (for deaf or hard of hearing people)
Helpline: 0845 600 2757

PRESS COMPLAINTS COMMISSION REPORT ON SUBTERFUGE AND NEWSGATHERING, 2007

1.0 Introduction

1.1 The Press Complaints Commission has conducted an investigation into the use of subterfuge by the British newspaper and magazine industry, with particular reference to phone message tapping and compliance with the Editors' Code of Practice and the Data Protection Act.

1.2 The inquiry followed the convictions in January 2007 of News of the World journalist Clive Goodman and inquiry agent Glenn Mulcaire for offences under the Regulation of Investigatory Powers Act 2000 (RIPA) and Criminal Law Act (1977). They had speculatively tapped into private mobile phone messages and used the information they discovered for stories in the News of the World.

1.3 This type of snooping has no place in journalism, and the Chairman of the Commission has publicly deplored it on a number of occasions. The Commission as a whole condemns such behaviour.

1.4 Despite the police inquiry, court case and convictions, the Commission considered that there were a number of outstanding questions that arose under the Code of Practice, which sets out the required professional standards for UK journalists and, as such, supplements the law. Last November, before the verdict was reached, the Chairman of the PCC had already put the then editor of the News of the World, Mr Andy Coulson, on notice that, depending on the outcome of the trial, the PCC might wish to pursue matters with him.

1.5 On January 26 2007, Mulcaire and Goodman were sentenced to 6 and 4 months in prison. Mr Coulson resigned his post, saying that he had "decided that the time has come for me to take ultimate responsibility for the events around the Clive Goodman case". Mr Colin Myler was appointed editor in his place.

1.6 Despite Mr Myler's appointment, the question arose whether the PCC should ask Mr Coulson to give an account of what had gone wrong. The PCC decided not to do so. Given that the PCC does not - and should not - have statutory powers of investigation and prosecution, there could be no question of trying to duplicate the lengthy police investigation. Furthermore, Mr Coulson was, following his resignation, no longer answerable to the PCC, whose jurisdiction covers journalists working for publications that subscribe to the self-regulatory system through the Press Standards Board of Finance.

1.7 As a result, that part of the investigation involving the News of the World was conducted by the Director of the PCC with Mr Myler. The Chairman of the Commission also discussed the matter on a number of occasions with the Chief Executive of News International, Mr Les Hinton.

1.8 In a statement on 1st February 2007, the Commission said that "the public has a right to know that lessons have been learned from this episode, both at the newspaper and more generally". It announced that it would be:

- Writing to the new editor of the newspaper for detailed information on what had gone wrong and to find out what steps would be taken to ensure that the situation did not recur;
- Conducting a broad inquiry across the whole of the press to find out the extent of internal controls aimed at preventing similar abuses;
- Publishing its findings.

1.9   There was a further point for consideration. The arrests and conviction of Mulcaire and Goodman coincided with a campaign by the Information Commissioner to raise awareness of the terms of the Data Protection Act, which applies to journalists but which also contains an exemption for some journalistic activity. The Information Commissioner was concerned that information provided to journalists by inquiry agents had been obtained by "blagging" or bribery in breach of the Act.

1.10 As part of its inquiry, the Commission therefore also asked the industry what was being done to raise awareness of the Data Protection Act, including its public interest defences.

1.11 In its approach to this matter, the Commission has also been concerned not to obscure or undermine the legitimate role of subterfuge in journalism that is in the public interest.

1.12 This report is therefore concerned with two main subjects: events at the News of the World in relation to Clive Goodman and Glenn Mulcaire, how the situation developed and how repetition will be avoided; and what the industry as a whole is doing to ensure that lessons have been learned from this incident so that British journalism is not brought into similar disrepute in the future.

2.0   The News of the World inquiry

2.1   Clive Goodman was a full time member of staff at the News of the World. The court heard that Glenn Mulcaire was an inquiry agent who was paid a retainer of £104,988 per annum by the newspaper. The court also heard that he had received £12,300 in cash from Clive Goodman.

2.2   The Director of the Commission wrote to the new editor of the News of the World, Colin Myler, on 7th February 2007. He said that the Commission had been especially concerned whether the employment of Mr Mulcaire represented an attempt to circumvent the provisions of the Code by sub-contracting investigative work to a third party. There are no loopholes in the Code in this regard, which says that "editors should take care to ensure it is observed rigorously by all editorial staff and external contributors, including non-journalists".

2.3   The Commission asked a number of questions with regard to the Mulcaire and Goodman situation and also what the newspaper proposed to do to ensure that it would not happen again.

2.4   With regard to Goodman specifically, the PCC said that it seemed from the evidence submitted to the court that he had repeatedly breached the Code as well as the law. The Commission therefore required the clearest reassurance that the paper made its staff journalists fully aware of the requirements of the Code and the law with regard to subterfuge, including when it would be justified.

2.5   The Commission informed the newspaper that it would be broadening its inquiry to involve the industry at large. It invited the News of the World to make any points, based on its experience and understanding of what went wrong, that might be helpful in this context.

3.0   The News of the World response

3.1   The editor, Mr Myler, replied to the Commission on the 22nd February. He described how the situation with Goodman and Mulcaire had developed and detailed what action was now being taken to minimise the chances of repetition. He urged the Commission to see the episode in perspective as it represented "an exceptional and unhappy event in the 163 year history of the News of the World, involving one journalist". Moreover, two people had been sent to prison, Goodman had been dismissed from the paper and the previous editor had resigned.

3.2 He emphasised the newspaper's commitment to the Code of Practice, drawing attention, by way of example, to an episode where a reporter had been dismissed for breaching its terms. He said that "every single News of the World journalist is conversant with the Code and appreciates fully the necessity of total compliance".

4.0 Goodman and Mulcaire

4.1 The editor told the Commission that it was important to distinguish between the aberrational Goodman/Mulcaire episode which resulted in the prosecutions and the paper's day to day contract with Mulcaire. It had emerged during the trial that Mulcaire had been paid a retainer by the newspaper. The editor confirmed to the Commission that this had been for £2,019 per week. Cash payments of £12,300 from Goodman to Mulcaire were in addition to this.

4.2 Because of the convictions, questions had been raised about the nature of the services provided by Mulcaire for which he was paid almost £105k per annum. The editor told the Commission that there had been a 'great deal of inaccurate media speculation' concerning this contract. In fact, the work was entirely 'legal and legitimate'. The police had thoroughly investigated the retainer, and the prosecution had made clear to the judge that they were not suggesting that the retainer agreement involved anything illegal. This had been accepted by the judge.

4.3 The editor accepted that the retainer paid to Mulcaire may have seemed 'substantial', but argued that the cost to the paper would have been much greater had the work been contracted out on an ad hoc basis. He contended that Mulcaire's hourly rate probably averaged less than £50. The editor added that there was nothing unusual about the employment of outside investigators; and that the practice was shared by solicitors, insurance companies, banks and many commercial organisations as well as newspapers.

4.4 The editor told the Commission what services Mulcaire provided. They were: gathering facts for stories and analysing the extent of the paper's proof before publication; confirming facts and suggesting strategies; credit status checks; Land Registry checks; directorship searches and analysis of businesses and individuals; tracing individuals from virtually no biographical details, including date of birth searches, electoral roll searches and checks through databases; County Court searches and analysis of court records; surveillance; specialist crime advice; professional football knowledge (Mulcaire was a former professional footballer); contacts in the sports and show business worlds; and analysis of documents and handwriting.

4.5 The editor hoped that it would be clear from this evidence that Mulcaire was not employed by the newspaper in order to circumvent the provisions of the Code, but to carry out legitimate investigative work.

4.6 But Mulcaire had a second, clandestine relationship with the paper through Clive Goodman. This was described to the Commission as a 'direct and personal' relationship, and involved cash payments amounting to £12,300 between November 2005 and August 2006, when the arrests took place.

4.7 Questions have been raised about how the newspaper could have allowed such payments to have been made, and whether anyone else at the newspaper was aware of Mulcaire and Goodman's illegal activities, which also breached the terms of the Code. The editor told the Commission that the paper has a standing policy on cash payments and transparency, something that was reiterated in a written memo to department heads and senior staff in 2005, and repeated at the start of 2006. Goodman was aware of this.

4.8 Despite this, the Commission was told that Goodman deceived his employers by disguising Mulcaire's identity and hiding the true origin of the information. Goodman claimed that the payments were for a confidential source on royal stories, identified only as 'Alexander'.

4.9 The Commission heard that "the identity of that source and the fact that the arrangement involved illegally accessing telephone voice mails was completely unknown and, indeed, deliberately concealed from all at the News of the World". The editor added in his submission that "it was made clear at the sentencing hearing that both the prosecution and the judge accepted that".

5.0 Action to prevent repetition

5.1 As to the Commission's questions about what would be done to avoid a repetition of the incident, the editor said that a number of steps were being taken.

5.2 With regard to external contributors, he had written to them to emphasise the absolute requirement that they abide by the Code and the law. The editor supplied the Commission with a sample copy of the letter that had been sent. In it, the editor set out to contributors that their contracts would now include 'a clause robustly reflecting [the paper's] fundamental commitment to the letter and spirit of the Code'.

5.3 The clause reads:

"The Contributor agrees that it is the Contributor's responsibility to review the Standards [the News Corporation Standards of Business], details of applicable rules, policies and procedures and the Code of Practice. The Contributor acknowledges that the Standards, such rules, policies and procedures and the Code of Practice may change or be updated from time to time and that these changes or updates will be notified to him or her by the Company from time to time. The Contributor agrees that, having been so notified by the Company, it is the Contributor's absolute responsibility to ensure that he or she is conversant with any such changes and updates and to observe them fully.

"The Contributor understands and accepts that failure to comply with the requirements of this clause may lead to termination of the contract".

5.4 With regard to staff journalists, the editor told the Commission that it had long been the practice of the paper "to make clear to staff the importance of fundamental observance of the Code, with emphasis on the fact that the use of third parties to circumvent the Code is unacceptable and may be illegal". The editor told the Commission that, in light of this, the Goodman case appeared to have been a 'rogue exception'.

5.5 The editor said that, following Goodman's conviction, he had e-mailed every member of staff individually, and written to them at home, with the Code of Practice. Staff had been informed of a new clause in their contracts, replacing a long-standing one which had said that "the employer endorses the Press Complaints Commission Code of Practice and requires the employee to observe the terms of the Code as a condition of his employment".

5.6 The new clause states:

"The employee agrees to comply in full with the News Corporation Standards of Business Conduct (the "Standards") and all other applicable rules, policies and procedures of the Company and its Associated Companies including News Group Newspapers, and the Press Complaints Commission Code of Practice (the "Code of Practice") which are included herewith and are available on the News International intranet and on the PCC website.

"The employee agrees that it is the employee's responsibility to review the Standards, details of applicable rules, policies and procedures and the Code of Practice. The employee acknowledges that the Standards, such rules, policies and procedures and the Code of Practice may change or be updated from time to time and further agrees that it is the employee's absolute responsibility to ensure that he or she is aware of any such changes or updates. The employer is responsible for notifying the employee of any such changes and/or updates. The employee agrees that having been notified by the employer it is the employee's absolute responsibility to ensure that he or she is conversant with any such changes and updates and undertakes to observe them fully.

"The employee understands and accepts that failure to comply with the requirements of this clause will lead to Disciplinary Proceedings which may result in summary dismissal".

5.7 With regard to cash payments, the editor had written to all members of staff to reiterate the paper's clear policy on cash payments: "they are only permitted in exceptional circumstances. Every such payment requires a compelling justification and must be fully recorded".

5.8 In response to questions from the Commission about what further controls on cash payments were being developed, the editor said that the following protocol and policy was now in place:

- Cash payments are to be kept to a minimum and regarded as the exception;
- Requests for cash payments must be accompanied by a compelling and detailed justification signed off by the relevant department head;
- Information supplied on Cash Payment Request documents must be accurate and comprehensive;
- In the exceptional event of a requirement for a cash payment to a confidential source, the following would apply:
  1. If the department head/staff member requesting the payment asserts that the identity of the source must be withheld, he/she is required to demonstrate clear and convincing justification for such confidentiality;
  2. A memo detailing the reason for making the payment to a confidential source has to be provided to the Managing Editor's office.
- Every cash payment request must be signed off by the relevant Department Head;
- Details of the intended recipient's name and address are then verified via the electoral register/other checks to establish that they are genuine;
- Any journalist requesting a cash payment is required personally to endorse, with their signature, each page of the relevant documentation;
- Each request for a cash payment must be accompanied by the appropriate supporting documentation with a copy of the relevant story attached.

5.9 Turning then to the question of continuous professional training for his staff, the editor told the Commission that the paper had conducted a regular training programme in legal and PCC issues for some time. The latest series, starting on 20th February 2007, would focus on undercover journalism and its ethical and legal dimensions in light of the Goodman case; and highlight the requirements of the Regulation of Investigatory Powers Act, the Data Protection Act, the Computer Misuse Act and the PCC Code. For the first time, a representative of the PCC would attend and address each seminar. Attendance by staff would be mandatory.

6.0 The Commission's findings

6.1 The offences for which Goodman and Mulcaire were convicted were deplorable. Members of the Commission deprecated what had happened. The Commission has always made clear that subterfuge is justifiable only when there are grounds in the public interest for using it. Undercover investigative work has an honourable tradition and plays a vital role in exposing wrongdoing. It is part of an open society. But it risks being devalued if its use cannot be justified in the public interest.

6.2 In this case Mulcaire and Goodman paid a high price for their breach of the law (and in Goodman's case of the Code of Practice as well). They were sent to prison. Goodman, who had compliance with the Code written into his contract of employment, was dismissed from the News of the World. The editor left his post. The case attracted a large amount of negative publicity.

6.3   No evidence has emerged either from the legal proceedings or the Commission's questions to Mr Myler and Mr Hinton of a conspiracy at the newspaper going beyond Messrs Goodman and Mulcaire to subvert the law and the PCC's Code of Practice. There is no evidence to challenge Mr Myler's assertion that: Goodman had deceived his employer in order to obtain cash to pay Mulcaire; that he had concealed the identity of the source of information on royal stories; and that no-one else at the News of the World knew that Messrs Goodman and Mulcaire were tapping phone messages for stories.

6.4   However, internal controls at the newspaper were clearly inadequate for the purpose of identifying the deception.

6.5   It was therefore right for the new editor to introduce a series of measures aimed at preventing repetition. These included: a revised contractual relationship with external contributors and staff members, with a new and robust reference to the Code, including a reminder that failure to comply with it could result in dismissal; a review of the policy on cash payments, and a reminder to staff about the current approach; and a renewed programme of mandatory training seminars aimed at raising awareness of the Code and the law. Commission officials have now completed seven 2 ½ hour seminars on undercover investigations and the Code of Practice at the paper.

6.6   The Commission endorses this approach and welcomes the seriousness with which the editor and the company evidently take this matter. The review that the newspaper carried out has, in the Commission's view, thrown up examples of good practice – in particular in relation to the new reference in contracts to compliance with the Code of Practice, the new arrangements with external contributors, and the initiative of inviting Commission staff to help with the training seminars. The Commission also welcomed the tighter internal controls on cash payments.

6.7   The Commission's role here has been additional to the law, which has already investigated, prosecuted and punished the people responsible for the phone message tapping. The Commission has a duty to promote high professional standards and to hold editors responsible for the implementation of the Code on their publications by editorial staff and external contributors. It has ensured that the background to the episode, and the solutions that the newspaper proposed, would be ventilated publicly and be subject to scrutiny. Journalists and contributors to the newspaper can now be in no doubt of the serious consequences that will arise if there is any repeat of this highly regrettable incident.

7.0   Wider inquiry

7.1   The convictions of Mulcaire and Goodman raised questions about press practice in this area generally, and threatened to undermine confidence in journalism. The Commission believes that the public has a right to be reassured that this behaviour is not tolerated and that other publications have learned the lessons from what went on and have sufficient internal controls to prevent something similar happening elsewhere.

7.2   The Director of the Commission wrote to newspaper and magazine editors, with copies to their managements, to inquire about the extent of internal controls and what they did with regard to educating journalists about the requirements both of the Code and the law. The Data Protection Act was highlighted. The Commission wrote directly to national newspapers and to magazine companies. It was grateful to the Newspaper Society for disseminating the questions through the regional press.

7.3   The Commission received a large number of responses, which contained a varying degree of detail. Some simply told the Commission that they did not and would not engage in telephone message tapping. Others went into some detail about the various measures that were in place at their publications to ensure compliance with the Code and the law. Perhaps understandably, the Commission received greater detail from the national press than the regional press.

8.0   Current practice

8.1   There were a number of instances of good practice. Contractual compliance with the Code of Practice is widespread, with further references to the necessity to abide by its requirements to be found in staff handbooks, and in regular internal reminders to journalists – both written and during meetings with heads of departments. Many newspapers told the Commission that the Code of Practice was available on the company's intranet or that the editor wrote to journalists with copies when they joined the company or when the Code was updated.

8.2   Some publications also provided formal legal training for journalists or had updated their contracts with journalists to make explicit reference to the Data Protection Act.

8.3   There was a reference to the PCC's own series of training seminars for journalists which have, among other things, raised awareness of when the Commission considers subterfuge to be appropriate. Some publications had had, or planned, internal 'master classes' on particular issues to achieve similar results and update journalists on the legal position.

8.4   One company had a 'Review Group' of editors which reported to the Chief Executive on matters of editorial policy and which was responsible for raising awareness of the Code and the law among journalists across the company.

8.5   There was less specific feedback about the circumstances when subterfuge might be acceptable or how journalists would know when the public interest exceptions to the Data Protection Act might apply. There was an assumption that such occasions would be rare, and when it was referred to in the responses the Commission was told that journalists would be expected to consult with the publication's lawyers, editor or managing editor.

8.6   One newspaper told the Commission that, in addition to the internal controls that were in place, the threat of negative publicity along the lines of that experienced during the Goodman case would be a sufficient deterrent.

9.0   Data Protection Act

9.1   The Commission had specifically highlighted the DPA in its letter to the industry following the publication by the Information Commissioner of two reports titled *What price privacy?* and *What price privacy now?*

9.2   In those reports, the Information Commissioner published details of newspapers and magazines that had been paying inquiry agents for information. There was a suspicion that some of the information may have been obtained in breach of the Data Protection Act. The Information Commissioner called on the industry to bring forward proposals to clamp down on the illegal trade in information. He also called on the government to increase penalties for breaching the Act to two years' imprisonment. There would be no exemption from such a penalty for journalists.

9.3   The Commission condemns breaches of the DPA – or any law – when there are no grounds in the public interest for committing them. However, it has said before that it does not consider that the case for stronger penalties has been made out. Jailing – or threatening to jail – journalists for gathering information in the course of their professional duties is not a step to be taken lightly, and would send out a worrying message about the status of press freedom in the United Kingdom.

9.4   It seems to the Commission from the exercise it has just carried out that the DPA is taken seriously across the industry. As highlighted above, some companies have rewritten their journalists' contracts specifically to make reference to the DPA. Others had specific training on the Act. There were numerous references to the Information Commissioner's work.

9.5   The industry has also been working together to draw up a practical note for journalists on how the DPA works and applies to them.

10.0 Conclusions and recommendations

10.1 It is essential that the type of snooping revealed by the phone message tapping incidents at the News of the World is not repeated at any other newspaper or magazine. Such events threaten public confidence in the industry, despite the considerable change in culture and practice that has undoubtedly occurred over the last decade and a half, leading to greater accountability and respect by the press for the privacy of individuals.

10.2 But it is similarly important that the industry guards against overreaction. There is a legitimate place for the use of subterfuge when there are grounds in the public interest to use it and it is not possible to obtain information through other means. It would not be in the broader public interest for journalists to restrain themselves unnecessarily from using undercover means because of a false assumption that it is never acceptable.

10.3 This balance will be achieved when journalists are confident about where the line is drawn. The Commission welcomes the numerous initiatives that are underway to raise awareness of the Code's requirements on subterfuge and the law; and it endorses the decision by the industry to draw up guidelines on compliance with the Data Protection Act. These will complement those drawn up by the PCC itself in 2005.

10.4 The Commission believes very strongly that the impact of these initiatives should be assessed before the government proceeds with its proposals to increase the penalties for journalists who breach the DPA to two years in prison. Such a move would be difficult to reconcile with notions of press freedom. The mere threat of a custodial sentence could be enough to deter journalists from embarking on legitimate investigations, despite reassurances about the public interest exemption from the Information Commissioner.

10.5 As a result of this inquiry, the Commission has a number of specific recommendations, drawn from the News of the World episode and best practice around the UK. In particular:

- Contracts with external contributors should contain an explicit requirement to abide by the Code of Practice;
- A similar reference to the Data Protection Act should be included in contracts of employment;
- Publications should review internal practice to ensure that they have an effective and fully understood "subterfuge protocol" for staff journalists, which includes who should be consulted for advice about whether the public interest is sufficient to justify subterfuge;
- Although contractual compliance with the Code for staff journalists is widespread, it should without delay become universal across the industry (the PCC will be pursuing this further);
- There should be regular internal training and briefing on developments on privacy cases and compliance with the law;
- There should be rigorous audit controls for cash payments, where these are unavoidable.

10.6 The PCC recognises that it has a key role to play in assuring the high journalistic standards that are the cornerstone of a free press and a credible system of self-regulation. To that end, the Commission will continue to offer free training seminars to UK publications. It will invite all national newspapers to attend a seminar in July 2007 specifically on subterfuge and the public interest. It will continue its training courses for budding journalists around the UK. It will, increasingly, take part in and promote seminars and debates on the great issues surrounding freedom of expression and journalists' responsibilities in a digital age.

10.7 Finally, the industry, and the general public, should be in no doubt that the Commission will continue to take the severest view of any publication which uses inquiry agents to gather news in a manner that would otherwise breach the Code.

APPENDIX 8

REPORT OF THE HOUSE OF COMMONS CULTURE, MEDIA AND SPORT COMMITTEE ON PRESS STANDARDS, PRIVACY AND LIBEL, 2010

Summary

The UK is a country which values the freedom of its press to report and comment on events, public figures and institutions, to be critical of them and to be a platform for dissenting views. These are important freedoms which are not available in all countries. In return, the public expects that members of the UK press will uphold certain standards, be mindful of the rights of those who are written about, and, as far as possible, be accurate in what they report.

The current system of self-regulation of the press, under the auspices of the Press Complaints Commission (PCC), came into force in 1991, following the Calcutt inquiry of 1990. Since then there have been times when events have led the public and politicians to question the integrity of the methods used by the press, and the competence of the PCC as an industry regulator.

Our inquiry was primarily prompted by the persistent libelling by the UK press of the McCann family and others, following the disappearance of their daughter Madeleine in Portugal in May 2007, the limited intervention of the PCC and its failure to launch an inquiry into the industry's failings in the case. We also sought to address concerns that the operation of libel laws in England and Wales and the impact of costs were stifling press freedom in the UK, as well as considering the balance between personal privacy and press freedom.

This Report is the product of the longest, most complex and wide-ranging inquiry this Committee has undertaken. Our aim has been to arrive at recommendations that, if implemented, would help to restore the delicate balances associated with the freedom of the press. Individual proposals we make will have their critics - that is inevitable - but we are convinced that, taken together, our recommendations represent a constructive way forward for a free and healthy UK press in the years to come.

Privacy and breach of confidence
In this section we examine the case brought by Max Mosley against the News of the World, as well as considering other recent case law and the impact of injunctions and super-injunctions on freedom of speech. We also comment on the operation of the Human Rights Act, which incorporates the European Convention on Human Rights in UK law. The European Convention includes both the right to freedom of expression and the right to a private and family life, rights that must be balanced against each other.

That being the case, we make a number of recommendations designed to ensure that the balance between the two Convention rights is appropriate. We do not consider however that it would be right, at this time, to legislate on privacy. We rule out mandatory pre-notification. We recommend however that the PCC should amend its Code to include a requirement that journalists should normally notify the subject of their articles prior to publication, subject to a 'public interest' test, and should provide guidance for journalists and editors on pre-notifying in the Editors' Codebook. We also recommend that failure to pre-notify should be an aggravating factor in assessing damages. To balance this, we recommend the development of a fast track procedure for a final decision where an interim injunction banning publication of a story has been granted, or where a court refusal has been appealed.

We comment on the recent events surrounding the imposition of a 'super-injunction' obtained by Trafigura, a company trading in oil, base metals and other items, preventing the publication of a report on alleged dumping of toxic waste in the Ivory Coast, and subsequent debate over reporting of Parliamentary Questions relating to that report. We express our concern at the confusion over the level of protection provided to the reporting of Parliamentary proceedings by the Parliamentary Papers Act 1840 and recommend that these important elements of freedom of speech should be put beyond doubt through the enactment of a modern statute.

We also recommend that the Lord Chancellor and the Lord Chief Justice act on concerns regarding injunctions more generally in cases of both breach of privacy and confidence.

Libel and press freedom

In this section we focus on the operation of libel law in England and Wales and its impact on press reporting. We consider important recent cases and developments since the 1996 Defamation Act, including 'responsible journalism', the government's consultation on the issue of 'multiple publication' in the internet age and legislation to abolish criminal libel. We consider the fairness of the 'burden of proof' being on the defendant, but in relation to individuals conclude that in order to satisfy natural justice the defendant should still be required to provide the proof of his allegations. However, with regard to corporations and defamation, we recommend that the Government should consider reversing the general burden of proof.

We discuss the damage 'libel tourists' have caused to the UK's reputation as a country which protects free speech and freedom of expression, especially in the United States, where a number of states have enacted legislation to protect their citizens from the enforcement of libel settlements made in foreign jurisdictions. We also comment on bills currently before the US Congress which are designed to afford similar protections. We conclude that it is a humiliation for our system that the US legislators should feel the need to take steps to protect freedom of speech from what are seen as unreasonable incursions by our courts. We note that neither the Lord Chancellor nor his officials have sought to discuss the matter with their US counterparts, and urge that such discussions should take place as soon as possible. We further suggest that, in cases where the UK is not the primary domicile or place of business of the claimant or defendant, the claimant should face additional hurdles before being allowed to bring a case.

We consider whether the statute of limitations and the multiple publication rule are fit for purpose in the internet age, and recommend that the Government should introduce a time limitation of one year for defamation cases relating to publication on the internet, subject to the test of when the claimant could reasonably have been aware of the article's existence.

We welcome the Lord Chancellor's establishment of a 'Working Group on Libel' to consider reform of the defamation laws. We also urge the Government to consult further, in particular over placing a broadened defence of 'responsible journalism' on a statutory footing.

Costs

Throughout our inquiry we have been mindful of the over-arching concerns about the costs of mounting and defending libel actions, and the 'chilling effect' this may have on press freedom. The evidence we have heard leaves us in no doubt that there are problems which urgently need to be addressed in order to enable defamation litigation costs to be controlled more effectively. We find the suggestion that the problem confronting defendants, including media defendants, who wish to control their costs can be solved by settling cases more promptly to be an extraordinary one. If a defendant is in the right, he should not be forced into a settlement which entails him sacrificing justice on the grounds of cost.

All the evidence which we have received points to the fact that the vast majority of cases brought under a Conditional Fee Agreement (CFA) are won. We therefore see no justification for lawyers to continue to demand 100% success fees which are chargeable to the losing party. We recommend that the recovery of success fees from the losing party should be limited to no more than 10%, leaving the balance to be agreed between solicitor and client. We further recommend that the Government should make After the Event Insurance premiums irrecoverable.

Press standards
In this section we discuss press standards and the level of public confidence in the press, which we explore through two recent cases - Madeleine McCann's disappearance; and the suicides in and around Bridgend in 2008. We also consider the impact of the Guardian's revelations regarding phone-hacking and blagging - the practice of obtaining information through deception.

With regard to the McCanns we conclude that competitive and commercial factors led to an inexcusable lowering of standards in the gathering and publishing of "news" about the case. While the lack of official information clearly made reporting more difficult, we do not accept that it provided an excuse or justification for inaccurate, defamatory reporting. We conclude that in this case self-regulation signally failed.

We reopened oral evidence to consider the allegations contained in the Guardian in July 2009 that the News of the World's parent company had paid over £1m in damages and costs to settle three civil actions relating to phone-hacking. We took these claims very seriously as they cast doubt on assurances we had been given during our 2007 inquiry Privacy and media intrusion that the phone-hacking at News of the World had been limited to one 'rogue reporter', Clive Goodman.

We find that it is likely that the number of victims of illegal phone-hacking will never be known, not least because of the silence of Clive Goodman and Glenn Mulcaire, their confidentiality settlements with the News of the World and the 'collective amnesia' at the newspaper group which we encountered during our inquiry. It is certainly more than the 'handful', however, cited by both the newspaper and the police.

There is no doubt that there were a significant number of people whose voice messages were intercepted, most of whom would have been of little interest to Clive Goodman as the paper's royal editor. The evidence, we find, makes it inconceivable that no-one else at the News of the World, bar Mr Goodman, was aware of the activity. We have, however, not seen any evidence that the then Editor, Andy Coulson, knew, but consider he was right to resign. We find, however, that the newspaper group did not carry out a full and rigorous inquiry, as it assured us and the Press Complaints Commission it had. The circumstances of pay-offs made to Messrs Goodman and Mulcaire, as well as the civil settlements with Gordon Taylor and others, also invite the conclusion that silence was effectively bought.

The readiness of all concerned - News International, the police and the PCC - to leave Mr Goodman as the sole scapegoat without carrying out full investigations is striking. The verdict of the PCC's latest inquiry, announced last November, we consider to be simplistic, surprising and a further failure of self-regulation.

In seeking to discover precisely who knew what among the staff of the News of the World we have questioned a number of present and former executives of News International. Throughout we have repeatedly encountered an unwillingness to provide the detailed information that we sought, claims of ignorance or lack of recall, and deliberate obfuscation. We strongly condemn this behaviour which reinforces the widely held impression that the press generally regard themselves as unaccountable and that News International in particular has sought to conceal the truth about what really occurred.

Self-regulation of the press

Finally we consider the future viability of self-regulation of the press, and set out a considered programme of reform aimed at making regulation of the press in the UK more effective.

We recommend that the PCC should be renamed the Press Complaints and Standards Commission, reflecting its role as a regulator, not just a complaints handling service, and that it should appoint a deputy director for standards. We further recommend that the PCC should have the power to fine its members where it believes that the departure from the Code of Practice is serious enough to warrant a financial penalty, including, in the most serious of cases, suspending the printing of the offending publication for one issue.

In the future the PCC must also be more proactive in its work. If there are reasonable grounds to believe that coverage of a case means that serial breaches of the Code are being made or are likely to take place, then the PCC should not wait until a complaint is received before it investigates and makes contact with the parties involved. We suggest that a convenient test as to whether a proactive inquiry is appropriate might be that three lay members of the Commission had indicated to the Chairman that, in their view, a proactive inquiry would be in the public interest.

We suggest that the membership of the PCC should be rebalanced to give the lay members a two thirds majority, making it absolutely clear that the PCC is not overly influenced by the press, that there should be lay members of the Code Committee and that one of those lay members should be the Code Committee's Chairman.

We recognise that there must be some incentive for newspapers to subscribe to the self-regulatory system, and suggest that the Government should consider whether proposals to reduce the cost burden in defamation cases should only be made available to those publications which provide the public with an alternative route of redress through their membership of the PCC.

For full report see *http//www.publications.parliament.uk/pa/cm201011/cmselect/cmc4meds/ 352/35102.htm*

APPENDIX 9

EXAMPLE OF AN ANONYMISED INJUNCTION JUDGEMENT

Neutral Citation Number: [2011] EWCA Civ 439

Case No: A2/11/0569

IN THE SUPREME COURT OF JUDICATURE
COURT OF APPEAL (CIVIL DIVISION)
ON APPEAL FROM QUEEN'S BENCH DIVISION
MR JUSTICE COLLINS
HQ11D00848

Royal Courts of Justice
Strand, London, WC2A 2LL

Date: 19th April 2011

Before :

LORD JUSTICE WARD
LORD JUSTICE LAWS
and
LORD JUSTICE MOORE-BICK

- - - - - - - - - - - - - - - - - - - -

Between:

ETK	Appellant
- and -	
News Group Newspapers Ltd	Respondent

- - - - - - - - - - - - - - - - - - - -
- - - - - - - - - - - - - - - - - - - -

Mr Hugh Tomlinson QC (instructed by Schillings Solicitors) for the appellant
Mr Anthony Hudson (instructed by Farrer & Co) for the respondent

Hearing date: 10th March 2011
- - - - - - - - - - - - - - - - - - - -

Judgment

Lord Justice Ward:

1. On Saturday 5th March 2011 the applicant made an application on short notice to Collins J. to restrain News Group Newspapers Ltd, the publishers of the News of the World, from publishing or communicating or disclosing to any other person:

   "(a) any information concerning the facts of this case and the individuals involved (including, in particular, any information identifying or in any way tending to identify the Applicant as being the person who has applied for this order), save for that contained in this order and in any public judgment of the court given in this action;

   (b) any information concerning the fact or details of the sexual relationship between the Applicant (who is a male working in the entertainment industry) and the person named in the Confidential Schedule (who is a female working in the entertainment industry)."

2. Having heard the matter in private, Collins J. dismissed the application, refused permission to appeal but granted temporary relief in the terms set out above on the applicant's undertaking expeditiously to apply for permission to appeal. That was done, Sedley L.J. adjourning the application to be heard by two Lord Justices on notice to the respondent. Given the urgency, I directed that the full court should sit on Thursday 11th March to be able to hear the appeal if permission were granted and the parties were content for the appeal to follow.

3. The case was listed to be heard in private. When it was called, Mr David Price Q.C. intervened on behalf of that well known figure, Mr Benjamin Pell, who is regularly seen in the press benches of these courts reporting especially on matters in this field in which he has become quite an expert, to the extent even of his occasionally prompting learned counsel with references to relevant authority of which counsel was ignorant. Mr Price sought to persuade us to hear the matter in open court but we ruled that since the main argument would be fact-sensitive, it was necessary for the preservation of confidentiality to sit in private.

4. We granted permission to appeal, heard the appeal, and although we indicated the result, we formally adjourned in order to hand down this judgment in open court.

The background

5. In about November 2009 the appellant, who is a married man, began a sexual relationship with another woman whom I shall simply call "X", who is herself married. The source of the News of the World's information suggests that this relationship became obvious to those with whom the appellant and X were working. Towards the end of April 2010 the appellant's wife confronted him with her belief, formed either intuitively, or from information conveyed to her, that he was having an affair. He admitted it. This was deeply distressing for the wife but she and her husband determined, not least for the sake of their two teenage children, to rebuild her trust and their marriage. To that end the appellant accepted that he would end his sexual relationship with X and he so informed her.

6. Continuing their working relationship was obviously awkward and in discussion with his employers, the appellant told them that he would prefer in an ideal world not to have to see her at all and that one or other should leave but both accepted that their working commitments did not then make that possible. They agreed to conduct themselves with due decorum and to continue to perform their duties in a professional way as in fact they did.

7. In December 2010 their employers informed X that her services would no longer be required, explaining publicly that it was a convenient moment to make this change. She was, understandably, upset and angry and may even have threatened to take proceedings against the employer. The appellant only became aware of her departure whilst he was on holiday with his family over Christmas.

8. News of these events leaked to the News of the World whose enquiries alerted the appellant to its wish to publish the fact of the affair and that the affair was the real cause of X leaving her employment. He moved accordingly for this injunction, supported not only by his wife, but also by X.

The judgment under appeal

9. Collins J. gave a short ex tempore judgment. He found there was a reasonable expectation of privacy. He conducted a balancing exercise between the right of the newspaper to freedom of expression under Article 10 of the European Convention of Human Rights and the appellant's right to respect for his private and family life under Article 8 and he recognised that by virtue of section 12 of the Human Rights Act 1998 the appellant had to show that it was more likely than not that at trial the balance would come down in favour of Article 8. He held that there was public interest in the effect of the adultery and so refused the injunction because the respondent intended to go no further than reporting the fact of the affair with the resultant dismissal of X . His "last concern" related to the children. As I shall show he held that the adverse effect on them could not tip the balance.

Discussion

10. The principles which govern an application like this for an interim injunction to restrain publicity of private information are by now well established.

> (1) The first stage is to ascertain whether the applicant has a reasonable expectation of privacy so as to engage Article 8; if not, the claim fails.
> (2) The question of whether or not there is a reasonable expectation of privacy in relation to the information:
>
>> ". . . is a broad one, which takes account of all the circumstances of the case. They include the attributes of the claimant, the nature of the activity in which the claimant was engaged, the place at which it was happening, the nature and purpose of the intrusion, the absence of consent and whether it was known or could be inferred, the effect on the claimant and the circumstances in which and the purposes for which the information came into the hands of the publisher": see *Murray v Express Newspapers* [2009] Ch 481 at [36].
>
> The test established in *Campbell v MGN Ltd* [2004] UKHL 22, [2004] 2 AC 457 is to ask whether a reasonable person of ordinary sensibilities, if placed in the same situation as the subject of the disclosure, rather than the recipient, would find the disclosure offensive.
>
> (3) The protection may be lost if the information is in the public domain. In this regard there is, per *Browne v Associated Newspapers Ltd* [2008] QB 103 at [61],
>
>> ". . .potentially an important distinction between information which is made available to a person's circle of friends or work colleagues and information which is widely published in a newspaper."
>
> Whether what may start as information which is private has become information known to the public at large is a matter of fact and degree for determination in each case depending on its specific circumstances.
>
> (4) If Article 8 is engaged then the second stage of the inquiry is to conduct "the ultimate balancing test" which has the four features identified by Lord Steyn in *In Re S (A Child) (Identification: Restrictions on Publication)* [2005] 1 A.C. 593 at [17]:
>
>> "First, neither article [8 or 10] has *as such* precedence over the other. Secondly, where the values under the two articles are in conflict, an intense focus on the comparative importance of the specific rights being claimed in the individual case is necessary. Thirdly, the justifications for interfering with or restricting each

right must be taken into account. Finally, the proportionality test must be applied to each." (It should be noted that the emphasis was added by Lord Steyn.)

(5) As *von Hannover v Germany* (2004) 40 EHRR 1 makes clear at [76]:

"the decisive factor in balancing the protection of private life against freedom of expression should lie in the contribution that the published photos and articles make to a debate of general interest."

(6) Pursuant to section 12(3) of the Human Rights Act 1998 an interim injunction should not be granted unless a court is satisfied that the applicant is likely – in the sense of more likely than not – to obtain an injunction following a trial.

A reasonable expectation of privacy?

11   Collins J. found in the appellant's favour. Mr Anthony Hudson, who appears for the respondent, undertakes to file a respondent's notice to challenge that finding. He submits that the manner in which the appellant and X conducted their relationship was such that it became known to those with whom they worked with the result that knowledge spread in the workplace, reaching to the higher echelons of management. Thus, he submits, the fact of the relationship was "naturally accessible to outsiders". He relies on observations of Eady J. in *X v Persons Unknown* [2007] E.M.L.R. 10 at [38] distinguishing between "matters which are naturally accessible to outsiders and those which are known only to the protagonists". That was a very different kind of case where the judge was drawing a distinction between a couple whose marriage was encountering difficulties (the "protagonists") and their acquaintances (the "outsiders") who knew of the marital tensions not from private revelation (which would be protected) but from some public manifestation of the discord e.g. an actual separation (which probably would not entitle the protagonists to a reasonable expectation of privacy). Here the sexual relationship was essentially a private matter. One way or another it became known to work colleagues but their knowledge does not put the information into the public domain – see *Browne v Associated Newspapers Ltd* cited at [10(3)] above. In my judgment the appellant was reasonably entitled to expect that his colleagues would treat as confidential the information they had acquired whether from their own observation of the behaviour of the appellant and X or from tittle-tattle and gossip which larded the office conversation or from a confidential confession to a colleague. A reasonable person of ordinary sensibilities would certainly find the disclosure offensive.

12.   In my judgment the judge was correct to hold that the appellant's Article 8 rights were engaged. I would therefore dismiss the respondent's cross-appeal.

The ultimate balance to be struck between Article 10 and Article 8

13.   As for Article 10, everyone has the right to freedom of expression but the ones with the greatest need for this constitutionally vital freedom are the organs of the media. In the interests of our democratic society we – and that includes the judges – must ensure that the press are freely able to enquire, investigate and report on matters of public interest. The press is the public watchdog. That freedom is, however, not unrestricted as Article 10(2) itself makes so clear that it is worth repeating:

"2. The exercise of these freedoms, since it carries with it duties and responsibilities, may be subject to . . . restrictions . . . as are prescribed by law and are necessary in a democratic society . . . for the protection of the reputation or rights of others or for preventing the disclosure of information received in confidence . . ."

This restriction can only be justified if it is a proportionate and is no more than is necessary to promote the legitimate object of the restriction. To restrict publication simply to save the blushes of the famous, fame invariably being ephemeral, could have the wholly undesirable chilling effect on the necessary ability of publishers to sell their newspapers. We have to enable sales if we want to keep our newspapers. Unduly to fetter their freedom to report as editors judge to be responsible is to undermine the pre-eminence of the deserved place of the press as a powerful pillar of democracy. These considerations require the court to tread warily before granting this kind of injunction.

14. As for Article 8, weight must be given not only to the right to respect for the private and family life of the appellant himself, but also to the rights of X and, in addition, the rights of the appellant's wife and his children. It is not at all clear to what extent if at all, Collins J. had regard to the Article 8 rights of anyone bar the appellant. He did say of X:

> "8. The first question is whether there is a reasonable expectation of privacy. There was certainly a reasonable hope of privacy shared by the claimant and [X]. The fact that the relationship was adulterous does not mean that privacy was lost. Prima facie the relationship should be protected by Article 8. . . ."

This suggests her rights were taken into account but other passages can be read as limiting his focus to the rights of the appellant alone for he said:

> "9. Thus, I have to consider the balancing exercise between the right of the newspaper under Article 10 and the right of the *individual* under Article 8. . . .
>
> 11. The News of the World argues that their rights outweigh those *of the Claimant*." [I have added the emphasis.]

15. As for the wife and children, the judge said this:

> "13. My last concern relates to the claimant's children. As Mr Tomlinson rightly points out, there is likely to be an adverse effect on them if the News of the World discloses the fact of the adultery. One recognises the concerns that this issue raises but unfortunately if one parent behaves in a way that attracts adverse publicity it will affect the children. This is not something which can tip the balance if there is otherwise no good reason to grant an injunction."

16. Every allowance must be made for the fact that this was an *ex tempore* judgment delivered on a Saturday morning in an urgent application when no-one can expect verbal exactitude or detailed reasoning on every point of the argument. The exigencies of life as the out-of-hours applications' judge shackle perfection. That said, I cannot but conclude that in this instance the judge erred. First, X's rights were at the very forefront of the story the News of the World wished to publish, namely that it was the fact of their adultery, not any lack of professional competence, that led to the termination of her services. She did not welcome the intrusion of the press, has made it plain to this Court that she has no intention of bringing proceedings either against her employer or the appellant who is associated with the employer and supports the application. The evidence before the court is that X has made clear that she did not wish her privacy to be invaded at all.

17. The position of the appellant's wife is equally clear: she opposes publicity. Then there are the children. The purpose of the injunction is both to preserve the stability of the family while the appellant and his wife pursue a reconciliation and to save the children the ordeal of playground ridicule when that would inevitably follow publicity. They are bound to be harmed by immediate publicity, both because it would undermine the family as a whole and because the playground is a cruel place where the bullies feed on personal discomfort and embarrassment. In another context, in *Beoku-Betts v Secretary of State for the Home Department* [2008] UKHL 39, [2009] A.C. 115, Lady Hale commented at [4] on the risk of:

> ". . . missing the central point about family life, which is that the whole is greater than the sum of its individual parts. The right to respect for family life of one necessarily encompasses the right to respect for the family life of others, normally a spouse or minor children, with whom that family life is enjoyed."

18. Collins J. may not have recognised the rights of the appellant's wife but he certainly did accept that the adverse effect on the children was relevant. Regrettably I cannot

agree that the harmful effect on the children cannot tip the balance where the adverse publicity arises because of the way the children's father has behaved. The rights of children are not confined to their Article 8 rights. In *Neulinger v Switzerland* (2010) 28 EHRC 706 the Strasbourg court observed that:

> "131. The Convention cannot be interpreted in a vacuum but must be interpreted in harmony with the general principles of international law. Account should be taken . . . 'of any relevant rules of international law applicable in the relations between the parties' and in particular the rules concerning the international protection of human rights. . . .
>
> 135. . . . there is currently a broad consensus – including in international law – in support of the idea that in all decisions concerning children, their best interests must be paramount."

Support for that proposition can be gathered from several international human rights instruments, not least from the second principle of the United Nations Declaration of the Rights of the Child 1959, from article 3(1) of the Convention of the Rights of the Child 1989 (UNCRC) and from article 24 of the European Union's Charter of Fundamental Rights. For example, article 3(1) of the UNCRC provides:

> "In all actions concerning children, whether undertaken by public or private social welfare institutions, courts of law, administrative authorities or legislative bodies, the best interests of the child shall be a primary consideration."

19. Thus it seems to me just as "the court's earlier approach to immigration cases is tempered by a much clearer acknowledgement of the importance of the best interests of a child caught up in a dilemma which is of her parents' and not of her own making" so too must the approach of the court to these injunctions have regard to the interests of children. The quotation is taken from paragraph 20 of the speech of the Baroness Hale of Richmond with whom Lord Brown and Lord Mance agreed in *ZH (Tanzania) v Secretary of State for the Home Department* [2011] UKSC4 which was a case concerned with the weight to be given to the best interests of children who are affected by the decision of the Home Secretary to remove or deport one or both of their parents from this country, more specifically with the question: in what circumstances is it permissible to remove or deport a non-citizen parent (here the mother whose immigration history was described as "appalling") where the effect will be that a child who is a citizen of the United Kingdom will also have to leave? I appreciate that the issue is far removed from that with which this Court is concerned but since the interests of the appellant's children are undoubtedly engaged, the universal principles cannot be ignored. The proper approach is, therefore, neatly summarised by Lord Kerr of Tonaghmore at paragraph 46 of that decision, namely:

> "It is a universal theme of the various international and domestic instruments to which Lady Hale has referred that, in reaching decisions that will affect a child, a primacy of importance must be accorded to his or her best interests. This is not, it is agreed, a factor of limitless importance in the sense that it will prevail over all considerations. It is a factor, however, that must rank higher than any other. It is not merely one consideration that weighs in the balance alongside other competing factors. Where the best interests of the child clearly favour a certain course, that course should be followed, unless countervailing reasons of considerable force displace them. It is not necessary to express this in terms of a presumption but the primacy of this consideration needs to be made clear in emphatic terms. What is determined to be in a child's best interests should customarily dictate the outcome of cases such as the present, therefore, and it will require considerations of substantial moment to permit a different result."

However this learning must, with respect, be read and understood in the context in which it is sought to be applied. It is clear that the interests of children do not automatically take precedence over the Convention rights of others. It is clear also that, when in a case such as this the court is deciding where the balance lies between the article 10 rights of the media and the Article 8 rights of those whose privacy would be invaded by publication, it should accord particular weight to the Article 8 rights of any children likely to be affected by the publication, if that would be likely to harm their interests. Where a tangible and objective public interest tends to favour publication, the balance may be difficult to strike. The force of the public interest will be highly material, and the interests of affected children cannot be treated as a trump card.

20. How then does this approach square with the way Lord Steyn advised in *In Re S* that the ultimate balance should be struck, see [0(4)] above. He was confining himself to articles 8 and 10 and not ranging more widely to take note of the other Convention rights of children. He expressed his opinion long before *Neulinger* called for a re-appraisal of the position. In any event, the emphasis he added makes it clear that he was concerned strictly with the balance between article 10 and article 8 *"as such"*, i.e. where the only rights in balance were those conferred by articles 8 and 10. If, as he requires, an intense focus on the comparative importance of the specific rights being claimed in the individual case is necessary, then the additional rights of children are to be placed in the scale. The question then is whether the force of the article 10 considerations outweigh them given what I have said in paragraph 19.

21. Here there is no political edge to the publication. The organisation of the economic, social and political life of the country, so crucial to democracy, is not enhanced by publication. The intellectual, artistic or personal development of members of society is not stunted by ignorance of the sexual frolics of figures known to the public. As Lord Hope said of Miss Campbell (paragraph 120 of *Campbell v MGN Ltd*),

"... it is not enough to deprive Miss Campbell of her right to privacy that she is a celebrity and that her private life is newsworthy."

22. In my judgment the benefits to be achieved by publication in the interests of free speech are wholly outweighed by the harm that would be done through the interference with the rights to privacy of all those affected, especially where the rights of the children are in play.

The decisive factor

23. The decisive factor is the contribution the published information will make to a debate of general interest. Is a debate about the reasons why X's employment terminated a matter of such public interest? Both the appellant and X will be known to a sector of the public though it is impossible to measure how large – or how small – that sector is. Certainly some members of the public will have noticed the end of her employment: a proportion of them will even have speculated why she left. But the reasons for her leaving give rise to no debate of general interest. The reasons for her leaving may interest some members of the public but the matters are not of public interest. Publication may satisfy public prurience but that is not a sufficient justification for interfering with the private rights of those involved.

Conclusion

24. I have come to the firm conclusion that the judge erred and that this is a case where it is more likely than not that an injunction would be granted following a trial. In my judgment the appeal should be allowed and interlocutory injunctions granted in the terms sought.

Lord Justice Laws:

25. I agree.

Lord Justice Moore-Bick:

26. I also agree.

BIBLIOGRAPHY

WEBSITES

5 Raymond Buildings: *www.5rb.co.uk*

Attorney General: *www.attorneygeneral.gov.uk*

British and Irish Legal Information Institute: *www.bailii.org*

British Broadcasting Corporation: *www.bbc.co.uk*

Campaign for Press and Broadcasting Freedom: *www.cpbf.org.uk*

Court Service: *www.hmcourt-service.gov.uk*

Crown Prosecution Service: *www.cps.gov.uk*

Department for Constitutional Affairs: *www.dca.gov.uk*

Families Need Fathers: *www.fnf.org.uk*

International Federation of Journalists: *www.ifj.org*

International News Safety Institute: *www.newssafety.com*

Judicial Studies Board: *www.jsboard.co.uk*

Legislation: *www.legislation.gov.uk*

Ministry of Justice: *www.justice.gov.uk*

Media Lawyer: *www.medialawyer.press.net*

Press Complaints Commission: *www.pcc.org.uk*

Procurator Fiscal, Scotland: *www.copfs.gov.uk*

Office of Communication: *www.ofcom.org.uk*

Scottish Legal Officers: *www.scotland.gov.uk*

Sentencing Council: *www.sentencingcouncil.org.uk*

BOOKS

Addis, M, and Morrow, P, *Your Rights: The Liberty Guide to Human Rights,* 8th edn, (Pluto Press, 2005).

Banks, David and Hanna, Mark, *McNae's Essential Law for Journalists,* 20th edn, (Oxford University Press, 2009).

Barendt, Eric, *Freedom of Speech,* (Oxford University Press, 2007).

Barendt and Hitchens, *Media Law: Cases and Materials,* (Longman, 2000).

Beales, Ian, *The Editors' Codebook, the handbook to the Editors' Code of Practice,* 2nd edn, (Newspaper Publishers Association, The Newspaper Society, Periodical Publishers Association, The Scottish Daily Newspaper Society and Scottish Newspaper Publishers Association, 2009).

Bloy, Duncan, *Media Law,* (Sage Publications, 2007).

Brooke, Heather, *Your Right to Know: How to use the Freedom of Information Act and other access laws,* (Pluto Press, 2005).

Brooke, Heather, *The Silent State,* (Windmill Books, 2011).

Caddell, Richard and Johnson, Howard, *Blackstone's Statutes on Media Law,* 3rd edn, (Oxford University Press, 2010).

Carey, Peter, *Media Law,* 5th edn, (Sweet & Maxwell, 2010).

Gunning, Jennifer and Holm, Soren, ed., *Ethics, Law and Society,* (Ashgate, 2005) Vol 1.

Hadwin, Sara, Real readers, real news: the work of a local newspaper editor, in Franklin, Bob ed., *Local Journalism and Local Media,* (Routledge, 2006).

Hargreaves, Ian, *Journalism: Truth or dare?* (Oxford University Press, 2003).

Kovach, Bill and Rosenstiel, Tom, *The Elements of Journalism,* (Atlantic Books, 2003). (Updated).

Kung, Lucy, Picard Robert G, Towse, Ruth, *The Internet and the Mass Media,* (Sage, 2008).

Lapping, Brian, *The bounds of freedom,* (Constable in collaboration with Granada Television, 1980).

Mayes, Ian, *The Guardian: Corrections and Clarifications,* (*Guardian* Newspapers, 2000).

Mill, John Stuart, *On Liberty & Others Essays,* (Oxford World Classics, 1991).

Milmo, Patrick and Rogers WVH, ed, *Gatley: On Libel and Slander,* Sweet & Maxwell, 11th edn (London, 2010).

Nicol, Andrew QC, Millar, Gavin QC, Sharland, Andrew, *Media Law and Human Rights,* 2nd edn (Oxford University Press, 2009).

Quinn, Frances, *Law for Journalists,* 2nd edn (Pearson Longman, 2011).

Randall, David, *The Universal Journalist,* 3rd edn (Pluto Press, 2007).

Robertson, Geoffrey and Nicol, Andrew, *Media Law,* 5th edn, (Penguin, 2008).

Rozenberg, Joshua, *Privacy and the Press*, (Oxford University Press, 2004).

Warby, Mark, Moreham, Nicole, Christie, Iain, Tugendhat, Sir Michael, ed, *Tugendhat & Christie: The Law of Privacy and the Media,* 2nd edn, (Oxford University Press, 2011).

Wilson, Des, *The Secrets File: The case for Freedom of Information in Britain today*, (Heinemann, 1984).

INDEX

LEGAL TAXONOMY
FROM SWEET & MAXWELL

This index has been prepared using Sweet and Maxwell's Legal Taxonomy. Main index entries conform to keywords provided by the Legal Taxonomy except where references to specific documents or non-standard terms (denoted by quotation marks) have been included. These keywords provide a means of identifying similar concepts in other Sweet & Maxwell publications and online services to which keywords from the Legal Taxonomy have been applied. Readers may find some minor differences between terms used in the text and those which appear in the index. Suggestions to *sweetandmaxwell.taxonomy@thomson.com*.

(All references are to page number)